TEACHING MULTI-CULTURAL POPULATIONS

FIVE HERITAGES

Edited by

James C. Stone
University of California at Berkeley

Donald P. DeNevi
Merritt College

D. Van Nostrand Company
New York • Cincinnati • Toronto • London • Melbourne

D. Van Nostrand Company Regional Offices:
New York   Cincinnati

D. Van Nostrand Company International Offices:
London   Toronto   Melbourne

Copyright © 1971 by Litton Educational Publishing, Inc.

Library of Congress Catalog Card Number 75-146600   ISBN: 0-442-27912-4

Published by D. Van Nostrand Company
450 West 33rd Street, New York, N.Y. 10001

Published simultaneously in Canada by
Van Nostrand Reinhold Ltd.

10   9   8   7   6   5

Cover design by Saul Schnurman
Cover photographs by Richard Bellak

A child goes to school to wonder. The school is where he enters the Anglo world with shy curiosity; it is a magical microcosm of society to him. The teacher is his sorcerer, a mother who is worldly-wise, knowing all sorts of facts and magic, powerful as the policeman, but human as an aunt or uncle. In the beginning that is how school seems to the child.

He is lost at the thought that he cannot enter that wonderful world because he speaks the wrong language or is the wrong color. The child is proud of his father; he boasts of his barrio heritage. He doesn't know that he is supposed to be "culturally deprived."

Stan Steiner, *La Raza: The Mexican Americans*, p. 213.

To Dorothy and Heather

Preface

Among American educators today there is a growing consciousness that revolutionary action needs to be taken to make school experiences meaningful for students whose racial, social, religious, and cultural backgrounds differ from those of so-called mainstream students. But the problem of materials looms very large.

The present book is an attempt to help fill the tremendous gap that presently exists between teachers' will to become more skillful with multi-cultural student populations and the as-yet short supply of the quality materials they urgently need in order to do so. We hope the volume will prove useful in all manner of pre-service courses as well as in on-the-job settings where the teacher is already interacting with multi-cultural classes.

Our organizing principle is that, inasmuch as America is an immense living laboratory for interaction among diverse peoples, it ought to be possible to assemble a book that mirrors this plurality—in a way that will sensitize present and future teachers to the needs and the opportunities created by cultural pluralism in the classroom. Accordingly, we have found that valuable social scientific knowledge—albeit in tentative form—now exists which can assist teachers in utilizing the rich cultural heritage of America's varied ethnic groups. We have therefore selected essays which provide information, realism, and insight and have arranged them under five headings corresponding to America's leading ethnic minorities: black, Puerto Rican, Mexican-American, American Indian, and Asian-American. We have sought especially to present material which is pragmatically based rather than purely descriptive, recognizing that, for the teacher of minority group children, the question of what actions and attitudes one adopts is of greater consequence than knowledge alone, although knowledge is a prerequisite for effective, informed behavior.

In general, each ethnic heritage is explored according to a scheme whereby we begin with a broad cultural-historical view of the group; then narrow to a more contemporary social and familial focus; and finally move with the child of this generation into the educational context of present-day American schools. The reader will note certain exceptions to this scheme, signifying that no appropriate material could be located—and suggesting that teachers acquainted with the groups little studied might consider making contributions to the literature.

In compiling the appendix of further resources at the conclusion of the volume, we tended to pull out all the stops, listing a rich diversity of materials that had come to our attention which seemed potentially enriching for the educator. No time-honored bibliographies have yet grown up in this area, and we rather welcomed the opportunity to mix classic anthropological texts with applied educational theory. Here too there is some lack of balance from section to section reflecting the disparity of materials available.

Looking back over the growth of this volume, we see a chain of colleagues, students, and others far too numerous to mention who contributed much to our thinking and our resources while we worked. We are also grateful to Nancy Bragdon and Francesco Cordasco for reading and reacting to the manuscript as it progressed. But most of all we look eagerly ahead—to the interactions, the debates, the discoveries, the experiments, the new teaching methods and materials, the new articles and books that we believe will come out of American education as it embraces the challenge which is the subject of this book.

J.C.S.
D.P.D.

Contents

Introduction   1

new The Mandate for an Innovative Educational Response
to Cultural Diversity/**Jack D. Forbes**   5

done Educational Enlightenment Out of Texas: Toward
Bilingualism/**Francesco Cordasco** ~~28~~ 3 13   19 —

Part 1   The Black Heritage   25

What Is Your Black Culture Quotient?   27

Who Are the Afro-Americans?/**Jack D. Forbes**   29

Community and Class Realities: The Ordeal of Change/
G. Franklin Edwards   36

Race and Reconciliation: The Role of the School/
John H. Fischer   55

How to Integrate Your District's Curriculum   73
A Talk to Teachers/**James Baldwin**   80

How Baseball Integrated a Hotel/**Melvin Durslag**   87

Working with the Afro-American Pupil/**Jack D. Forbes**   89

Black Is Not a Color of the Skin, It Is a State of Mind/
Ellen Holly   94

On Misunderstanding Black Militancy/**Faith Berry**   99

Part 2   The Puerto Rican Heritage   107

from A Study of Slum Culture: Backgrounds for *La Vida*/
Oscar Lewis   111

from *Spanish Harlem*/**Patricia Cayo Sexton**   118

The Lower Status Puerto Rican Family/**Joseph Bram**   130

The Puerto Rican Child in the American School/
Francesco Cordasco   141

The Losers/**Richard J. Margolis**   148

Part 3   The Mexican-American Heritage   163

What Is Your Chicano Culture Quotient?/**Felix Elizalde**   167

Social Characteristics and Problems of the
Spanish–Speaking Atomistic Society/**Charles B. Brussell**   169

Mexican Americans in School: A History of
Educational Neglect/**Thomas P. Carter**   197

Cognitive and Intellectual Functioning of
Spanish–Speaking Children/**Charles B. Brussell**   247

Teaching a Second Language to Spanish–Speaking
Children of the Southwest/**Herschel T. Manuel**   262

Where to from Here?/**Thomas P. Carter**   272

Part 4   The Indian Heritage   285

Toward a Background for the Teacher of Indian Students/
Edward P. Dozier   289

The Indian Child and His Culture/**Robert A. Roessel, Jr.**   294

The Indian and Civil Wrongs/**Jack Charles**   311

Red Man's Plight: 'Uncle Tomahawks' & 'Apples'/
Barbara Isenberg   318

The Powwow of The Young Intellectuals/**Stan Steiner**   324

American Indian Education: Time to Redeem an Old
Promise/**Estelle Fuchs**   339

Intelligence and Achievement of the Indian Student/
Robert A. Roessel, Jr.   348

Good Day at Rough Rock/**Paul Conklin**   358

School Problems of Indian Youth/**Frederic R. Gunsky**   365

Part 5 The Asian-American Heritage   369

Asians in America/**Asian Americans of the Third World
Political Alliance**   371

The Remarkable Evolution of a Japanese Subculture/
Harry H. L. Kitano   376

San Francisco's Chinatown/ **Mary Ellen Leary**   389

Sociopsychological Aspects of the Acculturation
of Japanese in America/**Harry H. L. Kitano**   397

The New Yellow Peril/**Tom Wolfe**   402

Conclusion   433

A New Model for the Teacher Preparation We Need/
James C. Stone   435

Appendix

Sources on the Education and Study
of Multi-Cultural Populations   447

Index   471

INTRODUCTION

This is probably a brash book.

It grew from our feeling that it ought to be possible to put together in the pages of a single book significant pieces which:

> deal with the wide variation and variability among America's cultural minorities

> do this in a way that is helpful for teachers and teachers-to-be

> reveal American minorities as part of the total context of international cultural variation

> do this without the easy generalizations of the kind-hearted liberal or the hard cynicism of the condescending conservative

Whether this is brash is one thing. That an attempt in this direction is imperative, we think, cannot be denied much longer.

It is certainly time for American educators to take an informed look at each of the large ethnic minority groups sending children into the schools. It ought to be a long enough and hard enough look so that each minority group is understood as being a unique people with unique characteristics, contributions, and concerns. In this sense, any part of the book can function as partial first-aid for the educator working with the particular minority group under discussion.

But in a larger, more therapeutic sense we hope the book will be read in its entirety by people in all parts of the country—people who may never see an American Indian child, people living in areas where the Puerto Rican subculture is unknown. For only by viewing cultural diversity *in its entirety*, we submit, can one hope to gain a true appreciation of multi-culturalism in today's schools. We try in these pages to promote that larger consciousness through in-depth ex-

1

plorations of each of the five ethnic minorities spotlighted. We examine the distinctive historical and cultural roots of each, its infusion into the American experience, its unique values and social mores, its varying economic and linguistic bases and, above all, the unique relationship of each to our educational institutions and assumptions.

At the outset of such an inquiry, it is useful to recall that educational problems posed by the culturally unique are confined to neither this nation nor this century. Virtually all complex societies, beginning with the cosmopolitan, multilingual empires of the Mediterranean-Mesopotamian-Indian subcontinent, have possessed heterogeneous populations. As just one example of early cross-cultural education, ancient Buddhist teachers are known to have traveled extensively throughout southern and eastern Asia, encountering and interacting with widely divergent languages and cultures.

At present most of the world's nation-states possess prominent cultural and linguistic minorities: Great Britain, France, Spain, Switzerland, Kenya, Fiji, the Soviet Union, China, India, Mexico, New Zealand, and Canada, to name but a few. Most such states have also been characterized at one time or another by low-income segments of the population that either evolved their own indigenous educational system (as in Vietnam before the French conquest) or participated successfully in mass education programs instituted by the dominant group (as in the great period of Islamic civilization prior to the fifteenth century).

Education has always been, in fact, an agency through which societies evolve. As such, it mirrors many of the forces astir in society at any given time. When that society is multi-cultural and in a period of rapid transition, as ours is, its educational institutions will inevitably be one of the arenas in which social change manifests itself.

It should probably be noted at the outset also that the phenomenon of cultural diversity and the teacher's understanding of it which forms the subject of this book are exceedingly complex, sensitive areas. What the book includes is only enough to start with, and it certainly will raise more questions than it answers. Added to this is the dilemma posed by continuous changes in terminology in this area. What was an accepted term yesterday is obsolete or an affront today. The *culturally disadvantaged* of last year are the *culturally different* of today, and the *culturally unique* of tomorrow! The language used by authors in these pages varies widely, like their perspectives. All can nevertheless contribute, we believe, to a broadening and deepening of the cultural awareness of teachers and teachers-to-be.

As a preface to the subsequent Parts of this book, the pieces following in this Introduction sound two notes: one of possibility, in Jack Forbes' essay; the other of promise, in Francesco Cordasco's article. Written several years ago, when the multi-cultural dimensions of the schools' problems were just beginning to be widely recognized, Forbes' article is an appropriate keynote. It touches on the major common concerns of minority populations and presents a synthetic, sympathetic overview of the mounting cultural conflicts in our society.

Emphasizing the beauty, romance, and contributions of minority cultures to the 1970 American melting pot, Forbes advocates full educational democracy for minority populations, and he makes a number of specific suggestions for moving the traditional educational establishment in that direction. To his points we would add these further emphases:

We possess in Americans' diverse cultural and linguistic heritages a tremendous untapped natural resource which is worth preserving and extending. Diversity of culture and language enriches all of us.

We ought to consciously encourage bilingualism in our schools. Teachers must become adept at interweaving non-Anglo contributions and material into the curriculum, to wherever they will enrich.

Non-Anglo literature, music, art, dance, sports, and games should become part of the curriculum.

Non-Anglo teachers must be sought, recruited, trained, retained, and supported in opportunities to work with non-Anglo pupils.

School information (and school meetings) intended for parents of minority group children should be made available in all appropriate languages.

Cordasco's article sketching the development of bilingual education, its antecedents, and its future promise, is also an appropriate prelude to the more specialized discussions that follow. There is little doubt in our minds that the key to improved instruction for culturally unique children is nothing short of bilingual education. Stop to consider the child who enters school knowing no English, speaking only his native tongue. If the school forbids him to speak anything but what is to him a foreign language, if it forces him to struggle along in that foreign language understanding it only dimly, if at all, this child—this member of any of the minorities considered in this book—is led to believe from his first day of school that there is something wrong with him because of his language. And because language is a function of life style, his fear soon spreads to the image that child has of his culture, the history of his people, the people themselves, and his own family in particular. This is a subtle, cruel form of discrimination, imprinting upon the consciousness of the young a degrading image which they may carry with them throughout their lives. Failure in school follows naturally. Rebellion comes close on its heels, with dropout or expulsion the logical end product.

Contrast what we just have described with the possibilities inherent in bilingual education. The child's first day in school is a rewarding one because his teacher speaks his native language and recognizes the traditions and folklore of his people. Instruction is in his native tongue. Books, toys, games, instructional aids, and pictures reflect his people, his heroes, his villains, his people's life style. School is but an extension of home for him just as "regular" schooling frequently is for the middle class child.

When children fail in school, or drop out—a particularly acute phenomenon with underprivileged blacks, American-Indians and Mexican-Americans, where the rate is as high as 50 percent—teachers are too often prone to write off such children as unteachable or lacking in aptitude. This reasoning is now being hotly challenged. Among the first challenges from within the educational system was the Robert Rosenthal and Lenore Jacobson study[1] which maintained that teachers' predictions of pupil behavior come to be realized. Children whom the teacher expects will make intellectual gains do in fact make them. Those the teacher considers "dumb" in fact behave this way. When the negative self image was eliminated, children were able to participate in the fun, excitement, and satisfaction of learning.

Providing bilingual education for all minority kids is a formidable job, but section VII of the Bilingual American Education Act seems to be a vehicle with the horsepower to make it go. When Congress passed the Act in 1967 it went on record as follows:

In recognition of the special educational needs of large numbers of students in the U. S. to whom English is a foreign language, Congress hereby declares it to be the policy of the U. S. to provide financial assistance to local educational agencies to develop and carry out new and imaginative programs designed to meet these special educational needs.[2]

In one sense, it is impossible to legislate changes in attitudes and exceedingly difficult to legislate changes in deep-seated habits and customs. The Act and those who set about implementing it have had their critics—frequently insightful critics genuinely frustrated by the slowness of any meaningful change. But generally speaking, the Act has opened the door to a host of new methods, concepts, and materials which hold promise not only for redressing old grievances among minority groups but also for rejuvenating an entire educational system. This means new teaching strategies, new multimedia paraphernalia, new teacher recruitment and training procedures, new efforts at bilingual classes, and even entire bilingual schools available on an individual choice basis through a federal voucher system,[3] as well as special instruction offered in schools by private corporations through performance contracts.[4]

In its efforts to make itself responsive to the needs of groups formerly neglected, the total system stands to gain greater efficiency and creativity.

---

[1]"Teacher Expectations for the Disadvantaged," *Scientific American* (April, 1968), later expanded into *Pygmalion in the Classroom,* New York: Holt, Reinhart and Winston, 1968.

[2]Section 7 of the Bilingual American Education Act, an amendment to the National Elementary and Secondary Education Act.

[3]*Education Vouchers: Financing Education by Grants to Parents—A Preliminary Report.* Prepared under federal grant CG 8542 for the U.S. Office of Economic Opportunity, Center for the Study of Public Policy. Cambridge, Massachusetts: March, 1970.

[4]Performance contracting is a service to schools rendered by a private corporation which guarantees to raise the achievement level of pupils a specified amount within a specified period of time for a specified amount of money. If the level is not achieved within the period allotted, the school does not pay for the service.

The Mandate
for an Innovative
Educational Response
to Cultural Diversity

Jack D. Forbes

The participation of urban Negro youths of school age in riots from Watts to New York, the confrontations between Negro parents and white school boards from Oakland to Boston, the school boycotts involving children of all ages, north and south, and the increased concern and agitation on the part of Mexican-Americans, American Indians, and Puerto Ricans: all have recently served to focus attention upon the problem of the culturally different and the poor as they relate to educational programs in the United States. And concurrent with this evidence of "grass-roots" dissatisfaction, the compiling of statistics and research-derived data has served to focus attention upon the "educationally short-changed" sectors of the population.

Evidence that something is seriously wrong with education as it involves racial and cultural minorities and low-income groups has been mounting for years. Decades ago, scholars such as Herschel T. Manuel and Paul S. Taylor documented the plight of the Mexican-American scholastic, but the "establishment" paid little heed. Scholars and leaders familiar with American Indians and Afro-Americans have been concerned with these groups' special educational needs for more than a century, and concern with weakness in traditional programs has been mounting for years. But it has taken the so-called "Negro Revolt" of the last decade, the recent "discovery" of the poor, and the launching of "New Frontier" and "Great Society" programs to force educators to take a new look at old assumptions.

Adapted from a lecture entitled "Educational Democracy and the Culturally Different," which later appeared as "The Education of the Culturally Different: A Challenge for Innovative Educational Agencies"—U.S. Government Printing Office, Washington, D.C.: 1968, pp. 1–20. Reprinted by permission of the author.

Major periodicals, such as *The New York Times,* continually reflect the grow-ing consensus that seems to be developing among the intellectual and govern-mental leadership of the nation. Increasingly these groups seem to agree that the major aim of current educational change consists in upgrading the schooling of low-income and culturally different children. R. Sargent Shriver, then director of the Office of Economic Opportunity, was one of the first to deliver remarks typical of this growing concern when he asserted that the present elementary school system is "critically inadequate to meet the needs of children of poverty." Worried over the long-term impact of "Head-Start" pre-school programs ap-parently being frustrated by poor follow-up kindergarten and first grade teach-ing, Shriver noted that Head-Start is "a short-term experience, and a shot of educational adrenalin whose effects can wear off in the grinding boredom and frustration of slum classrooms." The "war on poverty" director then called for a "Project Keep Moving" to transform slum classrooms, grade by grade (*The New York Times,* Nov. 20, 1966, p. 1).

Similar sentiments have since been echoed by leaders of varying sectors. James E. Allen, Jr., then New York State Education Commissioner, told the New York City Board of Education that it must improve schools in the slums imme-diately, back in 1966. Later he urged educators from a number of states, as-sembling for a meeting in New York City, to consider (*The New York Times,* Nov. 28, 1966, p. 1, 42):

What kind of schools will turn the tide of hope in the ghettos? What patterns of co-operation involving whites, Negroes, business, industry, labor and government can re-juvenate slum-area schools? What can be done to assure parents in slum areas of a more meaningful role in the schools and the education of their children?

Elsewhere, a conference sponsored by the Association on American Indian Affairs' education committee condemned the educational situation in Bureau of Indian Affairs' schools. "Thousands of American Indian children in Government-run schools are becoming hopeless 'no-culture people'," they said, and their executive director William Byler described the situation as "criminal." Indian children are not learning anything about the positive aspects of Indian history, said Mrs. Mary Lou Payne, a Cherokee, and the Rev. John F. Bryde, Jesuit super-intendent of Holy Rosary Indian Mission, asserted that there had been a drastic rise in mental health problems on the part of the Indian in recent years, partly because "He is not effectively identified with his Indian heritage, nor can he identify with the hostile, white world facing him" (*The New York Times,* Nov. 21, 1966, p. 38). Similarly, scholars attending the American Anthropological As-sociation's 1966 meeting that year condemned existing practices in poverty-area schools and called for changes which we shall discuss in a moment.

Ultimately, Congress and federal agencies have recognized the need to pro-vide better opportunities for the culturally different and the poor and have established a maze of new programs of an educational nature funded through the Office of Education, the Office of Economic Opportunity, the Department of Labor, the Interior Department, and the Department of Defense.

The statistics are, of course, alarming. That 67.6 percent of Negroes are failing the Selective Service mental tests (ranging from 25 percent in Washington to 86 percent in South Carolina) is one indication of the practical results of educational-societal failure. School dropout rates are another indication of failure, and these are notoriously high for American Indians (50 percent), urban Negroes, Mexican-Americans, and mainland Puerto Ricans. Although progress in recent years can be cited, the median school years completed for Indians twenty-five and older in Elko County, Nevada, stands at 7.9 years and for all non-whites in Nevada at 8.8 years (compared with 12.2 years for whites). Almost 17 percent of the Indian adults in Elko County have *never* been to school while only 0.7 percent of Nevada whites are totally without school experience. More than five percent of Nevada non-whites, as a whole, have never been to school (Elmer Rusco, *Minority Groups in Nevada,* 1966). The average educational level (years of schooling) for American Indians nationally stands at five years *(The New York Times,* Nov. 21, 1966, p. 38, and Dec. 4, 1966, p. 62).

As regards Mexican-Americans, Dr. Julian Samora early noted (*Southwest Conference Proceedings,* April 6, 1963, p. 19) that "they lag behind the non-whites and the Anglos regardless of what measure of educational achievement is used." A recent *Progress Report* of the UCLA Mexican-American Study Project (November 1966) has indicated that the gap between Anglo- and Mexican-Americans is narrowing but that the latter have five years less schooling if over twenty-five years of age and four years less if over fourteen years of age.

But perhaps of greater significance in illustrating the dimensions of the problem of the culturally different is the suggestion that the *quality* of the five to nine years of school to which they are ordinarily exposed is probably significantly poorer than that experienced by the majority Anglo-American population. In their study of education on the Pine Ridge Sioux Reservation (*Education in an American Indian Community,* Social Problems monograph, 1964) Murray Wax, Rosalie Wax, and Robert Dumont effectively document the thesis that, although Indian children may remain in school for a certain number of years, the last few years especially are educationally worthless and psychologically destructive. A major symptom of this process is "the 'withdrawal' or 'lack of response' of pupils in the late elementary grades and the high school" cited as their greatest problem by Pine Ridge Bureau of Indian Affairs teachers.

The phenomena of gradual alienation or "withdrawal" is also a noticeable experience in slum schools. James B. Conant (*Slums and Suburbs,* p. 26) quotes a Negro teacher as saying "We do quite well with those children in the lower grades. . . . But when they reach about ten, eleven, or twelve years of age, we lose them. At that time the 'street' takes over. In terms of schoolwork, progress ceases; indeed many pupils begin to go backward in their studies!" I. N. Berlin (*Saturday Review,* Oct. 15, 1966, p. 79), in working with largely non-Anglo delinquent high school students in San Francisco, noted that "their hate for their white teachers and other staff often seemed overwhelming."

Achievement test results also demonstrate that not only are non-Anglo groups exposed to fewer years of formal schooling than Anglos, but that the level of achievement involved is considerably inferior. When the Berkeley, California, Unified School District contrasted test results from ghetto (Negro) schools with those of white schools in 1964, the scores in predominantly non-white schools uniformly fell far below the white schools on both third and sixth grade tests.

Thus we may assert that, while minority group youngsters are now being exposed to a year or two of schooling more than were their parents, it is questionable that the "educational gap" has, in a qualitative sense, been narrowed. Results of Selective Service tests, in-depth studies of specific schools, and other data not cited here would tend to indicate that the "gap" is as great as ever and may, in fact, be widening for some groups. Despite massive rhetoric and programs, therefore, the problem presented by the education of the culturally different remains very much an issue in our society.

IN PURSUIT OF PANACEAS

The reaction of educators to the problem of under-achievement, alienation, and withdrawal as it relates to racial and cultural minority groups has been, in general, to intensify the use of traditional approaches and to focus the blame for failure upon the minority group. The concepts of "culturally disadvantaged youth" and "culturally deprived youth" have been coined, serving to suggest that the minority group pupil and his family are at fault, that the pupil and his subculture should be manipulated. This line of approach suggests that the traditional school is in effect a finished product which has served majority group pupils well and should, therefore, not be seriously challenged. Minority groups must adjust, must conform, must change, while the schools and their basically sound programs need no fundamental revision. As Reginald W. Major, former Chairman of the Education Committee of the San Francisco NAACP, has noted (*The Nation,* Sept. 12, 1966):

By accepting the premise of cultural deprivation, school administrators and school boards delude themselves and the public into believing that special programs designed to compensate for an inadequate home environment are all that is needed.

Operation Head-Start, the National Teacher Corps, and "compensatory" education programs are generally based upon the above assumption: that increased exposure to any school environment coupled with an intensified remedial approach will solve or at least ameliorate the problems of the "culturally deprived." This assumption may, however, be totally erroneous.

The National Advisory Council on the Education of Disadvantaged Children, reporting to President Lyndon Johnson on the effectiveness of 250 million dollars worth of summer education projects aimed at the poor, painted a "gloomy" picture (*The New York Times,* Dec. 1, 1966, p. 38):

For the most part, projects are piecemeal, fragmented or vaguely directed enrichment. It is extremely rare to find strategically planned, comprehensive programs for change. . . .

[Most of the programs] took place in ordinary schoolhouse classrooms and were, at best, mild variations on ordinary classroom work. . . . [In a Southern city] the program was as uncreative and unimaginative as I have ever seen. Pupils . . . dropped out in large numbers. Several teachers indicated that they felt that any kind of help which might be offered would not significantly change most of these kids.

Some of the programs were ingenious and sophisticated, but:

the aggregate of local efforts do not yet reflect a widely accepted strategy for creating a new, more effective educational climate for disadvantaged children.

It may be that those who wish to deal effectively with the culturally different child will have to revise their thinking about which end of the school-pupil continuum is "disadvantaged." Are "disadvantaged" pupils attending "advantaged" schools taught by "culturally enriched" teachers? Or is it possible that some culturally different pupils are more "enriched" than their "culturally deprived" teachers and schools—or that all are "deprived": schools, pupils, and teachers?

Cultural deprivation is not a new concept. For at least a century it has provided an expression for Anglo-American racism, chauvinism, and superiority. On the assumption that American Indian groups were "backward," young Indians were taken away from their parents and indoctrinated in white middle-class cultural values. The Indian child was assumed to have no culture except certain "savage" customs which had to be uprooted. Middle-class missionaries, secular or otherwise, were to civilize the aborigines by "giving" them a culture. The Waxes and Dumont describe this cultural vacuum doctrine as it is being applied today to both Indian and non-Indian children:

Especially in the slums inhabited by ethnic minorities the tensions of urban schools are markedly similar to those [at Pine Ridge Sioux Reservation] . . . Urban educators are isolated from the cultural and social milieux of their pupils, as are reservation counterparts. Knowing little of their pupils' life, and terrified or appalled by what they do discover, they justify their avoidance with a 'vacuum ideology' of cultural deficiency and deprivation which ignores or derogates the values and knowledge that the pupils have acquired in their homes and neighborhoods.

The concept of cultural deprivation as it has frequently been used is simply a belief that non-Anglo minority groups do not possess a "culture" which can be utilized or enhanced by the schools. The children of the minority group are "deprived" because they are not carriers of the Anglo middle-class heritage, and the task of the school is to make up for this deficiency. To put it another way, the school is a device for "assimilation," i.e., making the United States a homogeneous nation of multi-hued Anglo-Americans.

The notion of cultural deprivation, in short, is not merely an insult to the Mexican-American, Indian, Chinese-American, et cetera, but is also a continuation of the missionary urge of white, Anglo-Saxon Protestants ("WASPS") to demonstrate the superiority of their culture by making everybody else over into their image. Is this not a form of cultural imperialism, made possible only by the sheer political and economic dominance of the Anglo-American majority?

Confused Images

Not all educators who seek to force the culturally different student into an Anglo middle-class mold do so, of course, because of a conscious desire to implement a superiority complex or because of a compulsive monocultural prejudice. Many have simply never thought of the United States as a culturally heterogeneous nation and, secondly, have always assumed that minority groups must conform in order to compete in an Anglo-dominant society. But the reality of American life points in a different direction. The Chinese-American who speaks only English and who has lost contact with the Chinese community is *not* better equipped to make a living. On the contrary, he is competitively inferior to the Chinese-American who functions in a dual culture and can operate successfully either on Main Street U.S.A. or in Chinatown. And this is to say nothing of the advantages that a bicultural Chinese-American enjoys in other areas of life (access to a dual heritage in literature, philosophy, and art, for example) or in securing academic or governmental jobs which require two or more languages.

Educators seem often to operate in a mythical world created by the nature of their own middle-class contacts. Having little to do with non-Anglos or low-income people generally, they assume that the possession of Anglo middle-class skills and values will, in effect, enable one to function successfully everywhere and at every level of life. Anglo educators in much of the South-west live, for example, in self-created Anglo oases, cut off from the Indian-Mexican reality around them. They and their fellow refugees from the Middle-West or South have created middle-class spatial and attitudinal ghettos which experience little meaningful contact with large portions of the surrounding population. The educator fails to suspect that it may be *his* culture which is alien and regionally irrelevant. He therefore attempts to train young Navajos, Hopis, and Mexican-Americans to be middle-class Anglos. What kind of a social context will most of these non-Anglos have to make their living in? Certainly not an Anglo middle-class milieu!

Similarly, it is naive to assume that the majority of Afro-Americans will spend most of their time from now on in white middle-class settings. Urban or rural, the average Negro is likely for some time to be living in essentially a Negro subculture, in both socio-cultural and economic terms. In any case, a Negro youth will undoubtedly wish to maintain good relations with his family, relatives, and Negro contemporaries while growing up, and he does this, and will continue to do so, through the medium of his own subculture. The school-man who seeks to remake the young Negro (as a century of pedagogues, from the New England schoolmarm—reformer of the Reconstruction Era to the modern Anglo principal in a ghetto school have tried to do) ignores the realities of American Negro life and, worst of all, treats the rich Afro-American subculture as simply a tragic, but temporary, inconvenience to be gradually eliminated. Ultimately the Negro community as a whole will have more to say about this question than any group of educators, black or white.

NEW RECOGNITIONS OF ALIENATION

For at least a century, Anglo middle-class educators have had their own way: using Negroes, Indians, Mexican-Americans and other racial-cultural minorities as guinea-pigs for "experiments" in monocultural, monolingual, "vacuum ideology" "compensatory" education for as many as five or more generations, with a record that is not one to inspire confidence. What is needed today is not simply more and more of the same in greater doses (that too has already been tried) but a completely different conception of the function of the school and of its relationship to cultural heterogeneity.

Theresa M. Miller, a clinical psychologist, has stated (Saturday Review, Oct. 15, 1966):

It is obvious even to the untrained observer that when large numbers of children reject education and fail to learn the skills necessary for success in a society, there is evidence of maladjustment. There is some question, however, about where to find the primary patient. Is it always the child?

There are many scholars and laymen who would answer in the negative, as did Nathaniel Hickerson (Education for Alienation, Prentice-Hall, 1966):

The inability of affluent-oriented teachers in American society to understand or cope with the behavior of children from economically deprived families is often of paramount importance in alienating those children from the public schools. It is this clash of value commitments that, more than any other factor, drives our Negro, Mexican, Puerto Rican, Indian, and economically deprived Caucasian children out of the school and into the street. . . . They have been attacked at the point of great vulnerability, their own value structure.

Hickerson goes on to describe the process of pupil failure as he sees it. First, non-Anglo children are classified as "slow learners" and assigned to a remedial program.

All that is needed now to complete their isolation from affluent American society is to be driven away from the schools by a frontal attack upon their own systems of self-esteem and their most powerful commitments. . . . Commitment to family is belonging to something. . . . If their customs and habits are challenged by school and teacher, the children are placed in the position of having to choose between the ways of their families and a whole new set of suppositions. . . . Either father, mother, brothers, sisters, uncles, aunts, grandparents, friends, neighbors and their world is right, or the world of school and teacher is right.

The Waxes and Dumont observe that "given the abdication of their elders, and confronting teachers across a gulf of difference in age and culture, the slum [and reservation] pupils organize themselves into a cohesive society" which is anti–school and anti–establishment, particularly in the critical area of language:

The gulf between educators and pupils is deepened by differences in language or dialect of English. The children are subjected to courses designed to teach them a dialect of English that is considered 'correct' by pedagogues, but since few of the latter have any skill in linguistics or have the assistance of . . . electronic equipment . . . the course-work is usually more productive of classroom tension than of learning.

This position would seem to be borne out by a recent study of language in the Pittsburgh slums which revealed that slum children there used 3,200 words, including idioms, not recognized by their teachers or by educational tests. The persistence of these idioms is illustrative of the cultural vitality (and cultural separateness) of the urban poor. As such it offers a challenge to those teachers who can translate the slum language into formal linguistic channels (*Reno Evening Gazette*, Aug. 24, 1966, p. 28). The monocultural Anglo-American school is not merely alien to the cultural realities of many regions and communities, but it may well serve as a major *cause* for tensions which simultaneously thwart the avowed educational goals of the school and produce alumni unfit for participation in *any* culture. The reactions of minority groups to the little Anglo schoolhouse are instructive.

For many years, the typical school was both Anglo-American *and* Protestant. It was therefore rejected by Irish, Italian, and other Roman Catholics in favor of a separate school system, many schools which had (and still have) an Irish, Polish or other ethnic character. Other groups, such as Finns and Swedes, took over the public schools in areas where they were predominant and altered their character somewhat. Oriental and Jewish Americans either set up their own schools or, more commonly, established supplementary schools where Chinese language and culture, Japanese language and culture, or Hebrew language and culture could be made available to the youth of the community. Afro-American, Indian, and Mexican-American groups have sometimes done the same thing, but usually on an informal folk-group or ad hoc basis.

The trend, in other words, is clear. Group after group has been forced to establish its own educational institution—repudiating, in effect, the public schools. The only limitations upon this development have been the particular group's economic and educational ability and, of course, the receptivity of the local public school to multicultural reality. To establish one's own schools demands adequate financing and the availability of suitable teachers, but it also depends upon the existence of demonstrated need. Where the public school comes under the control of a non-Anglo group, or where a spirit of cosmopolitanism develops for one reason or another, the separate supplementary school may be deemed superfluous. In much of the United States, unfortunately, educational cosmopolitanism has never taken root, and separate educational programs flourish.

Rapport or Respect?

It is common nowadays for writers to assert, as Conant has, that

the nature of the community largely determines what goes on in the school. Therefore, to attempt to divorce the school from the community is to engage in unrealistic thinking. . . . The community and the school are inseparable.

Likewise, it is the fashion to stress the establishment of "rapport" between the school and its clients in order to enhance pupil motivation. Frank E.

Karelsen, then vice president of the Public Education Association and a member of the National Advisory Council for the Education of Disadvantaged children, has said this (*The New York Times,* Oct. 17, 1966, p. 34):

The most important element in the education of a child is the rapport between the child and the teacher. The parent-teacher relationship is vital to the development of the rapport. It is imperative to the educative process that parents and schools establish a close and on-going working relationship.

The council of which Karelsen was a member found that the most important single factor which distinguished successful summer "compensatory" programs from those that failed was "the difference in the quality of the relationship—the rapport—between teacher and child" (*The New York Times,* Dec. 1, 1966, p. 38).

But how does one make "inseparable" the non-Anglo community and the Anglo-dominated school? How does one establish "rapport" between students and teachers essentially at war with each other's values? The Waxes and Dumont suggest:

The test of a school is, not what its masters teach, but rather the atmosphere it creates, such that children do learn the significant subject matters from each other . . . one crucial condition for the creation of this educational atmosphere [is] a relationship of mutual respect between teachers and pupils. . . .

Goodwin Watson (in the "Foreword" to Frank Riessman, *The Culturally Deprived Child,* Harper & Row, 1962) agrees that the starting point for improving the teaching of urban slum children is respect. "Nothing else that we have to give will help very much if it is offered with a resentful, contemptuous, or patronizing attitude." The Waxes and Dumont provide a suggestion of how "respect," born of understanding, might help:

If educational specialists were thoroughly familiar with Sioux culture and willing to improvise experimental programs with the children and their parents, they might be able to devise educational materials and techniques that would result in high rates of scholastic achievement. . . . [At present] the educators believe the Sioux children are so lacking in culture that they cannot master scholastic materials, and the children regard the teachers and their subject matters as "White" and hence legitimate targets of their hostility and indifference.

AN EXPANDING VISION

The tide today is beginning to shift away from the whitewashing of cultural differences which prevailed in earlier years, toward a new acceptance and appreciation of cultural diversity in society and in the schools. The change will most certainly not be a painless one, for it requires the conscious rethinking by Anglo-Americans of their relationship to other groups with which they share this continent, a number of them indigenous to it. But the change is coming. It is being articulated in increasingly specific terms—in the demands of concerned non-Anglo parent groups and in statements by groups from the mainstream. One organization to champion multi-culturalism in education in recent years has been the American Anthropological Association, which at its 1966 annual meeting:

disputed the widespread assumption that children from poor neighborhoods have such limited cultural resources that they almost inevitably would achieve low grades in school. Instead, they argued that school should make more vigorous efforts to bring out the rich heritage of folk culture, especially among Negro and Puerto Rican children. This heritage is often hemmed in . . . by classroom conditions that are too impersonal or geared to the standards of children from more affluent homes (*The New York Times,* Nov. 19, 1966, p. 22).

Meanwhile, the Association on American Indian Affairs' education committee has proposed that "far greater emphasis" be placed on Indian values and history in order to give the children pride in their own race. The association's director, William Byler, has also called for "turning control of schools over to the various Indian tribes as long as they meet state and federal educational requirements" (*The New York Times,* Nov. 21, 1966, p. 38).

In a similar vein, others have called for the creation of neighborhood and community associations, *outside* of parent-teacher groups, which would involve parents in school activities.

Meanwhile, some public schools are already striving to establish red "rapport" with parents and pupils by following a multi-cultural program. Public School No. 1 on the border of New York's Chinatown is one such "intercultural" school. "We want to teach our children not to be ashamed of their group's own culture but to be proud of it," asserts Dr. Toby K. Kurzband, the school's principal since 1958. Almost half of the school's population is of Chinese background, about one-third are Puerto Rican, one-fifth are Negro, and one-tenth are Caucasian. A Puerto Rican Week was recently concluded, and similar "celebrations" are planned to stress the cultural values of other ethnic groups. Many of the teachers are of non-Caucasian origin. One of them, Pun-sun Soo, is a "Chinese auxiliary teacher" whose task is to help establish contacts with Chinese parents (*The New York Times,* Dec. 3, 1966, p. 41).

Minority groups themselves have definite ideas about how schools should manage multi-cultural situations. Mrs. Adelina Toledo Defender, a twenty-six year old Jemez Pueblo woman speaks for many Indians when she states (*Indian Voices,* Aug. 1966):

First of all and most important of all is to *understand the cultural background* of our wonderful Indian students. . . . Most teachers may not be aware of it, but most do discriminate against the Indian child. Most feel that here is a hopeless individual; this child action is to advance him onward whether he is capable or not. *This is when discrimina-*cannot be educated. . . . His culture is difficult to understand, so the only beneficial *tion arises because the teacher is trying to see the Indian child in the sense of his own values.*

Mrs. Defender urges, among other things, that

The Indian children should study Indian life pictorially in the first and second grades. Indian legends will create in the fresh minds of our Indian children the beauty of his culture. The fourth up to the ninth grades should have books on Indian history and legends presented to them as a required subject, and as part of their citizenship, in the high school level.

Finally, she argues:

The present system of teaching must not be effective for the results are so apparent. . . . There is much illiteracy on the reservations when there is no need. The difficulty does not lie in the lack of funds, but in the function of the educational system.

Mexican-American leaders, gathering at Occidental College in April of 1963, for a Southwest Conference on Social and Educational Problems of Rural and Urban Mexican-American Youth (Occidental College, April 6, 1963), urged among other things:

1. Bilingual children, or those whose cultural heritage is different from that of the broader community, must have special understanding and specialized course offerings in order that they may have successful learning experiences.
2. The child's home vernacular (Spanish should be considered a linguistic asset and not a 'language handicap.'
3. Schools should teach both English and Spanish in the elementary grades.
4. The school should develop a program to stimulate greater pride and understanding of the cultural heritage of the Mexican-American child.

From San Francisco to New York, Negro parents and community leaders are campaigning for integrated schools wherever feasible and for "quality education" everywhere. The programs being proposed vary from region to region but usually include a demand for coursework in black American and African history, greater use of material illustrating Afro-American life and culture, Negro principals in more schools, and greater participation by the community in overall school planning. In areas such as Harlem, Negro parents have been demanding virtual control of their own schools, in a manner similar to the wishes of many American Indians.

The Challenge of Implementation

Recognition is spreading that, although public education in the United States is theoretically "democratic" and responsive to community needs, in actual fact the Anglo-American controls the schools almost everywhere, either because of numerical superiority in a school district, gerrymandering of seats on the school board, control of the state educational apparatus, or simply because of the power and influence of the Anglo educational establishment. It is difficult to ignore the fact that American Indian children go to schools controlled either by a rigid federal bureaucracy or by local white school boards; that Negroes are either barred from control over their own schools by state action, as in parts of the South, or are a minority in a large metropolitan school district; that Mexican-Americans are in a position similar to the urban Negro, except in rural areas of the Southwest where they are, as of yet, submissive even when in a numerical majority; and that most other minority groups are in equally powerless positions. Most educators are not *obligated* to serve the interests of these groups, with the result that most non-Anglos still have little voice in educational affairs. Former Commissioner of Education James E. Allen, Jr., has frankly asserted that "most state education departments are geared to meet the needs of rural (white) children rather than those of big city slum areas because of the past orientation of state educational and legislative organs (*The New York Times,* Nov. 28, 1966, p. 1).

But the "social dynamite" represented by dissident, undereducated groups is now viewed as a threat to the interests of even the powerful and affluent. Self-interest thus demands that educators seek ways to establish mutual respect and intercultural understanding with minority group children.

As this endeavor proceeds, I would propose that the following set of propositions be used as bases for corrective action:

1. Each school must be responsive to the needs and interests of the community which it serves.
2. All sectors of the community must have a voice in educational planning and policy-making.
3. The school must concentrate upon essential learning, ceasing inadvertent and irrelevant attacks upon the cultural values of minority groups.
4. Freedom, tolerance, and cosmopolitanism must be exhibited by all school personnel as an example for the youth and adults of the community.
5. The cultural assets of the community and the skills of minority group persons must be utilized as positive educational forces by the school (for example, mariachi music taught in the school by local Mexican musicians).
6. The curricula of our schools should vary from region to region in order to reflect the rich diversity of American life.
7. Bilingualism must be regarded not merely as an asset but as a necessity in the twentieth century, and all pupils should be expected to master at least two languages in the elementary grades (Spanish and English in the Southwest and New York City; Chinese or Japanese and English in the San Francisco Bay area, for example).
8. All teachers and administrators must be required to receive training of an anthropological-sociological nature and must be expected to possess or acquire the linguistic skills necessary for communication with local students and their parents.

What would the implementation of these general principles mean in practice? It would mean that Sioux or Navajo children could no longer be "processed" at the whim of federal officials who ignore local community desires, or be "taught" by monolingual English-speaking teachers whose first instinct is to destroy the cultural heritage of native Americans. It would mean that schools serving Mexican-American pupils would have a Mexican flavor and a flourishing bilingual atmosphere. It would mean that black ghetto schools would have an Afro-American dimension, from mosaics on the walls to, very possibly, formal instruction in urban Negro dialect and advanced courses in Swahili, Yoruba, or Arabic. No more identical structures of cement and steel without character, and no more mass production of a single culture and language under the guidance of educators conforming one to another as two peas in a pod! We need to render impossible the kind of situation described by Dianne Gannon (*Liberation,* July 1966):

The Harlem child comes to school and discovers that the school is not about life as he knows it at all. It doesn't have pictures of the kinds of people he knows. It doesn't help him develop the skills he needs for the world in which he lives. . . . The world of school is irrelevant at best. It forces an alien linguistic and learning style on him, and if he cannot make the adjustment of being one person in school and another in Harlem, it abandons him to the street. . . . The school is a harshly foreign institution, and the Harlem child reacts pretty much like the Indian child at the government school, or like a conquered people. School is a waiting game, an endurance contest.

Moshe Smilansky has written (*Saturday Review,* October 15, 1966) that for educational programs aimed at the "culturally deprived" to succeed two conditions are necessary: "The child must have a clear picture of the meaning of the school, and the home must give its support to the school." He adds that, in order for the home to be able to support the school, the school must:

1. accept the home as a home
2. try to understand and support its particular functions
3. not try to change the home or to undermine it
4. seek a union with the home at the point of common concern—the successful progress of the child in school

School personnel in the United States, if they intend to deal successfully with the *education* of the culturally different must abandon their irrelevant attack upon the *culture* of these populations. The function of our public schools should be to help individuals develop their potential for self-realization, not to serve as an instrument for coercive culture change. The educational goal and the culture-change goal ("assimilation") are fundamentally contradictory and antagonistic. To concentrate upon forcing change is, of course, to invite the kind of withdrawal, hostility, and alienation described earlier, and to increase the likelihood that learning of a desirable sort will cease. But the argument for culturally heterogeneous schools is not totally dependent upon pedagogical needs, for any society which values democracy and individual freedom cannot consistently utilize the school as an instrument of enforced culture change. What kind of a democracy would utilize public schools to suppress the heritage of a minority simply because it is a minority (or because it lacks power)? For that matter, what kind of a free society would use the schools as a means to diminish individual freedom and enforce conformity?

A final result of the implementation of programs designed to enhance cultural diversity in the schools—and perhaps the most significant of all—will be the passing of the mass-produced monocultural schools which are damaging not merely to the self-confidence and self-knowledge of students from the various cultural and racial minority groups but to majority group pupils as well. Anglo children are being cheated in our schools when they master (and I mean master) only one language, when they learn about only one side of American history, when they are exposed to only one musical tradition, when they read only one kind of literature, when they experience only one approach to the visual arts, and when they are exposed to a curriculum which has no deep roots in the soil of their region and of America (I refer to roots that go back 20,000 years beyond St. Augustine and Santa Fe, New Orleans and Vincennes). It is not foolish to consider whether every American student should be expected to do what every Navajo child in the elementary grades is expected to do: i.e., master a new language. And why not a second new language in the secondary grades? It is not naive to suggest that pupils in the Southwest should become immersed in the rich Indian-Spanish-Mexican heritage of that region, or that pupils in Louisiana should be given special access to an understanding of the Indian-French-African heritage of that state. The mandate to design education for the culturally different is, then, a mandate to educate *all* pupils in such a way that the school is relevant both to the individual and to the full heritage of the region and the nation. True education is always cross-cultural and always cosmopolitan.

Perhaps we have now arrived at a stage sufficient to allow us to proceed with true education and to dispense with a fixation upon conformity and Anglo-Americanism. If this is the case, it will entail radical innovative measures, experimentation, demonstration, and leadership on the part of educational agencies.

Educational Enlightenment Out of Texas: Toward Bilingualism

Francesco Cordasco

It has long been an ethnocentric illusion in the United States that, for a child born in this country, English is not a foreign language and virtually all instruction in the schools must be through the medium of English. Some of our states (New York included) have mandated this ethnocentrism in a plethora of statutes which expressly forbid instruction in any language but English. Of course this is not difficult to understand. Despite the ideals of a democratic society in which the schools were to serve as a basic vehicle of cohesion, the schools instead became the agencies of social disaffection, cultural assault, and enforced assimilation. How could it have been otherwise, since the schools had to minister to children who brought with them myriad cultures and a multiplicity of tongues? More often than not (almost always in the urban immigrant citadels) the American schools found their children in poverty and neglect. If there is a common denominator which must be sought in the millions of American children who presented themselves to a society's schools, it is poverty. And its ingredients (within the parameters of this poverty) were cultural differences, language handicaps, social alienation, and disaffection. In this sense, the Negro huddled in the urban ghettos, the Puerto Rican poor in search of economic opportunity on the mainland, and the Mexican-American poor, largely an urban minority, are not newcomers to the American schools, nor do they present American educators with new problems. The American poor, traditionally, are the ingredients out of which our social institutions have fashioned the sinews of greatness.

In its efforts to "assimilate" all of its charges, the American schools assimi-

From *Teachers College Record*, May 1970, Vol. 71, No. 4, pp. 608–612. Reprinted by permission of the author and *Teachers College Record*.

lated (and in consequence very often destroyed) the cultural identity of the child; it forced him to leave his ancestral language at the schoolhouse door; it developed in the child a haunting ambivalence of language, of culture, of ethnicity, and of self-affirmation. It held up to its children mirrors in which they saw not themselves, but the stereotyped middle-class, white, English-speaking child who embodied the essences of what the American child was (or ought) to be. For the minority child, the images which the school fashioned were cruel deceptions. In the enforced acculturation there were bitterness and confusion; but tragically, too, there was the rejection of the well-springs of identity, and more often than not, the failure of achievement. The ghettoization of the European immigrant is, in substance, exactly analogous to the ghettoization of the Negro, Puetro Rican, and Mexican-American poor. Louis Wirth, a long time ago, called attention to the vitality of the ghetto in its maintenance of the life-styles, languages, and cultures of a minority people assaulted by the main institutions of a dominant society.

When the Congress discovered poverty in the enactment of the Economic Opportunity Act of 1964, and fashioned the cornucopia out of which the schools have plunked endless "goodies," the schools largely fashioned programs born out of this new federal largesse which reflected their continuing pursuit of the stereotyped middle-class, white, English-speaking child in whose image all of our children were to be cast. And so Head Start taught its children middle-class table manners; the Neighborhood Youth Corps took its social adventurers to museums and opera houses whenever they could be found; Upward Bound, too, became preoccupied with the cultural refurbishing of its charges and took for granted miraculous cognitive blossoming; and Title I Programs of the Elementary and Secondary Education Act did a whole host of things which were designed to elevate "culturally deprived" children to levels of middle-class conformism, de rigueur.

THE NON-ENGLISH SPEAKING CHILD

Those of us who have been concerned with Puerto Rican children in our major cities have for some time struggled with what was actually a very old problem. If all children presented themselves to the American schools with many differences, how graphic was the immediate difference epitomized in the non-English speaking child. The history of the American school has not been the evangelical triumph which the New England sage and historian Ellwood Cubberley sketched in such bold relief; rather, the non-English speaking child (almost inevitably in a context of poverty) was the easy victim of cultural assault, and his ancestral language was at once a target against which the school mounted relentless resources.

Against this tragic background and quixotic effort, largely unnoticed, has been a "sleeper" amendment to the Elementary and Secondary Education Act which in essence would propose that we wash away the haunting ghosts of ethnocentrism and cultural affectation, and turn to the meaningful cultivation of individual differences which better reflect the pluralistic base out of which the children of an open society truly come.

THE SLEEPER AMENDMENT

The history of this "sleeper" amendment is a good illustration of what Kenneth Clark has characterized as "the dilemmas of power." Where would one have sought the power in the Congress to recognize the particular needs of Puerto Rican children, if previous Congresses had chosen largely to ignore those millions of children who were non-English speaking who had passed through the portals of the school? The tactic here was obviously to relate the Puerto Rican child to the needs of another group long indigenous in our society but equally long disenfranchised, and for whom English was not the native language. In the five state area of the Southwest (Texas, New Mexico, Colorado, Arizona and California) there are at least 1.75 million school children with Spanish surnames, whose linguistic, cultural and psychological handicaps cause them to experience, in general, academic failure in our schools, or at best limit them to only mediocre success. The Mexican-American child classically demonstrated that an almost inevitable concomitant of poverty was low educational achievement. Thus, it was out of unlikely Texas that an extraordinary amendment to the ESEA was proposed: an unlikely provenance, since one would have expected that the provisions of this liberal and enlightened amendment would have been born in the great egalitarian citadels of the North.

On January 17, 1967, Ralph Yarborough (D.-Texas) introduced in the Senate of the United States S.428, which proposed "To amend the Elementary and Secondary Education Act of 1965 to provide assistance to local educational agencies in establishing bilingual American education programs and to provide certain other assistance to promote such programs." At long last the Congress had before it legislation which would legitimatize the cultivation of individual differences in our schools. Understandably, Senator Yarborough was concerned with the problems of his Mexican-American constituents, but his bill explicitly noted that: "For the purpose of this Title, Spanish-speaking elementary and secondary students means elementary and secondary school students born in, or one or both of whose parents were born in, Mexico or Puerto Rico, and, in states for which such information is available, other students with Spanish surnames." The very proposal of the bill was tantamount to the recognition that Mexican-American children had been neglected by American schools. But Senator Yarborough's legislation went far beyond this elemental recognition. It proposed (1) bilingual educational programs; (2) the teaching of Spanish as the native language; (3) the teaching of English as a second language; (4) programs designed to impart to Spanish-speaking students a knowledge of and pride in their ancestral culture and language; (5) efforts to attract and retain as teachers promising individuals of Mexican or Puerto Rican descent; and (6) efforts to establish closer cooperation between the school and the home. What extraordinary proposals! Those millions of children who had been denied what a mature society was now proposing might well have served as a Greek chorus intoning social amens.

As was to be expected, Senator Yarborough's bill (which had as co-sponsors both Mr. Javits and Mr. Kennedy of New York) created a flurry of activity in the House (though largely unnoticed outside the Congress) and a veritable spate of companion House bills were proposed, chief amongst which was H.R. 9840 mounted by James H. Scheuer (D.-New York). Congressman Scheuer would have everything that Senator Yarborough had proposed, but he chose not to accept the Yarborough bill's limitation of its provisions to Spanish-speaking students. For Congressman Scheuer the school would respond in much the fashion that Yarborough proposed, no matter what the student's native language might be, and Congressman Scheuer simply chose to increase five-fold the allocations which Senator Yarborough had proposed ($25,000,000 as against $5,000,000 for fiscal 1967–68), and further to allow participation by full-time nonpublic school students (children in parish schools).

TOWARDS BILINGUALISM

There are of course some objections which have been raised against the legislation. Some linguists have objected to the pegging of the bill to the poverty context, and have been adamant in proposing that the bill be unrestricted in its provisions and allow the cultivation of a vast bilingual resource. But this is truly another problem. What the legislation has really proposed (no matter how awkwardly, and with full cognizance of all the programming intricacies which will have to be worked out) is that the social institution which is the school and which serves the children of an open society must build on the cultural strengths which the child brings to the classroom: to cultivate in this child ancestral pride; to reinforce (not destroy) the language he natively speaks, to cultivate his inherent strengths; and to give this child the sense of personal identification so essential to his social maturation. We can only lament the lost opportunities of other eras. The legislation proposes that there is no excuse for failure at this juncture in our society. Senator Yarborough's "sleeper" legislation will have thrust greatness upon him, and Texas will have become in educational history as illustrious as Massachusetts. In August, 1967, his Senate Bill 428 was unanimously reported out of the Senate Sub-Committee on Education, and in the closing sessions of the 90th Congress became law. In the long interim which followed, a reluctant Congress finally authorized $7.5 million for fiscal 1969.

Secretary of Health, Education, and Welfare Robert H. Finch said on February

12, 1969, that he considered prompt, massive upgrading of bilingual education one of the major imperatives confronting HEW. He announced at the same time that he was establishing a new post, Special Assistant to the Commissioner of Education for Bilingual Education, as a first step in meeting this challenge. Proposals requesting some $47 million were received prior to the December 20, 1968, deadline from local agencies in 40 states, the District of Columbia, and Puerto Rico. Following review of the proposals by a panel of outside experts, selected applicants were asked by the Office of Education to submit formal proposals by May 5, 1969, for final evaluation. From a $7.5 million budget for the program for fiscal 1969, direct grants are to be made to those agencies that propose programs and activities which present innovative solutions to bilingual education problems. Projects must focus on schools that have a high concentration of children of limited English-speaking ability and who come from families earning less than $3,000 per year. Emphasis may be on planning and developing research projects; conducting pilot projects to test the effectiveness of plans; developing special instructional materials; and providing training for teachers, teacher aides, and counselors. Bilingual educational activities may be designed to impart to students a knowledge of the history and culture related to their languages; establish closer cooperation between the school and the home; and provide preschool and adult educational programs related to bilingual education.

Seventy-seven public school agencies in 27 states have been invited by the U.S. Office of Education to prepare formal proposals for grants under the authority of the $7.5 million Bilingual Education Program, Title VII of the Elementary and Secondary Education Act, as amended. These education agencies were selected from 312 which submitted preliminary proposals to the U.S. Office of Education by the December 20, 1968, deadline. Approved projects will be operating during the 1969–70 school year.

1 THE BLACK HERITAGE

Despite the judicial decisions and legislative enactments of the last two decades, the integrating of black people into American life is far, far, from complete. If anything, the extent of the separation of the races seems wider now to many than at the time of the 1954 Supreme Court decision on school desegregation. As a result, Afro-Americans are becoming leaders among all other minority populations in militancy and agitation for change. The schools are one of the main items on their agenda, yet many teachers today are still largely unaware of ways in which the black American and his family are isolated and victimized.

It is indisputable that numerous failures of our present educational system are deeply rooted in the racist character of our country. Through the centuries-old glorification of the white race, Western culture, America's "manifest destiny," and the corresponding denial of the historical and cultural existence of other people, American education has deprived many of dignity and of self-knowledge. If this trend is to be reversed, it will be because American education reaffirms its commitment to foster socially responsible individuals conscious of their obligation to create an environment in which all people can live and interact with one another. With black leaders who had largely been subdued prior to this past decade now asserting a new sense of pride, self-reliance, and impatience, teachers must address themselves directly to this problem.

One means of developing new understandings is the teaching of Afro-American studies, currently the fastest-growing new academic area in U.S. colleges and schools. Prodded by militant black student groups, concerned white students, and/or faculty consciences, many of the nations' two-year and four-year colleges, secondary schools, and elementary schools are rushing to add courses and units in black history, literature, anthropology, psychology, music, and art. As an academic discipline, black culture is so new that there are inevitable disagreements over what should be taught and who should teach it, with many insisting that only a black can fully appreciate and convey the depths of black culture. Any series of articles on the Afro-American should have as its primary purpose to foster understanding and appreciation, clear up misconceptions, and tell it like it is. This section tries to do just that. We begin by asking the teacher to undergo a black culture test in order to demonstrate that many educators don't know literally the first thing about blacks in America.

The first full-scale article in this section then reaches back to trace the introduction of Afro-Americans to this hemisphere. From this overview we move to a black sociologist's analysis of the present-day black community. Edwards paints a scholarly, accurate picture of a situation which is actually deteriorating, of blacks caught in a situation from which they seem unable to escape.

Is desegregation the answer? Fischer's article, "Race and Reconciliation: The Role of the School," examines complexities of desegregation, especially the question of whether it leads to better learning. If desegregation is an answer (and we are convinced it is), it will depend heavily upon community economics, teacher preparation, and the kinds of appropriate curriculum and instructional materials, techniques, and tools available. "How to Integrate Your District's Curriculum" touches on this problem and points out the bias in many of today's school textbooks. Adding this bias to community and teacher bias, one begins to sense the multiple dimensions of the desegregation issue.

James Baldwin's "A Talk to Teachers" is a classic. First published in 1963, it has been widely reprinted and quoted, for Baldwin was the first black to tell teachers on a national scale of the tremendous injustice and hate rampant among young blacks. As a poignant footnote to Baldwin's generalization we offer Durslag's graphic piece on the indignation suffered by American baseball heroes who happened to be black.

Specific ways in which students, parents, and teachers can transform the schools into centers for the rejuvenation of the community are offered in Forbes' second article in this section: "Working with the Afro-American Pupil."

The next-to-last article by Holly, "Black Is Not a Color of the Skin, It Is a State of Mind" contains an important warning against easy generalizations by whites about the black experience—even in their eagerness to undo old wrongs. Faith Berry's concluding article, "On Understanding Black Militancy," brings this Part round to the present day phenomenon of revolutionary action on the part of the black movement in the United States, which has moved from a struggle for rights to a struggle for power, from hope for reform to realization of a necessity for a revolution having as its purpose certain fundamental changes in the social, economic, and political institutions of America. As a corollary to our hypothesis that Afro-Americans will lead other groups in the struggle for equality, we therefore advance the suggestion that teachers and teachers-to-be must come to grips with what it means to be black in America today and with the strength and purposefulness of the black revolutionary movement. We offer the hypothesis that Afro-Americans will lead the rest of the groups in our search for equality—educational, cultural, economic, social.

What Is Your Black Culture Quotient?

Taking this test should give you some idea of how much or little you know about Afro-American history and culture.

1. According to recent[1] national surveys, the designation acceptable to the majority of people of African ancestry in America is:
   a. Black
   b. Afro-American
   c. Negro
   d. Afram
   e. Colored

2. The *currently* accepted symbol of status in the black community is ownership of:
   a. A Honda
   b. An English racer
   c. A "Hog"
   d. A Deuce-and-a-Quarter

3. *Soul on Ice* is about the life of:
   a. "Rap" Brown
   b. Stokely Carmichael
   c. Malcolm X
   d. Eldridge Cleaver
   e. Martin Luther King, Jr.

4. A soul-food dinner would most likely include all but one of the following:
   a. Collard greens

From *Today's Education*, February 1970, Vol. 59, No. 2, p. 27. Reprinted by permission of the National Education Association.
   [1]1910.

b. Candied sweet potatoes
c. Corn bread
d. Chitterlings
e. Green peas and carrots

5. The term "the man" has frequently been used by black people to refer to:
   a. Any member of the white establishment
   b. Local authority
   c. Any white man
   d. The police
   e. All the above

6. Negroes fought in which of the following wars:
   a. The French and Indian War
   b. The American Revolutionary War
   c. The Civil War
   d. The War of 1812
   e. All of these
   f. None of these

7. The man who by his pronouncements and influence on education and race relations provoked much controversy among black people in the United States during the late nineteenth century was:
   a. Ralph Bunche
   b. Booker T. Washington
   c. Benjamin Banneker
   d. George Washington Carver

8. "Playing the dozens" involves:
   a. Shooting marbles
   b. Throwing dice
   c. Exchanging nasty remarks with referrals to maternal parentage
   d. Harassing the police

9. The people of African ancestry who were brought to America in 1619 served as:
   a. Workers with the Spanish explorers
   b. Indentured servants
   c. Slaves
   d. Traders

10. Translate the following paragraph: Man, I just seen Joe, talk about rigid. Somebody eased into his crib and swung with his vee, all his vines, his sides, even snatched some old roaches he was saving for hard times.

Answers—1.(b) 2.(d—means a 225 Buick) 3.(d) 4.(e) 5.(e) 6.(e) 7.(b) 8.(c) 9.(c) 10. Man, I just saw Joseph, and he was angry! Somebody broke into his apartment and stole his television, all his clothes, his records, and even some old marijuana butts he was saving for hard times.

Who Are the Afro-Americans?

Jack D. Forbes

THE SIGNIFICANCE OF THE AFRO-AMERICAN PEOPLE

Americans of African descent, or Afro-Americans, comprise one of the most significant groups of people to be found in the Americas. Perhaps one hundred million strong, Afro-Americans dominate the population of most of the Caribbean republics and constitute a sizeable proportion of the citizenry of Brazil, Surinam, Guyana, Venezuela, Colombia, Panama, and the United States. Significant strains of African ancestry are also to be found among the people of Argentina, Peru, Ecuador, Costa Rica, Guatemala, Mexico, and elsewhere, but in these countries the African component is often already absorbed or is rapidly disappearing into the general population.

The Afro-American people, considered in the larger dimension, do not comprise a single "ethnic" group. People of part-African descent, often with American Indian and European as well as occasional Asiatic ancestors, are ordinarily to be classified with the national population of the country in which they reside. Thus, a part-African Brazilian is in no sense ethnically Afro-American (and still less, "Negro") but rather is simply a Brazilian. The same is usually also true for persons who are of predominantly African ancestry. A dark-skinned Cuban with "Negroid" characteristics is simply a Cuban who happens to be Negro (i.e., black).[1]

In discussing Afro-Americans, then, we are making reference to a large mass of people who have only one thing in common—the possession of some degree

---

From *Afro-Americans In the Far West: A Handbook for Educators,* Berkeley, California: Far West Laboratory for Educational Research and Development, 1968, pp. 1–7. Reprinted by permission.
[1]The word *negro* means black in the Spanish language.

29

of African ancestry. Most such people are simply to be identified as Venezuelans, Puerto Ricans, Dominicans, or Colombians, and have so thoroughly mixed with Indians and Europeans as to have lost any black identity. Others, while still remaining "Negroid" in physical appearance, have also become part of a national culture and are now also simply Haitians, Jamaicans, Panamanians, or Cubans.

The cultural legacy from Africa, rich as it is in the region from Haiti to Brazil, does not always provide any kind of Afro-American identity. All of the national cultures in the region have become Africanized to such an extent that all citizens, whether of African descent or not, share an African cultural legacy. For example, there is no Afro-Brazilian culture which belongs exclusively to Brazilians of African descent. All Brazilians live a way of life which is a complex mixture of African, American Indian, and European traits, and one which varies primarily from region to region or class to class rather than from racial strain to racial strain.

The United States would seem, at first glance, to present an exception to the above generalizations. It is true that in an "official" sense the United States is composed of people who are "Negroes" and people who are "whites" and often the dividing line is made to seem rather sharp. In the United States, an "American Negro" identity has developed and, to some degree, at least there also exists a "Negro subculture" or "black culture" which is not shared by the balance of the population. On the other hand, the situation in the United States is not altogether distinct, since millions of United States citizens of part-African ancestry are currently classified not as "Negroes" but as Puerto Ricans, Mexican-Americans, American Indians, Cubans, Louisiana Creoles, or simply as "whites."

Likewise, the African cultural heritage of the United States, from yams and coffee to jazz and calypso, is shared by all citizens and not merely by persons of African descent.

The significance of the Afro-American people is, then, a much larger subject than would be the significance of the "American Negro." A new race is being created throughout the Americas, a race which is amalgamating African, European, and American Indian strains, as well as Asiatic elements in certain regions. This new "cosmic" or "universal" race will vary in the relative proportions of African, Indian, and European background but in the region from Brazil through much of the United States and all around the Caribbean the African element will be of great significance.

In a similar manner, the cultures of the Americas are becoming composites of traits derived from Africa and other portions of the world. The African impact upon Europe has always been considerable, from at least the beginnings of civilization in ancient Egypt to the legacy of the Muslim civilizations and the impact of non-Muslim black Africa, and thus the culture brought by Europeans to the "New World" (especially by the Portuguese and Spaniards) was already part-African. In the course of the last five centuries this European-Middle Eastern-African legacy has been still further enriched by cultural elements introduced by black Africans and by their Afro-American descendents.

Throughout the Americas then, regional-national cultures are developing which are unique composites of world-wide legacies. From Brazil to the United States the African component in these composites looms very large indeed.

But the significance of the Afro-American people cannot be summarized solely by reference to racial and cultural contributions. For five centuries Americans of African descent have labored alongside their fellow Americans to produce the modern civilizations of this hemisphere. Serving as explorers, sailors, unpaid slaves, soldiers, artisans, architects, statesmen, revolutionaries, diplomats, musicians, poets, novelists, and in a multitude of other capacities, Americans of African descent have made major contributions whether functioning within the framework of an Afro-American cultural legacy or within the context of the larger national cultures.

In the United States, for instance, it can be conservatively asserted that the wealth of the southern states, and most of the architectural, literary, and artistic accomplishments springing therefrom were built up through the efforts of black labor, free or slave. Without the Negro slave and the free Negro artisan there never would have been any "aristocratic" culture in the Old South and no "country gentlemen" of the type of Thomas Jefferson and George Washington. Similarly, modern Southern economic development and wealthy-class "leisure" society rests upon a base of low-wage labor, principally Negro. When one considers that the Negro (and Indian) slaves were never paid over a period of three centuries and that since the Civil War Negro laborers have been largely underpaid, it becomes quite obvious that the *financial* debt which the white Southerner owes to the Negro (and Indian) is large indeed.

But the Afro-American's contribution in terms of labor was never confined to the South. New York and Rhode Island, among other northern colonies, always had large numbers of slaves and underpaid free persons of color. As in the South, the financial debt due these people for centuries of toil looms very large.

Elsewhere, Afro-Americans played crucial roles in the development of Spanish Florida, French and Spanish Louisiana, Spanish-Mexican Texas, and the balance of the West. Without the participation of people of color, whether slave or free, French-Spanish Louisiana and Spanish Florida would doubtless have never existed or, at the very least, would have remained extremely underdeveloped. Especially by the late seventeenth century, and all through the eighteenth century, Spanish soldiers of "mulatto" or other mixed-blood racial character were absolutely essential to the defense of the territory from Florida (where they fought against the English and Scots of South Carolina) to California (where they helped to control the Indian population).

In summary, the Afro-American legacy of the United States and of the balance of the Americas is of profound significance and has become, in great part, the collective legacy of all Americans. We may not all be part-African in terms of ancestry, but we are all participants in a part-African historical and cultural heritage.

Afro-American Population Statistics

The following figures are for 1940[2] and indicate only persons of recognizable African ancestry, i.e., those counted as "Negroes" or "mulattos" in national censuses. Millions of part-Africans (such as many Puerto Ricans) are not included.

	NEGROES	MULATTOS	PERCENTAGE OF TOTAL POPULATION
United States	13,500,000	(included in Negroes)	12%
Caribbean Islands	5,500,000	3,000,000	61%
Belice (British Honduras)	15,000	20,000	60%
Panama	83,000	271,000	56%
Colombia	405,000	2,205,000	29%
Venezuela	100,000	1,000,000	31%
Guyana	100,000	80,000	53%
Surinam	17,000	20,000	21%
Brazil	5,800,000	8,280,000	34%
Balance of Americas	330,000	414,000	—
Totals	25,850,000	15,290,000	—
Total Afro-Americans	41,140,000	—	15%

The above totals relate to a population estimate for the Americas of 275,000,000. Current estimates for the latter are in excess of 400,000,000. Thus one should multiply the figures in the list by one-third to obtain minimum approximations for the 1960's. This calculation would yield a total of 55,000,000 persons of African ancestry, an extremely conservative estimate since: (a) The Afro-American population tends to increase at a faster-than-average rate; (b) Light-skinned persons of part-African ancestry are largely excluded from these totals; and (c) American Indian and mestizo (Indian-white) groups with some degree of African ancestry are not included at all.

WE ARE ALL AFRICANS

The cumulative evidence of archaeology is indicating more and more that the human species first appeared in Africa. In that sense, as well as in a cultural sense, we are indeed all of African origin.

It is also important to state that we are all humans and that there is only one race—the human race or *homo sapiens*. There are indeed no such entities as the Mongoloid, Negroid, Caucasoid, Australoid, Americanoid, or Veddoid "races," and this is perhaps the first thing that a student of the Afro-American needs to learn.

Laymen and, later, scholars developed the concept of three or more major human "stocks" or "races" in order to be able to supply some degree of order to their early efforts to understand the complexity of human differences. But these concepts are *only* useful as very crude tools for initial comprehension. Why?

The idea of there being several major human stocks was developed prior to

[2]*Editors' note:* the last hemisphere report available when this essay went to press.

extensive, scientific observation of human types and resulted primarily from the uncritical reports of travelers, soldiers, and missionaries. Unfortunately, when scholars began to scientifically analyze physical characteristics they at first sought to force their empirical data into the mold created by laymen. Now, when most anthropologists and biologists would dispense with, or radically alter, the idea of "races" they face the difficulty of re-educating millions of laymen who have been taught the old concepts.

To understand the complexity of human types one must always begin with the individual tribe or ethnic group (i.e., a "people"). Generally speaking, each people, such as the Tuareg, Hausa, Yoruba, Masai, or Kikuyu, is a unique group with a unique cluster of physical characteristics. This does not mean that all of the individuals in the group will identically resemble one another but it does mean that there will tend to be a predominant "type" which serves to differentiate, say, the Zuni from the Navajo.

To begin with, then, we must speak of people as being Hopi or Papago instead of American Indian, Yoruba or Ashanti instead of African Negro, and Greek or German instead of Caucasoid. But we can usually also discover that the members of a given tribe or people have not married exclusively from within their own group. That is, they have constantly "exchanged" genes with outsiders, usually neighbors. From this circumstance we tend to find that neighboring peoples often resemble each other, except where recent migrations have introduced dissimilarities.

Ignoring, however, the recent migrations of the last few centuries, it is generally true that *one finds a gradual change as one moves from one people to another.* Thus, as one moves from north China and Mongolia westward to eastern and northern Europe one discovers a gradual change from "Mongoloid" types to "Caucasoid" types. There is essentially no place where one can say that one has passed from "Mongoloid" groups to "Caucasoid" groups, except where movement has been recent (i.e., within the last few hundred years). Whether one considers straight "black" hair, the elliptical eye-fold, the so-called "Mongoloid spot," high cheek bones, or blood types, one discovers that the progression is gradual and that the individual traits in question have an irregular distribution. Thus straight "black" (brunette) hair is very common throughout western Europe while the elliptical eye-fold is not. What this probably means is that the latter is of much more recent appearance in human history and that, therefore, the cluster of traits associated with "Mongoloid-ness" did not all evolve at the same date and probably not in the same area.

What exists in actuality is a "genetic pool" including genes favoring the development of the elliptical eye-fold in east Asia, other "genetic pools" including genes favoring the development of straight brunette hair in all of Eurasia, parts of Africa, parts of Oceania, and in the Americas, many "genetic pools" including genes favoring the development of brown or light brown skin color throughout almost all of Asia, the Americas, much of Oceania, parts of Europe and Africa, and so on with other characteristics.

The same generalizations can be made about the relationships existing between "Negroids" and "Caucasoids." It is true, of course, that if we place a Swede and a Yoruba side by side we will note some marked differences in outward physical characteristics. But if we proceed northward gradually, from Nigeria to Sweden via the Sudan, the Sahara, North Africa, Spain, France, the Netherlands, and Denmark what will we find? That by and large each tribe or people blends in with the next so that the progression is an almost imperceptible, gradual one.

In short, there is no Negroid race distinct from the Caucasoid race or the Mongoloid race, et cetera. We must talk in terms of specific peoples, for example, the Yoruba, and an extremely complex system of genetic relationships beyond that level.

But then is there no meaning to the term "African Negroid?" Yes, there is meaning if we realize that what we are talking about is a large number of tribal peoples, from Senegal to Angola (large along the coast) who possess certain similarities among themselves but who possess these similarities *not because they are a separate race* but because: (a) they have exchanged genes more often with each other than with outsiders, and (b) their predominant type tends to possess a unique cluster of non-unique genes.

For instance those characteristics which are commonly thought to comprise "Negroid-ness," such as dark brown or near-black skin, short tightly-curled hair, flared nostrils, and prominent lips are in no sense "Negroid" traits, considered individually. Each one of these characteristics has a wide, irregular dispersal in areas beyond West Africa and, to a lesser degree, in southeast Asia-Oceania. (This is true, of course, only prior to modern migrations).

But not all of the individuals of West Africa possess the above characteristics. West African "Negroids" may be found with aquiline noses, lighter skin, et cetera, thus illustrating that we are speaking only of a "predominant type" or "predominant genetic tendency" and not of a "race."

We must also bear in mind that most of the people of South Africa, East Africa, and Central-North Africa do not exhibit the "Negroid" cluster of traits but rather are intermediate between the "Negroid" and Mediterranean-Middle Eastern "Caucasoid" types, except in southwest Africa where certain unique and "Mongoloid" type features are found.

The complexity of human relationships has been greatly increased by modern migrations. Isolation was probably a major element in the former development of unique genes, but now isolation is largely being replaced by constant movement of peoples and this increases the importance of a second element in genetic transformation, that of intermarriage. Many new physical types have undoubtedly developed in the past as a result of the coming together of previously isolated peoples, but that process is currently especially significant (as in Latin America, Hawaii, the South Pacific and elsewhere, where new hybrid "races" are now coming into existence).

The process of intermarriage is, of course, a very ancient phenomenon and suggests another sense in which "we are all Africans." From documentary evidence it is known that significant numbers of Africans of "Negroid" and partially "Negroid" character have often been present in North Africa, the Middle East and Mediterranean Europe. The Egyptian people have had a noticeable "Negroid" strain since very ancient times and black Africans have also been present in considerable numbers in Europe itself. Ancient Greece and the Roman Empire absorbed many people of "Negroid" ancestry and Roman troops of African origin were stationed as far north as the British Isles. Other Africans moved about much of southern Europe as part of invading Muslim armies at a later date. From these and other sources it would appear likely that small amounts of African ancestry are the common possession of large numbers of modern-day Europeans, albeit having little or no effect upon outward physical characteristics.

Community and Class Realities: The Ordeal of Change

G. Franklin Edwards

One of the paradoxes of American life is that though the Negro is an old-line American he is not yet fully American. His presence in this country antedates that of most immigrant groups, but his career and community life are greatly different from those of immigrants from northern and southern Europe. In terms of the basic socialization processes and the community contexts in which they occur, differences between the Negro and these immigrant groups, including the most recent large-scale arrivals, the Puerto Ricans, are apparent.

Immigrant groups from Europe have followed a somewhat typical process as they moved into the main stream of American life. Most members of these groups entered the work force at the bottom of the economic ladder, as small farmers and as unskilled, semiskilled, and service workers. They lived initially among fellow immigrants in small village communities or in poorer city neighborhoods in which communal institutions helped cushion the cultural shock induced by the differences between life in their countries of origin and life in the United States. Family, church, the foreign language press, and mutual aid organizations helped in the adjustment process. Members of the second and succeeding generations acquired increasing amounts of education and the skills necessary to take advantage of available opportunities; eventually the Americanization process was fairly complete. By and large, members of these groups have assimilated American values and today experience little physical and cultural isolation based upon ethnicity. Although individual members of these groups continue to experience discrimination in the areas of admission to educational institutions, job promotions in industry, and acceptance into voluntary associations, a consciousness of group rejection does not exist. In those instances

From *Daedalus*, Winter 1966, Vol. 95, No. 1, pp. 1–21. Reprinted by permission.

where strong in-group community life exists, it is owing more to the persistence of group cohesion than to restraints from without.

In contrast to the pattern of immigrant groups, the Negro has remained socially and morally isolated from the American society. At no time in the almost three and a half centuries of his history in this country has he been "counted in." His caste-like position is owing more to restraints from without than to any centripetal force serving to keep him separated from other groups. He has lived, according to E. Franklin Frazier's characterization, as "a nation within a nation."[1] Robin Williams recently has referred to the general Negro community as "a world in the shadow,"[2] and James Silver, in describing an extreme instance of a local community's exclusion of Negroes, has referred to the "closed society."[3]

One basic difference between the Negro and these immigrant groups is that the former served for nearly two centuries as slaves. Although succeeding generations of Negroes acquired increased amounts of education after the Emancipation, access to opportunities commensurate with formal training often was denied because of color. The failure to learn certain basic skills to qualify for jobs in the world of work placed serious limitations upon the horizontal and social mobility experienced by members of the group. As a matter of fact, the social mobility of Negroes up to the present has been determined more by conditions within the Negro community than by those of the broader society. The number and distribution of Negroes within the professions, for example, have been related more directly to the needs of the Negro community for certain types of services than to the demands of the broader society.[4] It is for this reason that clergymen and teachers, functionaries required by the segregated Negro community, have represented at least one-half of all Negro professional persons at any given period.

The segregation of Negroes from the main stream of American life has produced institutional patterns and behavior which have a bearing upon contemporary efforts to eliminate inequalities between the two major racial groups. The behaviors are expressed as deviations of Negroes from many normative patterns of American life and suggest something of the magnitude of the differentials which must be dealt with if reconciliation, rather than further alienation, is to be achieved.

The contrasts in background experiences between the Negro and immigrant groups raise the fundamental question of whether, given the promise of recent changes, the Negro will now be integrated into American society in much the same manner as have these other groups. Any strict analogy between the future course of the Negro's relationship to American society and the processes which occurred in the experiences of immigrant groups, however, is subject to serious limitations and error.

[1]E. Franklin Frazier, *Black Bourgeoisie* (New York, 1957), p. 15.
[2]Robin M. Williams, Jr., *Strangers Next Door* (New York, 1964), p. 252.
[3]James W. Silver, *Mississippi: The Closed Society* (New York, 1963), p. 164.
[4]G. Franklin Edwards, *The Negro Professional Class* (Chicago, 1959), pp. 23–26.

The long history of oppression has profoundly affected the Negro's self-esteem. The fears, suspicions and feelings of inadequacy generated in the Negro by his subordinate status are not duplicated in the experiences of immigrant groups. Moreover, color and other physical traits distinguish the Negro sharply from other groups in the society. In the past, these characteristics were taken as physical stigmata which reinforced negative attitudes toward the Negro. Sharp physical differences were not present to complicate the relationships of immigrants to American society, although differences in this regard can be observed between the northern Europeans, on the one hand, and southern Europeans and Orientals, on the other.

The attitudes of the Negro toward himself are merely reciprocals of the attitudes of other groups toward him. There always have been serious reservations on the part of American whites regarding the Negro's capacity to live on a basis of equality with other Americans. Such reservations about the potentialities of immigrant groups for assimilation were not held in the same serious way.

Finally, it should be observed that significant advancement in the status of the Negro comes at a time when economic conditions are quite different from those faced by immigrant groups. The great influx of immigrants came at a time when there was a market for agricultural labor and unskilled work and mobility through these avenues was still possible. The Negro today has been displaced from the farm and must now compete for work in an urban market which requires a somewhat higher degree of education and technical skill than was the case a half century ago. Given the present educational and occupational inadequacies of a large segment of the Negro population, the task of overcoming these deficiencies is formidable.

While it is clear that further changes in the status of the Negro will occur in years ahead, moving the Negro nearer to equality with other Americans, the processes by which this will be achieved are certain to be difficult and tortuous. The remainder of this essay is an elaboration of this viewpoint.

Foremost among the indicators of the social isolation of Negroes is the Negro ghetto. It represents at once the restrictions placed upon the living space of the Negro minority and, as Kenneth Clark recently has pointed out, a way of life with a peculiar institutional patterning and psychological consequences.[5] Unlike most immigrant ghettos, which show a tendency to break up, the Negro ghetto, especially in Northern cities, has become more dense.

Karl Taeuber and Alma Taeuber, on the basis of an examination of segregation indices in 109 American cities from 1940 to 1960, note that in 83 of the 109 cities the segregation index was higher in 1950 than in 1940. Between 1950 and 1960, only 45 of these cities showed an increase. But it was observed that cities with already high levels of segregation were prominent among those with in-

[5]Kenneth Clark, *Dark Ghetto* (New York, 1965), pp. 63–80.

creases. A most significant observation is that in recent years Southern cities have had the highest increases in the physical segregation of Negroes, and the South now has the highest index of any region.[6] This is important inasmuch as in earlier periods Negroes were less segregated in the older Southern cities than in cities located in other regions.[7]

The concentration of Negroes in the central cities of our metropolitan areas and within the inlying cores of these central cities is too well documented to warrant elaboration here. Our concern is with the fact that the areas inhabited by Negroes are inferior in terms of housing quality, recreational facilities, schools, and general welfare services, and that all of these deficiencies contribute to crime, delinquency, school dropouts, dependency, broken families, excessive deaths, and other conditions which represent the "pathology of the ghetto." The pathology is most evident in housing. In 1960, for example, 44 percent of all dwelling units occupied by Negroes were substandard. Though nonwhites occupied only 10 percent of all dwelling units, they occupied 27 percent of those classed as substandard. Thirteen percent of nonwhites lived in units which were seriously overcrowded, and there was an increase of 85,000 such units occupied by Negroes between 1950 and 1960.[8]

Efforts to break up the ghetto, and hence to ameliorate the pathological conditions generated by it, have not been productive. Attempts by Negroes to leave the ghetto run afoul of a most formidable network of relationships involving brokers, builders, bankers, realtors, and citizens' organizations serving to restrict Negroes to certain neighborhoods.[9] There is, indeed, a vast profit to be made from slum housing, and this accounts for much of the behavior of some realtors. One study demonstrates that a slum landlord receives fifteen dollars more monthly if a substandard unit is rented to a Negro family than if the same unit were rented to a white family.[10] Myths regarding neighborhood deterioration following Negro occupancy persist, despite empirical studies which expose their fallacious character.

By and large, our urban renewal programs, designed to revitalize the older, more dilapidated areas of our cities, have not succeeded in providing better accommodations in the renewal areas for most Negroes, the majority of the displacees. They have succeeded very largely in having Negroes move into public housing and blighted areas. While in many instances the physical accommodations to which displaced populations moved represent an improvement over their former dwellings,[11] segregation has not been lessened. In our metropolitan

[6]Karl Taeuber and Alma Taeuber, Negroes in Cities (Chicago, 1965), pp. 37–43.
[7]Ibid., pp. 43–53.
[8]Our Nonwhite Population and its Housing: The Changes between 1950 and 1960, Office of the Administrator, Housing and Home Finance Agency (Washington, D.C., 1963), pp. 13, 15.
[9]A discussion of the supports for housing segregation is given in the Report of the Commission on Race and Housing, Where Shall We Live? (Berkeley, Calif., 1958), pp. 22–34.
[10]Beverly Duncan and Philip Hauser, Housing a Metropolis (Chicago, 1960), p. 208.
[11]Statistics on improvements in the quality of housing received by relocated families is given in The Housing of Relocated Families, Office of the Administrator, Housing and Home Finance Agency (Washington, D.C., 1965).

centers, for example, despite recent efforts to build small, scattered public hous-ing units, most projects constructed under this program have been large in size and have contributed to segregation as they became either nearly all-white or nearly all-Negro.

It is clear that the Negro ghetto, unlike other ghettos, has had great external pressure to keep it "hemmed in." While some of the greater concentration of Negroes in the older areas of our cities stems from income differentials between Negroes and whites, the Taeubers, using data for the city of Chicago, found that income differentials accounted for only 14 percent of the observed racial segre-gation in housing in 1950 and 12 percent in 1960.[12] They further observed that "on every measure—the Puerto Rican population [of Chicago] is less well off— it is less educated, of lower income, more crowded, less likely to be home-owners, less well housed, and lives in older buildings, yet the index of residential segregation for Puerto Ricans is sixty-seven as compared to eighty-two for Ne-groes."[13] There is now considerable evidence, also, that after two generations of strong community solidarity Chinese and Japanese communities in our cities show a considerable dispersion.[14]

Although in recent years some moderation of the tight housing market has occurred within the central city—thus permitting Negroes to obtain housing left by the whites who moved to the suburbs—the proportion of the suburban population which is Negro has declined steadily since 1900. Negroes have be-come increasingly locked in the central city, giving rise to the observation that there is a white noose around our central cities. In 1960, Negroes were less than 5 percent of the population of metropolitan areas outside central cities, but they made up 17 percent of the central city population of these areas.[15]

There is some hope that Executive Order 11063, issued by President Kennedy on November 20, 1962, banning discrimination in housing insured by agencies of the federal government, will have a salutary effect in reducing the degree of concentration and segregation of the Negro population. But skeptics point out that the Order does not cover all home-mortgage insuring agencies of the fed-eral government, the Home Loan Bank Board constituting an important excep-tion, and in recent years a smaller proportion of new construction has been built with federal insurance. Most importantly, the Order is not retroactive, leaving unaffected the housing stock existing at the time of its issuance.

Access by Negroes to much of the newly constructed housing must depend upon the supplementation of the national Order against discrimination by state and local ordinances having the same objective. In recent years there has been an increase in the number of such ordinances. By and large, however, the basic

[12]Karl Taeuber and Alma Taeuber, "Recent Trends in Race and Ethnic Segregation in Chi-cago," Proceedings of the Social Statistics Section, American Statistical Association (Wash-ington, D.C., 1962), p. 14.
[13]Ibid., p. 13.
[14]Where Shall We Live?, op. cit., p. 248.
[15]U.S. Bureau of the Census, U.S. Census of Population: 1960. Selected Area Reports, Standard Metropolitan Areas, Final Report PC(3)-ID (Washington, D.C., 1963), Table 1.

approach of local communities is conciliation of disputes, and much depends upon the vigor with which these local ordinances are enforced if they are to have any significant effect in countering discrimination and reducing segregation.

But significant moderation of Negro concentration and segregation depends upon more than laws against discrimination, however important these may be. The attitudes of both Negroes and whites toward integrated community life are important determinants of the extent to which deconcentration will occur, given enforcement of even the most severe sanctions against discrimination. There is abundant evidence, as mentioned earlier, that myths exist regarding the lowering of housing values and the maintenance of community patterns following invasion by Negroes, and many whites are inclined to move, so that in time complete succession, or turnover of neighborhoods from white to Negro, occurs. On the other hand, there is some resistance on the part of Negroes to moving into areas, especially the suburbs, where few Negroes live. This is particularly characteristic of families with children who must attend school and are dependent on neighbors for play and other social experiences. The well-founded fear of rejection by white neighbors leads to a foregoing of economic advantages which purchases in white areas represent or, in the case of suburban purchases, of a style of living consistent with one's social and economic level. Though numerous white liberal groups, mainly in suburban communities, have organized to encourage Negroes to purchase homes in their neighborhoods, they are often disappointed with the responses to their sincerest solicitations. The centripetal forces tying Negroes to the Negro community are the products of fear and isolated living and are likely to discourage any large exodus of Negroes to suburban communities in the immediate future. Doubtless open-occupancy patterns will result in a significantly larger number of Negroes residing in mixed areas at some future period, but the pattern of increase is likely to be exponential rather than linear.

This continued physical separation of the major racial groups has an impact upon social relationships between them. It limits the number of intimate contacts and the possibilities for understanding which grow out of association. Robin Williams, on the basis of an examination of the patterns of interracial contact in a large number of communities, concludes that the presence of a Negro subcommunity limits Negro interaction with whites, and barriers to communication between the two groups lead to inadequate understanding and to a perception of the other groups as hostile.[16] Duncan and Lieberson make the same point in a somewhat different way when they state that segregation is inversely related to assimilation.[17]

The growing awareness of the limitations of life in the ghetto, as a result of the influence of mass media, increased physical mobility, and better education, has played a vital part in precipitating the "Negro Revolution." The mass dem-

[16]Robin M. Williams, Jr., op. cit., p. 248.

[17]Otis Dudley Duncan and Stanley Lieberson, "Ethnic Segregation and Assimilation," American Journal of Sociology, Vol. 64 (January 1959), p. 370.

onstrations for equality of treatment in places of public accommodations, for access to better quality schools, for equal employment opportunities and voting rights are thought of as efforts by Negroes to achieve first-class citizenship. In another sense, they are efforts to overcome the barriers which have isolated Negroes from aspects of American life.

The difficulty of overcoming the problems created by the physical fact of the ghetto is indicated by attempts to improve the quality of education of schools in slum areas. In our large metropolitan cities, because of the segregation in housing and the traditional neighborhood concept of school attendance, a disproportionate number of schools, particularly at the elementary level, becomes predominantly Negro or predominantly white, with the Negro schools being inferior. Opposing theories for dealing with this situation, generally regarded as undesirable, have generated serious community conflicts. There are those who feel that the efforts should be concentrated upon improving the quality of education in these depressed areas by larger allocations for plant improvement, remedial work, new curricula, and better trained teachers. Other students of the problem contend that substantial improvement of slum schools cannot be achieved until such schools lose their predominantly Negro or predominantly white character. It becomes necessary in the thinking of the protagonists of this latter view to develop methods for overcoming racial imbalances in the schools. While a variety of techniques have been proposed, each has generated rather serious opposition. It is patent that this problem, one of the serious concerns of the leaders of the Negro Revolution largely because it is tied to segregation in housing, will not be easily solved.

As mentioned previously, the ghetto has not only restricted the interaction of Negroes with other members of the society, and hence symbolized the isolation under which Negroes have lived; but it has also been a primary force in the generation and persistence of atypical institutional patterns which are viewed as dysfunctional in any effort at reconciliation. Doubtless the foremost of these institutions is the Negro family which, because of historical circumstances connected with slavery and the isolated conditions under which Negroes have lived in both urban and rural areas, is characterized by rather significant variations from the dominant American family pattern. It is not so much the differences per se, or any mere deviation of Negro family characteristics from those of white middle-class families, but the variations in structural and interactional features known to be desirable in family living which become causes of concern.

The most salient feature of Negro family life which captures the attention of those concerned with integration of Negroes into American life is the degree of disorganization represented by structural breakdown. In only three-quarters of all Negro families, as compared with approximately nine-tenths of all white families, were both spouses present. One Negro family in five (21 percent) was headed by a female and 5 percent had only the male head present. Thus one

Negro family in four, as compared with one white family in ten, was headed by a single parent. This differential in the percentage of families headed by one parent accounts in part for the fact that in 1960 only one-third of Negro children under eighteen years of age, as compared with one in ten white children of comparable age, lived in families in which only one parent was present.

The assumption underlying the desirability of family unity—the presence of both spouses—is that on balance the economic, social, and affectual roles may be best discharged when both mates are present in the home. Divorce, desertion, and separation follow the generation and expression of tensions which, even before rupture occurs, reduce the effectiveness with which the mates can discharge the duties and obligations of family life, as well as deny the satisfactions derived from the intimate sharing of experiences and attainment of goals. In essence, the organized and unified family becomes at once a matrix for the personal satisfaction of the marital partners and for the protection, proper socialization, and well-being of their children. This is not to deny that the basic goals of family life, regarding child-rearing and other functions, may not be achieved by the single-parent family. Given the complexities of modern urban life and the established normative values around which the modern family is organized, however, the discharge of family functions may best be achieved when the family is unified.

In analyzing the statistics on the Negro family one becomes aware that the instability of the Negro family unit is greater than is represented by statistics on the percentages of males and females enumerated as widowed or divorced. In 1960, 15 percent of all Negro males and 20 percent of all Negro females, though enumerated by the Census as married, were living apart from their mates. The percentage of Negro males separated from their mates is four times as large as the comparable percentage for white males, and for Negro females four and one-half times as large as for white females.

The instability of Negro family life is explained only in part by the historical conditioning of attitudes toward family life, beginning with slavery, when strong family ties were not encouraged and Negroes, as Elkins has suggested, were made dependent upon whites.[18] The phenomenon arises also from forces of contemporary American life which place limits upon the possibility of successful family organization. These are reflected in the statistics on characteristics of the heads of Negro families.

As reported by the [1966] Census, approximately one-half, 48.5 percent, of the heads of nonwhite (mainly Negro) families had not finished elementary school. Even in urban areas where access to educational opportunities is somewhat greater and school-attendance laws somewhat better enforced than in rural farm and nonfarm areas, two out of five nonwhite family heads failed to reach the last year of elementary school. Of nonwhite heads living in rural nonfarm and rural farm areas, 70 and 80 percent, respectively, had failed to attain

[18]Stanley Elkins, *Slavery* (Chicago, 1959), pp. 115–133.

this level of schooling.[19] The low level of educational achievement for such a large proportion of nonwhite family heads has obvious implications for the cultural life to which the Negro child is exposed in the home and doubtless for the type of motivation the child receives for achievement in school. It also is related to the labor-force participation and income of nonwhites.

In an economy in which automation is rapidly introducing changes in the demand for certain types of labor, the heads of nonwhite families were disproportionately represented in those occupational categories in which fewer workers are required and monetary returns are small. Only 13 percent of all nonwhite family heads, as compared with 40 percent of white heads, were in professional, managerial, and clerical occupations for which labor demands are increasing. One in five white heads, but only one in ten among nonwhite, was a skilled worker. Thus, one in four nonwhite heads, as compared with three in five white, were white-collar and skilled workers.[20] The heavier identification with semiskilled and unskilled work accounts in part for the nonwhite employment rate being twice as large as the comparable rate of whites and for greater underemployment among nonwhites.

The type of job and both underemployment and unemployment influence the relatively low income of nonwhite family heads. The median nonwhite family income of $3,465 in 1963 was only approximately 53 percent of the white family income of $6,548. More than two-fifths of all nonwhite families (41 percent) earned less than $3,000 in 1963, which placed them at the poverty level, and only one in twenty earned $10,000 or more in the same year.[21] It is significant to note, in line with our previous discussion regarding the desirability of family closure—both parents in the home—that in 1959 families in which both husband and wife were present in the home had a median income of $3,633 as compared with a median of $1,734 for families having a female head.[22]

The problems of the Negro family, then, in terms of its instability and the associated phenomena of crime, delinquency, school dropouts, high morbidity and mortality are related to a complex of interwoven factors, of which level of educational attainment and income are important components. The President of the United States, in a historic speech at Howard University in June 1965, pointed to the complexity of the problem by stating that the provision of jobs, decent homes, welfare and social programs, care of the sick, and understanding attitudes are only partial answers to the conditions of the Negro family.[23] "The breakdown of the Negro family," he stated, "is related to centuries of oppression and persecution of the Negro man. It flows from long years of degradation and discrimination which have attacked his dignity and assaulted his ability to

[19]The statistics in this section are taken from G. Franklin Edwards, "Marriage and Family Life Among Negroes," The Journal of Negro Education, Vol. 32 (Fall 1966), pp. 451–465.
[20]Ibid., p. 463.
[21]Current Population Reports, "Income of Families and Persons in the United States: 1963," Series P-60, No. 43 (Washington, D.C., 1964), Table 1, p. 21.
[22]U.S. Census of Population: 1960, U.S. Summary, Detailed Characteristics, Final Report PC(1)-ID (Washington, D.C., 1963), Tables 224 and 225, pp. 594–603.
[23]The Howard University Magazine, Vol. 7, No. 4 (July 1965), p. 7.

produce for his family."[24] The President added that though we know much about Negro family life, other answers are still to be found. For this reason he indicated he would call a White House Conference in the fall to explore the problem further.

A definitive study by Hylan Lewis of child-rearing practices among low-income Negro families in the District of Columbia reveals that there is, indeed, still much to be learned about the operating dynamics and underlying causes of disorganization among such units.[25] What often is accepted as knowledge about these families is in fact mythology. It is noted, in the first instance, that these families are not homogeneous as regards their organization, functioning, and ambitions for their children. In many of them considerable strength is to be noted, but the exigencies of daily living often deny the achievement of the parents' most ambitious plans. Though parents set training and discipline goals for their children, these are often undermined by influences beyond their power, and the actual control over their children may be lost as early as the fifth or sixth year.

Investigation reveals that many of these parents, particularly the mothers, are warm, human, and concerned individuals who, despite deprivation and trouble, are persistent in their desires to have their children become respectable and productive citizens and in their willingness to sacrifice for them. The picture contrasts with the common belief that in an overwhelming majority of low-income families parents reject their children and are hostile to them.

Lewis' study raises questions regarding assigned reasons for alleged male irresponsibility toward family obligations and the degree of family concern with pregnancy out of wedlock and illegitimate births. There does appear to be a greater degree of concern by the male regarding his responsibilities and by family members regarding the sexual behavior of their offspring than is commonly recognized. What in fact emerges is that the behavior of these lower-income families is a practical response to untoward circumstances which undermine the well-intentioned, but often unattainable, goals of these units.

The major problems of the Negro family are experienced in urban areas where more than 70 percent of such families now live. There has been a heavy migration during the past twenty-five years from farms and small towns to large metropolitan areas. The limited extent to which many of these families can cope with the demands of urban life, given the low educational level and obsolescent skills of the adults, raises serious questions for the American society as well as for the families themselves. The War on Poverty, youth opportunity programs, medicare and other changes in our social security program are certain to exercise some influences in ameliorating existing conditions. But the deep-seated nature of many of those conditions and the personality damage they have pro-

---

[24] Ibid.
[25] Lewis' study, conducted over a period of five years, is now being prepared for publication. The references in this paper were taken from various reports which the investigator made available to the writer.

duced, as expressed in feelings of powerlessness, hopelessness, and forms of anti-social conduct, give rise to the prediction that no easy solution to problems of the Negro family may be found. This is especially true of those "hard core" or multi-problem families in many of which at least two generations have been dependent on public assistance programs. Present efforts to focus upon the young, as evidenced in Project Head Start and programs for youth, on the assumption that this population is most amenable to change, are based upon sound theory. There remains, however, the complex problem of improving the skills and enhancing the self-esteem of the adult members whose personalities are crystallized and whose levels of expectation have been shaped under an entirely different set of conditions. What is apparent is that the problems of the Negro family are intimately tied to those of the larger community.

The elimination of many of these difficulties depends upon a commitment to invest a great deal more of our resources in improving educational and social services, including more effective family limitation programs. What is indicated is that by opening the opportunity structure and providing both formal and informal education on a more extensive scale through diverse programs, key figures in many Negro problem families will be enabled over time to develop self-esteem and a "rational" approach to urban life, which many students regard as indispensable for successful adjustment to the urban environment. This can hardly occur as long as the present constraints and limitations continue to operate against a large segment of the Negro population or, to put it differently, as long as the isolation of the Negro is continued.

The difficulty of changing existing patterns is evident in a number of current efforts. The Manpower Retraining Program, for example, has encountered difficulty in working with enrollees with less than an eighth-grade education, which would exclude large numbers of Negro males from successful participation. Of all projects started under the Manpower Development and Retraining Act in 1963, 3 percent of the enrollees had less than eight years of schooling, while 36 percent had between eight and eleven years. Fifty-one percent were high-school graduates, and another 10 percent had gone beyond the high-school level.[26] Educational levels must be raised considerably before some of the disadvantaged can benefit from available training opportunities.

The problems of developing motivation, rather than supplying specific job skills, appear to be even harder to overcome. Charles Silberman, among others, has pointed out that the effort to eliminate poverty must involve the poor in action programs if the motivation to improve their lot is to be realized. Recent controversies over involvement of the poor in strikes, boycotts, and pickets and the use of other techniques to dramatize their condition and counteract feelings of apathy and cynicism have been sharply criticized by local citizens, especially those in the power structure.[27]

Finally, the bold program advanced by Whitney Young, Executive Director of

[26]Manpower Report of the President (Washington, D.C., 1964), Table F-3, p. 253.
[27]Charles E. Silberman, Crisis in Black and White (New York, 1964), pp. 309 ff.

the National Urban League, calling for a "Marshall Plan" for Negroes as a means of upgrading the competency and well-being of the Negro family, encounters serious opposition.[28] The charge of preferential treatment is raised, and this runs counter to the ideology of equal treatment. What is more important is that the practical operation of such a program would encounter difficulty from institutionalized patterns. To request preferential treatment for Negroes in apprentice programs and preferential hiring after completion of training, for example, cross-cuts seniority and other established principles of union organization and practice.

All of the above are mere illustrations of the complications involved in any effort to strengthen the Negro family in particular and to upgrade Negro life in general. They should serve to introduce some caution into the thinking of those sanguine persons who are persuaded that broad-scale and rapid changes are likely to occur in a short period of time. (The position taken here is not an apology for the gradualist position regarding race relations changes. It is, indeed, understandable that civil rights groups must inveigh continuously against the gradualist perspective as a matter of strategy. Our concern is with traditional and countervailing influences which have the effect of slowing the pace at which change might occur.)

The disabilities of the Negro family discussed in the preceding paragraphs are most characteristic of low-income units. Not all Negro families are affected by inadequate income, education, and employment opportunities, and many of them do not lack strong family traditions. There is a considerable differentiation within the Negro community in terms of status groups and social classes.

E. Franklin Frazier observed that as late as World War I the Negro middle class was composed "principally of teachers, doctors, preachers, trusted persons in personal service, government employees, and a few business men."[29] He stated further that:

This group was distinguished from the rest of the Negro population not so much by economic factors as by social factors. Family affiliation and education to a less degree were as important as income. Moreover, while it exhibited many middle-class features such as its emphasis on morality, it also possessed characteristics of an upper class or aristocracy.[30]

The urbanization of the Negro population, beginning with World War I and continuing to the present, resulted in the formation of large ghettos in Northern and Southern cities and provided the condition for greater occupational differentiation within the Negro community. The differentiation was more pronounced in Northern communities where Negroes had a substantially

[28]Whitney Young, Jr., To Be Equal (New York, 1964), pp. 22–33.
[29]E. Franklin Frazier, "The New Negro," in The New Negro Thirty Years Afterward (Washington, D.C., 1955), p. 26.
[30]Ibid.

greater opportunity to enter clerical and technical occupations than was true in Southern cities, and where the large population base provided economic support for a sizeable corps of professional functionaries. Education and income became more important than social distinctions in determining class membership.

The Negro middle class today includes a still relatively small, but expanding, number of persons. If occupation is used as a criterion for determining membership and those in professional and technical, clerical, sales, and skilled occupations are included, only approximately 26 percent of all nonwhite workers belong to the middle class. White workers in these above-mentioned categories represent 64 percent of all whites in the labor force.[31] The contrast between the two occupational structures is further indicated by the fact that the percentage of white workers, taken as a proportion of all white workers, is twice as large as the comparable percentage of nonwhite workers in professional and kindred occupations, and in clerical and skilled work; four times as large in managerial occupations; and three times as large in the sales category.

In none of the specific occupational categories associated with the middle class did nonwhite male workers achieve parity with white males in median income. The nearest approximation to parity in 1959 was in clerical and kindred occupations in which the nonwhite male median earnings of $4,072 was approximately 85 percent of the white male median of $4,785. In none of the other categories did nonwhite male workers receive so much as 70 percent of the median income of white males in the category.[32]

The expansion of the Negro middle class has been most marked by accretion of persons in professional, technical, clerical, and sales occupations. This expansion by approximately 300,000 persons since 1940 has been influenced in part by government policy which prohibits those business firms holding contracts with the federal government from discriminating against workers on the basis of race, religion, creed, or national origin. In engineering, architecture, and the natural sciences, occupations oriented to the wider world of work rather than to the Negro community, the increases among Negroes, though small in absolute numbers, have been rather dramatic. Between 1950 and 1960, there was a three-fold increase in the number of Negro engineers. The number of Negro architects increased by 72 percent, and the number of natural scientists by 77 percent.[33] This expansion comes at the end of a half century in which Negroes could hardly expect to earn a living in these fields and thus were not encouraged to prepare for entering them.

The number of Negroes in medicine, dentistry, and law, whose services traditionally have been oriented to the Negro community, has begun to increase

[31]Computed from U.S. Bureau of the Census U.S. Census of Population: 1960, U.S. Summary, Detailed Characteristics, Final Report PC (1)-1D, Table 208.
[32]Ibid.
[33]Computed from U.S. Census of Population: 1940, Vol. II, Characteristics of the Population, Part 1, U.S. Summary, Table 128, p. 278; and U.S. Census of Population: 1960, Vol. I, Characteristics of the Population, Part 1, U.S. Summary, Table 205, p. 544.

rather significantly. During the 1950's, physicians increased by 14 percent, dentists by 31 percent, and lawyers by 43 percent.[34] More substantial fellowship and scholarship aid, ability to pay for professional education, as well as the opening of the segregated professional schools in the Southern states, have contributed to this result.

It is not only the increase in number of these professionals which deserves attention; the improved opportunities for advanced training and learning experiences are also of importance. On the basis of increased opportunities for internships and residency training, the number of Negro physicians who became diplomats of medical specialty boards increased from 92 in 1947 to 377 in 1959.[35] Negro physicians, lawyers, and dentists are admitted today to membership in local societies of national professional organizations in larger numbers and enjoy the privileges these societies provide for continued professional growth.

It should be remembered, however, that these gains, while significant in terms of what has occurred in Negro life heretofore, are relatively small. The ratios of the actual to expected numbers of Negroes in middle-class occupations, as measured by the total labor force distribution, are extremely small.[36]

The differences between Negro and white community life cannot be measured solely by variations in income, occupation, education, and other objective indicators. In assessing the differences, it is important to recognize that the Negro class structure and institutions have emerged in response to segregation and represent adjustments to the isolation under which Negroes have lived. The meaning of relationships within the community and the values placed upon them must be considered.

Frazier has observed, for example, that in the absence of a true upper class based upon old family ties and wealth, the Negro middle class simulates the behavior of the white upper class without possessing the fundamental bases upon which such behavior rests.[37] Moreover, segregation has provided a monopoly for many Negroes in business and the professions and has introduced, in many cases, differential standards of performance. This has important consequences for any consideration of desegregation, for those who enjoy a vested interest in the segregated community are not likely to welcome competition from the broader community. The Negro church represents an extreme instance of vested interest in the Negro community and, at the same time, is the most important institution giving expression to the Negro masses. For this reason no degree of acceptance of Negroes by white churches is likely to bring about the dissolution of Negro churches.[38]

[34]Ibid.

[35]From data supplied the writer by W. Montague Cobb, M.D., editor of the Journal of the National Medical Association.

[36]Ratios for many of these occupations are supplied in Leonard Broom and Norval Glenn, Transformation of the Negro American (New York, 1965), Table 5, pp. 112–113.

[37]This is the thesis of E. Franklin Frazier, Black Bourgeoisie (Chicago, 1957). See, especially, pp. 195–212. See, also, Frazier, "Human, All too Human," Survey Graphic: twelfth Calling America Number (January 1947), pp. 74–75, 99–100.

[38]E. Franklin Frazier, "Desegregation as a Social Process," in Arnold Rose (ed.), Human Behavior and Social Processes (Boston, 1962), p. 619.

The Negro community doubtless will be the source of social life of Negroes for some time into the future. Sororities, fraternities, clubs, and other organizations will continue to serve a meaningful function. The acceptance by whites of Negroes as fellow workers often bears little relationship to their willingness to share social experiences with them outside the plant or office or to have them as neighbors.

The importance of the Negro community as a source of social life is indicated by the fact that, though the majority of the members of a Negro professional society felt that its members should identify with the local chapter of the national organization representing the profession when the opportunity became available, one quarter had some reservation about joining and another 5 percent were opposed to joining. The underlying reasons for reservations to becoming members of the formerly white organization were that, though Negroes may be accepted as professional colleagues, they would not be treated as social equals and that opportunities for leadership roles would be lost if the Negro association were dissolved.[39] What is patently indicated is that most members thought they should have the *right* to membership in the local chapter of the national organization, but they should retain their own association for social and professional reasons.

Despite the effort to conserve the conceived advantages of the Negro community, the larger social forces are introducing changes. Already the small Negro entrepreneurial group is threatened by these forces. Speaking to a group of Negro businessmen in Detroit, the Assistant Secretary of Commerce for Economic Affairs referred to the disappearance of the monopoly Negroes formerly held in certain businesses.[40] The impact of desegregation is being felt, he said, in the Negro market, for, as the income of Negro consumers expands, white businessmen become more conscious of the Negro's purchasing power. To this end they have added a cadre of professional Negro salesmen to their payrolls for the specific purpose of developing the Negro market. The success of this undertaking is indicated by the fact that many of the unemployed Negroes have risen to top executive posts in these organizations. Moreover, Negroes have begun to buy in increasing amounts from shopping centers serving the Negro community and have begun to patronize places of public accommodations other than those traditionally operated by Negroes. This change in consumer behavior represents a steady and gradual erosion of the position of the Negro businessman. The cruelest blow of all, the Assistant Secretary stated, is that "the large life insurance companies serving the market at large are bidding away Negro life insurance salesmen at an increasing rate."[41] These and other changes are certain to influence the structure of the Negro community.

[39]Martha Coffee, "A Study of a Professional Association and Racial Integration," unpublished Master's Thesis, Department of Sociology, Howard University, Washington, D.C., 1953.
[40]"Desegregation and the Negro Middle Class," remarks of Dr. Andrew F. Brimmer, Assistant Secretary of Commerce for Economic Affairs, Detroit, Michigan, July 16, 1965.
[41]*Ibid.*, p. 8.

THE ORDEAL OF CHANGE

From observing current developments in race relations and the operation of the larger social forces in our society, it is evident that several basic conditions operate to influence the pattern and pace at which change is occurring. These provide some insight into what may be expected in the future in regard to the general status of the Negro minority; they document the theory of slow and gradual change for some time to come in most areas and somewhat more rapid change in others.

A first consideration, not prominently mentioned heretofore, is the opposition to change by segments of the white community. Beginning with the school desegregation decision, there has been a mobilization of white community efforts to prevent the attainment of desegregation in many aspects of community life. This opposition has taken a variety of forms: the closing of schools, violence visited upon Negroes, intimidation of Negroes and threats to their job security, the rise of some hate groups—such as Citizens' Councils and Night Riders—and the strengthening of others—such as the Ku Klux Klan—the resurrection of racial ideologies having the purpose of establishing the inferiority of the Negro, and a variety of other techniques designed to slow the desegregation process.[42]

What is important in this connection is that many of the organizations connected with the opposition have had the support, if not the leadership, of prominent persons in the power structure; many governors, majors, legislators, and prominent businessmen have all given support to the resistance efforts, owing to political and economic expediency, if not to personal sentiment. Moreover, persons with some claim to scientific respectability in the academic community have contributed to the questioning of whether differentials between Negroes and whites stem from the former's disadvantaged community life or from the Negro's innate biological inferiority.[43]

There is no doubt that these forces have served to slow the process of desegregation. As late as December 1964, only 2 percent of Negro pupils in eleven Southern states formerly having segregated school systems were attending schools with whites. If the six Border states where desegregation did not encounter the same serious opposition as in the other eleven states are included in the count, only 11 percent of Negro pupils attend schools having a mixed population.[44] This has led to one student's referring to developments in this area as "ten years of prelude," suggesting that the pace may be somewhat more rapid in the future.[45]

[42]A good discussion of these hate groups is given in James W. Vander Zanden, *Race Relations in Transition: The Segregation Crisis in the South* (New York, 1965), pp. 25–54. See, also, Arnold Forster and Benjamin Epstein, *Report on the Ku Klux Klan* (New York, 1965).
[43]See the following: Wesley C. George, *The Biology of the Race Problem* (A report prepared by commission of the Governor of Alabama, 1962); and Dwight J. Ingle, "Racial Differences and the Future," *Science*, Vol. 146 (October 16, 1964), pp. 375–379.
[44]Figures from *Southern School News*, Vol. 11 (December 1964), p. 1.
[45]Benjamin Muse, *Ten Years of Prelude: The Story of Integration Since the Supreme Court's 1954 Decision* (New York, 1964).

There does appear to be a lessening of the opposition in many areas as a result of several important factors. These include self-interest on the part of prominent businessmen, many of whom have spoken out against violence and have used their influence otherwise. The passage of important legislation within the past year—the Civil Rights Act of 1964 and the Voting Rights Act of 1965— are certain to have an influence in softening open resistance. But doubtless resistance to change will continue in subtle ways, perhaps under a blanket of legitimacy, as in the instance of the large-scale discharge of Negro teachers in Southern states in recent months following the necessity of having to comply with the Commissioner of Education's "Statement of Policies" for enforcement of Title VI of the Civil Rights Act, by which Southern school systems are expected to make a substantial start toward complete desegregation by September 1965 and to complete the process by the fall of 1967.

A second important force affecting change is inherent in the nature of the phenomenon itself, especially the contribution made by the accumulated disabilities of the Negro family, and in individuals in terms of inadequate education, job skills, housing, patterns of dependency, and low self-esteem. The advancement toward a more equalitarian society depends upon how fully these disabilities can be overcome or eliminated. Any analysis must consider the generational problem, for the extent to which the education and job skills of many adult family heads—those over forty-five, for example—can be improved is problematic.

A stronger basis of hope rests with the generation which begins school under improved educational conditions and whose levels of aspiration will be shaped by a social context which varies considerably from that of the past half century, and may be expected to vary even more in the future. But even under the most favorable circumstances, the improvement of educational qualifications of Negroes to a position of parity with those of whites, an essential factor for job equality, may not be easily achieved. One prominent sociologist on the basis of statistical calculations concluded:

Whatever the future may hold with respect to the on-coming cohorts of young Negroes, the performance to date, together with the postulate that educational attainment is a "background" characteristic [for employment], enables us to make a most important prediction: the disparity between white and nonwhite levels of education attainment in the general population can hardly disappear in less than three-quarters of a century. Even if Negroes in their teens were to begin immediately to match the educational attainment of white children, with this equalization persisting indefinitely, we shall have to wait fifty years for the last of the cohorts manifesting race differentials to reach retirement age.[46]

The achievement of educational and occupational equality is far more difficult to attain than equal treatment in public accommodations. Many civil

[46]Otis Dudley Duncan, "Population Trends, Mobility and Social Change," a paper prepared for the Seminar on Dimensions of American Society, Committee on Social Studies, American Association of Colleges for Teacher Education, p. 52. (Quoted with the permission of the author.)

rights leaders recognize this and, now that the public accommodations struggle has been successful, consider that the movement has entered a new and much tougher phase.

A third force affecting change is the attitudes held by certain Negroes who either have a vested interest in segregation or are generally fearful of the deleterious consequences desegregation will bring. This has been discussed in an earlier section, and only a further example will be furnished here. As early as 1954 Negro teachers in South Carolina registered great fear over the possible untoward effects of desegregation of the public school system on their professional status as teachers. The chief fears expressed concerned the large amount of possible job displacement, new ways to evade the granting of equality in pay, employment, and benefits, greater demands for professional preparation, and the employment of fewer couples in the school system. Though most of these teachers were ideologically committed to desegregation, their fears regarding their jobs and community relationships with whites suggest that many of them, of necessity, were ambivalent toward desegregation.[47]

It is not likely that these attitudes strongly counteract tendencies to change. Their significance lies more in the manifest desire of Negroes to maintain social distance from whites in community relations as a result of their perception of the adverse use of power by whites.

The most significant influence in determining the pattern and pace of race relations changes is the federal government. The early court decisions, particularly in the area of public accommodations, orders by the executive, and recent legislation by the Congress have had salutary effects in altering disability-producing conditions. With more rigorous enforcement, they are likely to have an even more important influence in the future. The Civil Rights Act of 1964 provides a wedge for undermining, or at least neutralizing, much of the support for denying the constitutional rights of Negroes. The sanctions provided in Title VI of the Act, relating to nondiscrimination in federally assisted programs, is certain to produce a high measure of compliance. Under the Voting Rights Act of 1965, it is expected that between 50 and 70 percent of eligible Negro voters in the five Deep South states (Alabama, Georgia, Louisiana, Mississippi, and South Carolina) will be registered to vote by the time of the 1966 elections.[48] This result, along with the greater political consciousness of Negroes throughout the country, is certain to improve the power position of the group and result in the election of large numbers of Negroes to public office.[49]

The change in the position of the government in respect to the status of

[47]Hurley Doddy and G. Franklin Edwards, "Apprehension of Negro Teachers Concerning Desegregation in South Carolina," *Journal of Negro Education*, Vol. 24 (Winter 1955), Table 1, pp. 30–31.

[48]*The Washington Post*, September 6, 1965, p. 1.

[49]For a list of the growing number of Negro office holders, see Harold F. Gosnell and Robert E. Martin, "The Negro as Voter and Office Holder," *Journal of Negro Education*, Vol. 32. (Fall 1963), pp. 415–425.

Negroes results from the altered position of this country in world affairs since the end of World War II and to a substantial shift in public opinion regarding the position of the Negro during that period. It is important, therefore, to view contemporary changes as a part of broader social movements toward improved welfare for the disadvantaged within the country and in the world. These broad forces tend to override resistances, but they are subject to challenges and counter pressures. If viewed in this broad perspective, it is clear that more significant changes which will bring the Negro greater opportunities for participation in our society lie ahead. When, in fact, basic equalities will be achieved cannot be predicted.

Race and Reconciliation: The Role of the School

John H. Fischer

I

When George Counts asked in 1932, "Dare the schools build a new social order?" the response could hardly have been called resounding. A frightened few took the query for a Marxist threat, the Progressive Education Association spent a year reaching a split decision, but the majority even of those who gave it any attention at all dismissed the challenge as educationist hyperbole. Whatever it was the country needed, not many expected to find it in the schools. Two wars, a technological revolution, and a massive social upheaval have put a different face upon the matter. No longer is education the optional affair it was a generation ago. The easy rhetoric about the nation's reliance on its schools has become an uneasy reality.

President Johnson reflected the discovery when he said that "one great truth" he had learned is that "the answer for all of our national problems, the answer for all the problems of the world comes down, when you really analyze it, to one simple word—education."[1] Mr. Johnson is not the first President to speak well of learning. The dependence of democracy on popular education has been a continuing theme in our history. But it was not until the end of World War II that the country began seriously to consider the full implications of that relationship, and later still that it officially acknowledged the corollary proposition that to limit a man's education is to limit his freedom.

The rationale for improving the Negro American's chance to be educated derives from basic principles and well-established practice, but merely to

From *Daedalus*, Winter 1966, Vol. 95, No. 1, pp. 24–43. Reprinted by permission.
[1]Lyndon B. Johnson, Address delivered at the 200th Anniversary Convocation, Brown University, September 28, 1964.

proclaim a new policy of equality is not enough. Steps to equalize the Negro's educational opportunities must be accompanied by prompt and vigorous action to improve his access to those opportunities and to increase the inducement for him to use them. Until, in all three respects, he is brought to full parity with his white neighbor, the Negro citizen will continue to depress the composite level of American society, and the society to diminish his standing as a man.

As the struggle to secure the Negro's proper place in that society gains headway and success, it becomes steadily more clear that the two great educational handicaps he has suffered—segregated schools and inferior instruction—are so closely interrelated that they can be attacked successfully only when they are attacked simultaneously.

This is not to argue that segregation is the sole deficiency Negro children suffer in school or that only Negro pupils receive inferior education. Nor is it true that every Negro child is being poorly taught or that effective learning is possible only in the presence of white children. It is important to set the facts, the probabilities, and the proposals straight. Not every Negro child lives in deprivation: each year more Negro families join the middle class. Nor is every white child raised in a good home. Slums are often ghettos, but the two are not always the same. Poverty of purse and poverty of spirit often go together, but the exceptions are numerous and important. Yet when all the differences have been explained and all the exceptions admitted, the hard facts of racial discrimination remain to be faced.

Until the present generation, almost every action affecting Negroes as a group in this country, whether taken by the government or by private agencies, has been to some degree discriminatory and quite often hypocritical. The Negro's just cause for pride in the fortitude of his ancestors in no way alters the fact that from the moment of his birth he becomes the product and the victim of his people's history. The scars he carries are difficult to hide and slow to heal.

Assuring the Negro his proper place in American society involves more than opening a few doors, giving everybody his choice, and waiting for what is certain to come naturally. Many of the trends that have influenced the Negro individually and collectively have carried him not toward but away from the main currents of American life. The momentum that has been built up suggests a sociological analogue of Newton's first law of motion. Unless the course that the Negro race has followed for three centuries is altered by the application of external energy, its direction cannot be expected to change. The heart of the integration question is to determine what forms of energy are most appropriate and how they may be applied to bring the separate courses together. For some Negroes the process is already under way, but for many more significant change awaits intervention on a scale commensurate with the forces that must be checked and redirected. To serve this purpose no agency offers greater promise than the school.

We can begin on the educational task by considering some facts. One is that a school enrolling largely Negro students is almost universally considered of lower status and less desirable than one attended wholly or mainly by white students. Regardless of the quality of the building, the competence of the staff, or the size of classes, a school composed of three-fourths Negro children and one-fourth white children is viewed by members of both races, virtually without exception, as inferior to one in which the proportions are reversed. Whether all such appraisals are valid remains, at least for the time being, beside the point. So often are "Negro" schools inferior and so long have Negro students been assigned the hand-me-downs that unhappy memories and generalized impressions must be expected to persist despite the occasional presence of really good schools in Negro neighborhoods.

The contention that no school of Negro pupils can under any circumstances be satisfactory unless white students enter it is absurd. The argument insults every Negro child and credits white children with virtues they do not possess. But the effort to establish genuinely first-rate schools in Negro communities has been so long delayed that anyone undertaking to demonstrate that an institution known as a "Negro" school can produce first-rate results must be prepared to accept a substantial burden of proof.

A second impressive fact, closely related to the first, is the unfortunate psychological effect upon a child of membership in a school where every pupil knows that, regardless of his personal attainments, the group with which he is identified is viewed as less able, less successful, and less acceptable than the majority of the community. The impact upon the self-image and motivation of children of this most tragic outcome of segregated education emphasizes the dual need for immediate steps to achieve a more favorable balance of races in the schools and for every possible effort to upgrade to full respectability and status every school in which enrollment cannot soon be balanced.

The destruction of the legal basis of segregation by the *Brown* decision in 1954 marked the climax of an obviously necessary first campaign, but the new problems to which *Brown* gives rise are even more complex than those which preceded it. The task now is not only to end segregation but to correct the effects it has generated. There is little profit in debating whether *de jure* or *de facto* segregation is the greater evil. It was the consequences of the fact of segregation that convinced the Supreme Court that "separate schools are inherently unequal" and led the Court to strike down the laws supporting high schools. Only by a curious twist of logic could it be argued that segregation statutes having been declared unjust, the practice itself may now be condoned.

This is not to deny significant differences between segregation established by law and that resulting from other causes. As the Court itself pointed out, "The impact is greater when it has the sanction of the law." But underlying this greater impact is the Court's finding that "Segregation of white and colored children in public schools has a detrimental effect upon the colored children."

Imperative as the need for prompt desegregation is, it would be irresponsible to attempt to deal with a condition so deeply rooted in practice and custom, and so often due to causes lying beyond the school, without taking account of its complexity. The need for intelligence, imagination, and wisdom in effecting fair and workable reforms can hardly be overstated. Yet, however complicated the situation or the final solutions may be, a firm and forthright confrontation of the problem is essential and is everywhere possible.

Some of the most bitter attacks on school authorities have been occasioned not by their failure to integrate every school, but by their unwillingness even to accept integration as a desirable goal. Among the reasons offered in support of this position, two are especially prominent. One is that the only acceptable basis for school policy is simple and complete nondiscrimination. Unless the school is color-blind, this argument runs, the spirit of the *Brown* decision and the 14th Amendment is violated. What this approach overlooks or attempts to evade is that the consequences of earlier discrimination cannot be corrected merely by ending the practices that produced them, that without corrective action the effects inevitably persist. To teach anyone in a way that influences his further development it is invariably useful and usually necessary to take account of the background he brings to the classroom. So often are the disabilities of Negro students directly traceable to racial factors that a refusal on grounds of equality to recognize such factors in the school is not only unjust; it is also illogical. A physician reasoning in the same way would deliberately disregard his patients' histories in order to assure them all equal treatment.

A second justification commonly offered for not taking positive action to integrate schools is the lack of evidence that better racial balance leads to better learning, and it must be conceded that solid, objective evidence on this question is difficult if not impossible to find. The number of Negro children from deprived circumstances who have attended schools that were both integrated and educationally sound is still so small and the period of integration so brief that neither provides more than a limited basis for study. Because the Negro children with the longest experience in good integrated institutions have more often come from relatively fortunate and upwardly mobile families, their performance, although interesting, is only partly relevant to the task of equalizing opportunities for those who are both segregated and otherwise disadvantaged.

Moreover, even when better statistical data become available, it should not be expected that they will furnish, *per se*, a firm basis for policy. The purpose of school integration is not merely, or even primarily, to raise the quantitative indices of scholastic achievement among Negro children, although such gains are obviously to be valued and sought. The main objective is rather to alter the character and quality of their opportunities, to provide the incentive to succeed, and to foster a sense of intergroup acceptance in ways that are impossible where schools or students are racially, socially, and culturally isolated. The simplest statement of the situation to which school policy must respond is that few if any American Negro children can now grow up under conditions comparable to those of white children and that of all the means of improvement subject to public control the most powerful is the school. The Negro child must have a chance to be educated in a school where it is clear to him and to everybody else that he is not segregated and where his undisputed right to membership is acknowledged, publicly and privately, by his peers and his elders of both races. Although his acceptance and his progress may at first be delayed, not even a decent beginning toward comparable circumstances can be made until an integrated setting is actually established.

Some important gains may come rather quickly in newly integrated schools, but lasting changes in the deep-seated behavior patterns of children and parents of both races cannot realistically be expected to take place overnight. The effects of fourteen generations of discrimination, deprivation, and separation are not likely to disappear quickly. What a school has to boast about at the end of the next grading period is somewhat less crucial than what happens to the quality of living in America during the next generation. School integration will, of course, be more productive when parallel improvements are made in housing, economic opportunities, and the general social condition of Negro Americans; but the absence of adequate effort elsewhere only increases the urgency that prompt and energetic action be taken by the school.

The effort to identify and define *de facto* segregation, particularly where school enrollment is predominantly if not wholly of a single race, has led to the concept of racial "balance." While no single ratio of races can be established as universally "right," there is no doubt that when the number or proportion of Negro children in a school exceeds a certain level the school becomes less acceptable to both white and Negro parents. The point at which that shift begins is not clear, nor are the reasons for the variation adequately understood, but the results that typically follow are all too familiar: an accelerated exodus of white families; an influx of Negroes; increased enrollment, frequently to the point of overcrowding; growing dissatisfaction among teachers and the replacement of veterans by inexperienced or unqualified junior instructors.

Although there are no completely satisfactory measures of segregation or imbalance, several tests are applicable. The simplest is to ask whether a particular school is viewed by the community as a "Negro" school. Whether the school is assumed to "belong" to a Negro neighborhood or merely to be the one that Negroes "just happen" to attend, whether it has been provided expressly *for* a Negro population, or has gradually acquired a student body disproportionately composed of Negroes, the typical consequences of segregation can be predicted.

In gauging the degree of segregation or imbalance, the percentage or number of Negro students in a given building is usually less important than the relation of the school to the entire system of which it is a part. As Robert Carter has so cogently argued, it is the substantial isolation of Negro and white students from each other rather than the numbers involved that produces the implication of differential status and prevents the association that is the indispensable basis for mutual understanding and acceptance.[2]

One set of guidelines for correcting such situations has been proposed by the New York State Education Commissioner's Advisory Committee on Human Relations and Community Tensions:

In establishing school attendance areas one of the objectives should be to create in each school a student body that will represent as nearly as possible the cross section of the population of the entire school district but with due consideration also for other important educational criteria including such practical matters as the distance children must travel from home to school.[3]

Although it would be impossible in a sizable district to create or maintain in every school a student body that reflects precisely the racial composition of the total district, the cross section criterion offers an appropriate yardstick.

Most of the proposals for dealing with the issue attempt to strike workable compromises between desirable ideals and practical possibilities. The same Committee in a 1964 report[4] defined a school in New York City as segregated when any single racial group comprised more than 90 percent of the enrollment.

A more flexible criterion was used by Robert Dentler in a 1964 study.[5] Using the borough as the reference point, he proposed that a school be considered segregated if the proportion of any racial group in its student body is less than half or more than twice the proportion that group represents in the total population. Thus, in Brooklyn, where Negroes comprise 15 percent of the population, a school would be classified as "Negro segregated" when Negro enrollment reached 30 percent. Since Puerto Ricans form about 8 percent of the borough population, a school would be "Puerto Rican" segregated if it enrolled 16 percent or more pupils of that background. Conversely, a school enrolling fewer than 6 percent Negro students or 2 percent Puerto Rican students would be designated as "white segregated." Dealing with the issue in Chicago, Robert Havighurst[6] defines an integrated school as one enrolling at least 60 percent white students.

---

[2]Robert L. Carter, "De Facto School Segregation: An Examination of the Legal and Constitutional Questions Presented," *Western Reserve Law Review,* Vol. 16 (May 1965), p. 527.

[3]New York State Department of Education, "Guiding Principles for Securing Racial Balance in Public Schools," Albany, N.Y., June 17, 1963.

[4]New York State Education Commissioner's Advisory Committee on Human Relations and Community Tensions, *Desegregating the Public Schools of New York City* (Albany, N.Y., 1964), p. 2.

[5]Robert A. Dentler, *A Basis for Classifying the Ethnic Composition of Schools,* unpublished memorandum, Institute for Urban Studies, Teachers College, Columbia University, December 1964, p. 1.

[6]Robert J. Havighurst, *The Public Schools of Chicago* (Chicago, 1964).

II

The dilemma of definition cannot be entirely avoided, but far more important is the creation and retention of student bodies that will be considered acceptably integrated by the largest possible number of persons in both races. As the New York City report pointed out, an essential test of any plan for desegregation "must be its mutual acceptance by both minority group and whites. It should be obvious, but does not always appear to be, that integration is impossible without white pupils. No plan can be acceptable, therefore, which increases the movement of white pupils out of the public schools. Neither is it acceptable, however, unless it contributes to desegregation."[7]

Of the administrative schemes for bringing children of both races together the most widely used is "open enrollment," under which pupils are allowed to transfer from schools that are segregated or overcrowded to others in the district. The receiving school may be one with a better degree of racial balance, or its enrollment may simply be smaller than its capacity. While open enrollment reduces congestion in the sending schools, allows parents wider choice, and improves integration in the receiving schools, its usefulness, especially for poor children, is sharply reduced unless transportation is furnished at public expense. Freedom of choice is also more effective when it is supplemented by special counseling services and by the careful preparation of pupils, teachers, and parents of the receiving school.

In large cities open enrollment plans have uniformly been found to affect only a small percentage of Negro students. In Baltimore, where relatively free choice of schools (subject to legal segregation) was standard practice before 1954, open enrollment became the sole basis for desegregation following the *Brown* decision. In the school year 1954–55 only about 3 percent of the Negro students transferred to formerly white schools.[8] In subsequent years the number of integrated schools and the percentage of pupils enrolled in them steadily rose, but much of the change was due to the continued expansion of the Negro residential areas.

For readily understandable reasons, the free choice policy affects younger and older pupils differently. Most parents, and especially those in restricted circumstances, prefer to send elementary-age children to the nearest school, regardless of its condition. Families in more affluent circumstances are ordinarily willing to accept the added inconvenience and expense of transportation to get their children into better schools, but the regrettable fact is that if opportunity is to be equalized by traveling it is invariably the slum children who must accept the inconvenience of going to where the more fortunate already are.

At the secondary level, distance is less of an obstacle. This is one of the

---

[7]New York State Education Commissioner's Advisory Committee, *op. cit.*, p. 14.
[8]Maryland Commission on Interracial Problems and Relations, *The Report of a Study on Desegregation in the Baltimore City Schools* (Baltimore, Md., 1956), p. 10.

reasons that in New York City in 1963, when 22 percent of the elementary schools and 19 percent of the junior high schools were found to be segregated, by the same criteria only one of the eighty-six senior high schools was segregated.[9]

The most tightly structured approach to desegregation, the Princeton Plan, achieves racial balance by pairing adjacent imbalanced schools, the combined attendance areas being treated as a single unit and the pupils being divided between the schools by grade rather than by residence. The advantages are clear: Both schools are integrated, and each is enabled to concentrate upon a narrower span of grades. There are also disadvantages. Travel time is increased for approximately half the children and transportation may be required, each school's established identity and its relations with its neighborhood are altered, and large-scale faculty transfers may be required. In addition, the possibility that white families will choose to leave the community becomes an uncertain hazard in every such situation.

Early and largely impressionistic evaluations of pairing suggest that the device may be more appropriate in smaller communities with only a few elementary schools than in larger places where neighborhood patterns and rates of residential change are more complex. One analysis[10] of the probable result of pairing twenty-one sets of elementary schools in New York City showed that, at most, the proportion of segregated schools would have been reduced from 22 to 21 percent.

A more comprehensive method of correcting imbalance is the re-zoning of all the attendance areas of a school system in order to obtain simultaneously a viable racial balance and reasonable travel time for all the pupils. Re-zoning and the related practice of revising the "feeder" patterns by which graduates of lower schools move on to junior or senior high schools are usually more practicable in closely populated communities than in less compact suburbs where travel distances are greater.

Among the more recent innovations is the "educational complex" proposed for the New York City schools.[11] The term denotes a group of schools serving differing racial constituencies and consisting typically of one or two junior high schools and their feeding elementary units. The attendance areas of the individual schools are not changed, but within the complex a variety of joint activities may be undertaken to bring the pupils, teachers, and parents into closer association. Programs and services that cannot be offered uniformly in all of the schools may be centered in one or two of the buildings and pupils transported to them as necessary. Faculty specialists may be shared by more than one building and common problems met cooperatively. Parents of two or more of the schools working together may bridge over old neighborhood lines that inhibit communication and joint action. The "complex" offers unusual

[9] New York Education Commissioner's Advisory Committee, *op. cit.*
[10] *Ibid.*, p. 40.
[11] *Ibid.*, pp. 18–20.

possibilities for countering the effect of segregated housing. By retaining the advantages of neighborhood schools while introducing the social opportunities of a more diversified community, it offers children and parents a chance to try new experiences without totally abandoning the security of their familiar attachments.

Of all the schemes proposed for desegregating urban schools, the boldest and most imaginative is the educational park.[12] The rationale of the park rests on the hypothesis that the effect on the school of pockets of segregated housing will be offset if an attendance area can be made large enough to include white and Negro populations in balanced proportions. Thus, all the pupils of a greatly enlarged zone, perhaps 10,000 or more (in a medium-sized city, the entire school population), would be accommodated on a single site or park. Within the park, which could range all the way from a 100 acre campus with many separate buildings to a single high-rise structure covering a city block, students would be assigned to relatively small units, each maintained as a separate school in which teachers and pupils would work closely and continuously together. The distribution of students among the smaller units would be made without regard to the location of their homes but with the purpose of making each school as well integrated as possible.

Beyond these general outlines, there is little agreement on what an educational park should be. One view is that the full grade range should be included, from nursery school to community college. Others propose that a park serve one or two levels, perhaps elementary and junior high schools, or a comprehensive secondary program of three, four, or six years. New York City has examined the feasibility of using middle-school parks for grades five to eight, retaining small neighborhood schools for pre-kindergarten, kindergarten, and primary programs.

With such a combination, children and parents would be introduced to the public schools first in their own neighborhoods, where familiar relationships, short distances, and close home-school ties would be at their maximum. In these primary centers each child, depending on his age at entry, would spend four to seven years, and some children a longer period, receiving fundamental preparation that primary education at its best should provide. Remedial services, compensatory curricula, and enriched programs would be available to all who need them. At the fifth grade, each pupil would move on to the middle-school park where for the first time his classmates, now drawn from a much wider area, would reflect the diversity of a truly common school and, hopefully, a genuinely integrated one. All high schools, under this proposal, would operate under a city-wide policy of free choice for all students, subject only to such restrictions as were needed to prevent overcrowding and to respect requirements for admission to specialized programs.

[12]Nathan Jacobson (ed.), An Exploration of the Educational Park Concept (New York, 1964). The papers included in this report of a conference on the educational park contain the most perceptive appraisals of the concept currently available.

One criticism of the educational park is the excessively high costs that some associate with it. A single site and the construction required to house 10,000 pupils need be no greater, however, than the combined cost of ten sites and buildings for a thousand pupils each. Indeed, a larger site located on relatively open and cheaper land might well be less costly to assemble than comparable acreage in congested sections. The total operating costs for a single, well-managed park should be lower than those for several separate units. In almost every case, however, a large proportion of the pupils would have to be transported and the cost of that service financed as a new expense. As in any other new venture, the increased outlay required must be set against the anticipated return. In a well conceived educational park the better education and the improved social situation that may be expected offer future assets of substantial value.

Beside the possibilities for accomplishing school integration must be set the deterrents that currently retard the process, of which the most visible and powerful is the concept of the neighborhood school. Although the close identification of a school with its immediate community produces results beneficial to both, the battles now being fought in the name of that relationship, and sometimes for virtual possession of particular schools, obscure fundamental principles. The public school is the property not of its neighborhood but of the school district. Since the district itself is created by the state, it is quite reasonable to argue that both title and control rest ultimately with the people of the state as a whole. However commendable the interest of a neighborhood in its school may be, concern is not to be confused with proprietary control. Subject to the state's supervision, the school board alone is legally empowered to determine for any school whose children shall be admitted and whose excluded.

The neighborhood school is essentially an administrative device designed to assure all the children of a district equal educational opportunity and equal access to it. When the device ceases to serve those functions, and especially when its use is so distorted that it frustrates rather than furthers the primary purpose, it is the device rather than the purpose that must give way.

It is a curious coincidence that during the very period that city and suburban neighborhood schools have been gaining an almost sacrosanct status, the rural sections in which such schools were first established have been abandoning them. The neighborhood school in its original and most authentic form, the one-room schoolhouse, has been disappearing from the United States at the rate of 3,000 a year for the last half century. Despite understandable misgivings about school consolidation, rural parents by the millions have exchanged their nearby schools and the intensely local form of control many of them embody for the superior instruction and broader educational experiences more comprehensive institutions offer. They have learned that, despite its relative remoteness from the neighborhood, the consolidated school not only provides a broader curriculum, better books and equipment, and abler teachers, but, by drawing its pupils from a wider and more varied attendance area, also furnishes them an outlook upon the world that is impossible in the more homogeneous society of the local school.

City and suburban schools meanwhile have gone in quite the opposite direction, becoming steadily more segregated not only by race but also by social and economic level. The momentum of this movement creates one of the principal forces opposing integration in schools and communities. Combined with more common forms of racial prejudice, segregated housing, and repressive economic practices, the growing social stratification of the public school carries the most serious implications for the future of American society.

Despite the generous lip service that the common school has traditionally received, it is a clear fact that, in many parts of the country, substantial minorities of American children at both extremes of the social scale have not been educated in schools that could, by any reasonable criteria, be called inclusive. Yet the complementary truth is that the vast majority of our citizens, the white ones, at any rate, have been brought up in schools that "everybody" was expected to attend. Whether the connection between such childhood experiences and the health of a democratic society is still or ever was as close as Horace Mann held it to be, is beyond explicit demonstration. But whether an open society can be maintained and, even more to the present point, whether a hitherto excluded group can be brought into the full enjoyment of citizenship without the instrumentality of the common school, are questions this country cannot much longer evade. On so complex a matter, clear causal relationships are difficult to establish, but the correlation between the rise of the common school and the development of an open society in the United States is, to say the least, impressive. Before we accept by default or support by intent the trend toward stratified public education it would be well at least to project and appraise the probable consequences.

A second force impeding integration, in certain respects the first writ large, is generated by the growth of solidly white suburban communities around the heavily congested urban centers into which the Negro population finds itself channeled and confined. The "white noose" not only prevents the outward dispersion of Negroes but equally, if less directly, discourages white families from remaining in the city. As population density and neighborhood depression worsen, larger numbers of families with the freedom to choose and the power to act abandon both the city and its schools.

The steady increase of urban segregation, the growing ghettos, and the declining attractiveness of the city for all groups produce problems whose magnitude and complexity carry them beyond the control of separate localities. Every day the deteriorating situation emphasizes more strongly the need for a total reapproval of city-suburban relationships. If the present trend is allowed to continue, the difficulties that now plague the central city can be expected inevitably—and soon— to trouble entire metropolitan areas. The almost total segregation of the incorporated area, the political entity officially called the city, is hardly an acceptable alternative to the systematic desegregation of the total social and economic network that is in fact the city. It becomes constantly more evident that, unless steps are taken to bring about a better dispersion and integration of Negro citizens throughout metropolitan areas, direct action will be required to equalize educational opportunities and the process of school integration between the cities and their suburbs. This responsibility for re-examining urban-suburban racial imbalance and its locus is implied by a sentence in the *Brown* decision: "Such an opportunity [to secure an education] where the state has undertaken to provide it is a right which must be made available to all on equal terms." If the right to equal treatment in the schools, including freedom from racial segregation, overrides, as it does, statutes placing children in particular schools, the question naturally arises whether that right is to be restricted immediately by statutes that fix lines between local jurisdictions.

III

Imaginative and forthright action to bring as many children as possible into integrated schools as rapidly as possible is an urgent necessity, but it would be grossly unrealistic to assume that integration can be accomplished everywhere in the foreseeable future. In the borough of Manhattan, 78 percent of the public elementary-school pupils are Negro and Puerto Rican. Immediate and total integration could be accomplished there only by closing most of the schools in Manhattan and distributing their pupils among the remaining boroughs or by setting up a vast "exchange" system to move hundreds of thousands of children daily in both directions between Manhattan and other parts of the city. Quite aside from the sheer administrative and teaching problems such an operation would pose, little imagination is needed to predict the virtually unanimous objection of parents.

Important progress can be made, however, on the periphery of segregated communities, through the procedures described earlier and by energetic efforts to concentrate on the possible instead of deploring the impossible. When all the possibilities are exploited and new ones ingeniously devised, there will still remain many ghetto schools in which integration is simply not feasible. In those places, the only reasonable action is the massive improvement of schools to educate children where they are.

It is unhappily true, as Kenneth Clark points out,[13] that to ask for good schools in the ghetto is to risk the charge that one acquiesces in segregation. Yet, even though supporting better schools in ghettos has become a favorite ploy of the advocates of separate equality, that fact does not justify neglecting ghetto children. Indeed, many of these children are already so badly victimized by depriva-

[13]Kenneth B. Clark, *Dark Ghetto* (New York, 1965), p. 117.

tion and neglect that, if integration were instantly possible, strong remedial and compensatory programs would still be necessary to give them any reasonable chance to compete or to succeed.

In designing educational strategies to meet the special needs of Negro ghetto children the public schools are undertaking tasks they have never really faced up to before. The curricula of slum schools have almost invariably been no more than adapted versions of those designed for middle-class pupils. Even now, a number of the changes being introduced into slum schools involve little more than efforts to apply to the ghetto, although somewhat more effectively and more intensively, the characteristic practices of middle-class schools: smaller classes to teach traditional subjects; more time for reading, using standard readers; increased guidance service employing the customary techniques.

Such projects to multiply and intensify established procedures are by no means wholly wasteful or necessarily wrong. Kenneth Clark[14] insists with considerable justification that the change most needed in slum schools is an elevation of the teachers' expectations of the children. The main reason, he argues, that Negro students rank low academically is that too many teachers and the "system" as a whole consider them uneducable.

However much ghetto children could gain from proper motivation and a decent respect for their potentiality, strong encouragement and high expectation are not enough. No teacher can hope to teach effectively or fairly unless he differentiates between the child whose environment re-enforces the school's influence and the one whose out-of-school world is rarely even so good as neutral and more often is severely damaging. While much can be said for holding both children to the same level of expectation, it is hardly realistic to assume that both will reach it with equal personal effort and the same assistance from the school. The child suffering unusual deprivation would appear obviously to require—and to deserve—unusual attention. The extent to which the special help should be compensatory, or remedial, or unusually stimulating is, of course, a suitable subject of investigation and debate; but that it must be particularly adapted to the child who is victimized by his environment would seem self-evident.

A growing volume of research not only documents the relationship between a child's cultural environment and his school success but also illuminates with increasing clarity the crucial importance of the early years. Benjamin Bloom[15] has examined many of the pertinent studies in the field and estimates that the difference between a culturally deprived and a culturally abundant environment can affect a child's IQ by an average of twenty points, half of the difference being attributable to the influences of the first four years and as much as six points to the next four. After another comprehensive survey, J. McVicker Hunt[16] concludes

[14]*Ibid.*, pp. 131–133.

[15]Benjamin S. Bloom, *Stability and Change in Human Characteristics* (New York, 1964), pp. 68–76.

[16]J. McVicker Hunt, "The Psychological Basis for Using Pre-School Enrichment as an Antidote for Cultural Deprivation," *Merrill Palmer Quarterly*, Vol. 10 (July 1964), p. 236.

that while the notion of cultural deprivation is still gross and undifferentiated, the concept holds much promise. He considers it entirely possible to arrange institutional settings in which culturally handicapped children can encounter experiences that will compensate for what they may have missed. Martin Deutsch,[17] whose work has included extended experimentation with such children, has found that those with some preschool experience attain significantly higher intelligence-test scores at the fifth grade than do children of the same background who did not have the experience.

Opinions differ as to the type of preschool program that offers the most fruitful compensation to slum children. One approach assumes that ordinary home-supplementing nursery schools designed for middle-class children will also help the deprived youngster. A second concentrates on preparing the culturally deprived child for school by teaching him to follow directions and to use such things as toys, pencils, crayons, and books. A third approach begins with the view that the culturally deprived child differs fundamentally from others in self-concept, language values, and perceptual processes and offers specialized programs to compensate for the deleterious effects of his lean environment.

While there are still no systematic comparisons of the relative effectiveness of these different programs, two generalizations can be stated with some assurance. One is that preschool programs do appear to be effective in raising intelligence test scores, vocabulary level, expressive ability, arithmetic reasoning, and reading readiness.

The second is that the results do not run uniformly in one direction. A study made in the Racine public schools[18] reports that:

Potentially the most useful conclusion which can be drawn . . . is that "one shot" compensatory programs would seem to be a waste of time and money. The fact that differences between groups disappeared and that in several areas the rate of growth of both groups regressed during the traditional first grade years supports this contention.

If these implications are supported by future research, it would seem that curriculum revision over the entire twelve year school curriculum is a necessary part of any lasting solution to the basic problem of urban public school education.

The Racine finding bears out what anyone experienced in slum schools would probably have predicted. Any such teacher knows that the moment the child steps outside, at whatever age, he is caught again in the cultural downdraft of the street and all too often of the home itself. Efforts to compensate within the school must, therefore, begin at the earliest possible age and continue with steady and strong consistency throughout the whole length of the child's school career.

One outstanding example of what may be done in the upper grades was the

Demonstration Guidance Project,[19] initiated in 1956 in New York's Junior High School 43 located on the edge of Harlem. The principal aim of the project was to identify and stimulate potentially able pupils and to help them reach levels of performance more nearly consistent with their capacities. The project students, all selected because they were thought to possess latent academic aptitude and most of them from disadvantaged backgrounds, were placed in small classes, given double periods daily in English, and tutored in small groups. Intensive counseling, clinical services, and social work were provided, and regular contact was maintained with the parents. Scholastic achievement was stressed and special efforts made to prepare the students for college or jobs. Visits were conducted to museums, theaters, concerts, the ballet, and places of special interest in New York and elsewhere. The program was continued into the George Washington Senior High School and the last experimental group graduated in 1960. After three and a half years of this special attention, these students, most of whom would ordinarily have been considered poor academic risks, showed substantial gains over their own earlier records, and over the usual performance of students from the same school. Of one hundred five in one group, seventy-eight showed an increase in IQ, sixty-four gaining ten points or more. The median for the entire group rose in the three-year period from 92.9 to 102.2. Against a previous average for their school of 47 percent, 64 percent earned high-school diplomas. Three students ranked first, fourth, and sixth in their class; two and one-half times as many as in previous classes went to college, and three and one-half times as many to some form of further education.

On a modified and reduced scale, the Demonstration Guidance Project was subsequently introduced as the Higher Horizons Program to other schools in New York City with results that have been comparably positive if somewhat less spectacular.

IV

Special programs to meet the needs of deprived children have been undertaken in a number of school systems. A project in the Banneker Group of the St. Louis school system has stressed the teaching of reading, English, and arithmetic. Particular attention was directed to the motivation of the pupils, to setting standards of performance. The support of parents was solicited, and their pride in their children's accomplishments was stimulated. By the end of the third year of the project the achievement of Banneker eighth graders equalled or exceeded national norms in reading and language and fell only one month short in arithmetic. In the years immediately preceding, the comparable scores had ranged from one to two years below the national norms. The theme of the Banneker

[19]Board of Education of City of New York, *The Demonstration Guidance Project, Fourth Annual Report, 1959–60*, pp. 2–15.

project is expressed by Samuel Sheppard, the administrator who conceived it, in his instructions to teachers: "Quit teaching by IQ and the neighborhood where the child lives. Teach the child all you can teach him."[20]

Detroit set up a new effort during the 1960–61 academic year with some 10,000 elementary and secondary pupils, mainly in the Negro residential areas, concentrating not only on the children but also on work with parents and teachers. A principal aim was to modify teachers' perceptions of children with limited backgrounds. The program included curriculum revision, re-organized teaching schedules, tutoring, home visiting, and supplementary activities for pupils during after-school hours and summer months.

A Pittsburgh project centered in the "Hill" district employed team teaching to improve instruction in reading and the language arts.

Virtually every large school system in the country and many of the smaller ones are now attacking the problem of the culturally deprived child, but the volume of well-intentioned activity still substantially exceeds the amount of imaginative and well-designed research that is being done to analyze and appraise the innovations. Until the quality of experimental design and research matches the quantity of sheer energy being devoted to the task, much of the energy is certain to be wasted and potentially valuable information and insights to be lost.

A field in which further study and fresh thinking are badly needed is vocational education, where the long-standing practice of separating vocational students from those in academic programs has more recently been compounded by the effects of racial imbalance. The result has been to render vocational programs in some schools all but useless. The field has suffered also because many schools have adhered too long and too closely to the concepts of curriculum and organization developed forty years ago. The tragically high rate of unemployment among Negro youth is only one of urgent reasons for the early and thorough reform of this essential part of American education.

In higher education impressive progress in some institutions has diverted attention from the massive obstacles that remain to be overcome. While a detailed discussion of this situation is beyond the scope of this paper it is relevant to emphasize the reciprocal relationship between accomplishments by Negroes in colleges and universities and the improvement of elementary and secondary schools, a prominent element in this relationship being the supply of well-prepared Negro teachers. Hard facts on the relative competence of white graduates and Negro graduates of teacher education programs are not easy to secure, but such evidence as has come to light, most of it subjective, suggests that much remains to be done to equalize the quality of programs and the availability of places in first-rate schools. Despite the fact that thousands of Negro teachers have attained high levels of professional competence and status, many others who hold teaching certificates are unable to obtain employment even in schools that want

[20]William K. Wyant, Jr., "Reading: A Way Upward" in *Civil Rights USA, Public Schools, Cities in the North and West* (Washington, D.C., 1962).

Negro teachers, because of their inability to compete with other applicants. A largely similar situation prevails in graduate-school admissions.

McGrath's study of Negro colleges[21] provides part of the explanation and suggests directions in which some of the answers must be sought: the prompt and substantial upgrading of faculties, curricula, libraries, laboratories, and physical facilities of the colleges that serve predominantly Negro student bodies and enroll more than half the Negro college students of the country.

Another important part of the solution must be found in programs in high school and between high school and college to furnish the supplemental instruction that many Negro students require in order to qualify for first-rate institutions. The encouraging reports of such programs as those conducted by the National Scholarship Service and Fund for Negro Students,[22] as well as by a number of the institutions themselves, indicate what special effort and thoughtful planning toward that end can accomplish.

"A grand mental and moral experiment," Horace Mann once called free schools,[23] "whose effects could not be developed and made manifest in a single generation."

For the Negro American, the development of those effects has taken a good deal longer—far too much longer—than was required to make them manifest for his white countrymen. The knowledge that the Negro's right to education has been restricted is no new discovery, but what is new is the growing consciousness that what has been withheld from him has impoverished the whole people.

The argument for enlarging the opportunities and enhancing the status of the Negro minority goes far beyond extending a modicum more of charity to the poor. The appeal to equity and to the humane principles that undergird the democratic enterprise is the heart of the matter, to be sure, but the evidence is now irrefutable that until each American has full access to the means to develop his capacities every other American's chances and attainments will continue to be diminished.

That this relationship should become so critically significant in a time characterized by technological progress may seem paradoxical; yet it is that progress and the insatiable demand it generates for intellectual competence that now re-enforces our long-standing moral obligation to re-examine the standards by which we live as a society.

The detailed problems of procedure which flow from this obligation impose a complex array of tasks upon the network of the arts, the sciences, the humani-

[21]Earl J. McGrath, *The Predominantly Negro Colleges and Universities in Transition* (New York, 1965), pp. 21 ff.
[22]Kenneth B. Clark and Lawrence Plotkin, *The Negro Student at Integrated Colleges* (New York, 1963), pp. 7 ff.
[23]Horace Mann, "Intellectual Education as a Means of Removing Poverty and Securing Abundance," Twelfth Annual Report, *Annual Reports of the Board of Education of Massachusetts for the Years 1845–48* (Boston, 1891), p. 246.

ties, and the professional specialities that contribute knowledge and skill to the educational establishment. But here, too—here especially—the prior question and the transcendent issue are moral: What ought we to be doing?

If the educational and political leadership of the country can muster the strength of conscience to face that query forthrightly and honestly, there are abundant grounds for optimism that the subsidiary tasks will become both more clearly visible and more readily feasible.

How to Integrate Your District's Curriculum

[A] quick quiz on the Negro in American history:

Can you name "the first martyr of the American revolution"—a black man who was gunned down by Redcoats, along with four others, in a protest against taxation without representation?

Do you know what Negro woman led more than 300 slaves to freedom on the Underground Railroad?

Who performed the world's first successful open-heart surgery?

Who developed the blood bank system?

What Negro author was a close advisor to President Lincoln and a key leader in both the Abolitionist movement and the civil rights movement of Reconstruction?

If you haven't done well on this quiz, don't toss it off to poor memory. Your U.S. history students would probably flub these questions, too—and so would their teachers. Everyone forgets facts—but you *can't* forget facts you haven't been taught.

And this is the problem.

- The American Negro has been deprived of his heritage, his history and his heroes.
- Equally tragic, the *white* American has been deprived of knowledge about, and understanding of, the Negro race and its past.
- The nation's public school system must shoulder a major share of the responsibility for rectifying this situation.

Clearly, there is an urgent need to integrate the nation's curriculum, as well as its classrooms; to wipe out the stain of racism that leads to the standard portrayal of U.S. history as a lily-white drama, with a few black bit players in the background, strumming banjos; to restore to America's past the black men who sailed with Columbus, explored with DeSoto and roamed the western frontiers with Buffalo Bill and Wyatt Earp.

Increasingly, schoolmen are demonstrating an awareness of this need—and a healthy appetite for meeting it.

And, happily, the task is not as tough as it might, at first glance, seem:

You do not have to create a Negro history and culture. It is there. And it is a fascinating history: with heroes and villains, great men and small; with inventors, artists and scientists; with leaders and rebels.

You do not have to write a Negro history. It has been written and rewritten; for all grade levels; for all ability levels. It is available in hardcover books, paperbacks, film strips, recordings, movies and programed courses.

You do not have to devise new curriculum guides that show how to integrate the available Negro histories into present courses. Good ones have been developed, used, tested, and found workable.

However, in order to integrate your curriculum, you *do* have to:

1. Correct distortions in present American history textbooks.
2. Supplement information that is now lacking in your courses.
3. Fill in the Negro "vacuum" in areas other than history; for example, in reading, literature, art, music, science, and in the school library.
4. Seek out extra-curricular activities that will help make up for the deficits inherent in an all-white or segregated community.

WHERE TO START

Probably the best way to begin is to find out what is wrong with your present curriculum.

One of the better critiques of current history textbooks, and one that has received national recognition, is written by Irving Sloan, a former attorney and now a social studies teacher in Scarsdale, N.Y. In the introduction of his "The Negro in Modern American History Textbooks,"[1] Sloan says that his purpose is to "determine how the Negro is represented in the latest editions of a selected group of secondary school American history textbooks."

By pinpointing the myths and gaping holes that exist in current texts, Sloan has both diagnosed problems and prescribed antidotes. His book does more than damn the bad: it praises the good, fills in the gaps and shows how the subtle powers of ignorance can lead to prejudice.

Says Sloan: "Negroes have never fared well in history textbooks. True, there has been progress through the years—including some startling changes. But even today, there's plenty of room for further improvement."

[1]*Editors' note:* For this and other books mentioned in this selection, see the "Appendix" of sources and references at the end of this book, pages 447–470.

One example: the myth, common to many texts, that Negro slaves were uncommonly "well off" and, on the whole, devoted to their white masters. Sloan quotes from a 1962 revised edition of *The Growth of the American Republic,* by Morison and Commager:

. . . the Negro was a great success as a slave. He did not, like the Indians enslaved by the Spaniards, mope or die; he did not infiltrate and 'take over,' like the Greeks and Asiatic slaves in the Roman Empire. Between him and his southland he acquired so strong a love that even under freedom, it was long before any appreciable number would move to other sections or countries . . .

But even this is an improvement over the following passage from a 1950 edition of the same text:

As for Sambo, whose wrongs moved the abolitionists to wrath and tears, there is some reason to believe that he suffered less than any other class in the South from its 'peculiar institution'.

Summing up his short book—it takes him only 95 pages to comment on virtually every reference to Negroes in 25 junior and senior high school texts—Sloan says: "In most texts, it can be said that the Negro is considered only as a slave before the Civil War and a problem since the Civil War." His conclusion is reinforced by more than a score of similar studies.

Setting the Record Straight

How can you compensate for the racial inadequacies of textbooks which, in every other respect, may be excellent teaching tools?

One of the best of more than twenty curriculum guides that show how to integrate history texts is by William Loren Katz: "Teachers' Guide to American History."

It presents a compact history of the Negro in America and a step-by-step analysis of how to correlate this information with that given in presently inadequate texts. Up-to-date bibliographies are extensive and well-annotated, with specific references, for teachers and students, relating to each chapter. Annotations include comments on the value of various references for various grade and ability levels.

Some of the "holes" in textbooks that Katz's book helps to fill:

1538: Estevanico, an African with the Spanish explorers, opens up Arizona and New Mexico.

1770: Crispus Attucks, a runaway slave, is the first to fall in the Boston Massacre.

1844: George W. Bush leads white settlers into the Oregon territory.

1846: Free Negro Norbert Rillieux devises a vacuum pan that revolutionizes the world sugar refining industry.

1861-65: More than 200,000 Negroes serve in the Union Army and Navy; 22 win Medals of Honor.

1883: Jan Matzeliger invents a machine that manufactures a complete shoe, revolutionizing the entire industry.

1876: Negro cowboy Nat Love, who rode with the James gang and Billy the Kid, outshoots everyone in the Deadwood Rodeo to earn the title of "Deadwood Dick."

1893: Dr. Daniel Hale Williams performs the first successful open-heart operation.

1917: Henry Johnson and Needham Roberts, two of 100,000 Negroes sent to France, become the first two Americans to earn the Croix de Guerre in World War I.

1941: Dr. Charles Drew develops the blood bank system.

1950: Dr. Ralph Bunche is awarded the Nobel Peace Prize for his part in bringing peace to the Holy Land.

1954: Negro attorneys, led by Thurgood Marshall, win U.S. Supreme Court reversal of a half-century of legal school segregation.

1964: Dr. Martin Luther King, Jr. receives Nobel Peace Prize.

1967: Thurgood Marshall becomes the first Negro Supreme Court Justice.

Teaching the Teachers

Ultimately teachers, not textbooks, must strike racism from the heart of the nation's curriculums.

Fortunately, a wealth of teacher reference material is available and some progress can be made by simply getting a few of the right materials into the hands of the right people. Teachers who are given the books by Sloan and Katz, for example, will be off to a good start.

The next step: bring in supplementary curricular materials and organize them to fit into existing courses.

Says Katz:

There is *no special methodology* to be used in teaching about the Negro role in our history. A teacher can use any methods that he has successfully employed in the past—developmental lessons, homework, class discussions, outside reading assignments, committee work, dramatizations, charts, movies, filmstrips, bulletin board displays, research projects.

This material need not be highlighted; rather it should be *painlessly* made part of the lesson or single course of study. This will vary from teacher to teacher, class to class, grade-level to grade-level.

For additional teacher background in the general subject, Katz highly recommends these two histories: John Hope Franklin's *From Slavery to Freedom* and Langston Hughes' and Milton Meltzer's *A Pictorial History of the Negro in America*. From there, he says, the list of good reference materials stretches out almost endlessly.

Inservice training for teachers can vary, says Sloan, from regularly scheduled seminars, under the direction of a department chairman, to full-dress courses for credit.

Getting the teachers to handle their own inservice work, if it is not possible to develop an arrangement with a nearby college, might entail sending a staff member to one of the several institutes conducted throughout the nation on this subject. This staff member can then guide others in his district. State departments of education, which are becoming increasingly aware of this problem, are a good source to turn to for other leads to teacher training, too, says Sloan.

Integrating Other Subjects

Not surprisingly, curriculum areas other than history also fail to adequately deal with Negro contributions to our culture.

For the most part, Negro authors, musicians, artists and scientists are ignored in the English, music, art and science courses.

A useful bibliography here is one by Erwin A. Salk, *A Layman's Guide to Negro History*.

Salk's book lists and annotates over 150 books on Negro culture, including the works of novelists, poets, song writers, dramatists and painters. One chapter deals only with books and pamphlets on race, which would be suitable for either science or social studies courses. Both Salk and Katz list AV materials as well as books.

The school library can make a real contribution to your district's program for integrating curriculum. It can acquire Negro histories, magazines such as *Ebony*, and biographies of Negro leaders. For that matter, entire *series* of inexpensive paperback and hardcover books on minority groups are being published. One such series, published by Zenith Books, a division of Doubleday & Co., is written on a sixth-grade reading level. But it is also of interest to older students and adults. Most of the books in the series deal with Negroes; some, however, present stories of American Chinese, Mexicans, Puerto Ricans and Indians.

All book purchasers in a district should be aware of a recent development called "multi-racial textbooks," which attempt, through illustrations of children with different ethnic backgrounds, to give a more representative outlook on our racially mixed society. An annotated bibliography of 399 pre-school and elementary texts, "Integrated School Books," is available from the National Association for the Advancement of Colored People.

Extra-curricular activities, too, have been used by school districts to reinforce the integration of their curriculum. These activities include student visitations between predominantly white and predominantly Negro schools; assemblies featuring Negro civic and business leaders; and summer camp projects that promote biracial discussion and recreational programs.

Another possibility: elective courses devoted exclusively to Afro-American history. Such courses are being introduced in many big-city districts that have large

Negro populations. This type of course is often demanded by "black power" groups and this will probably not diminish until regular American history courses become fully integrated, Sloan predicts. Until then, he says, each district should consider whether a Negro history course is warranted and feasible.

I'm Willing—But Are They?

All right—fine and dandy. You can see the need to act and you can see what must be done.

But what about your community? Specifically, what about those who may seize upon your efforts to integrate curriculum as an opportunity to stir up trouble? Do you have to drag your district, kicking and screaming, into the 20th century? Or can it be done quietly and efficiently—no muss, no fuss?

As a matter of fact, there appears to be little cause for concern about possible community reaction. Districts that have initiated efforts to rectify racial inequities in curriculum have met little, if any, hostility.

In fact, one of the pioneers in this area—the Thornton township high school, in Harvey, Illinois—reports that, after four years of developing and implementing an elaborate "integration" program, there were no problems from parents and very few from students.

N. Franklin Hurt, a history teacher in Harvey, a racially mixed suburb of Chicago, says there has been no backlash whatsoever. "Of course, members of the black community are terribly enthusiastic about it," Hurt says. "But history courses have taken on a new excitement and interest for all students—black *and* white. It makes history *relevant* to today's student."

Hurt stresses the importance of an *active* role for administrators in the development of an integrated curriculum.

It's too easy to hand a teacher a bunch of supplementary materials that will just sit in the bottom drawer of the teacher's desk. A good administrator, however, knows how to turn on the pressure to overcome apathy.

One district faced with a different problem, White Plains, N.Y., recently went through a period of demonstrations and strife until demands for integrated studies and extracurricular activities, spearheaded by Negro students, were met. This occurred despite the fact that, unknown to the community, the school system had been preparing an integrated K-12 social studies program several months *before* the student boycotts and other incidents took place!

Carroll F. Johnson, White Plains superintendent, cautions school districts to expect a few problems—and to take them in stride. Says Johnson:

While we may not like the abrasive and anti-social tactics employed by various pressure groups to further their causes, we can't lose sight of the possible validity of their goals.

A few years ago, we of the over-30 generation were deploring youth's 'lack of involvement.' But now young people, both black and white, are at the center of the social forces that are causing us to re-examine our customs, our conventions and our creeds.

The demand for more information about the Negro contribution to our history is a legitimate demand. It can hardly be questioned by any reasonable adult. Naturally, it would be better for the schools to lead the students, rather than the other way around. But no matter who does the leading—or who *seems* to lead, and who *seems* to follow— enlightened school leadership will ultimately channel the forces of social change into constructive paths.

Only if we administrators are capable of helping our students accomplish legitimate objectives can we be in the position of insisting upon orderly conduct and the use of democratic processes, rather than revolutionary tactics.

A Talk to Teachers

James Baldwin

Let's begin by saying that we are living through a very dangerous time. Everyone in this room is in one way or another aware of that. We are in a revolutionary situation, no matter how unpopular that word has become in this country. The society in which we live is desperately menaced, not by Khrushchev, but from within. So any citizen of this country who figures himself as responsible —and particularly those of you who deal with the minds and hearts of young people—must be prepared to "go for broke." Or to put it another way, you must understand that in the attempt to correct so many generations of bad faith and cruelty, when it is operating not only in the classroom but in society, you will meet the most fantastic, the most brutal, and the most determined resistance. There is no point in pretending that this won't happen.

Now, since I am talking to school-teachers and I am not a teacher myself, and in some ways am fairly easily intimidated, I beg you to let me leave that and go back to what I think to be the entire purpose of education in the first place. It would seem to me that when a child is born, if I'm the child's parent, it is my obligation and my high duty to civilize that child. Man is a social animal. He cannot exist without a society. A society, in turn, depends on certain things which everyone within that society takes for granted. Now, the crucial paradox which confronts us here is that the whole process of education occurs within a social framework and is designed to perpetuate the aims of society. Thus, for example, the boys and girls who were born during the era of the Third Reich, when educated to the purposes of the Third Reich, became barbarians. The paradox of education is precisely this—that as one begins to become conscious

From *Saturday Review*, December 21, 1963, Vol. 46, No. 51, pp. 42–44. Copyright © 1963, James Baldwin. Reprinted by permission of the author.

one begins to examine the society in which he is being educated. The purpose of education, finally, is to create in a person the ability to look at the world for himself, to make his own decisions, to say to himself this is black or this is white, to decide for himself whether there is a God in heaven or not. To ask questions of the universe, and then learn to live with those questions, is the way he achieves his own society. But no society is really anxious to have that kind of person around. What societies really, ideally, want is a citizenry which will simply obey the rules of society. If a society succeeds in this, that society is about to perish. The obligation of anyone who thinks of himself as responsible is to examine society and try to change it and to fight it—at no matter what risk. This is the only hope society has. This is the only way societies change.

Now, if what I have tried to sketch has any validity, it becomes thoroughly clear, at least to me, that any Negro who is born in this country, and undergoes the American education system runs the risk of becoming schizophrenic. On the other hand he is born in the shadow of the stars and stripes and he is assured it represents a nation which has never lost a war. He pledges allegiance to that flag which guarantees "liberty and justice for all." He is part of a country in which anyone can become President, and so forth. But on the other hand he is also assured by his country and countrymen that he has never contributed anything to civilization—that his past is nothing more than a record of humiliations gladly endured. He is assured by the republic that he, his father, his mother, and his ancestors were happy, shiftless, watermelon-eating darkies who loved Mr. Charlie and Miss Ann, that the value he has as a black man is proven by one thing only—his devotion to white people. If you think I am exaggerating, examine the myths which proliferate in this country about Negroes.

Now all this enters the child's consciousness much sooner that we as adults would like to think it does. As adults, we are easily fooled because we are so anxious to be fooled. But children are very different. Children, not yet aware that it is dangerous to look too deeply at anything, look at everything, look at each other, and draw their own conclusions. They don't have the vocabulary to express what they see, and we, their elders, know how to intimidate them very easily and very soon. But a black child, looking at the world around him, though he cannot know quite what to make of it, is aware that there is a reason why his mother works so hard, why his father is always on edge. He is aware that there is some reason why, if he sits down in the front of the bus, his father or mother slaps him and drags him to the back of the bus. He is aware that there is some terrible weight on his parents' shoulders which menaces him. And it isn't long—in fact it begins when he is in school—before he discovers the shape of his oppression.

Let us say that the child is seven years old and I am his father, and I decide to take him to the zoo, or to Madison Square Garden, or to the U.N. Building, or to any of the tremendous monuments we find all over New York. We get into a bus and we go from where I live on 131st Street and Seventh Avenue downtown through the park and we get into New York City, which is not Harlem.

Now, where the boy lives—even if it is a housing project, is in an undesirable neighborhood. If he lives in one of those housing projects of which everyone in New York is so proud, he has at the front door, if not closer, the pimps, the whores, the junkies—in a word, the danger of life in the ghetto. And the child knows this, though he doesn't know why.

I still remember my first sight of New York. It was really another city when I was born—where I was born. We looked down over the Park Avenue street-car tracks. It was Park Avenue, but I didn't know what Park Avenue meant *downtown*. The Park Avenue I grew up on, which is still standing, is dark and dirty. No one would dream of opening a Tiffany's on that Park Avenue, and when you go downtown you discover that you are literally in the white world. It is rich—or at least it looks rich. It is clean—because they collect garbage downtown. There are doormen. People walk about as though they owned where they were —and indeed they do. And it's a great shock. It's very hard to relate yourself to this. You don't know what it means. You know—you know instinctively—that none of this is for you. You know this before you are told. And who is it for and who is paying for it? And why isn't it for you?

Later on when you become a grocery boy or messenger and you try to enter one of those buildings a man says, "Go to the back door." Still later, if you happen by some odd chance to have a friend in one of those buildings, the man says, "Where's your package?" Now this by no means is the core of the matter. What I'm trying to get at is that by this time the Negro child has had, effectively, almost all the doors of opportunity slammed in his face, and there are very few things he can do about it. He can more or less accept it with an absolutely inarticulate and dangerous rage inside—all the more dangerous because it is never expressed. It is precisely those silent people whom white people see every day of their lives—I mean your porter and your maid, who never say anything more than "Yes Sir" and "No Ma'am." They will tell you its raining if that is what you want to hear, and they will tell you the sun is shining if *that* is what you want to hear. They really hate you—really hate you because in their eyes (and they're right) you stand between them and life. I want to come back to that in a moment. It is the most sinister of the facts, I think, which we now face.

There is something else the Negro child can do, too. Every street boy—and I was a street boy, so I know—looking at the society which has produced him, looking at the standards of that society which are not honored by anybody, looking at your churches and the government and the politicians, understands that this structure is operated for someone else's benefit—not for his. And there's no room in it for him. If he is really cunning, really ruthless, really strong —and many of us are—he becomes a kind of criminal. He becomes a kind of criminal because that's the only way he can live. Harlem and every ghetto in this city—every ghetto in this country—is full of people who live outside the law. They wouldn't dream of calling a policeman. They wouldn't, for a moment, listen to any of those professions of which we are so proud on the Fourth of

July. They have turned away from this country forever and totally. They live by their wits and really long to see the day when the entire structure comes down.

The point of all this is that black men were brought here as a source of cheap labor. They were indispensable to the economy. In order to justify the fact that men were treated as though they were animals, the white republic had to brainwash itself into believing that they were, indeed, animals and *deserved* to be treated like animals. Therefore it is almost impossible for any Negro child to discover anything about his actual history. The reason is that this "animal," once he suspects his own worth, once he starts believing that he is a man, has begun to attack the entire power structure. This is why America has spent such a long time keeping the Negro in his place. What I am trying to suggest to you is that it was not an accident, it was not an act of God, it was not done by well-meaning people muddling into something which they didn't understand. It was a deliberate policy hammered into place in order to make money from black flesh. And now, in 1963, because we have never faced this fact, we are in intolerable trouble.

The Reconstruction, as I read the evidence, was a bargain between the North and South to this effect: "We've liberated them from the land—and delivered them to the bosses." When we left Mississippi to come North we did not come to freedom. We came to the bottom of the labor market, and we are still there. Even the Depression of the 1930's failed to make a dent in Negroes' relationship to white workers in the labor unions. Even today, so brainwashed is this republic that people seriously ask in what they suppose to be good faith, "What does the Negro want?" I've heard a great many asinine questions in my life, but that is perhaps the most asinine and perhaps the most insulting. But the point here is that people who ask that question, thinking that they ask it in good faith, are really the victims of this conspiracy to make Negroes believe they are less than human.

In order for me to live, I decided very early that some mistake had been made somewhere. I was not a "nigger" even though you called me one. But if I was a "nigger" in your eyes, there was something about you—there was something you needed. I had to realize when I was very young that I was none of those things I was told I was. I was not, for example, happy. I never touched a watermelon for all kinds of reasons. I had been invented by white people, and I knew enough about life by this time to understand that whatever you invent, whatever you project, is you! So where we are now is that a whole country of people believe I'm a "nigger," and I *don't*, and the battle's on! Because if I am not what I've been told I am, then it means that you're not what you thought *you* were *either!* And that is the crisis.

It is not really a "Negro revolution" that is upsetting this country. What is upsetting this country is a sense of its own identity. If, for example, one managed to change the curriculum in all the schools so that Negroes learned more about themselves and their real contributions to this culture, you would be liberating not only Negroes, you'd be liberating white people who know nothing about their own history. And the reason is that if you are compelled to lie about one aspect of anybody's history, you must lie about it all. If you have to lie about my real role here, if you have to pretend that I hoed all that cotton just because I loved you, then you have done something to yourself. You are mad.

Now let's go back a minute. I talked earlier about those silent people—the porter and the maid—who, as I said, don't look up at the sky if you ask them if it is raining, but look into your face. My ancestors and I were very well trained. We understood very early that this was not a Christian nation. It didn't matter what you said or how often you went to church. My father and my mother and my grandfather and my grandmother knew that Christians didn't act this way. It was as simple as that. And if that was so there was no point in dealing with white people in terms of their own moral professions, for they were not going to honor them. What one did was to turn away, smiling all the time, and tell white people what they wanted to hear. But people always accuse you of reckless talk when you say this.

All this means that there are in this country tremendous reservoirs of bitterness which have never been able to find an outlet, but may find an outlet soon. It means that well-meaning white liberals place themselves in great danger when they try to deal with Negroes as though they were missionaries. It means, in brief, that a great price is demanded to liberate all those silent people so that they can breathe for the first time and *tell* you what they think of you. And a price is demanded to liberate all those white children—some of them near forty—who have never grown up, and who never will grow up, because they have no sense of their identity.

What passes for identity in America is a series of myths about one's heroic ancestors. It's astounding to me, for example, that so many people really appear to believe that the country was founded by a band of heroes who wanted to be free. That happens not to be true. What happened was that some people left Europe because they couldn't stay there any longer and had to go some place else to make it. That's all. They were hungry, they were poor, they were convicts. Those who were making it in England, for example, did not get on the *Mayflower*. That's how the country was settled. Not by Gary Cooper. Yet we have a whole race of people, a whole republic, who believe the myths to the point where even today they select political representatives, as far as I can tell, by how closely they resemble Gary Cooper. Now this is dangerously infantile, and it shows in every level of national life. When I was living in Europe, for example, one of the worst revelations to me was the way Americans walked around Europe buying this and buying that and insulting everybody—not even out of malice, just because they didn't know any better. Well, that is the way they have always treated me. They weren't cruel, they just didn't know you were alive. They didn't know you had any feelings.

What I am trying to suggest here is that in the doing of all this for 100 years or more, it is the American white man who has long since lost his grip on reality. In some peculiar way, having created this myth about Negroes, and the myths about the world so that, for example, he was astounded that some people could prefer Castro, astounded that there are people in the world who don't go into hiding when they hear the word "Communism," astounded that Communism is one of the realities of the twentieth century which we will not overcome by pretending that it does not exist. The political level in this country now, on the part of people who should know better, is abysmal.

The Bible says somewhere that where there is not vision the people perish. I don't think anyone can doubt that in this country today we are menaced—intolerably menaced—by a lack of vision.

It is inconceivable that a sovereign people should continue, as we do so abjectly, to say, "I can't do anything about it. It's the government." The government is the creation of the people. It is responsible to the people. And the people are responsible for it. No American has the right to allow the present government to say, when Negro children are being bombed and hosed and shot and beaten all over the deep South, that there is nothing we can do about it. There must have been a day in this country's life when the bombing of four children in Sunday School would have created a public uproar and endangered the life of Governor Wallace. It happened here and there was no public uproar.

I began by saying that one of the paradoxes of education was that precisely at the point when you begin to develop a conscience, you must find yourself at war with your society. It is your responsibility to change society if you think of yourself as an educated person. And on the basis of the evidence—the moral and political evidence—one is compelled to say that this is a backward society. Now if I were a teacher in this school, or any Negro school, and I was dealing with Negro children, who were in my care only a few hours of every day and would then return to their homes and to the street, children who have an apprehension of their future which with every hour grows grimmer and darker, I would try to teach them—I would try to make them know—that those streets, those houses, those dangers, those agonies by which they are surrounded, are criminal. I would try to make each child know that these things are the results of a criminal conspiracy to destroy him. I would teach him that there are currently very few standards in this country which are worth a man's respect. That it is up to him to begin to change these standards for the sake of the life and the health of the country. I would suggest to him that the popular culture—as represented, for example, on television and in comic books and in movies—is based on fantasies created by very ill people, and he must be aware that these are fantasies and have nothing to do with reality. I would teach him that the press he reads is not as free as it says it is—and that he can do something about that, too. I would try to make him know that just as American history is longer, larger, more various, more beautiful, and more terrible than anything anyone has ever said about it, so is the world larger, more daring, more beautiful, and more terrible, but principally larger—and that it belongs to him. I would teach him that he does not have to be bound by the expediencies of any given Administration, any given policy, any given time—that he has the right and the necessity to examine everything. I would try to show him that one has not learned anything about Castro when one says, "he is a Communist." This is a way of *not* learning something about Castro, something about Cuba, something, in fact, about the world. I would suggest to him that he is living, at the moment, in an enormous province. America is not the world and if America is going to become a nation, she must find a way—and this child must help her to find a way—to use the tremendous potential and tremendous energy which this child represents. If this country does not find a way to use that energy, it will be destroyed by that energy.

How Baseball Integrated a Hotel

Melvin Durslag

Ernie Banks reflected on his first road trip in Major League baseball. As a member of the Kansas City Monarchs, he had done a measure of traveling, as a second class tourist, but now it was 1953 and he had hit the big casino. He was shortstop for the Chicago Cubs.

The first town we were to visit was St. Louis, he recalls. I had been there with the Monarchs. We stayed at an old Negro establishment called the Olive hotel. But now I was traveling with the big boys.

When the Cubs arrived in St. Louis, Banks and his teammate, Gene Baker, were informed that this was the only town in the National League requiring segregated housing. They would have to be sent to a place for Negroes.

And damned if Ernie wasn't back at the Olive hotel.

Don Newcombe, now director of community relations for the Dodgers, listened to the story with great delight.

When the Dodgers used to hit St. Louis, said Newk, they would send us to the Olive, too. There was Robinson, Campanella, Gilliam and one or two others, besides myself. Summers used to boil in St. Louis, and the air hung so heavy in our rooms at night that we could hardly breathe. We used to soak our sheets in cold water and wrap them around us when we went to bed.

The whites, meanwhile, were stopping at a rather fashionable hotel that featured air conditioning.

By 1954, continued Newcombe, We couldn't stand it any longer. Jackie (Robinson) and I went to the manager of the hotel where the whites stayed and we told him we

---

From *S. F. Examiner*, June 19, 1970, p. 54.

were tired of sleeping in sheets we soaked with cold water. We asked if he would take us in.

He said he would under one condition. We had to promise not to use the swimming pool. I said to him, I don't want to swim. All I want to do is sleep. We finally got rooms—on that side of the hotel that didn't face the swimming pool.

For Newcombe and his roommate, Roy Campanella, it was like landing on an island in heaven.

"We never left the room, except to go to the ball park," he said. "We didn't want to leave the air conditioning."

Eating in hotel dining rooms was the next problem confronting the Negro players, according to Newcombe.

In hotels on the road, he said, we had been asked to eat our meals in the room. We were told to order anything we wanted and to sign the check, but to stay in the room. The clubs didn't want any trouble with the hotels.

In 1955 in Cincinnati, Robinson's wife came to visit him. He announced to the rest of the Negro players that he was going into the dining room. And he did.

Afterward, we waited anxiously to find out what happened. Jackie said that he and his wife were served like anyone else. We didn't believe him and we went to the hotel manager. He said he had no objection to our eating in the dining room. It's just that no one before had tried.

As absurd as it may have sounded, Newk tended to believe him because of what he termed automatic attitudes of the time.

"When I was a platoon sergeant in the Army," says Don, "I told a Negro kid from Georgia to do something. He answered. 'I don't take orders from Niggers.' He was a little guy, and I could have squashed him like a cockroach. But I turned him over, instead, to a white officer, who told him he had better do what I say. The point is this—in the frame of mind that then prevailed, the kid couldn't conceive of anyone being his boss except a white man."

As Newcombe reflects on the dining room situation in Cincinnati, he is seized by the terrifying thought that it was only fifteen years ago. "Negro kids playing ball today don't realize the great changes that have taken place in a short while," he says. "There is no serious problem for the Negro in sports anymore. Those of my era aren't looking for credit, but we do like to feel we had just a little something to do with making things better for the kids today."

In other words, when they visit St. Louis, they can observe a moment of silence for Newk, Campy, Jackie, Junior and the others who slept in soaked bedsheets at the Olive.

Working with the Afro-American Pupil

Jack D. Forbes

SUGGESTIONS FOR TEACHERS AND ADMINISTRATORS

A school serving Afro-American pupils should serve as a bridge between these students and the adult world which they will subsequently enter. This adult world will sometimes be Anglo in character, but more often it will be of a mixed Anglo-Negro culture. In any case, the school, if it is to be a bridge, must serve as a transitional experience and not as a sudden leap into a foreign set of values and practices.

Additionally, American Negroes live within the margins of a society which has treated them in an almost unbelievably repressive manner for three hundred years, and more terribly still, has attempted (consciously or otherwise) to instill in the Negro a sense of inferiority. The school must address itself to the task of bolstering the self-image of black pupils and adults in order to overcome the psychological effects of centuries of discrimination. This is a doubly difficult task in view of the continuing reality of life in the United States, but it must be undertaken as a central function of any school serving Afro-Americans.

For all of the above reasons such a school needs to develop a set of strategies, in close collaboration with the local black community, which will make the school truly belong to the people being served, rather than to the people who operate the school system.

The following are suggestions which hopefully will help to bring about such a change.

From *Afro-Americans In the Far West: A Handbook for Educators,* Berkeley, California: Far West Laboratory for Educational Research and Development, 1968, pp. 58–64. Reprinted by permission.

1. The school environment should have some element of Afro-American character, subject, of course, to the desires of the local black community. Such character can be created by means of murals depicting aspects of the Afro-American or African heritage, the erection of statues depicting outstanding leaders of African ancestry, displays of African and Afro-American arts and crafts, bulletin boards depicting black people and their accomplishments, and by the adoption of a name for the school which is relevant to our Afro-American past. The expense involved in the above will not necessarily be great, as adults in the local Afro-American community might well become involved in projects which would have the effect of making the school "their" school.

2. Teachers and administrators in such a school should be familiar with the dialect spoken by the pupils and should be encouraged to utilize this language wherever appropriate in order to enhance communication both with pupils and with parents.

3. Imaginative administrators and teachers may wish to further linguistic development by using the local dialect as an initial means for introducing language concepts and for developing bi-dialectical skills.

4. If the local dialect is sufficiently different from standard English, the latter will need to be taught with an "English as a second language" technique.

5. Where the local community is interested, non-European languages spoken in Africa (such as Arabic, Swahili, or Yoruba) might be offered along with, or in place of, European languages at the secondary level. The United States needs persons able to speak African native languages and likewise certain Afro-American groups are interested in having such idioms taught.

6. Supplementary materials utilized in the classroom, as well as library resources, should include numerous Negro-oriented items (magazines, newspapers, books, phonograph records, films, et cetera), in order to provide cross-cultural experiences for all pupils and to provide an atmosphere relevant to the black pupil's heritage. Afro-American periodicals used in the school should cover the full range of opinion, including, for example, *Ebony* magazine with its basically Negro middle class orientation, militantly separatist *Liberator* magazine, and *Mr. Muhammad Speaks,* an organ of the Nation of Islam. The issues which cannot be ignored by a publication are often real issues which cannot be ignored by a school designed to be involved with the community and its concerns.

7. Every effort should be made to acquaint pupils and visiting parents with the rich literature now available pertaining to Africa and Afro-Americans. Many techniques are useful, including a permanent display case near the main entrance to the school, a paperback library operated by students or parents, a paperback bookstore, and an extensive use of supplementary soft-cover books as a part of regular classwork. Books by black authors should be given special prominence, as in a display case where photographs of the author can be placed next to the book being exhibited.

8. Curricula in the school should possess a Negro dimension wherever appropriate. In social science courses where the development of the western United States is being discussed, attention should be given to the black pioneers of the Southwest, to Negro governors, explorers and soldiers, and to more recent Afro-American developments. Courses in Afro-American history should be offered in all schools attended by pupils of African ancestry and these courses should not limit their attention to United States English-speaking Negroes.

9. Courses in literature should include readings in African and Afro-American literature (in translation, if necessary) and works by and about Negroes.

10. Curricula in music and "music appreciation" should give attention to all classes of Afro-American music, including folk-"blues", jazz, Afro-Brazilian, Afro-Cuban, Calypso, and other forms. In many schools, instruction in Afro-American musical forms might well replace or supplement the standard band and orchestra classes, in order to take advantage of one of the important assets brought to school by many Negro pupils.

11. The dance would appear to be an area where many black young people can

readily contribute to the enrichment of a school's program. While it would be a mistake to hold that all youth of Negro background are "good dancers," it is nonetheless true that black culture encourages the development of this skill. African and Afro-American dance styles should be included in any dance curriculum, along with other forms of the art.

12. Arts and crafts courses should acquaint all pupils with African and Afro-American art forms and should provide a close tie-in with the various "Black Arts" movements developing in ghetto communities.

13. Southern Negro cooking should be available as a part of the school's programs in home economics wherever sufficient interest exists.

14. Since one of the primary objectives of educators should be the linking of the school with the local adult community, it follows that Afro-American adults and youth should be involved in the life of the school as resource people, supplementary teachers, teacher's aides, and special occasion speakers.

Additionally, local advisory committees should be asked to help develop policy either for a neighborhood school or for a Negro-oriented cultural enrichment program in a district-wide or regional school. *No elements of African or Afro-American culture should be introduced into any school without the active participation of local black people in the development of the program.*

15. Our Afro-American cultural heritage, whenever brought into the school, should be treated as an integral and valuable part of our common legacy, and not as a bit of "exotica" to be used solely for the benefit of black pupils.

16. In a school composed of students from diverse cultural backgrounds every effort should be made to bring a little of each culture into the school. A part of this effort might involve incorporating each major ethnic celebration into the school routine (focusing on Chinese-Americans at Chinese New Year, Mexican-Americans during the Cinco de Mayo, Negroes during Negro History Week, et cetera).

17. School personnel should receive special training in Afro-American culture and history and should have some background in anthropology and/or sociology. It may well be that school personnel hired for employment in ghetto-area schools should have several weeks of intensive pre-service training in cross-cultural dynamics not unlike that received by Peace Corps and VISTA trainees. Such training should actively involve persons from the local community to be served.

18. A school serving a ghetto neighborhood should become closely identified with the aspirations of the local community and should function, in so far as is possible, within the framework of the local culture. This may call for much reorientation on the part of middle class school personnel, whether of African or non-African ancestry. It will also call for a revamping of the curricula so that course content deals with the real world perceived daily by ghetto children. For example, courses in United States Government should describe the manner in which political action actually takes place and not an idealized version of what might be the case in some non-existent utopia. Perhaps one appropriate manner in which to teach governmental concepts might involve training secondary-level students as community organizers or community service workers.

19. School personnel who believe that it is important to examine pupils periodically in order to provide data on "ability" for future counseling or "tracking" should wish to obtain accurate information by the use of tests which are relatively unbiased. It is difficult to ascertain the potential of dialect-speaking youth by means of standard English-language tests, nor can that of low-income students be predicted on the basis of tests oriented toward middle-class paraphenalia or concepts. On the other hand, biased tests will substantially predict the formal achievement level of culturally different or low-income pupils attending biased schools. Therefore, a change in tests will accomplish little unless accompanied by changes in the school, which serve to realize and enhance the potential revealed by the new test.

20. Maximum use should be made of techniques which are designed to enhance self-concept and involve the community in the life of the school, including the use of parent teaching aides, older pupils as tutors for younger pupils, and college students of minority background as para-professional counselors.

The above suggestions are basically designed to change the atmosphere of the school so as to provide greater motivation for all concerned, as well as to impart useful knowledge. In addition, many curricular and methodological innovations are available which are expected to improve learning for *all* students and these new programs should certainly be made available to Afro-American youngsters. It is to be suspected, however, that a school which is basically indifferent or hostile toward the local black culture will not succeed in stimulating greater learning merely by the use of methodological innovations unaccompanied by a change in the general orientation of the school.

Attention should be given to African and Afro-American history and culture in all schools, regardless of ethnic composition. Anglo-American young people grow up in a "never-never" land of mythology as regards the Negro and it is crucial for our society's future that anti-Negro myths be exposed and eliminated. We must bear in mind that the "white problem in America," the tendency of Anglo-Americans for three centuries to exploit and denigrate non-whites, is probably still the major hurdle blocking the advancement of the black population. White young people, growing up in a mythic world of prejudice against Negroes and knowing nothing of black contributions, may well, as adults, frustrate many of the goals of educational programs directly involving Afro-Americans. *The multi-cultural reality of American life and history should be a part of every school's curriculum.*

In many urban settings, it may be that the creation of "Community Education Centers" in place of age-segregated secondary, continuation, and adult schools will contribute to the solution of a number of problems. Many urban centers lack sufficient facilities for "adult education," have essentially unsatisfactory "continuation schools" for their most difficult students, and experience serious discipline and motivation problems in the ordinary secondary schools.

For the above reasons, it is herein suggested that urban secondary schools be transformed into multi-purpose "educational centers" for the total community which they serve, after the pattern of the junior college. To eliminate the segregated "teenage" and "adult" schools, to add to the total educational resources of a community, and to improve school-community relations, the following specific changes in secondary schools are suggested:

1. Open up all classes in the regular day program to any student, regardless of age, who might benefit from the class.
2. Open up all evening "adult" classes to any student, regardless of age, and develop evening programs where none exist.
3. Combine the regular day and evening programs, along with new late afternoon and Saturday classes, into a continuous day program.
4. Provide a nursery and a pre-school so that mothers of small children may enroll for classes.
5. Provide a social lounge and center, perhaps in a partially used basement area, to be decorated by the students and kept open until 10:00 p.m.
6. Provide areas, if space is available, for sewing centers, et cetera, for adults as well as youth.
7. Utilize teenage students as much as possible in working with the nursery, pre-

school, and other projects, so as to provide opportunities for the development of self-confidence and other desirable qualities.

8. Abolish all age-grading systems, so that each class consists of students capable of doing the work regardless of age.
9. Allow older teenagers to carry a partial load and still remain involved in the school's program.
10. Encourage work-experience programs.
11. Encourage the teachers, parents, adult and "regular" students to elect an advisory board to develop school policy, innovations, and enrichment experiences.
12. Alter the curriculum and orientation of the school so as to make it fully relevant to the language, culture, and desires of the community served.
13. Conduct a series of intensive community-teacher workshops to develop a full awareness of the contributions which both groups can make, and of the character and social dynamics of the local community.

Accompanying the opening up of classes to all and their extension into the evening hours and to weekends should also be the following:

1. The development of an adequate bookstore in each school, making available a significant proportion of current educational paperbound books and periodicals.
2. Allowing instructors to offer at least one seminar-type course each semester, perhaps on a topic of their choice, but with the approval of their faculty colleagues and based upon community relevance.
3. Allowing instructors to establish their own class schedules, using the extended day period and Saturday if so desired, subject primarily to the approval of their faculty colleagues.
4. Encouraging faculty to keep abreast of new knowledge in their fields by providing scholarships which would enable teachers to take additional subject-matter course work or pursue research-literature review interests during the non-teaching months.

In summary, it seems a shame indeed that in many urban areas where non-scholastics are in obvious need of the opportunity for additional secondary-level schooling, that the only schools in their areas or neighborhoods capable of meeting these needs arbitrarily restrict themselves to certain kinds of potential students or segregate by age-groups and thereby diminish the educational opportunities of all concerned.

The physical facilities and most of the personnel needed for community education centers are already available. All that is needed now is a willingness to experiment and innovate.

Black Is Not a Color of the Skin, It Is a State of Mind

Ellen Holly

Black is not a color of the skin or a bangle. It is a state of mind. The time has come for someone to make this very clear as *The Times* "Drama Section" makes its contribution to the pernicious idea that the only kind of Negro actor that should be hired is one whose skin is black and whose features are 100 percent African, and that any other choice represents a compromise, "cop-out," or tokenism on the part of those doing the hiring.

In his article about the new TV season, "Will the Blacks Say, 'Too Little, Too Late'?" Robert Dallos supports the view with a quote from *Variety* as follows:

A touch of black has come to "Peyton Place," but upon close examination the hue turns out to be a magic color designed not to offend the most sensitive white eye. The new hue is cast by Percy Rodriguez, a dark actor with definitely un-African features.

Obscuring the Issue

He has the facial structure that makes him look like a white man in blackface. . . . The result is that ABC has injected a Negro into the cast of "Peyton Place" without integrating the show. White viewers can identify with any number of the different levels of white society portrayed on the show, but the Negro watchers are going to find it hard.

For *Variety* to write this in the first place and *The Times* to reprint it in the second place is appalling because it permits two white writers with pseudo-liberal concerns to further obscure, rather than illuminate, an issue that they do not understand—namely, what "black" is about.

Let's examine the quote and all its ugly implications, but first let's look at a basic reality: while the African Negro has had the good fortune to exist in circumstances that have allowed him to retain his purity, the American Negro has become so diluted and bastardized—after wholesale miscegenation during slavery times and partial assimilation into a predominantly white society in the generations that followed—that an American Negro of 100 percent African appearance is rare.

It is conservatively estimated that more than three-fourths of the Negroes in the United States have one or more white ancestors, and their appearance reflects that fact.

Patently Absurd

Percy Rodriguez is an American Negro actor functioning in America. To criticize him for looking like an American Negro (i.e., having an appearance that reflects racial mixture) rather than an African Negro (whose appearance reflects racial purity) is patently absurd.

If African criteria are to be the yardstick by which American blacks are hired, few Americans will qualify, and we must consider importing actors from Uganda. Diana Sands, Earle Hyman, Gloria Foster, Billie Allen, Bill Gunn and James Earl Jones are all much too light-skinned.

Cicely Tyson is sufficiently dark but her facial structure is almost identical to Gene Tierney's so she fails as well. So do Ruby Dee, Barbara Ann Teer, Ena Hartman and Gail Fisher.

Sidney Poitier, Al Freeman, Jr., Moses Gunn and Clarence Williams III are also too sharp-featured. Never mind the fact that they are some of the most brilliant actors in this country. Lena Horne, Barbara McNair, Dionne Warwick, Diahann Carroll and Leslie Uggams will not serve either, and Harry Belafonte looks like Tab Hunter with a tan and an Afro wig.

State of Mind

Then you have the case of people like Hilda Simms, Osceola Archer, Jane White, Harold Scott, Janice Kingslow, Isabelle Cooley and myself, who find it virtually impossible to find work because we are considered to lack both the proper color and features.

That we are all able and gifted is of no importance. That we have each spent over a dozen years learning our craft is considered immaterial. We are told that we are not black enough, that we look too white. But we are black. It is enough for us, why isn't it enough for you?

Black is not a color of the skin, it is a state of mind.

However white I might appear to some myopic white writer, I am black because my experience has been a black experience. From the time I first went to school, got called the usual ugly names and learned the brutal realities of being an outsider, no day has been without its traumas—jobs I could not qualify for because I was black, apartments I could not rent, opportunities I was denied.

In Maryland I was thrown out of a diner and told to "get your black . . . around back and eat with the dogs." In St. Louis a waitress asked my race and, when told, said, "Oh, you're a nigger," and charged me $2 for a glass of orange juice.

In New Orleans I was forcibly prevented from performing with a modern dance company because I was black and the rest of the company was white and it was against the law for a black to appear on the same stage as a white. The list is endless.

Whatever individual color we happen to be, all of us who are Negro have been black enough to qualify for all the kicks in the head this country has had to offer, just as Percy Rodriguez with his "un-African" features was only recently considered quite black enough to be viciously discriminated against when he was making the movie "The Heart Is a Lonely Hunter" in the Deep South.

Now that there has been an about face and a few bouquets are in the offing, like a plum part on a TV show, how ironic that suddenly some of us are not black enough to qualify.

It is officious of a white writer to assume that Negro viewers are going to have a hard time relating to Percy Rodriguez. Why on earth would we? Among ourselves as a race, we're used to being every color of the rainbow and relating to each other without strain.

Running the Gamut

In my own family we run the gamut from an aunt who's a blue-eyed blonde to a brace of uncles who are "black as the ace of spades."

We all consider ourselves black and feel that we're all trapped in the system to sink or swim together, and the only time we become aware of color grada-tions is when we are forced to deal with "white" society and its psychotic orientation in the matter. "Magic hues," indeed.

Is everyone who hires Percy Rodriguez to be accused of tokenism? If so, where is this fine actor to work? Does it ever occur to anyone that he might have been hired on the basis of ability?

In half the Broadway plays I've been in, the odious moment has always arisen when the white management has come back all sweaty-palmed and apologetic to ask me to get out my paint pots and "darken down" because, although they hired me for having given the best reading, their motives are being misconstrued and they're being accused on all sides of "tokenism."

"Whitelisted"

Are managements to be blackmailed into making a "Whitelist," i.e., a list of Negro actors who are to be considered, in spite of prodigious gifts and skills and decades of experience, too "white" to be employed?

There is a depressing tendency on the part of entirely too many people—black militants and white "liberal" writers in particular—to pervert the concept of "blackness" into something as restrictive and exclusive as a country club to which you can belong only if your skin is black, your features generous, your hair worn Afro, your neck ringed with a jangling assortment of bones and trinkets, and your behavior tailored to follow certain rigid rules.

I believe with all my heart that black is beautiful, but let's not so restrict our interpretation of what black means that virtually everybody but a chosen few gets elbowed out of the race.

All my life I've identified as a black woman and I deeply resent an increasingly hysterical state of affairs which makes that more and more difficult for anyone who does not fit a certain stereotype to do.

"A Great Day"

It will be a great day when a Negro can look any kind of way God happened to make him and behave any way he pleases without losing his franchise on the right to identify and relate to himself as black and demand of others that they respond to him as such. Then and only then will the Negro be free.

As far as behavior is concerned, we do not accuse the Kennedys of turning their backs on their Irish heritage because they don't wear green clothes, brandish shillelaghs, believe in leprechauns and pepper their conversation with begorrahs. Yet any Negro who shines his shoes, wears a business suit, has a decent education or makes good money is accused of turning his back on his heritage and metamorphosing into a white man. What a hideous mistake to regard these things as intrinsically "white!"

The Negro who chooses to live his life as a negative response to whiteness—who says of every move he makes, "What's Whitey going to do? Get an education? Then I'm going to stay dumb. Wear blue? Then I'm going to wear yellow. Jump up? Then I'm going to jump down"—is hardly free but, on the contrary, shackles himself into the most oppressive kind of slavery.

Besides, how absurd to devote one's lifetime to the utter boredom of "Whitey-watching" that such a stance entails.

Where It's At?

Does no one understand what freedom really means?

In the name of black "freedom," a handful of black militants, enthusiastically aided and abetted by white "liberal" writers, have moved in like the Gestapo and staked out a territory called Where It's At, Man that so narrowly limits blackness that it can fit on the head of a pin.

The clever and the watchful, however, will see the same old ugly enslaving forces at work as American racial progress limits itself to the exchange of one stereotype for another. Uncle Tom is being replaced by the angry, young black skinned male from the ghetto, and if—like me—you happen, instead, to be an angry, thirtyish, beige-skinned female from the suburbs, your life is judged as somehow unauthentic and unreal.

The truth of the matter is that there is no one place where it's at. There are 22 million different, highly individual Negroes in this country and, therefore, 22 million different places Where It's At, Man, and it is a cynical comment on the nature and quality of human life to assume that any single one is somehow more valid than the next.

Internecine Warfare

The white press has played a historic role in fostering internecine warfare among Negroes. From time immemorial it has taught the rural Negro to be suspicious of the urban Negro, the Northern Negro to be suspicious of the Southern Negro, the dark Negro to be suspicious of the light Negro, the illiterate Negro to be suspicious of the educated Negro, the rich Negro to be suspicious of the poor Negro, and vice versa.

It is a part of the pattern that a new category crops up as the blunt-featured Negro is alerted to be on guard against the sharp-featured Negro (Percy Rodriguez).

In my more paranoid moments I suspect a plot because I think that the white man knows that if we ever stopped tearing each other to pieces, as we have been so beautifully computer-programmed to do, and joined together against the real enemy, he'd be in for a bad time of it.

A Kind of Bravery

"Black" is not a color of the skin. It is a unique experience shared by Negro Americans, however varied they may be, that sets them apart from any other group and results in a certain kind of psychological adjustment that no other group has to make—namely, the adjustment of learning how to survive, and perhaps even to flourish, in an atmosphere that is almost totally hostile.

It involves, among many other things, a certain peculiar kind of bravery, a certain kind of "soul" and an occasional vague nostalgia for the brilliant land-scape of a lost homeland that can't be returned to because one is separated by time rather than distance and one can't turn back the clock.

I don't mean to seem superior and make a mystique of being black, but I do mean to suggest that it is, at once, something infinitely more subtle and profound than the color of one's skin or the shape of one's nose or the bangle one wears around his neck.

To those who move to nullify the identity of some of us with the accusation that we don't look black, all I can say in reply is that we are black. It's enough for us. Why isn't it enough for you?

On Misunderstanding Black Militancy

Faith Berry

I think I may always associate Martin Luther King's "I Have A Dream" speech with a certain incident that related to it the day of the March on Washington, August 28, 1963.

Unable to get off from work to attend the March, I watched parts of it via television in Manhattan from the office of *The New Yorker* magazine where I was then employed. At the end of Dr. King's speech, one staff member, a young Jewish woman in her late twenties, obviously moved by the oration, went about the hallway of one of the floors, raving that the speech was the most marvelous she had ever heard in her life. When she said it to me, I added that indeed it was a stirring declaration. Then, in what I recall now as a somber tone, I said: "I wish Du Bois could have been there; this day was his dream. If he could have lived one more day to hear. . . ."

"Du Bois," she spoke up, "who's that?" Taken aback, I answered as briefly as possible who Du Bois was, what he had done; that he had died in Ghana the eve of the March. Roy Wilkins, I told her, had paid him tribute during his speech at the March; likewise an obituary was in that morning's *New York Times.* Looking at me in a manner that seemed to say if this man Du Bois were important enough she would have heard about him, the subject didn't seem to interest her. She happened to be a book reviewer, a product, I later learned, of Bryn Mawr and Harvard.

It occurred to me then that many well-meaning white people throughout the nation would pass through the day of the March lacking the sense of history to bring to bear on the events; and that Dr. King's speech, for all its ringing tones, would actually bring nothing more than a I-have-a-dream sense of empathy and emotion to those who had little or no knowledge of other black

From *The Crisis,* June-July 1970, pp. 219–223. Reprinted by permission of the author and *The Crisis.* Copyright © 1970 Faith Berry.

leaders who had antedated him or of the issues that made the "March for Jobs and Freedom" necessary.

In these years since the late Dr. King's speech, many of those same people have wondered what happened to interrupt the racial rapport seemingly apparent back in 1963. Why, they wonder, are so many black people now so "militant" when so many then appeared so peaceful.

Though calm compared to now, 1963 was not really a placid year. Demonstrations took place in over 800 cities and towns, climaxed by the March on Washington. The demonstrations that year in Birmingham were met by white violence and frequent bombings of black property, including a church where four little girls were killed. Medgar Evers was shot to death by an ambusher in Jackson, Mississippi. Furthermore, the year 1964 was not without less pain: the bodies of three COFO workers were found beneath a dam in Philadelphia, Mississippi; the search for them turned up the mutilated torsos of two black male Alcorn A & M students floating in the Mississippi River; the shooting of a black teenager by a white off-duty police lieutenant set off a Harlem civil disorder lasting five days. Then in 1965 came the death of Malcolm X; within weeks a March from Selma-to-Montgomery, to secure voter registration, was disrupted before its end by Alabama state troopers using tear gas, cattle prods, dogs and whips. The year 1966 brought the Mississippi March Against Fear in which James Meredith was shot, and Stokely Carmichael issued the call for "Black Power."

It was only part of the decade that signaled in a new militancy—South, North, East and West. In comparison to what flared up in ghettos of many cities throughout the nation, the earlier years may have seemed peaceful. But had so much happened so fast that many were trying to forget how many lynchings, how many gunshots, how many bombings, how much discrimination make people stop being "peaceful"?

I have thought upon hearing the question "what happened?" that not only does present racial polarity stem in part from a misunderstanding of black militancy and the issues, but likewise from a lack of knowledge of Afro-American history. It has taken more than the events of the 1960's to make black militancy evident. The fact that it only now seems obvious is perhaps because very often it has been buried in both a myth and a conspiracy—the myth of the docile darky and the conspiracy of those perpetuating it. At the same time, it has also buried itself—partly in fear, partly in patience. And for all such reasons, it has also been buried in history.

Being a black reader more than glad that many long overdue books on Afro-American life and history are now easily available—since for so long seeking and finding them outside a special library collection was like trying to dig for archaeological objects—I am also one who believes that this current black book rush might have done more towards creating racial understanding had one-half the books been in print long before the late 1960s. (To say the least, the recent unrest among black students would have been abated if not avoided.)

But except for a few lone historians and outspoken leaders, this is a nation which has hushed up the story of slave revolts, silenced or ignored black spokesmen considered too radical, and deleted the black experience almost entirely from the context of American history. Additionally, many important early works by Afro-Americans have been allowed to go out of print. It was thus not seen necessary by many publishers that such a mass of material be rushed into print until it could no longer be held back.

In such an atmosphere, when inner city rebellions—better known as "riots"—occurred in the mid-1960s, many were the confused who believed such incidents to be the first insurrectionary acts by blacks in the United States; and when Malcolm X first appeared, he was thought by some of the same people—including some blacks—to be the first such "militant" to express racial beliefs in quite the same rhetoric. Rarely if ever had they heard the names Nat Turner, Denmark Vesey, Gabriel Prosser, Robert Alexander Young, David Walker or Henry Highland Garnet—to cite only a few. And never, until perhaps recently, were lines such as part of the following poem by Claude McKay suggested reading in an American literature course:

Think you I am not fiend and savage too?
Think you I could not arm me with a gun
And shoot down ten of you for every one of my black brothers murdered, burnt by you?

As I soon learned, unfamiliarity with Afro-American thought and history has also included people from Harvard unfamiliar with the writing and work of W.E.B. Du Bois—a Harvard Ph.D., and without a doubt one of the most militant black men who ever lived. During his lifetime spanning nearly a century . . . hardly an issue pertaining to civil rights, civil liberties, or the life of black people, was left untouched by his voice or pen. Whether it was about the black family, the black man and unions, rural life, city life, the Negro in the North, the Negro in the South, disenfranchisement, education, employment, the Negro church, black people and the arts, black pride, Afro American history, a search for the African past, Pan-Africanism, socialism, the issue of world peace, or his long association with the NAACP and *The Crisis* he was always writing, lecturing and organizing; and hardly a problem exists today that he did not challenge or foresee. That he died at 95 and throughout his life was not sufficiently understood by the power structure because he was considered too militant is testimony to why many younger black Americans might now appear even more revolutionary than he did while he lived.

But as black militancy—however one cares to define it—is not new, neither are so-called "riots" new. Though some interpreters deludingly prefer to think of these recent events not as acts of black defiance against the system, but rather as violent black-white street confrontations—similar to racial clashes of earlier years—they are much less racial feuds than they are acts of black revolt. When slaves set fires to plantations (and they did) they acted not only out of enmity towards a white slave master, but against the inequities of the slave system. Accordingly, when urban blacks set fires it was against oppression and exploitation in the ghetto.

In such a mood, many American blacks—both young and not so young—have come to express dismay not only with the methods and ideas espoused by the NAACP and the Urban League, but also to advocate all-black organizations. This concept actually is not so new either. As only one example, at the turn of the century, Monroe Trotter—fiery editor of the Boston-based *Guardian,* and one of twenty-nine organizers of the 1905 Niagara Movement—objected to integrated conferences forming the NAACP. "I don't trust white folk," he said. Although he was an active, though highly critical member of the NAACP until 1913, he preferred to continue the spirit of the Niagara Movement through the National Equal Rights League, an exclusively black organization he formed shortly after the original Niagara Movement conference.

Similarly, little that is currently being said about black liberation or resistance to oppression has not been said by other black people in this country in previous times. But few have made history for it, and not often has it been told. David Walker, an escaped slave who went to Boston and there became agent for the black abolitionist publication *Freedom's Journal,* wrote in 1829 *Walker's Appeal in Four Articles: Together With a Preamble to the Coloured Citizens of the World, But in Particular and Very Especially, to those of the United States of America.* It was later published as a pamphlet. "If you commence," he wrote, "make sure work—do not trifle, for they will not trifle with you—they want us for their slaves, and think nothing of murdering us in order to subject us to that wretched condition—therefore, if there is an attempt made by us, kill, or be killed. . . ."

In 1843, at the Negro Convention held in Buffalo, Henry Highland Garnet, a black abolitionist minister, told his listeners in a message called "An Address to the Slaves of The United States:"

You should . . . use the same manner of resistance as would have been just in our ancestors when the bloody foot-prints of the first remorseless soul thief was placed upon the shores of our fatherland. . . . Let your motto be resistance! *resistance,* Resistance! No oppressed people have ever secured their liberty without resistance.

If for making such statements in 20th Century America Rap Brown is arrested for "inciting to riot" (and later listed as one of the FBI's "most wanted men") and other black men have fled into exile or been assassinated, it takes little imagination to guess what 19th Century black "militants" making such speeches or writing slave narratives went through in their day. Many fled the country or were killed. (When in 1830 David Walker was caught in Richmond, Virginia, distributing his pamphlet, he was arrested and never seen alive again.)

But history repeats itself in such a way that some black spokesmen once considered too radical to be heeded, or too incendiary to be heard, soon turn up looking like moderates. The list of those in this category is as long as this page. It does not include Booker T. Washington who was always more than moderate to begin with. It does include many of those some of us now call "Uncle Toms," because while disagreeing with their ideas and strategy, we fail to take into consideration what they have endured and contributed on behalf of the civil rights struggle.

There are also those militant voices so far ahead of their time that, not many, black or white, have the ability to hear them. Finally, they can no longer be heard for being lost in the multitude. When in 1962 Robert Williams in *Negroes with Guns* was using the term Afro-American—a term at the time few people were using—writing that "The Afro-American militant is a 'militant' because he defends himself, his family and his dignity;" and advocating that "as a tactic, we use and approve non-violent resistance" few appeared to listen. Many—including almost all his constituents in the NAACP—thought he was wayout. His advocacy of answering "violence with violence" met with official NAACP disapproval. (An NAACP pamphlet published in 1959, *The Single Issue in the Robert Williams Case*, sums up the Association position.) But hardly a day now goes by when we don't hear some of the same pronouncements Williams made in his book less than a decade ago. The Black Panther Party did not rise in an Oakland ghetto and spread to cities throughout the country because Williams wrote a book. Now back in the U. S. after nine years in exile, he is only one among many voices.

The belief that if revolutionaries are silenced or eliminated the ideas they exhort will die, is one of the fallacies of human history—especially of Afro-American history. In spite of all those who sought to deny him while he lived, no greater hero, dead or alive, now exists for the majority of young blacks than Malcolm X. Many however, preferring not to stress that his attitude toward whites underwent a profound change after his trip to Mecca, remember him as representing the symbol first of a man who dared—who told us not to challenge the white man's conscience, but to put his life on the line.

Although many whites cringed when he spoke and many blacks insisted he represented only a small minority, his now-famous 1964 "Ballot or the Bullet" speech stressed three concepts which now seem more than acceptable to many who would not have thought of listening six years ago: black political power, community control, and black business enterprise. "The black man," he said:

should control the politics and politicians in his own community. . . . We should own and operate and control the economy of our own community. . . . Our people not only have to be re-educated to the importance of supporting black business but the black man himself has to be made aware of the importance of going into business.

This was revolutionary advocacy until ghettos began to burn down. Now such thoughts would even bring agreement from Richard Nixon.

Because it has taken us so long to come such a short distance, the demands of black people by some standards now seem unreasonable. From many sides we hear repeated the belief that we live in a democratic system with no need for an escalation of black rhetoric and assertiveness. We are reminded of all the "gains" made, all the black officials recently elected. For those who need to be reminded, many of the gains would have not been made without some of the rhetoric and assertiveness many describe as undesirable. The 1965 Voting Rights Act—the most sweeping voting rights bill passed in 90 years, and the first to provide direct Federal action to enable blacks to register and vote— would not have been gained without the March from Selma to Montgomery.

It has been this way longer than some would like to agree. The threat of a march on Washington in June, 1941, by A. Philip Randolph and other black leaders, caused President Franklin D. Roosevelt by Executive Order to establish the Committee on Fair Employment Practices (later killed in 1946 through an appropriation bill rider and not until 1964 was made part of a civil rights act). Roosevelt, however, recommended no civil rights legislation during his Administration and none was enacted by Congress.

Relatedly, it would be false to assume that the 1964 Civil Rights Act—the most all-encompassing civil rights legislation then passed since Reconstruction— would have come without the far-reaching demonstrations and events of 1963 and 1964.

Keeping the pressure on—"being militant," if that is what it has to be called —is the only way most black people throughout the country have discovered brings any results. Out of disbelief action would result otherwise arose the slogan from many ghetto youths: "To bring America around we gotta burn it down." The apprehension took on credibility more and more in every sector; and the pressure is still on.

For those who would forget we now have a conservative in the White House there are many ways for black people to be constantly reminded. Not only has the present Executive leader exerted most of his efforts toward courting the white South and the "Silent Majority" (besides widening the war in Indochina); he has also tried unsuccessfully to dilute the 1965 Voting Rights Act, substituting it with a new *Nixon version* of proposed amendments. Finally, on June 17, after six months of continuing debate, Congress completed action to extend the Voting Rights Act to 1975, with Richard Nixon agreeing to sign the bill June 22. According to the Metropolitan Applied Research Center and the Southern Regional Council, an estimated 1,500 black elected officials now hold office—52 of them black mayors, 26 of whom are in the South; obviously, too many in number for the present Administration.

But blacks are continually told to "work within the system." For those who also forget that this is what has usually been tried, the records of the NAACP and Legal Defense Fund are ample proof. All those advocates, though, who still believe in the justice of the court system can only be said to have a high degree of idealism—one less shared by many than in previous years, and certainly not so by the Black Panthers. Corresponding to the latter view, Yale University President Kingman Brewster, Jr., on April 23 announced that:

I am appalled and ashamed that things should have come to such a pass in this country that I am skeptical of the ability of black revolutionaries to achieve a fair trial anywhere in the United States.

If the Executive and Judicial branches have not always acted as effectively as possible to protect civil rights of black citizens, so might the same be said of the Legislative Branch. Although nine black members presently occupy seats in the House, and one is in the Senate, almost without exception, all the powerful committees of both houses of Congress are chaired by southerners. This is the legislative body vested with power by Article I, Section I of the Constitution—a Constitution which, when it was written, provided not one proposal for the civil rights of black people. It is this legislative body which could never succeed in bringing any anti-lynching legislation to the Senate floor, although this same issue in the House has a slightly more favorable record in comparison. (Anti-lynching bills were passed by the House at least twice—the Dyer bill, January 27, 1922, by a vote of 230–119, and the Gavagan bill, April 13, 1937, by a vote of 277–120.) The Senate, however, from 1938—when the first effort was made to vote cloture on a civil rights measure—until 1964, was unable to shut off southern filibusters on any of eleven civil rights measures. The year 1964 thus marked the first time cloture was successfully invoked to close off long debate (usually by southerners) on civil rights legislation. Cloture was likewise necessary and successful for the Civil Rights Act of 1964, the Voting Rights Act of 1965, and Open Housing in 1968, even though the Civil Rights Acts of 1957 and 1960 were passed despite filibusters.

Outside the White House, the courts and Congress, black people traditionally have not had much sympathy from the FBI, the director of which since 1924 has been J. Edgar Hoover. In addition to making many hostile and unfair racial remarks over the years, one of his more recent was his public reference to Martin Luther King, Jr., as a "notorious liar." Moreover, although the National Advisory Commission on Civil Disorders found the underlying causes of urban unrest to be white racism, poverty, inferior housing, unemployment and poor housing, the Hoover contention was "the riots and disturbances have been characterized by spontaneous outbursts of mob violence by young hoodlums. . . ."

If many blacks in the streets of the nation cannot cite the facts as to exactly why the system doesn't work, the results can nevertheless be felt. If we have any feeling at all, we all can feel them. Black "militancy" is thus acting accordingly. It does not only mean wearing an Afro, a dashiki, giving a black power arm salute, or killing a cop. It says in effect, take the pressure off us, and put it where it belongs. It means, finally, bringing a way of life to bear and suffering any consequences necessary—none of which, as we have all discovered, could be any worse than all the struggle that has gone before.

2 THE PUERTO RICAN HERITAGE

The island of Puerto Rico, as a self-governing commonwealth in union with the U. S., is still run largely *by* Uncle Sam[1]—and, most Puerto Ricans would add, *for* Uncle Sam. As they have immigrated to the U. S.—especially to New York—Puerto Ricans differ in one major respect from most other minority groups who preceded them: they come as American citizens. Despite this advantage, however, the pattern of response to earlier waves of immigration has been repeated: they come as strangers, they are not accepted, they face barriers of color, custom, habits, language, and in many cases the great adjustment required to change from rural to urban life and from a warm humid climate to one having four seasons.

Cultural awareness of this unique group of transplanted Americans of second class citizenship has been promoted by Oscar Lewis' well-known vivid, scholarly picture of the movement from Puerto Rico to the mainland, *La Vida* (the life). In the background essay reprinted here, Lewis finds that many Puerto Ricans now cling "to their native language and customs and to their dream of returning to Puerto Rico." What happened to "the American dream" of the school as a ladder of vertical mobility in an open society?

In her study *Spanish Harlem* (referring to the New York City neighborhood to which Puerto Ricans frequently migrate), Patricia Cayo Sexton analyzes the unique characteristics of the Puerto Rican's culture, with interesting observations on the Puerto Rican's uneasy coexistence with nearby blacks and Italians. She underscores the point that, while many Anglos unfortunately lump Puerto Ricans and blacks together because they may resemble one another superficially and because they live adjacent to and among one another in many

[1]The U.S. obtained the island from Spain in 1898, and U.S. citizenship was granted in 1917. Since 1948, Puerto Ricans have elected their own governor.

eastern ghetto neighborhoods, both Puerto Ricans and blacks view themselves as very distinct. This lesson holds great import for teachers, and the following Part of our book attempts to provide a basis for recognizing and appreciating the unique cultural heritage of Americans of Puerto Rican descent.

The Puerto Rican's distinctiveness is well-documented in a research résumé by Bram, "The Lower Status Puerto Rican Family," which analyzes the life-style of today's U. S. urban Puerto Rican, in comparison with that of his former homeland. In effect, Bram finds that the Puerto Rican has traded an unstable and insecure poor, rural existence on the island for an unstable and insecure urban ghetto existence on the mainland.

Turning next to "The Puerto Rican Child in the American School," by Cordasco, who has served as educational consultant to the Commonwealth of Puerto Rico, we find, not surprisingly, that school achievement is low, with Puerto Rican children caught in a web of deprivation, poor housing, and high unemployment. Cordasco reviews the two major educational problems he identifies in this web: 1) how to teach English effectively as a second language to Puerto Ricans, and 2) how to promote better adjustment between Puerto Rican parents and children, on the one hand, and the community, on the other hand. In sum, Cordasco makes an eloquent plea for what has come to be called bilingual education.

This Part concludes with a report titled "The Losers" by Margolis. Prepared to serve as a common starting place for those attending a 1968 national con-ference on "Meeting the Special Educational Needs of Urban Puerto Rican Youth," the report was designed to raise questions, not to answer them, and to provoke discussion between Puerto Rican community leaders and those responsible for educational policy making. We believe it is equally provocative in raising questions for teachers to ponder. One of its most hard hitting points is that the Puerto Rican community must have the opportunity to share in deciding which approaches are most effective in working with their own children. This presupposes effective organizations which authentically represent Puerto Ricans and are capable of influencing the educational establishment.

Like most of the other documents in this volume, the Margolis piece is careful to point out that all minority groups are both *like* and *unlike* one another. He notes that black and Puerto Rican school children endure many of the same inequities and that much of the literature on minority problems assumes that solving the problems of the black child will at the same time solve those of the Puerto Rican child. In many areas of education this is true but Margolis also stresses that Puerto Rican children face unique educational problems which demand unique solutions. He identifies many of these problems, ranging from language deficiencies and cultural mores, to the virtual absence of Puerto Rican teachers in public school systems.

Complicated by rapid population growth and shifting locales, partly obscured by lack of hard data, the picture which emerges from these articles is a grim one—mitigated somewhat by the new developing roles of parents and private agencies. One might also mention the emergence of the Young Lords Party, a loose confederation of Puerto Rican youth in urban centers who are active and articulate in dramatizing and alleviating Puerto Rican community issues and problems.

But for the 400,000 Puerto Rican children in public schools today who are "the losers," the pace of change is still woefully inadequate. The magnitude of the challenge is such that radical change in public schools and other public agencies will be required. Teachers' awareness of the characteristics of Puerto Rican culture is one important step. This, in turn, will have to be followed by a major moral commitment on the part of all Americans to provide every child, regardless of race or origins, with the opportunity to fulfill his potential.

Until America makes this commitment fully, all of us will be "the losers." With pride in the Puerto Rican's heritage and an informed dedication to his education, we have an opportunity to make *all* of our children the winners.

from A Study of Slum Culture: Backgrounds for La Vida

Oscar Lewis

SUMMARY OF MAJOR FINDINGS IN NEW YORK

Although the majority of our sample families had lost track of relatives who had gone to New York, when our informants were planning to migrate, they usually managed somehow to get into contact with at least one relative there. Upon arrival, the first thing most Puerto Ricans did was look up a kinsman. Some 48 percent of our New York and Puerto Rican families were related by sibling ties; two-thirds of the New York families came from the same slum as their Puerto Rican relatives.

The majority of the migrants lived with a relative when they first arrived, but friction often developed, ending in the establishment of an independent residence. There was a strong general feeling that the family in New York was not as close or as helpful as in Puerto Rico.

The predominant type of household among our New York families was nuclear, but 20 percent of the households were extended, usually horizontally; that is, including a person of the same generation, such as a brother or sister who might contribute income to the household. However, a relatively small number of migrants were in their most productive years; over half of the New York sample was under age twenty. When they went to New York, 44 percent were between fifteen and twenty-four; the average age at the time of migration was twenty-eight.

The average household size was four. Whereas 44 percent of the household heads were legally married and 22 percent lived in free unions, 26 percent

From Oscar Lewis, "Summary of Major Findings in New York and Some Comparisons with Puerto Rico," A Study of Slum Culture, New York: Random House, 1968, pp. 203–213.

were separated, abandoned, or divorced, 6 percent were single, and 2 percent were widows.

The Puerto Ricans in our New York sample lived in Puerto Rican neighborhoods that formed little islands within the city, perpetuating their native language and many of their customs. The process of adjustment and of assimilation was slow and difficult. Contacts with North Americans were few and often limited to landlords, government officials, and other functionaries. Most of the migrants were disillusioned when they arrived because of the cold, the ugliness of the city, and the difficulties of finding employment and a decent place to live. Many retained a negative attitude toward the city, its people, and its customs even after many years of residence.

The motives for migration to New York were generated by low incomes and unemployment, but often the precipitating factor in leaving Puerto Rico was not directly economic in nature but rather psychological or personal. Most informants denied that their New York relatives had influenced their decision to migrate. Higher welfare payments in New York did not appear to be an important factor in migration.

Migration from Puerto Rico to New York usually involved two stages. The New York families were mostly of rural origin and had left their place of birth during their younger years to move to San Juan. Most of them had lived in a city slum for a number of years before leaving for New York. Of the families in our New York sample 82 percent had come from a Puerto Rican slum.

The Puerto Rican migrants did not look upon the decision to migrate to the United States as irrevocable. Only one of every four migrants in our sample stated that he planned to remain in New York permanently. Often, they came to work and save money in order to go back and buy a house or establish a small business, but they usually discovered that this was not easy. The majority of migrants were able only to make one or more return visits to their native land. Nevertheless, for the most part, they were glad they had come to New York.

The migrants changed dwellings in the city fairly frequently (an average of four moves per family), but the moves were restricted in geographical area, usually within the same borough and often within a block or two of the previous residence.

All the migrants lived in apartments, usually in dilapidated tenement buildings, but some had acquired leases in public housing projects. All but four families lived in unfurnished apartments. The median rent was $62.50 a month. Adjustment to apartment living was often difficult for the Puerto Rican migrants, who were accustomed to living in free communication with their neighbors in open-door, open-window, slum dwellings.

Most of the Puerto Ricans worked in factories in New York, and all but a few held low-prestige jobs. A higher proportion (40.6 percent) of the wives worked, also mostly in factories. Some 80 percent of the working adults belonged to a union. Occupationally, the families in our sample ranked at the very bottom of the scale, being in an even worse position than the New York Puerto Rican community as a whole.

The median annual income of the sample families was $3,678, a figure that again placed them in the lowest rank in New York.[1] The per capita monthly income was a little over $100.

Unemployment was about 9 percent, and 20 percent of the families were on relief. The jobs acquired by the migrants lasted an average of only three years. The lowest income families in our New York sample had an associated history of separation, abandonment, and divorce.

The educational achievement of the migrants was low, an average of 6.5 years completed by each adult. This is the lowest educational level of any of the major ethnic groups in New York. In general, there was a correlation between income and education.

"Dropouts" were a problem in New York; very few of the younger generation went beyond the ninth grade. In our sample of adults above eighteen years of age, over 90 percent had not completed high school. The majority of these had dropped out of school in Puerto Rico. The advantages to attaining a high school diploma were outweighed in most cases by the advantages of immediate employment. Almost no one had gone to night school.

The family heads complained about problems in disciplining the children and the fear, sometimes realized, that their youngsters were joining gangs. This delinquency was attributed to working wives whose absence from the home affected the ability of the parents to control their children.

Marital conflict increased in New York as a result of the changing role of the Puerto Rican wife. The working wife was less subject to the close surveillance of her husband, family, and neighbors and had greater financial independence. Their independence was resented by husbands and led to quarrels and sometimes to physical violence. The strict sanctions in New York against wife beating only increased the men's deep feelings of frustration.

The household inventories revealed that the families owned an average of $1,664 worth of household and related goods (not including clothing), most of which had been purchased in the five-year period preceding the study. Installment buying and the purchase of new, rather than secondhand, goods was the general pattern. The annual indebtedness averaged $128 per family. Clothing represented a large investment. Complete inventories of the clothing of selected families showed that a third more was spent on clothing than on all other household possessions.

English was learned more quickly by the men and children than by the women. Over half the men had achieved some degree of fluency in English, but two out of every three women in the sample knew little or no English, even though they might be employed. English was used by all informants almost exclusively as a utilitarian tool, to communicate with the foreman, to

[1] The median income would have been lower had we not included two families with annual incomes of over $10,000.

get about the city, and to make themselves understood in visits to hospitals and similar situations. Many purchased an English-language newspaper in addition to a Spanish newspaper. Little English was spoken in the home, but there was much concern that the children were forgetting Spanish. Since almost all the children attended New York public schools, most of them were bilingual to some degree. There was a tendency to give American names to children born in New York City.

Visiting relatives in the city was fairly frequent and regular, depending upon the distance of their homes. However, there was a general feeling among our informants that kin ties had weakened in the United States. We also found a reluctance to take *compadres* in New York, although many families still felt obligated to do so.

Church attendance, the practice of spiritualism, and the use of herbs declined in New York.

In general, the migrants believed that they had changed little since living in New York City. Our data tended to corroborate this. To most of them, the main advantages of living in New York were of an economic nature. The disadvantages were high rents and poor housing conditions, lawlessness in the city, racial or ethnic discrimination, and climate. There was marked hostility toward American Negroes and a strong resistance to being classified with them. Puerto Ricans seemed to be well aware of their competition with Negroes for a higher status in the city. On the other hand, there was a lack of unity among the Puerto Ricans and an inability to organize for common goals.

COMPARISON OF FINDINGS IN PUERTO RICO AND NEW YORK

On the whole, there was little important change in the customs and culture of the sample families that migrated from Puerto Rico to New York. However, they were much better off economically than their relatives in Puerto Rico. Many had an income three or four times greater and spent about three times more. The median income per family in New York was $3,678, as compared with $1,703 in Puerto Rico. Although the New York families enjoyed a generally higher standard of living, they did not spend proportionately more on household articles. The families in our Puerto Rican sample had invested an average of $1,379 in household and related goods, while the New York average was $1,664, only $285 higher.

There are several factors that explain the low differential in expenditure. First, the prices of furniture and appliances were lower in New York; and second, two major items, the stove and refrigerator, were usually provided by the landlord. All the New York families lived in rented apartments, but 80 percent of the Puerto Rican sample were homeowners; and, in any case, in Puerto Rico all the families had to buy their own stove or refrigerator, which made a significant difference in the total outlay. Most of the New York Puerto Ricans had not made a total commitment to remain there permanently and therefore hesitated to invest heavily in household furnishings.

Despite the small difference in expenditure, a comparison shows that the New York families had far more of each of the luxury items listed, with the exception of automobiles. Only two (4 percent) families in New York, compared with twelve families (12 percent) in Puerto Rico, owned an automobile. Some 80 percent more New York families had gas or electric stoves, 71 percent more had dining-room sets, 55 percent more had phonographs, 54 percent more had fans, 48 percent more had TV sets, 35 percent more had living-room sets, 34 percent more had refrigerators, and about 25 percent more had radios, wristwatches, sewing machines, and washing machines. Thirteen families owned typewriters in contrast to none in our Puerto Rican sample.

Investment in clothing was much higher in New York than in Puerto Rico. In Puerto Rico, the mean outlay for clothing was $657 per family, while in New York it was $1,560 per family. New York winters required expensive warm clothing, and more was spent on women's clothing because a large number of women worked outside the home. There was less resistance to the purchase of clothing than of household goods because clothing could easily be taken back to Puerto Rico. Finally, even for very poor Puerto Ricans, clothing was an item of conspicuous consumption, and the higher income in New York made it feasible to buy more.

On the whole, spending and saving patterns tended to remain the same in New York. Indebtedness for installment purchases was $128 per family in New York, compared with $110 in Puerto Rico. There was an absence of savings in both cases, except saving for occasional trips between the island and the mainland. In addition, many New York families sent expensive gifts to their relatives in Puerto Rico. In New York there was a greater tendency to budget expenditures and to buy food less frequently and in larger quantities, paying with cash rather than buying on credit and patronizing supermarkets as well as neighborhood Hispano-American grocery stores.

Another factor affecting the income and standard of living of the families in New York was the smaller size of family and the higher proportion of individuals in the productive age group. In New York, only 4 percent of the total sample population were sixty years of age or over and 51 percent were under twenty, whereas in Puerto Rico, there were 22 percent over sixty and 65 percent under twenty. The average size of household in our Puerto Rican group was six; in New York it was less than four.

Family composition and marital status did not change significantly in the New York sample except for a higher proportion of persons (26 percent) who were divorced, separated, or abandoned, compared with only 14 percent in the sample group in Puerto Rico. The tendency toward matrifocality was seen in approximately one-third of the families in both groups, although it was somewhat more pronounced in Puerto Rico.

There is little evidence of any marked difference in family life, but certain definite trends are discernible. The weakening of extended family and *compadrazgo* ties and reciprocity and the combined pressures of racial and ethnic discrimination, higher aspirations, improved standard of living, higher income, and higher expenditures tended to make the nuclear family more unified, independent, and self-reliant. The increased independence of women reportedly made for more marital discord and contributed to a lessening of parental control over children, but despite their differences, husbands and wives depended more upon one another and were more cooperative.

In both Puerto Rico and New York, most of the working adults in our samples were employed in low-prestige jobs, although in New York factory work was much more common and fewer persons worked as craftsmen and laborers. There was a higher incidence of female employment in New York. Outside employment of wives increased from 16 percent in Puerto Rico to 40 percent in New York. In New York far more women worked in factories and none took in washing and ironing, as women often did in the Puerto Rican slums.

Unemployment dropped from 23 percent in Puerto Rico to 9 percent in New York. In both New York and Puerto Rico, 20 percent of the families were receiving government aid in the form of relief payments. However, the income and standard of living of relief clients were much higher in New York. Most of the families that had been on welfare in Puerto Rico were self-supporting in New York.

There was a significant correlation between income and education in both Puerto Rico and New York, but it was more pronounced in New York. The educational level, like the income, was higher in New York; adults averaged 6.5 years of schooling, compared with 3.6 years for their relatives in Puerto Rico. School dropouts were a problem in both places, but the average number of grades completed by dropouts in New York was 9.5, compared with 5.9 in Puerto Rico.

In Puerto Rico, one in five working adults belonged to a union, whereas in New York, four out of five were union members. The New York sample families showed a greater tendency to join voluntary organizations than the sample families in Puerto Rico. Of the New York adults, 12 percent belonged to school groups and 7.2 percent to religious organizations, compared with 4 percent in Puerto Rico for both. Church attendance, however, declined in New York.

The presence or absence of the traits of the culture of poverty can best be determined by means of intensive family case studies. Because the present report is based primarily upon our questionnaire data rather than upon our family case studies, which have yet to be completed and analyzed, it is difficult to assess what happened to the culture of poverty when our Puerto Rican families moved to New York. Moreover, the frequency of visiting back and forth between Puerto Rico and New York further complicated the picture. At this point we can make only a few tentative comparative observations.

Certain traits of the culture of poverty, particularly those related to marriage and family life, such as the presence of free unions, unstable marriages, infidelity, multiple marriages, early marriages, illegitimacy, and matrifocality, were equally present in New York and in Puerto Rico. The higher incidence of broken marriages in New York may not be too significant because of the factor of selectivity. Many of the families had left Puerto Rico primarily because their marriages were shaky or had already dissolved. Other traits such as wife beating, the use of physical punishment in the training of children, and abandonment and neglect of children were subject to the stricter laws of New York, which had some deterrent effect.

Although our New York sample families had improved their standard of living, worked at higher status jobs; joined more voluntary organizations; used banks, airports, and airplanes; belonged to unions; received hospital, medical, unemployment insurance compensation, and more adequate welfare and were more subject to the mass media, their sense of marginality to the larger society was, if anything, greater than in Puerto Rico. Because the mainland society was predominantly middle class, white, and Protestant, with strong racial prejudices and discriminatory practices and a different language, morality, and standard of behavior, low income Puerto Rican migrants felt more than ever like second-class citizens. To a large extent they were physically set apart by being classified with Negroes and subjected to discrimination and segregation in housing, schools, jobs, churches, entertainment, and social life. This factor increased their sense of inferiority and, to some extent, their hostility toward those in authority. The total effect was to make them withdraw from the larger society and to activate their sense of nationality and ethnic identity. They clung to their native language and customs and to their dream of returning to Puerto Rico. They took little interest in United States politics and rarely participated in affairs outside their Puerto Rican community. They were further disillusioned and alienated by the lack of unity among themselves, particularly among the more successful middle-class Puerto Ricans.

from Spanish Harlem

Patricia Cayo Sexton

NEIGHBORS—PUERTO RICAN, NEGRO, ITALIAN

East Harlem cuts deep into Manhattan, on two square miles of the highest priced rock in the world, running from the East River to Central Park, and roughly from 96 to 130 Streets on Manhattan's east side.

Its borders are always shifting. So are its neighborhoods, or subareas. Some have their own identity. When the European immigrants dominated East Harlem they referred to it as "the neighborhood." It was then more a neighborhood simply transferred from some European town to the New World, with the same culture. Though Italians still talk about "the neighborhood," social workers and the new migrants—Puerto Ricans and Negroes—know that physical togetherness alone does not make people neighbors.

The community is divided, says a City Planning Commission report, into several social areas. A commuter's railroad track on Park Avenue, the former site of an elevated line, a hill on 102 Street are natural borders that create subareas. These may, like national boundaries, isolate one group from another and give rise to separate patterns of living. Often the borders separate the more from the less desirable areas.

Public housing can be a more formidable barricade than streets, tracks, and lines of transportation. The giant projects tend, like barbed wire, to shut off communications. Projects midway in East Harlem stretch across its whole width and cut it in two. To the north and west of this barrier are the dominantly Ne-

---

gro neighborhoods. To the south on one end is El Barrio, the oldest Puerto Rican settlement in the states.

Mixed in with El Barrio's Spanish residents are some West Indians, Irish, Russians, Hungarians, and Negroes. Its nerve center is the enclosed market under the Park Avenue railroad tracks. Here goods and information are exchanged. Some claim that prostitution and the narcotics trade are rife in El Barrio, on 110 and 111 Streets, for example, west of Park Avenue. Two active community groups also work there: the Taft Neighborhood Development Committee and the East Harlem Reform Democrats. Along Fifth Avenue and in a different world is a towering row of public institutions facing Fifth Avenue and Central Park, their backs turned to the slum.

The "Triangle" at the northern end of East Harlem between 125 and 130 Streets is probably Harlem's poorest spot. Though it has a number of stable residents, its present, predominantly Negro population includes many recent arrivals from the rural Deep South. It stands in a corner by itself, isolated, ignored by many agencies that tend to the southern tier. The Triangle is the end of the line for many hard-core cases. The bulldozers have pushed them about, like gravel, from one spot to another, and now they are here, many of them too down-and-out to qualify for public housing. Again the bulldozers may push them out. The next step in their line of march seems to be the East River.

> Better a neighbor that is near than a brother far off.
> —PROVERBS

East Harlem is now brimming with a mixture of dark and volatile people: Puerto Ricans who give it a Spanish accent (41 percent), Negroes (38 percent), Italians and others (21 percent).

The most significant recent population change is the increase in Negro residents. Many of them came in with the new public housing projects. In 1940 Negroes were only 20 percent of East Harlem's population. In each recent decade Negroes increased by roughly 10 percent. As in other cities, New York City's Negro population has been dispersing. The increase of Negro population now comes mainly from natural increase rather than new migration. The migrations have merely slowed, not stopped, and newcomers in undetermined numbers still arrive from the most backward rural areas of Puerto Rico and the deepest South.

Puerto Ricans have also increased. They were only 30 percent of the total in 1950. The Italians, until recently dominant, are still leaving for Long Island and other suburban points. Both East and Central Harlem have been losing population very rapidly. East Harlem's loss was 17 percent in the 1960 census. Central Harlem's was about 14 percent, most of it in the 21 to 44 age group. The young grow up and leave when they marry and start work.

East Harlem's residents have known upheaval and change. About half of its population moved from one place to another during one five-year period. In Central Harlem only one out of three moved.

Woe unto him that is alone when he falleth.
—ECCLESIASTES

Cultural differences have been overplayed in discussions of the disadvantaged. Idiosyncracies of culture are of more interest and use to the tourist than to the advocate of progress and change. What is most significant about the culture of the disadvantaged is that its essentials are much like those of the advantaged, minus the material comforts and self-respect that are their by-products. A brief tour of East Harlem's culture . . . will suffice, with a pause for a taste of its special Puerto Rican flavor.

The cultural attitudes of the Puerto Rican and Negro segments toward authority are in direct contradiction to each other, Preston Wilcox observed as director of the East Harlem Project. Puerto Ricans tended to be submissive toward authority and thus easily came under the domination of a single leader who did little to develop their potential. The Negro segment tended to be aggressive toward authority—the result being that they continued to receive 'guarded' reactions from authority figures with little goal achievement.[1]

Submission from one group, aggression from the other; neither gets the most out of authority. Puerto Ricans, it is claimed, favor the "maximal leader," the unquestioned leader that all follow: a corollary in everyday life is that "If they like you, they'll accept anything from you." Protest leaders in East Harlem are critical of Puerto Ricans for accepting social inequities and for their "failure to join Negroes in protest." It is said that Puerto Ricans are "more American than Americans," and that anything in the United States goes with them; they do not complain.

An estimated one-fourth of Puerto Ricans are Negro. Though Puerto Ricans tend to be racially unbiased, by mainland standards, the dark-skinned Puerto Ricans say they are treated as the "lowest" in their families, and it is said that the Puerto Rican drug addict is almost always the darkest member of his family.

Though conflict is still open, Puerto Ricans are closer in life style, religion, and attitudes to their Italian rather than their Negro neighbors. Italians, an exclusive and "cornered" community in East Harlem, accept neither group, but Puerto Ricans are less rejected and some intergroup dating and marriage do occur. Only a few Puerto Ricans and even fewer Negroes are to be seen in the Italian's last major preserve: La Guardia Neighborhood House. A mixed dance was once held there (Italian and Puerto Rican), but the boys fought over mixed couple dancing, and the attempt at friendship through youth socializing was all but abandoned. La Guardia House still sponsors a fairly active Italian—Puerto Rican friendship group (which Negroes say should include them too) to reduce violent conflict and help in neighborhood improvement.

[1]Preston Wilcox, "Grassroots Participation, a Step Toward Better Mental Health," *Realizing the Mental Health Potentials for Children and Youth in City Living.* Proceedings of a conference held by the Manhattan Society for Mental Health, October 2–4, 1961, p. 46.

All three groups are fond of music and dancing. While the Puerto Rican youth retain much of their "folk music," the Italian youth are almost submerged in the pop music of the larger "youth culture" and rarely speak Italian or sing Italian songs in public.

Sex is a favorite subject if not activity, though strong restraints on girls are found among Italians and Puerto Ricans. One youth worker, who has lived or worked in East Harlem all his life, claimed that "all the kids can think of is sex;" he referred to all three ethnic groups. "No wonder they can't learn anything in school," he said, "they have sex on their mind 24 hours a day."

One teacher described her Puerto Rican and Negro children as "very active" physically. "They love to dance and move their bodies. They can't sit still. The ones that do well in school usually don't like to dance or move around. When I had a group to my house, they all danced wildly, except one girl who was the best student in the school. She didn't dance at all."

"The children here," she said, "can do so much on their own—sewing, and painting, and creative work. The middle class children always have to be taken care of. They want you to do everything for them." East Harlem's children tend to take on responsibility and independence at an early age, and to "do for themselves."

Teachers and others claim that Puerto Ricans keep their children close to home and off the streets, while the Negro children are permitted much more freedom of the streets and sidewalks. Puerto Rican girls, in particular, are closely watched and sheltered, and are rarely permitted out at night without an adult escort. This restriction is breaking down with time. Italian girls too are very closely watched by their parents, and many are continually in trouble with parents about keeping late hours or not being home on time. Negro girls are given much more freedom.

While Italian youths express open and profound racist feelings, Puerto Ricans, themselves a racial mixture, tend to feel that "everyone is equal" and that they should not talk against Negroes. Some, in unguarded moments, will express fear of Negroes. One sixth grader said:

The Negro people, they all act tough. The colored people, if we walk down the street and if a Negro were walking by and we looked at them, they just start a fight. If we're walking down the street, my grandmother says, and I see a Negro walking down the street, he could talk anything he want, I would look down not to see his face because the Negro people act tough. They say 'what are you looking at?'

Their relations are better with Spanish Negroes:

Where I used to go there was some nice Negro people. I used to always be with them and take them to my house and give them candy or anything what I had. I had a friend, she was real nice with me. She used to always, you know, stick with me, and another girl named Margie, you know, she was colored people. Colored, yeah, but she was Spanish, she was just like me. She lived in the same building and we three used to always stick together. I think sometime that Negro people are generous too.

The dark-skinned Puerto Rican child tastes mainland racial prejudice and doesn't like it at all; it helps him understand, however, what American Negroes have to live with. A sixth grade Puerto Rican girl tells this story of discovery:

I went to Lane's about two weeks before Easter, and I looked all over the place, and my mother is light skinned and I was with her. So I looked all over the place like that and I didn't see nobody my color and I said to my mother, "I'll wait out here," and she said, "No, you come in here." We went up to the top part to find the hats, so I got on the escalator and there was these light-skinned people on the escalator going down and I was going up and they were looking at me and I had this badge that said about the Beatles "I like Paul," and they looked at me, and this lady stuck her tongue out at me. And I asked my mother and my mother said, "You don't live with her, keep walking," but they were all looking at me and I thought because I was the only dark-skin in there. I looked all over the place and I was the only one dark skin.

Race and ethnicity underlie much of the open and hidden conflict in East Harlem, as it always has in the slums of New York's melting pot. The poor, consumed by conflict with the new poor who are moving in on top of them, often ignore "enemies without" and those at a distance who pull the strings that manipulate their lives.

Typically, in the old tenement housing, these groups will not live together in the same building, though they may live in adjacent buildings or at opposite ends of a block. In the new public housing projects, they at least share the same roof, however little they may communicate under it. In the old blocks, one side of the street may be Italian and the other side Puerto Rican. The melting down of these new migrants, the effort of learning to talk and share and work together, is a slow and troubled process.

Politically, the Puerto Ricans in East Harlem have tended to form alliances with Negroes rather than with Italians within the Democratic party, and they have now successfully taken over much of the party's control from the Italians.

The rapidly diminishing Italian community tends to live in the old row houses rather than the projects; a number of Italians are home owners who are aging and want to stay in their old neighborhood. Italian youths of dating age are boxed in, constrained from dating Puerto Ricans and Negroes, and unable to find a big enough matrimonial field in their own community; Irish boys from other neighborhoods are desirable to the girls but not very accessible. The Italians are more prosperous than the other groups and the Puerto Ricans least prosperous. Negroes tend to favor project living, and they now constitute a fairly large upwardly mobile and unusually sophisticated group in East Harlem, though there are also large numbers of destitute people.

The Italian community is tightly sealed against outsiders; many of East Harlem's "Italians" are Sicilians, some of whom have been (some claim still are) close to the Sicilian underworld; nobody talks about it to outsiders. This underworld may have been, in fact, East Harlem's most earnest "self-help" effort—a community project that serviced people in a variety of legal and illegal ways, gave assistance, welfare, and protection, enriched some and helped others rise out of poverty. Neither Puerto Ricans nor Negroes have had any comparable organization.

> I have shut my balcony
> because I do not want to hear the lament,
> but from behind the grey walls
> I hear nothing else but the lament.*
> —GARCIA LORCA

The gray poverty of the old Spanish section of East Harlem, roughly marked by 96 and 112 Streets on the south and north and Fifth and Third Avenues on the west and east, contrasts with the green poverty of the homeland, Puerto Rico.

The island, once a U.S. colony, is now a commonwealth. It elects its own government and pays no taxes to the United States. Yet it receives the benefits of U.S. citizenship and limited U.S. federal services and funds. Recent economic growth has made it the most prosperous Latin American territory, though it is still a long way from prosperity as we know it.

The Puerto Rican migration to Neuva York, unchecked by immigrant quotas, is a major source of the island's prosperity. It upgraded the migrants, converted them from rural to urban people, relieved the island of some of its labor surplus, and sent lots of cash back home.

The commonwealth government plays many improvisations on the mixed economy theme. It built much of the industry on the island and still operates some of it. It also gives substantial tax exemptions to private enterprises that have been brought in from the states, and feverishly encourages private investment.

In Puerto Rico the outsider is aware of a national spirit amid residual poverty. A spirit that is busy and buzzing and wide-eyed rather than shrewd, ruthless, competitive. It is a lyric and a creative excitement rather than a highly organized or mechanized one. Many people, very modest people, seem to think it is their job to do something: first for their people, second for themselves. It seems the reverse of what they run into in New York City. The rural campesinos are still impoverished, however, and 13 percent of the labor force is unemployed.

For an industrializing people, many Puerto Ricans have an incongruous bubbling of good spirits. Mainland visitors usually love the island and wonder why Puerto Ricans left this lovely place to live in El Barrio.

The simple answer of course is poverty. They left in search of a job, food, good shoes, a phonograph, a chance to succeed—just like everyone else. New York is cold and gray; Puerto Rico is green and warm, an island paradise. It is so close to New York by air coach that Puerto Ricans continue to have some of the best of two worlds and, unlike any previous migrants, keep one foot in the green homeland and the other in gray El Barrio or south Bronx.

The migration to New York City, where 60 percent of the migrants (over

* Federico Garcia Lorca, Selected Poems. Copyright 1955 by New Directions Publishing Corporation.

650,000) came is said to have stopped.[2] It is harder to get jobs in the states and easier for those with skills to get jobs in the island than before. So many return to their "rich port" or never leave in the first place. Some learn skills on the mainland and go home to use them, or acquire capital and go home to set up a business.

Meanwhile Puerto Ricans helped those back home. In 1954, $3 million went from New York to Puerto Rico by postal money order alone. In 1940 bank deposits in Puerto Rico were $76 million; in 1961, $674 million. About half the capital invested in new manufacturing now comes from Puerto Rico itself. Political power has changed hands. Once dominated by sugar lawyers, the legislature came to be heavily influenced by labor leaders and spokesmen. It is this political change that produced economic change. The great Governor Luis Muñoz himself was influenced by the U.S. labor movement, as were many of the new Puerto Rican leaders.

In the 1930s, after some thirty-five years of American colonial status, Puerto Rico was impoverished, illiterate, diseased, congested. About one-third of all births were illegitimate. It was almost wholly dependent on sugar and had little industry. In other words, it resembled most of Latin America. With its commonwealth status came new life and prosperity. . . .

Nominally Roman Catholic, about ten times as many Puerto Rican children go to public as to parochial school, though the New York archdiocese has about 250 Spanish-speaking priests. There are some 4,000 Puerto Rican-run businesses in New York.

El Diario—La Prensa, a Spanish daily paper in New York that prints Puerto Rican news, is owned by Roy Chalk, of Trans-Caribbean Airways, a non-Puerto Rican. The paper is called the "patron" of many Puerto Ricans; some say it is a Puerto Rican equivalent of Tammany Hall. Others criticize its "conservatism" and influence on Puerto Rican opinion.

Some Puerto Ricans have moved up rather fast in New York. In 1950, only 24 percent of mainland-born Puerto Rican women were in sales and clerical occupations. A decade later, 43 percent held these jobs.

Many Puerto Rican women marry and bear children while *they* are still children. The birth rate for girls younger than 20 is *five times* higher among Puerto Ricans and Negroes than among non-Puerto Rican white groups. The effect of the combination of large families and low wages is visible in the ethnic make-up of the New York City Welfare Department's recipients of supplementary assistance, assistance given those who have jobs but whose wages do not cover their

---

[2]About 50,000 Puerto Ricans are going north each year, but there has in the past few years been a great increase in the number returning. The return migration went up to 33,000 in 1963 and is expected to be over 50,000 in 1964.

In 1960 Puerto Rican per capita income was just below $700 a year, the highest in Latin America, but less than half that of Mississippi.

Of new professional jobs created in Puerto Rico between 1955 and 1960 (3,000), 28 percent were taken by returned migrants. Of 6,000 new merchant and commercial openings, 36 percent were filled by returnees

minimum needs. One-half of all families in New York who receive this assistance are Puerto Rican. Thus government subsidizes the hundreds of marginal businesses in the city that do not pay a living wage.

Birth control is a big issue with Puerto Ricans, as it is with others. The women so want to keep down family size, says Elena Padilla, in her book *Up from Puerto Rico*,[3] that "abortions and other forms of discontinuing pregnancies may be attempted," such as castor oil, quinine pills, strong purgatives and teas. Abortions, carried out by women *(comandronas)* who do them for small fees, "are closely guarded secrets, for, reported one informant, 'a woman who has an abortion can be sentenced to death in the electric chair.' " Sterilization, obtained without great difficulty in Puerto Rico, is said to be preferred to contraception.

Many Puerto Ricans, she reports, regard other Puerto Ricans as "worthless" because of their "lack of unity" and because in New York they do not "help each other as they do in Puerto Rico."

"Americans" are highly regarded by Puerto Ricans. They are said to be "nice, honest, beautiful, and funny." "Americans," as defined by Puerto Ricans, are nonimmigrant whites. The second-generation New York Puerto Ricans interviewed gave a "high" rating to Americans, Cubans, Italian, Jewish and other European immigrants; a "medium" rating to American Negroes including West Indians; and a *"low" rating to the new Puerto Rican migrant.* "For some Hispanos it is openly accepted and unquestioned that Hispanos are undesirable persons." One Puerto Rican voiced his feelings when he said, "Our race, the Latin race, has spoiled this country by the use of drugs. That is why the Americans hate us."

Such feelings are not usually reciprocated. Only American Negroes, West Indians, and Cubans rated Puerto Ricans "high." Italians rated them "medium." Others rated them "low."

Though Puerto Ricans are a mixed race, ranging from blonde to black, the "mainsprings of intergroup tensions in the neighborhood lie between recent Puerto Rican migrants and American Negroes." Puerto Ricans speak of Negroes as "bad, dangerous, and capable of violence against them." The Negroes and Puerto Ricans who have lived in the neighborhood for years however "have learned to associate with each other in small groups, become close friends, visit each other, and share in real comradeship."

In East Harlem the beginnings of a close alliance between Negro and Puerto Rican can be seen, but there is still tension and fear. Many Puerto Rican and Negro parents keep their small children close to home or inside the apartment even in hot summer months. The streets are dangerous, they say; they are filled with youths whose parents do not try or cannot keep them home; they are filled with young men who are too old to be told what to do and who, in their tragic idleness, have a way of teaching "bad things" to the young or getting in trouble with other ethnic groups.

[3]New York, Columbia University Press, 1958.

Among Puerto Ricans the family is stressed as the "center of an adult's obligations," while individuality and "doing things just for oneself are discouraged as being of no value."

Success and achievement are encouraged only as ways to help the family. The person who does not succeed can expect help from the family. As one person put it: "A good life is when we work and we have the things we need for all the family." Independence and self-reliance "are not to be encouraged in a child." Good children are defined as "obedient, respectful, and docile."

For recent migrants, prized values are: being a "good" worker, formal schooling, learning English while not forgetting Spanish, desiring "progress" and getting ahead ("get the feet off the dish") especially through the education of children, not letting anyone "take you for a ride," being quiet, being careful in choosing friends, and trusting only a few people.

It is considered "an essential quality of a good and worthwhile person that he "have sentiment." Women may express grief by an "attack"—loud screaming, shaking, falling to the floor with arms rigidly extended and hands clenched. Attacks are regarded as a "demonstration of intense grief and great affection for the person in danger." A man is not criticized for crying or having an "ataque."

In El Barrio, says a City Planning Commission report, Puerto Ricans "are extraordinarily gregarious and have greatly suffered the loss of the small shop. The *bodega*, the barber shop, the small Puerto Rican luncheonette and the township club were and are, in the cases of the few remaining ones, the meeting grounds for Puerto Ricans of all ages."

As a group they would rather take "every precaution to hide and shelter a relative for years than reveal the exact number of occupants in an apartment to a building inspector or landlord."

One young Negro, president of a public housing tenant council in El Barrio, complained that Puerto Ricans are hard to talk to about tenant meetings.

"Fear is everything," he said. "It's the only thing that works. I used to go to their door and they'd close it in my face. Now I canvass with a Puerto Rican fellow and they talk to him. He goes to the door and says: 'Do you want to be shot? Do you want to be robbed? If you don't, you'd better support the tenant's council—because we're going to get rid of crime around here. Otherwise, there's no telling what will happen to you.' He signs them up."

Up farther, in the Triangle, organizers say the few Puerto Ricans there are much easier to organize than Negroes and much less afraid. Perhaps Puerto Ricans living in slum housing are less afraid and feel less strange than those living in new projects.

El Barrio's streets and life are tied into the blood stream of the city. They are not detachable. Many people do not seem to have this clearly enough in mind; East Harlem seems to them almost a separate duchy, which can go it alone.

Even less clear, and further from view, is the connection of the community with the state and federal systems. In these distant centers most of the strings are pulled that manipulate the lives of slum dwellers.

The neglect of the slum, and discrimination against it, come out of the city's neglect by the state and federal systems. The city, and increasingly its suburbs, stand against the state system, which is controlled by rural and business interests. And, when the "state system" and its political conservatism control the federal system, the city stagnates and suffers. It is always in need of massive transfusions from the federal system. Its own money-raising powers are limited by the state, and contributions from anticity state legislatures are not generous.

Neglect of the city has spawned East Harlem's slums. It has produced massive pathology in the whole city. The wounds of East Harlem and El Barrio will probably never heal while the city's sores are raw.

NEW YORK'S LOWER DEPTHS

But is the whole of East Harlem a slum? In its low income housing projects, families on welfare range from 13 percent in one to 21 percent in another. Still, the majority of families are self-supporting.

The Triangle is an American Casbah, loaded with troubles and despair, but even there can be found much hope. In the Triangle's thirty-six acres, more than half the families are stable enough to have lived there for from eleven to twenty-one years. In a study done by a local group, 15 percent of the residents were found to have criminal records and 10 percent to be narcotics addicts. The reverse is that even in this trouble spot only a small minority were addicted and relatively few had criminal records.

On a warm summer day the broken and derelict men are visible on the Triangle streets, sodden with despair and whatever they take to make their internal escape from the slum. But far more numerous at some hours of the day are the spirited and attractive young men and women. While some of the Triangle's citizens look sullen and resentful, many do not. No stereotype fits; and, what outsiders would call a slum, many insiders would not.

One young Puerto Rican described East Harlem this way:

I'm 23 years old, and I've been living here all my life. I never been out of this neighborhood. To me this neighborhood is all right. People who have money—maybe it's a dump, as they call it, but this is my home.

It is not a slum to everyone.

The relevant facts about East Harlem's poverty were turned up by a mayor's study. They showed that one in five New Yorkers lives in conditions of poverty. Though more than half of the poor are white, nonwhites are 29 percent of the poor and Puerto Ricans 19 percent. The poor are largely confined to sixteen of the seventy-four recognized communities of the city—one of them East Harlem, the poorest of the poor.

Nothing more meaningful about East Harlem can be found than the fact that its median family income of $3,700 is $2,300 a year lower than the median for the city, or that jobless rates for Negroes run about 50 percent above the norm of whites and for Puerto Ricans about 100 percent.

About half of all private dwellings in East Harlem are dilapidated. Almost one in three is overcrowded. It is possible that crowding alone may produce much of the slum's stress. Experimental biologist Dr. Hudson Hoagland has found that overcrowding in animal society can produce stress-induced maladies—liver disease, heart trouble, sexual deviation—that serve as natural population controls. When crowded, animals die off despite adequate food; rats show abnormal sexual and social behavior. It is part of the "acute stress syndrome," he suggests, that results from the overactivity of the pituitary adrenal system, which regulates the release of hormones during stress.

Slum dwellers may be reacting in the same physiological way as the biologist's animals. Most people need and want privacy, at least on occasion—a room of one's own, an escape from family demands, noise, conflict. Because of the continuing bombardment of the senses, day and night, many slum children wake up nervous and tired. But the children are not lonely, and they are less likely than the more isolated "only child" of the middle class family to commit suicide.

A Negro woman in East Harlem expressed a common opinion:

We're in such crowded tenements down here, that it's hard to live privately. Your neighbors can't move—because of the salaries that are being made—into a decent neighborhood. The mix is good. You have to mix in order to get along with people. But the living so close together, that's a bit too much.

In East Harlem tuberculosis rates are high and venereal disease (VD) rates are more than twice the city average. Crowding helps spread disease. So does the inability of the poor to pay for decent medical care.[4]

Crowded rooms and lack of privacy no doubt help persuade East Harlem's youths (indeed the poor everywhere) to marry younger than do their middle class peers. Since the young are even less able to buy medical care, one out of three pregnant mothers gets no prenatal attention. Not surprisingly then, infant mortality is 37 per 1,000 live births (compared with the city average of 26), and 50 percent of the infant deaths occur on the first day of life.

The typical East Harlem resident has never been to high school. Median school years finished are 8.2. Only one out of five has graduated from high school. Only one out of twenty has had any college. Of all residents in upper Manhattan who have had no formal education, 50 percent live in East Harlem, and most are Puerto Ricans.

In East Harlem few residents (and those mainly Italians) own their own homes.

---

[4]More than 90 percent of East Harlem school children depend on institutional medical care. New York's Health Commissioner, Dr. George James, said that "poverty is the third leading cause of death" in the city. He attributes 13,000 deaths a year to it, including cancer, diabetes, pneumonia, influenza, cardiovascular diseases, and accidents, along with tuberculosis and VD.

By contrast, nationally 38 percent of Negroes and 64 percent of whites in 1960 owned their own homes.[5]

The typical New Yorker is a tenant. As such he is denied the status, power, and stability that the American's chief property assets can offer: a home and the car that usually goes in its garage. The New Yorker, the poorer one in particular, typically has neither. Many like it this way and prefer apartment living when there are no young children in their families. But it is not clear what the effect the total denial of these assets has on the poor and others. The lack of these major creative and recreational outlets may result in significant psychological deprivation. Though caring for a house and car is simply a chore for many middle class people, manual workers often find in it a major source of satisfaction. If a worker is handy with his hands he will spend much of his time with his house and car, finishing the basement or attic, building a fence or porch, repairing his car. Do-it-yourself attitudes and skills are by-products of car and home ownership. So is the sense of control over the environment and the machine. It is a vital part of the American style of life that is missing in East Harlem and other rental areas. If the residents of East Harlem owned these buildings they would not permit them to remain in their present state of decay. They would be moved to clean, paint, and fix. As it is they think it is the landlord's responsibility—and almost always it is. In the rental slums of New York, apartment ownership may offer a substitute for home ownership.

In other cities, even the poor, unless they are desperate, often buy their homes if only on land contract. In New York the poor rent. As renters they usually contend with absentee landlords, who neglect their property. The tenants complain. The landlords ignore them. The city investigates; nothing happens. Tenants are helpless, unable to move either landlords or the city to action. Since a serious housing shortage still exists in the city, they are unable to move out to better housing.

---

[5]The typical owner-occupied Negro home was valued at $6,700 in 1960, compared to $12,230 for the white home. In 1950, 35 percent of Negroes and 57 percent of whites owned their homes; thus the rate of increase has been greater for whites.

The Lower Status Puerto Rican Family

Joseph Bram

In discussing the Puerto Rican family, one must remember at all times that the society of this West Indian island is part of a wider Spanish-speaking world, which in turn is part of our Western civilization. Thus, in the final analysis, the family in Puerto Rico should be expected to have a great deal in common with the family in Spain, Ireland, Sweden, the United States, et al.

Our interest in this discussion, however, is focused on Puerto Rico, and consequently we shall deal with specific local-historical peculiarities found in Puerto Rican society. In so doing one should be careful not to overstate the significance of these peculiarities, as over against the more widely shared characteristics of family life in the total European-American culture area.

In concentrating on one particular national society out of several dozen constituting the European-American world one runs into more differences of *degree* than those of structure. Thus all societies of that area are monogamous. Some of them, however, are more rigorous in opposing adultery, concubinage, divorce and pre-marital experimentation than others. None of the Western societies has placed the wife's and mother's authority legally or socially above that of the father's and husband's. Yet it is known that male authority is weaker in Denmark than, let us say, in Greece.

It is also important to keep in mind that statements regarding national or class characteristics are at best probabilistic in nature. When we say that the cult of gastronomy is typically French, we actually mean that we are likely to find more individuals valuing the refinements of *cuisine* among the French than, for instance, in England. Thus all statements about Puerto Rican modes of behavior

From F. Cordasco and E. Bucchioni, *Puerto Rican Children in Mainland Schools*, New Jersey: Scarecrow Press, 1968, pp. 116–126.

made in this essay must be understood as referring to their relative frequencies.

The title of this article points out that our concern here is with the lower status Puerto Rican family. One knows that comparative social status can be defined in terms of numerous criteria, such as income, housing, occupation, education, clothes, manners, peculiarities of speech, racial origins, church membership, etc. In most cases the identification of social status must be based on several such criteria, which occur in consistent and meaningful clusters.

When dealing with the social status of an immigrant group one must consider one at a time the standards of status rating applied to it by the majority society (mainland Americans in our case) and those of the immigrant group itself. To many prejudiced mainland Americans *all* Puerto Ricans in the United States are low status people with just a few individual exceptions. A member of the Puerto Rican community, on the other hand, may be keenly aware of a wide range of status differences among his fellow islanders.

The status rating of individual immigrant families by their own community is never identical with the one they enjoyed on native grounds. When moving from the island to New York City many a Puerto Rican family undergoes a loss of "accumulated social assets." In its new position as occupant of a cold-water flat on Tenth Avenue in Manhattan it finds itself down-graded, with no neighbors aware of the good social standing it enjoyed in the native environment.

The same process, however, may operate in reverse and be described in terms of a loss of "accumulated social blemishes." Thus a family which at home had labored under an established unfavorable reputation, may, under the protection of metropolitan anonymity, be able to make a fresh start and move upwards on the socio-economic ladder.

Of the many criteria of lower social status listed above, poverty seems to us the most significant one. If one excepts the cases of recent and accidental reverses of fortune, poverty is most meaningfully related to other such earmarks as housing, clothes, manners, level of literacy, etc.

How much poverty is there on the island of Puerto Rico today? The economic advances made by the island society since the establishment of the semi-autonomous Commonwealth of Puerto Rico in 1952 have been quite spectacular. At the same time, the well-deserved publicity given them by the press has obscured the picture of mass destitution which remains widespread. Here are some figures based on the population census of 1960: (Based on *Boricua,* La Revista de Puerto Rico. Diciembre 1962, p. 31)

18.2 percent of the families have an annual income of more than	$3,000
33.8 percent of the families have an annual income between	$3,000-$1,000
16.9 percent of the families have an annual income between	$1,000-$500
31 percent of the families have an annual income of less than	$500

The extreme forms of poverty are alleviated by various Commonwealth programs: free school lunches, free shoes for impecunious school children, free outpatient clinics, free hospitalization, visiting nursing services, pension and relief plans, low income housing and the distribution of surplus food made available by the Federal Government.

Well-planned and generous as these policies have been they have not done away with mass poverty and all its usual concomitants.

It is sometimes assumed that the cost of living in Puerto Rico must be much lower than in the continental United States. This is only partially true. The climate of the island, of course, makes it unnecessary to own warm clothes or to spend money on heating the homes. The alimentary needs of the body are also somewhat lower in the sub-tropical Caribbean area. On the other hand, Puerto Rico is dependent on imported foods including such national staples as rice, beans, wheat flour and dried codfish (bacalao). The cost of freight is added to the prices of these staples. Clothes, domestic appliances and cars also cost more on the island than in the United States.

One could claim, nevertheless, that extreme poverty is a bit more bearable in a place where temperature is never below 68°. Children have no lack of natural playgrounds; the aged lounge on benches around the plaza of their community, neighbors spend long hours socializing outside their small and inadequate dwellings, and many a homeless man may find a shed or a driveway where no one would disturb his sleep. Streams and water-holes in the mountain areas and the beaches along the coast provide accessible facilities for bathing and swimming. Cooking can be done on open-air improvised stoves (fogon). Furthermore starchy fruits such as panapen (breadfruit) are plentiful and inexpensive as emergency resources. There is no intent in these remarks to play down the drama of poverty, disease and loneliness to which many human beings fall prey in Puerto Rico. Yet for purely comparative purposes attention is being called to the relatively less tragic fate of the poor in the less inclement climate of the Caribbean area.

The poor of Puerto Rico are of two basic types—urban and rural. Rural folk are in turn divided into those of the lowlands of the coast, and the dwellers of the highlands. The urban poor may be either of recent rural origin or with an older urban background.

Town people tend to call all rural folk jibaros. Coastal rural groups feel insulted by this term and apply it to the farmers of the mountainous interior. But even these farmers would sometimes use the term in referring to another hamlet or community while excluding themselves from this category. Thus not many people openly identify themselves as jibaros while the term is used loosely with regard to a wide range of socio-economic types.

The reluctance to regard oneself as a jibaro conflicts with the idealization of this type by the literati and intellectuals of the island. The jibaro has been portrayed by them as the true carrier of the Puerto Rican folk tradition. He was the authentic native "son of the earth" marked off by his own inimitable sense of humor, practical wisdom, shrewdness in his dealings with city people, and a strong spirit of independence. All *jibaro* proverbs, sayings, songs, games, super-stitions, tales of supernaturalism and works of craftsmanship (e.g. home-made string instruments, figures of saints, i.e. *santos,* carved out of wood, et al.) have been reverentially collected and enshrined in the public mind or in public collections.

What sober statements can one make about this sizable and yet elusive element in the population of Puerto Rico? "True" *jibaros* appear to be descended from the predominantly white early settlers of the interior of the island. Geographical isolation combined with poverty has made them the least literate element in the insular society, and the least familiar with the urban way of life. Not many true *jibaros* have had the daring, for instance, to migrate to New York City. Those who did had spent first a few years in one of the coastal shanty-towns or slum suburbs in Puerto Rico, where they underwent a bit of accultura-tion to city ways.

The well-known drama *La Carreta* (1952) by René Marqués portrays the social fate of such a family. In the first act they are shown leaving their home in the mountains under the pressure of economic circumstances. In the second act we witness their trials and tribulations in the coastal slums of Puerto Rico. The third and last act of the play portrays them as "adjusted" to the urban ways of the Bronx as well as victims of unscrupulous individuals and of industrial accidents.

Many *jibaros* are landless and propertyless agricultural workers who meet their subsistence needs by selling their labor power. Some of them own their homes but do not always own the lot on which the dwelling is located. Others live rent-free in the home provided by their employer. Occupying a house erected on lands belonging to another person qualifies them as "squatters" (*agregados*) and implies various customary obligations with regard to the owner of the holding.

Those *jibaros* who are agricultural wage-earners without property or any out-side income are often forced to play a subservient role with regard to their potential or virtual employers, the storekeeper from whom they buy their gro-ceries on credit between the harvest seasons (*zafras*), the wealthier neighbors who may give a temporary job to their wife or son, and to many others. They teach their children to behave with proper humility and to render services to their more powerful neighbors and even playmates.

In a somewhat different category are those *jibaros* who own enough land to depend for survival on subsistence farming. They raise marketable crops of fluc-tuating value (such as tobacco or coffee) and supplement cash income with some vegetables, fruit, chickens and pigs grown and raised by their own efforts. In *jibaro* families of this type the father finds himself in the role of task-master and foreman, whose job is to extract as much work as he can from his small family group. At the same time, he also controls the family expenditures and is thus cast in the role of an occasional "kill-joy." The same function, however, gives him a chance to make a show of generosity and affection by buying things for the home or clothes for his wife and children.

Halfway between the wage-earner and the small land holder is the sharecropper. In the tobacco growing area he splits with the owner of the land the costs of production and shares in the half of the proceeds. Traditionally share-croppers press the members of their family into work in the fields or into serv-ices to the landlord and thus they are found in the role of task-masters and dis-ciplinarians.

As elsewhere in the Spanish-speaking world, the Puerto Rican *jibaro* family is also governed by male authority. The *jibaro* man who has limited claims to social and economic prestige is strongly dependent on his wife's and children's deferential attitudes (particularly in the presence of outside observers) for his ego-gratification. Many a *jibaro's* wife does not begrudge her husband this privilege since indirectly it enhances her own social standing as well. She feels that there is no honor attached to being married to a weak and unmanly hus-band. In fact, she may even tend to exaggerate his dictatorial masculinity and portray herself as a masochistic victim in the hands of a strong virile tyrant.

Where male authoritarianism appears to be a socially recognized norm, women quite commonly evolve indirect methods of defense and compensation. The ailing wife and mother (without being an outright malingerer) often uses her afflictions to secure sympathy and a more lenient treatment. Threats of suicide and frequent unsuccessful attempts at suicide (*suicides manqués*) by Puerto Rican women have been diagnosed by careful observers as attention-getting de-vices. Quite often, however, suicide in Puerto Rico is committed in an irretriev-able manner. The Anglo-American imagination is particularly struck by those cases where the victim soaks her clothes in gasoline and sets herself on fire. Several such cases occur every year along with more numerous but less spec-tacular forms of self-destruction.

The *jibaro* mother makes up for her inferior social position by gaining her children's (her sons' in particular) affection and attachment. She may do that by protecting the guilty boy from his father's anger, by passing small amounts of spending money to him and in many other ways. The image of his "suffering mother" has been found deeply embedded in the mind of many a Puerto Rican adolescent boy or grown man. Most Puerto Rican men regard themselves as natural protectors of their mothers when they are victims of desertion, widow-hood, poverty or social abuse.

The *jibaros* are known to be proud of their numerous progeny, which sym-bolizes the father's procreative vigor and also represents the poor man's only "wealth." It is indeed a proud day in an individual *jibaro's* life when he walks to a fiesta in the nearest center surrounded by his small flock of four or five children.

The rural folk of the coastal plains are not drastically different from the *jibaros* of the highlands. Nevertheless, several points of distinction should be brought out. To begin with, most of them are employed by either government operated or privately owned sugar cane plantations. They thus are landless laborers en-tirely dependent on their wages for a living. They more than often live in primi-tive barracks where each family occupies a one or two-room dwelling (without indoor cooking or toilet facilities) or a section in a similarly inadequate multiple dwelling. They are surrounded on all sides by temporary tenants like themselves and have no illusions of independence that go along with the ownership (by a *jibaro*) of a small home in the relatively inaccessible mountain fastness. The comparative crowding which characterizes their life deprives them of all privacy and affects their sense of dignity.

The family of a sugar cane worker is more a unit of consumption than of production. The head of the family does not have to act as a task-master since he rarely has access to any gardening or poultry raising facilities where members of his family might be engaged in productive work. As soon as his sons or daughters reach the age of marriage or become employable they tend to strike out for themselves and drift away to wherever work can be secured.

Workers in the cane and their families are also in a much less personal relationship with their employers (private owners, corporation representatives, supervisors, foremen, et al.) than the rural folk of the highlands. For practical and traditional reasons the *jibaros* of the interior have to live up to the standards of conduct acceptable to wealthier neighbors on whose goodwill they often depend, i.e. the storekeepers who sell to them on credit, landowners on whose land they build their homes, local politicians and other power-wielders. This may account for a somewhat higher rate of the more respectable church weddings and for more regular attendance at church services in the mountain area, also for a somewhat stronger resistance to the inroads of Protestantism.

Correspondingly, the sugar-cane workers of the coast have a much higher incidence of the less respectable consensual or common-law unions and have proven more receptive to the appeals of Protestant proselytizers.

The urban poor of the island are much more open to observation on the part of the middle class and upper class people of the cities than are the *jibaros*. The slums and shanty-towns of Puerto Rico are adjacent to the more respectable neighborhoods and no one can escape the sight of human misery which they harbor. The city poor more often come to the attention of medical men, hospital personnel, social workers, police authorities, school teachers, members of the clergy and other professional people. This being the case it is rather surprising to discover that sociologists and other researchers in Puerto Rico have given them less attention than to rural populations.

This element in the population of the island is of course much more diversified than anything one would observe in the countryside. We find among them widows with or without dependent children, abandoned wives, jilted girls, orphans, invalids subsisting on small pensions, uprooted *jibaros*, unemployed and unemployable individuals of every possible origin, mentally inadequate persons, women of easy virtue, and many aged people (single or in couples); et al. They survive by engaging in a wide variety of small and often temporary occupations as pedlars, delivery men, unskilled repairmen, gardeners, part-time domestics, lottery ticket salesmen, newsboys, etc. Some of their activities conflict with municipal regulations, police rules and law in general. This would be true of illegal number games (bolita), the sale of privately manufactured rum (canita), prostitution, etc. Centuries of existence under indifferent and inefficient administrations combined with widespread poverty have resulted in much more lenient attitudes toward these "marginal" and outlawed occupations than a moralist conditioned by life in prosperous democratic communities would expect. Here is an area where one has to approach human behavior with a bit of historical perspective and the faculty of empathy.

Government relief, municipal aid, private charity and sporadic contributions by relatives keep many of these city poor not only alive but less unhappy than one might imagine them to be. In part this is due, as pointed out earlier, to the climate of the island, but also to the gift of sociability with which the people of Puerto Rico are so richly endowed.

One of its expressions is their extreme fondness for children. In giving their care and affection to children, the Puerto Ricans are less proprietary than other Europeans and Americans. They easily make room in their poor and crowded homes for children of divorced parents, illegitimate offspring, orphans, abandoned children and foster children (hijos de crianza) in general. Many people enter marriage while having children by previous common law or legalized marriages. It is not unusual to have a family with three or four children none of whom are the offspring of the married couple. As a rule such adopted children or children by previous marriages are treated as well as their adoptive parents' joint progeny.

A special type of relationship known as godparenthood (compadrazgo) can also be considered as a partial corrective to poverty and loneliness among lower status Puerto Ricans. A person sponsoring a child at baptism and christening becomes his life-long godfather (padrino) or godmother (madrina). Where two godparents (compadres) preside over the same ritual this co-participation establishes a special social tie between them. Similarly all godparents are bound in a special way to the biological parents of their godchild. Thus most Puerto Ricans have ritually sanctioned friends, allies, protectors and confidants. The practical value of such a relationship may vary from case to case. Nevertheless, the institution of godparenthood obviously extends the individual's trust and reliance beyond the immediate family, and in some cases provides a person with a substitute for a defaulting family group.

The love of children so common in Puerto Rico appears in a somewhat less idyllic light if viewed against the background of demographic statistics. In 1940 the population of the island was 1,869,255. In 1950 it had reached the figure of 2,210,703 and in 1960 it was 2,349,544. The total land area of the island being 3,421 square miles, the population density of Puerto Rico is nearing the ratio of 700 per square mile, one of the highest in the world. Considering the slender natural resources of the island, the situation is rapidly reaching the point of critical intensity.

There are three basic ways of relieving this growing population pressure: birth control through contraception, emigration and industrialization. All three have been encouraged by the government of the Commonwealth, unfortunately with inconclusive results. Contraception has met with strong opposition on the part of the Roman Catholic Church, which has, however, failed to reverse its growing popularity. Industrialization, combined with tourism, has created numerous jobs and indirect sources of income for the island treasury with its heavy programs of social welfare. And, finally, migration has relieved some of the immediate pressure on the island economy by reducing the number of unemployed and encouraging the flow of subsidies by emigrants to their needy kin.

The advocacy of contraception has also run into nonreligious opposition. Some Puerto Rican men have been reported as feeling that the use of contraceptives was humiliating to their wives or to their own male dignity (or both). Other observers have claimed that shyness and awkwardness in communication between married people made the use of contraception difficult. The provisional figures of birth rate for 1961 give 23.4 (per 1,000 population) for the United States, 31.0 for Puerto Rico. Nevertheless there has been a steady decline in the successive birth rate figures over ten years. The much sharper rate of decline in the rates of mortality, however, has neutralized the limited gains made by the application of birth control.

We have mentioned earlier the frequency of common law (consensual) marriages among lower status Puerto Ricans. Dr. Sidney Mintz in focusing on one specific rural area (which he calls Barrio Jauca) has established the fact that out of 183 marital unions 134 were of the consensual variety. (1) For the island at large the ratio of such common law marriages has been variously estimated between 25 percent and 35 percent of the total. The historical roots of this practice go too far to be examined here. The phenomenon is not restricted to Puerto Rico but has been observed throughout the Caribbean area and in parts of South America.

Dr. Mintz shows very closely that such marriages are as a rule initiated by means of a socially standardized procedure (a "ritualized elopement") which is viewed by the community as equivalent to more traditional legal and religious observances. (2)

Children born to such unions suffer only minor social disadvantages in their home areas, but run into inconveniences and embarrassments when they migrate to the cities or to the mainland of the United States. This is due to the growing importance of pension plans, social security benefits, veteran pensions and insurance policies, all of which have to rely on properly legalized relationships between spouses and between parents and children.

In the meantime people say that "vale mas un buen amancebado que un matrimonio mal llevado" (a good consensual union is worth more than a bad marriage). The prohibition of divorce by the Roman Catholic Church has also been used to justify consensual unions where the two parties are not tied to each other for life. The growth of Protestant congregations in Puerto Rico may be in part due to the toleration of divorces by most of them, even though their strong emphasis on personal morals obviously checks the trend toward easy divorces.

From the Anglo-American point of view one of the striking features of Puerto Rican marriage relationship is the prevalence of jealousy. As could be expected, male infidelities are somewhat more frequent and less rigorously condemned by the community. When the woman's husband shows a decline of personal interest in his wife she is likely to seek "professional" advice from a spiritualist medium or a practitioner of folk-medicine (or folk-magic).

When a man suspects his wife of growing indifference he looks around for a possible rival and is very likely to challenge and even assault the presumed seducer. Painful and dramatic as they are these tensions and actions are indicative of somewhat higher romantic and erotic expectations on the part of married lower status Puerto Ricans than what we observe in our more placid and sedate society.

The Puerto Rican family as we find it in New York (or Philadelphia, Chicago, Boston, etc.) should not be expected to be a duplicate of its counterpart on the island. To begin with, mainland Puerto Ricans are keenly aware of the social prejudice they encounter on the mainland. Two conflicting reactions to social hostility may take place. The members of a family group may, so to say, "close their ranks," i.e. experience an intensified sense of solidarity and view their home as a haven of refuge. The other possible reaction is that of resentment against the group to which they belong, whose characteristics are the alleged cause of its rejection by the outside world.

Where local prejudice against Puerto Ricans assumes racialist undertones (which seems to be always the case), it may have a divisive effect on family unity and solidarity. Puerto Rico is a land of racially mixed marriages (particularly in the lower social strata), and children in many homes run the whole gamut of pigmentation from the very dark to the Mediterranean light. In the North American social environment lighter-complexioned youngsters have a better chance of social and occupational acceptance than their darker siblings. Brothers and sisters are thus separated by differential opportunities, and envy and resentment enter their life.

The same factors may invade the relationship between two differently colored spouses or in-laws, or grandparents and grandchildren. The dark grandmother who hides in the kitchen while her lighter granddaughter, a high school girl, entertains her classmate in the living room, could serve as a symbol of the impact of race prejudice on the Puerto Rican family in New York.

Another source of anxieties among mainland Puerto Ricans is constituted by their gradual loss of influence over their children. In the natural course of events, Puerto Rican children learn English better and faster than their parents.

With the language they acquire a whole world of values, attitudes and rules of adolescent etiquette which remain incomprehensible to their elders. Before long, the English-speaking child may serve as an interpreter in his mother's or father's dealings with the outside world and may come to feel that his parents are unsuited to the American way of life, or even "inferior."

Quite often Puerto Rican women have an easier chance of finding employment than their husbands in our city economy, and thus become principal family providers. With this economic change goes a re-definition of male authority, and many a family head feels that something has gone wrong in his domestic life. Some accept their new dependence on their more successful wives and turn to a half-way justifiable idleness. In the meantime, the unemployed man's children lose their traditional respect for him, and refuse to accept his attempts at reasserting his authority.

Many other changes take place in Puerto Rican family life in the new social environment. At home they lived under what sociologists call "primary social controls," i.e. in small close-knit communities, where neighbors, relatives, storekeepers, school teachers and all others exercised a restraining influence on individual behavior. The anonymity of New York life makes them feel uncomfortably free, "on their own," and also fearful of how this might affect those loved ones (wife, daughters, sons, etc.) whose behavior they would like to supervise.

The easy and casual sociability of the island has also been affected by the new urban world. The climate of the mainland and big city traffic have made street life of the Caribbean type next to impossible. Instead of occupying small family homes with doors and windows open on the outside world, New York Puerto Ricans find themselves living in isolated apartments behind closed doors.

Numerous other material details undergo far-reaching changes, e.g. methods of laundering, patterns of cooking, sleeping arrangements, shopping practices, etc. ad infinitum. None of these taken by itself may be viewed as profoundly significant; in combination they change the whole style of living. Eventually the values of the island give way to something new and different.

When an entire ethnic group is undergoing such a change, it should not be assumed that its individual members will change, it should not be assumed that its individual members will move along at the same pace or will react to the challenges of transformation in the same manner. Family circles may thus be expected to be torn between nostalgic homesick old-timers, ambitious and pushing opportunists and the more rational synthesizers between the old and the new. The island home which was left behind becomes idealized and/or vilified quite realistically, just as the urban world of mainland America is extolled or run down in accordance with the fluctuating circumstances and changing moods. The influx of new migrants from the island keeps alive the overall ambivalent attitudes of the Puerto Rican community. Numerous individuals get tempted by the short distance and the low airplane fares and go home, only to turn around and come back to New York.

Trying to describe and understand the lower status Puerto Rican family of our day is on the whole not easy. The island society is undergoing numerous changes, briefly identifiable by such terms as urbanization, industrialization, secularization, welfare economy, diffusion of literacy, growing life span, increasing population, etc. When individual Puerto Rican families fly over to the mainland and attempt an adjustment to the new socio-economic world of the United States, they find themselves subjected to numerous additional pressures. Neither back home nor here in the States can their existence be described as stable and secure. Thus in order to understand any specific Puerto Rican family group one has to "locate" it on the total map of social change which this national society is undergoing at this time.

SELECTED BIBLIOGRAPHY

Bram, Joseph	Spirits, Mediums and Believers in Contemporary Puerto Rico, *Transactions of the New York Academy of Sciences*, Ser. II, Vol. 20, No. 4, pp. 340–347, February 1958
Hansen, E.	*Transformation: The Story of Puerto Rico*, 1955
Hatt, R. K.	*Backgrounds of Human Fertility in Puerto Rico*, 1952
Landy, David	*Tropical Childhood*, Cultural Transmission and Learning in a Rural Puerto Rican Village, 1959
Mills, C. W., C. Senior and R. Goldsen.	*The Puerto Rican Journey*, 1950
Mintz, Sidney W.	*Worker in the Cane. A Puerto Rican Life Story*, 1960
Roberts, L. J. and R. L. Stefani	*Patterns of Living in Puerto Rican Families*, 1949
Rogler, Charles	*Comerio. A Study of a Puerto Rican Town*, 1940
Sereno, R.	Cryptomelanism: A Study of Color Relations and Personal Insecurity in Puerto Rico, *Psychiatry* 10: 261–269, 1947
Steward, J. H. et al	*The People of Puerto Rico*, 1956
Stycos, J. M.	*Family and Fertility in Puerto Rico*, 1955
Tugwell, R. G.	*The Stricken Land*, 1947
Wolf, K. L.	Growing Up and Its Price in Three Puerto Rican Subcultures, *Psychiatry* 15:401–433, 1952

|3

Notes

1. Sidney W. Mintz,—*Worker in the Cane. A Puerto Rican Life Story*. Yale Life Story. Yale University Press. 1960. pp. 89–92.
2. *Ibid.*

[1]Sidney W. Mintz, *Worker in the Cane. A Puerto Rican Life Story*. Yale University Press. 1960. pp. 89–92.
[2]*Ibid.*

The Puerto Rican Child in the American School

Francesco Cordasco

THE MIGRATION

In 1960 some 900,000 Puerto Ricans lived in the United States including not only those born on the island but also those born to Puerto Rican parents in the states. Until 1940, the Puerto Rican community in the United States numbered only 70,000, but by 1950 this had risen to 226,000, and over the decade to 1960 the net gain due to migration from the island amounted to nearly 390,000. The census of 1950 began the recording of second generation Puerto Ricans (those born on the continent to island born parents) and counted 75,000; in 1960, the figure stood at 272,000, so that by 1960 three out of every ten Puerto Rican residents in the United States were born in the states.

Although there has been a dispersal of the migration outside greater New York City, the overwhelming number of Puerto Ricans are New Yorkers; the 1960 census showed 612,574 living in New York City (68.6 percent of the United States total). New York City's proportion had dropped from 88 percent in 1940 to 83 percent in 1950 and to 69 percent in 1960.[1] If there is no serious setback in the American economy the dispersion will undoubtedly continue.[2]

From *The Journal of Negro Education,* Spring 1967, Vol. 36, pp. 181–186. Reprinted by permission of the author and *The Journal of Negro Education.*

[1]U. S. Bureau of the Census. *U. S. Census of Population:* 1960. *Subject Reports. Puerto Ricans in The United States.* Final Report, PC (2)-1 D. U. S. Government Printing Office, Washington, D. C. 1963.

[2]The 1960 census reported Puerto Rican-born persons living in all but one (Duluth-Superior) of the 101 Standard Metropolitan Statistical Areas of over 250,000 population. Particular concentrations were reported (1960) as Chicago, 35,361; Paterson-Clifton-Passaic (N.J.), 6,641; Los Angeles-Long Beach, 7,214; San Francisco-Oakland, 4,068. For an illuminating study of Puerto Rican dispersal in New Jersey, see Max Wolff, *Patterns of Change in the Cities of New Jersey: Minorities—Negroes and Puerto Ricans Affected by and Affecting These Changes,* N. Y. mimeo., 1962.

The Commonwealth of Puerto Rico neither encourages nor discourages migration. As an American citizen, the Puerto Rican moves between the island and the mainland with complete freedom. If his movement is vulnerable to anything, it fluctuates only with reference to the economy on the mainland. Any economic recession or contraction graphically shows in the migration statistics.[3] It is at best invidious to suggest that "The Puerto Rican migration to *Nueva York*, unchecked by immigrant quotas, is a major source of the island's prosperity," but there is truth in the appended observation that the migration ". . . upgraded the migrants, converted them from rural to urban people, relieved the island of some of its labor surplus, and sent lots of cash back home."[4]

For the American schools, the Puerto Rican migration presented a distinct and yet in many ways a recurrent phenomenon. With the imposition of immigration quotas in the early 1920s, the non-English speaking student had gradually disappeared. The great European migration and its manifold educational problems had in a manner been resolved. With the increasing Puerto Rican migration and the recurrent pattern of the ghettoization of the new arrivals, the migrant child, non-English speaking and nurtured by a different culture, presented American schools with a new yet very old challenge.[5]

PUERTO RICANS AND MAINLAND SCHOOLS

The Puerto Rican "journey" to the mainland has been (and continues to be) the subject of a vast literature.[6] For the most part, the Puerto Rican child reflects a context of bitter deprivation, poor housing, high unemployment, and a record of disappointing educational achievement. It is the poverty context to which the Puerto Rican community has been relegated in our cities that explains its prob-

---

[3]See in this connection migration figures for 1953-54. The best source on Puerto Rican Migration is the Migration Division of the Department of Labor, which maintains a central mainland office in New York City and offices in other U.S. cities. It also maintains an office in Puerto Rico to carry out a program of orientation for persons who intend to migrate to the states.

[4]Patricia Sexton, *Spanish Harlem: Anatomy of Poverty*. (New York: Harper & Row, 1965), p. 15.

[5]Although one of the greatest achievements of the American common school has been the acculturation and assimilation of the children of non-English speaking immigrants (largely European), it has received little study. See F. Cordasco and L. Covello, *Educational Sociology: A Subject Index of Doctoral Dissertations Completed at American Universities, 1941–1963.* (New York: Scarecrow Press, 1965). Of over 2,000 dissertations listed, only a few clearly concern themselves with the non-English immigrant child, or generally with the educational problems of the children of immigrants.

[6]One of the best accounts is Clarence Senior, *The Puerto Ricans* (Chicago: Quadrangle Books, 1965), which includes an extensive bibliography. See also Christopher Rand, *The Puerto Ricans* (New York: Oxford, 1958); Don Wakefield, *Island in the City* (Boston, Houghton-Mifflin, 1959); Elena Padilla, *Up From Puerto Rico* (New York: Columbia University Press, 1958); Jesus Colon, *A Puerto Rican in New York And Other Sketches* (New York: Mainstream Publications, 1961); an older but invaluable documented study of Puerto Ricans in New York City is that of C. Wright Mills, Clarence Senior, and Rose Kohn Goldsen, *The Puerto Rican Journey* (New York: Harper and Row, 1950).

lems and graphically underscores its poor achievement in the schools. Not only is the Puerto Rican child asked to adapt to a "cultural ambience" which is strange and new, he remains further burdened by all the negative pressures of a ghetto milieu which educators have discerned as inimical to even the most rudimentary educational accomplishment.[7]

How the Puerto Rican child has fared in the mainland schools is best illustrated in the experience in New York City, where Puerto Ricans have the lowest level of formal education of any identifiable ethnic or color group. Only 13 percent of Puerto Rican men and women 25 years of age and older in 1960 had completed either high school or more advanced education. Among New York's nonwhite (predominantly Negro) population, 31.2 percent had completed high school; and the other white population (excluding Puerto Ricans) did even better. Over 40 percent had at least completed high school.[8]

In 1960 more than half (52.9 percent) of Puerto Ricans in New York City 25 years of age and older had less than an eighth grade education. In contrast, 29.5 percent of the nonwhite population had not finished the eighth grade, and only 19.3 percent of the other whites had so low an academic preparation.[9]

If the schools in New York City were to correct all of this (the numbers in the second generation who have reached adult years is still small, only 6.4 percent of persons 20 years of age and older in 1960), there is still evidence that Puerto Rican youth, more than any other group, is severely handicapped in achieving an education in the New York City public schools. A 1961 study of a Manhattan neighborhood showed that fewer than 10 percent of Puerto Ricans in the 3rd grade were reading at their grade level or above. The degree of retardation was extreme. Three in ten were retarded one and one-half years or more and were, in the middle of their third school year, therefore, reading at a level only appropriate for entry into the second grade. By the eighth grade the degree of retardation was even more severe with almost two-thirds of the Puerto Rican youngsters retarded more than three years.[10]

Of the nearly 21,000 academic diplomas granted in 1963, only 331 went to Puerto Ricans and 762 to Negroes, representing only 1.6 percent and 3.7 percent, respectively, of the total academic diplomas. In contrast, Puerto Ricans received 7.4 percent of the vocational school diplomas, and Negroes 15.2 percent. For the Puerto Rican community, these figures have critical significance since Puerto Rican children constituted in 1963 about 20 percent of the public elementary school register, 18 percent of the junior high school register. In keeping with long discerned trends, Puerto Rican youngsters made up 23 per-

[7]For a graphic commentary on the debilitating environmental pressures and the "ghetto milieu" see David Barry, Our Christian Mission Among Spanish Americans, mimeo. Princeton University Consultation, February 21–23, 1965. The statistical indices of Puerto Rican poverty (and the related needs) are best assembled in The Puerto Rican Community Development Project (New York: The Puerto Rican Forum, 1964), pp. 26–75.
[8]See The Puerto Rican Community Development Project, p. 34.
[9]Ibid., pp. 34–35.
[10]Ibid., p. 39. The study was undertaken by the Research Center, Columbia University School of Social Work.

cent of the student body in vocational schools and 29 percent of that in special (difficult) schools.[11]

Clearly, the critical issue for the Puerto Rican community is the education of its children, for the experience in New York City is a macrocosm which illustrates all the facets of the mainland experience.[12]

EDUCATIONAL PROGRAMS TO MEET THE NEEDS OF PUERTO RICAN CHILDREN

In the last decade a wide range of articles have reported special educational programs to meet the needs of Puerto Rican children;[13] although many of these have been of value, the more ambitious theoretic constructs have largely come from the school boards and staffs which have had to deal with the basic problem of communication in classes where a growing (and at times preponderant) number of Spanish-speaking children were found. As early as 1951 in New York City, a "Mayor's Advisory Committee on Puerto Rican Affairs" turned its attention to this major problem of communication;[14] and this problem was periodically re-examined during the years which followed.[15]

In New York City (as in other cities)[16] the Board of Education turned its attention to the Puerto Rican child because communication *had* to be established, and (in this context) the most ambitious study of the educational problems presented by the Puerto Rican migration became (for New York City):

. . . a four-year inquiry into the education and adjustment of Puerto Rican pupils in the public schools of New York City . . . a major effort . . . to establish on a sound basis a

---

[11]*Ibid.,* p. 41, and tables, pp. 43–44.

[12]The situation would not be significantly different in other cities where the Puerto Rican community is encapsulated in poverty, e.g., Camden (N.J.), Philadelphia, Chicago. A different dimension would be added in the educational problems presented in those areas where Puerto Rican migrant workers, contracted for agricultural labor, live for varying periods of time. The best source of information on the Puerto Rican agricultural migrant worker is The Migrant Division, Commonwealth of Puerto Rico. See footnote #3, *supra.* The N.J. Office of Economic Opportunity completed a study of the needs of migrant workers in that state in terms of its projected programs.

[13]Typical is Jack Cohn, "Integration of Spanish Speaking Newcomers in a 'fringe area' School," *National Elementary Principal* (May 1960), pp. 29–33. See also F. Cordasco, "Helping the Language Barrier Student," *The Instructor,* XLXXII (May 1963), 20; S. L. Hlam, "Acculturation and Learning Problems of Puerto Rican Children," *Teachers College Record,* LXI (1960), 258–264; James Olsen, "Children of the Ghetto," *High Points,* XLVI (1964), 25–33; John A. Burma, "Spanish Speaking Children," in Eli Ginzberg, *The Nation's Children,* III (1960), 78–102.

[14]"Puerto Rican Pupils in the New York City Schools, 1951." *The Mayor's Advisory Committee on Puerto Rican Affairs. Sub-Committee on Education, Recreation and Parks.* This was a survey of 75 elementary and junior high schools as well as a report on day classes for adults, evening schools, community centers and vacation playgrounds. The report was directed by Dr. Leonard Covello, principal of Benjamin Franklin High School in East Harlem. See in this connection, Covello's *The Heart Is the Teacher* (New York: McGraw Hill, 1958), *passim.*

[15]See Martin B. Dworkis (ed.), *The Impact of Puerto Rican Migration on Governmental Services in New York City* (New York: New York University Press, 1957).

[16]Particularly Philadelphia, Chicago, Newark, and Camden (N. J.).

city-wide program for the continuing improvement of the educational opportunities of all non-English speaking pupils in the public schools.[17]

If the major emphasis of *The Puerto Rican Study* was to have been the basic problem of language (English), its objectives were soon extended to include the equally important areas of community orientation and acculturation. The *Study's* objectives were summed up in three main problems:

1. What are the more effective ways (methods) and materials for teaching English as a second language to newly arrived Puerto Rican pupils?
2. What are the most effective techniques with which the schools can promote a more rapid and more effective adjustment of Puerto Rican parents and children to the community and the community to them?
3. Who are the Puerto Rican pupils in the New York City public schools?[18]

For each of these problems, *The Puerto Rican Study* made detailed recommendations (Problem III, largely an ethnic survey, resulted in a profile of characteristics of pupils of Puerto Rican background and fused into Problems I and II).[19]

Problem I:

How to teach English effectively as a second language. The Puerto Rican Study concluded that an integrated method (vocabulary method, structured or language patterns method, and the functional situations or experiential method) was to be employed, and it developed two series of related curriculum bulletins, keyed to the prescribed New York City course of study.[20] But in the course of its considerations, it dealt with the ancillary (and vital) need ". . . to formulate a uniform policy for the reception, screening, placement and periodic assessment of non-English speaking pupils."[21] It recommended (until such time as the Bureau of Educational Research may find or develop better tests or tests of equal value) the use of *The USB Test—Ability to Understand Spoken English; The Gates Reading Test—Primary and Advanced;* and *The Lorge-Thorndike Non-Verbal Test.* It proposed, too, three broad categories of class organization, considered the need of adequate staffing (Substitute Auxiliary Teachers [SAT], Puerto Rican Coordinators, School-Community Coordinators and Other Teaching Positions [OTP], and guidance counselors, particularly in the senior high

[17]J. Cayce Morrison, Director, *The Puerto Rican Study* (1953–1957): *A Report on the Education and Adjustment of Puerto Rican Pupils in the Public Schools of the City of New York* (New York: Board of Education, 1958), p. 1.
[18]*Ibid.* See New York City Board of Education, *Summary of Recommendations Made by the Puerto Rican Study For the Program in the New York City Schools,* December 8, 1958.
[19]The profile was separately published in 1956, and reprinted in the final report (1958).
[20]A series of nine *Resource Units* and four *Language Guides.* Each *Resource Unit* bulletin contains three or more resource units. See *Puerto Rican Study* [Publications of the Puerto Rican Study] for list.
[21]See *Summary, supra,* p. 3.

schools), and found essential the ". . . coordinating [of] efforts of colleges and universities . . . to achieve greater unity of purpose and effort in developing both undergraduate and graduate programs for teachers who will work with non-English speaking pupils. . . ."[22]

Problem II:

How to promote a more rapid and more effective adjustment of Puerto Rican parents and children to the community and the community to them. In its recognition of this problem, *The Puerto Rican Study* struggled with providing answers to the basic anxieties and preoccupations of a group of people beset with problems of housing, adequate employment, health, and "assimilation." That the *Study* found difficulty in providing answers is perhaps explained by its inability to relate the answers it found most effective to the mandate of the school. If it was possible to revise curricula and discern the problems implicit in the learning experience of the Puerto Rican child, it remained an altogether different matter to attempt the solution of broad socio-economic problems, or to attempt the amelioration of community ills. In essence, the following statement suggests how far the schools have retreated from the community:

On the relation of Puerto Rican parents to schools, *The Puerto Rican Study* holds that because Puerto Rican parents are pre-occupied with problems of learning English, finding apartments, finding employment, and with problems of providing their families with food, clothing, and proper health protection, they are not ready to set a high priority on their children's school problems. The schools can't wait until they are ready.[23]

If *The Puerto Rican Study* is not thought of as a *finished* guide to the solution of the problems it investigates but rather as a beginning, it must be characterized as the best assessment of the educational challenges which the Spanish-speaking child poses to the American school. In this sense, it is both a guide and a blueprint for effective reform.

A POSTSCRIPT

Basically, the Puerto Rican child is not a newcomer to the American school. In many ways he presents himself to a school and a society whose very nature is heterogeneous and variegated and to which the non-English speaking child is no stranger. In this sense, the acquisition of English for the Puerto Rican child (if necessary and inevitable) is not a great problem; certainly, it is a soluble problem to which the American school brings a rich and successful experience and *The Puerto Rican Study* affirms how successful and resourceful American schools can and have been. What is more important to the Puerto Rican child (and to American society) is the process of acculturation. How does the Puerto Rican

[22] *Ibid.,* p. 5.
[23] *Ibid.,* p. 7.

child retain his identity, his language, his culture? In substance this remains the *crucial* problem, and in this crucial context, the role of the school in American society needs to be carefully assessed. If the Puerto Rican child is sinned against today, the tragedy lies in the continued assault against his identity, his language, and his cultural wellsprings. In this sense, his experience is not fundamentally different from that of millions of other children to whom the American school was a mixed blessing. This is in no way a deprecation of the egalitarianism of the American "common school," but rather a reaffirmation of the loss of the great opportunity that a free society afforded its schools to nurture and treasure the rich and varied traditions of its charges. The "melting pot" theory is at best an illusion measured against the realities of American society, and a true discernment of its strengths.[24]

In another light, the Puerto Rican child is the creature of his social context: its opportunities or lack of opportunities. If his needs are to be met, they can only be effectively met insofar as the needs of this context are met. A school which is not community-oriented is a poor school. If this is so for the middle-class suburban school, it is even more so for the urban school which is the heir of the myriad complexities of a rapidly deteriorating central city. More important than the Puerto Rican child's lack of English is the lack of that economic security and well-being that relates him to a viable family structure. If the Puerto Rican child's major disenchantment does not result from the segregated schools into which his poverty has placed him,[25] still one would have to deplore the school's inability to cope with the alienation that segregation spawns, and the bitter destitution that poverty brings to its children. Perhaps, the "great society" really emerges from a strengthening of the school by its joining hands with all the creative agencies of the community.

[24]See Milton M. Gordon, *Assimilation in American Life: The Role of Race, Religion and National Origins* (New York: Oxford University Press, 1964); and review, F. Cordasco, *Journal of Human Relations,* XIII (Winter 1965), 142–143.

[25]See Joseph Monserrat, "School Integration: A Puerto Rican View" Conference on Integration in New York City Public Schools. Teachers College, Columbia University, May 1, 1963.

The Losers

Richard J. Margolis

This report examines the predicament of Puerto Rican children in our public schools: what they are learning and what they are not learning, what the schools are doing and what the schools are not doing. The report lists no specific conclusions—although several implied ones are there for the taking—and makes no explicit recommendations. Its purpose is to put the problem in sharper focus and on wider display, not to promote any single set of solutions.

Our public schools of late have provided such a large and comfortable target for the slings and arrows of reformers that one hesitates to pierce them with yet another. I have tried to be more thought-provoking, and if my judgments at times strike some as unduly harsh it is because the lives of so many schoolchildren strike me as unduly sad.

The title of this report—"The Losers"—refers to us all. The children are losing all hopes of learning or succeeding; the schools are losing all hopes of teaching; and the nation is losing another opportunity, perhaps its last, to put flesh on the American dream.

Much has already been written on this subject. In his preliminary bibliography Professor Francesco Cordasco[1] lists some 450 articles and studies devoted to "Puerto Rican Children in American Schools." More recently the *IRCD Bulletin* has published a helpful "Selected Bibliography" on the same subject.[2] Many of the studies are worth reading, but none surveys the current scene, particularly

From Richard J. Margolis, *The Losers: A Report on Puerto Ricans and the Public Schools,* New York: Aspira, 1968, 17 pp. Reprinted by permission.

[1]Frank M. Cordasco and Leonard Covello, "Studies of Puerto Rican Children in American Schools: A Preliminary Bibliography," in F. Cordasco and E. Bucchioni, *Puerto Rican Children in Mainland Schools* (New Jersey: Scarecrow Press, 1968), pp. 435–460.

[2]January, 1968. The *Bulletin* is a publication of the ERIC Information Retrieval Center on the Disadvantaged, Yeshiva University, New York.

the scene beyond New York City. My assignment from Aspira[3] was to fill the gap.

The result is by no means definitive, but it does offer at least an outline of the major challenges today confronting the public schools and the Puerto Rican community. In gathering material I visited sixteen schools in seven cities: Bridgeport, Connecticut, Chicago, Philadelphia, Newark, Hoboken, Paterson and New York. Wherever I went and whomever I talked to—teachers, administrators, children and parents—I was warmly received and meticulously enlightened. One hopes the report, the [subsequent] conference and the long-range results will justify the trouble they went to.

THE CHILDREN

Our children are not being taught to read or do their arithmetic.
—*a Puerto Rican parent in Chicago*

No one can say precisely how many Puerto Rican children are enrolled in public schools in the United States, but anyone who has examined their predicament knows they tend to learn less, lose heart more and drop out sooner than their classmates. It is true that their classmates, mostly poor and often black, fare none too well either. The Puerto Rican child and the Negro child share many humiliations, not the least of which is a system of even-handed injustice dispensed by big-city school administrations throughout the North. But the Puerto Rican child carries additional burdens all his own, his status as a stranger in our midst being perhaps the heaviest, and these have been sufficient to keep him at the very bottom of the educational pyramid.

The observer can but dimly discern the everyday frustrations which many Puerto Rican schoolchildren have come to take for granted: their imperfect grasp of English, which often seals both their lips and their minds; their confusion about who they are (what race? what culture?), a confusion compounded by the common ravages of white prejudice;[4] their sense of being lost, of traveling through a foreign country with a heedless guide and an undecipherable map. The list of frustrations is long. They may not reveal the whole truth, but they do illuminate many of the consequences.

They Learn Less

The many Puerto Rican parents who complain that their children "are not being taught to read or do their arithmetic" are usually right. No new study is required

[3]*Editors' note:* an organization of the Puerto Rican community.
[4]An exchange, during a routine shakedown on the streets of Philadelphia, between a white policeman and a Puerto Rican teenager may shed light on this subject. "Are you a spic or a nigger?" the policeman asked.
"I'm a Puerto Rican, cop."
The policeman hit him. "Don't you know you're not supposed to call me a cop?"
"Excuse me, officer, don't you know you're not supposed to call me a spic?"
The teenager told this story, on tape, to a white interviewer. It may or may not be accurate in every detail, but the message is clear.

to confirm their anxieties; findings in the Coleman Report on *Equality of Educational Opportunity*[5] are sufficiently eloquent. They indicate that Puerto Rican children in the United States lag behind both urban whites[6] and urban Negroes in verbal ability, reading comprehension and mathematics.

Test scores of sixth grade students, for example, place the average Puerto Rican child about three years behind the average white child in all three categories of achievement, and about one year behind the average Negro child. In the later grades, the gap between Negroes and Puerto Ricans narrows, but the gap between whites and the two minority groups becomes wider. Relatively speaking, the longer a Puerto Rican child attends public school, the less he learns.[7]

They Lose Heart

The less he learns, the more he despairs. One of Coleman's tests, designed to assess the student's sense of control over his life, contained this statment: "Every time I try to get ahead, something stops me." Almost a third of the Puerto Rican children agreed with the statement, compared to about a fifth of the Negroes and only one-eighth of the whites.

Answers to another test statement—"Good luck is more important than hard work for success"—were just as revealing. Nineteen percent of the Puerto Rican children agreed; nine percent of the Negroes; four percent of the whites.

"Shallow men believe in luck," wrote Emerson. So do deeply hurt children. If many Puerto Rican children feel they lack control over their environment—and

[5]by James S. Coleman & Associates, U.S. Government Printing Office, Washington, D.C., 20402, Catalogue #FS 5.238:38001, 1966. $4.25. For a pertinent summary, see Robert A. Dentler's "Equality of Educational Opportunity" in *Urban Review*, December 1966. All subsequent references to the Coleman Report will be based on Dentler's summary unless otherwise noted.

[6]It requires no uncommon eyesight to see that some Puerto Ricans are dark, many are white and others are inbetween. But the tortured nomenclature of ethnic studies has decreed that "Puerto Rican" be neither "white" nor "Negro"—in effect, that it be its own color. The ambiguous terms do nothing to clarify matters, but since I am making use of some of the studies, I have sorrowfully adopted some of their categories. (The U.S. Census Bureau defines a Puerto Rican as anyone who was born on the island or who has at least one parent who was born on the island.)

[7]Dentler summarizes the overall results of the three tests as follows:

TEST	GROUP	6TH GRADE	9TH GRADE	12TH GRADE
Verbal Ability	White	6	9	12
	Puerto Rican	3.3	6.1	8.4
	Negro	4.4	6.6	8.7
Reading Comprehension	White	6	9	12
	Puerto Rican	2.9	5.7	8.3
	Negro	4.2	6.4	9.1
Mathematics	White	6	9	12
	Puerto Rican	3.2	5.6	7.2
	Negro	4	6.2	6.8

therefore over their own destinies—the reasons are not hard to find. Here are some very routine examples of helplessness, chosen from many I came across while visiting schools and families:

- A six-year-old was roundly scolded by his teacher for wetting his pants. All morning he had been trying to tell her—in Spanish!—that he had to go to the bathroom.
- Jose Gonzales, a kindergartener, has given up trying to tell his teacher his name is not Joe. It makes her angry.
- An honor student asked her counsellor for a chance to look at college catalogues. "Is that Italian or Spanish?" asked the counsellor, looking at the name on the girl's card. "Spanish? Now this is just my opinion, but I think you'd be happier as a secretary."[8]
- A vocational student hoping to become an electrician did the same wiring job for four consecutive years, over and over and over again.
- A "phys ed" instructor noticed that one of the girls was wearing a new gym suit. "Oh," he said loudly, "did the welfare check come?"
- A junior high school student was accused by his teacher of lying because he averted his eyes when speaking to her, a sign of respect on the island.
- A little girl couldn't wait to get her first report card. But when she got it there was nothing written on it except two big letters: "LD". Language Difficulty.
- A teenager told his principal he would have to drop out if he wasn't given protection from assaulting gangs whose turf lay between home and school. The principal referred him to a psychiatrist.[9]

But I am running ahead of my story.

They Drop Out

Things being what they are, it is not surprising to hear from some teachers and administrators that Puerto Rican schoolchildren have nowhere to go but up. Yet there is little support even for that faintly comforting notion. It would be more accurate to say that Puerto Rican children have nowhere to go but *out*—out of the schools and into a world for which they are unprepared. This they are doing in large numbers. The public schools are like a giant sieve, sifting out all but the strongest, the smartest or the luckiest.

Many school administrators insist they have no serious dropout problem among Puerto Rican students. Some attribute the low high school enrollment totals to the newness of the Puerto Rican community. "Their kids haven't reached high school age yet." High school principals also like to say that Puerto Rican students who leave school are not really dropouts—they are simply "transfers" to another school. "We have a mobility problem, not a dropout problem."[10]

There is probably something to be said for both these explanations, but not much. Experience in cities where the Puerto Rican community has had time to

[8]In yet another of Coleman's tests, high school seniors were asked: "Have you ever read a college catalog?" A "Yes" response was given by 45 percent of the Puerto Ricans, 59 percent of the Negroes and 73 percent of the whites.
[9]After enduring more beatings, he did drop out—a healthy response to a most unhealthy situation.
[10]"How blind must he be that he can't see through a sieve?"—*Cervantes*

produce its share of teenagers makes it clear that the dropout syndrome cannot be explained away. For example, in 1966 in New York City public schools, Puerto Ricans comprised more than one-fifth of the total enrollment but less than one-eighth of the academic high school enrollment. On the other hand, non-Puerto Rican whites accounted for about half the total enrollment and about two-thirds of the academic high school enrollment.[11]

Plainly, a lot of Puerto Rican elementary students are disappearing before they reach high school. The picture is similar in Newark, where there are more than five thousand Puerto Ricans in public schools. They account for eight percent of all elementary students but only four percent of all high school students. The comparable figures for non-Puerto Rican whites is 18 percent for elementary school and 36 percent for high school.

As for the claim that dropouts are really transfers to other schools, one must ask: What schools? Surely none of those I visited. Somewhere in America there may be a Shangrila high school into which Puerto Rican teenagers drop. If so, it is overcrowded.

The widespread policy of putting back teenage Puerto Ricans to lower grades (because of their language difficulties) is one reason they drop out. The teenager is likely to feel both foolish and bored among children three and four years his junior. Rather than be left back he may prefer to be left out altogether.

We get an inkling of these difficulties by looking at Hoboken's dropout figures for 1967. Of the 149 students who dropped out, 131 "left to seek employment." *Almost half the dropouts left before the tenth grade.* We have no way of knowing how many of these were Puerto Rican—they comprise more than a third of the overall school population—but it seems likely that only a Puerto Rican would be old enough to drop out of the eighth grade in order to look for a job.[12]

Not all school systems deny that dropouts exist—New York and Hoboken, if not exactly outspoken on the subject, at least don't look the other way—but

---

[11]The figures suggest an accumulated total of more than 20,000 Puerto Rican dropouts who would otherwise have been attending academic high schools in 1966. Nevertheless, the figures show a slight improvement:

% Puerto Ricans in New York City's
Academic High Schools and in All Schools

	All Schools	Academic High School
1957	14%	5%
1966	21%	12%

(All enrollment figures in this report have been supplied by the local school administrations.)

[12]The 1967 dropout totals by grades are as follows:

12th	13
11th	35
10th	32
9th	25
8th	20
7th	13
below 7th	11
total	149

many prefer obfuscation to clarity, apparently on the theory that what they don't know can't hurt them.[13]

The picture becomes still murkier when we try to discover how many Puerto Rican high school students go on to college. No school system I visited has bothered to count, but in some high schools they answer not by the numbers but by the names. So few Puerto Ricans are going on to college that a principal can usually count them on one hand.[14]

All of which suggests that today's ghetto school, in its commerce with Puerto Rican children, is failing to do the job which the nation has traditionally assigned to it: that of assimilating newcomers into the American mainstream. The long-range implications of this failure are depressing in the extreme. The Puerto Rican population is swelling, and it is rapidly moving out of New York City into other metropolitan areas throughout the North. In 1960 the Puerto Rican population on the mainland was about 856,000 eighty percent of whom lived in New York City.[15] Today the population is approximately 1.5 million. New York City's share may be as low as 62 percent.[16]

One immediate consequence of the Puerto Rican diaspora is the strain it is putting on urban school systems already bent double under a combined burden of "deprived" children, deprived budgets and, in some cases, deprived imaginations. There are close to 400,000 Puerto Rican children enrolled in public schools. How are the schools responding to this latest challenge?

THE SCHOOLS

Del dicho al hecho
hay un gran trecho

(Between the saying and the
doing there is a great distance)

The schools *are* responding—but feebly, haphazardly and slowly, oh so slowly. Most school systems with growing Puerto Rican enrollments point with pride to the progress they are making; and if the number of new programs is an indicator of progress, then a measure of pride is justified. ("Come see our demonstration" is the sort of invitation a visitor usually gets.) But while the schools may be making progress, the children, for the most part, are not. This is because most of the

---

[13]"The most vicious attribute of urban school systems, until recently," observes Peter Schrag, "has not been their consistent failure with the disadvantaged, but their refusal to produce honest data on that failure. In case after case, they pretended . . . despite statistical evidence to the contrary, that it was individual children, not schools, that failed."

[14]Those holding high school degrees are often ill-prepared to compete in the job market. In Newark a group of volunteer lady tutors found that many Puerto Rican girl graduates who had majored in secretarial studies were incapable of filling out a job application form.

[15]U.S. Census, 1960.

[16]Dr. Francesco Cordasco puts the New York City Puerto Rican population at 69 percent *School & Society*, Feb. 18, 1967.

programs either miss the target entirely or else focus on such a tiny part of it that one must weigh their triumphs in milligrams. "Our attempts at solutions," observed. Juan Cruz, a human relations specialist for Chicago schools, "are like trying to cover the sky with one hand." He could have added that what one actually covers on such occasions are one's eyes.[17]

The programs are a mixed bag. There are after-school tutorials and before-school breakfasts; teaching English as a second language and teaching English as a first language; bilingual approaches and non-lingual approaches; teacher visits to Puerto Rican homes and teacher "visitations" to Puerto Rico; efforts to make parents feel welcome and efforts to make parents feel guilty; seminars to convince teachers that Puerto Rican children have "special cultural needs" and seminars to convince teachers that Puerto Rican children are "just like everybody else." Every program boasts its own point-of-view; and every point-of-view seems to boast its own program.

The upshot, more often than not, is a considerable amount of random activity that creates an illusion of progress. Sorting out this tangled skein, we find three salient threads: one leads to teachers; one leads to children; and one leads to parents.

Changing Teachers

Every Puerto Rican parent has more than one angry story to tell about teachers who urge children to "go back to Puerto Rico," teachers who are not above using "spic," and teachers who mimic a child's accent in front of his classmates. But the problems, and the prejudices, are usually a good deal more subtle than these "atrocity" stories imply, and the solutions a good deal less obvious.

"You can't imagine how bigoted that man was only a couple of years ago," my Puerto Rican guide said of a school principal I had just interviewed. "Now he can't do enough for us. Attitudes do change." They do indeed, and some of the schools' efforts have been so directed.

The target of these efforts, the teacher, is likely to be white, middle class and eager to teach. Doubtless she would have less trouble with students who were white, middle class and, according to her lights, eager to learn. Not that she has it in for anybody—if she is prejudiced in fact, she is "against prejudice" in theory—only that she "can't be expected to work miracles" on children who are "disadvantaged." The message, of course, is that the children are unteachable; and, as Kenneth Clark and others have pointed out, the message is self-fulfilling (similar to voting against a candidate because "he can't win").

Because she subscribes to the great American abstraction that "prejudice is bad," she abhors the more barbarous symptoms of bigotry and allows herself the luxury of feeling tolerant. The tolerance often turns to condescension. "Look

---

[17]In their anxiety to make known how overwhelming is the "Puerto Rican problem," educators sometimes grope for similes: "It's like trying a car in a sand dune." "It's like trying to bail out a sinking ship with a teaspoon."

at those glowing Spanish faces," a teacher in Chicago said to her visitor. "I think all Spanish children are beautiful, don't you?"

Denying her prejudices, the teacher also denies genuine differences among her students. In each city I asked teachers if their Puerto Rican pupils differed from the others in any way besides language. The denials were vehement.

There is, of course, something to be said for the egalitarian belief that all people are basically similar; but teachers who deny authentic cultural differences among their pupils are practicing a subtle form of tyranny. They are saying, "All people should pretend to be like everyone else when they are not." That is how the majority culture imposes its standards upon a minority— a cruel sort of assimilation forced onto children in the name of equality. "They drink *coffee* for breakfast," a teacher whispered to me. "I'm trying to break them of that." José must become Joe.

Many school systems have recognized this problem and have made efforts to solve it. The two methods most in vogue are teacher tours of Puerto Rico (Hoboken's "Operation Assimilation thru Cultural Understanding" is one such) and teacher seminars (for example, Philadelphia's series of conferences aimed at "Building Bridges of Understanding"). Both these ideas have their merits, but one is less impressed by their potential than by their limits. The trips to the island, usually taken during winter, cannot escape a slightly touristic tinge no matter how serious the sponsor's intent. A look at some typical itineraries, complete with visits to El Yunque and St. Thomas, is not reassuring.

The seminars would be more valuable if more teachers attended them. Most administrations are compelled to pay, in either cash or credit-hours, in order to bring the teachers out. The Philadelphia experience is typical. Teachers are being paid $5.50 per hour to attend occasional half-day seminars on Saturdays, and attendance is far from good. Many of those who do show up offer no opinions and ask no questions.

The Philadelphia seminars were conceived by imaginative leaders in an effort to speak directly and frankly to the classroom teacher, and to encourage her to speak just as frankly about her problems with Puerto Rican children. Doubtless they have helped some teachers, but in general I am inclined to agree with Carmen Dinos' dictum, uttered at one of the seminars: "We don't want to change attitudes, we want to change behavior."

Perhaps closer to the mark are those programs which teach a smattering of Spanish to classroom teachers. Most cities offer such courses, and those who have taken advantage of them—again, the number is small[18]—usually find the going easier with their Puerto Rican pupils. A teacher who can greet her class in Spanish can start the day right. The children feel good about it (more at home?). In one class a teacher hurled a Spanish insult—"sinverguenza" (without shame) —at an obstreperous child. The boy thanked her, saying it had been a long time since he's been insulted in Spanish.

---

[18]In Newark, for example, fewer than one percent of the teachers—20 out of 3,500— have signed up for in-service courses in Spanish.

Obviously, the sense of estrangement that often baffles both the teacher and her students would be relieved by the presence of a Puerto Rican teacher. The sooner we get Puerto Rican teachers into our schools, the sooner we will make headway. The current picture is discouraging. Many school systems have no Puerto Rican teachers; some have a few. New York may have more than 100, no one seems to know for certain.[19] Over-strict language requirements in New York and elsewhere have discouraged many applicants.

Few Puerto Rican teachers move up to administrative positions, and those who do usually get there by virtue of their specialty: being a Puerto Rican. New York has five Puerto Rican supervisors, all of them connected in some way with the bilingual program. I did not find a single Puerto Rican high school counsellor in all the cities I visited. The high school counsellors I did find—some white, some black—were without exception uninformed, unsympathetic and unintelligent in their dealings with Puerto Rican children. A Puerto Rican student at Temple University in Philadelphia says he and his Puerto Rican college-mates were all advised by their counsellors not to try for college. They were told to get jobs in a factory.[20] The story is not atypical.

Teaching Children

On the floor of an elementary classroom in the Bronx is painted a large, colorful map of Puerto Rico. The teacher says, "Now everyone stand on the place where he came from," and there is a noisy scurrying of feet in the direction of Ponce, San Juan, Arecibo and Caguas.

The self-evident proposition that a child should know where he comes from, and be able to stand on it, dawned on most school systems only recently and is just beginning to make headway. A few social studies teachers are mentioning Puerto Rican history; a few school systems are planning a curriculum unit about the Caribbean islands; a few publishers are putting out pertinent materials. The position of Puerto Ricans today, in their efforts to establish themselves and their history as legitimate curriculum topics, is similar to that of the Negroes ten years ago.

On the other hand, schools have been quick to recognize that many Puerto Rican children have a "language problem," and they have come up with the traditional response: they have instituted all kinds of tutorials, orientation courses[21] and other short courses designed to submerge Spanish in a torrent of English. The idea behind all these special classes is that a child can hardly be expected to learn anything in school until he has first learned the school's language. In other words, the medium is the message.

[19]Whatever the precise figure, it is miniscule in contrast to the number of Puerto Rican pupils. The school staffs in District #7 in the Bronx, for example, are two percent Puerto Rican; the enrollment is 65 percent Puerto Rican.

[20]This sort of callous put-down may in part be due to the training counsellors get. A check of three standard college textbooks on student counselling did not yield a single reference to Puerto Ricans, Negroes or any other minority group.

[21]Sometimes, alas, called "citizenship classes."

Reasonable as this notion appears to be, the results have been most disappointing. More often than not the child is returned to the regular classroom knowing only a smattering of English—enough to get by sometimes but nowhere near enough to deal intelligently with the regular curriculum. His Spanish is inhibited and his English is sketchy. As more than one teacher has remarked, "He becomes illiterate in two languages."

He also becomes confused and anxious. In their eagerness to erase Spanish from the child's mind and substitute English, the schools are placing Puerto Rican children in an extremely ambiguous role. They are saying, "Forget where you came from, remember only where you are and where you are going." That is hardly the kind of message that inspires happy adjustments.

Now a growing number of educators are saying it may be easier and more profitable in the long run to change the school's language instead of the child's. That is an oversimplification, but the basic assumption behind bilingualism is that children learn more when taught in their native language. The other assumption is that children can gradually learn a second language—in this case, English—if it is introduced in the context of other subject matter. A few months ago the Congress of the United States in effect bought both these assumptions when it appropriated about $50 million, over a three-year period, to help local school systems set up bilingual programs, with Spanish taught as a native language and English as a mandatory second language.

The bilingual approach seems to make sense, but since nearly all new approaches in education shine with a glossy credibility, we have a right to ask for supporting evidence. Some new studies and my own observations provide some:[22]

- Dr. Nancy Modiano of New York University, studying children in a remote region of southern Mexico, found they read better when first taught to read in their original Indian languages and later exposed to Spanish. "The evidence of this study," she said, ". . . points to the efficiency of approaching reading in the national language through the mother tongue."
- In a three-year study of Spanish-speaking junior high school students in New York City, it was found that those who were taught science in Spanish performed better than those who were taught science in English. The first group also scored higher on city-wide reading tests and displayed "a more positive attitude toward self and background culture . . ." The investigators surmised that "A student who can see the language of his home applied to the high prestige area of science study may hold himself and . . . his background in higher esteem."
- At Conners Elementary School in Hoboken, which is 48 percent Puerto Rican, Spanish-speaking first-graders in a demonstration program are being taught to read and write in Spanish. Their classroom teacher is Cuban and their teacher aide is Puerto Rican. According to the school principal, who concedes he had at first been dubious of the program's value, the children are learning at a faster rate than comparable children in English-speaking classrooms. Moreover, he says, they are learning English, because it is being taught in the context of other subject matter. For example, the label on the color chart says both "roja" and "red," and the child is free to learn either. He usually learns both.
- Several years ago at P.S. 192 in Manhattan it was decided that "the best way to help

[22]For what it is worth, some of the older studies do not.

our Puerto Rican children to achieve their potential was to place them in a special class with a specially trained teacher who can speak and teach in Spanish." This was done, and it is one of the reasons—though hardly the only one—why the average reading level among children there is very close to the national average. "If you put a Spanish-speaking kid into an English-speaking class," warns principal Seymour Gang, "he just vegetates." Two-thirds of P.S. 192's enrollment is Spanish-speaking.

The bilingual approach does not provide all the answers to all the problems, but it is the most promising technique available today. Its strengths are psychological as well as linguistic. A Spanish-speaking teacher in the classroom does more than speak Spanish. She creates a familiar climate which lessens the child's anxieties and frees him to concentrate on his main job, which is learning.

There has been some objection to bilingualism from Puerto Rican parents who fear it may be another excuse for segregating their children, and who complain that their children are supposed to learn English, not Spanish. But there is no reason to segregate, certainly not in the early grades. *All* the children can become bilingual: Spanish-speaking children can learn English and English-speaking children can learn Spanish. With a little luck and earnest attention, the schools can make growing up inside a melting pot the positive experience historians have always claimed it to be. But it is up to the schools to sell this idea to the parents.

Reaching Parents

Schools have a tendency to include parents in their list of frustrations and to exclude them in their deliberations. They often preach parent participation but what they are usually after is mere cooperation. PTAs in schools that are predominantly Puerto Rican are frequently more dead than alive. An elementary school principal in Chicago, after expounding on the importance of parent involvement, conceded that the school had no PTA because, "To be frank, it's a hell of a nuisance." Principals complain that Puerto Rican parents take no interest in the school and seldom come to meetings—"even when we print the notices in Spanish."

The complaints have some basis in fact, but PTAs are so commonly an instrument of the principal's policies, rather than of the community's will, that one can understand why parents stay home. A principal in Bridgeport told me, "My PTA is slow this year. I can't seem to find officers for it." She will doubtless continue to have trouble as long as she considers it *her* PTA.

As for the Puerto Rican parents, they often begin by thinking the schools can do no wrong and end by suspecting the schools can do no right. They thus proceed, over the disillusioning years, from a respectful reluctance to interfere to an angry readiness to protest. The path leads somewhat circuitously from authoritarianism to militant democracy, but the vital intervening stages—cooperation and participation—are usually missing.

In Bridgeport I took an informal survey among Puerto Rican families in a public housing project. No adult I interviewed among eleven families knew the name of any principals at the schools their children were attending, and only one person could name a teacher. No one was aware of having ever been invited to a parents' meeting at the school or of having been given any instructions on how they could best assist the school.

I mention this because the schools to which these parents send their children all say they believe in parent participation; their eagerness to involve parents in school programs is a point of pride. Obviously, the road from the school to the public housing project needs to be paved with more than good intentions.

Some school administrators have given up trying to make Puerto Rican parents feel welcome, on the grounds the parents don't stay in the neighborhood long enough. And it is true that "mobility" is a problem. Being poor, many Puerto Rican families are constantly on the move in search of better jobs and more livable housing. And being Puerto Rican, they are often on their way back to the island. In one typical week in Chicago, 105 children, direct from Puerto Rico, entered public schools, and 27 left to return to the island.

Schools sometimes distribute leaflets in Spanish dwelling on the virtues of "remaining in your school district," but the tone is usually sermonistic and the effects are apparently negligible. More effective, it seems, is P.S. 192's "method." P.S. 192 is one of the few ghetto schools where children are learning to read and do their arithmetic. Not only do families remain in the district, some families who don't live in the district say they do, so they can send their children to P.S. 192. One gets the impression that Puerto Ricans, like anyone else, will stay put if there is something worth staying for.

Education ranks high on the list. "On the island," observed a Puerto Rican educator in New York, "the teacher is second in prestige only to the priest." On the mainland the tradition carries over. Parents treat teachers with great respect (their notes sometimes begin, "Dear Esteemed Teacher . . .") and often look upon them as "second parents." The teacher is expected to handle all problems that might arise during school hours.

But the American teacher would rather be a professional than a surrogate parent, and when a child presents more than the usual difficulties her first inclination is to call in the parents. This is common procedure in American schools, but it strikes many Puerto Rican parents as an uncommon nuisance. "Yesterday I had to leave my job and go to the school," a mother in Chicago complained recently, "because they said my boy was acting up. If he was acting up, why didn't they stop him? Isn't that what they're there for?"

The point can be argued either way. The problem is that it is seldom argued at all—there is seldom a decent dialogue taking place between parents and schools.

Many schools are trying hard to break through the sounding-off barrier. In Chicago some of the schools now have community representatives—appointed, unfortunately, by the principals—who act as bridges between the neighborhoods and the schools. Parents with complaints often seek redress through their community representatives. Schools in Philadelphia and elsewhere have enlisted the interest of many mothers by organizing projects which bring Puerto Rican culture into the schools—for example, a school display of Puerto Rican art.

New York's community relations program has 148 bilingual specialists, and among their responsibilities is that of "mediating" between the schools and the communities. The specialists can be helpful in interpreting the community's wishes to the school system; but as with so many other ethnic "representatives" employed by school systems, there is always a question of whom he is supposed to represent, the communities or the schools. His ambiguous position is similar to John Alden's, for while serving as spokesman for one party he is constantly being pressed to court the other.

THE FUTURE

School systems are not in business to foment disorder or to invite organized attacks upon themselves. In the final analysis, it would be most surprising if the Puerto Rican community were to find its voice through programs sponsored by, or spokesmen hired by, local boards of education. As one such spokesman remarked recently, "The communities ask me why I'm not doing more for them. I ask them why they're not *forcing* me to do more. I have to be able to go to my superiors and say, 'This is what the people want, and they won't get off your back until they get it.' "

Borne on a fresh current of concern, some Puerto Rican parents are sensing the wisdom of such counsel. They are beginning to organize, to ask questions, to show up at board of education meetings. They are forming new Aspira clubs in Chicago, Waterbury, Rochester and throughout New Jersey. In Philadelphia Puerto Rican college students have launched a program aimed at encouraging Puerto Rican high school students to go on to college, and at discouraging high school counsellors from saying it can't be done. About a year ago a group of irate Philadelphia Puerto Rican mothers and college students succeeded, by picketing, in forcing the resignation of a nay-saying counsellor.

The new spirit, tentative as it is, has already started to pay off. It is hardly a coincidence that school systems like Chicago and Philadelphia have recently included Puerto Rican children in their ethnic enrollment totals. Their awakened interest in Puerto Rican pupils is a direct result of pressure from an awakening Puerto Rican community; and if counting the children remains a far cry from teaching them, it is nevertheless the first essential step on the path to reform.

It seems clear that one key to improvements inside the school is informed action from outside the school. Free-floating pressure has its uses, but if the Puerto Rican community is to make a major impact on the schools it will have to be through specific recommendations supported by specific data. No school system, no matter how humane its intentions, is likely to come up with a comprehensive program aimed at saving Puerto Rican children unless the community suggests one and presses for its enactment. The New York experience has already made this clear. In response to strong but non-specific pressures from the Puerto Rican community, the New York school system has "jumped on its horse and ridden off in all directions." It appears to be true that education is too important to be left entirely to the educators.

At the same time it would be a pointless cruelty for educators to delay reforms until parents demand them. Professional pride and self-respect should be sufficient goals. We have said much during the sixties about children who don't learn; what are we to say now about educators who don't educate and school systems that don't notice? If the protests of parents are growing more frequent and more strident, it is not because the parents *know* more than the educators, it is because they *care* more. School systems that don't care, no matter their expertise, are hardly school systems at all, because very little "schooling"—teaching and learning—occurs within them. Things will get no better until the schools face up to their obligations and decide that what needs improvement is not their image but their performance. Meanwhile, they forfeit their responsibilities, just as the children forfeit their hopes and the nation forfeits its future. We are all the losers.

THE PUERTO RICAN DIASPORA: A SPECULATION ON ITS SIZE

Making population estimates is a tricky enterprise—we have no complete figures later than the 1960 Census—but it is possible to hazard some interesting guesses. The 1960 Census lists the Puerto Rican population in the United States as 855,-724. Four out of every five mainland Puerto Ricans lived in New York City and one out of every four Puerto Ricans in New York City was attending public school.

Assuming this one-in-four ratio holds in other school systems, we can make deductions about Puerto Rican dispersion and population increases by examining current public school enrollment figures around the country. Here is a sample:

CITY	P.R. PUBLIC SCHOOL ENROLL- MENT, 1967-68*	P.R. POP., 1960**	EXT. P.R. POP. 1968	INCREASE
New York	244,458	612,574	977,832	60%
Chicago	25,500	32,371	102,000	208%
Philadelphia	6,299	14,424	25,196	73%
Hoboken	2,500	5,313	10,000	88%
Newark	5,300	9,698	21,200	118%

*figures were supplied by local school administrations
**U.S. Census, 1960

Other cities throughout the North—including Rochester, Bridgeport, Cleveland and Jersey City—have reported similarly astonishing increases in their

Puerto Rican school enrollments.[23] In view of all this, it would seem far from illogical to assume that the Puerto Rican population outside New York City has more than doubled during the sixties, probably increasing by 2.5 times. If so, we can estimate the current mainland population at 1,586,397, 62 percent of whom live in New York City. The breakdown between New York City and elsewhere would be as follows:

New York City	977,832 (62%)
Elsewhere	608,565 (38%)
Total	1,586,397 (100%)

Given these figures, we estimate the number of Puerto Rican children attending mainland public schools at 396,599 (one out of every four).

These speculative estimates of increases pose difficult problems of explanation. Official figures for net in-migration for the period in question account, at best, for an added 100,000 people. Granted that Puerto Rican families tend to be unusually large, it seems almost incredible that population growth of this dimension could have come about through natural increase. Perhaps part of the answer is to be found in the U.S. Census Bureau's recent report that, in ghetto areas, difficulties in collecting statistics may have resulted in substantial gross underestimates of "non-white" population.

[23]These current school enrollment figures alone range from 45% to 90% of the 1960 Census total Puerto Rican population figures.

3 THE MEXICAN-AMERICAN HERITAGE

Although somewhere in the neighborhood of five and one-half million Mexican-Americans reside in the United States, they have long considered themselves America's "forgotten" minority. At this writing, however, more and more Mexican-American communities are beginning to view themselves as vital, functioning societal units with the ability and power to shape their own destiny and to pass on their heritage to their children. Although the art, music, and dance of the Mexican-American is appreciated in some circles, his historical and recent accomplishments, often superficially recorded in English, remain generally distorted or ignored. A realistic view of Mexican-American history and cultural contributions is especially rare among present-day teachers.

Although present-day Mexican-Americans play a vital role in the industrial, agricultural, artistic, intellectual, and political life of the Southwest, the significance of this group cannot be measured solely in these terms. It is certain that the Southwest as we know it would not exist without the Mexican-Spanish contributions. That which sets New Mexico off from Oklahoma and California from Oregon is in large measure the result of the activities of the ancestors of our fellow citizens of Mexican descent. The so-called American west has been and is being enriched immeasurably by their presence north of the present-day international boundary with Mexico.

As with other groups of culturally unique children, Anglo teachers have too often viewed the Mexican-American child as "culturally deprived"—in need of having this "cultural vacuum" filled with Anglo-American ways. Only recently have educators begun to realize, largely through prodding from the Mexican-American community, that Mexican-American youth bring to school varied experiences and skills which can be utilized as mediums for both the development of the Mexican-American pupil and the enrichment of school experiences for

Anglo children. As a matter of fact, the Mexican-American child has a head start over the Anglo-American because of his familiarity with two languages. (A few Mexican-Americans speak or understand an Indian language as well). Often, it is true, the knowledge of both Spanish and English is imperfect, but nonetheless that most precious of linguistic skills, the ability to switch back and forth from one language to another and the "feel" for being comfortable in two or more languages, is present as either a fully or partially developed resource.

Teachers are just beginning to recognize the value of bilingualism. It can enrich their total classroom program at the same time that it makes full use of the Mexican-American child's language advantage. A truly bilingual learning experience will not only allow the Mexican child to develop both of his languages but will make it possible for monolingual English-speaking children to actually *master* a second tongue.

Mexican-American children also bring to school a variety of bi-cultural experiences which are also full of potential for enriching almost every facet of the school's program. Their knowledge of folk arts, cooking, music, literature, games, sports, and dances can be utilized as vehicles for cross-cultural education. The quality and richness of any school's program can be greatly enhanced if teachers are concerned enough to guarantee that all of their pupils are exposed to a multi-cultural experience which truly reflects the meaning and diversity of the Southwestern legacy.

Before reading the six articles in this section, it is important to clarify the terminology in this area, which is confusing not only to the general public but to many teachers. A *Chicano* is a person of Mexican descent. A *Latino*, on the other hand, is one whose origins stem from Central and South American countries—the "Latin" countries of the Southern Hemisphere. Neither of these terms is to be confused with *Gachupinos,* a term used by both Chicanos and Latinos for persons who are from Spain. All have one thing in common: they are Spanish speaking people. But there are many ramifications involved. "Chicanismo," for example, is a philosophy that tries to embrace all Spanish speaking people with a somewhat common identity of language and, sometimes, religion. In New York and San Francisco, Latinos far outnumber Mexicans, who in turn are sensitive to overbroad use of terminology.

Points to remember: Chicanos generally don't mind being called Latinos, although most Latinos dislike being referred to as Chicanos. Today, there is almost no Latino movement, although there is a strong Chicano movement.

Just as we began our Afro-American section with a cultural quotient test, so we begin this section with one developed by Felex Elizalde for the Mexican-American culture. Directly following is a broad overview by Brussell of the Mexican-American's historic culture: particularly his family and community structure; his view of Anglos and vice-versa; his perception of time, achievement, and illness; some insights into his language skills and how they affect education; and some concluding remarks about his acculturation in America.

From this overview, we move to Carter's analysis of Mexican-Americans in school, which reviews the segregation-separation issue, using excellent data from the Southwest. Carter offers special insights into the subtleties of teacher-student interactions and the assumptions each makes about the other. Viewed openly, the author urges, these assumptions can become a basis for developing mutual understanding.

The use of nationally standardized tests with widely divergent groups of students has long been an issue in American education. When one considers the use of these Anglo middle class measures applied to culturally unique children the practice seems questionable indeed. Brussell's article, "Cognitive and Intellectual Functioning of Spanish-speaking children," makes an excellent case for not using standardized tests on Spanish-speaking children. Part of the unfairness of standardized tests stems from the language problem, which Manuel's article subsequently explores.

This Part concludes with Carter's second article, aptly titled, "Where to from Here?" In a closely-reasoned plea for proceeding rationally—studying those programs of instruction that are effective, analyzing why they work, and seeing how they can be duplicated and improved—Carter cautions against the all-too-human tendency to do otherwise, i.e., to grasp solutions that suit us because they fit our preconceptions. This is a sobering note on which to end this or any other Part of our book. For what has motivated so much of Americans' ineptitude in teaching multi-cultural populations if not a tendency to assume that anything *different* ought to be re-educated into something not different?

What Is Your Chicano Culture Quotient?

Felix Elizalde

Taking this test should give you some idea of how much or little you know about Mexican-American history and culture.

1. Black is to Negro as Chicano is to:
   a. Chinese
   b. Latin
   c. Mexican-American
   d. Chicago

2. On May 5 Chicanos celebrate:
   a. Mexico's Independence from Spain
   b. The battle of Puebla
   c. Chinese New Year
   d. The death of the Frito Bandito

3. The first "wetbacks" crossed into America:
   a. At Ciudad Juarez in 1846
   b. At Tiajuana in 1922
   c. At Plymouth Rock in 1620
   d. At Nuevo Laredo in 1882

4. To Chicanos *carnal* means:
   a. Butcher
   b. Used car salesman
   c. Sports car
   d. Brother

Reprinted by permission of the author.

5. *La Jura* refers to:
   a. An Anglo jury
   b. A popular people's song of the '30s
   c. The cops
   d. A freedom fighter in Mexican history

6. The 12th of December is:
   a. Cesar Chavez' birthday
   b. The day of the Virgen de Guadalupe
   c. Mickey Mouse's birthday
   d. The anniversary of the "pachuco" riots in Los Angeles

7. A *frajo* is a:
   a. Short handled hoe
   b. Cigarette
   c. Car
   d. Drink made with tequila

8. Of the four-year college enrollment in California about ＿＿ percent consist of Chicanos:
   a. 02
   b. 15
   c. 30
   d. 05

9. The Chicano equivalent of "ghetto" is:
   a. el gato
   b. el barrio
   c. el rancho grande
   d. the east village

The correct answers to the questions are: 1.(c) 2.(b) 3.(c) 4.(d) 5.(c) 6.(b) 7.(b) 8.(a) 9.(b). Based upon the number of correct responses you can determine how close you are to Chicano culture: (8 to 9) you are probably a Chicano; (7 to 8) high-scoring for a non-Chicano; (4 to 6) contact your nearest Chicano Studies Department; (0 to 5) you are culturally deprived.

Social Characteristics and Problems of the Spanish-Speaking Atomistic Society

Charles B. Brussell

Rubel (25) has suggested that the social system of the Spanish-speaking peoples may be described as an "atomistic society." He defines this type of society as one in which the social system is characterized by an absence of close coopera- tion between nuclear families, in which such qualities as contention and wariness figure into the perceptions which nuclear families hold of each other, and in which such social behavior and emotional qualities are consonant with normative expectations (p. 207). The social system of such a society may be described in terms of three organizing factors. First, the nuclear family is considered the basic unit in terms of which one should pursue economic and social ends. Second, the relationships beyond the range of the family are between one individual and another, rather than between an individual and a group of others. Third, the relationships between one person and others are characterized by a high degree of personalism. This viewpoint emphasizes the high importance placed upon the family; and, since the young child's first significant relationships are formed almost entirely within the realm of his family, the literature concerning the family structure of Spanish-speaking peoples may be the most worthwhile place to begin a review of the social characteristics of Spanish-speaking peoples.

INTRA-FAMILIAL RELATIONS AND ROLES

Madsen (16) states that the most important role of the individual is his familial role and that the family is the most valued institution in Mexican American

From Charles B. Brussell, *Disadvantaged Mexican American Children and Early Educational Experience*. Developed and published by the Southwest Educational Laboratory, Austin, Texas, 1968, pp. 25–44 and 93–95.

society. It is the main focus of social identification in all classes of Mexican American society, and to violate one's obligations to one's parents or siblings is a very serious offense. Authority within the family is invested in the father (Heller, 12). He is conceived as the ruler of his household, and the maker of all important family decisions (Edmondson, 10). Ideally, the Mexican American male is entitled to unquestioning obedience from his wife and his children. He is conceived as having "superior" strength and intelligence, which places him above criticism (Madsen, 16). Thus, within the home, interpersonal relations, especially with the father figure, are characterized by decorum and respect. The ideal male role is highlighted by the concept of *machismo*, or manliness. The male needs to make of his life a validation of the assumption that the male is stronger, more reliable, and more intelligent than the female. The concept of "manliness" outweighs all other aspects of prestige next to devotion to the family.

The father is the disciplinarian of the family. He sees that the children stay in line, and he punishes transgressions (Madsen, 16). The father, however, does not lack tenderness for his children, for both fathers and mothers express deep affection and concern for their children (Clark, 8). At times the father will play with his children, but such displays of sentiment are usually confined to very young children, and take place mainly within the home. The father's role as an authoritarian figure becomes clearly crystallized as children experience the onset of puberty and "reason," at which times the father withdraws from the role of playmate to that of dignified master of the home. The father may appear to the child as an aloof enforcer of proper behavior, and tenderness is always deeply colored with respect (Edmondson, 10).

Generally, the world outside the home is a man's world. In relation to the female, the Mexican male is in a position of prestige, freedom, and super-ordination. He does not usually entertain friends in his own home. Demonstrating his sexual prowess by seeking extramarital affairs is viewed as an affirmation of his "manliness" and is a means of winning him prestige among his male acquaintances (Madsen, 16; Edmondson, 10). The only requirement is that such affairs be handled discreetly enough that he does not get caught. Maintaining a mistress in a second household known as a *casa chica* is the most convincing way of proving his *machismo* and his financial ability (Madsen, 16).

On the other hand, the woman must ideally be a model of purity. The wife owes her husband absolute sexual fidelity, and is to be tolerant of his pastimes and extramarital affairs (Madsen, 16). Her place is within the home, and her role is subordinate and restricted. A woman's primary obligation as a wife is to please her husband, and make a home for him. As a mother, her responsibility is the well-being of her children. Her marriage is her career.

The mother has the principal charge of caring for children under six and the education of the girls in the family. While the father is away at work, the mother is the unquestioned authority in the family, but obedience is less likely to be enforced by physical punishment than by invoking paternal authority or feelings of love and duty (Edmondson, 10). While either parent may administer physical punishment to smaller children, mothers avoid administering such punishment to older children, if possible (Clark, 8). Either parent may punish an older daughter, but an older son is usually disciplined only by the father. Mother-child relationships tend to emphasize tenderness more than respect and authority (Edmondson, 10).

In return for adult domination which is not to be questioned, children receive much love and attention (Tuck, 33). They experience the warmth and security of many close personal relationships. But children are generally considered to be past infancy when a younger sibling is born, and they are then often left to their own devices to amuse themselves. At this time they are often placed in the care of older siblings (Clark, 8). Small children may have a few toys, but they seem to show less interest in them than Anglo children of the same age. Older infants may be given a toy to play with, but just as frequently they may be given a comb, compact, cigarette case, or key ring. Boys and girls may play together until they are seven or eight years old, but they are then encouraged to play separately. Although parents do not seem to be "bothered" by having children around, they talk very little to their small children except to answer questions and to give instructions.

A son owes his parents respect and obedience, but as the boy moves into puberty his ties to the home become looser, and he may spend most of his free time with male friends away from the home. He may tend to form loosely knit play associations with other Mexican American youth, known as *palomillas* (Madsen, 16). The membership in these groups may be constantly changing, and they lack formal organization and leadership. Common interests and the pleasure of social interaction hold these groups together. It is within these groups that Mexican American boys may learn the terminology and techniques of sex through informal discussion, since sex instruction within the home is rare. Rubel (25) believes that these groups may contribute to the atomistic nature of Mexican American society since these groups are little more than aggregations organizing a minimum number of individuals into loose relationships, in which a sense of obligation between associates is absent, and in which participants are unable to exercise leadership over one another.

In contrast, at the onset of puberty a daughter is pulled more tightly into the home in order to protect her purity (Madsen, 16). She is not allowed to be alone with a boy. Girls of all ages are expected to help their mothers with the housework and the care of younger children. These obligations increase as the daughter's age increases, and she is pulled more tightly into the sphere of the home. Ideal relationships between the daughter and her mother become especially close, due in part, according to Madsen (16), to the female tendency to group together in a male-dominated world. The relationship between a daughter and her mother is of great importance and lasts throughout a woman's married life (Rubel, 25).

Older siblings are encouraged to develop a sense of responsibility toward the younger children in the family. They have authority over younger ones, and an older child may be punished if a younger brother or sister in his care misbehaves (Clark, 8; Madsen, 16). Due to this hierarchy of authority, an older sibling, particularly an older brother, may be feared by his juniors. A brother is expected to feel strong obligations of mutual support toward his siblings of both sexes (Edmondson, 10). A boy must protect his younger brothers, and should seek advice from his older brother. Brothers must stand together in time of trouble, and together protect their sisters. The older brother must always be obeyed and respected (Madsen, 16). Edmondson (10) feels that the relatively strict hierarchical structure of sibling relations within the Spanish-speaking family may serve to control manifestations of sibling rivalry.

The authority and responsibility of an older brother, and to a lesser degree of an older sister, are quasi-parental (Edmondson, 10). In fact, if the father is deceased or absent, the oldest son is expected to become his surrogate (Rubel, 25). Thus, ideal relationships between an older and a younger brother call for patterns of respect similar to those expected between father and son. As brothers grow, their relationship becomes formalized, and they do not play or engage in frivolity together. Madsen (16) believes these respect patterns governing the relationships between brothers account for an older boy's association with a different set of friends outside the home, and the formation of palomillas.

A sister occupies a place of special tenderness—she often cares for younger children when she herself may be no more than five or six years old (Edmondson, 10). A brother has a special obligation to protect his sister and her honor, and this obligation is usually taken quite seriously. Sisters are very close, a tie usually maintained even after marriage. The bond between sisters is so strong that sisters' husbands are separated from all other relatives-in-law by a special kinship bond known as the concuno relationship (Rubel, 25).

The Mexican American family, persisting in traditional forms, continues to be an extended type of family evidencing strong ties which spead through a number of generations in a large web of kinship (Heller, 12). Obligations of mutual assistance and reciprocal favors prevail among kinsmen, and a diffuse solidarity may be extended to include almost any degree of blood or affinal relationships (Edmondson, 10). Outside the nuclear family, relationships to individuals in kinship roles may be viewed as variations on themes set up in the roles of father, mother, son, daughter, brother, and sister. Clark (8) states that children live and mature in a wide circle of kinsmen.

Particularly important to an individual is his mother's sisters (Rubel, 25). An individual's relations with aunts and uncles tend to be somewhat formal and very respectful (Clark, 8). Children are close to their grandparents, but they are less formal with them than their own parents. Grandparents may demonstrate affection for their grandchildren more frequently than parents do. The respect accorded to grandparents, however, is not extended to siblings of the grandparents (Rubel, 25). First cousins (primos hermanos) are considered to be somewhat like one's sisters or brothers—they are conceptually separated from all other degrees of cousinship in one's own generation. This distinction is lost, however, in the generation of the cousin's children.

The institution of *compadrazgo* or coparenthood extends the range of kinship beyond genetic links. Madsen (16) defines *compadres* or coparents as ". . . sponsors who assume carefully defined roles in relation to the other participants in a religious ceremony establishing ritual kinship." Clark (8) notes that *compadrazgo* is a significant social institution throughout the Catholic folk cultures of southern Europe and Latin America. The most important *compadrazgo* relationship is initiated at the time of baptism, and the baptismal godparents of one's children become the most important *compadres* (Rubel, 25; Madsen, 16).

Ritual kinsmen are expected to respect each other and to help each other materially (Rubel, 25). Godparents *(padrinos)* are expected to furnish ceremonial clothing for the sponsored child *(ahijado)* and to defray the costs of the rite. They have a social obligation to the child to see that he does not lack the necessities of life, and they are expected to provide goods and money for the child's rearing if the parents are unable to make such provisions. They may give advice and administer discipline to the child whenever they think it necessary, with or without the invitation of the parents (Clark, 8). *Compadres* may be selected from among one's own relatives, such as an uncle, aunt, or cousin. It is, however, considered bad taste to choose a *compadre* having higher social or economic status than oneself (Madsen, 16).

Relationships between *compadres* are warm and friendly, but formal and dignified. One never gossips about his *compadres* nor does he tease or joke with them (Clark, 8; Madsen, 16). *Compadres* are considered as close as blood relatives, visit each other frequently, and have the right to call on each other for help and advice. Clark (8) believes that the *compadrazgo* relationship serves the three functions of formalizing and extending the kinship group, enhancing kinship ties in order to minimize antagonism and conflict, since those so related are expected to treat each other with respect and deference.

For the child, his ritual kinsmen, in addition to his nuclear family, constitute an extension of his security system (Rubel, 25). The relationship between a godparent and his godchild may be much like that which exists between uncle and nephew. *Padrinos* will also be chosen for a child at the time of his confirmation and the godparents of the child's confirmation are the next most important *compadres* of the child's parents. *Compadrazgo* relationships also may be established at weddings or other occasions, but these are not regarded as significant.

INTER-FAMILIAL AND EXTRA-FAMILIAL RELATIONSHIPS

Rubel (25) concludes that one of the most important aspects of the ethos of the Spanish-speaking individuals in the community he studied is a fear of invidious sanctions of neighbors directed against one's family. The author comments that the people in the community he studied ". . . peer out from the security of their homes at a society which they view with distrust, suspicion, and apprehension . . . Only within his or her own home is the Mexican American in an environment in which he or she trustingly participates with others (p. 99)." Madsen (16) finds a similar phenomenon in his study. He notes that a proper relationship between experienced persons in the Spanish-speaking society must preserve the dignity and individuality of each. To question the beliefs of another is to belittle the other, and a person may also feel belittled when another questions his accomplishments or compares them with greater successes achieved by others. Madsen states that the most common way of belittling others is to attain greater material or social success than one's friends. To do so is dangerous, for it may arouse envy.

The Spanish-speaking regard envy to be so powerful an emotion that it is difficult or impossible to suppress, and envy may be aroused by success in almost any kind of activity (Madsen, 16). It may result in hostility toward the person or family envied. Thus, leveling mechanisms such as gossip and ridicule may be employed by the person envying against the objects of his envy. Since a successful individual expects to be envied, he may imagine that there is more hostility directed against him than actually exists. He may come to fear not only the envy of others, but their suspected greed, dishonesty, and treachery. Madsen states that the child, early in life, learns that he lives in a threatening and hostile universe, where the motives of others are open to suspicion. This fixation, believes Madsen, enhances the value of social distance, and teaches the Mexican American to keep his defenses high. It alerts the individual to see to it that the proper relationship of dignity and individuality is maintained between individuals. Polite social distance will preclude direct involvement in the affairs of others, and the educated person will display polish and courtesy (urbanidad) in his social relationships.

The machismo of the male demands that he represent his family with honor, especially since it may be open to the envy and the belittlement of others. In the world outside his family, he must tolerate no overt offense to his family's honor, which he will fight to defend (Madsen, 16). A man's first loyalty is to his family, and Rubel (25, p. 55) comments: "The strength to which a person is bound to his family so overshadows all other bonds in importance that it contributes to the atomistic nature of the neighborhood. Socially, each house stands alone, separated from all others."

SOME PROBLEMS OF SPANISH-SPEAKING PEOPLE

Social or cultural problems are relative things. A particular set of circumstances experienced by a group of people is likely to raise problems only when set against a different, but not necessarily better, set of circumstances. When reviewing the literature that discusses the problems that Spanish-speaking people encounter, the only reasonable conclusion is that these problems largely arise because circumstances, values, and standards that guide the lives of individuals in the smaller, or minority, group are viewed in the light of the circumstances, values, and standards that guide the lives of individuals in the larger, or dominant group. Heller (12, p. 34) says: "The kind of socialization that Mexican children receive at home is not conducive to the development of the capacities needed for advancement in a dynamic industrialized society." Thus, a large number of the problems Spanish-speaking people face may exist in relation to function within the "dynamic industrialized society" of the dominant group. Heffernan (11) sees eight specific problems: (1) low level of aspiration on the part of Mexican American students which results in failure to achieve commensurate with ability; (2) lack of parental aspiration and support of educational effort; (3) economic insecurity; (4) lack of feeling of belonging to the peer group; (5) inadequate facility in the use of the English language; (6) failure to recognize education as an avenue of social and vocational mobility; (7) differences in cultural values between the Mexican American culture and the culture of the dominant group; (8) low community standards. Manuel (17) sees four specific problem areas: (1) division of communities into contrasting groups, each with a lack of understanding of the other; (2) differences in culture which tend to perpetuate the isolation of one group from the other; (3) difficulty in language, the Spanish-speaking child typically having to learn English as a second language; (4) privations of low family income. The following is a review of some of the major problems identified by the literature.

Spatial Separateness

Mexican Americans tend to live together in one section of town. In smaller towns, this section is often set apart from other residential sections by a railroad track, a highway, or a river (Kibbe, 10, Section 1). Such a section is known as a *colonia* or *barrio*. Burma (3) defines the *colonia* as "a satellite community, separated from the parent community by psychic and social isolation, with definite if unverbalized barriers between it and the parent community." Generally, the Spanish-speaking group will occupy buildings in the older and more neglected parts of town, where rent and ownership costs are low and community services and facilities are at a minimum (Saunders, 29). While the dwelling types for urban Spanish-speaking people vary considerably, probably the most common is the small two or three room house, which typically may be in a state of partial disrepair. Streets in the *colonia* are less likely to be paved than in the Anglo sections, and alleys may serve the functions of streets (Burma, 3).

A number of reasons have been offered to explain Mexican American residential segregation. Kibbe (10, Section 1) believes that this spatial separation is due in part to the fact that the Spanish-speaking are a gregarious people and like to live close to one another. Another factor is the language handicap which makes it more convenient to live near those who speak the same tongue.

However, Kibbe says that often the Spanish-speaking are not permitted to rent or own property anywhere except in the "Mexican Colony" regardless of their social, educational, or economic status. On the other hand, Clark (8) believes that the spatial separation is less the result of Anglo discriminatory policies than of poverty. Saunders (29) believes that in some areas spatial separateness is the result of Anglo descriminatory policies, but that in other areas it results from the concentration of a Spanish-speaking peoples in certain types of occupations. Saunders believes, however, that this separation is mostly a manifestation of the free choice of the Spanish-speaking—"free" within the limits of the fact that poor people in general have only a limited range of choice with respect to where they will live. In addition, he feels that the Spanish-speaking may find it more comfortable to live among people like themselves than among those who are, in many respects, culturally alien and possibly hostile.

In their study of residential segregation in 35 Southwestern cities, Moore and Mittelbach (19, Section 1) established an "index of residential dissimilarity" in which 0 meant that there was no segregation of a subpopulation from another (members of both populations were randomly distributed throughout the city), and a score of 100 meant that two populations were totally segregated (all members of each population were concentrated in separate areas). For the 35 cities studied, the mean index of dissimilarity for the Anglo-white versus the Spanish-surname population was 54.5, ranging from a low of 30 in Sacramento, California, to a high of 76 in Odessa, Texas. While Galveston, Texas, was found to have an index of 33.3; Austin, Texas, had an index of 63.3; San Antonio, an index of 63.6; and Houston, an index of 65.2. Intra-minority segregation of foreign-born and native-born persons of Spanish-surname ranged from a low of 9 in Austin, Texas, to a high of 50 in Colorado Springs, Colorado. The index was 14 for Houston and 17 for San Antonio.

The cultural factor most highly correlated with the segregation of Mexican Americans from Anglos was found to be large households, indicating traditional familial characteristics. This factor was found to be correlated with income. In other words, when large proportions of Mexican Americans begin to have small families, they tend to become residentially integrated with Anglos. The direct economic factor (ratio of each minority to total median income) was found to be the least important in the segregation of Mexican Americans from Anglos. Demographically, the size of the city was found to be very significant in the segregation of Mexican Americans from Anglos—the larger the city the greater the segregation.

Stereotypes and Discrimination

There is evidence that both Anglos and Mexican Americans hold notions of the other group which amount to stereotypes. In his study in South Texas, Madsen (16) finds that the two ethnic groups are keenly aware of the differences that divide them, and that feelings of resentment issue from a mutual lack of understanding. Each group believes that the other does not behave properly, and each feels superior in some respects. Clark (8), writing in California, finds that Anglos, on the whole, know little about Mexican American customs and values, speak no Spanish, and share many popular misconceptions concerning the Mexican American people. Burma (3) states that few Anglos know anything of what goes on inside the *barrio,* and that this ignorance makes possible the belief of inaccuracies, misinformation, and contradiction.

In his study of a community in South Texas, Simmons (31) noted the existence of a dual morality in the notions Anglos held of Mexican Americans. On the one hand, they expressed the belief that Mexican Americans should be accorded full acceptance and equal status in the larger society, because this is the "American creed." On the other hand, regardless of whether or not they expressed this ideal, they also expressed the contrasting assumption that Mexican Americans are inferior. They admitted the existence of a "high type" of Mexican American characterized by occupational achievement, wealth, and command of Anglo American ways. Simmons encountered notions of the Mexican Americans which characterized that group as indolent, improvident, irresponsible, childlike, undependable, unclean, and immoral. Both Madsen (16) and Burma (3) have noted the existence of similar stereotypes.

Simmons (31) found that adherence to a number of these stereotyped beliefs justified practices of exclusion and subordination in the community he studied. He feels, however, that Anglos often base their conclusions on what they observe in common labor situations. Many Mexican Americans work as field hands or work in packing sheds, and this is never clean work. He further feels that the strong sense of loyalty and obligation that Mexican Americans evidence in their interpersonal and familial relationships indicates that a charge of immorality is baseless. He attributes the hostility that some Anglos allege on the part of Mexican Americans to a projection of the Anglo American's own feelings.

Saunders (29) also feels that few if any of these stereotyped generalizations are valid, and that none of them are demonstrably due to any genetic inheritance, as many of these beliefs imply. Like Simmons, Saunders feels that many of these stereotyped beliefs are based on observable behavior traits that are characteristic of some members of the Spanish-speaking group in some situations. Observers may tend to evaluate behavior and approve or disapprove it on the basis of their ideas of what kind of behavior is appropriate in the observed situation. They fail to take into account that the persons being observed may have dissimilar ideas about proper behavior due to their participation in another culture. From their standpoint, they may be acting in accordance with these ideas. But, continues Saunders, stereotypes have the merit, for those who accept them, of providing easily understandable reasons for the status and the behavior of Spanish-speaking persons. They may provide an easy rationalization for maintaining the status quo, and make unnecessary any attempts to improve conditions for the Spanish-speaking group.

But Clark (8) states that Anglos have no monopoly on misconcept and group prejudice. Simmons (31) finds that Mexican Americans also have stereotyped images of Anglos. Mexican Americans conceive of Anglos as belonging to one or two types. One type is unprejudiced, friendly, warm, and just, but these are the minority. Most Anglos are braggarts, conceited, inconstant, insincere, mercenary, exploitative, and unkind. Madsen (16) notes similar stereotypes. Simmons (31) finds that these stereotypes reflect Anglo American stereotype patterns of exclusion as experienced by the Mexican Americans.

However, Simmons notes that since Anglos are dominant in society and monopolize its accomplishments and rewards, their belief that Mexican Americans are inferior may cause the Mexican Americans also to believe that they are inferior. There is a tendency to concede the superiority of Anglo ways, and, while Mexican Americans may impute hostility to Anglos, they do not impute inferiority to the dominant group. Perhaps this may be seen in part as a reflection of the self-fulfilling prophecy.

Through a wide-spread acceptance of a false assumption that one is inherently inferior, the person caught up in the self-fulfilling prophecy comes to desire to fulfill what is expected of him, and the false concept passes from generation to generation (Naegele, 20). This is apparently the view of Parsons (Brickman, 2) who investigated school bias toward Mexican Americans. Sociometric tests indicated to him that Mexican children come to share the view of themselves held up to them by the Anglos. Being constantly told that they are inferior, they begin to behave in that pattern.

However, Carter (6) finds that the results of his study do not support the belief that Mexican American youngsters see themselves more negatively than Anglo students see themselves. Junior high school and senior high school students were asked to rate themselves on a five-point scale containing four sets of differentials: intelligence, goodness, happiness, and power. Twenty-one percent of the Mexican American students rated themselves on the good side of the good-bad differential, while only 13 percent of the Anglo students did so. The Mexican Americans also saw themselves as more wise than the Anglos, although they saw themselves as a little less happy than the Anglos. Carter notes, however, that the area he studied is rural and agricultural, and that different results may be obtained in an urban and industrial setting.

Burma (3) indicates five reasons why there may be discrimination against Mexican Americans. First, he feels that color may enter somewhat into the discrimination, for Mexican Americans are often darker than the Anglo population, and darkness of skin was considered a sign of inferiority long before Mexicans came upon the scene in great numbers. Second, they are predominantly poor, and thus suffer from a class discrimination. Third, their culture is different, and may be looked upon as inferior. Fourth, they are mainly Catholics in a predominantly Protestant country. Fifth, they speak a different language, and when it is used in public, Anglos may feel excluded, or fear insult.

Concerning Burma's first point, it is interesting to note that Moore and

Mittelbach (19, Section 1) found in their study that whenever there are relatively few Mexican Americans in comparison with Negroes, segregation of either group from Anglos may be accentuated. Mexican Americans may suffer from being classified with the Negro minority, since discrimination against Negroes may become diffused to encompass Mexican Americans. Each minority seems to affect the other's chances for movement in the system. Burma's second point, that of class, is especially interesting. Heller (12) claims that analysis of the 1960 Census data shows the Mexican Americans to be an unusually homogeneous ethnic group, generally ranking very low as measured by standard socio-economic characteristics. Rubel (25) says that the ethnographic evidence reveals the lack of clearly defined social classes among the Mexican Americans. In his study, Burma (3) finds two classes, lower and middle, but notes that to the Mexican Americans there are three classes, since the Mexican Americans may divide the group that the Anglos consider the "middle" class into a "middle" and an "upper" class.

Clark (8) accepts four social classes: the high society, the middle class, the lower class, and the braceros. Madsen (16) distinguishes five class levels among the Mexican Americans: the lower-lower class, the upper-lower class, the lower-middle class, and the upper-middle class, and the upper class. However, no matter how finely a particular investigator may wish to discriminate between various class levels within the Mexican American population, the 1960 Census data reveal that a large number of Mexican Americans are poor, and would fit, at least in socio-economic terms, into a lower class. Saunders (3) believes that much of the so-called problem behavior that Anglos note among Mexican Americans derives from the culture of a lower class rather than from an Hispano cultural heritage or the fact that these people are Spanish-speaking. Lower-class Anglos tend to behave in much the same way as do Mexican Americans when viewed through the notions of popular stereotypes. Saunders believes that attention should be focused on social class differences rather than on ethnic differences.

Cultural Differences and Differences in Value Orientations

The Spanish-speaking hold views of life which are characteristics of their culture and which are different in certain respects from the views held by Anglos. Luna (15) believes that Mexican Americans have not fully accepted Anglo values relating to time, change, success, efficiency, education, and modes of communication. Edmondson (10) holds that there are six general value orientations that stand out in the culture of the Spanish-speaking with some degree of clarity: traditionalism, familism, paternalism, personalism, dramatism, and fatalism. Familism and paternalism, both traditional values of the Mexican culture, extend throughout the culture and furnish organizational models for relationships outside the sphere of kinship. A man's position and prestige is largely dependent upon his basic qualification as head of a household, and the familistic orientation may help to explain the quasi-parental authority of older over younger siblings. Feminine roles are oriented to the primary familistic roles. The concept of friendship on the kinship model illustrates the familistic tendency, since extended use may be made of the terms *primo* or *compadre* when speaking to friends. Paternalism is seen in the superordination of the male sex, and in the relationship of older brothers to younger ones. Edmondson sees these values as being in contrast with Anglo values, for where the Spanish-speaking may emphasize traditionalism, the Anglo culture tends to emphasize progress and change; where the culture of the Spanish-speaking is paternalistic, that of the Anglos is egalitarian; where the culture of the Spanish-speaking values familism, that of the Anglo emphasizes individualism.

The Spanish-speaking do emphasize individuality, but in a manner different from the way in which Anglos emphasize it (Edmondson, 10). While Anglos emphasize individual initiative, it is a socialized initiative calling for self-expression within certain limits. The Spanish-speaking individual may transcend these limits, and, emphasizing the element of personalism, place loyalty on an individual basis. The Spanish-speaking individual is, first, himself and second, a social entity. Kluckhohn (14) found much the same thing in her study. She found that among the Spanish-speaking the individualistic principle (in which individual goals have primacy over the goals of specific collateral or lineal groups) ranked slightly higher than the lineal principle (in which group goals have primacy).

Rubel (25) sees this emphasis on personalism as affecting the political activity of Mexican Americans. He holds that the importance of personalism in elections is a converse of the absence of special-interest groups organized to exert pressure for group advantage. The Spanish-speaking are likely to vote for the candidate who seems most likely to respond favorably to instrumental activities characterized by personalism. Personal relationships tend to take the place of abstract applications of principles (Edmondson, 10). Again, where the Spanish-speaking culture is personalistic, the Anglo culture values a group orientation and abstract morality.

The attitude toward fatalism marks a distinction between the culture of the Spanish-speaking and the culture of the Anglo. Madsen (16) states that it is generally believed that the fortune of the individual is predestined, and that every occurrence in human existence comes to pass because it was fated to do so. Kluckhohn (14) found that the Spanish-speaking group she studied was oriented toward a Subjugated-to-Nature position (in which the inevitable is accepted) rather than a Mastery-over-Nature position (in which natural forces are to be overcome and put to use for the benefit of human beings). To the Anglo, the environment is something to be manipulated and changed to suit his needs; the Spanish-speaking person, on the other hand, is likely to meet difficulties by adjusting to them rather than by attempting to overcome them (Saunders, 29).

This fatalism, according to Edmondson (10), may manifest itself in a number of ways. In language, the Spanish-speaking typically use the impersonal passive reflexive form of verbs where the English-speaking would use the active voice with a definite agent. The Spanish-speaking will say "It broke itself" (se rompio) or "It lost itself" (se perdio) instead of "I broke it" or "I lost it." Through this usage the speaker appears as the helpless object to whom things happen, rather than the master of his fate with an active part in his own destiny. Fatalism may manifest itself in politics. The Spanish-speaking do not tend to view politics as an arena in which moral and ethical values take place for the building of a progressively better world. Corruption in politics may be viewed as inevitable, and political and administrative justice may be viewed as accessible only through friends and relatives. Fatalism does manifest itself in religion. Madsen (16) states that most Mexican Americans believe that fate is a mechanism of God's will.

The concept of fatalism is strongly tied with the Mexican American's concept of time. Since God, rather than man, is seen as controlling events, Mexican Americans lack the future orientation of the Anglo and his passion for planning ahead (Madsen, 16). Kluckholm (14) found that the Spanish-speaking prefer a present alternative (in which there is little concern with the past, and the future is regarded as vague and unpredictable) to a future alternative (in which the future is anticipated to be "bigger and better" and in which a high evaluation is placed on change). Saunders (29) points out that the Anglos are very much preoccupied with time. They consult watches and calendars frequently. The present is not important for itself, but for the opportunities it affords to engage in activities that can affect the future. Activities are not seen as ends in themselves, but rather as means to ends, the attainment of which lies somewhere in the future.

The Mexican American, on the other hand, feels that the present cannot be ignored (Saunders, 29). He does not look upon the future with vision, nor does he brood over the past. God plans the future, and many Mexican Americans would consider it presumptive for a man to plan for tomorrow (Madsen, 16). The Mexican American is dedicated to living the moment to its fullest extent in the roles he finds assigned to him by God.

These concepts of fatalism and of time are related to concepts concerning change, efficiency, and desirable types of activity. Saunders (29) contends that newness among the Anglos has come to be valued for its own sake. New things are attractive because they are thought to be better somehow than the old, and the notion of progress becomes associated with the fact of change. Saunders believes that there probably is nothing that the Anglo more completely accepts than the notion that change is good and progress inevitable. But to the Spanish-speaking, the future is uncertain, and, in any event, is not of his making. Uncertainty, and perhaps danger, comes with the new, the unfamiliar, the untried. Simmons (31) says that Mexican Americans will accept new ways, but only if the new ways appear more meaningful and rewarding than the old.

Allied to the Anglo notion of progress and change, is the Anglo concept of efficiency. Anglos like to keep busy—they are doers (Saunders, 29). As a group, they see industriousness as a virtue. Work is a value in itself, and if it has any meaning beyond itself, it is that it is a road to success. Idleness is considered to be very close to sinfulness, and every moment of time must be utilized, for "time is money." To the Spanish-speaking, however, work is simply the lot of man—a necessary burden (Heller, 12). The belief of the Spanish-speaking that a day's work is only a day's work, whether performed now or at a later time, is in direct conflict with the Anglo premise that time and money are interchangeable. The Spanish-speaking feel that the ceaseless push for advancement has fettered the Anglo's integrity and intellectual ability (Madsen, 16). The Spanish-speaking home stresses the notion that inactivity and leisure are in themselves worthwhile goals (Heller, 12).

Heller (12) notes that few Mexican American homes stress higher education or intellectual effort, and attributes this partly to the parents' belief that higher education is useless for their children, and may not result in achievement but rather may lead to frustration and humiliation. But Madsen (16) points out that the "educated" person in a Spanish-speaking home is one who has been well-trained as a social being. He displays polish and courtesy in his social relationships. Thus, informal education within the family is viewed as being more important than formal schooling. Whatever factor dominates in a given situation, achievement is not usually stressed in the Mexican American home, and Heller (12) sees this lack of emphasis upon "making good" in conventional terms as being consistent with the themes of fatalism and resignation that run through Mexican American culture.

These attitudes toward fate, time, and achievement on the part of the Mexican American are reflected in his choice of desirable activities. Kluckhohn (14) found that the Spanish-speaking in the group she studied favored a Being orientation rather than a Doing orientation in their choice of desirable activities. She defines the Being orientation as the preference for "the kind of activity which is a spontaneous expression of what is conceived to be 'given' in the human personality." She further states that this orientation might be phrased even as "a spontaneous expression in activity of impulses and desires. . . ." Heller (12) notes that the Mexican American home does not tend to cultivate in children the ability to defer gratification, and sees this as a reflection of the Mexican American's present-time orientation. In contrast, the Doing orientation, characteristic of the Anglo culture, demands activities in which accomplishments result that are measurable by standards conceived to be external to the acting individual.

Edmondson (10) also has named dramatism as an outstanding value orientation of the Spanish-speaking. Madsen (16) points to the concepts of proper relations between individuals within the culture of the Spanish-speaking, and indicates that Mexican American social relationships are highly formalized and that life itself is seen as dramatic and ceremonial. Edmondson (10) points to the Spanish-speaking peoples' love of fiestas, and especially to religious ritual as evidence of the sense of dramatism. But if it is dramatism that may add attraction to religious ritual, then perhaps this source of dramatism is more attractive to the Mexican American woman than the Mexican American man, for the women have a better record of church attendance. While daughters will continue to attend church regularly throughout their lives, boys go less and less regularly after the age of 13 (Madsen, 16). Madsen indicates that male attendance at church seems to increase with vertical social mobility.

He also believes that Protestantism holds appeal for those members of the Mexican American middle class who are seeking closer identification with Anglo ways of life. Burma (3), it may be recalled, believes that one reason discrimination may be leveled against Mexican Americans is that they are Catholic in a predominantly Protestant country. But in their study of social mobility among Mexican Americans, Penalosa and McDonagh (21) found that Catholics were more upwardly mobile than Protestants, giving no support to the belief that retaining Catholicism hinders upward mobility.

In addition to the differing value orientations mentioned, there is a body of literature that discusses differing medical concepts held by Mexican Americans. Such studies are offered by Saunders (29), Clark (8), Madsen (16), and Rubel (24, 25). Clark (8) believes that medical systems are affected by most major categories of culture, and Rubel (25) believes that by focusing attention on topics of illness and health one can discover a new vantage point from which to view the social system and the emotional qualities that are found within it.

The folk theories of medical disorders found among the Mexican Americans are based on a hot and cold theory of balanced relationships. This theory is derived from the Hippocratic theory of pathology, which postulated that a human body in the state of health contained balanced qualities of the four "humors" (phlegm, blood, black bile, and yellow bile), some of which were thought to be innately hot and others innately cold. If the hot and cold body essences became disproportionate, the body became ill (Clark 8). This belief is a legacy from colonial Mexico where the Spaniards introduced the system in the 16th Century. In the Mexican American folk concepts of disease, largely based upon this notion of hot and cold imbalance, diseases are generally classified in two major categories: first, there are the "natural" illnesses *(mal natural)* which come from violating the balance of the natural world controlled by God. These may be corrected by restoring the balance that was disrupted. Second, there are the "unnatural" diseases *(mal puesto)* which result from bewitchments sent by human adversaries. These may be cured by countermagic or by removing the immediate source of harm (Madsen, 16). Mild sicknesses may be treated at home by the mother or other female relatives having a knowledge of folk medicine. Severe illnesses may be referred to *curanderos,* or folk healers.

Certainly Mexican Americans accept many "scientific" Anglo medical beliefs, and Clark (8) points out that the number of scientific medical disorders familiar to the Spanish-speaking is constantly increasing as they have more and more contact with the English-speaking community and those in the Spanish-speaking community who are conversant with Anglo medical terminology. However, there appears to exist among the Spanish-speaking a number of diseases whose etiology and treatment differ markedly from Anglo concepts. A number of these diseases are of special interest because they may affect children.

Fallen fontanel, or *caida de la mollera*, probably is the most common ailment of infancy, and occurs in children under three years of age (Madsen, 16 and Rubel, 25). The concept of balance again is important here, for the fontanel and the palate are believed to be correlated so that the imbalance of one affects the other. Jarring the baby must be avoided since a fall or a jolt can dislodge the fontanel causing it to collapse. It is recognized by such symptoms as excessive crying, insomnia, digestive upsets, loss of appetite, and possibly fever. Treatment may consist of gently pushing upward on the palate while cradling the child or while holding the child upside down on the theory that gravity will help to push the fontanel back in place. Gently sucking the baby's fontanel may also be employed.

Mal ojo, or evil eye sickness, unintentionally may be inflicted by a person who possesses "strong vision." Such persons are conceived to have a strong power over weaker individuals, and the seat of this power is his visual apparatus. Covetous glances or excessive attention paid one person by another expose the individuals involved to the dangers of an unnatural bond in which the weaker is drained of his will to act and the power of the stronger enters his body (Madsen, 16; Rubel, 25). While anyone may be susceptible to *mal ojo,* women and children are especially likely to succumb due to their weaker nature. Symptoms may consist of severe headaches, fretfulness, high temperatures, and, in the case of children, inconsolable weeping (Rubel, 25). Because the power of the stronger individual is beyond his control, he is considered guiltless unless he refuses to break the bond. He may do this by simply passing a hand over the victim's forehead, or patting the victim about the temples. If the illness is allowed to progress, however, it is potentially fatal, the last stage of the illness being a violent coughing fit. A common treatment consists of rubbing the patient's body with an unbroken raw egg in order to draw out the evil force (Madsen, 16). The egg may then be broken and poured into a glass of water. The formations of the egg in the water can indicate whether the diagnosis was correct and the cure successful. The glass containing the egg mixture may be left under the patient's bed for a night in order to remove any remaining sickness.

Rubel (25) notes that in the illness of *mal ojo,* social relationships are conceptualized as being inherent dangers to the equilibrium of the individual. Madsen (16) believes that the evil eye is, to some extent, a reflection of envy. Unconscious hostility may also be expressed in attributing strong vision to another person, and desired avoidance may be rationalized on the grounds that the individual possesses the evil eye. Thus, concepts of social relationships seem to be reflected in this concept of disease.

Empacho, a form of indigestion, also may affect a child. A ball of undigested food is believed to form on the wall of the stomach, which blocks the normal digestive processes (Madsen, 16; Rubel, 25). It may be caused by a severe emotional experience, or by requiring the individual to eat against his will; that is, the individual is placed in a situation of conflict and stress. While it is potentially fatal due to dessication, it is easily treated. The back of the patient may be carefully stroked and kneaded along the spinal column and around the waist. A penetrant may also be administered in order to break up the ball that has formed.

Children also may suffer from *asustado*, or fright sickness, although it is more often associated with adulthood (Madsen, 16). In this disease, a part of the self, the *espiritu*, may leave the body. The precipitating experience may be one in which the victim cannot cope with circumstances, even though he wants to do so. It is often of a frightening nature (Rubel, 25). The symptoms may be exhaustion, restlessness, and loss of appetite (Madsen, 16). Effort is devoted to coaxing the soul of the patient back into his body during curing. This may be accompanied by a sweeping motion with some instrument such as a tree branch or a broom.

If a disease reaches a more serious stage or fails to respond to treatment by a female member of the family, the family may seek the help of a *curandero*, or folk healer, rather than a medical doctor. There are a number of reasons for this. Clark (8) believes that Mexican Americans may resent the authoritative stance of the Anglo physician, his objective approach, and his quick, impersonal, efficient examination. Rubel (25) believes that there is a communication gap between Mexican American patients and Anglo doctors, since Mexican American patients often do not understand the medical terminology used by Anglo doctors. He also believes that Mexican Americans resent the Anglo doctor's fee-for-service arrangements, believing that the doctor practices to enrich himself while the lay healer practices to help people.

Also, Anglo doctors are ignorant of entire sectors of the health concepts Mexican American patients may hold. Mexican Americans, notes Clark (8), expect a curer to reassure them, to show that he sympathizes with them and cares what happens to them. A folk healer may do these very things where an Anglo doctor may not, and Madsen (16) notes that several cases of mental illness that previously failed to respond to psychiatric treatment have been cured by *curanderos*. He feels that many *curanderos* are unrecognized by highly skilled social workers. However, Rubel (25) believes that to the Mexican American the individual who cures is less important than whether the healing has been successful: "The cure is the thing."

At least one study has been made of mental health problems among Mexican Americans in an urban community (Crawford, 9). Four samples were surveyed to determine the nature and incidence of mental health problems. One sample consisted of 24 selected children from a larger sample of 399 first grade children. The smaller sample was divided into a group described by teachers as "having no problems of school adjustment" and a group considered to represent varying types and degrees of school adjustment problems. The parents of the "no problem" group shared responsibility for their children more equally than did parents of the "problem" children who were father-dominated. Parents of "no problem" children used many different types of discipline, and employed little physical punishment. Parents of "problem" children showed less diversity in the kinds of action used to discipline, and used physical punishment more frequently. Families of the "no problem" children were not disturbed by influences exerted by relatives, while families of the "problem" children reported friction with the "wife's relatives." Mothers of the "no problem" children reported very few contacts of any sort with neighbors, while mothers of the "problem" children reported intensive contacts with neighbors, often of a conflicting nature. The "problem" children were in most instances "roamers" who played all over the neighborhood without supervision. Generally, the families of the "no problem" children had a more cohesive nature, maintained strong family ties, and were acceptably orientated toward relatives. Families with "problem" children were less integrated, experienced friction with relatives, and relied upon neighbors for many social contacts.

Clark (8) points out, though, that life to the Mexican American is full of countless pains and traumas. Suffering is the lot of the Spanish-speaking, and must be borne with courage and dignity. Not wishing to be thought "inferior," the Mexican American does not readily succumb to illness. The adult must be stoic. Children, however, are less frequently expected to ignore their physical symptoms, and the younger the child, the less stoic he is expected to be. But some of the adult emphasis on strength and stoicism may carry over into attitudes toward sick children, and children may often be sent to school with colds, ear infections, or other difficulties. They may be expected to carry on their normal activities until the disease becomes incapacitating.

The Language Difference and the School Experience

The fact that the Mexican American's primary language is usually Spanish may cause complex social problems for the Mexican American child when he enters school, and Madsen (16) sees the language problem faced by Mexican American children as serious.

The linguistic problems of Spanish-speaking individuals who also speak English are several. A number of writers seem to agree that the patterns of speech and thought inculcated by the use of the primary language, Spanish, interfere with the correct speaking of English. Chavez (7) mentions differences in sounds and in concepts between the two languages. For instance, the short *i* in *miss* may be pronounced by the Spanish-speaker as the *ee* in *meet,* since *i* carries the sound of *ee* in Spanish. Similarly, the *sh* of the English word *show* may be pronounced by the native Spanish-speaker as the *ch* in the English word *church*. In addition, a difference in concepts between the two languages may cause the listener to note a difference even when no accent is present. In Spanish, some words are plural, but their English counterparts are singular, such as the word nose. In speaking English, the Spanish-speaker may say, "I hit them against the door." Or, the native speaker of Spanish may utilize direct translations of Spanish phrases when speaking English, producing such phrases as *peach bones* for peach pits and *train houses* for train cars. Nor is it without significance, holds Saunders (29), that in English a clock runs, but in Spanish a clock *walks*. This may be seen as one example of the way in which differing value orientations are reflected in speech.

Beberfall (1) mentions hypercorrection, omission of the final consonant, and the use of the future tense as language problems. Hypercorrection occurs when the Spanish-speaking individual makes a linguistic correction that extends into other areas where it is not needed. Thus, correcting the *i* of *miss* and the *sh* of show, the individual may extend his correction to such words as *chief,* producing instead *chiff,* and *church,* producing instead *shursh.* Omitting a final consonant in Spanish seldom is likely to affect the meaning of a word, but it may cause difficulty in English. When speaking English, the Spanish-speaker may say, "I hope it *rain* today." Then, too, the present tense is often used in Spanish where English will call for the future tense. Thus, the Spanish-speaker, employing his native language habits, may say, "I *see* you tomorrow."

Perales (22) mentions three problem areas the Spanish-speaking individual may face when speaking his own language: limited Spanish vocabulary that requires borrowing from an equally limited English vocabulary to complete his expressions; the use of *pochismos,* English words given a Spanish pronunciation and meaning; and errors in pronunciation and enunciation. Regarding the first problem area, students may use such expressions as "yo le dije que I wouldn't do it" (I said to him that I wouldn't do it) and "El fue, but I stayed in la casa" (He went, but I stayed in the house). Holland (13) explains this linguistic borrowing in this manner: due to their environment, Mexican American children develop only a small basic vocabulary of Spanish words and concepts which are directly related to restrictive in-group experiences.

Their first year in school brings them into contact with words and concepts in English for which they have no comparable terms in Spanish. They then have no alternative but to introduce English into their conversations when they need to use a concept which they have learned exclusively in contact with the English-speaking environment. Their typical speech patterns often become a complex mixture of both languages. Holland believes, therefore, that these children cannot really be thought of as fully bilingual, but rather that they are substandard or partial speakers of two languages. Their particular type of bilingualism interferes with the more thorough learning of either language and the result is that they may have fewer complex language symbols at their command than their Anglo classmates. The NEA-Tuscon Survey group (19) also comments that even if the child speaks both English and Spanish, he may be only nominally bilingual, not truly so, having a low level of literacy in both languages. He watches television and listens to the radio. He is soon speaking a language which is neither Spanish nor English, but rather a mixture of the two.

Concerning the second problem area cited by Perales (22), the native speaker of Spanish in an English-speaking environment may give an English word a Spanish pronunciation and meaning when speaking his own native language. For instance, the Spanish-speaker may use the word *huachar* (from the English verb *to watch*) instead of the correct Spanish verb *mirar,* or *chuzar* (from the English verb *to choose*) instead of the correct Spanish word *escoger.* The Spanish-speaking student in an English environment also may be hampered by lack of correct pronunciation of his own native language. For instance, he may say "Nos juimos con eos" for "Nos fuimos con ellos."

The NEA-Tuscon Survey group (19) indicates that the Mexican American comes to school knowing some English, but has used it infrequently. The language of his first years of childhood has been Spanish, and his personality and experiences have been shaped by it. Yet the language of instruction is English, and, when the child enters school, he finds himself in a strange and threatening environment. This survey group comments:

. . . He (the Spanish-speaking child) suddenly finds himself not only with the pressing need to master an (to him) alien tongue, but also at the same time, to make immediate use of it in order to function as a pupil. His parents, to whom he has always looked for protection and aid, can be of no help at all to him in his perplexity. Moreover, as a result of cultural and economic differences between the English-speaking and the Spanish-speaking segments of his community, many of the objects, social relationships and cultural attitudes presented to him in lessons, though perfectly familiar to an Anglo youngster, lie without the Latin American's home experience. Accordingly, the problem of learning English is, for him, enormously increased by his unfamiliarity with what objects and situations the no less unfamiliar words and phrases stand for (pp. 8–9).

Sanchez (28) also comments on this problem:

Imagine the Spanish-speaking child's introduction to American Education! He comes to school, not only without a word of English but without the environmental experience upon which school life is based. He cannot speak to the teacher and is unable to understand what goes on about him in the classroom. He finally submits to rote learning, parroting words and processes in self-defense. To him, school life is artificial. He submits to it during class hours, only partially digesting the information which the teacher has tried to impart. Of course he learns English and the school subjects imperfectly! (pp. 31–32).

Heller (12) points out that until the late forties, Mexican American children were segregated formally in separate buildings or separate schools from the time of their first arrival. This was largely based on the rationalization that these children knew little or no English on entering school, and could not compete on an equal basis with Anglo American children. Therefore, it was best for both groups to be separated. In 1947, in California, the courts decided, in the *Mendez* case, that enforced segregation violated the Fourteenth Amendment of the United

States Constitution. A similar decision was rendered in Texas in 1948, in the *Delgado* case. These cases and their implications are reviewed by Sanchez (27), who points out among other things that Spanish-speaking children seem to learn English best and most quickly when they participate in mixed classes with English-speaking students. However, Heller feels that today the schools are still largely segregated on a *de facto* basis, since the schools attended by the Mexican Americans are in the poorest areas. The existence of *de facto* segregation also appears to be the view of the NEA-Tuscon Survey group (19).

The Spanish-speaking child also encounters psychological barriers related to linguistic barriers when first entering school, according to the NEA-Tuscon Survey group (19). Being suddenly immersed in English at six years of age in an environment lacking the plasticity and warmth of human relationships found in the home may create within the Spanish-speaking child psychological barriers that may not disappear for a lifetime. The teacher may sense these barriers and erect his own in an attempt to compensate for a sense of inadequacy in dealing with the child. The Spanish language may then become a refuge into which the child may retreat at every opportunity. The Survey group sees the Mexican American child as also encountering a different set of cultural patterns than those he has learned at home, an accelerated tempo of living, and possibly a teacher, who, although sincere, has little understanding of the culture, beliefs, and sensitivities of the Spanish-speaking. Heller (12) sees such lack of knowledge as making it more difficult for teachers to instruct Mexican American children, and to proceed in a way that would make it easier for the children to identify with the teacher.

The Mexican American may encounter at school the additional confusion of being forbidden to speak Spanish both in the classrooms and on the playground. Students may even be punished for lapsing into Spanish, according to the NEA-Tuscon Survey group (19). This group sees this prohibition against the speaking of Spanish as breeding withdrawal and damaging the Mexican American's self-image. Language is an intimate part of culture. Of language, Saunders (29) says:

. . . Language enables us to make sense out of reality. It provides for each of us a way of isolating, categorizing, and relating phenomena without which experience could only be a confused succession of sensations and impressions. Our perceptions, to the extent that they represent anything more than crude sensation, are organized around concepts, each of which is represented by one or more verbal symbols. What a person "sees," the meaning it has for him, and how it is related to other phenomena are determined by the concepts he has, and these in turn are learned from the social groups into which he was born and with which he lives (p. 116).

Concerning the prohibition against the speaking of Spanish by Mexican American children in the schools, the NEA-Tuscon Survey group (19) comments:

. . . In telling him that he must not speak his native language, we are saying to him by implication that Spanish and the culture which it represents are of no worth. Therefore (it follows again) this particular child is of no worth. It should come as no surprise to us, then, that he develops a negative self-concept—an inferiority complex (p. 11).

Various writers comment upon the results of these linguistic and psychological barriers that the Mexican American child meets when first entering school at age six. Holland (13) devised a special administration of the Wechsler Intelligence Scale for Children which yielded an English Verbal IQ and a Bilingual Verbal IQ. In testing 36 Spanish-speaking children ranging from the first grade level through grade five, credit for an English response was given when a correct answer in English was given to a question stated in that language. Credit for a bilingual response was given if the testing situation had to be supplemented with Spanish, which was done only when the instructions were not understood or were only partially understood in English. The difference between the two types of IQs obtained by the system was called the *language barrier,* whose size, Holland claimed, is directly related to a student's difficulty in classroom achievement. The subjects were found to have an average barrier of 4 to 6 IQ points per student. The English Verbal IQ, it should be noted, was conceived to be indicative of the subject's present level of functioning in English language skills, while the Bilingual Verbal IQ was conceived to be indicative of the subject's future potential for verbal skills when his knowledge of English might become approximately equal to his knowledge of Spanish. Holland further found that this *language barrier* was most evident at the first grade level and diminished with each successive year of schooling, but that it was still present among fifth grade students. He concludes that these children have learned enough English by the fifth grade to compete with their Anglo classmates, but by this time they are unable to "catch up" and the classroom becomes more bewildering.

Heller (12), on the other hand, believes that a number of studies have shown that Mexican American children tend to start out on much the same level as Anglo children, both in IQ scores and scholastic achievement. Yet, pointing to one of her own studies of Mexican American high school seniors in Los Angeles, she notes that after 11 years of schooling their IQ distribution curve did not correspond to the normal IQ curve. Almost half of the Mexican American students, in contrast to 13 percent of the Anglo American students, were below average in IQ. Manuel (17) cites W. H. Sinninger of New Mexico Highlands University as saying that Spanish American pupils are up to or near the national norms in achievement in the primary grades, but that they start dropping below the norms in the fourth grade and lose ground in each of the succeeding grades. According to Sinninger, this drop is the result of inadequate meanings and vocabularies. Work in the primary grades is mechanical and concerned with developing a sight vocabulary and word recognition skills, which do not call for the word power demanded in the higher grades.

LA RAZA AND ACCULTURATION

Heller (12) notes that people of Mexican descent, as well as those born in Mexico, identify themselves with pride as members of La Raza (the Race), which is united by esoteric bonds of blood and custom. "La Raza groups together all those in the world who speak Spanish; it implies both a mystical bond uniting Spanish-speaking people and a separation of them from all others (Rubel, 25, p. 7)." It is the maintenance of this "racial" identification involving ties to language and custom, which seems to raise the problem of acculturation; that is, the absorption of the values of the dominant group by the minority group.

Perhaps one reason for the retarded acculturation of Mexican Americans is that they have maintained a rural, or folk, culture while the middle class culture of the United States is an urban culture (Naegele, 20). Clark (8) believes that what distinguishes a folk people from the more complex world in which they live is that they have a body of tradition passed orally from generation to generation which determines the pattern of their lives. Almost everyone conforms to it. Tradition sets the pattern, and it is seldom questioned. The child in such a society receives his education for life in the circle of the extended family, not in a school. Life may be hard, but it is stable. Things change slowly. Campa (5) also sees the conflict between the American urban culture and the folk culture of the Spanish-speaking as the main barrier to the acculturation of the Spanish-speaking community. He seems to feel that the folk culture has not yet evolved to the status of a complete society, and that this makes acculturation more difficult since there must be an approximation of cultural level between them. Clark (8), however, points out that a folk culture is not necessarily simpler than other types of cultures, and in some aspects actually may be infinitely more complex.

Saunders (29) sees four factors retarding acculturation. First, there is the proximity of Mexico. The enormous traffic that moves back and forth across the border each year provides continuing links between the Spanish-speaking people of the border states and of Mexico. Not only people move across the border, but also printed materials, material goods, and motion picture films. Radio programs in Spanish are received not only from across the border, but also from many Spanish-language stations within the border states. The need to learn English is lessened and the need to conform to Anglo ways is minimized when one lives surrounded by people who follow other ways and speak mainly Spanish. And, as Spanish-speaking people acquire the characteristics of the dominant society, their places tend to be taken by immigrants from Mexico who have few, if any, Anglo traits.

Second, segregation, which has been mentioned previously, retards acculturation. Saunders believes that spatial separation is both a cause and an effect of retarded acculturation. Separate communities will tend to minimize cross-cultural contacts. A lack of Anglo cultural traits will tend to create a continued awareness of differences and a continuation of the tendency to live apart.

Third, there seem to be relatively few persons in the Mexican American group able to provide models of success or effective leadership for any considerable part of the Spanish-speaking population. Heller (12) notes that as persons of Mexican American descent advance substantially in the social scale, they tend to sever their relations with the Mexican American community. Social mobility, she says, has been synonymous with renunciation in the minds of many Mexican Americans. Burma (3) points out that leaders must have one characteristic in common to be successful: They must have the welfare of La Raza at heart. They must try always to help their people and not be ashamed of them. Penalosa and McDonagh (21) found in their study, however, that upwardly mobile Mexican Americans retained their Mexican ethnic identification. Heller (12), too, feels that the pattern is changing, and that Mexican Americans who have achieved prominence in various fields in recent years have not severed, but rather have stressed, their ties with the Mexican American community.

The fourth factor mentioned by Saunders (29) as retarding acculturation is an attitude of suspicion and mistrust which operates primarily against Anglos, but may also be directed by some Spanish-speaking individuals against others of their own group. These attitudes may undermine sincere efforts at organization and leadership from within the Spanish-speaking group, and may create an unwillingness to cooperate with Anglo individuals, agencies, or organizations in programs that are intended to benefit Spanish-speaking people.

However, Saunders (29) also points out four factors that promote acculturation. First, there is the size of the Spanish-speaking population. The smaller group, he believes, is certain to be attracted toward the ways of the larger group, especially since contacts with the larger group cannot be entirely avoided, and since adoption of Anglo ways may be psychologically or materially rewarding. Nonetheless, the Spanish-speaking population is a big minority group, and Naegele (20) believes that the larger the percentage of the minority in the total population the greater the time needed for assimilation to take place.

Saunders also sees urbanization as promoting acculturation. The shift from rural living to city living has tended to be disruptive of old ways and has brought new pressures. New family and community relationships have developed. More divorces occur, as do more marriages outside the group. New patterns in recreation have appeared, and increasingly the focus of attention of children is away from the home. Class divisions have grown sharper, and the group is no longer as homogeneous as it once was. Even though impersonal, contractual relationships which characterize urban life are unsatisfactory to many Spanish-speaking persons, they nonetheless must enter into them. In doing so, the Mexican American becomes increasingly at ease with them, loses part of his cultural heritage, and acquires a part of that of the Anglos.

Tied with increasing urbanization is increasing mobility, which Saunders names as the third factor promoting acculturation. The Spanish-speaking people of the Southwest move about more freely today in increasing numbers, and are able to change their social status within a lifetime. Wherever the Spanish-speaking person goes, Anglo culture tends to intrude, bringing changes which may not be welcome but which are inescapable.

Lastly, Saunders believes that education itself promotes acculturation. Spanish-speaking people are increasingly participating in formal education, and are thereby subjecting themselves and their children to a powerful acculturative experience. The schools expose Spanish-speaking children to Anglo concepts, ways, and values, and the child who finishes 8 or 12 grades of school has had an extended exposure to Anglo cultural elements, through the English language, the curricula they study, and the association with English-speaking students.

One may hypothesize that intermarriage with Anglos may also promote the process of acculturation. Believing that the study of intermarriage is also a study of "social distance," Mittelbach and Moore (18) have studied 7,492 marriage licenses issued in Los Angeles in 1963 which included all marriages in which one or both spouses carried a Spanish surname. They find that intermarriage with Anglos is increasing. Their study indicates that the third generation Mexican American, rather than the first or second generation Mexican American, is more likely to marry outside the ethnic group, and that Mexican American women are more likely to marry outside the ethnic group than men. The rate of marriages outside the ethnic group seems to increase with each generation, and a rise in school status for both men and women leads to favor marriages outside the Mexican American group. As Mexican Americans move into the middle class, they seem to select spouses in terms of class in addition to, or instead of, ethnic considerations, and this was most typical of the third generation. The author finds that the social distance between generations of Mexican Americans is even greater than the social distance between some Mexican Americans and Anglos. In addition, the third generation evidences less Catholic practice than does the second, and the third generation tends to marry younger than either the second or first generation. These patterns suggest to the authors the dim outline of an anti-traditionalist younger generation. However, Mexican Americans still tend to marry other Mexican Americans, and the authors do not see assimilation through intermarriage as imminent. Nonetheless, they do believe that the data raise serious questions about the perpetuation of the ethnic group and the "Mexican culture," at least in Los Angeles. Their findings do indicate a gradual assimilation of the Mexican American population, and indicate to the authors a growing dynamic change.

But the question remains of whether the Mexican American group wishes this "growing dynamic change," and to what degree they themselves may desire assimilation. The NEA-Tuscon Survey group (19) points out that the schools, reflecting the dominant view of the dominant culture, wish the Mexican American child to grow up as another Anglo. This the Mexican American child cannot do unless he tends to deny his family and his culture. Madsen (16) comments that in the school the Mexican American child hears the teachings of his parents contradicted, and is urged to behave in ways that may be uncomfortable for him. Simmons (31) comments that what the Mexican Americans advocate is a fusion of the two cultures in which the best of each would be retained. Manuel (17) believes that the development of a common culture which includes the best of both cultures and yet permits wide individual variations is a reasonable goal.

Naegele (20), on the other hand, believes that since Mexican American culture resists complete conformity to Anglo patterns, that it may be worthwhile to entertain the idea of a dual culture in which Mexican Americans may have the right to be themselves within the Anglo American culture. Yet Simmons (31) points out that the basic demands of living in the United States have required some change on the part of the Mexican Americans. Although original family organizations have persisted, patterns of traditional authority have witnessed major changes. Still, believes Simmons, even the acculturated Mexican American will retain in some degree the more subtle aspects of his culture, such as conceptions of time, fundamental value orientations, and modes of participation in interpersonal relations. Thus, if full acceptance of Mexican Americans by Anglos depends upon the complete disappearance of the Mexican American's cultural differences, full acceptance will not be accorded in the foreseeable future. Yet, as has been noted, Simmons believes Mexican Americans will exchange old ways for new, but only if the new ways appear more meaningful than the old ones, and then only if they are given full opportunity to acquire and to use the new ways.

BIBLIOGRAPHY

(1) Beberfall, Lester, "Some Linguistic Problems of the Spanish-Speaking People of Texas," *Modern Language Journal,* February, 1958. Vol. 42, pp. 87–90.

(2) Brickman, W. W. (ed.), "School Bias Toward Mexican Americans," *School and Society,* November 12, 1966. Vol. 94, p. 378.

(3) Burma, J. H., *Spanish-Speaking Groups in the United States;* New York: Duke University Press, 1954. Chapters 3 and 4.

(4) Campa, A. L., "Individualism in Hispanic Society," in Moseley, J. E. (ed.), *The Spanish-Speaking People of the Southwest;* Indianapolis, Indiana: Council on Spanish American Work, 1966. p. 11–19.

(5) Campa, A. L., "Culture Patterns of the Spanish-Speaking Community," in Moseley, J. E. (ed.), *The Spanish-Speaking People of the Southwest;* Indianapolis, Indiana: Council on Spanish American Work, 1966. pp. 20–35.

(6) Carter, T. P., "The Negative Self-Concept of Mexican American Students," *School and Society,* March 30, 1968. Vol. 96, pp. 217–219.

(7) Chavez, S. J., "Preserve Their Language Heritage," *Childhood Education,* December, 1956. Vol. 33, pp. 165 +.

(8) Clark, Margaret, *Health in the Mexican American Culture;* Los Angeles: University of California Press, 1959.

(9) Crawford, F. R., *The Forgotten Egg: An Exploration into Mental Health Problems among Urban Mexican American Families and Their Children;* Austin, Texas: Texas State Department of Health, Division of Mental Health, 1961.

(10) Edmondson, M. S., *Los Manitos: A Study of Institutional Values;* New Orleans: Tulane University, Middle American Research Institute, 1957.

(11) Heffernan, H. W., "Some Solutions to Problems of Students of Mexican Descent," *The Bulletin of the National Association of Secondary School Principals,* March, 1955. Vol. 39, pp. 43–53.

(12) Heller, C. S., *Mexican American Youth: Forgotten Youth at the Crossroads;* New York: Random House, 1966. Chapters 2 and 3.

(13) Holland, W. R., "Language Barrier as an Educational Problem of Spanish-Speaking Children," *Exceptional Children,* September, 1960. Vol. 27, pp. 42–44.

(14) Kluckhohn, F. R., and Strodtbeck, F. L., *Variations in Value Orientation;* Evanston, Illinois: Row, Peterson and Company, 1961.

(15) Luna, E. G., "Spanish-Speaking People of the Southwest," in Moseley, J. E. (ed.), *The Spanish-Speaking People of the Southwest;* Indianapolis, Indiana: Council on Spanish American Work, 1966.

(16) Madsen, William, *Mexican Americans of South Texas;* New York: Holt, Rinehart and Winston, 1964. Chapters 2–12.

(17) Manuel, H. T., *Spanish-Speaking Children of the Southwest: Their Education and the Public Welfare;* Austin: University of Texas Press, 1965. Chapters 1, 4, 8, 9, and 10.

(18) Mittelbach, F. G., Moore, J. W., and McDaniel, R., *Intermarriage of Mexican Americans,* University of California at Los Angeles, Mexican American Study Project, Advance Report No. 6; Los Angeles: University of California at Los Angeles, Graduate School of Business Administration, Division of Research, November, 1966.

(19) NEA-Tuscon Survey on the Teaching of Spanish to the Spanish-Speaking, *The Invisible Minority . . . Pero No Vencibles;* Washington, D.C.: National Education Association, Department of Rural Education, 1966.

(20) Naegele, V. A., "Sociology," in *Americans of Mexican Descent—An In-Depth Study;* San Antonio, Texas: a publication of the Human Resources Development Institute, held July 31-August 11, 1967, at St. Mary's University.

(21) Penalosa, F., and McDonagh, E. D., "Social Mobility in a Mexican American Community," *Social Forces,* June, 1966. Vol. 44, pp. 498–505.

(22) Perales, A. M., "The Audio-Lingual Approach and the Spanish-Speaking Student," *Hispania,* March, 1965. Vol. 48, pp. 99–102.

(23) Rowan, Helen, "A Minority Nobody Knows," *The Atlantic Monthly,* June, 1967. Vol. 219, pp. 47–52.

(24) Rubel, A. J., "Concepts of Disease in Mexican American Culture," *American Anthropologist,* October, 1960. Vol. 62, pp. 795–814.

(25) Rubel, A. J., *Across the Tracks: Mexican Americans in a Texas City;* Austin: University of Texas Press, 1966.

(26) Samora, Julian, "Educational Status of a Minority," *Theory into Practice,* June, 1963. Vol. 2, pp. 144–150.

(27) Sanchez, G. I., "Concerning Segregation of Spanish-Speaking Children in the Public Schools," *Inter-American Education Occasional Papers,* December, 1951. Vol. 9, Chapter 1 and Appendix.

(28) Sanchez, G. I., *Forgotten People: A Study of New Mexicans;* Albuquerque, New Mexico: Calvin Horn Publishers, Inc., 1967.

(29) Saunders, Lyle, *Cultural Difference and Medical Care: The Case of the Spanish-Speaking People of the Southwest;* New York: Russell Sage Foundation, 1954.

(30) Saunders, Lyle, "Anglos and Spanish-Speaking People: Contrasts and Similarities," in Moseley, J. E. (ed.), *The Spanish-Speaking Peoples of the Southwest;* Indianapolis, Indiana: Council on Spanish-American Work, 1966.

(31) Simmons, O. G., "The Mutual Images and Expectations of Anglo Americans and Mexican Americans," *Daedalus,* Spring, 1961. pp. 286–299.

(32) Soffietti, J. P., "Bilingualism and Biculturalism," *Journal of Educational Psychology,* April, 1955. Vol. 46, pp. 222–227.

(33) Tuck, R. D., *Not With the Fist: Mexican Americans in a Southwest City;* New York: Harcourt, Brace and World, 1946.

(34) Woods, Sister Frances Jerome, C.D.P., *Cultural Values of American Ethnic Groups;* New York: Harper and Brothers, 1956.

Mexican Americans in School: A History of Educational Neglect

Thomas P. Carter

Some educators take the position that much of the school curriculum and many school policies and practices inhibit learning and promote culture conflict, emotional problems, and the eventual flight of children from school. They believe that the school is at fault because of its inability to adjust realistically to serve culturally different groups, that there is nothing per se bad or deficient about Mexican Americans, but that the school has failed to capitalize on the "good and sufficient" child. These educators denounce the argument that Mexican American children are culturally deprived and see their background as full of meaning, order, and significant experiences. Recognizing these points, Lopez stated in an address to schoolmen concerned with the education of Spanish-speaking people (1964, p. 16):

I take exception to the word 'problem' when referring to the Mexican American community or the youngster, or so referring to any youngster regardless of his racial background. It is not a minority problem . . . not a problem of the child and so forth. It is a problem of the school, of the total community, of society. So, consequently . . . as we seek solution to these problems, let us not look within little Juan—let's see if we can find the solution to his problem within us.

While it is true that the school, as an institution, reflects or mirrors its parent society and probably has little effect on changing the nature of that society—the school cannot build new industries, destroy castes, eliminate racial or ethnic discrimination, change the roles of men or women, change power distribution, and so forth—it is not unreasonable to assume that the school can eliminate or modify practices that are detrimental to certain children. Whether or not the elimination of school practices or conditions that discourage Mexican American children will ultimately affect the nature of the local society must await the passage of time.

Following the same theme, but concentrating on institutional factors, a prominent Texas school administrator argued that the "traditional school" has "crippled" many Mexican American children:

We have expected the impossible of the Mexican American child when he comes into our school system. In the first grade we have always spent a great deal of time preparing a child for formal school experience in reading. We call this reading readiness, but we have not taken into consideration that the Mexican American child, coming from a different cultural and language background, is completely unable to benefit from the little nice things we do because he is unable to conceptualize in the Anglo culture and language. From the day he enters school he begins to lag behind in acquiring information because the only medium of communication is English. Eventually if he sticks it out he arrives at junior high school two to three years overage. If something isn't done at this age the child will not tolerate too many frustrations and becomes a dropout. These are the kids we have crippled because of the bungling methods we have used in attempting to instruct them in the traditional American school.

Few take as strong a stand. However, a significant number of educators would generally concur; many advocate radical institutional changes.

The present school is inappropriate for many Mexican American youngsters. Factors particularly disadvantageous are de facto segregation, isolation in its various forms, the dependence on English, and inadequate teachers. Less obvious factors include rigidity of school practices and policies, curricular irrelevancy, culture conflict, and the negative perceptions of educators. The aggregate of these factors produces a generally negative school social environment or climate—a factor recognized as crucial to school survival and success. Social climate includes every aspect of the environment in which a child "learns" and "lives" in school. "School environment of the child consists of many things, ranging from the desk he sits at to the child who sits next to him, and including the teacher who stands in front of his class" (Coleman, 1966, p. 37). These things are difficult to measure objectively. The on-site observations, teachers' comments, interviews, and findings reported in the few objective studies that have been done are all open to question. However, a description of the school environment for many Mexican American children is attempted in this chapter.

SEPARATION AND ISOLATION

Many Mexican American children attend schools where they form the ethnic majority. While de jure segregation has been declared unconstitutional, isolation of minority-group children from sustained contact with other groups continues. The school does little to promote full and equal-status interaction among ethnic groups and reflects instead the ethnic separateness of the community.

De Jure and De Facto Segregation

No Southwestern state legally provided for the segregation of Mexican American children, yet the widespread practice had the force of law. In the mid-1940s, this Southwestern form of de jure segregation was terminated by recourse to the courts.

Separate "Mexican schools" were maintained in the past on the grounds that the separation was beneficial to Mexican American children. Reasons for segregation espoused in official school pronouncements included the Mexican American child's language handicap and his need to learn English, his need to be Americanized before mixing with Anglos, and his slowness in school, which would hinder the progress of Anglos. Mexican Americans were reported to be dirty and disease-ridden and to have low moral standards. Separate schools gave Mexican American children the opportunity to overcome these deficiencies and protected them from having to compete with Anglos and thus feeling inferior, as well as from the Anglo practice of "hazing" and other discriminations reported prevalent before the 1950s. (See Carpenter, 1935; Clinchy, 1954; Taylor, 1934.)

Segregation practices, however, implied other reasons than those given by educators. Although no definite or uniform practices were evident, certain actions and conditions raised the question of motives. These included: (1) The tendency for "Mexican schools" to have vastly inferior physical facilities, poorly qualified teachers, and larger classes than Anglo schools. (2) The practice of placing all Spanish-surname children in segregated schools, even though some were fluent in English. The fact that Negro children were sometimes assigned to "Mexican schools" suggests a racial rather than language basis for segregation. (3) The lack of effort to enforce the often weak attendance laws. (4) The failure to demand enrollment and attendance of Mexican American children while counting them on the school census. This Texas practice was abolished when the state shifted to "average daily attendance" as a basis for financial support. (5) In numerous cases the discouraging of individual children from attending school at all, especially in secondary-level institutions. Such practices were not universal in the Southwest, but they were common. Some still are. (See Calderón, 1950; Ceja, 1957; Common Ground, Winter 1947; Rubel, 1966; Strickland and Sánchez, 1948; Taylor, 1934; Trillingham and Hughes, 1943.)

The amount of Mexican American de jure segregation and its quality are difficult to assess. Little, in his 1944 study of Texas school districts he assumed to be representative, found that segregation was widespread but was not always practiced at the same grade levels. The large percentage of districts segregating at the higher grade levels, as shown in Table 1, is another encouragement to the belief that reasons other than "the language problem" and "pedagogical justifications" were behind segregation practices.

Attitudes revealed in public pronouncements and conversations indicated strong racist and economic biases on the part of both educators and laymen.

TABLE 1   School Segregation at Different Grade Levels, Texas

NUMBER OF DISTRICTS SEGREGATING	GRADES SEGREGATED
9	1–2
16	1–3
23	1–4
27	1–6
13	1–7
17	1–8

Source: Little (1944).

Comments like these were reported commonly: "If the Mexicans get educated, they will go to the cities where they can get more money. Some Mexicans are very bright, but you can't compare their brightest with the *average* white children. They are an inferior race. . . . Most of the schools here take the money out of the Mexican allotment and use it for the whites" (Taylor, 1934, pp. 196, 200, 203). In general, segregation seemed to be maintained out of fear of intermarriage with inferior people and a feeling that if Mexican Americans were educated, they would not be so easy to manipulate and would no longer work for low wages. Such attitudes still prevail and probably underlie the widespread desire to maintain neighborhood schools and de facto segregation.

As in other sociopolitical areas, World War II stimulated Mexican Americans to demand change. Becoming more aware of their rights, privileges, and duties as American citizens, they demanded an end to separate schools and other discriminatory practices. Although it was illegal in all Southwestern states, segregation of Mexican Americans had gained the force of law and required legal action to terminate it. In 1946, with Mexican American organizational support behind them, a group of Mexican American parents initiated legal action against four Southern California elementary school districts. In *Westminster School District et al.* vs. *Mendez et al.*, the plaintiffs, on behalf of their minor children, claimed that the school districts discriminated illegally against children of Mexican descent by maintaining separate facilities. The plaintiffs contended that such practices violated their Constitutionally guaranteed rights to "due process and equal protection of the law." They did not argue that "Mexican schools" were inferior; rather, they agreed that they were as good as the Anglo institutions or perhaps superior to them. The court ruled in favor of the parents and enjoined the districts from segregating. The decision was appealed in a higher court, but the lower court decision was sustained. This case laid the groundwork for subsequent desegregation decisions in the 1950s, which were argued also on the basis of the First, Fifth, and Fourteenth amendments to the Constitution. (See Cooke, 1948, pp. 417–421; Sánchez, 1951.) In 1948, legal redress was sought to end school segregation of Mexican Americans in Texas. In *Delgado* vs. *The Bastrop Independent School District*, a federal court ruled that such segregation was illegal. The decision, like that in California, was based on Constitutional guarantees. Legally sanctioned segregation was ended.

De facto segregation continues. Schools are ethnically and racially out of balance in metropolitan areas, as well as in smaller urban and rural areas, because housing patterns continue to influence the placement of new schools and of the boundaries within which children must live to attend them. The end of legal segregation has not markedly affected concentrations of low-income Mexican American children in segregated schools. As families that become better off economically move from the traditional *barrios*[1] to mixed neighborhoods, the group that remains becomes more homogeneously poor and culturally disadvantaged. Those who leave are replaced by new rural or Mexican immigrants. Few Southwestern towns or cities are without their Mexican American sections. The situation is changing somewhat, but residential segregation remains the common pattern (see Moore and Mettelbach, 1966). With few exceptions, schools reflect this segregation.

California is the only Southwestern state to publish statistics relative to the concentration of ethnic groups in schools. In October 1966, the State Department of Education collected data from all but six of California's 1,162 school districts. Racial imbalance was found to characterize many of the schools. Although this fact had long been recognized, the degree of ethnic isolation was somewhat startling. For the purpose of analysis, school districts were divided according to size of enrollment. The eight largest districts, with enrollments of 50,000 or more, and a representative sample of 56 smaller districts were analyzed separately. A method to determine whether a school was *majority, minority,* or *mixed* was established:

A simple integregation scale was applied to each of the 2,340 schools in the study groups, comparing each school's percentages of the three largest racial and ethnic groups (Spanish surname, "other white," and Negro) with the corresponding percentages of the districts in which the school is situated. Allowing a deviation of as many as 15 percentage points above or below the appropriate district percentage, it was possible to classify each school as high concentration, mixed, or low concentration with respect to each of the three racial or ethnic groups. When the basis of comparison was "other white" percentage, the term *majority* school, *mixed* school, or *minority* school could be substituted (California State Department of Education, 1967a, p. 10).

The California survey indicates that Negro children are more segregated than Mexican Americans in both the largest and smallest districts of the state. In the eight largest districts, 17 percent of Spanish-surname children attend *minority,* 28 percent *mixed,* and 15 percent *majority* schools. Eighty-five percent of Negroes attend *minority* schools, 12 percent *mixed,* and 3 percent *majority.* In the smaller districts 30 percent of the Spanish-surname students attend *minority,* 63 percent *mixed,* and 7 percent *majority* schools. In these districts also, Negro children are more segregated.

These figures are perhaps adequate for the statewide picture, but they distort

[1]*Barrio* is a term used in many ways in the Southwest. "Neighborhood" is perhaps the best translation. It does not necessarily mean a slum, but it has this connotation in some areas. In this [material] it means simply Mexican American area or neighborhood.

the real situation. There are fewer minority secondary schools than minority elementary schools, and to lump them together is misleading. The recent study by Coleman et al. (1966) of educational opportunity sheds some light on the elementary—secondary school differences: "A substantial number of Indian-American and Mexican American first graders are in schools in which they are the majority group. This is not true at the 12th grade" (p. 41). The report also says (p. 212):

While the average Negro elementary child is in school where 16% of the students are white, the average percentage of white classmates is . . . 53% for Mexican-Americans. At the secondary level, the average Negro is in a school where 24% of the students are white, while the average percentage of white classmates is . . . 68% for Mexican-Americans. . . .

An educational executive in Texas commented:

I would say that more Mexican American children generally attend elementary school with other Mexican American children and when it's not that way, generally the ratio will be decidedly in favor of the Anglo—the proportion will be much larger Anglo.

This informant implied that there are two types of schools. One is almost exclusively Mexican American, the other almost exclusively Anglo. Mexican American children generally are not interspread with Anglos, but when they are, Anglos predominate. This situation is quite common in elementary schools throughout the Southwest. The "Mexican school" serves the lower social class; the mixed (but usually predominantly Anglo) school serves the middle class.

The California survey (1967a) indicates that in minority schools one finds overrepresentation of compensatory education programs:

On the integration scale, 27 percent of the Title I (ESEA) target schools . . . in the 56 district sample are *minority* schools, and 2 percent are *majority* schools: 79 percent of the Title I target schools in the eight largest districts are *minority* schools, and 1 percent are *majority* schools. Funds from a special California compensatory education act go also almost exclusively to *minority* schools . . . 81 percent of the Senate Bill 28 [a California compensatory education program] special aid schools in the sample are *minority* schools . . . 92 percent of the Senate Bill 28 special aid schools in the eight largest districts are *minority* schools. . . . (pp. 12–13).

Specifically mentioning Mexican Americans, the survey says: "In compensatory education target elementary schools (Title I-Elementary and Secondary Education Act), Spanish surname pupils comprise 54% of the enrollment. 48% of all Spanish surname elementary pupils in the State attend these target schools" (p. 5). Mexican Americans tend to go to minority elementary schools, and these schools receive a disproportionate share of compensatory education funds. Mexican American poverty and minority schools are associated.

In the Los Angeles School Study it was found that the composition of the school population was of great importance to the success in school of Mexican American children. A number of elementary schools and junior and senior high schools were categorized according to the number of children in various ethnic and socioeconomic groups. The categories are roughly analogous to the minority, mixed, and majority categories used in the California survey. It was found that: "School type contributed substantially to the performance of Mexican-American elementary and junior high levels, but not at senior high levels" (Gordon et al., 1968, pp. 134–135). In other words, if other factors are constant, minority-group children perform better in schools that have a low percentage of minority-group pupils. However, "The performance of Anglo pupils is not affected by school context at any level." Although tentative, these findings strongly suggest that mixed or majority schools improve Mexican American academic achievement.

In spite of the law, theoretical arguments, and some empirical evidence against segregated schools, there is a strong and widespread desire to retain neighborhood schools (see Coleman et al., 1966). While few educators interviewed for this study were overtly segregationist, most defended the neighborhood-school concept and contended that the closing of "Mexican schools" would work to the disadvantage of the children. Their arguments are similar to those previously used in defense of de jure segregation:

. . . the Mexican children are often at a disadvantage . . . in segregated schools Mexican children experience no such invidious comparisons. They compete against other Mexican children, with far better results ensuing. Even Mexican parents who have been opposed to segregation have been converted to its merits. For the first five grades, segregation is advocated . . . on the ground that the children make better progress and have a chance in that time period to learn the English language and thus to compete with American children on a fairer level than would be the case in an earlier grade level. They acquire a confidence in their own abilities, which helps them to go ahead creditably with American children (Bogardus, 1928–29, pp. 276–283).

Another frequently heard argument for maintaining "Mexican schools" is that parents are perfectly content with the status quo; there have been few pickets or objectors—"Mexican Americans like to be among their own kind, just as Anglos do."

California, responding to pressure from the civil rights movement, is moving to desegregate its schools. The California School Boards Association stated in 1965 that school districts should be "encouraged to analyze the extent of racial imbalance in their district and take steps to ameliorate any imbalances which are found to exist" (California School Boards Association, 1965, p. 4). The California State Department of Education also is encouraging the ending of racial imbalance. Schoolmen are generally aware of this imbalance in their schools and, encouraged by Department of Education consultants, are proposing plans for desegregation.

A number of California cities, including Sausalito, Garden Grove, Berkeley, Livingston, and Riverside are implementing plans to overcome ethnic imbalance. Riverside is desegregating its minority-group children by sending them by bus to assigned schools. Two schools almost exclusively composed of Mexican American and Negro children were closed in the fall of 1966; a third, a *barrio* school, was closed in the fall of the following year. Some members of the Mexican American community served by the *barrio* school were in favor of keeping their neighborhood school. The movement to desegregate Riverside and other California schools was first led by Negro elements, but now Mexican American leadership is also vocal. However, Mexican American and Negro advocacy of desegregation may be lessening, as more members of these groups stress ethnic and racial "nationalism" and separateness. This trend will undoubtedly be supported by many middle-class Anglos who adhere to racial isolation and perhaps to a racist ideology.

A seven-year study of the effects of desegregation on the achievement, attitudes, and behavior of children of all three groups has been undertaken. An interdisciplinary team from the University of California at Riverside, and members of the staff of the school district, are collecting data from children and parents. The findings of this study have not yet been published (see Singer and Hendrick, 1967, pp. 143–147).

In spite of governmental pressure in California, much reluctance to desegregate is still evident among educators and within both the majority- and minority-group communities. Pressure probably will eventually cause districts to modify the status quo. However, the percentage of educators interviewed for this study who desired to end segregation was higher in California than in Texas. Many Texas Mexican American teachers desire desegregation but feel that it is utterly impossible for the present. Anglo Texas schoolmen interviewed say that they are trying to do their best with the present school programs, that desegregation may some day be forced upon them, but that community opinion is strongly opposed to "mixing the races." This attitude may be assumed to characterize also those areas of New Mexico and Colorado that are under strong Texas influence (see Chambers, 1949). Barring massive protest by Texas minority groups, or strong state-level intervention, continued de facto segregation for many years may be foreseen. California and Colorado may be slowly moving toward desegregation and probably will continue to do so, perhaps with increasing resistance from many sources. Advocates of all positions, with varying degrees of influence, are found in all five Southwestern states. School systems and staffs of each area strongly reflect the local social environment.

Mexican American School Districts

History and geography have isolated Mexican Americans from contact with Anglos. In all five states there are districts that are predominantly Mexican American; in many the percentage is over 85, and in some it approaches 100. These districts are concentrated in counties along the border, in California's rich agricultural valleys, and in northern New Mexico and southern Colorado. Extremely high percentages of Mexican Americans are particularly evident in the small Texas cities along the Rio Grande River, especially in Starr, Kenedy, and Zapata counties. Describing this in 1957, a Texas Education Agency report stated (p. 1):

The heaviest concentration of Spanish surname pupils was reported from the counties bordering Mexico . . . a total of 31 counties, about 12% of the total number in the State, reported an enrollment of 50% or more Spanish surname pupils. Schools in eight counties reported more than 75%, and one county, Kenedy, reported 100%.

In many cases, the percentage of Mexican children in school would be higher if it were not for the large number of them who drop out.

In some communities, two school districts exist: one Mexican American, the other either mixed or predominantly Anglo. Del Rio, Texas, and Las Vegas, New Mexico, are examples. Las Vegas is two incorporated cities, each with its own school district. Del Rio is one city with two school districts. While there are other and different kinds of reasons for the existence of the two school systems, strong segregationist overtones are evident. A number of school districts visited are virtually 100 percent *pura raza* (Mexican American).

Free-Choice Policies

Many school officials interviewed commented that their districts have a free transfer plan. This plan allows for free choice of school by parents; those desiring to place their children in predominantly Anglo schools are permitted by school policy to do so. Educators argue that this is a step toward compliance with the "spirit of desegregation." The function of this policy may be seen two ways: it permits Mexican Americans to attend predominantly Anglo schools and allows Anglos to flee from schools with large percentages of Mexican Americans. It appears that very few lower-class Mexican Americans transfer to other schools, because of their lack of desire, their lack of knowledge of school procedures, or because of intimidation by school officials. In order to transfer, students usually must have permission from either the school board or the superintendent. One Texas interviewee replied to a question on this point as follows:

The parent says, well, look, I don't want my kid going to this school where I live. He can apply for a transfer, and then the transfer comes before the Board of Trustees and they say, "What's the reason for the transfer?" "Well, I don't like that school." "What's wrong with it?" Who among these people [low-status Mexican Americans] is going to push a request of that type?

Responding to a question about whether middle class Mexican Americans would have any problems, the same informant stated:

They probably wouldn't live in that area. I know some who have done it and they know their way around. They come in, it's no problem for them. They're accepted every year.

On the other hand, a sociologist, a specialist in Mexican American affairs, commented on the flight of Anglos:

They do have a free transfer policy; for example [a certain high school], up until five or six years ago was the high school of the elite. This is the school to which the wealthiest families and the old families sent their children. Then in the last 10 years, you had a very heavy movement of Mexican Americans into the geographical area covered by [this school] so at the present time, perhaps the Mexican Americans number more than 60 percent of the student body. The wealthy Anglo American families now transfer their children to [another school].

Whether the free-choice policy maintains segregation or encourages mixing of the groups remains to be seen. However, it appears evident that the "good Mexican" has little difficulty in gaining permission to transfer his child, and that de facto segregated minority-group schools are becoming more homogeneously lower class. What was once segregation according to ethnic group is increasingly becoming separation according to social class. The bottom social group in much of the Southwest is made up of Mexican Americans, who remain isolated from "better off" Mexican Americans, as well as from Anglos.

Brain Drain

As movement of rural Mexican Americans to the cities continues, another form of isolation may be developing. In one school district in rural northern New Mexico administrators discussed what they called the "brain drain":

. . . there is a kind of cycle, a continuum of migration from the rural areas to the more urban and this drains off the more qualified people at all levels so that the more qualified semi-urban are moving to Albuquerque and the more qualified of the unqualified rural are moving to the small city, so that you constantly are faced with a lowering quality of aspiration [etc.]. The intelligent, relatively speaking, the well-educated, the ambitious, leave the more rural areas [etc.]. But what it means to teachers and superintendents in the small city is that they are constantly dealing with children of a less ambitious group of people or less upwardly mobile.

Whether the effect on the quality of students is as described is open to question. Logically, it might be assumed to be so. Whether this is reality or educators' perception of reality may be of little importance: it can be argued that because they think it is true teachers' expectations are lowered and efforts lessened.

Roman Catholic schools may act as a brain drain also. It is reported that parochial schools principally enroll Mexican American children of upwardly mobile or middle-class families. Comments by informants for this study varied greatly on this point. Each parochial school is different, as is each community and its public schools. The degree to which Catholic institutions take the best academic prospects must be determined by local study.

Mexican American Teachers

The assignment of Mexican American teachers to minority schools functions to isolate children from contact with Anglos. It is strongly argued that, having gone through a similar life pattern, Mexican American teachers understand their charges and are the best possible role models for their group's children. Mexican American spokesmen encourage school administrators to hire bilingual teachers and to assign them to "Mexican schools." "Bilingual" is almost invariably translated as "Mexican American" by administrators. A Colorado source states:

> . . . given equal academic or even lower academic qualifications, the Spanish-surnamed teacher applicant deserves special consideration because of two special qualifications he possesses . . . (1) his example or presence in the school can encourage Spanish-surnamed students, and (2) his ability to understand and give special counsel to many Spanish-surnamed students. . . . The second qualification may not always be valid. . . . Mexican American teachers . . . from upper-middle-class-urban culture may have nothing in common with a poor working class Spanish-surnamed student (Colorado Commission on Spanish-Surnamed Citizens, 1966, p. 62).

In spite of qualifying conditions, this kind of statement is usually interpreted to mean that Mexican American teachers should be hired for Mexican American children. Administrators tend to comply whenever possible.

As rules of thumb it can be stated that Mexican American teachers are generally (depending somewhat on the state or area): (1) highly desired by districts that have large Mexican American populations; (2) employed in numbers proportional to the Mexican American population of the school in which they teach; (3) concentrated at the elementary level; and (4) rarely found in Anglo elementary schools (except as Spanish teachers).

Except in districts in which the population is almost wholly Mexican American, there are very few Mexican American administrators in any field. In the vast majority of districts, Mexican Americans fill only the teaching positions. The few administrators are almost invariably principals of predominantly Mexican American schools, or language (often Spanish) consultants. In a few districts there are district-level administrators in charge of business, physical education, health, school social workers, and federal projects. In general, Mexican American administrators are found at all levels in the almost purely Mexican American districts, are low-level administrators in Anglo-controlled districts—even where the majority of students are of the minority group—and are associated with activities that bring them into contact with the ethnic community. Regardless of the advantages, such practices tend to isolate Mexican American communities and children from contact with Anglos and vice versa.

One almost wholly Mexican American district reflects the type of placement pattern characteristic of such areas. "A" School District consists of 12 elementary schools, 1 junior high school, and 1 senior high school. Its total enrollment for 1966–67 was about 2,600. The central office staff of 16, the 5 board members, and the 14 principals were Mexican Americans, as were all counselors and assistant principals. Of the teaching staff of 126, all but 10 had Spanish surnames. The student population was about 99 percent Mexican American.

A large metropolitan district demonstrates another and much more common placement pattern. "B" School District contains 9 regular high schools, 20 junior high schools, and 79 elementary schools. Its total enrollment for the 1966–67 school year was approximately 74,000. The Mexican American school population was about 60 percent of that total. Table 2 indicates the staff breakdown for 1966–67. Almost half of the Spanish-surname teachers were assigned to schools that approximated 100 percent Mexican American enrollment; the others were sprinkled throughout the system. However, it is reported that the percentage of Mexican teachers approximated the percentage of Mexican American children in the other schools. Of the 10 Spanish-surname building administrators, 8 were in *minority* schools.

"C" School District serves a smaller city. Although approximately 80 percent of the students in the district are Mexican American, its placement pattern is similar to "B" District. Of the 30 principals, assistants, and counselors, 3 have Spanish surnames; only 1 is in a secondary school in the capacity of assistant principal of a junior high. No central office administrator has a Spanish surname. Of the 425 teachers, 106 have Spanish surnames. These are concentrated in schools with large Mexican American student populations. No Spanish-surname teacher is placed in the one predominantly Anglo school (85–90 percent). Sixty-six percent of the Spanish-surname teachers are in elementary schools and 34 percent in secondary schools.

Districts "B" and "C" described above are representative of districts that are strongly under the control of the dominant Anglo society but are eager to procure as large a Mexican American staff as possible. While Mexican American teachers are hired and placed, few are promoted to the administrative ranks.

In California, during the 1966–67 school year, there were 3,866 teachers and 153 principals with Spanish surnames (California State Department of Education, 1967b). This represented 2.25 percent and 1.68 percent respectively of the state totals for these two categories (p. 8). Of the certified Spanish-surname teachers in the large districts, 51 percent taught in *minority*, 24 percent in *mixed*, and

TABLE 2 Spanish-Surname and Non-Spanish-Surname Staff Members of "B" School District

	NON-SPANISH SURNAME	SPANISH SURNAME	TOTAL
Board of education	6	1	7
Central office administrators	32	1 (Reading consultant)	33
Business and other services	10	1 (Head nurse)	11
Secondary school principals, assistants, deans, and counselors	88	6 (4*)	94
Elementary school principals and counselors	72	4*	76
Teachers	2,625	289†	2,914

Source: "B" School District Staff Personnel Directory.
*Number employed in schools approximating 100 percent Mexican American enrollment.
†49 percent in schools approximating 100 percent Mexican American enrollment.

25 percent in *majority* schools (p. 28). In the sample of 56 smaller districts, 66 percent of Spanish-surname teachers taught in *mixed*, 12 percent in *majority*, and 22 percent in *minority* schools (p. 29). Approximately 55 percent of the Spanish-surname certified personnel taught at the secondary level (p. 13). According to this California survey, "There is little likelihood that a Spanish surname student will be taught by a teacher of his own ethnic group"—since there are too few Mexican American teachers (p. 31). Yet, in most cases observed, the general rule holds: Mexican American teachers, especially elementary school teachers, are placed in schools that have high percentages of Mexican American students.

Colorado Spanish-surname elementary school teachers appear to be in larger percentages in districts that have smaller percentages of Mexican Americans. Whether such teachers are placed in predominantly Mexican American schools within these districts is not known. At the secondary school level, the tendency appears to be to concentrate Spanish-surname teachers in districts that have larger percentages of Mexican American students. In Denver, 1.33 percent of elementary school, 2.38 percent of junior high school, and 1.43 percent of senior high school teachers have Spanish surnames. However, their number is small. Of Denver's 3,687 teachers, only 65 have Spanish surnames; of these, 57 percent are at the secondary level. It is reported that most of these are probably Spanish teachers (Colorado State Department of Education, 1967, p. 61).

At the state department of education level, Mexican American educators fill numerous staff positions. In every state included in this study, Mexican Americans hold responsible positions; most deal with intergroup, migrant, compensatory, or related educational activities.

SEPARATION IN MIXED SCHOOLS

In ethnically mixed institutions, many minority-group students are nonetheless isolated from sustained equal-status interaction with Anglos. Naturally there are numerous exceptions. The *agringado* middle-class student usually mixes quite well with his Anglo peers. (An *agringado* is an Angloized Mexican American. The term is not used here in any depreciatory sense.) He tends to achieve and react in ways similar to other middle-class children, even though he may suffer from a more than normal identity crisis. The majority of Mexican Americans, however, have lower-class status and are not acculturated to middle-class orientations and norms; they are carriers of low-class (perhaps caste), traditional or transitional cultures. Even though these Mexican Americans attend mixed schools, in reality they may be isolated from their Anglo and *agringado* peers. School policy and practice contribute to this isolation, tending to reinforce the ethnic and social class cleavage that exists within most of the Southwest. The school reflects the community and tends to perpetuate the separation of Mexican and Anglo roles and expectations.

Ethnic Cleavage

In most of the Southwest, two separate castelike social structures exist. Two communities, the Anglo and the Mexican American, exist side by side. This castelike relationship is characterized as dominant-submissive: the Anglo segment is superordinate, the minority subordinate (Simmons, 1952). The school mirrors and is a microcosm of the community it serves. Whatever ethnic cleavage and castelike social structures are locally extant are present also in the community's educational institutions. Loomis (1943, p. 25) concluded in his early study:

The measures of cleavages used indicate strong tendencies for Spanish-American and Anglo students in the two New Mexico high schools studied to choose associates within their own ethnic groups. Some tendency was manifest from members of the minority ethnic group, whether English-speaking or Spanish-speaking, to reject the members of the majority ethnic group relatively more frequently than the reverse.

Parsons reports that ethnic cleavage characterizes the small California farming community of "Guadalupe" and that the school reflects and teaches separate roles to the children (1965, pp. 386–387):

. . . ethnically differentiated social patterns and associated stereotypes are learned by village children quite early. After the second grade, Anglo and Mexican-American children increasingly restrict their social choices to members of their own ethnic group. By the time they reach the upper elementary grades, there is virtually complete social separation between the two groups. That the children are aware of Anglo dominance is reflected in their leadership and prestige choices. Both Anglo and Mexican-American children choose Anglos as sources of prestige and both groups made significant choices of Anglos for positions of leadership. One of the most impressive features of the Guadalupe social structure is the high degree of functional integration exhibited by its major institutions in the maintenance of the traditional ethnic patterns. Whether they are at home, in church, at school, on the playground, shopping with parents, attending scout meetings, or watching the artichoke festival activities, children are provided with examples of the social positions they are expected to occupy and the roles they are expected to play. They are frequently shown that Anglos are best in everything and the Mexicans are the worst. Mexican-American children are rewarded in school and in church when they look and act like Anglos and punished (or ignored) if they look and act like Mexicans.

To what degree school personnel act to reinforce and perpetuate this cleavage differs with each institution and community. Interviewees support the contention, however, that teachers do reflect the stereotyping and expectations of Mexican Americans that characterize their community. Mexican American students interviewed report that teachers' behavior appears to reflect such attitudes. Students mention teachers asking the class "Why are you Mexican kids so lazy?" Others report that teachers show preference for Anglos and regularly choose them for school leadership roles. Parsons describes such a situation (1965, pp. 38–39). An Anglo boy was placed in charge of a small group of Mexican American boys after they had rushed from a classroom. He quotes his interview with the classroom teacher:

Teacher: Usually the kids are pretty good, but that day those boys were in a hurry to get out to the playground. . . . I remember thinking that the Mexican boys were going to make trouble if I didn't catch them—you know, they just can't follow directions. You always have to tell them what you want done. They seem to have a hard time remembering the rules. Anyway, I thought that if I told Johnny [the Anglo boy] to take the lead, they would have a good example of how to act.

Interviewer: Was there some reason why you chose Johnny specifically?

Teacher: Yes. He was right there of course. Besides that, I think Johnny needs to learn how to set a good example and how to lead others. His father owns one of the big farms in the area and Johnny has to learn how to lead the Mexicans. One day he will be helping his father and he will have to know how to handle the Mexicans. I try to help him whenever I can.

Physical education activities also reflect the school's isolationist and separatist actions: teams are divided on ethnic lines. Teachers responding to questions concerning this procedure commented:

Most said that it was "traditional" for the PE activities to be arranged along ethnic lines. Several said that ". . . most everything in Guadalupe is set up this way. It just seems like the natural thing to do. Anyway, the kids are more comfortable when they are playing with their own group." Many agreed that there was likely to be less "trouble" if the two ethnic groups were kept separate (Parsons, 1965, pp. 300–301).

Parsons contends that teachers and administrators "share the general Anglo stereotypes of Mexicans and . . . use these as the basis for organizing their perceptions of, and programs for, the Mexican pupils." In the summary of his dissertation, he mentions the following practices, among others, that contribute to ethnic differentiation of pupils and stereotyping with the school (pp. 306–307):

1. posting achievement charts (there is a tendency for students to use charts as a basis for judgments about classmates)
2. sending Mexican American pupils who "smell" out of the room
3. (establishing and continuing formal teacher-student relationships between Anglo teachers and Mexican American students, in contrast to the less formal relationship between Anglo teachers and Anglo students
4. placing the Mexican American students in a subordinate position to Anglo students by saying that Mexican Americans lack intelligence and need "the guidance of Anglos who know better" than they do

It is strongly recommended here that the Parsons study be read in its entirety for full understanding of its significance.

From recent observation and interviewing relative to interethnic relationships in school, one major, although perhaps unsurprising, conclusion can be reached: ethnic separation is general in Southwestern schools, its degree and nature determined by community social patterns and their reinforcement of educators. What control educators have over school intergroup relations reflects the views of the more conservative and powerful members of the Anglo community.

Where contact is permitted in mixed schools, adolescents are experimenting in new relationships; perhaps these youth are responding to the national climate of ethnic acceptance instead of reacting solely to the local social climate.

Students are, with varying degrees of success and speed, reported to be breaking down ethnic distinctions. This is particularly true in regard to inter-ethnic social contact between the sexes. Interviewees for this study commented that "serious" interethnic dating is increasing; adolescents seem to be more and more prone to date members of the other ethnic group. Mexican American-Anglo dancing is rarely openly discouraged by the school authorities, as it was reported to be formerly. Yet, the most "traditional" Mexican American students are reported to feel that such close contact is "bad." The same would be true of more "traditional" Anglo youth. A small number of Angloized Mexican Americans are acceptable as steady dates to the Anglos. Anglo boy and Mexican American girl (usually Angloized and "non-Mexican" appearing) is mentioned as being a common dating arrangement. Popular Mexican American boys date Anglo girls, but some stigma seems to be attached in this case. Even in the most castelike communities, "thrill dating" is reported to be practiced, usually as a clandestine activity that involves both sexes of both groups. Anglo girls test the "Latin lover" stereotype attributed to Mexican American boys; Anglo boys conversely investigate the "immorality" of Mexican American girls, a dating arrangement reported to be highly unacceptable to "traditional" girls. In spite of the increasingly permissive racial and sexual attitudes of today's youth, the majority of both ethnic groups seem to restrict their serious activities to members of their own group. Numerous teachers interviewed for this study mentioned their dislike of mixed dancing and dating. They contended that while the school can do little to discourage it, they themselves "take the offenders aside" (almost invariably the Anglo partners) and inform them of the stigma ascribed to such activities. Suffice it to say that boy-girl activities, perhaps the last stronghold of ethnic separation, are gradually changing. The more urban the environment, the more interethnic dating is evident.

Even in the communities that have the most rigid ethnic cleavage, there is a general acceptance by educators that any school-sponsored activity is open to all students. Academic and sports activities are rarely, if ever, closed to students because of their ethnic background. In only one school did an informant comment that certain sports activities were closed to "Mexicans:" tennis was "lily white," but in other sports, Mexican Americans were welcomed. In this same school, until a few years ago, debate and drama activities were open only to Anglos, but these restrictions were broken down by ambitious Mexican American students. It must be stressed that it is rarely school officials who encourage the breakdown of ethnic barriers; it is usually the case that they respond belatedly to the fact that students have already destroyed the obstacles established by tradition.

Social class barriers still exist and appear to be replacing some ethnic distinctions. School policy requiring fees or expenses to enter certain activities discourages lower-class students. In one school, for example, band is reported to be an elite activity. The school provides instruction only on an advanced level, thus excluding children who have not had private lessons. In other schools, students are required to buy equipment before they can go out for certain sports. While poor Mexican American star performers may be given such equipment by local athletic buffs, often the beginner desiring to try out is not. Acceptance into the Anglo or middle-class ethnic peer groups is usually associated with acceptable dress, again discouraging the entrance of otherwise acceptable poor Mexican Americans. Because most Mexican American children in most areas come from lower socioeconomic levels, economic factors discourage their full integration in school and student life. The degree and nature of these conditions depend on the actions of educators and the local community social climate, and variations among areas are great.

A few Mexican Americans in every mixed school are breaking down the ethnic barriers and are fairly well integrated socially. Even in many of the most conservative communities, these few children are on the fringe of acceptance into Anglo peer societies, but in some cases they remain essentially isolated or form small groups with equally marginal youngsters. In every secondary school observed during this study, however, clear lines of ethnic separation were visible in activities in which students were allowed free choice of associates.

Nothing stated or implied here is meant to refute the findings of those who have made empirical studies of ethnic cleavage in schools. Educational institutions continue, explicitly and implicitly, to teach children to conform to the expectations of the community. The previous paragraphs merely report that some of the more obvious sanctions of the school are probably disappearing. Implicit sanctions against ethnic "togetherness" are still evident; their full exposition must await detailed study of individual school and community situations.

Separation by Special Curriculum

Educators speak of the "special needs" of minority-group children and establish school programs to meet them. Most such needs are met by special classes or programs to overcome the "deficiencies" of Mexican American children. Such special compensatory education (usually remedial) programs are becoming almost universal in Southwestern schools. Because of institutional practices, however, some compensatory programs are tracks that tend to cause the isolation of Mexican American students. Compensatory classes that require attendance for a period or so a day (the child remains in regular mixed classrooms the rest of the day) are the most commonly encountered. This kind of program does not isolate the child to an unwarranted degree. Other compensatory programs do substantially isolate Mexican American children, who then tend to associate with their Mexican American peers and, in essence, attend a subschool within an ethnically mixed institution. Institutional organization and procedures can discourage or prohibit breaking out of such sections or groups.

Tracking

One of the prime functions of the school is to help society allocate status and role—that is, to separate individuals and treat them differently in order to fill the ever recurring social and economic slots. Few would argue that this sorting and sieving process is not essential. However, many educators and social scientists believe that present sorting practices are merely perpetuating status at birth—that members of the low social class leave school prepared to enter low-status social slots little different from those of their parents. If this is true, the school is indeed granting status on ascription rather than proscription, a situation that is counter to the values professed both by the school and by American society. Tracking is becoming an almost universal sieving device to treat students differentially. Great concern is manifest that the manner in which children are sorted into tracks, and the treatment they receive in them, almost predetermine their low achievement in school and their ultimate exit from school prepared only to assume low status.

In one form or another, rigid ability grouping is widely and increasingly practiced in Southwestern schools. For the purpose of this paper, a distinction is made between *grouping* and *tracking*. *Grouping* as used here refers to the practice of temporarily placing children in groups of like ability or interest— for example, "reading circles" within otherwise heterogeneous classrooms. These tend to be temporary and under the exclusive control of the classroom teacher. *Tracking* is an extreme form of ability grouping involving the permanent assignment of children to classrooms or sections (tracks) composed of individuals assumed to have like abilities, interests, or other characteristics. Tracking involves formal institutional decisions, planning, and curriculum organization; grouping does not. Grouping tends toward flexibility and student mobility and tracking toward inflexibility and student immobility. Track placement is usually institutionally determined on the basis of grades, teachers' observations, results of achievement and intelligence tests, counselors' observations, behavior records, or some combination of these factors. However, appraisal of intellectual capacity and achievement, whether by standardized tests or other means, is usually the principal determinant of track assignment. In these measured characteristics, Mexican American children tend to fall below school or national norms. The relationship between socioeconomic class and track placement is obvious; with few exceptions, families in lower socioeconomic classes rear children who score below average on the instruments that are used to predict or measure school achievement or intelligence.

Mexican Americans are greatly overrepresented in the lower-ability tracks of every mixed school I have observed; Anglos are overreppresented in the middle- and high-ability tracks. In one Texas "Mexican" high school, which serves very low income families, only the low and average tracks were found. In other district schools three or more tracks exist, including the accelerated. Tracking at the elementary school level is increasing; secondary school tracking is general and well established. Many tracked or homogeneous first-grade classes were observed. According to the Coleman report (1966, pp. 13–14), 37 percent of Mexican American children attend elementary schools where tracking is used, compared to 48 percent of the majority-group students. In the Southwest, 79 percent of the Mexican American secondary school students, contrasted to 82 percent of the Anglo secondary school students, attend schools that are tracked. Coleman et al. indicate (p. 112) that the percentages of Mexican American children in the highest and lowest tracks are almost identical to the "white" student percentages. This finding is opposed to everything that was observed in this study or reported to it. However, the degree to which Mexican Americans overpopulate low-ability tracks can only be determined by careful study of individual institutions.

It is common practice to divide children into two, three, or more tracks when they enter junior high school. At this level, vocational, occupational, and academic aspirations and aptitudes are usually considered. Aptitude and achievement, regardless of how they are determined, are matched with college or vocational requirements. Tracks are well established and stable by the end of junior high school. As in elementary school, Mexican American children are found to be in disproportionately high percentages in vocational and low-ability tracks (see Hickerson, 1962; Parsons, 1965). High school continues the practice; there it becomes almost impossible to move out of a track, principally because of institutional rigidity and the differing curriculums within tracks. Once a student is tracked at any level, movement upward is difficult. However, a first grader has a better chance to change tracks than a tenth grader.

Few educators interviewed in this study argued against tracking, the vast majority perceiving it as the fairest and most efficient way to handle intellectual difference and encourage maximum achievement. The general complaint was that present techniques to determine track placement are inadequate. A few informants saw tracking as a most insidious form of segregation and as a damning and self-fulfilling prediction. Educational institutions rely heavily on the results of group and individual psychometric instruments to sort children into tracks. Yet almost every educator interviewed argued that such instruments were neither reliable nor valid for culturally different children. A paradox exists. Most teachers and administrators argue that the school and the students would be better off, or equally well off, if they stopped relying on such instruments. But their institutions, well-oiled and self-perpetuating, continue to make decisions that affect the life chances of children on the basis of tests often agreed to be of questionable value. The difficulty in determining correct track placement for all children is obvious. Serious questions must be asked about the techniques used in "sorting" culturally different children. If the ethnic imbalance found in school tracks reflects valid innate intelligence appraisals, it would have to be concluded that Mexican Americans are indeed an "inferior race." But if intelligence is equally distributed among all groups of people, the techniques of measurement and placement must be rigorously examined.

Most educators contend that the practice of assigning students to tracks encourages maximum academic achievement, that tracking eliminates extremes of ability, thus providing a more "comfortable" learning environment, and that in the tracking system the curriculum can better be adjusted to "meet the needs" of students as a group and as individuals. Others argue against tracking, some contending that it has adverse effects on the attitudes, aspirations, and self-concepts of students. Still others say that it discourages students from reaching their maximum potential. No research concerning the effect of tracking on Mexican American students was found during the course of this study; other research on the effects of homogeneous grouping on student achievement and attitudes has been generally inconclusive.

A comprehensive survey of research relative to the effects of tracking was recently conducted by Goldberg, Passow, and Justman (1966). After carefully examining experimental research in Europe, as well as the United States, they concluded that:

Many of the issues concerning grouping [tracking] remain unresolved, and most questions are still unanswered despite 70 or 80 years of practice and at least 40 years of study. Insufficient and conflicting data are being used to support partisan views concerning the consequences of grouping, rather than to resolve the persistent issues (p. 21).

These researchers conducted their own carefully constructed and evaluated experimental study of elementary tracking in New York City. After analysis of the data collected, they stated:

. . . in predominantly middle-class elementary schools, narrowing the ability range in the classroom on the basis of some measure of general academic aptitude will, by itself, in the absence of carefully planned adaptations of content and methods, produce little positive change in the academic achievement of pupils at any ability level. However, the study found no support for the contention that narrow range classes are associated with negative effects on self-concept, aspirations, interest, attitudes toward school, and other non-intellective factors (pp. 167–168).

They concluded that tracking in itself is neither good nor bad:

Grouping can be, at best, ineffective, at worst, harmful. It can become harmful when it lulls teachers and parents into believing that because there is grouping, the school is providing differentiated education for pupils of varying degrees of ability, when in reality that is not the case. It may become dangerous when it leads teachers to underestimate the learning capacity of pupils at the lower ability levels. It can also be damaging when it is inflexible and does not provide channels for moving children from lower to higher ability groups and back again. . . . (p. 168).

Statements like the above are of particular relevance to Mexican Americans in Southwestern schools. It is the contention of this author, supported by observations and interviews, that most tracking adversely affects both teachers' and students' expectations and their subsequent behavior. Goldberg, Passow, and Justman found that tracking did not significantly affect the self-concept, attitudes, or aspirations of their middle-class sample. They point out that this may be true because low-track students did not differ socially or ethnically from high-ability sections, "thus did not perceive their status as socially or racially segregated with a concomitant degradation which such segregation may imply" (pp. 165–166).

Regardless of the effect on academic achievement, the track system, as commonly functioning now in the Southwest, unduly isolates Mexican American youth from equal-status interaction with others. The low-ability track status of most Mexican American children reinforces existing stereotypes. Mexican American children learn their future subordinate role in society by practicing it at school; Anglos reaffirm their superordinate position and find proof positive that Mexican Americans are indeed dull-witted, as stereotyped. Ethnic homogeneity in tracks supports group cleavage and maintains cultural difference and may in fact slow the process of acculturation. Thus the track system may run counter to the almost universally professed desire to Americanize foreign groups through the schools. Any practice that keeps two cultural groups apart inhibits one from learning the culture of the other.

Tracking is an ethical and legal, as well as an educational, dilemma. Critics ask whether it is the prerogative of the school to predict, and perhaps predetermine, success or failure in school and society. If American society is based on the inalienable right to succeed, can this right be abrogated by the practices of schools? Concomitant with the right to success is an equally inalienable right to fail. Some critics argue that as long as the school impinges on neither, American democracy is served. The track system may not be Constitutional. In a recent landmark decision, a United States District Court enjoined the city schools of Washington, D.C., from the practice. The decision was based on provisions of the Constitution insuring "due process" and "equal protection of the law." The court found that the track system deprived poor people and Negroes of rights guaranteed them and was, by its very nature, discriminatory. The information collected during the hearings, concerning the practice of tracking in Washington schools, could equally well describe the practice in most Southwestern schools. After extended hearings, the judge, in his closing remarks, said:

Even in concept, the track is undemocratic and discriminatory. Its creator admits it is designed to prepare some children for white collar, and other children for blue collar, jobs. Considering the tests used to determine which children should receive the blue collar special, and which the white, the danger of children completing their education wearing the wrong collar is far too great for this democracy to tolerate (United States District Court, Defendants' Civil Action No. 82–66, p. 177).

The impact of this decision on tracking in Southwestern schools can only be conjecture. To what degree Mexican American organizations will attempt recourse to the courts for redress depends on a multitude of social and political factors.

The previously widespread practice of assigning all Spanish-surname children to "Mexican rooms" within mixed schools is disappearing. Such extreme tracking is, in reality, a form of segregation, popular in areas where no "Mexican school" is maintained. Samora reported in 1963 (pp. 2–3): "Many communities have had their 'Mexican rooms' for years and years. This is segregation on pseudopedagogical grounds, the reasoning behind being that children who come to school who are Spanish-speaking should be placed in a room by themselves in order to learn English. One community in Colorado had such segregation through the first four grades as late as 1950. A neighboring community in Southern Colorado just abandoned their 'Mexican rooms' last year, after pressure was brought about by the local Spanish-speaking citizenry."

Some "slow" tracks in mixed schools are 100 percent Mexican American. It is difficult to determine whether this tracking is established for ethnic or "ability" reasons. A recent case in point involved a school district in the eastern part of New Mexico, an area with a long history of attempts at isolation or segregation of its Mexican American school population. Pressure from the G. I. Forum and other Mexican American organizations was brought to bear; state education department officials investigated, and explanation and solution were forthcoming. A Mexican American organization officer interviewed for this study inferred that the district will probably attempt the reestablishment of "Mexican rooms." This interviewee contended that such rooms were the result of ethnic prejudice rather than ability tracking.

"Special education" classes—that is, classes for children who are classified as mentally retarded—are an extreme form of tracking. Mexican Americans are greatly overrepresented in such classes. In the 10 California counties that have the largest number of Spanish-surname students, there were almost twice as many Spanish-surname children in special education as their percentage in the total school population would indicate. These 10 counties had an average Spanish-surname enrollment of 15.35 percent, and 30.09 percent of special-education students had Spanish last names. This figure includes one county, Alameda, in which 10.14 percent of the enrollment was Spanish surname and only 13.03 percent were in special education, thus lowering the percentage for all 10 counties together. In the California counties ranked 39 through 48 according to number of Spanish-surname students, it was found that the average enrollment of Spanish-surname students was 2.76 percent and there was an average of 3.63 percent in special education classes. The counties ranked 49 through 58 had so very few Spanish surnames that percentages were not calculated. Apparently the larger the Mexican American percentage within schools, the more likely it is that the children will be considered retarded. Perhaps when the number is small, minority-group children are considered more individually, and when the group is large stereotypes have more influence on judgments concerning individuals. Undoubtedly, a multitude of other forces are at play. For California as a whole, 13.30 percent of the school enrollment are students with Spanish surnames, and

26.62 percent of special-education students have Spanish surnames (California State Department of Education, 1967a). Observations made and questions asked during this study regarding the percentage of Mexican Americans in special-education classes throughout the Southwest revealed similar disproportions, although statistics are unavailable.

Although Mexican Americans are overrepresented in classes for the educable mentally retarded, they are not overrepresented in the lower levels of retardation. Mercer and other researchers are carefully compiling data on mental retardation in a California metropolitan area assumed to be representative of the nation. To date, much of their research is unpublished, but a letter of inquiry brought the following reply (1967):

When ethnic group was studied alone, there were disproportionately large numbers of identified mental retardates of Mexican-American and Negro heritage. The numbers ran almost five times higher among Mexican-Americans and three times higher among Negroes than would be expected from their percentage in the population. . . . However, when the data are analyzed by IQ level, the disproportionately high numbers in the Mexican-American and Negro populations are all concentrated in persons with IQ's over 50. They have, percentage-wise, no more mental retardates with IQ's under 50 than does the Anglo-American population. It appears from these preliminary findings that the higher rate of identified mental retardation among Mexican-American and Negro populations is accounted for by the so-called 'undifferentiated' types of retardation—the cultural-familial varieties which are highly related to social and economic deprivation.

The failure of standard psychometric instruments to measure Mexican American children validly is recognized as a principal reason for the overrepresentation of that ethnic group in special education, as well as in other low tracks. However, Palomares and Johnson conducted an experiment that demonstrated the crucial role played by the psychologist (1966, pp. 27, 29). Each author tested and interviewed a number of Mexican American children who had been recommended for EMR (Educable Mentally Retarded) class placement. After testing the children with standard instruments, "The non-Spanish-speaking psychologist [Johnson] found 24 of his 33 pupils (73 percent) eligible for EMR classes and recommended their placement. In contrast, the Spanish-speaking psychologist [Palomares] recommended that only 9 of his 35 pupils (26 percent) be placed in EMR classes. Clearly, examiners, as well as tests, differ, even though the pupils tested are similar and the tests used are the same." After a discussion of the psychometric instruments used, the authors concluded:

The importance of the psychologist as a variable in the evaluation process has received less attention than the tests. The results of this study indicate that the examiner is a most important variable. Whether the examiner does or does not speak Spanish may aid in his establishing rapport. . . . [The] examiner's years of experience and his understanding of school problems and cultural handicaps presented by those pupils are more important than his fluency with the language.

It is suspected that a larger-scale experiment would result in similar findings. As in so many educational endeavors, it is not so much a problem of the tools of the trade as it is a problem of the lack of understanding and skill of the workmen.

Teachers of special-education classes, and administrators in charge of such programs, were asked in the course of this study to estimate the number of Mexican Americans within such classes that were truly mentally deficient. Only one replied that all were; others estimated that from 50 to 80 percent rightfully belong in regular classes. An interesting point of view is espoused by a few educators, especially special-education teachers. While they recognize that most Mexican Americans in special classes are "sharp" and intelligent, they argue that it's better to allow them to stay where they are because in special education children receive the individual attention and psychological support lacking in regular classrooms.

CULTURAL EXCLUSION

Many educators in schools that have large percentages of low-status, non-Anglo-ized Mexican American students believe in rigid exclusion of all things Mexican. The higher the percentage of Mexican Americans in a given school, the more rigidly their culture, or the culture they are assumed to have, is excluded. Cultural exclusion takes many forms; by far the most obvious is the prohibition of anything that seems "foreign," including the carrier of culture itself, the Spanish language. A more subtle form of exclusion is curricular rigidity; schools with high percentages of Mexican Americans tend to adhere most carefully to state or local curriculum guides and grade-level requirements. Few institutions can thus modify their curriculums to include elements relative to the lives, expectations, experiences, or values of Mexican American children.

The culturally "Mexican" child has and does present the school with an extreme challenge to Americanize him and acculturate him, and do it as rapidly as possible: "The philosophy of the State and local school systems is imbued with the traditional middle-class Anglo-American value that all minority and immigrant groups should be required to abandon their native languages and cultures, give up their identity, and become absorbed as individuals into the dominant group, usually on a lower-class level. If any group resists full acculturation, it is regarded as somewhat uncivilized, un-American, and potentially subversive. There is a complete unwillingness to accept the idea that a native born American who happens to want to speak Spanish, German, or Polish, and to retain many of the values of his native culture, might well be a loyal American. As a result, the full force of the educational system in the Southwest has been directed toward the eradication of both the Spanish language and the Spanish-American or Mexican-American cultures" (Knowlton, 1965). In order to accomplish this eradication, almost every vestige of "Mexicanness" is excluded from the school environment. Christian and Christian (1966, p. 304) say that the Mexican American has been thought to be "a thorn in the side of educators" and that the

Spanish language and culture are "weeds to be uprooted so that English and 'our way of life' can flourish." To accomplish this uprooting a school must have a strong authority structure.

Authoritarianism

Schools with large percentages of Mexican American children tend to maintain order rigidly. "Mexican schools" tend to be less permissive than Anglo or mixed schools within the same district. Texas schools in general are more authoritarian than those of California, in part perhaps because California is less Southern in general attitude, its society is more open, and its educational philosophy is influenced to a greater degree by progressives.

The reliance on rigid control can be partially explained by recognizing that educators are insecure in their roles; their status is ambiguous or poorly defined. There is a perilous equilibrium of authority in the political structure of educational institutions. According to Waller (1932, pp. 10–11), the school:

. . . is a despotism threatened from within and exposed to regulation and interference from without. It is a despotism capable of being overturned in a moment, exposed to the instant loss of its stability and its prestige. . . . The authority of the school executives and the teachers is in unremitting danger from (1) students, (2) parents, (3) the school board, (4) each other . . . the members of these groups, since they threaten his authority, are to some extent the natural enemies of the person who represents and lives by authority. . . .

Culturally different students, especially adolescents, pose threats that are not encountered with other children. Their culture and language are unknown and "bad." It appears that the larger the percentage of Mexican American students the more necessary is the use of strong authority in order to control and "convert" them. Conforming behavior is insured by rigid sanctions against overt manifestations of "Mexicanness." Secondary school students are less tractable and more of a challenge than young children, and thus strong authority structures are most evident in junior and senior high schools.

The "No Spanish Rule"

The Southwest has a long history of prohibiting the speaking of Spanish in school. Social scientists and critics make a strong case that this is inferred by Mexican Americans to be a prohibition or negation of their homes and culture. The school curriculum, with few exceptions, is carried in English. Some educators believe that prohibiting Spanish encourages rapid acculturation. Institutional arguments for the "no Spanish rule" are well known and regularly stated: (1) English is the national language and must be learned; the best way to learn it is to prohibit Spanish; (2) bilingualism is mentally confusing; (3) the Spanish spoken in the Southwest is a substandard dialect; and (4) teachers don't understand Spanish. Although schools are undergoing change, the prohibition of Spanish is still widespread. The argument that Anglo staff cannot understand Spanish and therefore it should be prohibited is prevalent. Such statements as "I can't understand them" and "it's impolite to talk a foreign language in front of a person who doesn't speak it" are common. To what degree the institutional prohibition of Spanish speaking reflects these feelings is unknown. Perhaps the truth is that Spanish speaking is an extreme threat to authority: those in power don't know what the Mexican Americans are saying. Are they being disrespectful, impudent, using foul language, urging their peers to riot and revolt? The enemy is seen to be using undecipherable code and thus violating the established conventions of war (school regulations).

The constant and increasingly loud criticism of the "no Spanish rule," as well as the widespread advocacy of bilingual instruction, should have eliminated this problem by now. It has disappeared in some schools, yet still persists in many others. Many schools no longer actively prohibit Spanish—instead, they encourage English. Whether encouraging English is not prohibiting Spanish depends on the local situation. The difficulty of determining what is truly happening is obvious. In one all Mexican American junior high school in Texas the teacher's manual says: "Encourage the use of English. All teachers are expected to correct students using Spanish on school property." From observation and interviewing in this school, it appears that every effort is made to prohibit Spanish but that it is almost impossible to do so.

Numerous examples of imposing strong sanctions against Spanish are encountered. One almost wholly Mexican American district did so until recently when it received a substantial private grant to experiment with bilingual instruction. A state department of education official commented that apparently a principal consideration in awarding the grant was that English speaking was rigidly enforced in district schools.

"Spanish detention" still exists. At one Texas secondary school, students caught speaking Spanish are punished; if they persist, they are suspended and ultimately may be expelled. This school is approximately 100 percent Mexican American and serves a slum area. Commenting on this particular situation, a local university professor said: "They have what they call Spanish detention and if the child is caught speaking Spanish he is usually held after school for an hour, an hour and a half. If he persists, he may be spanked by the principal." In another Texas city, similarly strong sanctions were imposed by a Mexican American high school principal on his 99 percent Mexican American student body.

The younger the child, the less strict the rules; secondary schools appear to exert more pressure than elementary schools. Numerous Southwestern elementary schools are encouraging the speaking of Spanish, and doubtless the majority of Southwestern institutions no longer actively prohibit it. Many educators interviewed for this study saw the prohibition of Spanish as an anachronism and expressed hope that it would be universally abolished. Federal educational assistance under the Bilingual Education Act may encourage the elimination of such practices.

Other Behavioral Controls

The "no Spanish rule" is part of a whole syndrome of behavioral controls imposed by Southwestern schools. Institutions observed, with few exceptions, tend to prohibit other manifestations of "Mexicanness." As such manifestations are most prevalent among the unacculturated and the poor, strongest sanctions are found in schools serving that population. At the secondary level, Mexican American students often appear to be the very model of modern, middle-class teenagers. Elementary school students are much less so. In attempting to convert Mexican Americans to "our way of life," the school inadvertently creates an environment that does not reflect the real American culture. Rather, the climate is ideal middle class: the "unsavory" aspects of American culture, its diversity and controversial elements, are excluded. The enforcement of strict behavioral standards promotes serious culture conflict. Children learn a culture (language, values, expectations, roles, and so on) in their homes or from their peers. The school enforces another and different culture. In order to persist in the school, the child is required to drop the other culture, at least outwardly, and manifest the cultural characteristics demanded by the institution. Many cannot do this and flee the hostile school environment, removing themselves mentally in the elementary school years and physically as soon as local law or practice permits. (For more information about culture conflict and education see Allinsmith and Goethals, 1956; Spindler, 1963; Henry, 1960, pp. 267–305.)

Space does not permit full explanation of this rarely discussed topic. Suffice it to say that a rather extreme form of culture conflict may be apparent between the home and the school. The product of this conflict is usually the rejection of the new school values and mores, while the child remains essentially what his own culture dictates. However, with two sets of rules imposed, some children react negatively. Caught between two cultures, a significant number manifest signs of personal disorganization: "The conflict in directives is perhaps the source of the most serious difficulties in larger, less homogeneous societies, where the total educational process includes schooling as well as training in the home. Serious conflicts and deep-seated maladjustments may result from education [schooling] received at the hands of persons whose cultural or sub-cultural frames of reference differ" (Herskovits, 1957, p. 315). The student rejects one culture or the other; few can live with the internal conflict generated by two sets of values and mores. Since he has to live in a real society, he will often reject what he sees as the meaningless, artificial, and inappropriate culture taught at school.

Many subtle aspects of culture conflict affect Mexican Americans in school; examples of a few can be cited. Every culture or subculture teaches children what kind of man or woman they are expected to become. In some cases the male role learned by Mexican American boys is diametrically opposed to the behavior demanded by the middle-class-oriented school. Most secondary schools stringently prohibit boys from having long hair, sideburns, mustaches, wearing tight pants or shirts with more than the collar button open. Boys are suspended for violation of this code. Rubel (1966), in his study of a Mexican American community in Texas, indicated that rigid dress behavior is required in the local junior high school. An administrator stated that each Mexican American child is screened before he is permitted to enroll, and "if he wants to stay, he has to get a good haircut, cut off the sideburns." Another educator interviewed by Rubel concurred (p. 11):

We try to get kids' hair cut, get 'em to look like the rest; cut off the *pachuco* style . . . down in old Mexico they go around with their shirt unbuttoned all the way down to the navel, and then they tie it around their waist. They think it makes them look sexy. We can't have that here.

Rigid codes are enforced in most Southwestern schools. In a California junior high the vice-principal cut a seventh grader's long black locks:

Shame-faced and almost in tears, Mexican-born John Garcia took his seat in class. His head was bald in spots. He tried to hide the black tufts of hair that stuck out all over. There was an awkward silence. Garcia's humiliation was to serve as a warning to the other boys. Haircutting never works [John's English teacher commented later]. All this does is force them out of school; they've had this kind of treatment since the first grade. Why should they want to stay in? (Industrial Union Department, AFL-CIO, 1966, pp. 18–19).

The teacher pointed out that Anglo children are never given such treatment.

Children are regularly suspended, and ultimately excluded, for "non-American" physical appearance. A school social worker in Texas interviewed said this: "One of the biggest problems that I have in my job is to go and ask a father to tell his son to cut his hair in an Angloized way, with the short sideburns and no bush on top, and the father is wearing his hair exactly like the son. About the only thing you can tell him is that, 'Look we don't like this at school because children don't dress like that and we don't want the children to look like adults.' This is really stepping on eggshells." The implications of conflict are obvious. The school enforces a kind of conformity that may violate what some Mexican American boys accept as manliness. As dress codes appear to be more rigorously enforced in lower-social-class schools, the brunt of this practice falls on those most prone to adhere to divergent dress or grooming.

Psychologists say that a child's name is perhaps a first touchstone of self-identity. Yet schools continue to change the Spanish given names of children as they enter. Many parents do desire to use English names, but many see nothing improper about the Spanish Christian names conferred at baptism. Teachers apparently do. *Jesús* is almost invariably changed to Jesse; after all, good middle-class teachers couldn't say "Jesus, I want you to be quiet and sit down." One does wonder, however, why they couldn't use *Jesús*. *Maria* becomes Mary, *Juan*

John, *Roberto* Bobby, and so on. Although it may seem unimportant, it can be argued that the Angloization of Spanish Christian names may do psychic harm. Such practices reflect the way the school sees the Mexican American child and are part of the syndrome of culture conflict as encouraged by the school in its attempts to obliterate things Mexican. A question concerning Anglo perception of Mexican culture must be raised. If a little French boy named *Pierre* entered a Southwestern school, would teachers change his name to Peter? Probably not, on the grounds that the French are "cultured people." Mexican Americans are not and must be transmuted as soon as possible into full-fledged Americans.

Modesty, of a very special nature, is taught in some traditional Mexican American families. Girls learn not to expose their bodies. Medical examination by male doctors is abhorred, as is nudity in front of other females. Group showering is required in practically all secondary school physical education classes. To force a Mexican American girl who has been taught this kind of modesty to disrobe and shower in the presence of others is a direct affront to strongly ingrained beliefs. Girls are reported to form circles around their disrobing peers and use other devices and ruses to protect their modesty. In this case, the Anglo core value of cleanliness, institutionalized, confronts traditional Mexican modesty.

Ramirez and Taylor conducted research relative to the influence of identification with traditional Mexican American culture and student "success" in northern California junior high schools and senior high schools. In a preliminary report, Ramirez (1967b) contends that there is little doubt that some Mexican American negative feelings toward school and some of their poor achievement in school are attributable to culture conflict. He states:

By assessing attitudes toward education and reviewing the cumulative files of 300 Mexican-American students, the researchers were able to identify those students who are experiencing most difficulty in adjusting to school setting and, thus, seemed to be those most likely to drop out in the near future. . . . These students were interviewed, observed in class and were asked to tell stories relating to pictures depicting students, teachers, and parents interacting in a school setting. The stories told to these pictures were very revealing in terms of value conflicts and their effect on the adjustment of the student and his attitude toward the school.

While finding that all Mexican Americans do not hold traditional ethnic values, Ramirez did demonstrate that culture conflict was apparent in some students. With these students, the value orientations that cause the most conflict with the school's expectations include those previously mentioned plus the fact that the traditional culture:

. . . teaches the adolescent to be loyal to his family group. This frequently results in subordination of the student's educational goals when the family is in need of help. . . .

Ramirez concludes that traditional Mexican students bring:

. . . values with [them] to the school which in many cases are in direct opposition to those of their teachers, counselors and principals. Not only must the bicultural student face conflicts at school; he also meets conflicts in the home when the values he learns at school are opposed by parents. He is thus continually faced with the ominous choice of conforming or quitting. This usually results in feelings of insecurity and eventually in negative feelings toward the school which he comes to see as the source of his frustration and ambivalence.

The previous examples of conflict induced or encouraged by school policies and practices concentrate on children reared in the "traditional" Mexican American family. These families are becoming less common in much of the Southwest; perhaps most Mexican American children grow up in families that are themselves transitional. Minority-group families run the gamut from the traditional to the highly *agringado*. Between these poles, all number of possible variations of transitional culture exist. With the possible exception of the *agringado*, who meshes quite well with the school's expectations and often with his Anglo peers, traditional and marginal children manifest a strong proclivity to form tight ethnic peer groupings. Mexican American children reaching adolescence and caught between quite divergent cultures at home and at school tend to place great reliance on their peers for psychic support, value orientation, and roles. In a sense, these peer societies form their own transitional subcultures. The ethnic peer group exerts a tremendous influence on many Mexican American teenagers' lives and on their success in school. For many Mexican American youngsters, the peer group is a primary agency of socialization. The outward manifestations of peer-society membership are likely to be bizarre: new argots, unusual dress, "peculiar" behavior, and so on.

The ethnic peer group functions in numerous ways. It provides sanctuary and protection in schools, establishes acceptable and unacceptable behavior, ameliorates certain kinds of anxiety, defines male and female roles, and carefully prescribes the types of academic success and school participation deemed acceptable. Robles' 1964 study of a California junior high school that draws its Mexican American students from a *barrio* elementary school clearly describes how the ethnic peer group affects the upwardly mobile Mexican American student's school behavior. As a result of strong peer allegiance, there is:

. . . a noticeable lack of participation, avoidance and lack of interaction with the total student life of the school . . . this behavior stems from . . . peer group pressures because most of the mobility oriented students show a higher aspirational level [and more interaction] when the peer group is not present (pp. 66–67).

The effect of the ethnic peer group is often to set low school aspiration levels and thus adversely affect grades and achievement. Robles points out that conscientious school personnel can accomplish much to modify such situations if they understand the total social function of the ethnic peer group.

Attitudes and actions relative to ethnic peer groups vary in the Southwest. Most educators interviewed during this study indicated that they saw such groups as negative and detrimental to the school and the individuals involved. In most cases, the schoolmen see their role as suppressive, and strong regulations against outward manifestations of membership in these groups are exercised. In many secondary institutions there is literally a hot war in process between ethnic peer groups and the school. In many cases efforts are made to destroy, rearrange, or modify the groups; they are often held to be delinquent or involved in some form of antisocial behavior. Little understanding of the role such groups play in the lives of culturally marginal Mexican American adolescents was demonstrated by the schoolmen interviewed.

The ethnic peer group may be seen as another threat to stability and the authority structure of the school. The more divergent the group's behavior, the greater the threat is seen to be. The middle-class peer group, although it is not totally acceptable to school management, is not so threatening as the ethnic peer group so characteristic of urban slums: "While cars, dates, and athletic success are far more valued than scholastic competence, even in middle-class schools, still teachers find it easier to maintain order within the schoolroom and the children do manage to acquire more of the subject matter taught there. The big difference between the situation of slum and suburb is not the literacy of the parents, but the meshing of values of parents and teachers. By providing an understanding support of their children in school, parents reduce the necessity of the child to rely so heavily on his peers in his struggle with educational authority" (Wax, Wax, and Dumont, 1964, p. 97). The values of many Mexican Americans do not mesh with those of the school, and low-status Mexican American parents do not lend the essential support.

The roles, values, languages, and so forth learned from the ethnic peer society, like those learned in the "traditional" home, are regularly prohibited by schools, since the newly learned peer culture is often diametrically opposed to the middle-class expectations of many teachers and administrators. Again, conflict results: what is meaningful to the child is prohibited by the institution. Some institutions attempt individual counseling to "save the better youngsters" from their peers. This attempt, usually a you-know-what-is-right-and-good-for-you appeal by counseling staff, fails to recognize the tremendous social and psychological pressure on the child. The school's rigid prohibition of the outward manifestation of peer-group membership creates an intolerable situation for some adolescents. Rather than treat such manifestations of marginality as normal and useful, the school declares open warfare. In so acting, it denies or contradicts what the child is doing to find his place in society and learn his own identity. It drives the peer group underground and often drives its members from school.

Some educators, however, do see the strong ethnic peer group as normal, understandable, and useful. Counselors at one California high school visited are making a sustained effort to use the peer group itself as a tool to raise achievement and increase "positive" school participation. They are attempting through nondirective counseling techniques to reorient the groups without destroying their integrity.

Even in the most authoritarian institutions, some traces of Mexican culture are permitted and sometimes encouraged; items encouraged usually reflect the controlling Anglos' acceptance and perhaps idealization of certain aspects of the Mexican culture. Music, art, the celebration of certain Mexican festivals and holidays, and so on are often promoted. Thus the educator's stereotype of the quaint or picturesque Mexican culture is sustained, and Mexican American children are encouraged to become what educators think they already are.

The lower the social class of the student body, the more rigidly the child is expected to conform to the educator's image of the perfect middle-class Anglo teenager. The predominantly Mexican American secondary schools in Texas observed were extremely rigid in their prohibition of all but "perfect" (idealized middle-class) behavior. California schools were much less so. Yet, in all states visited, *minority* or *mixed* lower-class schools appeared more restrictive than middle-class institutions. Many Texas slum minority schools are ultraconformist, tending to operate by the book. Classroom discipline is rigid, children speak when spoken to, halls and playgrounds are patrolled and rigidly controlled, gum chewing can lead to suspension, dress codes are strictly enforced, hair is short, dresses long. The Mexican American teenager who cannot or will not conform is pushed out early in his junior or senior high school career. The rest of the children appear to be "ideal" middle-class teenagers. Unfortunately, rigidity of behavioral standards and the conflict such standards engender drive many traditional, transitional, or low-status Mexican Americans from school.

The Curriculum

The three components of the school curriculum—its content, method, and sequence—are drawn from the culture carried by a society. The content is drawn from the history, knowledge, skills, values, expectations, roles, laws, and so forth of parent generations. Teaching methods reflect how members of a given society commonly teach children, as well as how they teach their children to learn. Sequence is made up from analyses of the stages of development at which the children of a given society are exposed to and internalize certain cultural items.

In American society, school curriculum is based on an analysis of the middle class. The curriculum is usually somewhat dated, even for middle-class children, but it does appear to approximate at least the "ideal" culture of the average home. When this same curriculum is employed with culturally divergent children, severe reactions can be anticipated. What may well be relevant to the "normal" or "standard" American child may be irrelevant to another subsociety's child. In extreme cases, what is taught the "standard" child is directly contrary to what has already been learned by the "different" child. Many educators believe that the failure of the school curriculum to reflect and supplement the home curriculum (culture) is responsible for many Mexican Americans' failure in school.

A number of comparisons can be made between disadvantaged, predominantly minority, schools and more advantaged Anglo or mixed schools. Differences pertaining to behavior have already been cited. In general, the lower the social class and the higher the ethnic density in the school, the more rigidly teachers adhere to state or local curriculum guides and texts. Difference is equally apparent between high- and low-ability tracks within the same school. The lower the track level, the more bookish, less oral, more rote, more dogmatic, more memoristic the techniques of instruction appear to be. The higher the social class of the school, the more progressive the approach (or at least the more acceptable in contemporary education theory). The learning environment of many predominantly Mexican American schools or classes can best be characterized as dull and uninspired. Many Mexican American classes observed in this study consisted almost exclusively of recitation of facts, truths, values (the fable of the ant and the grasshoppr is popular for young children). At high schools, numerous "discussions" were observed; in reality they were usually only recitations.

Rigid adherence to local or state grade-level requirements contributes to the narrowness of the curriculum content so obvious in many disadvantaged classrooms. If it is required that certain first-grade texts must be read, for example, a supreme effort is usually made to get each child to read at that level. The skills of reading are emphasized and the time for other activities reduced. If a certain number of "concepts" must be learned in order to move to the next grade, memoristic methods are often resorted to almost exclusively. If an average child is deemed to need x number of words to be promoted to second grade, teachers tend to teach only these words. The long-established practices of inflexible grade-level requirements contribute to curriculum rigidity and memoristic teaching, and cause a large number of Mexican American children to repeat grades and thus become overage.

If it is thought essential to devote maximum time and effort to teaching those skills on which grade level and promotion are based, little time remains for teaching anything else that might be relevant and intrinsically rewarding. What little intrinsic reward in the form of relevant learning experience may be found in high-ability or middle-class classrooms is all too often lacking in the lower tracks. Low-status children are overrepresented in low-ability groups; in many areas, the lowest-ability group is the Mexican Americans, and they thus suffer most from the "good intentions" of teachers and the system.

Couple the above situation with the fact that learning experiences in school may be out of sequence for low-status minority-group children, and another problem is evident. The sequence of the curriculum is based on analysis of the children of the dominant society; Mexican American children may be learning cultural items in their subsociety at a different period in their lives. It may be true that middle-class children, as a group, are "ready" to read English at six but that Spanish speakers are not, and it may be true that many low-status children are "ready" to learn the decimal and money systems at five while middle-class children are not ready until later. Yet curriculum sequence is rarely substantially modified for culturally different learners. When the content is out of sequence for a group, the school inadvertently reduces the relevancy of the learning experience, making such "learning" unnatural and exclusively dependent on the rewards school or teacher offers. Intrinsic reward for school learning is reduced. It appears that this situation is all too common.

Regardless of the general rule, numerous oral, spontaneous, and exciting schoolroom situations were observed. However, these exceptions neither prove nor disprove the rule. Texas schools are again the extreme example; few such very "traditional" classes were observed in California and the other states. Yet, in all states visited it was generally true that the higher the ethnic density of the class, the more traditional the teacher-learner relationship and the more rigid the adherence to set curriculum.

Lack of connection between home and school culture has long been recognized as a problem. Curricular irrelevancy was seen as a principal problem to be solved as early as 1941: "Such subject matter as geography, history, and health, is taught in terms that are foreign to the [Spanish-Americans]. During the school year of 1939–40, the pupils of El Cerrito [a small rural New Mexico community] worked out posters and other projects based on such subjects as transportation in Boston and importance of navigation in the growth of Chicago. Under such a curriculum as this, it is small wonder that pupil interest is at a minimum and that progress is slow" (Leonard and Loomis, 1941, p. 53). Many educators continue the theme today, contending that low-status children's lack of interest in school is partially due to the fact that they see little or no connection between what they learn in school and live at home. As has often been reported, school readers tell stories about families of different color and culture. For example, stories about fathers going to the office and children returning to beautiful bedrooms and homes are seen as irrelevant to low-status children. Attempts are being made to rectify this situation, and many new texts and primers are being published. Admirable as this is, it is only a superficial remedy for the problem of irrelevancy and culture conflict. The curriculum of the school is rarely substantially modified by using "paint their faces brown" texts. To change the curriculum radically, to incorporate relevant and nonconflicting items from the Mexican American home culture may actually be impossible for the average middle-class teacher or school system. Many schoolmen would see incorporating culture they consider to be "bad," negative, or foreign as supporting the very life-styles they and their schools are dedicated to eradicate. A real quandary exists.

The curriculum is permeated with the assumed ideals, not necessarily the mores, of middle-class culture. Extreme cleanliness, respect for the law, unfamiliar manners and morals, and so forth continue to confront Mexican American children in school. They are expected to learn (memorize) these things in order to gain a grade or teacher approval. Perhaps such exercises are only irrelevant to the child and what is so learned will soon be forgotten. However, certain conflicts are created. For example, a Head Start teacher interviewed was appalled by the lack of respect for the police manifest in her Mexican American children. To overcome this, a large blue "Policeman Sam" some five feet tall was constructed of cardboard. Children were drilled on how Sam helped them, protected them, and was a friend of the family. The children observed seemed eager to please the pleasant teacher and were rewarded for their recitations of how good Sam was by her acceptance and praise. Policemen may be seen in a totally different way at home, and a child might be severely punished for his school-taught reply to his father's question about what he is learning in school. Children are taught the same nursery-rhyme stories that are used with middle-class children; the maxims of Anglo middle-class culture are drilled and drilled. Many of these are probably irrelevant; some may be conflicting.

Cleanliness is an obsession with many teachers, Mexican American as well as Anglo. It is taught to minority-group children by explaining the reason for it (to wash away germs), by having them constantly wash their hands, by drill in brushing teeth, and by rote memorization of information and maxims reinforcing cleanliness. Clean is translated into *limpio* (with little understanding that *limpio* does not carry the same cultural meaning as *clean; limpio* means clean in the scrubbed way while *clean* involves a whole set of moral connotations). No stone is left unturned to insure the Americanization of Mexican American children in this regard. One elementary school teacher interviewed advocated the forceful bathing of "dirty Mexican kids because it will teach them how nice it feels to be clean," a very doubtful result. A school social worker commenting on his district teachers said: "We have the type of teacher that wouldn't let a Mexican child hug her without looking at the hair to see if there are lice."

Nutritional practices of the children are causes for indignation and elicit strenuous efforts to modify food preferences. A Texas school principal, complaining about the children's refusal to eat vegetables, commented that beans and carrots seemed to be the only vegetables they would eat. In the same school, children were prohibited from access to hot pepper sauces; only the teachers' table had such condiments. "We don't serve children such highly seasoned food because it's bad for the digestion," commented the principal. The central cafeteria of a large district, about 85 percent Mexican American, served half an avocado and a carton of milk on the same lunch to its thousands of students. In this area, many believe that these two foods eaten together cause *empacho* (a digestive upset). Understandably, many children left one or the other item. The consternation over the waste can be imagined. An Anglo home economics teacher was observed in a junior high school as she explained a well-balanced dinner to a group of Mexican American girls. The children were confounded that the menu included a "hot" and a "cold" food, a practice they had been taught was guaranteed to produce *empacho*. The girls questioned the teacher concerning this and were answered with an "I never heard such superstitious nonsense" argument. This teacher as well as the others mentioned above seemed totally unaware of the influence of culture on the stomach. Proper dinner service is emphasized, as are table manners: "A person just can't eat with a *tortilla* among nice people." This may be in considerable conflict with what "nice people" do at home.

Inflexibility and rigidity of school practices and curricular irrelevancy or conflict are seen as interrelated aspects that function to the detriment of culturally different Mexican American children. Ungraded, or multilevel, primary grades are becoming increasingly popular as a solution to grade-level rigidity. Whether in fact this reorganization significantly modifies the present situation requires analysis of each school. If nine levels with rigid set requirements are substituted for the previous three grades, it is doubtful that any substantial change is made. However, if there are flexible requirements for the levels, there may be real change. A Texas superintendent interviewed implied that his newly instituted upgraded primary system was, in essence, a subterfuge. He said that it was essentially a tracking device, one of its advantages being that parents do not attach as much stigma to their children's repeating a level, or remaining there longer than normal, as they do to failing a grade and being retained.

An obvious aspect of rigidity is the traditional school year. The September-to-June calendar precludes many migrant and other agriculturally dependent families from sending their children to school for the full academic year. This fact, coupled with rigid grade-level requirements, is partially responsible for the large number of migrant children who fail to be promoted. Only recently are schools beginning to adjust to the migrants' calendar, but most migrant schools observed for this study appear not to be adjusting their regular grade-level requirements, curriculum, or school policies and practices.

Few educators interviewed are aware of the ramifications of curricular irrelevancy and conflict. However, many recognize such obvious problems as that the American history taught in school may be in serious disagreement with the history of Mexico and the Southwest taught at home. Many see the inherent problems of a curriculum taught solely in English, especially if little is done to teach Spanish-speaking children the language of the school. Unfortunately, thoughtful analysis of the effect on Mexican American children of curriculum, policies, and practices is rarely evident. The failure of most educators to recognize the influence of conflict on personality and behavior as well as the conditions permitting one cultural group to accept innovations from another causes a tremendous loss of time and energy. The school sees the children that won't accept "our way of life" as "stubborn," failing to understand the massive support of the diverse Mexican American subsocieties and subcultures that reinforce this "stubbornness."

DIFFERENCES IN PERCEPTIONS AND FACILITIES

Great differences exist among educational institutions in the Southwest as well as among schools within the same local administrative structure. This section delves into some of these differences. Little hard evidence can be presented in some of the areas discussed, and therefore much that is written here relies on impressions gained from observations.

Teachers' Views

Teachers are not unlike other middle-class citizens. They almost universally see their role and the school's to be one of encouraging the poor and foreign to become full-fledged middle-class Americans. They genuinely and willingly desire to help Mexican Americans, but they don't necessarily like them or like or accept them as they are. Friedenberg contends that (1967, pp. 194–195):

Between the traditions and staff of the public school, on the one hand, and the 'culturally deprived' among its clientele, on the other, there is real conflict and often enmity. It is frustrating to deal with these children who ignore, reject, or misinterpret the schools effort to transform them, who find its offerings meaningless, and are unmoved or annoyed by the arguments it offers on its own behalf; who cheerfully shrug off its pretentions. . . .

Indeed the "culturally deprived" and many Mexican Americans do reject institutional endeavors. They may be openly hostile to the school and what it teaches, and they may find its curriculum irrelevant. Many reject the best efforts of the institution by removing themselves mentally in the intermediate grades and physically at the earliest practical moment.

Such rejection encourages teachers' frustration and often covert dislike. Teachers, being human, tend to blame the student for his failure to "learn" what they "teach." Either the peculiar (abnormal) personality characteristics of the individual or the equally strange cultural characteristics of the group are seen to prohibit internalization of the curriculum presented or the social norms taught. Some teachers see the rejection of school as personal failure—they have not "reached the child." The two views are equally frustrating. On the one hand, the child is seen to reject the school because of his home culture or personality, two things exceedingly difficult to modify. On the other, the teacher sees herself as failing, which is particularly damning because she may feel she has conscientiously tried everything. The frustrations inherent in the attempt of one individual or institution to teach another person or group to modify values, modes of life, language, and so forth, can easily be translated into contempt. Poverty and foreignness are acceptable as long as they go away. It is exceedingly difficult to understand, accept, like, or treat as social equals the natives who reject the sincere efforts of the missionaries.

Two major views of the Mexican American exist among Southwestern teachers. The "failure of the culture" idea is gaining wide acceptance, as discussed earlier in this study. A few educators are able to grasp the full implication of the influence of the home culture on children's personality and school performance; but most use the concept of cultural difference to justify the school's failure. The other most common perception involves an undifferentiated view of all children.

Many teachers contend that children are generally alike, regardless of their backgrounds, and that school is equally meaningful to all. Many of these teachers have had little experience with diverse ethnic or poverty groups, nor has their training provided insights into such matters. In 1959, Ulibarri questioned teachers in New Mexico about their awareness and sensitivity to cultural differences and found that teachers generally manifest little real awareness of the differences among Mexican American, American Indian, and Anglo cultures or of the influence each has on children. Most teachers expressed the opinion that school was equally significant and meaningful to children of all three groups (Ulibarri, 1959, pp. 103–105). To what degree a repetition now of Ulibarri's formal research would reach the same conclusion is unknown, but many of the teachers interviewed for this study demonstrated practically no real knowledge of the influence of culture on children's personality and behavior.

The views that Mexican Americans' problems in school may be caused by their individual personalities, by the failure of the culture, or by the failure of teachers, all lead to frustration. The first two views tend to encourage continued and intensified efforts to modify the child; all encourage the development of the common teacher attitude that Mexican American children just can't learn. Too many well-intentioned teachers have given up, contending that failure will continue until the home environment changes, and that until that time there is little hope for all but the exceptional lower-class minority-group child. The pervading atmosphere of almost every school with a high concentration of Mexican Americans that was visited in this study was one of pessimism. Others have received similar impressions. Knowlton (1965, pp. 3–4) reports comments that Mexican American children lack the ability to learn. He writes that teachers have said, "Look, so many Spanish-American children have to repeat the first grade two or three times. They just can't learn as fast as Anglo-American children. They lack the native ability to do schoolwork. If you don't believe me, just check their test scores." Many educators have reached this point of view after years of sustained effort. As one California junior high school teacher interviewed for this study phrased it:

We will keep trying . . . but there is nothing you can do with these kids, they can't discuss, they can't talk, all you can do is give them seat work to keep them busy and keep them under control.

This perspective often provides justification for rote methods used, as well as for the rigid classroom control so often observed.

Only recently has empirical research tended to corroborate the widely held belief, or suspicion, that teachers' perceptions of children's ability is a crucial factor in academic achievement. Previous experimental evidence has indicated that animals perform better on tests of learning when the experimenters are falsely informed that certain animals have been bred for intelligence. Drawing on earlier research with animals and such phenomena as the placebo and Hawthorne effects (that is, the influence of nonspecific factors on behavior), Rosenthal and Jacobson (1968) studied the effect of teachers' high expectations on children's academic behavior, as measured by standardized instruments. A random sample of children in a south San Francisco low-social-status elementary school were falsely predicted to make dramatic gains in IQ and general class work. Only the teachers, not the parents, were informed of the "blooming" or "spurting" predicted for individual children. The researchers' carefully controlled study rather clearly demonstrated that the false predictions were self-fulfilling and that the experimental groups of children did make substantial gains in IQ.

In addition to the general findings of the rise in IQ for the "spurters," a number of points made in the Rosenthal and Jacobson study (pp. 174–178) are of special interest here.

1. The expectancy advantage—the degree to which IQ gains by the "special children" exceeded gains by the control group children—was particularly evident among younger children (first and second graders).
2. Older children who may have been more difficult to influence (did not demonstrate the same degree of expectancy advantage as younger children) may have been better able to maintain their advantage autonomously.
3. While it was anticipated that slow-track children (the school divided children into three tracks) would be most affected by teachers' expectations, it was found that the middle-track children "spurted" the most. However, the other tracks were not much behind during the first year.
4. "After the first year of the experiment and also after the second year, the Mexican children showed greater expectancy advantages than did the non-Mexican children, though the difference was not significant statistically. One interesting minority-group effect did reach significance, however, even with just a small sample size. For each of the Mexican children, magnitude of expectancy advantage was computed by subtracting from his or her gain in IQ from pretest to retest, the IQ gain made by the children of the control group in his or her classroom. These magnitudes of expectancy advantage were then correlated with the 'Mexicanness' of the children's faces. After one year, and after two years, those boys who looked more Mexican benefited more from their teachers' positive prophecies. Teachers' pre-experimental expectancies for these boys' intellectual performance were probably lowest of all. Their turning up on a list of probable bloomers must have surprised their teachers. Interest may have followed surprise and, in some way, increased watching for signs of increased brightness may have led to increased brightness."
5. "In addition to the comparison of the 'special' and the ordinary children on their gains in IQ it was possible to compare their gains after the first year of the experiment on school achievement as defined by report-card grades. Only for the school subject of reading was there a significant difference in gains in report-card grades. The children expected to bloom intellectually were judged by their teachers to show greater advances in their reading ability. Just as in the case of IQ gains, it was the younger children who showed the greater expectancy advantage in reading scores. The more a given grade level had benefited in overall IQ gains, the more that same grade level benefited in reading scores."
6. "All teachers had been asked to rate each of their pupils on variables re-

lated to intellectual curiosity, personal and social adjustment, and need for social approval. In general, children who had been expected to bloom intellectually were rated as more intellectually curious, as happier, and, especially in the lower grades, as less in need of social approval. Just as had been the case with IQ and reading ability, it was the younger children who showed the greater expectancy advantage in terms of their teachers' perceptions of their classroom behavior. Once again, children of the medium track were most advantaged by having been expected to bloom, this time in terms of their perceived greater intellectual curiosity and lessened need for social approval."

7. "When we consider expectancy advantages in terms of perceived intellectual curiosity, we find that the Mexican children did not share in the advantages of having been expected to bloom. Teachers did not see the Mexican children as more intellectually curious when they had been expected to bloom. There was even a slight tendency, stronger for Mexican boys, to see the special Mexican children as less curious intellectually. That seems surprising, particularly since the Mexican children showed the greatest expectancy in IQ, in reading scores, and for Mexican boys, in overall school achievement. It seemed almost as though, for these minority-group children, intellectual competence may have been easier for teachers to bring about than to believe."

The importance of this study cannot be overstated; however, as with other research, the questions raised are as important as those investigated. The specific items concerning teachers' expectations of and behavior toward Mexican Americans (especially boys) are particularly loaded.

Teachers' pessimism varies with the grade and the subject they are teaching and with the environment or morale of the particular school. Primary-grade teachers tend to be quite optimistic concerning Mexican American children's ability to learn; intermediate and secondary teachers more commonly have given up. Indeed during the primary years, minority-group children do tend to perform fairly well, appear to be quite "well adjusted," and seem to be "happy" in school. In the upper elementary grades, rejection of the school begins and "adjustment problems" become more evident. Teachers' pessimism is often allayed by introducing new curriculums or perhaps modifying the curricular content or teaching techniques. Teachers often respond to these changes with enthusiasm and optimism. Regardless of the nature of the innovation, a placebo effect may be engendered; if the children become involved in the experimental atmosphere, a Hawthorne effect may be implemented. If teachers' optimism persists, school social climate may well be modified to the benefit of the children's achievement. However exciting such situations are, they happen only exceptionally.

Other points of view discourage teachers' efforts and optimism. A few teachers take what might be called the "happy slave" perspective, arguing that the school should not attempt to modify Mexican Americans substantially since they are perfectly content with their way of life and their low socioeconomic status. They argue that the social distance between Anglos and the minority group is the natural order and should be maintained. Such teachers don't dislike "Mexicans"—they "understand" them and their "childlike" ways. Individuals subscribing to this view think that outside interference disrupts the natural order inherent in their castelike society. As one Texas school counselor interviewed for this study said:

Only a few days ago a teacher told me that these Mexican American children don't know their place: "Why they are just the rowdiest people I've ever seen—they don't act typically Mexican. Since you got all those Federal programs and all these aids, why they think they own this school.

According to the "happy slave" view, the school is a service to the Mexican American and the Anglo alike. The rudimentary literacy acquired by the average Mexican American is essential to his position as an efficient worker. The extreme variety of this view is blatant prejudice, dropping the "happy-go-lucky" idea and replacing it with strong convictions of racial or cultural inferiority. This kind of prejudice is not common, but it is encountered in some individuals, especially in areas strongly influenced by the Southern ethos. Neither of these two views encourages equal-status interaction between the groups; both encourage a fatalistic view of Mexican American children's potential in school or prospects for future "success" in society.

Tracking Mexican Americans into lower-ability sections encourages academic failing. Teachers' low expectations and subsequent rigid, rote, memoristic, and dull teaching promote students' rejection of school and what it teaches. Tracking encourages a ". . . sense of personal humiliation and unworthiness. [Students] react negatively and hostilely and aggressively to the educational process. They hate teachers, they hate schools, they hate anything that seems to impose upon them this denigration, because they are not being respected as human beings, because they are sacrificed in a machinery of efficiency and expendability. . . ." (Clark, 1965, p. 128). The track system fails Mexican American students, if not all students, and encourages them to reject the school. This rejection is usually rationalized by educators as the failure of the home and culture. Teachers argue that one can expect little from such backgrounds and react negatively and defensively to the hostility manifest in their students, a condition that in turn was at least partially engendered by such school practices as tracking. It is a vicious circle. Unfortunately, the most common teacher view of Mexican American children is at best one of pessimism and at worst one of contempt.

Mexican American Teachers

It would appear logical to assume that Mexican American teachers would, as a group, be accepting and understanding of their own group's children. Having gone through similar life situations, they would tend to understand the living and learning situations of their group's children. And it is logical to assume that Mexican American children would look up to such teachers and use them as social role models. However, observations of Mexican American teachers and interviews of students during this study encourage the questioning of such assumptions.

Spanish-surname teachers generally subscribe to the views of Anglo teachers. Even the racist position finds a few adherents who assume that the degree of Indian blood in an individual influences his intellectual capacity. Mexican American and Anglo teachers appear to be equally effective or ineffective with Mexican children. While bilingual teachers are certainly needed, the fact that they are of Mexican descent appears to be of little consequence. The ability to understand, to accept, empathize with, and constructively cope with individual and cultural diversity are the characteristics necessary. Many Mexican American and Anglo educators take strong exception to this point of view. To what degree burgeoning "ethnic nationalism" on the part of the Mexican Americans and racial prejudice and desire for separateness on the part of the Anglos affect their respective positions is unknown, but it seems likely that they are strong influences.

Perhaps some light can be shed on this controversial topic by analyzing the roles teachers play in schools. Southwestern teachers, of all ethnic groups, appear to fit into three broad and naturally overlapping categories as they function within, and relate to, their respective schools and students. These are the conformist, the "expecter," and the "system beater." Each group has a standard and a super category within it, and it is suggested here that Mexican American teachers tend toward the super side of each group.

In order to persevere within a rigid and authoritarian school system, teachers must conform. Teachers with widely divergent personalities or philosophies from those extant within a system have two alternatives: either outwardly conform or flee. Either they must learn to adjust by keeping their mouths shut, teaching children what they are supposed to learn, and showing appropriate deference to authority, or they must seek a position in a different system or occupation. This school social system unfortunately discourages many creative individuals of all ethnic groups and tends to perpetuate the school status quo. Many teachers, especially women, cannot flee to other systems or jobs; many are tied to a locale by their husband's occupation, their family, their love of the particular geographic area, and so on. They have to conform to exist. Of these, some become institutional or status personalities, internalizing the norms of the institution. Some conform even to degrees not demanded by the institution. A large percentage of Mexican American teachers appear to be in this super conformist group. They adhere strictly and rigidly to institutional demands, apparently in order to gain whatever financial, social, or political rewards the system provides. The fact that so many minority-group teachers seem to be of this type is completely understandable. The number of alternative positions (economic slots) available to Mexican Americans is more severely limited in many communities in the Southwest than are those for the minority-group teachers. A nonconformist Mexican American teacher may incur the wrath of authority for his divergence more than his Anglo counterpart. Thus, a Mexican American teacher may well be "forced" into conformity, because of the position afforded his group, or because of the expectations of those in educational power.

While adhering to the system's requirements and policies, many Mexican American teachers recognize the school's inadequacies. They understand many of the Mexican American child's school problems, but because of their precarious position they are unable to do anything to change the situation. Since few Mexican Americans reach authority positions within Anglo-dominated school systems, and fewer still who are promoted hold divergent views, another problem is created. The nonconformist Mexican American teacher, the one who wants change, has few advocates in power. These teachers are even less capable of fomenting change than are their Anglo peers within the conformist group. The vast majority of Mexican American teachers started their careers with zeal and determination to aid their group's children, but pressure from innumerable sources has dampened their enthusiasm. The few that can't conform flee to other occupations or become "system beaters."

Desire to help children and holding high expectations for them are characteristic of most teachers of all ethnic groups. Most teachers honestly want their students to excel in school and succeed in society. These characteristics seem especially applicable to the middle-class or upwardly mobile individual. Mexican American teachers with excessively high expectations for their group's children are encountered everywhere. Such teachers may honestly attempt to identify with their charges, contending that they are part of the same culture but have risen above it. This group seems to be super middle class. They seem to say "Look, you *chicanos,* I made it and you can make it too. The only thing wrong with you is your attitude." These teachers may also be conformists contending that there is nothing wrong with the system, only with the attitudes of their Mexican American students. Such Mexican American teachers seem to expect more of minority-group children and be harsher on them than are many Anglos, seeing this approach to be in the best interest of children.

Many Mexican American teachers are themselves the product of environments similar to their children's but are upwardly mobile, often accepting middle-class norms and values more thoroughly than their Anglo counterparts. Some of these "expecters" may harbor very negative feelings toward their poor relations. Clark finds the same conditions to exist among Negro teachers, arguing that such attitudes are understandable, though regrettable. He states (1965, p. 132): "Many of today's scholars and teachers come from 'culturally deprived' backgrounds. Many of these same individuals, however, when confronted with students whose present economic and social predicament is not unlike their own was, tend to react negatively to them, possibly to escape the painful memory of their own prior lower status."

Whatever the cause, negativism in one form or another seemed to this author to be a characteristic of many of the Mexican American teachers interviewed during this study. This negativism may manifest itself in the excessively high expectations and rigid demands for conformity characteristic of a great many of these teachers. One Anglo Texas superintendant indicated that he would never again place a Mexican American principal in a *barrio* school. He commented that his district "has fallen flat on its face in moving Mexican Americans into principalships. They have no sympathy for Mexican American parents." One such principal "expected a great deal more of Mexican American parents that he would have of Anglo parents," and the school district almost had a revolution on its hands. Other informants reported that students were particularly resentful of rigid and high expectations from minority-group teachers.

"System beaters" exist in all ethnic groups. As in the other categories, Mexican Americans seem to overpopulate the super side of this group. In this author's opinion the system beater does the most for minority-group children. System beaters of Mexican descent seem particularly efficient in raising achievement, encouraging acceptable behavior, and so on, and may perform a truly significant role in their schools. These teachers apparently deliberately attempt to identify with their students and often seem to succeed. They stress the identical nature of their own and their students' background and in so doing develop a joint conspiracy with students to evade the full force of the system's directives and sanctions. A mutual protection association is formed between teacher and student, each encouraging the other to evade the system while incurring as little disapproval and as much reward as possible. Such teachers are often censured by administrators but help to provide the kind of support essential for certain kinds of Mexican American students.

Many Mexican American principals and teachers of course do a magnificent job. Some of the most patient and understanding educators interviewed and observed in the course of this study were Mexican American. One such principal in particular seemed to be the antithesis of the principal described by the superintendent quoted above. Some of the most spontaneous classes observed were conducted by Mexican American teachers (this was rare at the secondary level, however). But numerous mechanisms within both the school and society appear to be operating to encourage overrepresentation of super conformists and super expecters. Changes in school hiring, placement, and promotion policies would undoubtedly affect this situation in a positive way.

Quality of Facilities

The allocation of financial resources to children through educational institutions can be an important, although terribly oversimplified, measure of educational quality. The five Southwestern states vary considerably in their ability or desire to support their school systems. Table 3 indicates the differences in financial

TABLE 3 Selected Statistics on School Attendance, Graduation, and Expenditures per State in Five Southwestern States, 1965-66

AVERAGE PERCENTAGE OF CHILDREN AGES 5-17 ATTENDING SCHOOL DAILY			NUMBER OF CHILDREN (AGES 5-17) PER 100 ADULTS (AGES 21-64)		
State	Rank order among all states	Percent	State	Rank order among all states	Number of children
California	5	93.8%	New Mexico	1	69
Colorado	6	92.0	Arizona	12	58
Arizona	21	84.7	Colorado	18	56
New Mexico	22	84.6	Texas	18	56
Texas	24	83.3	California	43	49

ESTIMATED EXPENDITURE PER ADA*			PUBLIC SCHOOL EXPENDITURE AS PERCENT OF PERSONAL INCOME, 1965		
State	Rank order among all states	Expenditure	State	Rank order among all states	Percent of personal income
California	9	$613	New Mexico	2	5.4%
Colorado	22	571	Arizona	5	5.0
Arizona	23	568	Colorado	10	4.6
New Mexico	24	556	Texas	24	4.0
Texas	39	449	California	32	3.8

PUPILS PER CLASSROOM TEACHER			ESTIMATED AVERAGE TEACHERS' SALARIES		
State	Rank order among all states	Pupils	State	Rank order among all states	Salary
Colorado	12	22.3	California	2	$8,450
Arizona	22	23.8	Arizona	15	7,230
New Mexico	26	24.4	New Mexico	20	6,630
Texas	31	24.9	Colorado	21	6,625
California	44	26.7	Texas	33	6,025

PUBLIC HIGH SCHOOL GRADUATES IN 1964-65, AS PERCENT OF NINTH-GRADE CLASS IN 1961-62			PERCENT OF DRAFTEES FAILING MENTAL TESTS, 1965		
State	Rank order among all states	ninth-grade Percent of Class	State	Rank order among all states	Percent
California	1	88.9%	Colorado	20	14.0%
Colorado	20	78.2	California	25	15.3
Texas	34	69.5	Arizona	26	20.5
New Mexico	38	68.0	Texas	35	23.3
Arizona	47	62.6	New Mexico	38	25.4

Source: National Education Association (1967, pp. 12, 21, 25, 29, 32, 54). *Average Daily Attendance unit.

effort and the results of that effort in the Southwestern states. No precise conclusions can be drawn from this table, but certain differences seem obvious. In general, California spends the most money, pays the highest salaries, has the highest percentage of children attending school, appears to have the fewest dropouts, and is second only to Colorado in lowest percentage of draft rejectees. Texas is at the other extreme with the poorest school attendance, lowest teacher salaries, and lowest expenditures per pupil; it is in the middle range in number of dropouts and has the next to highest percentage failing mental tests for the draft. When it is understood that a large percentage of the dropouts and draft rejectees in these states are in minority groups, in some areas almost exclusively Mexican American, the magnitude of the school's failure in regard to the disadvantaged is evident. While California expends the most money per pupil, it is the lowest of the states in percentage of total personal income used for public education. New Mexico and Arizona, with the largest number of children per 100 adults, seem to be making a strong effort by allocating to the schools the largest percentages of total personal income. Differences within states are perhaps as great as between them. However, it seems evident that California and Texas are at extreme poles on most, if not all, aspects of school.

In general, making comparisons within states, it can be stated that the lower the socioeconomic status of students, the poorer the quality of physical facilities. Schools in rural districts, which tend in the Southwest to serve large percentages of poor Mexican Americans, generally have less adequate plants than schools in metropolitan districts in the same state. Differences in physical facilities between high-status and low-status schools are much less obvious in California than in the other four Southwestern states studied.

The terrible physical condition of "Mexican schools," as described in the early literature, is still encountered, but it is not so prevalent as in the past and rarely so bad. Sánchez' report on New Mexico school conditions in the late 1930s, Taylor's description of Texas schools during the same period, and other reports from California, Arizona, and Colorado, documented the plight of these Mexican American schools. All these reports demonstrated that physical plants were run-down, badly maintained, overcrowded, poorly furnished, and lacked equipment. In general, they clearly failed to compare with Anglo institutions within the same school district. (See Calderón, 1950; Corona, 1955; Holliday, 1935; Kibbee, 1946; Lehman, 1947; Manuel, 1930; Rubel, 1966; Sánchez, 1966; Strickland and Sánchez, 1948; Taylor, 1932; Trillingham and Hughes, 1943.)

Contemporary conditions are much improved, yet one still finds schools with high percentages of Mexican Americans in deplorable physical condition. In many sections of the Southwest, the contrast between the physical facilities of predominantly minority schools and the middle-class institutions is immense. The minority schools are poorly maintained and dilapidated, often lacking in landscaping and outside play facilities. The present practice is to replace these older, previously de jure segregated, buildings with new modern facilities. This accounts for the fact that in some communities the barrio schools have by far the best facilities in the district. If this trend continues, the difference in quality will be eliminated. Often schools for migrant children occupy the oldest and poorest plants within a district. Some of them are miserable almost beyond description, especially in certain areas of Texas.

In school districts with very high percentages of Mexican Americans, school plants are generally inadequate. In some of these districts, many buildings in present use were not constructed as schools; conversions were made from convents, old homes, or military facilities. It is probably impossible to tax the population at higher rates in most of these areas, which are economically depressed. However, the economic base in some of them is industrial agriculture, and in these higher taxation is possible, the local politico-economic power structure permitting.

A Texas school administrator interviewed during this study, recognizing the poor facilities afforded Mexican Americans in his area, described the feeling of some of his fellow educators, and perhaps the Anglo community. He commented that many feel it best to provide inferior facilities, arguing that placing such children in beautiful schools with exciting surroundings would raise their expectations and ultimately encourage frustration, since "so few Mexicans can ever reach such levels during their lifetime."

School plants do not guarantee high quality education. Some of the most exciting, creative, and apparently dedicated teachers observed were working in unbelievably poor physical conditions. However, it is difficult to deny that size of class, length of teacher service, qualifications of teachers, and so forth influence quality of education. As with other aspects of Mexican American schooling, previous reports indicated that past conditions were much worse than those observed today. However, in some cases, discriminatory practices in regard to teacher placement and size of classes continue. Schools with high percentages of Mexican Americans received, and still receive, a disproportionate percentage of poorly trained teachers. It is a common practice for noncertified teachers to gravitate toward, or be placed in, these schools. In an unpublished study of 1,650 elementary teachers in the lower Rio Grande Valley of Texas, Ramirez (1966) reported that 10 percent of the teachers had no bachelor's degree, 13 percent were serving with emergency credentials, and 30 percent were on provisional credentials; only 57 percent were fully certified Texas teachers. A Rio Grande Valley superintendent reported that he was forced to employ some teachers with as few as 60 college credits. In other areas, the situation appears to be much better. The Governor's Committee on Public School Education in Texas (1968) found a strong relationship between Spanish-surname percentages in the population and teachers who are practicing without a bachelor's degree. It can be inferred that the higher the percentage of Mexican Americans the fewer fully certified teachers are in the schools. The Governor's Committee found that one characteristic of districts that have teacher shortages seems to be a high percentage of minority groups. During the three-year period from 1964–65 to 1966–67, teachers who did not have degrees and were teaching with emergency permits made up more than 14 percent of the total teaching staff in 9 of the Committee's 158 sample districts. Table 4 clearly illustrates the magnitude of the problem. Since areas with high concentrations of minority groups have low socioeconomic conditions and thus low school revenues, the relationship of poverty and assumed quality of schooling is also demonstrated.

The shortage of qualified teachers throughout the Southwest particularly influences the quality of Mexican American schooling. Noncertified teachers are often placed in schools serving low socioeconomic areas where little reaction can be expected from the adult community. Teacher shortages have a more adverse effect on minority schools or districts than on Anglo. It is commonly reported, but undocumented, that minority schools serve as training institutions: beginning teachers are often assigned there, and those who do well are subsequently moved to higher status (more Anglo) schools (see Trillingham and Hughes, 1943; Condit, 1946, p. 5). This is rarely the case with Mexican American teachers, however. As mentioned in previous sections, they are usually kept in schools with high percentages of minority children. Most school districts place few such teachers in high-status Anglo schools, but many transfer good Mexican American teachers to mixed schools.

Teachers who are considered to be troublemakers by local school administrators are said to be "punished" by being placed in minority schools. A number of interviewees contended that while they could not prove such statements, they were quite sure it was the practice. In some cases, this could prove to be a positive action; some troublemakers are creative noncomformists and work out very well in certain kinds of new settings.

Mexican American children tend to be in larger classes than their Anglo counterparts; the teacher-student ratio is higher. Although the nationwide statistics reported by Coleman et al. (1966) do not indicate significant differences, many excessively large Mexican American classes were observed during the course of this study. Such overcrowded conditions were reported to be very common in the past.

TABLE 4   Teacher Shortages in Texas Analyzed According to Population Characteristics, 1964-65 to 1966-67

District	Permits to teachers without degrees	Total permits	Percent of teachers without degrees	Percent of Spanish surnames in district population	1966-67 salary base
Edgewood [San Antonio]	591	1,024	57%	76%	$4,104
Rio Grande City	53	113	55	88	4,104
Brownsville	124	297	44	73	4,384
Laredo	85	204	41	82	4,204
Pharr–San Juan–Alamo	57	140	41	70	4,450
Harlingen	56	153	37	29	4,449
Harlandale [San Antonio]	76	302	25	40	4,504
Ysleta [El Paso]	190	1,048	18	36	5,000
San Antonio	135	995	14	45	4,900

Source: Governor's Committee on Public School Education in Texas (1968, p. 46).

In metropolitan areas, differences in the quality of physical facilities for the two ethnic groups will probably disappear within the decade. Old "Mexican schools" are being replaced with new modern facilities. Nonmetropolitan and rural districts that have high percentages of Mexican Americans will undoubtedly lag behind because there are insufficient funds to replace worn out or inadequate facilities. California has already succeeded in eliminating many of its older buildings, partly because state laws require earthquake-proof structures. More subtle discrimination, such as teacher placement policies, will probably continue. The elementary school teacher shortage will continue to cause hardship on low-status children. Unless the Mexican American community or the states themselves actively protest such discrimination, it can be predicted to continue.

SUMMARY AND CONCLUSIONS

The processes through which school practices, teachers' attitudes, and irrelevancies and rigidities in the curriculum have contributed to the low educational attainment of Mexican Americans have been touched upon here. These factors act in combination and probably in mutually reinforcing fashion. There is neither a theoretical framework nor empirical evidence that would make it possible to isolate and assess the impact of each of the numerous forces through which the school system contributes to deficient education for Mexican Americans. Hence, the influence of the school's inadequacies might best be seen by observing the results of its work.

One probable result is a negative school experience for the Mexican American child, causing him to reject the institution and, since it is often his first and most intensive encounter with an institution of the larger society, to transfer his rejection to society as a whole. When teachers' behavior or institutional procedures encourage a negative social climate within the school, the learner's general reaction will tend to be negative also. Though a certain degree of negativism toward school is common to all groups or classes of children, segregation and isolation of Mexican Americans tend to aggravate it. Negative attitudes toward school are particularly noticeable in segregated schools or among students assigned to low tracks. The individual child attempting to persevere and retain a positive view toward school finds it extremely difficult to counter the attitude of his relatively homogeneous peer group.

Another consequence of the school's inadequacies is the familiar culture conflict between home and school. Teachers drill minority-group children to accept middle-class norms of achievement, individual responsibility, and good manners in order to gain a good grade or the acceptance of the teacher. It can be argued that what is so "learned" may soon be forgotten, and it is also often the case that culturally different children do not see the symbolic reward of a higher grade as significant incentive. The norms taught may deviate from those at home and derogate the family and the peer group. Children learn one culture (language, values, expectations, and roles) in their home or from their peers, and the school enforces another and different culture. In order to stay in school, the child is required to drop the "bad" culture he has learned at home and at least outwardly manifest the cultural characteristics expected by the school. Many cannot do this and ultimately drop out—mentally in the primary or intermediate grades and then physically as soon as local law or practice permits. Others reject their home culture. Still others cannot cope with the situation at all, and caught between two sets of norms they may be subject to personal disorganization.

To make matters worse, the attempt to convert Mexican American children to "our way of life" inadvertently creates a school environment that does not reflect the reality of American culture. Thus, the school that has a high percentage of Mexican American students usually demands conformity to "super-middle-class" Anglo norms of behavior. Its curriculum tends to be more rigid than that of middle-class institutions in the same locale.

Tracking and other practices that isolate Mexican American children not only discourage equal-status interaction between them and their Anglo peers but also serve to reinforce the stereotypes each group holds of the other. The track system reinforces teachers' stereotypes as well, and affects their work: their expectations are lowered, and they may therefore make less effort, have lax achievement standards, and offer less encouragement.

Thus through innumerable practices and policies, the school inadvertently discourages Mexican American children from succeeding there. There is a crying need for objective institutional self-analysis as a step toward remedying this situation.

Cognitive and Intellectual Functioning of Spanish-Speaking Children

Charles B. Brussell

NEW VIEWPOINTS CONCERNING INTELLIGENCE

Before reviewing the literature concerning the performance of Spanish-speaking children as measured by standardized tests of intelligence, it may be helpful to place the concept of intelligence within the broader framework of the more recent thinking concerning the nature of intelligence. Before World War II, holds Hunt (11), most of the general textbooks tended to present the view that IQ scores derived from intelligence tests were essentially constant because intelligence was fixed, or predetermined at birth. Dissonant evidence, however, has led Hunt and others to re-evaluate the notion of fixed intelligence.

. . .

Where, then, does Hunt search for a precise definition of intelligence, and an explanation of its development? Although he draws ideas from many sources, he devotes considerable space to the concepts of the Swiss psychologist, Jean Piaget. This may reflect a current surge of interest in the developmental system of Piaget, noted by Flavell (7).

. . .

Hunt (11) believes that five main themes dominate Piaget's theoretical formulations. First, there is continual and progressive change in the structures of

From Charles B. Brussell, *Disadvantaged Mexican-American Children and Early Educational Experience.* Developed and published by the Southwest Educational Laboratory, Austin, Texas, 1968, pp. 45, 49, 51–60, 97–99.

behavior and thought in the child. Flavell (7) indicates that cognitive progress is possible in Piaget's system because accommodatory acts are continually being extended to new and different features of the environment. The feature to which accommodation has been extended will be assimilated into the individual's mental structure to the extent that it can fit somewhere within the existing structure. But once the feature has been assimilated, it tends to change the structure to some degree, and to make possible further accommodatory extension. And these structures are not static and unchanging even in the absence of environmental stimulation, for they are constantly becoming re-organized internally and integrated with other systems. Changes in structure due to assimilation direct new accommodations, and new attempts at accommodation stimulate structural reorganizations.

Second, these structures appear in an invariant order. However, the relationship between a behavioral landmark and the age at which it appears is no more than a convenient device. The rate of development is explained by the child-environment interaction. Honstead (9) notes that it is much more important to understand how development takes place than exactly when it can be expected to occur.

Hunt's third point is that the gradual diversification and differentiation of behavioral and thought structures derive from the invariant functions of assimilation and accommodation that operate in a child's continuous interaction with his environment. This concept of organism-environment interaction through the processes of accommodation and assimilation is neither hereditarian nor environmentalistic, but both. The first response of a child in a given situation is a behavioral structure (schemata) already present from past assimilation. Variations in environment, however, force the child to cope with these variations, and, in the process of this coping, to modify the structures. The more variations in reality with which the child has coped, the greater is his capacity for coping; that is, the more differentiated and mobile his structures become. Thus, the more new things that a child has seen and heard, the more things he is interested in seeing and hearing.

Fourth, intelligence increases as actions become internalized to become thought and as thought becomes "decentered" and dominant over a child's perceptions and activities. Simple reflexive schemata become coordinated into more complex schemata, which in turn become re-coordinated into mobile action-systems as the child's independence from immediate stimulation increases. Central neural processes that mediate or constitute thought become more and more autonomous and more and more dominant over receptor inputs and motor outputs.

Fifth, Piaget explains thought in terms of its logical properties. Reversing the explanation of thought as reflecting logical properties, Piaget sees logic reflecting thought. As man accommodates thought to the problems raised by electronic computers, atomic power, and interstellar travel, thought with new logical properties may result. In fact, Hunt (11) sees the electronic computer as supplying a model for brain functioning. Experience can be regarded as the programming of the intrinsic portions of the cerebrum for learning and problem solving, and intellectual capacity at any given time can be conceived as a function of the nature and the quality of this programming. It is possible that a review of the studies concerning the intellectual functioning of Spanish-speaking children will be more meaningful if placed in the context of these newer views concerning intelligence and intellectual development.

THE INTELLECTUAL FUNCTIONING OF SPANISH-SPEAKING CHILDREN

A review of the literature reveals an apparent lack of studies concerning the measured intellectual functioning of pre-school Spanish-speaking children, and there is clearly a need for more research in this area. However, there are a number of studies available that have concerned themselves with older Spanish-speaking children. Carlson and Henderson (3) conducted a longitudinal study in which a number of different intelligence tests were administered to 115 children of Mexican parentage whose IQs were found to be lower than the mean IQ of Anglo children by critical ratios that the authors did not feel could be attributed to chance. The gap between the two groups widened between the first and the third testing period, apparently due to a "dropping-off" of the Mexican American children's IQ scores rather than to an increase in the IQ scores of the Anglo children.

The authors admitted that they had not controlled the factors of urban-rural parental background, a possibly more limited vocabulary not only in English but also in Spanish for the experimental group, and differences in motivation at the time of testing. They did feel, however, that they had controlled the direct urban-rural factor, the socio-economic factor, the effects of prejudice, and the "total cultural complex." Pasamanick (22) replied to the study, calling the Carlson and Henderson implication that they had controlled the "total cultural complex" an unfortunate one. He then cited tables of education and work status, indicating a lack of socio-economic homogeneity among the five census tracts in Los Angeles from which Carlson and Henderson had presumably drawn their subjects. He also pointed out that the authors had not controlled the factor of the quality and quantity of parental education, and that the experimental and control groups differed in age 3.2 months at first testing and 9.4 months at third testing, a difference that probably was significant statistically. Pasamanick concluded rather grimly that none of the factors enumerated by Carlson and Henderson could be controlled at that time, and were "inherently uncontrollable" under the then existing circumstances.

Shortly afterwards, Cook (4) tested 97 Mexican American children from the St. Paul, Minnesota area on the Stanford-Binet and the Form I of the Point Scale of Performance Tests, a non-verbal intelligence test. The mean age of these children was 12 years and seven months, with their ages ranging from six years and seven months to 16 years and six months. On the Binet, the mean IQ of the children was 83.77, while on the PSPT it was 101.06. The author believed that the non-verbal scale revealed a high potential that the Binet did not, and stated that educational guidance for Mexican American children should be based on the results from a non-verbal intelligence test as well as upon the more commonly used verbal scales. The subjects, according to the author, appeared to be handicapped by lack of language facility on the Binet test, which was given in English.

Altus (1) attempted to investigate the problem of bilingualism as it affected intelligence test scores. He began by noting that previous investigations had indicated that, on the average, the measured IQ of Mexican American children was 10 to 15 points below that of their non-Mexican American school-age peers. He concluded, though, that this difference could not be considered real as long as such handicaps as bilingualism were left uncontrolled. He administered the Wechsler Intelligence Scale for Children to a group of bilingual Spanish-speaking children and a group of unilingual children on the grounds that the WISC had both a Verbal scale and a Performance scale, and that the Performance tests were largely self-explanatory. He believed that the Performance IQ would be a fairly good indicator of the Verbal IQ except in those instances where handicapping influences such as bilingualism were in operation. The mean age of these children was approximately 11 years for all subjects. The average difference in Verbal IQ turned out to be 17 points in favor of the unilingual group, and the greatest discrepancies between the two groups appeared on the Vocabulary, Information, and Similarities subtests of the Verbal scale. Since there was no significant difference between the Performance IQ of the two groups, the author concluded that the Spanish-speaking group's retardation on the Verbal scale was linguistic.

Johnson (17) also studied the relationship between bilingualism and intelligence test scores. He administered to 30 Spanish-speaking boys, ranged in age from 9 through 12, the Goodenough Draw a Man Test (non-verbal), the Otis Self-Administering Test of Mental Ability, and a Reaction-Time Test of Bilingualism. The mean on the Goodenough Test was 98.77, while the mean Otis intelligence quotient was 86.37. The Reaction-Time Test of Bilingualism required the subjects to recall as many English words in five minutes as they could, and then as many Spanish words as they could in the same length of time. It was found, at a high level of statistical significance, that there was an inverse relationship between performance on the Otis and knowledge of Spanish in comparison to English. That is, the higher the Otis IQ, the less knowledge the child had of Spanish in comparison to English.

On the other hand, a greater knowledge of Spanish was found to be associated with superior performance on the Goodenough, although this relationship was not statistically significant. The author also found that the greater the knowledge of English in comparison with knowledge of Spanish, the more nearly the Goodenough and the Otis scores approached each other. The author concluded that an intelligence test employing the English language was probably not a valid instrument when used with subjects deficient in the assimilation of the culture of which English is reflective, and that measuring the intelligence of bilingual subjects presented complex problems which possibly render both performance and linguistic tests invalid.

Keston and Jimenez (18) tried to determine if an intelligence test is best administered to Spanish-speaking students in English or in Spanish. They administered Form *M* of the Stanford-Binet Intelligence Test to 50 Spanish American children in the fourth grade. A month later, they gave the same children a Spanish translation of Form *L* of the same test. On the average, these children were about 10 years old. The mean IQ of these children on the English version was 86.0; but on the Spanish version it was only 71.8. The correlation coefficient of the IQ scores on the English and on the Spanish versions was .36; and since Terman and Merrill had reported a correlation between the scores obtained on the two forms of .93 when both were delivered in English, the authors concluded that factors other than the effects of translation were operating to lower the correlation. One factor that they pointed out was that probably the children tested had a higher level of development in English than in Spanish. The examiners had noted that in their Spanish conversation these children had speech habits similar to pre-school children. They also manifested limitations in vocabulary and complexity of expression when using Spanish.

The authors concluded that development in the use of the Spanish language came to a virtual standstill when these children entered grade school and began their formal education in English. On the other hand, many of the English expressions of common usage in the earliest grades had not yet been mastered by these children, indicating to the authors that there is some confusion in the language habits of children in a bilingual situation, and that even the English version of the test does injustice to these children when the resulting IQ scores are interpreted too literally. There was a .62 correlation between the English IQ test scores and grade point average, but only a .11 correlation between Spanish IQ test scores and grade point average. In other words, the children performed better in the language in which they had had formal instruction. The authors decided that even though the norms of the test were determined from an English-speaking population and were therefore not really applicable to these students, that the norms were as good as any available and that the test was best administered in English. On the other hand, they did not find the Spanish version a fair measure of the children's intellectual abilities either, since their variety of spoken Spanish contained many contaminations and Anglicisms.

Jensen (13) tried another approach to the assessment of the intellectual abilities of Spanish-speaking children. He noted that both verbal and non-verbal intelligence tests generally classified the majority of Mexican American children below the average of the predominantly Anglo American groups on which the tests were standardized, and that standard intelligence tests can be inappropriate for children who have not had much exposure to the Anglo American culture of the normative group, since standard intelligence tests are actually static measures of achievement which sample the knowledge and skills that the child has acquired in the past. He therefore attempted to measure the educational potentialities of Mexican American children by using tests that provided direct measures of *present* learning abilities. He utilized two types of materials consisting of familiar and abstract objects. The familiar objects consisted of such things as a bar of soap, a toy car, a ball, etc. The abstract objects consisted of plastic forms of various shapes and colors. There were three types of learning tasks: an Immediate Recall task in which subjects were asked to recall objects after they had been studied and then removed from sight; a Paired Associates Learning task, in which the children were required to associate one object with another and then recall one object of the pair when it was hidden from view; and a Serial Learning task in which objects were hidden from view under small boxes and the children were required to guess what was under each box, turning it up to see if they were right. A child had not met the criterion until he had learned the entire serial order from left to right. Several experiments were run utilizing fourth and sixth grade Mexican American and Anglo children who had been matched for socio-economic status and IQ level.

The author found that Mexican children of low IQ performed significantly better than Anglo children of low IQ. The Anglo children of low IQ were actually slow learners compared to Mexican American children of the same IQ level. There was no significant difference between the learning abilities of children of either ethnic group who had above average IQ scores. The author concluded from his total work that the IQ test is a valid measure of learning ability for Anglo children, but not for Mexican American children against whom the test discriminates on some other basis than inherent poor learning ability. Mexican American children of low IQ as measured by an intelligence test appeared to be quite normal in learning ability. These children, however, might not have acquired in their environment the kinds of knowledge, habits and skills that are tapped by IQ tests, and which provide a basis for school learning. The author also concluded that non-verbal intelligence tests probably discriminate against Mexican American children as much as verbal intelligence tests since non-verbal performance tasks actually require verbal mediation.

Rapier (26) studied the effects of verbal mediation upon the learning of Mexican American children. In one experiment, 40 children were selected and paired for IQ, there being 10 Mexican American and 10 Anglo children in an "average" group. The experiment attempted to study the effects of supplying the necessary mediating links on paired-associates learning. The children learned to pair an ordered series of pictures with another ordered series of pictures, and then learned to pair these with a third ordered series of pictures. There were no significant differences found in the learning abilities of either ethnic group. These children were then asked to learn to pair the first series with pictures from the third series, but an experimental group was allowed a common connecting link between pictures in the form of the second series, while a control group had to learn to pair the first series with pictures from the third series that had been randomized. In both ethnic groups mediated learning occurred.

However, dull Mexican Americans used mediating links in learning new connections better than dull Anglo Americans. The author thus concluded that Mexican Americans will profit from the opportunity to use verbal mediators for the facilitation of further learning, and that their learning disability might not be due to the inability to verbally mediate, but rather to a lack of reservoir of verbal associations which they could invoke in any new learning situation.

Johnson (14, 15, 16) and Demos (5) have studied ethnic attitudes of Mexican Americans. Piaget (25) has pointed out that affective life and cognitive life are inseparable although distinct, because all interaction with the environment involves both a structuring and a valuation. One cannot reason without experiencing certain feelings, and conversely, no affect can exist without a minimum of understanding or discrimination. Johnson (14) began by devising an experimental projective technique for the analysis of racial attitudes which he called the Projective Test of Racial Attitudes. He selected six pictures which generally covered most of the social situations that individuals of four, eight, and 12 years of age would ordinarily meet.

The pictures contained life situations which portrayed behavior most easily emphasized by the subjects such as a boy with a bat, two cowboys approaching each other, and a girl crying. Each picture had a hero figure with whom the subject could identify, thus projecting something of the dynamics of his own personality into the depicted situations. The cards were relevant to ethnic situations. For example, in one picture an Anglo child would be holding a bat while a Mexican boy stood near, and vice versa. Children's responses to viewing the cards were scored on five variables: effect of the environment, adequacy of the principal character, fate of the hero, conclusion of the story theme which the subjects were asked to furnish; and subjects' opinion of the other ethnic group as stated immediately after the testing. The initial study indicated that there was a tendency for four-year-old Spanish-speaking children to be prejudiced in favor of the Anglo group, but the prejudice seemed to be coupled with resentment. On the other hand, four-year-old Anglos who preferred the Mexican stereotype were least prejudiced. There was an insignificant tendency for the Spanish-speaking children to become more moderate in their opinions of the Anglo as age increased, but Anglo dislike of the Spanish-speaking group increased markedly from the four-year-old to the eight-year-old level.

Johnson used this instrument to study the origin and development of the Mexican attitude toward the Anglo and the Anglo attitude toward the Mexican (15). He found that four-year-old Spanish-speaking children seemed to be less prejudiced than were Anglo children of the same age. During the years from four to eight, Spanish-speaking children developed a negative attitude toward Anglos which reached approximately the same level as that demonstrated by 12-year-old Spanish-speaking children. In other words, there was a leveling off process in negative attitude development between the ages of 8 to 12. On the other hand, negative attitudes of Anglo children toward the Spanish-speaking developed little during the years from four to eight, but during the years from eight to 12 their negative attitudes greatly increased. At age 12, Anglo children had the highest level of prejudice of all groups and ages studied. Further analysis indicated that the origin of the Spanish-speaking child's prejudice toward the Anglo originated at about the three-and-one-half year age level, while Anglo children's prejudice developed somewhat before this time. The author took this to indicate that the instilled attitude of one group may contribute to the attitudinal development of the other. As age increased, Spanish-speaking children's reactions to the Mexican-Anglo environment in the pictures became less satisfactory, and they indicated less feeling that this environment was helpful.

Johnson (16) administered the Hoffman Bilingual Scale to children of the four, eight and 12-year-old age groups to determine their degree of bilingualism. He then administered the Protective Test of Racial Attitudes and correlated a prejudice score, derived from that test, with the bilingual score of the Hoffman Scale. Four-year-old Spanish-speaking children with the greatest and the least bilingual background were found to have the least prejudice. Apparently a great amount of knowledge of the Anglo culture or no knowledge of it at all yielded the least bias toward it. Spanish-speaking subjects at the eight-year-old level having highest and lowest bilingual scores had equal prejudice. Spanish-speaking children at the 12-year-old level having the greatest and least bilingual scores tended to furnish unsatisfactory conclusions to themes in their response to the pictures. However, correlations between the adequacy of the principal character and bilingualism, and the fate of the hero and bilingualism, indicated that as age increased there was less tendency for children with high bilingual background scores to attribute subordination and defeat to the hero in the picture.

Demos (5) devised an attitude scale of 29 items thought to deal with Mexican American attitudes toward education, and administered it to a Mexican American group, an Anglo group randomly paired with the Mexican American group, and an Anglo group matched with the Mexican American group on age, grade, sex, social class, and intelligence. The children were in the seventh through the twelfth grades. While the random Anglo group differed from the Mexican American group on 10 items, the matched Anglo group differed from the Mexican American group on only 6 items. Since matching reduced the number of significant differences from 10 to 6 items, the author concluded that these 6 differences were a result of Mexican American group membership. On five of these differences, the Mexican Americans had the less favorable attitude. These differences included attitudes on the importance of an elementary education, the staff's concern about students, the desirability of dropping out of school, the desirability of a gang, and the importance of good school attendance. On the sixth item, the value of a college education, the Mexican American group had the more favorable attitude. The author offered no rationale for these differences, but noted that several of the issues where significant differences were involved dealt with human relations.

Another problem is the content of the intelligence test. Hunt (11) writes:

. . . In traditional tests, what is sampled is typically named in terms of such skill categories as verbal or arithmetic skill. The attempts by factor analysis . . . to specify what is sampled . . . yield what is probably best conceived as systems of coordinates which simplify the comparing of people in their test-performance and, perhaps, facilitate making predictions about the efficiency of people. These systems of coordinates, regardless of the names given to them, may—yes, probably—have little or nothing to do with the natural structures, schemata, operation, and concepts organized within individuals that determine their problem-solving (p. 311).

These structures, schemata, operations, and concepts are, in Piagetian theory, learned through a continual organism-environment interaction; and the environment with which one interacts may be important in determining what type of accommodations and assimilations will take place—that is, what the phenotype of the intelligence will be at any given moment. It has been noted that Jensen (13) believes that Mexican American children may not have acquired in their environment the kinds of knowledge, habits, and skills that are tapped by IQ tests. Yourman (32), in speaking of a decision made several years ago in New York City to abandon group IQ testing in the city's public schools, notes that almost half of the city's public school pupils might be called culturally deprived, having home and community experiences not comparable to those of the representative children of their ages against whom their native learning ability is measured. The problem of the normative group and the problem of the content are related. The types of questions asked and the types of performances required by standardized intelligence tests may adequately sample the intelligence of those similar to the individuals upon whom the norms were based, but may be completely inadequate for the purpose of sampling the intelligence of individuals who are dissimilar in learning patterns and in environment from those upon whom the tests were standardized.

Another problem is the adequacy of non-verbal tests of intelligence for the purpose of sampling the intelligence of Spanish-speaking children. While the Spanish-speaking children's scores on non-verbal tests of intelligence have generally been higher than their scores on verbal intelligence tests, Johnson (17) believes that measuring the intelligence of bilingual subjects presents complex problems which possibly render both performance and linguistic tests invalid. Sanchez (25, Section 1) says: ". . . investigators, proud of their recognition of the 'language handicap' of Spanish-speaking children, have chosen to test these children with 'nonverbal' tests, overlooking completely that the nonverbal tests are as culturally-based as the verbal tests and that neither can test what is not there." Jensen (13) also concludes that nonverbal intelligence tests probably discriminate against Mexican American children as much as verbal tests, since nonverbal performance tasks actually require verbal mediation.

Stablein, Willey, and Thomson (30) have evaluated the Davis-Ells Test of General Intelligence or Problem Solving Ability, a test which is nonverbal except for the instructions. Their subjects were 83 Anglo children about nine years of age and 127 Spanish American children about ten years of age. In addition to administering the Davis-Ells test to these children, they also administered the Metropolitan Achievement Test Battery, the Primary Mental Abilities Test, and a vocabulary test. On each test, the Spanish-speaking group scored lower than the Anglo group. The Spanish-speaking group was as different from the Anglo group on the Davis-Ells test as on tests reputed to be heavily loaded with cultural items—it discriminated as much between the two groups as other measures. This may have been due to the particular construction of the particular test, or to any of a number of other factors; however, it would seem impossible to construct any completely nonverbal test since a modicum of verbal mediation would need to be involved, especially with younger children.

Another problem concerns the use of translated tests. Even after translation, cultural factors may remain which may render the test invalid for Spanish-speaking children despite the fact that it is administered in their own language. Roca (28) discusses the problems encountered by the psychologists of the Division of Research and Statistics of the Department of Education of Puerto Rico when they attempted to translate and adapt for use in Puerto Rican schools three standardized intelligence tests: the Wechsler Intelligence Scale for Children, the Revised Stanford-Binet Scale, and the Goodenough Test. They attempted not merely to translate the tests, but also to adapt the tests to the needs of Puerto Rican children. On the two verbal scales, they found that this required not merely a change in the wording of many questions, but also a change in the order of difficulty of the questions. In order to compensate for cultural factors the question "Who wrote *Romeo and Juliet?*" which appears in the Wechsler-scale was changed to "Who wrote *Don Quixote?*" Another question in the Arithmetic subscale of the Wechsler concerned buying oranges. However, buying oranges was such a common activity in Puerto Rico that the question had to be moved to an easier level of difficulty.

It should be reasonably obvious that such changes play havoc with the structure of the tests. Therefore, the psychologists involved in this study attempted to standardize the translated and adapted tests on Puerto Rican children, for which purpose they used several hundred children. The results are informative. On the translated and adapted scales, the average IQ for Puerto Rican children was about 87. Even on the nonverbal Goodenough Draw-a-Man Test, the test norms for different age groups of Puerto Rican children were found to be lower than the norms of corresponding American children. The author attributes these lower test results on the adapted scales to cultural differences, and points out that no matter how well an intelligence scale is adapted from one culture to another, cultural differences still remain which will cause the children from the second culture to score lower than those from the first.

Another problem that may merit some consideration is the level of verbal competency of the Spanish-speaking children taking the standardized intelligence test, especially when it is administered in Spanish. Keston and Jimenez (18) concluded from their study that the Spanish version of the Stanford-Binet was not a fair measure of the intellectual ability of the children in their study, since the Spanish spoken by these children contained many contaminations and Anglicisms. Perales (22, Section Two) found that Spanish-speaking students tend to encounter three difficulties when speaking their own language; they tend to borrow from a limited English vocabulary to complete expressions begun in Spanish, because their Spanish vocabulary is limited; they may tend to give English words Spanish pronunciations and meanings; and they may have difficulties in pronunciation and enunciation. If a child has any of these difficulties, there may be a reasonable question as to whether or not giving him an intelligence test in Spanish would handicap him. Manuel (19) states that if the child knows only Spanish, the obvious procedure is to test the child in Spanish. He feels, however, that when the Spanish-speaking child enters the English-speaking school that the situation changes rapidly, and that by the second grade the children will do about as well on a group test of general ability when the directions are given in English as when the directions are given in Spanish. He also feels that school achievement can be tested best in the language in which learning has occurred. For preschool children who know little or no English, however, there would seem to be no alternative but to test in Spanish, if tests are required. Manuel believes that many of the tests used with English-speaking children are really quite appropriate for Spanish-speaking children, if the results are interpreted correctly. He states that the "unfairness" of a test is more likely to be in the interpretation than in the test itself.

The interpretation is an important factor. Until fairly recently it was commonly held that intelligence was an innate capacity fixed at birth by genetic determination. Therefore, it was easy to believe that the IQ, a purported measure of this fixed capacity, was itself constant, and that any fluctuations in the IQ score were the result of errors of measurement. When based on this philosophy, IQ score interpretations tended to conclude that the IQ score was a fairly reliable measure of innate capacity which could be little changed, and that it was a fairly reliable predictor of future behavior. Hunt (11) writes:

. . . It would appear to be outside the realm of scientific possibility . . . to predict with precision the future characteristics or phenotypic fate of any organism from knowing merely its present characteristics, without being able to specify the future conditions under which it will live. Since it is impossible to specify what any person's future en-

counters with his environment will be, attempting to predict his future behavior from test performances alone is at best a matter of statistical empiricism. At worst it smacks of occult prophecy.

This is not to say that standardized intelligence tests do not have some predictive value in certain areas under specified conditions. Intelligence tests are known to correlate with grade point average attained in school. For instance, it may be recalled that Keston and Jimenez (18) found that English test scores of Spanish-speaking children in their study correlated .62 with grade point average. For English-speaking children whose experiences and environment are more nearly similar to those of the normative group, this correlation can be expected to be higher. If it is realized that this is a correlation and not a direct correspondence, then perhaps a tentative prediction in a limited area such as grade point average may be made for children similar to the normative group from the score on an intelligence test. But applying such an interpretation to the scores obtained by Spanish-speaking children on a standardized test may, as Manuel (19) has indicated, constitute the "unfairness" of the test.

One possible way to make a beginning toward overcoming the problems of invalid interpretation is to construct tests in such a manner that they give truly comparable results whether delivered in English or in Spanish. Such has been the approach of the Guidance Testing Associates, which, under the directorship of Dr. H. T. Manuel of the University of Texas, issues the Inter-American series. This series offers Tests of General Ability at five levels, an individually administered Preschool Test of General Ability, and Tests of Reading at five levels, in comparable Spanish and English editions (see the manual, 21, and the catalogue, 8). The manual for the Inter-American Series states that the comparability of the English and the Spanish editions is the unique contribution of the Series. Each child can be tested in his native language, and the scores derived from either language will be comparable. The technical report (20) indicates that items in the tests were constructed with three criteria in mind: (1) selection of materials common to the cultures of the Spanish-speaking and the English-speaking peoples of the Western Hemisphere, but not necessarily of the same frequency within the cultures; (2) use of the same pictures, drawings, and numbers in the non-language parts of the test booklets; (3) use of the same directions and the same verbal content, expressed for one edition in standard English and for the other in standard Spanish of similar difficulty. There are limitations, however. The manual (21) states that the materials are too limited in breadth to include the many abilities which should be summarized in order to provide an adequate measure of general intelligence. In addition, no national norms have been developed based on a national standardization sample. The recommendation is that those who use the tests prepare their own local or regional norms. Undoubtedly this would be ideal. It is, however, no easy task.

Stanford (31) has suggested another way of avoiding improper interpretation of intelligence test scores when applying standardized intelligence tests to Spanish-speaking children. He indicates that it may be more accurate to say that what is being measured by intelligence tests when applied to Spanish-speaking children is their *operational* level in an English-speaking society at a given point in time. Therefore, the author would not discard intelligence tests when they fail to work with Spanish-speaking chlidren, but rather would encourage teachers to view these test results as flexible indicators of expected operational level at a given time rather than established mental ability. These scores, according to the author, can be expected to improve as the Spanish-speaking child becomes increasingly socialized in the English-speaking classroom.

BIBLIOGRAPHY

(1) Altus, G. T. "WISC Patterns of a Selective Sample of Bilingual School Children," *The Pedagogical Seminary and Journal of Genetic Psychology,* December, 1953. Vol. 83, pp. 241–248.

(2) Birch, H. G., "Sources of Order in the Maternal Behavior of Animals," *American Journal of Orthopsychiatry,* April, 1956. Vol. 26, pp. 279–284.

(3) Carlson, H. B., and Henderson, N., "Intelligence of American Children of Mexican Parentage," *Journal of Abnormal and Social Psychology,* July, 1950. Vol. 45, pp. 544–551.

(4) Cook, J. M., and Arthur, G., "Intelligence Ratings for 97 Mexican Children in St. Paul, Minn.," *Journal of Exceptional Children,* October, 1951. Vol. 18, pp. 14–15.

(5) Demos, G. D., "Attitudes of Mexican American and Anglo American Groups Toward Education," *The Journal of Social Psychology,* August, 1962. Vol. 57, pp. 249–256.

(6) Dennis, Wayne, "Causes of Retardation Among Institutional Children: Iran," *Journal of Genetic Psychology,* March, 1960. Vol. 96, pp. 47–59.

(7) Flavell, J. H., *The Developmental Psychology of Jean Piaget;* Princeton, New Jersey: D. Van Nostrand Company, Inc., 1963.

(8) Guidance Testing Associates, *Catalogue, Educational Tests, Inter-American Series, 1967–68.* Austin, Texas.

(9) Honstead, Carole, "The Developmental Theory of Jean Piaget," in Frost, J. L. (ed.), *Early Childhood Educational Rediscovered;* New York: Holt, Rinehart.

(10) Hughson, Arthur, "The Case for Intelligence Testing," in Frost, J. L., and Hawkes, G. R. (eds.), *The Disadvantaged Child: Issues and Innovations;* Boston: Houghton Mifflin Company, 1966. pp. 126–130.

(11) Hunt, J. McV., *Intelligence and Experience;* New York: The Ronald Press Company, 1961.

(12) Hunt, J. McV., "How Children Develop Intellectually," in Frost, J. L., and Hawkes, G. R. (eds.), *The Disadvantaged Child: Issues and Innovations;* Boston: Houghton Mifflin Company, 1966. pp. 83–95.

(13) Jensen, A. R., "Learning Abilities in Mexican American and Anglo American

Children," *California Journal of Educational Research,* September, 1961. Vol. 12, pp. 147–159.

(14) Johnson, G. B., Jr., "An Experimental Projective Technique for the Analysis of Racial Attitudes," *Journal of Educational Psychology,* May, 1950. Vol. 41, pp. 251–278.

(15) Johnson, G. B., Jr., "The Origin and Development of the Spanish Attitude Toward the Anglo and the Anglo Attitude Toward the Spanish," *Journal of Educational Psychology,* November, 1950. Vol. 41, pp. 428–439.

(16) Johnson, G. B., Jr., "The Relationship Existing Between Bilingualism and Racial Attitude," *Journal of Educational Psychology,* October, 1951. Vol. 42, pp. 357–365.

(17) Johnson, G. B., Jr., "Bilingualism as Measured by a Reaction-Time Technique and the Relationship Between a Language and a Non-Language Intelligence Quotient," *Journal of Genetic Psychology,* March, 1953. Vol. 82, pp. 3–9.

(18) Keston, M. J., and Jimenez, C., "A Study of the Performance on English and Spanish Editions of the Stanford-Binet Intelligence Test by Spanish American Children," *Journal of Genetic Psychology,* December, 1954. Vol. 85, pp. 262–269.

(19) Manuel, H. T., *Spanish-Speaking Children of the Southwest: Their Education and the Public Welfare;* Austin: University of Texas Press, 1965. Chapter 7.

(20) Manuel, H. T., *Technical Report, Tests of General Ability and Tests of Reading. Inter-American Series Forms CE, DE, CEs, DEs;* Austin, Texas: Guidance Testing Associates, 1967.

(21) Manuel, H. T., *Manuel—Tests of General Ability and Tests of Reading, Inter-American Series, Forms CE and DE, CEs and DEs;* Austin, Texas: Guidance Testing Associates, 1967.

(22) Pasamanick, Benjamin, "Intelligence of American Children of Mexican Parentage: A Discussion of Uncontrolled Variables," *Journal of Abnormal and Social Psychology,* October, 1951. Vol. 46, pp. 598–602.

(23) Piaget, Jean, "The States of the Intellectual Development of the Child," *Bulletin of the Menninger Clinic,* May, 1962. Vol. 26, pp. 120–128.

(24) Piaget, Jean, *The Origins of Intelligence in Children,* Translated by Cook, Margaret; New York: W. W. Norton & Company, Inc., 1963.

(25) Piaget, Jean, *The Psychology of Intelligence,* Translated by Percy, M., and Berlyne, D. E.; Totowas, New Jersey: Littlefield, Adams & Company, 1966.

(26) Rapier, J. L., "Effects of Verbal Mediation Upon the Learning of Mexican American Children," *California Journal of Educational Research,* January, 1967. Vol. 18, pp. 40–48.

(27) Rice, J. P., Jr., "Education of Subcultural Groups," *School and Society,* November 28, 1964. Vol. 92, pp. 360–362.

(28) Roca, Pablo, "Problems of Adapting Intelligence Scales from One Culture to Another," *High School Journal,* January, 1955. Vol. 38, pp. 124–131.

(29) Skeels, H. M., "Effects of Adoption on Children from Institutions," in Frost,

J. L., and Hawkes, G. R. (eds.), *The Disadvantaged Child: Issues and Innovations;* Boston: Houghton Mifflin Company, 1966. pp. 116–119.

(30) Stablein, J. E., Willey, D. S., and Thomson, C. W., "An Evaluation of the Davis-Ells (Culture-Pair) Test Using Spanish and Anglo American Children," *Journal of Educational Sociology,* October, 1961. Vol. 35, pp. 33–38.

(31) Stanford, M. R., "Don't Discard Those IQ Tests When They Fail to Work With Non-English-Speaking Children. A New Approach Can Make Them Meaningful," *Texas Outlook,* October, 1963. Vol. 47, p. 31.

(32) Yourman, Julius, "The Case Against Group IQ Testing in School with Culturally Disadvantaged Pupils," in Frost, J. L., and Hawkes, G. R., *The Disadvantaged Child: Issues and Innovations;* Boston: Houghton Mifflin Company, 1966. pp. 131–134.

Teaching a Second Language to Spanish-Speaking Children of the Southwest

Herschel T. Manuel

The problem of teaching English as a second language to large numbers of Spanish-speaking children will persist in the Southwest for as long a time as can be foreseen. Geographical position, migration across the border, and the tenacity with which people hold to their mother tongue assure continuation of the problem. Because the teaching of English as a second language is difficult, and because ability in English is so important for the welfare both of the individual and of the community, language must be given high priority in the education of Spanish-speaking children.

In a thoughtful approach to the problem of teaching English to Spanish-speaking children, a question of basic policy must be raised at once. To serve the best interests of the child and the community, what part should Spanish have in the school program? Ability in the Spanish language may be in itself a significant objective of education. There is no doubt that the ability to use Spanish effectively can be a great asset to an individual and to the community. As the world grows smaller, the ability to communicate in a language which is used by millions of other people becomes a matter of increasing practical importance from the standpoint of international understanding and cooperation. Too, competence in more than one language widens the horizon of an individual and makes a significant contribution to his intellectual life. It provides a source of deep personal satisfaction as well. From this point of view, the ability in Spanish which a child develops in his home is an asset to be cultivated rather than carelessly cast aside. The chief practical hope for conserving and developing this asset is found in the school.

From Herschel T. Manuel, "The Problem of Language," *Spanish-Speaking Children of the Southwest*, Austin, Texas: University of Texas Press, 1965, pp. 118–129.

The fact that Spanish is a desirable objective of education does not dispose of the matter. At every level of instruction there is keen competition for a place in the curriculum, and there is not enough time for everything which might profitably be taught. An intelligent decision concerning the place of Spanish must be based upon a consideration of relative values. Including one area of subject matter may automatically exclude or limit another.

The case for or against Spanish does not rest solely on its value as an objective of education. Its possible use as a tool of instruction should be considered also, and the question should be asked whether part of the instruction of Spanish-speaking children should be given in their home language. At present in the Southwest, it is the policy of the public schools to use English as the language of instruction throughout the school grades. Spanish is sometimes used in speaking with children who know little or no English at school entrance and sometimes later to help in understanding English. It is the general practice, however, to minimize its use and to use English almost exclusively. In fact, many teachers have little or no knowledge of Spanish. In some schools Spanish is taught as a separate subject in the elementary grades, and of course later in the high school.

From time to time theorists have suggested the possibility of starting the schooling of Spanish-speaking children in Spanish, with English as the second language. This policy is followed in Puerto Rico, for example. In schools conducted on this policy the child becomes accustomed to the school routine, learns how to behave in a group, and learns to read in Spanish while he is learning an English oral vocabulary and simple English speech. Theoretically this suggestion has much to commend it. The transition from home to school and the process of learning to read are difficult enough under the most favorable circumstances. It is more difficult if the child is deprived of communication in his mother tongue and is plunged into a second-language environment immediately on school entrance. There is no doubt that the frustration and feeling of insecurity which a child experiences when confronted with such difficulties can be serious from the standpoint of individual development and school progress.

Initiating a child into the school routine in his native language, it is pointed out, enables him to meet the difficulties of the first year under the most favorable conditions. If this policy were adopted, most of the Spanish-speaking children at the end of the first year would be reading Spanish. A long step toward conserving this important language resource would be taken, and an avenue for extending his concepts through reading in a language with which the child is already familiar would be opened. It is theorized that at the end of a year or so he would have acquired enough knowledge of spoken English to make possible a fairly easy transfer of his reading habits to English, and at the end of the third grade he would have a reading knowledge of two languages rather than one.

The picture is not as rosy as it looks at first glance. Puerto Rican educators have not found it easy to teach English as a second language. Nor would it be easy in the United States. The Puerto Rican parallel breaks down at a critical point. There it is expected that English will continue to be a second language.

There Spanish is the language of instruction in all grades of the schools and is the primary language of everyday life. The great handicap of children who are learning English in Puerto Rico is the lack of sufficient contact with English and the lack of practical motivation for learning it. In the United States' Southwest, on the other hand, English is the language of the majority of the people except in certain limited areas, and English is the language of instruction in all grades of the schools. If Spanish-speaking children are to learn English for effective use, they must have many contacts with it. In a policy of teaching Spanish first barriers might be placed to their learning of English by helping to preserve their Spanish-speaking background and by lessening both the motive and the opportunity for out-of-school use of English. It is possible also that less English would be learned in school if the time were divided between English and Spanish and if the children could meet their major needs in their mother tongue. According to the testimony of students in an earlier chapter, the learning of English is accelerated by placing a child in a situation where English must be used. It could be objected also that one group in Spanish and another in English would make it difficult to combine the two in the same working group and thus would tend to continue a social division which should be overcome as soon as possible.

The more generally applicable solution of the problem seems to lie in a very different direction—the teaching of English to Spanish-speaking children *before* they reach the age when reading is normally taught. This proposal puts a burden squarely on the shoulders of parents who know English. They can help their children a great deal by teaching them English and by helping them to have contacts with other English-speaking persons. The responsibility of the public is to supplement the efforts of the parents by providing formal school opportunities before the age of six, the customary age of school entrance. Preschool "education" could be organized to give such language and other experiences as would erase some of the handicap with which foreign-language children otherwise start their work in an English-speaking school.

TEACHING ENGLISH TO FIVE-YEAR-OLDS

A reasonable immediate goal is to make formal schooling available to all children of five years of age. What shall this year be called? "Kindergarten" is a possibility, but this name seems to set it apart from the schooling which is to follow. Unfortunately, we have committed ourselves to a numbering of school levels which starts with grade 1 for the six-year-old and the beginning of reading. It would be hard to start lower down and get accustomed to a new numbering. Perhaps the new year could be called the prefirst grade. In any case, it should have very definite educational objectives coordinated closely with the level to follow. Certainly, it should not be primarily an independent development or a place where children simply play and rest while their parents work. The idea that school properly begins at six years of age is an outmoded concept, and the whole primary division should be reconstructed to include children of ages five to eight instead of six to eight.

In California the provision of public schooling for five-year-olds is fairly common. Denver, Colorado, is an illustration of cities with well developed programs for five-year-olds. Texas has taken a long step forward in providing state aid for summer schools for non-English-speaking children who will be of school age the following September, but this is only a step toward the desired goal.

Before state aid became available, summer instruction for Spanish-speaking children was provided in a number of Texas communities, through the initiative of local school systems and to some extent through private support. With the assistance of the League of United Latin American Citizens, of which he was president, Felix Tijerina led a movement to provide privately financed summer schools for Spanish-speaking children who would enter the first grade in the following September. A modest goal of teaching four hundred English words was set. A few of these schools were established, providing a demonstration of the plan. In this effort Tijerina drew freely on his own resources. Also, as a member of a state committee considering educational legislation, he was a leader in the effort to get state sanction and public support for summer schools for preschool non-English-speaking children.

A decision to place the emphasis in the school upon English does not imply a lack of appreciation of Spanish, or a lack of concern that the transition to English be made with as little emotional shock as possible. Children may be led to have a high regard for both Spanish and English, and yet to give major effort to developing ability in the new language. Certainly, there is no place for a policy which makes a child ashamed of his mother tongue.

A SUGGESTED LANGUAGE PROGRAM

Although more research is needed for a better understanding of the learning problems of children whose home language is Spanish, enough is known to point the way toward fruitful experimentation. The following outline presents a program in which ability in both English and Spanish can be developed in accordance with the principles previously discussed.

1. Provide a full year of education for children five years of age, with a gradual transition from speaking Spanish to speaking English and an emphasis on preparation for reading English. This prefirst grade experience may be expected to prepare the children for more nearly normal progress with other children and thus diminish the retardation which in later years is a major cause of dropping out of school.
2. Begin instruction in reading English when the children have reached an adequate stage of readiness.
3. Begin instruction in reading Spanish when the children have mastered the basic techniques of reading English, and give instruction in Spanish as a language through the elementary grades to all who qualify. The "mastery" of basic reading techniques may be tentatively defined as the average-and-above level of achievement reached by children in general at the end of grade 3. If English-speaking children are en-

rolled in the same school, they may be given instruction in oral Spanish beginning in grade 1, in preparation for beginning to read Spanish when their achievement in English has reached the same level.

4. Encourage the more able pupils to continue the study of Spanish beyond the elementary level.

The children who demonstrate interest and ability in language are the ones to whom we can look with greatest confidence to conserve and develop the individual and community assets of knowing Spanish as the first language.

Increasing Contacts with Standard English

Although this is not the place to discuss detailed techniques of teaching Spanish-speaking children in the schools, some facts and principles the public and teachers alike should understand. For example, the urgent need of increased contacts with satisfactory examples of spoken and written English both outside the school and in the school itself is a matter of common concern. These contacts are of supreme importance in the preschool years and in the elementary grades while the child's language habits are being formed largely by imitation. If the child's chief contact with English is limited to the time which he has in a class recitation or which he has individually with a teacher of twenty to fifty pupils, the outlook is discouraging for a mastery of standard pronunciation, speech rhythm, accent, vocabulary, and usage. The record of accomplishment and the testimony of the students themselves support this statement.

The effort to increase the contacts with standard English should be a very practical one adapted to the conditions under which children must live, but it should be imaginative. The parents of Spanish-speaking children must make opportunities and take advantage of those that exist. To leave all to the school is to invite inferior and discouraging achievement. Sentimental attachment to the mother tongue and conformity with the language pattern of the group may be satisfying to a parent, but it will not prepare his child to live and compete in an English-speaking environment.

The public—both English-speaking and Spanish-speaking—can help by supporting the efforts of the schools and of outside agencies to increase favorable language opportunities. Television is already a powerful educational instrument in teaching language, and it can be made a much more effective instrument. Special television stations can be established to devote themselves entirely to programs in the public interest. It is not too much, however, to ask of commercial stations a little time for carefully prepared educational programs at an hour favorable to children. Regarding television programs, Ralph Long, a student of English as a second language, has offered a suggestion which has unlimited possibilities: that language programs be prepared with children (nonprofessional actors) as participants. Anyone who has witnessed the keen interest of children in the simple dramatizations of the primary grades must be impressed by the possibilities of arranging such presentations for a wider audience. The language would be simple, for it would be children's language, and the listening child would tend to identify himself with the children in the performance.

Within the school, modern technical advances make it possible to add greatly to the language environment. If a schoolroom is properly equipped with a laboratory of projection apparatus, sound equipment, and listening devices, children can look and listen during periods when the teacher is busy with another class. Horse-and-buggy equipment of schools is not satisfactory in a jet-airplane age! Fantastic equipment or equipment clearly beyond a school's means is not urged, but efforts in the conservation and development of human resources should be modernized. Naturally, it will require a little larger slice of the tax dollar.

Drill with Understanding

The matter of drill is another common concern of public and professional staffs. The first principle here is that language must be based upon experience and must be motivated by a desire to communicate—to know what someone else is saying or has written and in turn to say something one's self. Pupils must want to talk and to write, and they must actually talk and write something which they wish to say. Teaching, at home or elsewhere, which is too far from the child's world or which contains too much criticism of the child's efforts can only result in a relatively barren drill. Why should a child try to think of something to say just to illustrate how something *can* be said? Language situations must produce the desire to communicate.

On the other hand, there is no royal road to learning a language, for incidental listening and imitation are not enough. There must be drill, and drill often requires effort. A person does not get ahead by dreaming and wishful thinking. Hard work is necessary, and children should learn to give it and expect to give it. The idea of calling everything a game, even in the kindergarten, is absurd; it does not prepare for life in a real world.

Four important points need to be made with regard to drill. The first is that drill should be carefully planned to give correct practice. A child learns what he practices, whether right or wrong. The second point is that the drill should be organized in steps adapted to the child's ability and previous learning. Haphazard drill may be a kind of merry-go-round, going on and on but not ahead. The third point is that drill should be conducted with a maximum of effort and attention. Motivation is important, and the time given to drill in one period should not be too long. A spread of practice over periods in which maximum effort is given will be better than a single long period of gradually decreasing interest and effort. Naturally, the periods should not be too short, for it often takes a little time just to "warm up." The use of self-teaching devices increases the possibilities of distributed and effective drill. The fourth point is that the child should know when he has made a correct response in a learning situation. If a learning situation requires repeated trials to make a correct response (as in learning to speak another language), the knowledge that a response is correct reinforces the tendency to make it again.

TECHNIQUES OF TEACHING

For more than thirty years educators have given serious attention to teaching English to Spanish-speaking children, and many helps are available, especially for teachers in the primary grades. Both individual school systems and state departments of education have prepared outlines and other forms of assistance. The late L. S. Tireman published a systematic treatment, entitled *Teaching Spanish-Speaking Children,* covering many topics and including an extensive discussion of the teaching of language.

Reading different accounts and visiting different schools, one is impressed by the variety of emphases in point of view and method. The fact is that children can learn from quite different learning situations. A linguist once remarked regarding a teaching situation in another geographical area, "The teachers were doing everything wrong, but the pupils were learning!" Although a careful evaluation would find that some methods are better than others, there is a great deal of room for variation in effective teaching.

In 1938 the Office of Education published a bulletin by J. L. Meriam with the provocative title *Learning English Incidentally.* This was an account of an experiment in which the emphasis was upon experience rather than language. The author pointed out the difference in these words:

. . . the activity program of La Jolla School is not used, as in most schools, to *motivate* the learning of English. Whatever of English is acquired by these bilingual children is strictly incidental to the accomplishment of a larger objective—the improvement of the normal activities of children.

He advocated the use of English in its various forms as one of many tools for reaching greater efficiency in normal life. "English at its very best is of value as it functions."

Although most students of the problem would regard Meriam's position as extreme, his insistence on the close connection of experience and language is quite sound. He does not at all preclude attention to other aspects of the situation, such as careful choice of the words to be taught and attention to the language as well as to the situation in which it is needed.

Robert Lado's discussion of the similarities and differences between English and Spanish (in his *Linguistics across Cultures*) emphasizes linguistic considerations in teaching a second language. As he points out, the languages are alike at some points and are different at others. The points of difference are the places of greatest difficulty in learning. There are differences in the speech sounds, in the sequence of sounds, in stress and rhythm, in word form and meaning, in intonation, and in grammatical structure. The teacher of Spanish-speaking children should know the points at which the greatest difficulties occur. In general, methodology is far behind in its adaptation to linguistic factors.

The listing of a few differences in the Spanish and English languages will illustrate the difficulties in learning either of the two as a second language. In word order, the adjective more often precedes the English noun but follows the Spanish noun. Thus "large river" is *rio grande* (river large). In English, adjectives and the articles "a" and "the" are unchanged by the gender of the noun; in Spanish the endings of the articles and of many adjectives change with the gender of the noun, and many nouns which are neuter in English are either masculine or feminine in Spanish.

Except for emphasis, Spanish commonly omits the pronoun as the subject of a sentence, the subject being understood from the forms of the verb and the context. Thus "I tell a story" and "he tells a story" can be simply *digo un cuento* and *dice un cuento*. In English the pronoun "you" serves for both singular and plural, but in Spanish there is more than one word that means "you." *Usted* is used for singular and *ustedes* for plural; also, in more intimate relations *tú* (accented) is used rather than *usted*. To complicate matters further, *tu* (unaccented) is used for the possessive singular "your," and *tus* for the possessive plural; in English, on the other hand, "your" is either singular or plural.

Systematic differences in spelling may present some difficulty. Thus, "-tion" in English is *-ción* in Spanish; "nation' is *nación*.

Differences in the sound values of letters and syllables frequently lead to errors in pronunciation. The Spanish sound represented by *i* is close to that represented by *ee* in English. For that reason Spanish-speaking children will tend to say "leetle" for "little." The sound of *th* is not common in the Spanish of the Southwest. Children may need help in placing the tongue to get the differences between *t* and *th,* and between *d* and *th*.

Differences in rhythm and intonation in connected speech add to the difficulties of pronunciation and of understanding. Lado calls the rhythm of Spanish a "syllable-timed rhythm," in which each syllable tends to take the same time. In English on the other hand, the timing is more by phrases than by syllables. In both languages some syllables are stressed more than others, and differences in pitch are used in somewhat different ways.

In the elementary grades while speech habits are still flexible, it is rather easy to help a child produce a speech sound almost correctly by imitation, guided if necessary by suggestions on how to make a given sound. The difficulty is one of providing sufficient practice with that sound. Once the child leaves the teacher, he may practice a very different sound—and what he practices he learns. At this point recordings of correct sounds which may be used for practice away from the teacher can be very helpful. The purpose is to give the pupil almost constant contact with satisfactory models. The same principle holds when the child has learned to read. He must be encouraged to read a great deal. Whether he listens or reads, it must be with understanding.

Teachers sometimes become accustomed to nonstandard pronunciations, as do children, and do not hear them as errors. It is possible also to be too sensitive to errors and to be so critical that children are uncomfortable and avoid English as much as possible.

If children advance to the junior high school with glaring errors in speech, the correction of these errors is difficult. During these years, however, and even later much can be accomplished through special classes or individual help supplemented by increased contact with standard English. At this stage a special speech teacher who understands the difficulties of Spanish-speaking children can be of great value.

Other Problems

Two of the greatest difficulties in the teaching of English in the primary grades are (1) developing a program which leads systematically and at the right speed toward definite goals, and (2) giving sufficient content to the teaching. However interesting and valuable exercises may be in themselves, they should fit together in a sequence which leads toward some end. There was once a phrase "busy work" which still all too aptly describes many classroom activities. Giving content to language is difficult when the vocabulary is small. Take three hundred to five hundred words some time and try conducting an exhilarating conversation using only them!

In the higher grades it is sometimes difficult to find reading material of content appropriate to the maturity of the children and at the same time simple enough in language to allow the children to read without experiencing difficulty so great that they will give up the struggle. This, of course, is also true of English-speaking children, but the problem is especially acute with children who are learning English as a second language. There is another possible approach to the solution of the problem of difficult reading material. To a certain extent, instead of avoiding difficult selections or rewriting them to present the content in easier language, systematic help could be provided at the points where the difficulties are likely to be greatest. Difficult words and unfamiliar expressions can be explained in preparation for the reading, thus increasing the child's ability to deal with the material as written.

Sometimes Spanish can be used effectively in teaching English, particularly if it is hard to explain a word in simpler English or to develop its meaning through experience. For example, such a word as "however" may be explained quite simply by giving its Spanish equivalent. On the other hand, the use of Spanish can easily be overdone. Giving equivalent words in a language which a child already knows tends to make him translate rather than use the new language in his thought processes. Even Spanish-English dictionaries encourage translation. Thinking in English is stimulated by using as far as possible a dictionary in which the meanings of English words are expressed by pictures or by other English words already in the child's vocabulary.

Craftsmanship in Teaching

There is a certain craftsmanship in the work of the good teacher, a combination of skills which to some extent is individual. At the primary level, for example, a teacher who is musical and creative may make music of primary importance in learning language. Nearly any situation can have an appropriate song, sometimes composed for the occasion, to reinforce the learning. Similarly, a teacher talented in art may make the use of charts and illustrations especially effective. Another with a good literary background and the ability to tell a story may give the children an unusually rich experience in literature. A teacher with dramatic training may emphasize the role of make-believe and make common situations intensely interesting. Another with a scientific background may open a new world by helping the children to see the things around them through the eyes of science.

Where to from Here?

Thomas P. Carter

The socioeconomically disadvantaged and subordinate status of Mexican Americans has been recognized by Southwesterners for many years. Concomitant with this recognition was the belief that such a situation was the "natural order" and that "Mexicans" were somehow doomed by their genetic or cultural inheritance to second-class citizenship. Racists explained the minority group's position as being a result of its generally inferior intelligence. The less biased among the Anglos rationalized it in terms of the widely accepted stereotype of the lazy, apathetic, and noncompetitive "Mexican." Unfortunately, many social scientists inadvertently contributed to this stereotype by their repeated stress on the concept of a "folk" or traditional culture. Their research findings were over generalized, extended, and misinterpreted by laymen and educators. (For a strong indictment of social scientists see Romano V., 1968.) Although the concept of the ethnic or racial inferiority of the minority was and is erroneous, Anglo society was correct in one sense: the Southwestern social system (the "natural order") did function best with a pool of cheap and unskilled labor and a subordinate "caste." The low-skilled, poorly schooled "Mexican" fitted admirably into the rather distinctive social and economic systems of the region and helped to sustain them. Although it is a gross overgeneralization to assume that the five-state Southwestern region had one common social system, it is fair to say that certain elements were held in common.

SCHOOL AND SOCIETY

Most Mexican immigrants, as well as those of Spanish ancestry resident in the Southwest for generations, were well-integrated cogs in the social system. Most possessed the skills, experience, and perhaps temperament demanded to mesh into the rural agricultural economy. The economy was, and still is in certain areas, based on a *hacienda* and a dual "caste" system, reminiscent of the social arrangements of the plantation of the South. With the continuing disappearance of the *hacienda,* a new system emerged, agricultural industry. This newer system is socially not unlike the *hacienda,* except that the paternalism of the *patrón* is not continued by modern management. Mexican Americans who had not entered the agricultural system in earlier periods meshed equally well. They had the skills and knowledge essential for the closed social systems spawned by mining and railroad interests. In a sense, the Mexican immigrant never left home: the social, economic, and perhaps political arrangements on both sides of the Rio Grande were very much alike.

Society and its schools produced an adult Mexican American population prepared for participation in the agricultural economy of the traditional Southwest. The school was, and in many geographic areas still is, "successful" in equipping most Mexican Americans with the knowledge and skills appropriate to low status: minimum English language ability, rudimentary reading and figuring skills, and the values necessary to a law-abiding, although nonparticipating and essentially disenfranchised, citizen. The fact that the school failed to Americanize or to raise the group status of so many Mexican Americans was evidence of its success. Local society functioned well with an easily controlled, politically impotent, and subordinate ethnic caste. School practices evolved that functioned to perpetuate the social and economic system by unconsciously encouraging the minority group to fail academically, drop out early, and enter society at the low status traditional for Mexican Americans, thus producing the human types necessary to perpetuate the local society. Mexican American failure to achieve well in school contributed to the Anglos' belief that they had innately inferior intelligence, that they were lazy, passive, fatalistic, and lacked initiative. This self-reinforcing circle of circumstances became well established in the Southwest and persists to the present.

Social changes are occurring rapidly today, but the school is rarely able to keep up by modifying its practices or policies, or its teaching staff and their attitudes and perceptions. Too often school conditions "appropriate" to past social circumstances persevere into the present with devastating influence on minority-group children as well as on society in general. Some areas of the Southwest continue to follow the earlier ranch and small-town social patterns, even though most of the area has undergone rapid and profound change.

Since the beginning of World War II, the Southwest has: (1) become predominantly urban; (2) rapidly industrialized; (3) in the rural areas, replaced earlier occupational and socioeconomic arrangements with agricultural industry; and (4) placed much less emphasis on mining and railroading activities. The majority of Mexican Americans, like their Anglo counterparts, now live in metropolitan areas, and most compete in the urban industrial job market. Far too many Mexican Americans find it difficult or impossible to compete with other groups because of the substandard schooling they previously received. The stability of the older social system is disappearing. Radical and rapid demographic, economic, and social changes contribute to grievous personal, social, and economic maladaptations and malfunctions.

Leaders in the Southwest now recognize that maintaining a rapidly increasing Mexican American population with low status as a group and poor education represents a serious threat to societal stability. While such a population may have served the old rural Southwest well, presenting no threat to the social equilibrium, its persistence at present contributes to many undesirable and unsettling conditions. Even the more politically and socially conservative Anglo groups see these conditions as alarming and are exerting pressure on the schools to eliminate overt manifestations of the Mexican American's low social status. Society is directing the school to "raise the group" by insuring that the young achieve academically and persevere in school. With improved school achievement and increased years of schooling, higher group status is anticipated and the subsequent elimination of unemployment, unemployability, underemployment, dependency on welfare, juvenile delinquency, and adult crime. Pressures from within society are forcing action to resolve grave problems, problems partially created by the fact that schools inadvertently functioned to maintain the minority in a subordinate position. It must be acknowledged, regretfully, that it is not educators' altruism that is coming to the fore. Rather, it is the controlling political groups who see that societal peace and balance are threatened and encourage or demand whatever school action is evident. Society is slowly becoming concerned and is beginning to direct its institutional arms, especially the schools, to solve the problems created by radical changes in the Southwest. A low-status Mexican American is no longer functional; the "natural order" has changed.

The community and its formal educational institutions are inexorably interrelated. It is impossible to separate institutions from the society they serve; each functions for and contributes to the maintenance and continuity of society. The school reflects the sociocultural totality, incorporating the professed values as well as the mores, the good and the bad, the static and the kinetic, and the progressive and the conservative. The dependency of the American school on local society for direction as well as economic support almost guarantees that little initiative will be forthcoming from educators. While this local control is deemed essential in America's democratic society, it nonetheless discourages attempts by schoolmen to use their institutions as agents of directed, or even nondirected, social change. Educational leaders are all too often members of the conservative establishment or are dominated by them, impotent to counter their wishes. If these controlling elements manifest little interest or concern about the status of minority groups and see the situation as "natural," and if the minority groups remain mute and powerless, little initiative will be forthcoming from the educational establishment. If no group or problem is rocking the boat, the school comfortably assumes it is performing adequately. These conditions characterized the Southwest in the recent past—the few who raised their voices to advocate school reform found they had an unresponsive, though polite, audience.

Educators' concern about the low socioeconomic and educational status of Mexican Americans and pressure to raise the minority group's position are related to forces within society to a much greater degree than they are to the forces within the institution. Southwestern society has and does determine educational practices; as this society changes, slow but perhaps steady changes can be anticipated in the school. Many of the school's practices so perfectly mirror the local society's mores that any substantial modification must await changes in the community. Legal intervention to force local school mores (practices) into alignment with national values or mores are usually countervened, subverted, or evaded by local schools, as is exemplified by attempts at enforced desegregation. Other school practices are not so closely aligned with the mores but are nonetheless exceedingly difficult to modify because of "institutional habit" and the inability of the highly bureaucratized school to modify itself. For many reasons, educators and schools resist change, whether the force for change emanates from within or without institutional walls.

The School's Position

There is no one explanation of why Juanito can't read, is "poorly motivated," and flees the school early to assume the low status traditional for his group. Searching for the reasons for the low school achievement and years of schooling of the Mexican American minority has resulted in the isolation of three complex and interrelated sets of factors:

1. The nature of the diverse Mexican American subcultures and the socialization afforded Mexican American children
2. The kind and quality of formal education available to Mexican Americans
3. The nature of the local and regional social systems and the equal or unequal opportunity they afford the minority group

Unfortunately, most educators fail to recognize the latter two points and stress only the first, that the minority group's low status, lack of assimilation and acculturation, and failure in school are due to the group's distinctive Mexican culture. The widespread, if not almost universal, acceptance of this "theory" is easily understood, since it exonerates society and school from complicity in the situation. The low status and continued "foreignness" of minority groups are situations caused by innumerable social and economic factors within the dominant society as well as cultural characteristics of the minority. However, Americans generally tend to blame the minority for its own low status and for being the cause of its own "problem."

In rejecting this simplistic argument of "cultural distinctiveness," there may be a strong tendency to overreact and fail to understand the interrelationships between the three major factors involved. The nature of the minority subcultures or subsocieties is influenced in untold ways by local society and institutions, and vice versa. The complex whole is not amenable to facile separation or clear definition; a total social situation *causes* the Mexican American tendency to achieve poorly in school and drop out early.

One not-so-startling conclusion can be drawn from analysis of the kind of children who succeed in schools: those who do so tend to be children who are culturally and personally similar to what the school expects. They are almost invariably the "normal' children from "normal" homes, average middle-class American youngsters. The "different" child, whether he be Anglo, Negro, lower class, or whatever, rarely measures up at school entrance or exit to the normal or "standard" child. It is easy to conclude that the cultural, social-class, or personality differences of "different" children, faced with an undifferentiated or standard middle-class-oriented school, cause them to fail in school. Most educators, with the support of the vocal elements within the middle class, assume that the school is adequate and validly represents the core values and content of American culture. Therefore, it is not difficult to understand why school people, when given a choice between seeing Mexican Americans' poor school performance as attributable to either their home or the nature of the school, readily opt to blame the "deficient" home.

In order to support this position, educators have developed elaborate and detailed descriptions of the life-styles and personalities of Mexican Americans and their children, setting forth the assumed differences in world view and life-style that account for the minority-group child's lack of school and social success. Unfortunately, the common beliefs of educators about Mexican American children have these common failings:

1. They are based on little, if any, current objective evidence.
2. They are derived from older, though perhaps valid, descriptions of rural "folk culture."
3. They demonstrate little insight into the nature of culture, society, or language.
4. They describe one monolithic Mexican American ·culture, whereas in reality great diversity exists.
5. They picture a static minority culture changing little over time.
6. They correspond beautifully with the common Anglo stereotype of "Mexicans" in general.

Armed with this formidable arsenal of false or exaggerated beliefs, schoolmen find the reasons for Mexican Americans' school problems and in so doing put the burden on the minority—who unfortunately may sometimes believe that the educators' reasons are correct.

Having identified the Mexican American home and culture as the source of school problems, school personnel proceed to remedy the situation in the only way their logic allows: the school must eliminate cultural difference or "deprivation" and thereby insure institutional and social success. This position is fortified by the widespread belief among educators that the school was a principal agency in the acculturation of other "foreign" groups. Most educators argue that a prime function of the school is the rapid, perhaps ruthless, Americanization of children of foreign backgrounds. In this regard, the school supports the general American concept that members of minority groups are acceptable as soon as they cease to be culturally distinct and become indistinguishable from everyone else. Compensatory education and remedial programs to "meet the needs" of "deprived" Mexican American children (to reorient, reconstruct, retool, or remodel them) are undertaken and generally supported by most educators and civic leaders. Such programs and projects result from the combination of three prevalent assumptions: that the home culture is the cause of school failure, that the school is satisfactory as it is, and that a principal function of the school is to Americanize foreign peoples by eliminating their alien language and cultural orientation. This author contends that school programs based exclusively on these three highly questionable assumptions are doomed to failure and that there is little or no objective evidence indicating otherwise.

In spite of the dearth of evidence of success, vast sums of federal and local money have been and are being spent in efforts to reorient or modify the lowest social classes and "foreign" groups into what the middle-class school sees as desirable. In a sense, federal funds contribute to the highly questionable assumption that children of such groups are intellectually inferior or culturally deprived or both. Federal efforts also implicitly support the proposition that if the minority-group child is successfully remodeled into an "acceptable American," society will willingly embrace him and offer him equal opportunity. Federal financial assistance has only rarely resulted in substantial school reform or modification and instead tends to reinforce the local educational status quo.

There are two major factors that impede the Mexican American's ability to use the school to raise his socioeconomic status. The nature of the school discourages academic achievement and attainment; and discrimination and the limited number of statuses open to his group in much of the Southwest discourage his aspirations (which are usually high). Local society often does not reward Mexican Americans for their efforts upward. The school is now charged with raising the school achievement and years of schooling of the group in order to insure their incorporation into the rapidly changing society, but in many areas, the present society provides only limited social or occupational slots, thus eliminating the future reward so crucial to school perseverance, achievement, and motivation. In a sense, the school must produce Mexican Americans able to occupy statuses that are not now available locally and to learn roles that are not appropriate in many locales. This indeed is a big order. Few educators contend that the school can change the social system; it is too closely controlled by its parent society and interrelated with it. The school cannot provide the open statuses necessary to encourage postponement of reward; only changes in the socioeconomic order can do so. Nevertheless, the school could make school participation so intrinsically rewarding that it would encourage Mexican Americans to persevere in preference to withdrawing early. Attending school could be personally gratifying. Unfortunately schools are usually unable to change radically. It is difficult to modify conditions and practices, since many reflect local mores and attitudes. Not only are the attitudes of educators themselves conservative, but the practices and curriculums of the schools are also, reflecting the older and controlling generation's beliefs. Schools thus continue practices that tend to lower achievement and perseverance, encourage early mental and physical withdrawal, and in general cause school participation to be of little intrinsic reward.

Unfortunately, the school has reached or is reaching a stage that makes substantial modification most difficult. A contributory factor encouraging the maintenance of the institutional status quo is the fact that the practices that inhibit Mexican Americans in school tend to be supported as essential by the powerful conservative elements controlling schools. These groups usually demand the continuance of instruction in English only, strong reliance on IQ test scores, rigid tracking, de facto segregation, the inculcation of middle-class values, and strong authoritarianism within schools—practices that have become almost "core values" in the local educational scene. The aggregate of these and other practices creates the negative school social environment that is seen as a crucial factor in the failure of Mexican Americans in school. Although exceptions exist, the majority of Southwestern educators are unable either to analyze their schools objectively or to make the modifications necessary to encourage minority-group success. The majority of institutions seem static: "The structure has become too intricate, or too rigid, or the idea of function has faded from the minds of the functionaries" (Waller, 1961, p. 442). The functionaries of the school appear to be overly concerned with the maintenance of their own positions, which is guaranteed by the continuance of the institutional status quo. The professed objectives of American education (equal opportunity, reaching of maximum potential, and so forth) are increasingly voiced by educators, but all too often they seem little more than shallow utterances. The means by which such ends are to be attained are likely to function to impede their realization. School practices, curriculums, overreliance on testing, and rigid ability grouping can inhibit the reaching of such exemplary goals. These conditions are difficult to modify, especially since they are often the very foundations of an individual functionary's power, prestige, and income. Schools seem to be guided quite commonly by the need for self-preservation and self-justification.

A difficult situation exists, but the modification or elimination of certain practices or conditions and subsequent affirmative action could bring about improvement in the performance of Mexican Americans in school. Theoretically, educational leadership has three possible avenues toward accomplishing this improvement: attempting to change the children themselves, attempting to change the school, and attempting to change society.

CHANGING THE CHILD

In spite of the clamor for equality of educational opportunity and more efficient schools and programs for minority-group children, one is hard pressed to demonstrate that any of the almost universally recommended and used compensatory or remedial programs are producing the long-term results desired. While limited evidence suggests that some Mexican American children are reaching short-term goals of reading readiness, English language ability, and so forth, no proof is available to demonstrate that such readiness and ability result in sustained higher achievement, fewer school dropouts, or exit from school into higher-status positions than those held by their parents. There is little doubt that the school will continue its attempts to remodel children into facsimiles of middle-class Anglos. Although this author believes that compensatory or remedial education will not substantially improve the school success of Mexican Americans, there is as little hard evidence to support this position as there is to support the argument that it will.

Certain recommendations can be made about the collection of evidence bearing on this problem. It is essential to know exactly what kinds of programs reach both their short- and long-term objectives. Agencies financing such projects should make continued funding contingent on detailed study of a program's effectiveness. Guidelines for such programs must be reset to insure adequate objective data collection and analysis. Compliance must be insured. In order to overcome the widely divergent methods of evaluation now used, agencies should develop, or sponsor others to develop, standardized master proposal forms and data-collection and evaluation procedures. The standardization of forms and procedures should present little difficulty, since most compensatory and remedial programs for the disadvantaged are quite similar (almost identical) throughout the nation. These standard forms should require the delegate agency (usually the school) to describe clearly the short-term and long-term objectives of the program proposed, the methods (techniques) assumed to reach them, staff characteristics, the number and kinds of students involved, and the outcomes.

Every program has both short- and long-term objectives. For example, English-as-a-Second-Language programs have as their principal short-term objective competence in English, and their long-term or major goal is success in school. Both objectives are measurable, the short-term more easily than the long. To measure the short-term goal, federal guidelines and the standard form could demand measurement of children's English competency both before and after they have gone through the program. A standardized test for this purpose must be found or developed. All districts could employ the mandatory test(s) or substitute others that are agreed upon as comparable. Whether students reach or do not reach the long-term objective of success in school is much more difficult to measure, but it is nonetheless the crucial consideration. This is the obligation of the funding agency. Provision should be made for a continuing (longitudinal) appraisal of students' academic performance, school behavior, participation, and status after leaving school. Either the agency must provide funds for a term longer than the usual fiscal year, or future district projects must be required to put aside money for continuing research on students from prior years. With the data assembled and reduced for computer processing, the agency involved can make its analysis of program effectiveness. Without these or similar measures there will doubtless be a continuation of inadequate evaluation and inadequate decisions based solely on subjective rather than objective analysis. Evidence must be generated to show what works, when it works, with whom it works, and ultimately how it works. Such evidence *might* encourage educators to cut down the present waste of money and effort and perhaps curtail practices that are detrimental to minority-group children, but it must be recognized that information alone cannot be expected to change present school efforts. For example, assuming that traditional compensatory programs will indeed be demonstrated to accomplish little, it does not necessarily follow that schools will curtail or modify them. Such programs become institutionalized and as resistant to change as other school practices.

Concomitant with schoolmen's desire to "phase in" the out-of-phase Mexican American child is the less often expressed, but equally cherished, desire to change the child's parents. Common examples of this desire are schools' efforts to encourage English speaking at home, American or "modern" child-rearing practices, and changes in diet. The child is often used as the vehicle to encourage the rapid acculturation of his "foreign" parents. If the goal is to change cultural aspects of the home (and many authorities feel that it should not be), certain steps can be suggested. As with efforts to modify the child, present attempts to modify the home must be seriously evaluated. The conditions under which distinct groups of Mexican Americans will accept and incorporate cultural items transmitted to them from the school must be determined. This author questions the feasibility (and morality) of using the school in this way, but most schoolmen do not. They need to know what works. Careful objective studies of the school as a cultural innovator must be undertaken, but it is doubtful that most educators have the skills or insights necessary to carry them out. For this reason anthropologists or other social scientists should be commissioned to study the school in regard to this function; an objective analysis of the influence of the school on minority culture is essential.

The crucial question here is not one of approach but of ethics: should the school "change foreigners" or should it incorporate distinct cultures into the school and its curriculum? Objective information should help educators to improve the quality of not only their pragmatic but ethical decisions such as this.

CHANGING THE SCHOOL

Radical modification of the school to eliminate factors discouraging the success of minority-group children, or to incorporate factors assumed to encourage it, is rare. School conditions contributing to the success or failure of these children are not clearly spelled out, and much discussion of them is conjecture. How successful would bilingual schools be? No one really knows. Would the elimination of rigid tracking encourage higher academic achievement, discourage mutual stereotyping, and enhance the minority-group's self-concept, as suggested? Again no one knows for sure. One can continue in this vein, each question receiving essentially the same reply. In order to come to at least a partial resolution two steps are necessary:

1. Schools must make substantial changes in their staffs, curriculums, and organization.
2. Schools that do so must be studied carefully, objectively, and over long periods of time.

In other words, procedures must be implemented to encourage and support large-scale experiments, and these must be carefully and critically evaluated.

It is recommended here that outside funds be withheld from districts that fail to comply with standardized evaluation procedures or fail to modify conditions assumed or found to be detrimental to Mexican Americans. This might be a particularly valuable technique of governmental intervention, as many districts have come to rely very heavily on federal financial assistance. However, such intervention should be considered a last resort, as it is in the case of desegregation. It must be remembered that such action would be most likely to hurt the Mexican American children more than the Anglo children or the district as a whole. Perhaps reward would work better than punishment. Money could be used as a catalyst. Large amounts could be made available to districts or schools willing to undertake radical modifications and subsequent study of outcomes. One important outgrowth of relatively widespread experimentation would be objective information concerning the causes of change itself. It would be very useful to know what causes substantial institutional change and under what conditions certain approaches or interventions could be expected to result in less rigidity, more flexibility, and the minority group's greater success in school.

One approach to changing the school that is commonly advocated is attempting to prepare teachers more adequately. Certainly no one would argue against this, but it must be remembered that teachers are only one component of the institution. Without other institutional changes it is doubtful that even the best teachers could encourage the amount of minority-group improvement needed. In any case, improved teaching staff is a step in the right direction. Inservice reeducation of teachers could, if handled creatively, provide avenues leading to the overall improvement of the school. Whether attempts to improve teachers focus on the college or the school (preservice or inservice), a number of factors must be considered:

1. What are the weaknesses of teachers that need to be overcome?
2. What programs will best overcome these weaknesses?
3. How is it possible to convince or force the college or school to implement these programs?

In many ways it may be easier to modify inservice than preservice programs. The teacher-education "establishment" may well be more resistant to change, more rigid and formalized, than lower-level institutions. In any case, means to change teachers need to be found; if colleges of education are unwilling or unable to change their approaches, other institutions must be established to perform the needed functions.

Any program of preservice or inservice teacher preparation should include three essential components (Carter, 1969). First, the formal content of instruction must be relevant to the school problems of Mexican American children and to cross-cultural education. It must include such slighted disciplines as anthropology, sociology, psycholinguistics, and the psychology of cultural marginality. A second component crucial to any successful program is vastly increased student involvement with Mexican Americans. Students must be encouraged to interact with the real world within the school, the Mexican American community, and in activities that bridge the two. The third and perhaps most important of the components is small group seminars, modeled after T-group or sensitivity sessions. These seminars are catalysts; without adding any new ingredient, they should hasten the process of interaction, force a reconciliation, or at least a constructive encounter, between content taught by more formal methods and content learned through experience.

Regardless of the program, present or future teachers must:

1. Recognize the overwhelming influence of culture on personality and behavior.
2. Have a thorough knowledge of Mexican American culture.
3. Understand the function of the school *vis à vis* culturally different peoples.

To accomplish these objectives, some rather personal things must happen to teachers. Basic assumptions about themselves, the world they live in, and their explanations of both must be subjected to reappraisal. "Folk myth" explanations of such phenomena as race, achievement, social class, intelligence, and more have to be destroyed; too often such unsound explanations deter teachers' ability to cope with the very real problems associated with them. Sensitivity sessions may provide the framework from which teachers can gain the essential support as they reconstruct themselves and their beliefs. (For more information on this approach see Landes, 1965.) It is not possible to propose specific arrangements of content, seminars, and field exposure, since each situation is distinct. However, it is strongly suggested that each of these three components is equally important in any teacher education or reeducation program.

In the cases of schools that have extremely rigid practices, treat their students unequally, or show very poor results from their special programs, federal agencies could demand what might be referred to as "total" inservice reeducation. The total staff of a particular school, including everyone from principal to secretary, would study, evaluate, and remodel their school and themselves. To accomplish this reeducation, special teams of well-prepared "counterparts" would work with the staff of an individual school for a protracted length of time. Counterpart teams would probably be made up of specially prepared interdisciplinary university and public school personnel. These teams would work toward the three goals mentioned in the above paragraph. Changes in teaching techniques, school organization, curriculum, and teachers' behavior toward the Mexican Americans would be undertaken with the counterpart teams acting as guides to self-analysis. Theories would be exposed to local reality; rational adjustments of school to the local situation would be the objective.

Drastic approaches are probably essential in order to achieve the institutional self-analysis and change so crucial to the school success of Mexican American children. Ideally, the institution will accomplish these things without undo outside intervention. Realistically, however, increased minority-group pressure and governmental intervention will probably not only occur but be necessary. Educators need help to understand such pressure and to react constructively to it. Universities, under contract to government, might be of help. State governments could do more in this area, following the examples set by Colorado and California. However, if only token measures are taken to help educators understand the situation, it should be anticipated that schoolmen will fail to capitalize on the positive aspects of Mexican American pressure and desire for involvement. Educators can be predicted either to do nothing or to overreact if no help is forthcoming. All elements must work to insure constructive reactions to the impending confrontation.

Teachers and schools must change. It may be hoped that those in authority will implement the modifications themselves, but their progress to date has been far less than spectacular. Drastic measures are demanded; perhaps the time has come for taking the action one prominent educator suggests (Sullivan, 1968): "Maybe we should close down our schools for a while and retain our teachers . . . even if the children were on the streets they'd be learning more than from some of our teachers."

CHANGING SOCIETY

The extreme difficulty of legislating mores is readily evident to the careful analyst of school and society. The subterfuges, counterventions, and delaying tactics employed to circumvent desegregation are cases in point. While efforts to enforce the law should not be curtailed, it must be recognized that many laws run counter to local mores and that much resistance will be encountered. This is as true with desegregation of schools as it is with fair employment, equal opportunity, and other aspects of civil rights. However, the federal government can take advantage of an interesting situation: higher-level occupations appear more open to minority groups than do lower-level occupations. In fact society appears to be rapidly eliminating many of the manual and semiskilled occupations while creating more at the managerial or professional levels. At present, minority-group members face less opposition from the majority at those levels requiring higher education. As the lower-skilled occupations or economic slots become more restricted in number and kind as a result of mechanization, it can be expected that those holding them will more jealously guard their positions, and it seems logical to assume that discrimination against the Mexican Americans filling these lower-level jobs will increase (see Hill, 1966). While competition between ethnic groups for lower-level agricultural slots has been slight, it probably will be greater for industrial positions. A number of peculiar situations exist in the Southwest:

1. Mexican Americans face slight prejudice if they enter high-level (those requiring college education) occupations.
2. Competition for the disappearing low-skilled industrial occupations exists (with much variation throughout the five states) and may increase as it has in the South for Negroes. With competition increased, discrimination may result.
3. Discrimination is more prevalent in the castelike and rural areas than in the more socially open urban areas.
4. There seems to be less discrimination against Mexican Americans in areas where their percentage in the population is low, especially outside the five Southwestern states.

Certain steps could be taken to capitalize on these situations to the benefit of the minority group and society in general.

Mexican Americans must be brought to the schooling level required of higher-status and more open occupations. They must also be encouraged to leave the geographic areas of severe discrimination and move to other parts of the region or the nation. To accomplish these two objectives, government might: (1) Establish a "GI Bill" for the poor, guaranteeing the financial assistance necessary to complete the schooling required to enter higher-status occupations. Combined with the following steps (2) and (3), this would promote the motivation necessary to stay in school. (2) Provide information for Mexican Americans about the nature of opportunities open to them in other geographic areas; many know only their local community. (3) Provide financial and other assistance necessary to allow the relocation of individuals and families.

These steps would not change the societies where Mexican Americans are now concentrated (and where discrimination is most intense), but they would at least permit Mexican Americans to capitalize on the present situation.

4 THE INDIAN HERITAGE

Conquered peoples, and especially those who have experienced a brutal conquest, tend to isolate themselves from their conquerors, spatially where possible, and inwardly (psychologically) almost universally. They tend to develop styles of behavior which cause them to often be categorized as apathetic, withdrawn, irresponsible, shy, lazy and helpless in terms of managing their own affairs. Alcoholism and excessive personalistic factionalism seem to typify such defeated, powerless populations, and individuals exhibit signs of possessing serious inferiority complexes and a weak or negative sense of personal identity. This style of behavior tends not to be greatly ameliorated by paternalistic-elitist reform or welfare programs which may subsequently be administered by the dominant population, perhaps because such prodigious efforts serve simply to reinforce a sense of inferiority and incapacity.[1]

Considering that the median school years for an Indian student total 8.9, and that the dropout rate after that is 75 percent, one begins to sense that, having had their population reduced by 85 percent in the last 200 years, having been deprived of wealth and of protection from exploitation and denigration, the American Indian has suffered traumatic socio-psychological ill effects. Stung by the loss of his cultural heritage and his pride the Indian encountered the pains of frustration once again in education.

Yet for all people, as for all individuals, the time comes when they must reckon with their history. For many Indian students, the present is a time of such renaissance. At long last, the Indian people are beginning to express a new consciousness and a new resolve. Recognizing the historical tasks confronting them, and fully aware of the cost, Indian youths are today pledging themselves to activism.

Articles in this Part detail some of the factors and frustrations which have

[1]Jack Charles, "Introduction," *California Indian Education*, Modesto, California: California Indian Education Association, Inc., 1969, p. 2.

brought about this new ideology, and some of the things that understanding teachers can do about it. The first selection, by Dozier, provides an anthropological, historical, and linguistic review of American Indians, underscoring that all tribes are different. Building on this base, Roessel's article offers specific suggestions for phases of Indian culture which teachers can study as wedges to understanding this population. For any tribe, Roessel recommends an inquiry into aspects of the culture that he considers most fundamental: means of subsistence, values, and crafts. We suggest additional possibilities: religion, dance, sports, and games.

The piece by Charles, "The Indian and Civil Wrongs," presents a devastating sketch of the Indian's loss of his land which will be disturbing to those among us who have felt our government could do no wrong. Our collective guilt deepens in "Red Man's Plight," as Isenberg analyzes the employment problem —even among those Indians who have been specially trained, let alone the older Indians who have long had no role to play.

We shift gears with Steiner, from the old to the young Indians now breaking away from the strong traditions of the past to lead their tribes in a new movement. How many of us understood what had happened when a group of youthful Indians captured the infamous citadel of Alcatraz in San Francisco Bay which, in defiance of the U.S. government, they occupy to this day?

Young people witnessing their parents driven from reservations to cities and sometimes back again, all by poverty, insist that this harsh existence must stop, that it will not be a part of their own lives. Education has failed their parents; it will not fail them. In the old days, the Indian child was assigned to special classes. In both elementary and the higher grades, he was not really expected to compete with the white students of the larger society. At the same time, he was expected to divest himself of all his "inferior" cultural attributes, and to espouse values that were foreign to him. He was expected to speak English, the American language, when his native tongue was Indian. He was "placed" into classes or subdivisions of them according to his performance on biased tests—tests that had no bearing on his own cultural experience and context. Thus he was placed, in effect, in mentally retarded classes. He was taught that George Washington and Abraham Lincoln were his forefathers; he was taught to revere them at the neglect of his own ancestors.

Steiner's article underscores the massive reidentification with old Indian culture taking place today at all age levels. The "New Indians" are attempting to unite their brothers and sisters, their parents and cousins, into viable unions which will critically analyze how American institutions have historically been sources of many problems in the Indian community.

What can understanding teachers do? With "American Indian Education: Time to Redeem an Old Promise," Fuchs turns our attention to the young now in our schools. She makes the case for a pluralistic curriculum which will not whitewash the Red man, yet will bring him closer to others in America.

The three concluding selections in this section on American Indians take up various aspects of the modern classroom experiences of Indians and the new opportunities for their teachers. Roessel provides a sensitive examination of the cognitive styles of Indian children drawn from first-hand experience and observations. Conklin supplies a report on Roessel's own pioneering school for Indians, unique in this country, and Gunsky gives us a strictly practical set of possibilities for getting started.

Toward a Background for the Teacher of Indian Students

Edward P. Dozier

"Are there questions that teachers could put to themselves, no matter where or which Tribes they might be teaching, that would develop for the teacher a body of knowledge providing valid insights into the cultures of their students?" This was only one of many important questions put to this writer at a meeting of teachers held last year. The answer to this question logically falls into two broad categories: general, and specific.

Generally, there are certain considerations which any teacher should keep in mind no matter who he is teaching, whether Indian or non-Indian. The teacher must have respect for the *dignity* of the individual, regardless of the student's particular family, ethnic, or cultural background. Here would be included certain peculiarities of dress, hair style, etc., whether idiosyncrasies of the individual or the product of his particular cultural heritage. These aspects of appearance or behavior can be tolerated without injury to school authorities or the school environment. Secondly, a teacher must recognize that *identity* with one's specific heritage is natural, and is usually a cherished possession and hence cannot be demanded, discredited or devalued. Here may be listed such things as language, religion, values and so on, even though these cultural possessions are different from those held by the teacher.

Adverse criticism or disciplinary action by school authorities is likely to have a negative effect on the student. The result may be rebellion, withdrawal, and/or self hatred. Temporarily, there may be an attempt to identify with the teacher's culture and values, but the result is usually a warped personality. The sensitive student frequently becomes alienated from his own group and from that of the dominant culture as well, and develops a negative self-image which

From *Freedomways*, Fourth Quarter 1969, Vol. 9, No. 4, pp. 328–333. Reprinted by permission.

can be harmful to himself and others with whom he associates. Erik H. Erikson, the psychologist, describes and analyzes this phenomenon far better than I can in his new book: *Identity: Youth and Crisis* (Norton, New York, 1968). See also his article: "Youth: Fidelity and Diversity," reprinted in the book, *America Changing* (Charles E. Merrill, Columbus, Ohio, 1968).

There is ample documentation for the damaging effect to Indian personality in the Bureau of Indian Affairs schools of the first and second decades of this century, when both of these general points were flagrantly violated by teachers and school authorities. Unfortunately, abuses still go on in these schools despite changes in the Bureau. Teachers and administrators in the public schools also constantly violate these two principles.

Considering more specifically this question, the teacher must bear in mind the student's social and cultural background and particularly the historical background of Indian-White relations.

As to Indian social and cultural background, this involves a brief discussion of the social and cultural characteristics generally shared by Indian groups. The teacher ought to be aware of the fact that North American Indians (north of the Rio Grande), were all tribal peoples—hence they have certain general characteristics which they share with one another despite numerous local differences. It is only these general patterns that we can hope to help the teacher comprehend—for specific tribes the literature for local groups must be consulted. The importance of the rather large extended family and kinship ties is characteristic of Indian community life. Larger aggregates beyond the immediate local group were sporadic and relatively unimportant in the past. Despite occasional warfare (actually there were primarily skirmishes; large-scale warfare was unknown), there was an essential respect for other local groups. Strong alliances are the exception rather than the rule. For example, the Iroquois Confederacy and the Pueblos at the time of the Revolt of 1680.

Early childhood rearing practices everywhere among Indian groups were (and are still) characterized by permissive techniques and were the responsibility of the kin group.

The economy was largely hunting and gathering; where agriculture existed, it was in a relatively simple form and there was no development of extensive trade or markets. The Pueblos, as with other aspects of their society and culture, were a partial exception. They carried on a rather intensive system of irrigated farming practices and grew a surplus of foods. Still, no markets ever developed among them.

Religion was, and is, a simple form of animism, usually the only religious specialist was the Shaman or medicine man. Again, the Pueblos are an exception (partial exceptions are also the Northwest Coast Indians and some Indians in the Southeastern United States). In general, however, religious organization was simple and there is no evidence that any group ever attempted to impose its system of beliefs or organization upon another. There was considerable borrowing, but no coercion to force the religion of one group on another.

Within the local group—the village—the Pueblos did apparently force *their members to* participate in religious ceremonies. The Pueblos, because of their proximity to rather complex religious and political groups in Mexico (such as the Aztec) do seem to have been less tribal than others.

Linguistic diversification is tremendous, yet there seems to be ample evidence that in terms of concepts and meaning, Indian languages were organized in a remarkable similar fashion. In the past, Indians simply learned one another's language when the need to communicate across linguistic barriers arose—an essentially common level of sociocultural development (the tribal level) apparently made this possible. Languages are adjusted to the society and culture of its speakers and native Indian speakers have tended to have difficulty in adjusting to languages of highly complex cultures. But this is not a formidable task and the teacher with patience and understanding can develop good English speakers among Indians who retain knowledge of their own language. Bi-lingualism is no detriment—indeed the acquisition of several languages tends to enhance learning in other areas as well, in terms of latest findings of linguists and psychologists.

Indian society and culture have produced a series of values which contrast sharply from those of the dominant white group. In social interaction, Indians put the emphasis on good relations; good relations with relatives and good relations with neighbors. They stress the feeling or the emotional component rather than the verbal one. Characteristically, Indians are not extremely talkative. They convey their ideas and feelings largely through behavior rather than through speech.

Important contrasts also exist between whites and Indians with respect to attitudes toward work or activity. Work is, of course, a positive value in American culture. American Indians, on the other hand, emphasize a more relaxed attitude toward work and activity. Success, competition, "progress," and the accumulation of wealth and property—these values important to white Americans, are generally absent among Indians. For American Indians who stress good interpersonal relations and who freely exchange property and food, these values appear strange and selfish. For most Indians, these white American values can only be achieved by destroying good relations with relatives and neighbors and arousing anxiety in themselves; they are, therefore, not worth striving for.

A utilitarian philosophy among white Americans as against a contemplative one among Indians; the stress on youth among whites as against wisdom of age and experience among Indians, and many others, are also important contrasts between white Americans and American Indians. Sufficient examples, perhaps, have been cited to indicate the clash of values which ultimately derive from cultural differences. Yet it is important to be aware of these contrasts, for they inhibit the adjustment of Indians into our educational system.

The result of the shared characteristics sketched above is that personality-wise and in their response to Anglo-American schools and administrative programs, the reaction of North American Indians has been remarkably similar. This is not to say that American Indians all recognize a common destiny or are likely to organize together to achieve common ends. For yet another characteristic of American Indians is their individuality and independence— as we have noted above, larger political units beyond the local kin group were practically unknown in the past except temporary ad hoc type alliances. Pan-Indian participation as a purely entertainment or recreational activity may bring Indians together, but they shy away from political unions where a tighter organization and allegiance to effective leadership are demanded.

A teacher aware of the broad characteristics of Indian cultures will I believe be a better teacher. There is no convenient source of this information. Robert Redfield's work: The Little Community (c. 1955), Primitive Society and Its Transformations (c. 1957) are good sources for tribal characteristics. In lectures and discussions the social and cultural characteristics of general Indian society and culture have been drawn at the American Indian Development Workshop at Boulder. A recent article by Dr. Nancy O. Lurie, "The Enduring Indian," Natural History, Vol. 75, No. 9, pp. 10–22, is also pertinent. Personality structure of all Indians as essentially similar is described by Drs. George and Louise Spindler, in The Annals, Vol. 311, pp. 151–152 (1957). The entire volume which contains the Spindlers' article is devoted to American Indians and is a good source for the history and contemporary situation of United States and Canadian Indians.

Sources on Indian values have not been systematized, although Father John F. Bryde, S.J., Superintendent, Holy Rosary Indian Mission, Pine Ridge, South Dakota, has reproduced a list for student use. Indian values have also been discussed intensively in the American Indian Development Workshop, Boulder. We need a book on Indian social, cultural and value patterns.

The initial contact between whites and Indians, and the subsequent history of this relationship have also produced essentially similar responses from all Indian groups. The result is the development of a remarkably common set of attitudes toward governmental supervision and programs, including education.

In the initial contact period, there was deprivation in land and resources upon which the Indian depended, and a resulting disorganization in social and religious organization. Yet, because of the nature of Indian society and culture, and because of administrative inconsistency, there was not a wholesale destruction of Indian culture and society. There have been change and modification through the years, but unlike central Mexico, for example, much of the Indian way of life was permitted to endure.

But the adverse initial contacts and the later inconsistent Indian policies of the government have made Indians in general resentful, distrustful, and on occasion even hostile to all government programs. Despite the large number of tribes and the diversity of languages the attitude toward government control has been much the same among Indians. This attitude undoubtedly arose or rises out of a series of deprivations: the initial defeat in wars, the loss of lands and resources, confinement in reservations (particularly the associated ration system) attempts for most tribes to convert them into agriculturists once the game was gone, enforced recruitment of Indian children to schools miles away from home, and a host of other deprivations. The result was a resistance to acculturate—expressed by children in resentful attitudes toward schools, and frequently poor performances. While the young people of today have not directly experienced the deprivations suffered by their parents and grandparents, they have inherited the legacy of bitterness, feelings of inadequacy, and resentment to schools. High drop-out rates, poor performances, or the lack of motivation are the results of this attitude.

The teacher who is aware of the broad patterns of differences between his own culture and that of the Indian will develop the necessary patience and understanding to work with Indian students. Some behavior modification is essential, of course, to develop the adaptive and necessary skills in Indian students for a successful adjustment to the dominant school system and culture. Yet the transition can be accomplished without wholesale destruction of the Indian languages and the traditional patterns of Indian social and cultural life. After all, all peoples are in constant flux of change. In the usual non-disruptive social and cultural change situations it is a give and take on both sides. It need not be a complete one way change route in the Indian-White contact situation— there are a number of social and cultural patterns which the Indians can retain without hampering a smooth and satisfactory adjustment into the dominant American society and culture. We are already a heterogeneous society—look at our ethnic enclaves, our different religious denominations. Indeed, our very diversity should give our nation strength and provide the checks and balances needed to survive through the conflicts and challenges of the modern world.

The Indian Child and His Culture

Robert A. Roessel, Jr.

The Indian child today lives between two worlds. On the one hand, there is the traditional way of life represented by the culture of Indians prior to the coming of the white man. On the other hand, there is the modern American civilization with its own distinctive patterns and sets of values.

Education is the vehicle that may be used by the Indian to acquire the fruits and blessings of the white man's way of life. In order for educators to reach the Indian child and to instill within that child a desire to learn, it is necessary for that educator to have a basic understanding of the culture of the Indian.

Anthropologists define culture as the total way of life of a people. For example, we say the Navaho has a culture of his own because, from almost any point of view we observe him and see different practices and beliefs which are not found among other groups of people. The Navaho lives in a hogan, performs healing ceremonies which often include sand painting, attends squaw-dances and fire-dances, speaks a distinct language, wears turquoise jewelry, dresses in a prescribed manner, prepares particular kinds of food in special ways, his methods of greeting strangers, his ideas of hospitality, his beliefs about nature and the universe, his moral and ethical standards, his methods for educating the youth, etc. are peculiarly different from those found among other people. This Navaho way of life is even different from their neighbors, the Hopi Indians, who live in an area surrounded by the Navaho. In view of all this, we can safely declare that there is a Navaho culture and that it belongs to the people we call the Navaho.

From *Handbook for Indian Education*, Los Angeles, California: Amerindian Publishing Company, 1969, pp. 19–34.

A little thought will show that this phenomenon that is called Navaho culture is a great complex embracing the total life of the Navaho. A complete record of any culture would record in full their arts, industries, amusements, politics, family life, education, religion, etiquette, etc. Fortunately, it is not necessary that all data be gathered or all details understood for us to sense its meaning and to grasp its character.

Students of the American Indian tell us that there were between 300 and 600 tribes inhabiting the area we now call the United States.[1] Even in 1960 the Bureau of Indian Affairs was responsible for over 200 different tribes.

Each tribe has its own distinctive way of life or culture. The educator faced with the prospect of learning about 200 tribes may well throw up her hands in despair and renounce any effort to learn about the culture of the Indian.

Providentially, several factors combine to make the educator's task far from hopeless. If she is desirous of learning about the culture of a particular Indian student, or group of students in her class, the chances are that there is only one, or at most, several tribes involved. An educator teaching in the public schools of Casa Grande, Arizona, would probably have Pima and/or Papago Indian children in the classroom. In other words, the location of the school will definitely limit the number of tribes that might be represented at that school. So a teacher would have to become familiar with several tribes at most.

If a teacher wants to learn about Indian culture in order to teach a unit about the Indian she would probably limit her study to several of the better-known Indian tribes.

In addition, there are certain values and beliefs which are held in common by most Indian tribes. Generalizations are usually dangerous but just as we speak of our "American culture" so we can speak of our "Indian culture." These common values are discussed later in this [selection].

COMPONENTS OF CULTURE

Let us examine more closely the concept of culture and how knowledge of it can be an invaluable tool to the educator. The term "culture" may be sub-divided into at least these component parts: Subsistence, Housing, Clothing, Crafts, Social Organization, Political Systems, Religion, Mythology, Language, and Values.

Subsistence

The type of economy developed by a particular Indian tribe would definitely in-fluence the set of values that tribe accepted. For example, a tribe which was de-pendent upon agriculture might be expected to develop a set of traits which

[1]A. L. Kroeber, *Cultural and Natural Areas of Native North America* (Berkeley: University of California Press, 1947), pp. 134–41.

would emphasize the value of the crops and the importance of fertility. The Hopi Indians are such a tribe.

On the other hand, a tribe which was more nomadic and less dependent upon agriculture, and more dependent on livestock might be expected to develop a set of values stressing livestock. Health would become a matter of grave concern because the group couldn't move and follow the flocks if members of the tribe become ill. In such a culture, the Navaho for example, fertility is not nearly as important as health. In a nomadic pastoral tribe, ceremonies oriented around health and healing might become extremely important.

An educator, or anyone for that matter, who desires to understand the people, must become familiar with aspects of subsistence. What were the economic characteristics of the tribe in the years before the coming of the white man? What changes in subsistence have taken place over the years? What are the local community values on the various subsistence techniques? These are but a few of the questions that need to be asked and answered if understanding is to be realized.

Suggestions to the Educator—Subsistence:
1. Become acquainted with the means of subsistence.
   a. Travel and visit on the reservation(s).
   b. Read reports and books on reservation economy and potential.
   c. Talk to people who know something about the reservation and the land.
   d. Acquire pictures of the reservation showing the resources and needs.
2. Include items related to tribal subsistence in school work and class projects.
3. Become familiar with typical Indian food and be able to say that you've eaten some.

Housing

Past and present housing is influenced by the economy of the people. People following a flock of sheep are not going to live in homes located close together because there would be no forage for the animals. Tribes depending on agriculture can develop permanent homes which are constructed close together since their fields are used time after time.

Today, teachers should realize that home conditions influence the achievement of Indian students. In the first place, many Indian families have little understanding of the importance of education. They see only that education is slowly, but surely, divorcing the child from his parents and the home. Therefore, the Indian child frequently obtains no positive encouragement from his parents. In the second place, the home may be the kind where there are no lights to study by or no desks to study on.

Teachers and administrators need to know something about the homes of the Indian child. They need to know what study facilities are available to the student. Often the Indian child lives in one room with perhaps six or eight other family members. Homework may be an obstacle that will cause the Indian student to fail—not because he doesn't want to study, but because he has no place to study.

Many Indian homes have no running water. In a study conducted by the United States Public Health Service the following figures on running water in Indian homes were obtained:[2]

Hopi .... All mesa villages had no running water in homes
Papago ...... Less than 1 percent had running water in homes
San Carlos Apache .... 8.7 percent had running water in homes

This absence of running water might be reflected in the Indian child's clothes not being as clean as those of other children or the Indian student not being as clean as his white neighbor. A sympathetic teacher can do a great deal to reduce the Indian child's sense of inferiority in these areas.

Suggestions to the Educator—Housing:
1. Become acquainted with the housing need.
   a. Travel and visit the reservation.
   b. Read reports and books on reservation housing.
   c. Talk with people who have had experience with tribal housing.
   d. Take pictures of housing showing the difference in types and style.
   e. Visit the homes and go inside.
2. Use material collected to provide a unit or classroom decoration so small children feel at home.
3. Incorporate area of health in discussion of housing—but do not take the position that all native Indian homes are unhealthy—rather show how existing homes can be improved with tools and materials at hand.

Clothing

Many tribes even today dress distinctively and often colorfully. The teacher needs to understand the dress of the local Indians and should look upon that clothing not as something strange and unusual, but rather as something indicative of a rich cultural heritage. In this way the Indian child need not become ashamed of the way his parents dress.

Suggestions to the Educator—Clothing:
1. Become familiar with clothing worn at home by the school child and by his parents.
   a. Visit the reservation.
   b. Read books and reports.
2. Become familiar with problems of washing and repairing the Indian child's clothes.

[2]Files of the Division of Indian Health, United States Public Health, Phoenix Area Office, Arizona.

3. Understand the financial problems involved in the parents buying additional clothes.

Crafts

Indian arts and crafts are, perhaps, the best known area of Indian culture. People from all over the world collect historic or prehistoric Indian art. Navaho rugs and silver, Hopi katchina dolls, Papago and Pima baskets, Sioux bead work, Apache buckskins, and Pueblo pottery, are internationally known and admired.

The discerning educator should learn about the arts and crafts of the Indians in that area or in that state. Here is a field in which the Indian can excel. The wise teacher will draw upon this and build on this apparent natural gift of the Indian people. It would be ridiculous to ask a Papago Indian girl to tell the class members how to weave a rug. It would be foolish to ask an Apache student to describe the art of pottery working.

It is necessary for the teacher to know what tribes make and to ask an Indian student to discuss something that his tribe can do.

Often Indian students will profess no knowledge of a tribal craft. This may or may not be true. Regardless, the educator through his interest and desire to learn can instill in the Indian student an appreciation of the arts and crafts of the Indian cultural heritage. The Indian child is greatly influenced by the attitude and actions of his teacher. If the educator laughs at the tribal customs and culture, you may be sure that the educator may either be driving the Indian child away from his people or driving the child away from the educator— perhaps both.

If there is wisdom in the philosophy of building on strengths then Indian Education needs to direct more time and attention to encouraging an active arts and crafts program. The Bureau of Indian Affairs, in 1960, has extensively enlarged an Indian Arts and Crafts Program in Bureau Schools.[3]

A bridge of understanding may be partially constructed between the Indian parent and the school through the successful development of an Indian Arts and Crafts Program in the school. Local community specialists can be brought to school and teach the students their particular craft. The school benefits in improved school-community relations as much as do the students.

Suggestions to the Educator—Crafts:
1. Become familiar with local native arts and crafts.
2. If possible buy and wear some art object made by the Indian people in that area.
3. Encourage good Indian arts and crafts.

[3]In 1961 the B.I.A. opened the Institute of American Indian Arts at Santa Fe for Indian youth of high artistic talent. Comprehensive programs are provided both at the high school and post graduate level.

4. Invite Indian craftsmen to school to give talks and/or demonstrations.

5. Develop this aspect of the total educational program.

Social Organizations

Social organization includes the institutions that determine the position of men and women in society. The importance of social organization is seen in that it provides the means of organizing behavior and of providing for the inculcation in the coming generations in the prevalent sanctions and accepted behavior patterns of the group. In this way, the continuity and cohesiveness of the culture is insured.

The family is the most fundamental of all social groups and it is universal in its distribution.[4] However, as in all culturally determined social groups, there is a certain amount of variability in the types of family structure and organization.

The biological and social family may be quite distinct entities.[5] The biological family simply consists of two parents who produce offspring and the number of ancestors doubles with each generation. In our society we count descent in both the father and the mother. However, it is more common among societies of the world to count descent only on one side (unilateral). The Navaho, for example, count descent on the mother's side (matrilineal) when a person belongs to his mother's family. The Papago, on the other hand, trace their descent from their father (patrilineal) and a person belongs to his father's family.

Herskovits stated that there is no doubt that different traditions of descent greatly influence the psycho-social relationships between members of families in matrilineal and patrilineal societies.[6] We can readily see an aspect of the patrilineal emphasis in our society in the father's role. He is the family head, the arbiter and often controls the economic resources—"Father Knows Best." In our society the father is frequently the disciplinarian for the family—at least in more extreme cases.

Contrast this with a matrilineal society where the mother frequently is the family head and the mother's eldest brother often assumes many of the functions we usually associate with a father in our society. The mother's oldest brother often controls the finances, speaks for the family and is the disciplinarian. In such a matrilineal society the biological father is left the pleasant role of playmate, counselor, and friend to his children.

The importance of understanding something of the social organization of Indian children may be seen in the frequently observed fact that to many [people] all Indian children appear to be related. A teacher new to teaching Indians is usually impressed with the number of "brothers" and "sisters" and "cousins"

---

[4]E. A. Hoebel, *Man in the Primitive World* (New York: McGraw Hill Book Company, 1958), p. 318.

[5]Melville J. Herskovits, *Man and His Works* (New York: Alfred A. Knopf, 1949), p. 290.

[6]*Ibid.,* p. 291.

that are found in any given room. The Indian student, when identifying another child as his "brother," may not mean the same thing that the non-Indian means when he uses the term "brother." The Indian uses the term frequently to mean any member of the clan to which he belongs; there may not be any blood relationship.

The next object of our attention is the extended family. By extended family we mean a social group consisting of near relatives in addition to the mother and father and their children. In our society we do not utilize the principal of the extended family so as a whole we are unfamiliar with it. However, many of our Indian tribes are organized on this principle and we as educators must understand it if we are to understand the social and emotional background of the Indian child.

What then are the implications of this concept for educators? In the first place, the extended family surrounds the Indian child with constant love and attention. The child becomes accustomed to having numerous relatives around, many of whom treat him as their own child. In such an atmosphere a sense of security is developed.

When the Indian child is taken abruptly from an extended family situation, with all its psychological characteristics, and placed in a school situation, which may be a great distance from the home and family, the child becomes insecure, withdrawn, and unhappy. Where he once found love and understanding from members of his extended family he now finds indifference and misunderstanding from strangers.

Starting school is a difficult enough undertaking in our society where our values and emphasis are consciously directed at education. Think how much more difficult it must be in a society which still fails to grasp and accept the real functions and purposes of education and particularly when the school often destroys the only source of security the Indian child enjoys—his family and home!

The educator must be alert and alive to the importance of the extended family in the life and actions of the Indian child. He must make every effort to insure that the security provided by the extended family is not destroyed by the school but rather is strengthened and encouraged.

In the second place, the extended family provided the Indian child with a number of relatives whom he calls "mother" and "father." The child knows his biologic parents, but there are other relatives whom he calls "mother" and "father" and who treat him as their own child. This means that the death of a parent, separation or divorce does not necessarily have the same traumatic effect as it does in non-Indian society.

We have seen that the extended family structure gives the Indian child a strong feeling of security. The school may unconsciously and inadvertently destroy or materially weaken this security. To counteract this tendency, teachers and administrators must understand the functions of the extended family and strive to provide the necessary love and understanding.

Suggestions to the Educator—Social Organization:
1. Know something about the clan system of the tribe.
2. Know something about the organization of the family of the tribe.
3. Respect the Indian method of determining kinship and never ridicule.
4. Perhaps make a chart showing the clans of the tribe and the membership of class members in each clan.

Political Systems

No people are without ways and means of controlling conduct and directing the affairs of the group. The mechanisms for the regulation of affairs that concern the entire group as a whole are called political organization. The western world has developed the concept that in any given society there will be leaders and there will be followers: democracy, rule by the majority, representative government are among those elements considered vital to our political philosophy.

It is difficult to comprehend that certain Indian tribes traditionally had no "leaders" in our sense of the word. They had no individual or group of individuals who could speak for all members of the tribe. This presented many perplexing and tragic problems during the days of the Indian Wars. One small segment of a tribe may have signed a treaty of peace with the United States government and yet another portion of the same tribe may have staged a raid the day after the first group signed the treaty. Our government often felt that the tribe deliberately broke the treaty and consequently the Indian gained a reputation that he could not be trusted.

Even today many non-Indians fail to understand the unique political systems the various tribes enjoy. It is important to note that among many Southwestern Indians democracy is not the rule of the majority, which might result in 51 percent of the people for something and 49 percent of the people opposed; but rather the rule of consensus. In other words, everyone must be for something and none are opposed.

The author recalls an incident which took place on the Navaho reservation which reflects this desire for consensus. The people at Low Mountain, an isolated community in the heart of Navaho country, decided that they wanted to elect a school board. Although it was a Bureau of Indian Affairs School, and therefore was not legally operated and controlled by a Board of Education, the community felt that they should elect a group of interested adults who would work closely with the school personnel. A cold winter day was set for the meeting and nearly a hundred Navahos for miles around arrived by wagon, truck, and horseback. The group quickly decided that there should be three members chosen to the "school board." The meeting began about 10:00 a.m. and by noon they had unanimously selected two members of the board. The author felt that the third member would be chosen right after lunch and all would go home happy.

The group reconvened after eating and quickly voted by an overwhelming majority on the third member. But the meeting was not over. This was not acceptable until all present freely voted in his favor. The entire afternoon was spent in discussing this man and his strengths and weaknesses. Those few who were originally opposed to this individual stated their objectives and in time persuaded others that he was not the man for the job. At six o'clock that evening this man still had a majority who favored his selection, but the entire group agreed that this man would never command the support of the entire community—so he was dropped from consideration.

The group decided to camp overnight at the school and continue the meeting in the morning. That night one could see many camp fires encircling the school as the Navaho waited for morning. At this point the author was uneasy and unhappy. Perhaps the whole idea of a school board was foolish after all, none of the men selected spoke English, besides if it took this long to elect one man then you might never get things done and anyway the author wanted to go to town and do some shopping since it would be Saturday.

Saturday morning the group met once again: the only difference lay in the fact that word must have been sent out and there were nearly 200 Navahos present that morning. The same process began again. A man would be discussed; often he would rise and tell why he wasn't qualified. By noon not a single vote had been taken, but many men had been discussed. Finally a man was mentioned and all seemed to be interested. The group talked about this individual for over an hour and no one said anything against this person. A vote was taken and every single person present voted in favor of this individual. This, then, was an example of the principle of consensus at work.

In working with that unanimously elected body for nearly three years the author came to realize the advantages of such a method of selection. These three men spoke for the entire community, not just a segment of it. They were able to give unqualified support to the school and they had the unqualified support of their community.

To work successfully and to obtain optimum results in working with Indian tribes, the educator must understand the structure of the political organization of that tribe. The educator must be able to work within the framework of their system.

Suggestions to the Educator—Political Systems:
1. Understand something about the traditional method of tribal political organization.
2. Understand something about current tribal political organization.
3. Include existing tribal organization in social studies and civic classes.
4. Take students to visit tribal government in action.
5. Invite tribal leaders to the school to discuss tribal government.
6. Respect the Indians' method of selecting candidates and of holding meetings—regardless of time involved.
7. Work closely with tribal and community leaders.

Religion and Mythology

Religion is considered by anthropologists to be a universal cultural complex.[7] No known society is without some form of religion. "Religious attitude . . . characterizes all cultures and every stage of history."[8]

In the Southwest today many Indian tribes have retained a considerable portion of their own native religion. The Indian tribes of no other section of the United States have preserved their own traditional beliefs and practices as have the Indians of the Southwest. One has only to recall the Hopi Snake and Katchina Dances, the Pueblo Corn and Animal Dances, the Apache Bear and Crown Dance, the Papago Bean Dance, the Navaho Yeibechai and Fire Dances and many others to realize that age-old Indian ceremonies still contain a great deal of meaning and importance for many tribes.

The educator must have some understanding of the role of the native Indian religion in the lives of those living within the area served by his school. He must become familiar with basic elements of their religion.

On the Hopi reservation, in northern Arizona, school personnel have an unwritten agreement that Hopi children may be excused from school to participate in the necessary tribal rituals and ceremonies. In return tribal leaders and parents insure the attendance of their children at all other times.

An Apache girl, who reaches puberty and who is fortunate enough to have a Puberty Ceremony, has acquired stature and standing in the eyes of her tribe. The teacher or the principal who would refuse to excuse such a girl from school for the ceremony would arouse community bitterness and ill will. The girl would probably fail to attend school, regardless of whether she were excused or not.

. . .

Mythology is kindred to that of religion, but mythology is one that more teachers are aware of and concerned with. The educator who takes the time and makes the effort to learn certain myths and legends of the Indian groups with whom he is working will be taking definite steps toward better understanding and improved rapport. There are many authentic Indian legends available to the interested person. In addition to those in libraries and collections, there is the possibility of actually having Indians come to school and tell their stories to the children. Another method would be to have a collection of myths available in the room. There is probably no better way to motivate the Indian child to read than to have some of his well-known stories available to him in written form. The interested educator can take a complex story and reword it, using a controlled and appropriate vocabulary. In fact, a book of legends can be prepared which would contain a number of such stories. This book might well be illustrated by the children. The author has seen this done effectively by creative and alert teachers.

[7]Clark Wissler, *Man and Culture* (New York: Thomas Y. Crowell Company, 1938), p. 74. Herskovits, *op. cit.*, p. 347. Hoebel, *op. cit.*, p. 540.

[8]Wilson O. Wallis, *Religion in Primitive Society* (New York: F. S. Crofts and Company, 1939), p. 1.

Suggestions to the Educator—Religion and Mythology:

1. Become familiar with local Indian dances and ceremonies and respect them.
2. Attend local Indian dances and ceremonies.
3. Invite medicine men to the school and have them address the students in regard to myths and legends and traditions.
4. Respect individual Indian student's right to be absent from school to attend important ceremonies.
5. Be careful not to knowingly or unknowingly cause a child to lose face in regard to his or his family's belief in their traditional religion.
6. Use legends and myths in reading and in storytelling.
7. Prepare a booklet of myths and legends for each major tribe.

Language

Language has appropriately been called the vehicle of culture. Without language the accumulation of knowledge, that makes humans different from other animals, could not have been developed or maintained. We must constantly remember that one's thoughts are limited by one's language. The Hopi with their concept of time, as indicated in their language, are said to be much more able to comprehend Einsteinian Theories than are those of us whose language divides time into past, present, and future.[9]

In other words, the world view of any particular people will, in large measure, be controlled by their language. The language of one people may not permit the comprehending of fundamental principles of another people. Even the process of translation may prove unsatisfactory.

This is another area of concern for the educator teaching Indian children. It is necessary to have some knowledge of the type of language spoken by the Indians in that locality or school. What are some of the basic emphases of the language and what is the world view of the people?

A practical concern of the educator is what sounds of the native language are similar to English sounds and what English sounds have no counterpart in the Indian language. In this manner, the areas of difficulty are identified in advance and the teacher may make special preparation and effort to eliminate these problem sounds.

Suggestions to the Educator—Language:

1. Understand the general organization of the Tribal language.
2. Learn a few words of the language and use these words in class. Do not be afraid of mispronouncing because actually it is better if you do and if the Indian students laugh at your efforts. In this way unnecessary barriers are broken down.
3. Make a list of sound differences and sound difficulties—work especially hard on these.
4. Be aware of the problems of translation.

[9]Benjamin Lee Whorf, Language, Thought and Reality, ed. by John B. Carroll (Cambridge: Massachusetts Institute of Technology, 1956).

Values

The final culture component to be discussed is that of values. The entire area of values is of great importance to the educator. There are at least two extreme positions in regard to values that one could take: the first would be cultural ethnocentrism, the second would be cultural relativism.

Cultural ethnocentrism means that the values of one particular culture are superior to the values of other cultures and that therefore the superior values ought to supercede the values of the other culture. This philosophy prompted much of the conquest of America. The values of the white man were felt to be vastly superior to those of the "savages." Therefore, it was only fitting and proper that those values of the superior culture should be imposed on the inferior culture.

Cultural relativism means the opposition of the above. In other words, the values of any culture are relative to the cultural background out of which they arose. There are no superior or inferior cultures or sets of values. Under this philosophy mankind is seen as being everywhere equal and the values of western "civilized" man are in no way superior to those of the most "primitive" Indian. The criteria would be only as to how successful each value was in meeting problems faced in each particular culture.

Cultural ethnocentrism and cultural relativism are extreme and the educator may wish to take a more moderate position. But, the fact remains that any person who teaches Indian children and who fails to grasp or understand the Indians' set of values and who instead tries to impose the values of our dominant culture is in for considerable difficulty.

Our society places great importance on competition. In fact, many Americans believe that competition is an essential cultural trait found throughout the world. Such is not the case. Many of our Southwestern tribes place no importance on competition, but rather place a supreme value on cooperation.

When the author first began teaching Indian children, he felt that a good teacher in St. Louis would be a good teacher with Indians—a corollary to this would be that whatever proved to be successful with white children would prove to be successful with Indian children. The author began teaching Navahos at Crownpoint, New Mexico, located on the eastern edge of the Navaho reservation. Most teachers have used or at least are familiar with the use of gold and silver stars placed on a chart to reward children who have turned in a perfect paper. In non-Indian schools this device has been in successful use and the author constructed such a chart for use with his classroom of Navaho children. During the first several weeks a pattern became very apparent—no child ever got two gold stars. After a Navaho student once received the recognition of a gold star he never again turned in a perfect paper. This proved very frustrating and the author felt that these Indian children just didn't care and that perhaps they were "uneducable."

One day an adult Navaho friend came into the classroom and looked at the chart and laughed. The problem was explained to him and he laughed once again. The Navaho friend stated that many Navaho children are taught to cooperate—not to compete. They find their security in being a member of the group and not in being singled out and placed in a position above the group. In putting a gold star by the name of the Navaho student that turned in a perfect paper a conflict of values resulted. This group of children resolved this conflict in favor of the Navaho values of cooperation.

The chart was taken down and boxes of gold stars went on sale—cheap.

The successful educator must become acquainted with the values of the tribes with whom he is working. In this way he will avoid unnecessary conflict and eliminate needless operation. The next section discusses in greater detail some of the value differences between cultures.

Suggestions to the Educator—Values:
1. Respect differences in values.
2. Study the values of the Indian tribe and list those areas where there may be possible conflicts with our values.
3. Determine your philosophy of Indian Education which should include such things as objectives, who determines direction and rate of speed, etc.

BASIC DIFFERENCES BETWEEN CULTURES

Thus far we have been concerned primarily with the various areas of culture and have attempted to show how knowledge in such areas is important for educators working with Indian students.

[Table 1 presents] certain distinct cultural differences between the dominant non-Indian society and the Indian society. It must be emphasized, however, that the statements listed . . . are generalizations and therefore subject to exceptions.

DIVISIONS IN INDIAN CULTURE

Educators should be aware that all Indians, even in a single tribe, are not at the same cultural level. There is some logic for considering three separate sub-cultural groups within any one tribe.

Traditionalists

The first group may be called the Traditionalists or the Conservatives. Usually a large number of the older uneducated Indians fall into this category. The Conservatives still adhere to their own religion and the old cultural pattern. They believe that the problems their tribe has today are the results of the abandonment of the old way of life. The Gods are not happy because the Indian people have turned from their former beliefs toward the white man's way.

The membership in the Traditional segment need not be limited to the older generations. Upon examination one discovers that there are younger, even educated members of this group.

TABLE 1

NON-INDIAN WAY OF LIFE	INDIAN WAY OF LIFE
1. FUTURE ORIENTATED Rarely satisfied with the present. Constantly looking to the future.	1. PRESENT ORIENTATED Live in the present, living for today, not tomorrow.
2. TIME-CONSCIOUSNESS Governed by the clock and the calendar, living closely scheduled with certain amount of time devoted to each activity.	2. LACK OF TIME CONSCIOUSNESS Many tribes have no word for time: no need to be punctual or on time because there is always lots of time: concept "Indian time" which means that a meeting set for 8:00 may not start until 10:00.
3. SAVING Save today so can better enjoy tomorrow; hold back a part of wealth so can develop more things—"a penny saved is a penny earned"—school is looked upon as a system of long-term saving because it will increase earning power in the future.	3. GIVING Not concerned with saving: air and land was free, food could not be saved because it would spoil—no need to save. Respected person is not one who has large savings, but rather one who gives. Value placed on giving while the person who tries to accumulate goods is often feared.
4. EMPHASIS ON YOUTH The non-Indian society places great importance on youth; advertising, books and newspapers all stress the value of youth. How to look young, how to feel young, how to act young. Little consideration given to age.	4. RESPECT FOR AGE Respect increases with age and the tried and trusted leader is usually an older person. Youth is often a handicap with young educated Indian leaders frequently complaining that they are not given the positions of leadership that they feel they are qualified to hold.
5. COMPETITION The non-Indian believes competition is essential if not universal. Progress results from competition and lack of progress may be synonymous with lack of competition.	5. COOPERATION Indians place a value on working together, sharing and cooperating. Failure to reach selected objectives is felt to result from failure to cooperate.
6. CONQUEST OVER NATURE The non-Indian society attempts to control the physical world, to assert mastery over it: for example, dams, rain making, atomic energy, etc.	6. HARMONY WITH NATURE The Indian believes in living in harmony with nature. He accepts the world and does not try to change it. If it fails to rain or the crops fail to grow, it is, he believes, because the necessary harmony has been destroyed. Whenever harmony is restored, nature will respond.

The element that all Traditionalists have in common is the conviction that the old way is the right way. The size of this group in each particular tribe varies, with some tribes having far more adherents to this philosophy than other tribes.

Teachers and administrators should make every effort to discover whether or not the Conservatives constitute a minor or a prominent role in the life and actions of the tribe and the community. The intelligent educator should make every effort to consider the Conservatives in his plan and in his programs. There are many ways to obtain the cooperation and support of this group: inviting medicine men to come and talk at the school, having authentic legends told and taught, teaching aspects of the history of the tribe, encouraging older women to come and teach or discuss traditional arts and crafts, etc.

In the Southwest today this segment of the total Indian culture is more important than many realize. In many instances this cultural element is thought to be unapproachable and unpredictable. However, an adequate educational program must consider and make provisions for the needs of members of this group.

Moderates

The second division within most Indian societies may be called the "Moderates." This group is not only very proud of their Indian heritage and sincere in their desire to retain elements of the Indian way of life, but also they realize the value and need for many ways of the white man. They believe time will not stand still and that the Indians must adjust to the dominant pattern. The Moderates enjoy many of the blessings of civilization and believe that the Indian people need to obtain more of the fruits of progress without abandoning their heritage and customs.

In other words, the Moderates see good in the old and the new and are of the opinion that the future of the Indian lies in their ability to hold on to both. It has been identified by some as the "realistic position." The Moderates are probably the most numerous group among Southwestern tribes. Large numbers of educated Indians are advocates of this position. They believe that many of the problems facing the Indian tribes today are created or compounded by taking either of the two extreme positions—the desire to return to the old way of life (Traditionalists) or the desire to forget the past and live for the future ((Progressives).

The alert educator will attempt to utilize the strengths of this group. He should be informed as to the numerical strength of the Moderates and have an understanding of their middle-of-the-road position. This group frequently fails to capture the respect or support of followers of either of the extreme positions. Nevertheless, there is every reason to believe that the Moderates are more numerous and increasing more rapidly than either the Progressives or the Conservatives. In many Indian communities the adherents of the Moderate philosophy are non-vocal, while the followers of the other two beliefs are often extremely vocal.

Progressives

The third major cultural segment in most present-day Indian tribes is known as the "Progressives." The word does not have the same meaning as the word "progressive" as used in modern educational philosophy. Rather the word is here used to indicate that group of Indians who believes that the only true "progress" and advancement of the Indian is to come through the complete abandonment of the old cultural pattern and by replacing it with the modern white values and beliefs.

The Progressives believe that the present problems facing the Indian are due in large part to the fact that the Indian people are still living in the past and still trying to follow their outmoded beliefs and culture. The Progressives add that only when the Indian people turn away from the past and forget it, can progress result. The native religions, the ancient arts and crafts, the old type dwellings and many other items must be forever forgotten if the Indian is to be able to successfully enter the white man's world. These vestiges of the past are handicapping modern Indians and therefore must be discarded.

To members of this group, education becomes an end in itself and members make every effort to adopt white values. In general, this group is feared and mistrusted by members of the Moderates and especially the Conservatives.

The educator should determine how many Progressives live in the community serviced by his school. He must decide whether or not this group is very significant in that community. Certain Indians follow this philosophy because they believe that it is the accepted and desired philosophy by the non-Indians. In other words, there are Progressives who believe as they do because they think that they will gain stature and prestige from the non-Indians.

Often the interested teacher or administrator can "convert" members of this group to membership in the Moderate group by emphasizing the school's respect for the Indian's culture and contributions. In other words, in many instances the Indian acceptance of this Progressive role is influenced by a desire to do what he believes the white man wants and expects him to do.

SUMMARY

Educators, if they are desirous of maximum results, should inculcate or reinforce a sense of pride on the part of the Indian student in his own culture and heritage. Modern education will of necessity teach the Indian child the characteristics and fundamentals of western civilization. But, it is equally important that these Indian students recognize the values and contributions that their culture has made, and may continue to make, in the growth and development of this nation. Too often we are concerned solely with making non-Indians out of Indians. In the process we may create more problems than we solve. We must always be careful not to break the mold in which the Indian child was raised—because if we do, we may break or destroy the individual who was in that mold.

SUGGESTED READING

Beatty, Willard. *Education for Cultural Change*. Chilocco, Oklahoma: Department of Interior, Bureau of Indian Affairs, 1953.

Kluckholm, Clyde and Leighton, Dorothea. *The People*. Cambridge, Mass.: Harvard University Press, 1948. This is perhaps the best and most used book on the Navaho. It contains an excellent foundation to the understanding of Navaho culture, although certain material is presently outdated.

Leighton, Dorothea and Kluckholm, Clyde. *Children of the People*. Cambridge, Mass.: Harvard University Press, 1947. This book is the companion volume to *The People* and contains an excellent account of the life and personality characteristics of Navaho children. It includes test data from different sections of the reservation. A very helpful book for the teacher of Navaho children.

MacGregor, Gordon. *Warriors Without Weapons*. Chicago: University of Chicago Press, 1946. A good book dealing with the Sioux and problems they are faced with. It is somewhat outdated, but provides a useful frame of reference.

The Indian and Civil Wrongs

Jack Charles

While some Americans riot, march, or sit in, descendants of the original residents of this prosperous land watch and suffer in frustration and despair.

Protesters of one type or another, for one cause or another, get the headlines and the photographs. Most other Americans join the quieter, more intense drive toward membership in the "affluent society."

But American Indians get neither publicity nor wealth. There aren't enough of them to demonstrate and attract much attention; voter registration drives would be useless—even with full Indian registration, voting power would be negligible; whatever wealth might come their way is controlled finally by officials of the white-father-knows-best Bureau of Indian Affairs; and Indians, by and large, are too proud to scream for attention and help in a land they feel should belong to them by right of birth.

The average life span of Americans has lengthened to slightly under seventy years, but the average life span of an American Indian living on a reservation is about thirty-one years. On certain reservations, the average is about twenty years, and on one Hopi reservation in Arizona, an Indian child can look forward to less than seventeen years of life. The major causes of death are tuberculosis (at a rate seven times the national average), malnutrition and diseases closely associated with malnutrition and filth, or both.

Sociologists who devote time and study to the Indians and their situation advise us that Indians in their teens and early twenties sometimes become enthusiastic about the opportunities that await them in the outside world, but that most of them ultimately return to the reservation to live the rest of their lives in the company of cynicism and alcohol (if and when they can obtain alcohol

From *Christian Herald*, July 1968, pp. 1–7. Reprinted by permission.

under the white man's laws) or to commit faster and easier suicide. Sociological statisticians say that the suicide rate among Indians is the highest of any known group in the world today. The Bureau of Indian Affairs in Washington neither affirms this nor denies it.

We are still scalping the Indians, spiritually, ethically and materially. Odd as it may seem to some, the largest and most constant scalping takes place in the area of real estate. And the scalpers are the members of the Congress of the United States and its several agencies.

A good example of real-estate scalping took place not many years ago on Seneca Indian territory in Pennsylvania and New York.

Sometime near April 15, 1961, a corps of engineers received a go-ahead from the U.S. Congress—start building Kinzua Dam. Until this time, the Indians had not been too concerned about all the talk they heard, all the dam and lake talk. Their lack of concern was, in retrospect, a bit naive in view of the past handling of numerous Indian treaties by Congress, but the Senecas placed much confidence in the fact that they possessed a copy of an historic treaty negotiated in 1794 by Seneca chiefs and representatives of the U.S. Government.

The document was signed November 11, 1794, by Timothy Pickering on behalf of President George Washington. Pickering, the President's personal deputy, placed the Great Seal of the United States on the treaty which promised that "The United States will never claim the same (the lands deeded to the Senecas), nor disturb the Seneca Nation."

Beyond the written promise was a matter of honor based on gratitude. The treaty was signed at a time when our new nation was much in need of the assistance of the Senecas in protecting the land against foreign enemies, aid which later proved to be invaluable. The experienced and courageous warriors of that relatively small Indian group were responsible for making adequate the military forces of the United States. During the War of 1812, the aid of the Senecas was a major factor in our success.

It would be nice to think that the arrangements with the Indians were and are such that a white American might say that wisdom and honor have prevailed. That is not the case. Seneca tribal officials now describe the lake formed by the Kinzua Dam as the "Lake of Perfidy."

The Kinzua Dam and the lake that resulted from the dam's construction and operation have taken ten thousand acres of the thirty thousand that were granted in perpetuity to the Seneca Nation. According to a statement made last February by a public information official of the Bureau of Indian Affairs, all the Seneca families involved have been relocated in homes provided by the federal government and the governing body (tribal council) has been granted twelve million dollars in what the bureau official frankly describes as "conscience money."

A conference of American Indians convening in Chicago in June of 1961 sent the following telegram to then President John F. Kennedy as an expression of their concern:

This assembly of more than five hundred Indian people coming from sixty-seven tribes of American Indians respectfully urges you to give full and careful consideration to all possible alternatives to the Kinzua Dam Project. Only you can stop the United States from breaking the solemn treaty of 1794 with the Seneca Nation. We join the Seneca Nation in this final appeal that the United States honor the treaty signed by the first president of the United States.

American Indian, Chicago Conference
by Anthony Rivers, Jr., Acting Chairman

During a press conference a few days later, President Kennedy said, "The Supreme Court has passed on the question, so I guess there is nothing more to be done."

The Supreme Court did indeed rule that the Congress of the United States is free to arbitrarily and unilaterally do away with any treaty with an Indian nation for any reason it may deem sufficient. The ruling was based on a Supreme Court opinion of many years ago that the relation of American Indians to the United States Government is that of a child to a guardian and that the U.S. Congress is not required to deal with any Indian tribe within the borders of the United States as a governmental entity.

In a strong dissent from the majority opinion of the Supreme Court, Justice Hugo L. Black said, "Great nations, like great men, should keep their word."

No conference was ever held with any Indian on the matter of the Kinzua Dam. That structure is a monument to the dealing of a strong government with the weak.

Perhaps we twentieth-century Americans can pacify ourselves, if we think about such situations at all, with the fact that such dealings with the Indians are not without precedent, and that our present high-handedness is at least not tainted by bloodletting.

Andrew Jackson, regarded as a saint by many who have recorded the history of Tennessee, became a major military hero by virtue of his defense of New Orleans against a British attack in 1815. History, legend, novels and movies make much of the fact that Old Hickory won that battle against insurmountable odds because he was aided by quite a number of his backwoods sharpshooter friends. There were a few such white roughnecks at his side, but the sharpshooters who really swung the tide were mostly Seneca, Oneida and Cherokee Indian friends.

Jackson rewarded his "friends in combat" some twenty-three years later in the fashion Indians have now come to expect. It was decided that the United States needed Indian territories in Georgia, North Carolina and Tennessee for some purpose or other and that the seventeen thousand Cherokees inhabiting the needed lands should remove themselves to a section of Oklahoma selected by the U.S. Government.

When the Cherokees proved reluctant to leave their lands, President Jackson dispatched General Winfield Scott and seven thousand United States soldiers to the area to force the unarmed Indians into Oklahoma. Most of the Indians traveled on foot. During that trek, now known as "The Trail of Tears," approximately one-fourth of the Cherokees died of malnutrition, exposure, or from injuries inflicted by the armed soldiers.

There is nothing unique about taking Indian land anywhere in America for any given purpose, using any excuse; but a 1966 ill-fated (so far) foray in Tennessee *was* unique, unique because Tennessee citizens furiously objected to another dam—the Tellico—to be built by the Tennessee Valley Authority on Indian lands. This unique objection came in spite of the fact that every new dam constructed by the TVA has always meant a boost in the economy of the immediate area. In Tennessee bucking or talking against the TVA and its decisions is like opposing motherhood.

This time, strangely, no outcry of any proportion arose from Indians who might have been displaced by the dam and the resulting lake. The outrage came from white individuals and organizations, ostensibly because they were incensed about continued mistreatment of Indians right under the whites' collective nose. A reading and hearing of the numerous protests, however, revealed reasons that were more to be expected. It is striking that, after one sentence in the initial protest mentioning "inconvenience to the Indians," the Cherokees do not receive any sympathy or concern.

The Tennessee Planning Commission protest said: "We need to understand that a river can be economically beneficial to an area and remain a free-flowing stream . . . As a state, we have been slow indeed to . . . accept the responsibility for . . . preservation of a great heritage."

The Tennessee Outdoor Writers Association said, in part:

The dam will destroy an economic and recreational resource which is unique in the nation. Not only does the river in its natural state possess marked industrial advantages, it is also a treasure trove of archaeology, history, timber and scenic beauty.

Beside the economic-interests objectors, a petition to block construction of the dam was signed by Cherokee Indians living on a reservation situated mostly in North Carolina but extending into East Tennessee. It was coincidental that Justice William O. Douglas of the Supreme Court of the United States was in the area at the time, gathering material for an article for *National Geographic* magazine. Chief Jarrett Blythe, ruler of the Qualla Indian Reservation, the one which would be affected by the lake formed by the proposed dam, heard of the scheduled visit and presented the petition to Justice Douglas on April 4, 1966, at Chota, North Carolina.

The Indian petition would have meant little in itself without the protests arising from economic interests, such as the one from the Association for the Preservation of the Little Tennessee. This influential group asked the TVA to table plans for the Tellico Dam for ten years, pleading that the area's economy would develop during that time without TVA money if the threat of the dam was removed. Leaders of the association told their representatives and U.S. senators in

Washington that industries interested in potential sites lining the river were being frightened away.

The Association for the Preservation of the Little Tennessee soon found an ally in the Tennessee Planning Commission. Then the Tennessee Outdoor Writers Association chimed in, even more loudly and firmly than the first two groups. Before many weeks had passed, the groups joining in the protest became an impressive parade. Quickly falling in line for the march were the Tennessee Game and Fish Commission, the Tennessee Farm Bureau, the Chilhowee Rod and Gun Club, the Tennessee Conservation League, the Tennessee Duck Hunting Association, the Chattanooga Realtors Association, Boy Scout Troop 3057 (of Hixon), the Knoxville Men's Garden Club, the Knoxville Field and Creel Club and some thirty other organizations.

You can imagine the concern of Tennessee politicians when faced with such an array of voting potential. Needless to say, the project has not been mentioned, at least not publicly, for over two years.

Exit one dam, the paradox being that the reasons given by protestors are almost identical to the reasons supporting pleas for abatement in over one hundred Indian protests against actions of government. It is a sad commentary that the monkey wrench was thrown into a government plan to utilize Indian land by a rather large and vociferous group of white Americans who really couldn't care less about the rights of Indians, but who did and do care intensely about their own sports and commercial interests.

The ridiculous situations and dicta under which Indians must now live in our country are many, and perhaps seem inconsequential to us in our wide freedom, but these dicta reveal a collective attitude that seems inexcusable.

- In a day when the Supreme Court and most other courts zealously assure the freedom of Americans to have no religion at all and avoid even the appearance of religion in schools and other public institutions, a ruling issued a few years ago by the Bureau of Indian Affairs, and still in effect, prohibits the performance, even on reservations, of a traditional Indian religious ritual called the Sun Dance. The dictum says, in part, ". . . the reckless giving away of property . . . frequent and prolonged periods of celebration . . . in fact any disorderly or plainly excessive performance that promotes superstitious cruelty, licentiousness, idleness, danger to health and shiftless indifference to family welfare is illegal." (The ruling doesn't mention such things as cocktail parties.)
- Fewer than 10 percent of the adult Indians in America are eligible to vote because of literacy tests used in states with heavy Indian population.
- It is a violation of a federal statute for a white man to purchase an article of clothing or a cooking utensil from an Indian on a reservation. The fine is fifty dollars. (I don't know how this applies to the blankets and baskets the Indians sell to tourists in the mountains of Tennessee and North Carolina.)
- The U.S. Commissioner of Indian Affairs has absolute authority to license peddlers or traders who do business on reservations. He may specify the amount of goods that can be sold, and he can specify the quality and set the price.
- No Indian living on a reservation may enter into a contract of any consequence with anybody without the approval, in writing, of the Commissioner of Indian Affairs, and, in some instances, the Secretary of the Interior.
- An Indian, though technically a citizen of the United States, is prohibited from having so much as a bottle of beer in his possession if he resides on a reservation.

This in spite of the fact that whites and Negroes all around him have spiritous beverages legally available.
- Federal law grants an Indian unlimited hunting privileges, but it prohibits his possessing firearms.
- The ruling of the Supreme Court in 1954 that school facilities for Negroes equal to those of whites does not meet the guarantee of the Constitution was rendered on the basis of the fourteenth amendment. The same court, basing its decision on the same amendment, has ruled that "the states may separate schools for Indian children, provided such schools are equal in equipment to the schools provided for white children."

Remembering that President Lyndon B. Johnson's proposed budget for 1966 had included thirteen million dollars to build a high school for Indian students in Albuquerque, New Mexico, I called Ralph Looney, city editor of the Albuquerque *Tribune,* and inquired about the present status of the Indian School.

I was informed that seven hundred thousand dollars in federal money has been spent in planning for the school; a site has been selected within sight of two of the nine public high schools now in Albuquerque; $9,100,000 has been appropriated for the school; bids were to be received and contracts awarded in the spring of 1968.

Is this money wisely spent?

Even churches do not have a good record in dealing with and accommodating the Indians. A report on the Indian work done in Minnesota by the home missions section of the Lutheran Church in America states: "The Indian child grows up alerted to suspect dominant society, to resent the change of land ownership, and to question the ethics of the white storekeeper selling beans to the white man at two cents a pound and to the Indian at four cents. Today, the storekeeper simply adds ten dollars to the charge account of an Indian.

"The years that white Lutherans and Indians have been living in Northern Minnesota have been eighty years of pauperization and demoralization of the Indian."

Well, we have made some progress in our dealings with Indians since 1626. Perhaps the theme of those dealings is put all too well in the Congressional Record for June 13, 1964. Senator Strom Thurmond of South Carolina rose to address the presiding officer of the Senate. He said, "Mr. President, I call up my amendment number 1014, and ask to have the clerk read it." The gist of the amendment was stated in the first sentence:

No treaty or agreement of the United States with any tribe, band, or identifiable group of American Indians residing within the territorial limits of the United States shall hereafter be amended, modified or otherwise altered except in conformity with legislation hereafter enacted by the Congress.

Then Senator Hubert Humphrey of Minnesota arose and said, "Mr. President, this amendment applies to treaties with Indian tribes. I do not believe it is germane to the substance of the civil rights bill; therefore, I make the point of order that the amendment is not germane."

The chair ruled that the amendment was not and is not germane, and so American Indians were devoid of any specific mention in the Civil Rights Act or amendments thereto, until the Open Housing Act of 1968, which provided Indians with what has been overoptimistically called their own Bill of Rights. Whether it turns out to be the same one under which the rest of us exercise citizenship remains to be seen.

Red Man's Plight: 'Uncle Tomahawks' & 'Apples'

Barbara Isenberg

Drunk, the stony-faced young Indian weaves up the stairs, dragging a faded blue windbreaker in one hand. His eyes focus dully on a sign at the top. It says, "Indians Discovered America."

His feet carry him up and into the Indian Welcome House. Framed in the doorway, he blurts out all he has come to say. "I'm done for, no damn good," he cries. "I don't care about nothin'!" Then he is gone, back to the alien streets of an alien city.

Every year thousands like him come to the nation's cities, driven there by privation on the Indian reservations. Often arriving with no job, no training, no prospects, only with the name of a relative and hope for a new life, the newcomer finds the metropolis almost as harsh as—and sometimes more so than—the place he left.

He suffers from massive culture shock; Afghanistan would be no more strange to many American Indians than Los Angeles. This contributes to an extraordinary rate of alcoholism that makes it all the harder for the migrant to keep and find a job. But still the Indians come.

A Growing Bitterness

According to social workers, cultural anthropologists and others, Indians already have formed an urban poverty-stricken group that ranks as one of the most oppressed and least understood of all. Talks with urban Indians reveal a growing bitterness against the white man and his ways—and a growing militancy, recently exemplified by the Indian take-over of Alcatraz Island in San Francisco

From *The Wall Street Journal*, April 10, 1970, p. 1 and 19.

Bay and the growth of Indian organizations battling for Indian rights. "Urban Indians have become the cutting edge of the new Indian nationalism," says Vine Deloria Jr., former executive director of the National Congress of American Indians and author of the book *Custer Died for Your Sins*, a polemic against white society's handling of the Indian.

The activist spirit seems certain to grow along with urban migration. The 1960 census showed 48% of the American Indian population living in cities and towns; the 1970 count is expected to reveal anywhere from 55% to 65% living there.

Many make their way to cities in the Midwest and West, such as Denver, Minneapolis and Los Angeles. The Indian population of Los Angeles alone has tripled in the past 20 years to some 60,000; as many as one of every 11 Indians in the U.S. is believed to live in this area, and more keep coming every day. (The nationwide Indian population is estimated variously at from 650,000 to one million.)

"We are just transported from one poverty pocket to another, that's all," says Lehman Brightman, the militant president of United Native Americans, a San Francisco-based organization. His group, which puts out bumper stickers ("Custer Had It Coming") and backs the Indians holding Alcatraz, also is pressing for the ouster of Interior Secretary Walter Hickel, whose department oversees Indian affairs.

WHY KEEP COMING?

If the city is so unkind, why do Indians keep coming? Migrants reply that the reservation is even worse. Indian unemployment there currently runs about 40%; the income of many families is below $500 a year; the infant mortality rate is many times the national average; the average life expectancy is only two-thirds the national average, and the vast majority of reservation Indians are poorly housed and educated.

"There is no choice at all. If we want to work, to have some chance, we must go elsewhere; few of us would leave if opportunity existed on the reservation," says Jess Sixkiller, executive director of Chicago-based American Indians United, another activist group.

Many Indians have been resettled in cities under relocation and job training programs of the Bureau of Indian Affairs (BIA), an arm of the Interior Department—and a body accused by many Indians of bureaucratic fumbling and paternalism. (Ironically, the BIA itself is the nation's biggest employer of Indians. Its present commissioner, Louis Bruce, is the third Indian to head the agency.)

Critics maintain that BIA training programs are too heavily weighted toward manual skills in declining demand. James Wilson, an Indian who is director of the Indian division of the Office of Economic Opportunity, says too many Indians are being trained in trades like welding, which is being shoved toward obsolescence by automation, and too few are being trained in white-collar skills. He claims three of every four urban Indians he has come in contact with are underemployed.

Little Relationship

Many BIA-trained Indians are placed in jobs that have little or no relation to their training. The agency concedes that 22% of its trainees in fiscal 1969 "elected" to take such positions but says the rest were placed in jobs related to training.

Trudy Felix Brightman, an Indian in San Francisco, says the BIA brought her there for training as a dental technician, couldn't find her a job and finally sent her to work in a laundry as a clothes presser, Most of her friends, she says, left the dental training course only to wind up in factories. "That's one of the really criminal things the BIA does," argues a social worker familiar with Indian problems. "Bring somebody to the city, train him as a mechanic and then let him wind up doing something else."

Joe Vasquez, president of the Los Angeles Indian Center and a member of the city human rights commission, declares: "After 180 years, the Indian is still unable to find his place in a white-dominated society. All the BIA does is manipulate our assets." Replies a BIA spokesman in Washington: "Obviously, we have shortcomings. We just don't have enough money to train everyone who might want to be trained, and it is hard for us to recruit people for our own agency and train them in the complexities of Indian problems."

But deficient as the existing BIA programs may be, they do at least offer urban migrants the hope of learning some skill and the chance of finding a job that will pay a survival wage. BIA says graduates of its urban programs in fiscal 1969 found employment that paid an average of $2.70 an hour for men and $1.93 for women. Also, Indians relocated and trained by BIA get a monthly stipend until they are placed.

That is more than most Indian migrants to the cities can expect when left to their own devices. Besides their lack of job skills, many also lack proficiency in English, making the search for work all the more difficult. Often they are joined in their wanderings by washouts from BIA relocation programs who are unable to find or keep jobs.

The result is an aimless drifting of Indians back to the reservations or from city to city. The BIA doesn't know the extent of these wanderings; it keeps no track of them, and it doesn't even keep current figures on how long the people it relocates stay in their jobs and cities. But a 1965 BIA study showed 40% of the relocated Indians returned to their reservations.

The total for migrants coming on their own is probably much higher. UCLA anthropologist Theodore Graves, who studied Indian newcomers to Denver, found that less than half stayed more than six months. Many went to other cities, and the rest returned to the reservation—only to find themselves equally ill-equipped to work there and with even less opportunity. For many Indians, this began a cycle of urban migration and return, each phase ending in fresh personal failure.

Strangers to Competition

One of the first problems confronting many Indians making the transition from reservation to city life is the need to become familiar with the complexities of the modern world. Fred Connor, an Indian who came to Los Angeles five years ago, says he would bang on the back doors of buses, not understanding why they didn't open, and wander aimlessly through "the canyons whites call streets." In restaurants, he often found the menus incomprehensible.

But there are deeper-rooted problems. Anthropologists say that Indians are quick to share with fellow tribesmen whatever they have, place little importance on saving money for a rainy day and don't try to keep up with the Joneses. In the city, they are thrust into a society that frowns on what whites would call "handouts," where thrift is a virtue and where fierce individual competition for jobs and status is the rule.

Indian time is one of sun and season, and the clock watching and stress on punctuality that whites display are puzzling to tribesmen. A woman civil service employee in one big Midwestern city recently was fired because she couldn't get used to going to work at a regular hour, and sometimes she didn't show up at all. In Minneapolis, the American Indian Movement often sends members to Indians' homes to drag workers out of bed and get them to the job.

"OUR BRIGHTEST PEOPLE"

For an appalling number of Indians, alcohol is preferable to accommodation to the white world. All too quickly, Indian migrants seem to find their way to the urban Indian bars—the Ritz in Los Angeles, the Larimer Street bars in Denver, the Shamrock or Sammy's Reservation in Chicago. Whites are unwelcome in most. A visitor to the Ritz, packed with Indians on a recent weekday morning, drew baleful stares.

Drunkenness is not an urban problem alone, of course. Drunken reservation Indians can be found on the streets of Gallup, N.M., the "Indian Capital of the World," any Saturday night—particularly since a judge ruled recently that the local house of detention couldn't take in more than 60 inebriates. It had been handling more than 200 on weekend nights.

But the pressures of urban life in a strange society magnify alcoholism. No one knows the full extent of the problem, but all say it is enormous; a daytime walk through an Indian neighborhood in Los Angeles reveals many cases of drunkenness, and Indian leaders concede they are not isolated instances. "Many of our brightest people are in the bars," says Ernest Stevens, chairman of the California Inter-Tribal Council and himself a reformed alcoholic. "They know the truth, and they can't stand it."

"Uncle Tomahawks"

City Indians also complain that they are a forgotten minority. While antipoverty programs technically are designed to serve all the poor, Indians maintain that they are really geared to the needs of the larger minorities and often are controlled by these minorities at the local level. Surveys that statistically pinpoint the plight of the urban Indian and form a base for programs that might serve him are lacking.

In the face of such difficulties, many urban Indians become increasingly bitter toward white society. Those Indians who do adapt are called "Uncle Tomahawks" or "Apples"—red on the outside, white on the inside. But the urban experience is also teaching many Indians that they have to organize to make their voices heard.

Indian organization has been hindered by tribalism, which has tended to inhibit the formation of coalitions. But though tribal differences still divide city Indians, they are gradually overcoming them to form broader, stronger organizations.

American Indians Movement, the Minneapolis-based group, is one of the most active. It has set up an "Indian patrol" to police the Indian community, a move executive director Clyde Bellecourt says has sharply reduced arrests of Indians by city police. The group also has boycotted some Government programs it feels discriminate against Indians and has helped to get an all-Indian advisory board to counsel state and local educational authorities on problems of Indian education. It's currently planning a multipurpose Indian center to be built with Model Cities funds. In the meantime, the group has formed units in Cleveland, Denver, Seattle, and Rapid City, S.D.

Small Businesses

A national group, Chicago-based American Indians United, is planning various cultural programs around the country. In Los Angeles, the Urban Indian Development Association is trying to set up small Indian-owned businesses under Federal grants. Urban Indian centers are multiplying too, many of them joining in a loose confederation headed by American Indians United.

There are more than 70 centers now, compared with about 40 a year ago. Generally supported by donations and by OEO grants, they provide information about jobs and government services through volunteer staffs composed mainly of Indians. They also provide a place for urban Indians to meet and sometimes just relax.

There are some stirrings at the Federal level over the special problems of the urban Indian. The National Council for Indian Opportunity, headed by Vice President Spiro Agnew, has held hearings on urban problems in several cities, and Mr. Agnew has stressed the need to give priority attention to city Indians. But no big programs are under way or planned, and critics say the flow of cash into existing programs doesn't come close to filling the need.

The Powwow of
the Young Intellectuals

Stan Steiner

A few years ago, in the tribal newspaper of the Navajos, there appeared this classified advertisement:

> **SWAP, SELL, OR TRADE**
> Well trained roping horse. Rodeo
> experience. Weight 1150 lbs. 14
> hands high. Excellent condition.
> Will sacrifice. Owner in college.

He put his cowboy boots, his worn jeans, his one tie, his high school diploma, his rock 'n' roll records in his broken suitcase. He tied his suitcase with a rope—perhaps the lasso he had used in bulldogging calves in the Indian rodeos.

He walked in bare feet, one last time, down the dirt road to the blacktop road and onto the crossroad of the superhighway. Then he put on the new shoes he had bought. He looked back at the open country, he turned his back on his indecision, and he walked down the superhighway toward Albuquerque and the University of New Mexico.

The cowboy who had sold his horse was one of thousands of an entire generation beginning a journey between two worlds. Until then he may have been just another "invisible Indian," his thoughts, like himself, kept within the confines of his reservation. Now he was on the open road, where the white man could really see him. He had become visible.

He was the new Indian.

He might have been the Navajo boy Herbert Blatchford, one of the pioneers-in-reverse who journeyed from the reservation to the University of New Mexico in the early postwar years. The young Navajo was to become the scholarly voice of the university-educated, twentieth-century Indians. The quiet voice of the college Indians, articulate and confident, he was the founder of the National Indian Youth Council and is now the executive director and the editor of its journal, *The Aborigine*. But, like the cowboy's his was a long journey.

Young Blatchford is the descendant of an ancestral headman, the grandson of the brother of the great chief Manuelito. He had ridden, as a boy, to the summer pastures with his family's flock. Sheepherding was the old way of the Navajo and he had grown up in a tradition of which he was not the contradiction.

He had been educated in not one, but two, church schools: those of the Methodist and Christian Reform missions. He had entered what he termed the "no-man's land" of education. He had traded his sheepskin bed for a sheepskin diploma. In that unpresuming way he has—in the way of the Navajo—Blatchford said to himself, not modestly but impersonally: "He had experienced about all any sheepherder would. In retrospect he might be classed as a literate sheepherder."

The life of a young Indian, like Blatchford, on the reservation, before his journey to a university education, has been earthily described by a Navajo girl, Carol Bitsui. She was a student at the High School of St. Michael's and the president of the class of 1967, when she wrote of her "feelings of being a Navajo:"

I was raised on the reservation in a hogan with neither a running water, not a button to press for warm heat.
My bed was cradleboard, a sheepskin and the earth. My food was my mother's breath, goat's milk, berries, mutton, and corn meal. My play partners were puppies, the lamb and the lizards.
I ate with my fingers. I went barefoot at most time. I washed my hair with yucca roots. I combed my hair with strawbrush. I wore a hair knot.
I had to rise early. I herded sheep in the blazing desert of Coyote Canyon. I carried water from the water pit. I ground corn for my food. I carried wood on my back and in my arms. I carded wool for my mother.
I sometime went without eating because there was no food in the dish cupboard of my hogan.
I wore clothes that were made out of flour sacks. I sang songs as I tended my sheep. I rode a horse without a saddle. I rode in a wagon to the Trading Post.
I prayed to the Great Spirit of my people. I respected nature because it was sacred to me. I took part in my people's ceremonies. I went to squaw dances, fire dances, and Yei Bi Chai dances, not for fun, but to be the patient's guest. I listened to the legend been told by my grandparents. The medicine man was my doctor. The herbs were my medicine.
I did not speak English, for it was a strange language to me.

Going down the rough dirt road, from the earthy and easygoing tribal life on the rural reservations to the middle-class upmanship of university life in the cities, these young Indians were like refugees in an unknown country. The university was more than strange. It was foreign and alien.

"Very few of us crossed the gap between the two cultures," Blatchford said. "Those who found it difficult to indulge in the new culture developed into a hybrid group, belonging fully to neither culture."

Listening to the young Indians talk of pop sociology, the Beatles mystique, and "the lonely crowd," and seeing them dressed in properly improper collegiate costumes of tight jeans and loose shirts—the native costume of modern Indian youth—few of their classmates could have imagined the depths of the cultural abyss they had to cross to reach the campus malt shop. Journeys of this kind are too hazardous and frightening to talk about. The students do not often talk about them.

The rites of passage are treacherous. But these youths have one advantage their forefathers did not have; they are lonely but not alone.

"In the old days an Indian youth was singled out for education, as an individual, 'to divide him from his tribe,' " Blatchford said. "The Indian boarding schools divided and conquered. But we were a group. There was group thinking. I think that surprised us the most. We had a group world view."

In the years after World War II and the Korean War formal education in the white man's universities, long frowned upon by the tribal elders and skeptically ignored by the governmental educators, became a necessity. Youths who had seen the modern world in military service wished to know more about it, how it worked, where they, as Indians, would fit in. So, reluctantly, did their parents.

Educators of the Indians were now prepared to build elementary and secondary schools, in more than token numbers, for the tribal elite, and to encourage the graduates to go on to college. In the hope that the Indian youth would leave the tribal reservations at last and enter the "mainstream," the government made education the top priority in Indian affairs. The "social-cultural integration of Indians [is] a primary goal of formal education," the Assistant Commissioner of Indian Affairs, James Officer, told a university conference on "Research in Indian Education." He was echoing in the jargon of the academe what an Indian Bureau report in 1882 stated with cruder truth: the schooling of "the savages," it said, was to assure that "the children are taught to speak English, taught the manners and ways of the whites; in a word, Americanized."

The Americanization of the Indian began once more, but this time in the high schools and universities. Within ten years—from 1950 to 1960—the number of Indian high school students increased from 24,000 to 57,000. In that decade the Indian youth attending college for one year or more went up from 6,500 to 17,000.

Nowhere was the cultural trek of the young Indians to the schools more dramatic than among the Navajos of the Southwest. The "Long March" of

Navajo children to the schools zoomed from 5,308 (in 1939) to 13,883 (in 1951) to 30,650 (in 1961). In a single decade, after World War II, the number of high school graduates of this tribe increased from 185 to 1,840 annually, while the number of Navajo college students went up from a mere three dozen to more than 400 yearly in the early 1960's.

University education is, in a sense, the Indian's postgraduate course in education in the ways of the white man begun in the army barracks. In the barracks the GI Indian was often a loner. He was a stranger in the midst of strangers. He had no tribal way of understanding the exotic life of the military, and the experience was socially disturbing, no matter how individually rewarding.

In the universities the Indian student is one of many. He rooms with Indian youths like himself, and he belongs to an Indian club. There are even Indian "cultural evenings" to wash off the whiteness of the antiseptic classrooms.

Still the young Indian is troubled. The college dropout rate is high. It is not his academic rating but the academic life that unnerves him. Forty percent of the Indian students who dropped out of one college came from the upper third of their high school graduating classes. In fact, "Indians with high academic aptitude drop out of college as frequently as Indians with moderate academic aptitude," reported Dr. Bruce Meador in a study of Indian college students at five Southwestern universities, prepared for the U.S. Office of Education. "More intelligent Indians drop out of school (percentage-wise) for emotional reasons than non-Indians," Dr. Meador reported.

Blatchford was more specific. The anxieties of the university students, he thought, were not due to their tribal past, or university present, so much as to their fear of the educational "no-man's land" between the two cultures.

"The feeling got around that we students were not sure about our college and tribal future. We weren't," Blatchford said. "We decided to find out whether we were in, or out, or on the borderline, of our people. So we decided to hold a meeting and invite the tribal elders. And our parents. And to ask them.

"There wasn't a room to meet in at the University of New Mexico, in Albuquerque. 'Booked up,' they said. So we met in the auditorium of the Cathedral of St. Francis, in Santa Fe. That was in 1954. That was a historic year, remember?" he added.

Under the blessed hands of Saint Francis of Assisi the powwow of the young intellectuals gathered. It was an ironic setting for the creation of the modern movement of new Indians—the Red Muslims. On the site of the old church of the conquistadores of Spain, built in 1622 by Indian slaves, where the ground was bloodied with the history of Pueblo revolts, the students met.

The governors of the Pueblos came, wearing their tunics and jeans, and bearing their thousand-year-old dignity. The leaders of the Navajos and Apaches came in, business suits and sunglasses. The wizened, and sometimes wise, old men, in traditional dress, soothed by age, came together with the nervous young Indian college boys and girls, with their anthropology textbooks in their suitcases.

The young spoke first. And Herbert Blatchford spoke first among the young:

In our early childhood, we, as American Indians, have been taught the distinction be-significant factor in human environment. We are a deeply and uniquely religious people. tween the living and the lifeless. We have been taught to value the spirit of man as a

We, as Indian students, have been indoctrinated to the importance of education many times and by multiple measures. We have been educated to affirm one proposition: American cultural education. On the other hand, we have, under false pretenses, been encouraged to obliterate our own cultural values.

Our problem is: How can we, as young people, help to solve conflicts between cultures? What happens when a person graduates from college? Where can he go to further his training before attempting to hold tribal leadership? Can we, in some small way, fill this need?

Let the elders tell us what they say, Blatchford said; we have heard the professors, but they are not Indians. "Because of our cultural heritage, we, under the guidance of our elders, have become tolerant of all circumstances. And we have relied on the essence of time to give us proof of all encroaching sincerity."

The elders listened to the young. And then they said: Education is necessary. We will support you, if we can. We will send you dancers to perform in your Kiva Club at the university, to raise money for your scholarships.

The elders said: Come home when you are educated in the white man's ways. Your people need to know what you know.

> My child, come this way,
> My child, come this way,
> You will take home with you a good country—
> Says the Father,
> Says the Father,
> Ate heye lo! Ate heye lo!

> I love my children—Yeye!
> I love my children—Yeye!
> You shall grow to be a nation—Yeye!
> You shall grow to be a nation—Yeye!

Harmony between the old and young was unlikely. In the meeting of tribal minds the Indians did not close the gap between the generations. But they bridged it.

Wendell Chino, the president of the National Congress of American Indians, was to say five years later:

We are realizing the emergence of young, educated Indian leadership so that the reins of tribal destinies are being transferred to the college-trained, college-educated young leaders [who are] still availing themselves of the sage advice of the older people. . . .

It had been so from the beginning. "We owe a debt of gratitude to the youth" had been almost the first words of the keynote speech of the Choctaw leader Ben Dwight, at the founding convention of the first National Congress of American Indians in 1944. These young Indians "who have come from tribal schools, who have gone to colleges," the Choctaw had said, were responsible for that movement too.

The patriarch of that founding convention, Attocknie, the elderly longhair and religious man of the Comanche tribe, had nodded:

I am ignorant, but I have the interest of the young and educated Indians at heart. There are Indians like myself who are not educated, who are restricted, and who cannot exist under conditions that will work well with the young and educated Indians. Now, we are very proud of you, our children, that are so highly educated.

"It started with the old people," Blatchford said of the movement of new Indians.

It was never a disjointed venture. The youth, when they get together now, always meet on Indian land, always with the old tribal people. And we came from that very first meeting with the feeling that by going away to college we were not going away. We would be welcome home. So this gave us confidence. Let's start more Indian clubs in the universities, we said. We drew in kids from other colleges. The idea spread like wildfire.

These university clubs were the tribal fraternities of the collegiate Indians. Once they had set them up, the youth wished to bring the far-flung clubs together into a council—a powwow of all the young tribal intellectuals.

Enthusiastic but inexperienced, they sought the advice of Charles Minton, director of the Southwestern Association on Indian Affairs. He was a fatherly, if fitfully arbitrary, friend of the Indians, a refugee from corporate law, given to recitation of romantic poetry of the West, who had helped the youth hire their hall at St. Francis.

Minton, a white-haired iconoclast of the old school, had "gone Indian." Once a Pueblo governor had invited him to a religious ceremonial, but Minton curled his lips, "You know I am a pagan. I can't come." The old man was as enthusiastic as the young Indians about the idea and guided the formation of the Southwestern Regional Youth Conference.

Once more the Indians were to be saved from cultural oblivion by the holding of another conference. It was not exactly what the young Indians had in mind, but it was a beginning.

Conferences were held yearly. One of the largest was held at the University of New Mexico in 1960—then a gracious host to the 350 Indian students from 57 tribes. There were by then even foreign visitors: "the young African from Tanganyika" was mentioned in the conference notes, "who came to observe and take back with him a similar program for African youth."

The "sponsor," as the fatherly Minton thought of himself, was happily harassed. He described the "sponsor" as the one "who does the ground work, much of the leg work, acts as backdrop, fills in the gaps, and does what no one else has time for." He did not, however, speak at the conference. Instead, he sent lists of "suggested" topics to the would-be delegates, who were, in turn, selected, not elected, by school administrators. Nonetheless, the sponsor insisted that the Youth Conferences were "not directed, influenced, or censored. It was 'free,'" the sponsor said, "'speech.'. . ."

"His Indians," as Minton affectionately called the youth he chaperoned with paternal concern, were beginning to chafe under his fatherly strictures.

"There is a need for a freer movement," Blatchford told the faculty advisors of the Youth Conference in the spring of 1960. Let us have "whatever sparks enthusiasm and interest; rather than [this] more formal agenda," he pleaded.

The uprising of the new Indians was about to break out of the academic reservations. It was at yet another conference—the conference on Indian affairs was "our Western cultural rite," said Professor E. Roby Leighton, of the University of Arizona—that the emerging tribal nationalism of the youth was to crystallize into direct action.

In the summer of 1960, the turning point was reached. The unwitting host to this tribal explosion was Professor Sol Tax, the editor of Current Anthropology, who had organized an American Indian conference at the University of Chicago. The Indian establishment had gathered. Few of the venerated tribal leaders and government officials in Indian affairs were missing. There were so many anthropologists with portable tape recorders that they convened their own conference-within-the-conference to compare tapes.

Most of the young Indians who went to Chicago did so on their own. They were not invited. They represented nobody. They thumbed their way. "I was curious [to see] what Indian youth were doing nationally," Blatchford said. "We met for the first time as a group in Chicago," Mel Thom said.

The youthful ardor that they brought to the conference was dispelled by the routine rhetoric of those they called the "Uncle Tomahawks"—the official Indian leaders. "Just out of college, we were very young. So we looked on. We saw the 'Uncle Tomahawks' fumbling around, passing resolutions, and putting headdresses on people. But as for taking a strong stand they just weren't doing it," Mel Thom recalled. His restive voice was echoed by Clyde Warrior: "It was the old song and dance to a slightly new anthropological tune." Herbert Blatchford dismissed "the whole show:" "There was a lot of rigmarole about procedure and all that. We weren't interested."

The oratory of the Uncle Tomahawks droned on and the tape recorders of the anthropologists whirled on. But the youths had heard it all before. Little by little the young Indians began to voice their own opinions—at first to themselves. Hundreds of pages of conference notes, memos, committee reports, and meeting agendas poured out of the mimeograph machines. And on the backs of these sheets of "instant anthropology" the young Indians scribbled furious words of annoyance and disagreement.

In large, angry letters one youth wrote to himself: "Fellow American Indians, we the younger Indians are deeply concerned about the outcome of this conference. Within the years to come we will be directly affected by its result." His notes were passed from hand to hand. "It is agreed among ourselves that we [the youth] take a united stand," the handwritten message went on. "With due respect to our elders' learned expression and honorable deliberation . . ."

Neither the official Indians nor the university sponsors were aware of the youthful rebellion. The anthropologists were busily and happily "applying new methods of applied anthropology," as one said later. Conferees enthralled with their own eloquence did not hear the rumblings from the floor. But the conference was about to be host to the birth of the movement of Indian nationalism, the new tribalism.

The disquiet of the youth was voiced by a Navajo girl, Vivian One Feather. She said one day: "We're wondering what youth are doing at an adult meeting. Let's have a meeting of our own."

"We got together in a youth caucus," Herbert Blatchford said. "I chaired it. I told them, 'Look, you can't run and hide. You came all this way. You ought to talk about what you want.' So they talked all night! They talked for four days! I didn't get any sleep for four days! None of us did."

There were twelve youths in that "youth caucus." But these few were soon chairing many of the conference committees. So strong did this band of political warriors become that when the "Statement of Purpose" they wrote was almost tabled they talked of halting the conference by urging a "strike" of the committees they chaired.

"We had a battle. But the 'Statement of Purpose' the conference passed had mostly what we wrote," Mel Thom said.

Into the statement were written the first demands of the new Indian nationalism. "We, the majority of the Indian people of the United States of America," it began, have "the inherent right of self-government" and "the same right of sovereignty." The tribes "mean to hold the scraps and parcels [of their lands] as earnestly as any small nation or ethnic group was ever determined to hold to identity and survival," it declared.

"Our situation cannot be relieved by appropriated funds alone," it continued. "The answers we seek are not commodities to be purchased, neither are they evolved automatically through the passing of time. . . . What we ask of America is not charity, not paternalism, even when benevolent.

"The effort to place social adjustment on a money-time interval scale which has characterized Indian administration has resulted in unwanted pressure and frustration," the statement said. It reaffirmed tribal values—"a universe of things they knew, valued and loved." And it requested technical and financial assistance like "any small nation."

Word for word the incipient nationalism of the "Statement of Purpose" of the conference was identical to the scribbled thoughts of the youth caucus.

As soon as the Chicago conference ended the Indian youth were scattered to the four winds. Throughout that summer letters flew back and forth from reservation to reservation. Those who found letters inadequate tape-recorded their thoughts and air-mailed these. "Boy, the air was thick with tapes as with arrows that summer," one recalled. It was Herbert Blatchford who suggested that the young Indians gather once again, by themselves, and form their own youth movement.

Let us all gather "to maintain our unity" and talk of "possible circumstances for our destiny," Blatchford wrote in a round-robin letter. He suggested that the Inter-Tribal Ceremonial held in Gallup, New Mexico, in early August would be a symbolic and practical time for the young Indian intellectuals to powwow.

"We must use the moon as our mirror."

THE RED MUSLIMS

It began in a too small and stuffy room on the wrong side of the railroad tracks in the highway town of Gallup, New Mexico. On that August 10, 1960, the nondescript and dusty Indian Community Center was suffocated by the unbelievably hot, burnt morning air that seemed to evaporate in one's mouth. Ten young Indians, who were to be known as the Red Muslims, sat in a circle like a modern war council.

Whistles of the wailing freight trains drowned their words. In the streets tens of thousands of tourists and Indians milled about. They had come to see the ceremonials. Hour upon hour the ten young Indians talked—a Paiute, a Mohawk, a Ute, a Ponca, a Shoshone-Bannock, a Potawatomi, a Tuscarora, two Navajos, and a Crow. These university youths had come from diverse and distant tribes. One had written, "Of course I'll go into hock to meet with you. . . . I may be forced to travel by oxcart, but I shall be there." But, once there, seated in a circle of decision, with their angers and determinations, they were uncertain. This was not the Cathedral of St. Francis or the University of Chicago. Now their destiny was their own to decide.

"If we organize are we really trying to help our people, or are we going to seek status for ourselves?" asked Clyde Warrior.

The Mohawk girl Shirley Witt was troubled by this too: "Is there any way by which this organization can guard against political climbing? Can we prevent its being used as a lever to gain high position?"

The university Indians talked of their desire to "find a place for themselves, as a group, within the Indian world. Some of the members stated that, though their training in school would not be of direct help to the Indian people, nonetheless they felt a very strong need to serve those at home. Several members added their voices to this.

"Most of all," the minutes of that meeting concluded, "the group felt that it was vital to retain the beauty of the Indian heritage."

Little by little the image of the new Indians emerged. A Winnebago girl, Mary Natani, said that they "must identify themselves as Indian and still adjust to another culture. But not leave behind what is really Indian." The new Indians would be "hybrids," Blatchford said, and would create a synthesis of the two cultures in their Indianness.

On that day the idea of a new tribalism—red nationalism—began to take form. (One girl, at the meeting, admitted that she had never been to a "regular powwow.") The form was, however, still uncertain; the leaders were yet unchosen; and the organization was nonexistent.

It was the Paiute Mel Thom who proposed the organizational principles of the new Youth Council. He thought that "political climbing" was a concept of the white man that was inherent in the structure and goals of his society. It was not tribal nor Indian. Let us organize "in the Indian way" on the "high principles derived from the values and beliefs of our ancestors," he said. "[And let us] consider rules based on Indian thinking as being sufficient."

Thom later elaborated on these beliefs:

The movement grew in the Indian way. We had decided what we needed was a movement. Not an organization, but a movement. Organizations rearrange history. Movements make history. That's what we decided to do. That's what we did.

Long ago the Indians knew how to use direct action. You might say that was the traditional way that Indians got things done, Thom went on. We were concerned with direct action: Indians moving out and doing something. The younger Indians got together in the Youth Council because they didn't feel that the older leadership was aggressive enough. And we felt that Indian affairs were so bad that it was time to raise some hell.

"But it had to be done in the Indian way," he added.

In the bold and innocent conceit of youth the ten young Indians proclaimed themselves to be the National Indian Youth Council. They elected one another the officers—all ten of them. They were its entire membership. Within a few years they were to number thousands. But at that moment they were all chiefs.

The movement needed a leader. Mel Thom, who had been president of the Southwestern Youth Conferences, was elected to the council presidency.

"Little Bear" some have nicknamed him, and "Smokey, the Bear." There were friends—he thought they were friends—who named him "Mao Tse Thom." Physically he fits these nicknames. He is sturdy, short, and stocky. He has a tenacity and hard wit that are discernible in his intense dark eyes. There is something rocklike and unrelenting about him.

He "was born and raised" on the Walker River Reservation in Nevada. The land is a rocky wasteland, a desolate, dismal region of thorny undergrowth and scrawny trees. The barren land is inhabited by ghost towns and geological prehistory and by this Paiute people. Growing up on the desert, he had eaten "everything from jackrabbits to potatoes to chow mein." He had worked at everything from "cow-puncher to construction work through swampland and deserts to assistant resident engineer for the Federal Aviation Agency."

"Just a reservation Indian," Thom said of himself. He had left a "successful career"—he was a graduate civil engineer—to return to his reservation and become tribal chairman of his Paiute people, without pay.

"When you say, 'Did I go back to the reservation?' you are being a little naïve," Thom said.

Does that mean to physically go back and work? This is hardly the case. Our Indian community exists at every level of society—in the universities, in the cities, on the reservations, in the government. It doesn't matter where Indians are any more. They remain Indians. They are, in fact, becoming more consciously Indian. They are very much part of the larger Indian community. So we're finding a new type of young Indian. He fits into this total community.

The young Indians travel around a lot more. And there's an awareness coming among these young Indians, the more they get around, the more they travel, the more they see and understand how the white society and government work. . . .

In the country today we are undergoing some kind of revolution. The young people in the whole country are not satisfied. Being an Indian and being young means you are twice as dissatisfied. You can hold a people down just so long. Then, pretty soon, they are going to kick back. And that's what's happening with some of the Indian tribes. It has already happened with the young Indians.

Young Thom, as the leader of the Youth Council, and as tribal chairman, combines within himself the new and old tribalism. He was one of its political architects.

"The Indians are the only tribal people, really tribal people, in this country, who don't have the same system, the same values as urban America," Thom said.

And even though what exists in the Indian world is inconsistent with urban America, we've got to recognize this different way of life. If we continue to look at the Indian as a 'problem' that can be worked out by making him look like any other American, well, it wouldn't work.

The Indian way, or what you might call Indian culture, is the way the Indian people live today. The government and the people of this country seem to feel that the Indian heritage, or Indian culture, is the way we look, or dance, or sing. But Indian culture is the way people live today.

And there is a way! The young, educated Indian people know this way, this tribal way, and they like it.

Generations ago, in the last gasp of the "Indian revivalists," it was the Paiute prophet Wovoka whose religious visions of the rebirth of the old tribalism inspired the Ghost Dances. In the fading years of the nineteenth century his prophecy swept the defeated reservations like a prairie fire. Wovoka was a tribal ancestor of young Thom's on the Walker River Reservation. The old prophet's grave, where he was buried under his Christian name of Jack Wilson, lay not too far from the office of the new tribal chairman.

In his belief in a new tribalism, Mel Thom is heir to tradition. The Paiutes of Walker River were one of the last tribes to lay down their arms. It was not until 1911 that the final "battle" of the old Indian Wars had been fought on the alkali flats of the Nevada desert. It was known in history books as the "Paiute Outbreak," but the tribe itself called it "The Massacre of the Black Desert."

"My father knew two children who were caught by the U.S. Army in that massacre. They died. They died of heartbreak," Thom said. Like the tribal memory of Wovoka, these inheritances were in young Mel Thom's thoughts and in his bones.

He even spoke of modern "Indian Wars." His voice had that defiant, unflinching, but calm tone of a modern warrior: "Let us take a look around our great country and see what the red man of today is fighting," Thom said.

There is definitely a battle going on, no question about that. This is not a fictitious 'nothing fight' like that on TV and in the movies. This is a different kind of war—a cold war, one might say. Fortunately, for someone, this is not a hot war; otherwise the Indians might not have so many friends and experts.

The opposition to Indians is a monstrosity which cannot be beaten by any single action, unless we as Indian people could literally rise up, in unison, and take what is ours by force. We see, however, that our Indian is small, confused, and regretfully does not include all our Indian people. We know the odds are against us, but we also realize that we are fighting for the lives of future Indian generations.

The weakest link in the Indian's defense is his lack of understanding of this modern-type war. Indians have not been able to use political action, propaganda, and power as well as their opponents. Enemy forces have successfully scattered the Indian people and got them divided against themselves. The enemy has made notable gains; they deployed their forces well. But there is increased activity over on the Indian side. There is disagreement, laughing, singing, outbursts of anger, and occasionally some planning. Given some time, it looks like an effort can be put forth. If we can hold our ranks together, our chances of gaining in our modern campaign are good. There is growing hope.

"We are convinced, more than ever, that this is a real war. . . . No people in this world ever has been exterminated without putting up a last resistance," Thom said. "The Indians are gathering."

Like a familial father the Commissioner of Indian Affairs, Robert Bennett, reluctantly acknowledged this youthful turbulence. He was tolerant of it: "The attitude of the young Indians might, to some extent, be equated to the attitude of a lot of young people in the United States, as manifested by their strikes at universities, their burning of draft cards, their resistance to Vietnam. A lot of us like to indulge in this sort of thing once in a while."

Yet the Commissioner was cautionary. His paternal patience went just so far: "I hope the young people are not misguided in this. We still have reality to face. And the realities that the Indian people have to face require that they have a good education so that they can make a proper adaptation." His official attitude was one of patience—up to a point.

The revivals of old tribalism had lost their way in the labyrinths of nostalgia. Religious leaders of the past had looked to the past. When the reservation life offered no promise for the future and the present was empty and stagnant, it was inevitable that tribalism meant a desperate attempt to hold on to a disappointing heritage. Nostalgia was not a luxury. It was a necessity of nothingness and defeat.

But the young university Indians foresee a future. They do not wish to preserve the past as a museum culture, but wish to recreate their Indian way of life in a modernized twentieth-century version. "They are creating this culture," said Vine Deloria, Jr. These youths were born into an era of resurgent nationalism among dark-skinned people the world over. Having conquered their awe of the technology of Western civilization, the young wish to master it, but not be mastered by it.

The new Indians seek "proper adaptation." But to them it means adaptation of the non-Indian society to their modern Indianness. It means rejection of the melting pot. It means, most of all, rejection of assimilation by the consuming maw of mass urban society. And it means creation of what Mel Thom named "the Greater Indian America."

It was prophesied by Herbert Blatchford, the young Navajo who helped found the Youth Council, that the time of the new Indian had come:

Perhaps it is a remnant of the "Warrior Society" whose job it was to be aware of all threats to the tribal group. Well then, rise up—make haste—our people need us.

It was prophesied by young Richard McKenzie, the Sioux who led the "Raid on Alcatraz" to claim the abandoned prison as a site for a University of the American Indian. Sitting in the board room of the San Francisco Indian Center, the young man said:

Kneel-Ins, Sit-Ins, Sleep-Ins, Eat-Ins, Pray-Ins like the Negroes do wouldn't help us. We would have to occupy the government buildings before things would change.

It was prophesied by Guy Okakok, the Paitot leader of the Alaska Eskimos at the polar village of Point Barrow, who said almost in a whisper:

Eskimos still want to be peaceful and like and trust everybody, but the time has come when they must take a stand.

It was prophesied by the old leader of the Blackfeet of Montana, Walter Wetzel, an honored former president of the National Congress of American Indians:

We Indians have been struggling unsuccessfully with the problems of maintaining home and family and Indian ownership of the land. *We must strike*. We must have a new policy.

It was prophesied by the young leader of the Tuscaroras of New York State who turned back the bulldozers of Robert Moses when a dam was planned on Iroquois land. Wallace "Mad Bear" Anderson was thought by many to be a modern prophet, and his prophecies were revolutionary:

Our people were murdered in this country. And they are still being murdered. They used germ warfare against us, when they drove us into Kansas. My people crossed the rivers and waited. They promised us land, homes, tools. Wagons came filled with blankets and clothes. They were infected with smallpox. My people took them and died and they died and died. We do not want to be absorbed by a sick society. There is an Indian nationalist movement in the country. I am one of the founders. We are not going to pull any punches from here on in.

It was prophesied by Robert Thomas, the Cherokee anthropologist, who wrote in *Indian Voices:*

The Indian picture isn't any blacker than it always was. It is just that American Indians are trying to do something about their problems and injustices. They are speaking out more and making their wish known. They aren't laying quiet and doing nothing any more. Maybe a new day is dawning for the Indian.

It was prophesied by Robert Burnette, the leader of the American Indian Civil Rights Council and former director of the Indians' Congress. The fiery Sioux, of whom it has been said, "If he had been a war chief one hundred years ago the white man would have never crossed the Mississippi," declared:

There is a new mood. In the last few years there has been an upsurge of young Indians. And the old Indians are joining them. And they will drive the corrupt out of their lands.

It was prophesied by the Ojibwa Francis Le Quier, the chairman of the Great Council Fire, who in 1963 posted this proclamation on reservations throughout the country:

To the Chiefs and Spiritual Leaders of the Indians of the North and South American Continents: . . . This is the day when the Great Spirit calls to all men. This is the day all our Great Chiefs spoke of. This is the day when all Indian prophecies will be fulfilled. This is the day when all the tribes shall come together and be one nation. This is the day when a new race of men shall be raised up by the power of the Great Spirit. This is the day of the Great Justice.

You shall hear the voice of the Owl, the Fox, the Bear, the Coyote and the Eagle.

The young Chickasaw Kenneth Kale wrote:

> We know all about
> Our redskinned counterpart
> Of Martin, Gregory, and Stokely
> Rolled into one
> Like an angry "Red Muslim"
> With work to be done. . . .
> I've often wondered why it is said
> That the Indian Spirit is broken and dead
> When in their midst like a grizzly bear
> Is the sleeping redskinned giant
> Now on the prowl. . . .

The voice of the new Indian was heard in the land. What he had to say was a choral chant of tribal resurgence that was articulated in the themes and words of modern man. Yet what he had to say was old.

In the beginning there had been an educational explosion. Now the young Indians were lighting the fuse of a political explosion. "We in the National Indian Youth Council were looking for a target area. We were looking for a target area for direct action," Mel Thom said.

On the wild rivers of the State of Washington the new Indians found their target.

American Indian Education: Time to Redeem an Old Promise

Estelle Fuchs

The complexity of the issues raised by Indian education and the passion that pervades discussion of them can be understood only as part of the long and tortured history of Indian-white relations in this country. The Indian cannot easily forget the white man's attempts to exterminate his people, their forcible removal from ancestral lands, the efforts to convert them from their ancient religions, and the guarantees of rights to traditional homelands that were so often broken in practice. The record is varied; no one tribe's story is an exact duplicate of another's. But all share a history of subjugation and deliberate attempts to destroy their diverse cultures—sometimes by force, at other times by missionary zeal. And always their very identity and diversity (as Navahos, Pimas, Cherokees, Pawnees, etc.) were obscured by the common misnomer "Indian."

Concern for the education of American Indians appeared early in the history of the English colonies in the New World. Dartmouth was founded for the education of "youth of Indian tribes . . . and also of English youth and others." Harvard was established for the schooling of English and Indian youth and the campus of William and Mary still treasures an early building erected for Indians. But the issues raised by the white man's efforts to extend the benefits of his educational tradition to the natives of the New World were clearly defined at an early date—and still endure. Benjamin Franklin told of the response by Indian leaders to an offer of education for Indian youth:

You who are wise must know that different nations have different conceptions of things and will therefore not take it amiss if our ideas of this kind of education happen not to be the same as yours. We have had some experience with it. Several of our young people were formerly brought up at the colleges of the northern provinces; but

From *Saturday Review*, January 24, 1970, Vol. 53, No. 4, pp. 54–59. Copyright 1970 Saturday Review, Inc. Reprinted by permission of the author and Saturday Review.

when they came back to us, they were bad runners, ignorant of every means of living in the woods . . . totally good for nothing. We are, however . . . obliged by your kind offer . . . and to show our grateful sense of it, if the gentlemen of Virginia will send up a dozen of their sons, we will take great care of their educations; instruct them in all we know and make men of them.

Today, nearly a quarter of a million Indian children are in American schools. About half of them are the educational responsibility of the Bureau of Indian Affairs (BIA), which is an agency in the Department of the Interior. But the problems of education and cultural differences remain. After two years of exhaustive hearings on Indian education, a recent Senate subcommittee report was entitled "Indian Education: A National Tragedy—A National Challenge."

The dimensions of the problem are indicated by the record of absenteeism, retardation, and dropout rates in Indian schools. Yet, despite the dreary statistics, more Indian children are coming to school, and they are remaining in school longer. Thus, the issues in Indian education today cut to the core of the problems facing all American education—the quality of the educational environment, its responsiveness to the rich diversity of American life, the roles of federal and state governments in supporting the educational enterprise, and, perhaps most important of all, the degree to which the local community shall share in educational decision making.

The position of the Indian differs from that of other minorities, because Congress, as it extended its rule across the continent, recognized the Indian tribes as sovereign nations, and concluded some 400 separate treaties with them. Many of these agreements promised education as one of the federal services that would be provided in exchange for Indian lands.

From the beginning the federal government was uneasy about running schools itself and sought to turn over responsibility to other agencies. During the late nineteenth century, funds were distributed to various religious denominations to maintain mission schools. But public protest against federal aid to sectarian schools led the government to discontinue the practice. As a result, a system of federally operated schools was developed. (The government chose to close down two successful nineteenth century Indian school systems organized by the Cherokee and the Choctaw.)

Paying little attention to the multitude of linguistic and other cultural differences among the tribes, and the varied traditions of child rearing in preparation for adulthood in the tribal communities, the government entered the school business with a vigor that caused consternation among the Indians. The package deal that accompanied literacy included continuing efforts to "civilize the natives." Old abandoned Army forts were converted into boarding schools, children were removed—sometimes forcibly—long distances from their homes, the use of Indian languages by children was forbidden under threat of corporal punishment, students were boarded out to white families during vacation times, and native religions were suppressed. The practices were rationalized by the notion that the removal from the influence of home and tribe was the most effective means of preparing the Indian child to become an American.

The Carlisle Indian School in Pennsylvania, perhaps best known for its famous alumnus, the athlete Jim Thorpe, helped to usher in this ignominious period in the history of education for Indians. The policy might even have succeeded in obliterating Indian cultures and destroying Indian children, if it had not been for two factors. First, the facilities available were totally inadequate, leaving enormous numbers of children untouched by the policy's influence, and second, children resisted the system by running away, and lower echelon BIA personnel sometimes conspired with Indian families to keep the children at home.

Attempts to force Indians into the white man's mold extended to economic policy as well. The Dawes Act of 1887, ignoring the fact that the Indian had no tradition of private ownership of land, and that some tribes did no farming, distributed tracts of reservation lands, called allotments, in parcels of forty to 160 acres. The result was disastrous for the Indians, because the land left over after the allotments were made was declared surplus by the government, and some unsuccessful Indians lost even their allotments. But the result was extremely profitable for those who, by 1934, had managed to grab ninety million acres of former Indian lands.

Both the educational and the economic policies of this period led to the impoverishment of the Indians and to the shattering of their morale. The bitterness of that era remains in the living memory of many older Indians today.

The general pattern of corruption and intolerance of cultural differences that was characteristic of American society in the 1920s pervaded the Indian Service as well, and led to a Senate investigation that produced the best critical survey of federal Indian programs conducted to that date. The Meriam Report of 1928 called for a reversal of former policy in order to strengthen the Indian family and social structure rather than destroy it, to expand day schools and to humanize the boarding schools, to stimulate community participation, and to relate schooling more closely to the postschool needs of Indian youth.

The ensuing years ushered in a more humane and creative period in Indian affairs. It was the era of the New Deal and generally progressive legislation. John Collier, commissioner of Indian Affairs, was empathetic to Indian problems and a strong proponent of the value of cultural diversity and the rights of Indian peoples. The Indian Reorganization Act, passed in 1934, put a stop to land allotments. Tribal governments were formed, funds were pooled for the purchase of lost lands, and community schools were built. Although problems of poverty and economic development remained to be solved fully, it was a generally exciting and hopeful period.

World War II brought a cutback in federal spending for the New Deal Indian programs, and before they could be vigorously renewed another radical reversal in policy took place that today leaves its mark in anger, suspicion, and fear that will not be easily erased.

The new policy, known as "termination," was instituted in the 1950s and aimed to sever reservations from the services of the Bureau of Indian Affairs. Although different in form, it smacked of the allotment era and other previous attempts by the government to escape its obligations to Indians by forcing them into the general population. Even when they received large sums of money for their lands, the Indians enjoyed little lasting benefit, and many former reservation residents became city dwellers—too often lower-class, with their income from tribal resources gone. The experience of the Klamath of Oregon, who lost their timberland income, has served as a warning to all reservation Indians. They are wary of any program leading in the direction of hated termination.

Although the termination policy has been currently halted, all contemporary issues in Indian affairs—including Indian education—are interpreted in the light of possible relationship to the ending of federal services to Indians.

Within this shifting pattern of government policy, the federal school system for Indians has grown tremendously in size and complexity from its small beginnings at the turn of the century. At present, the BIA operates 226 schools located in Alaska, Arizona, New Mexico, North Dakota, and South Dakota—states where the greatest concentrations of Indians are to be found. There are schools also in California, Florida, Iowa, Kansas, Louisiana, Mississippi, Montana, Nevada, North Carolina, Oklahoma, Oregon, and Utah.

Most of the schools located off reservations are secondary schools with boarding facilities. The majority of elementary schools, both day and boarding, are located on reservations. Attending this far-flung school system are almost 35,000 Indian children in boarding schools, more than 15,000 in day schools, and nearly 4,000 who are housed in dormitories close to reservations, while attending local public schools. The BIA also administers federal funds under the Johnson-O'Malley Act for some 63,000 Indian youngsters attending public schools on or near reservations, runs programs for some 30,000 adults, and offers a modest scholarship program for 4,000 college undergraduates.

Like other growing school systems, enrollment in the BIA schools doubled from 1959 to 1967. The present rate of growth of the Indian population on reservations is 3.3 percent per year, three times the rate of increase for the national population at large. More than 200,000 Indians out of a total estimated population of fewer than a million are of school age, and the bureau is responsible for educating nearly half of them.

This natural population increase is compounded by the rather recent acceptance of universal schooling on the part of the Indians generally, and the growing expectation that it extend through secondary school and into college. At present, grades eight and ten have the highest dropout rates, but the numbers remaining in school longer appear to be growing yearly. A generation ago, for example, only one child out of four school-age Navahos was in school. Today, more than 90 percent of the children are, and dropout rates are no greater than the national levels. The Hopi too are making extraordinary progress. But in some tribes the picture is far less bright.

To keep pace with growing enrollment, the BIA has sought to provide classroom space by a crash program of building schools both on and off the reservations. And because the federal government has not instituted the kind of road building program that would have made school attendance more feasible in remote areas, an extensive pattern of boarding schools has been maintained, and transfers to public schools have been encouraged.

Like schools all over the country, those for Indians are a mixed lot. While older buildings with unattractive barracks-like dormitories remain, the newer BIA schools are modern structures that could sit comfortably in any of the more affluent suburbs of the nation. Complete with inviting cafeterias, spacious dormitories with semiprivate sleeping quarters, large social halls, and auditorium-gymnasiums, they include modern classrooms with the latest textbooks and equipment. If these new school plants are to be subjected to any criticism, it is that they are too conventional, too much like schools that might be anywhere. They have not been imaginatively styled for the communities they serve. While conditions vary depending upon the administration, often the interiors of these suburban-type school buildings offer no indication that the children within them are Indian. There are, of course, notable exceptions, among them the Indian Arts and Crafts School at Santa Fe, which, although in an older building, clearly honors the Indian heritage of its students.

It is characteristic, too, that the usual federal school sits apart from the Indian community it serves. Located on or off reservation, in a compound surrounded by a fence, it is an enclave of federal property. On reservation, the life of the staff tends to be quite separate from that of the local people. The schools are characterized by what has come to be called "compound culture," in which staff members generally socialize with one another rather than with the Indians. There is little visiting back and forth in the community.

The BIA system has its share of concerned professionals as well as those who find safety within the protective confines of a tenured civil service system. And staff turnover is high; the isolation and the compound culture do not appeal to many.

With rare exceptions, employment in the schools of the BIA is subject to the rules and regulations of the federal civil service system. Consequently, teachers in Indian schools meet national standards. The civil service requires at least a B.A. degree from an accredited university and training in education or relatively high scores on national teaching tests. Salaries have also risen to national levels, ranging at present from $7,649 to $12,119. These standards represent a vast improvement over the past, and there are generally few differences between BIA teachers and public school teachers in regard to educational background, sex, experience, and age.

However, the establishment of rigid requirements for certification within the system seems to be operating to keep Indians from easily entering the teaching ranks. Efforts to improve this situation by the employment of paraprofessionals are being made, but these do not solve the problem of moving increasing numbers of Indian professionals into decision-making positions within the schools themselves.

At present, 16 percent of the teachers in BIA schools are Indians. But fewer Indians are entering teaching now, compared with twenty years ago, and most Indian teachers are not assigned to teach in their home communities.

Controversy over goals for Indian education becomes evident in the area of curriculum. Inhumane, forced assimilationist practices are largely a thing of the past. Today, some would like to see the schools emphasize traditional Indian life, Others see the schools serving the function of teaching "Anglo" culture. Growing among Indians and educators alike is the desire to develop curricula that are pluralistic in emphases—retaining respect for the various Indian traditions and for Indian identity while teaching skills needed for life in urban, industrial America as well as on the reservations, where new economic and political developments are taking place.

The complexity of the curriculum problem is indicated by the fact that even today two-thirds of all Indian children entering BIA schools have little or no skill in English. There are nearly 300 Indian languages in use today; more than one-half of the Indian youth between the ages of six and eighteen use their native tongue. All Indians express a concern that the schools teach English, and experience indicates that programs in Teaching English as a Second Language (TESL) provide a more valid and humane way to teach English than to depend upon exposure. TESL programs have been developed and instituted, but funding language programs in both BIA and public schools is a perennial problem. Of the $7.5-million appropriated for the National Bilingual Education Act, only $300,000 is being spent on Indian programs benefiting 773 children.

Aside from the TESL program, curriculum and methodology for Indian children are little different from those employed in schools throughout America. Minimum or no attention is given to the Indian heritage, or to contemporary issues in Indian life. On the whole, attention to the pedagogical complexities of cross-cultural education has been neglected by educators despite their clear relationship to school success or failure, and very few social scientists have concerned themselves with Indian children and the preparation of teachers to work especially in this setting. It is usual for the schools to ignore the cultural heritage of the children as if it didn't exist—or worse, as if it required eradication.

An exciting departure in Indian education is provided by the program of the DINE (Demonstration in Navaho Education) experimental school at Rough Rock, Arizona. Instruction in Navaho language and culture is part of the curriculum, and the school itself is supervised by an all-Navaho school board. The newly organized first Indian college, the Navaho Junior College at Many Farms, is also gearing its curriculum to the special needs of Indian students. These are among the first tribal-run schools since the Choctaw and the Cherokee ran their own school systems during the last century.

Critics of the BIA and its schools are responding to conditions that are sometimes peculiar to the BIA, but in other cases are not unlike those found throughout American education: the discontinuity between teacher education institutions and the schools in which their graduates will be teaching; the inadequate number of Indians recruited into teaching; the lack of understanding and empathy for the culturally different and the poor; unsuitable instructional materials; inadequate professional leadership; and the lack of involvement of the communities being served.

Aside from its inheritance of distrust and suspicion stemming from an earlier era, the BIA is also beset with all the usual problems faced by an entrenched bureaucratic system. Official policy from above is often frustrated by inadequate execution in the field. Indeed, the educational staff in the field is responsible to BIA area offices concerned with many matters other than education, rather than to the director of educational programs.

Also, the system tends to encourage the maintenance of the traditional structure and methods; advancement into administration is through the ranks and encourages the promotion of those defensive of the system rather than those who are innovative or experimentally inclined. Most important, responsibility and accountability, at all levels, are to the bureau rather than to the Indian communities.

Part of the BIA's difficulty is due to the fact that, while it maintains an educational system of its own, it has been committed to the principle that, whenever possible, Indian children should be placed in public schools. This policy is in keeping with assimilationist goals, the general reluctance of the federal government to run a school system, and the unwillingness, except on a small experimental basis, to allow Indians to run their own schools. This ambivalent position of presiding over a school system dedicated to its own demise is not conducive to adequate Congressional funding, support, and planning.

States and local communities generally have been unwilling to assume educational responsibility for Indians living on reservations because the land is tax-free. Therefore, the federal government has provided subsidies to reimburse public schools for the education of Indian students.

But the transfer of Indians to public schools is a two-edged sword. On the one hand, it seems reasonable that public education allows the Indian child access to common schooling along with others. It appears to encourage integration, and it supports the rights of states to oversee education. It appeals to liberals as a means of rescuing Indians from the custodianship of the BIA, which smacks of a colonial service.

On the other hand, attendance at public schools has frequently placed the Indian child in the position of a minority group within a largely white institution. It often puts him in a position of economic and social disadvantage, especially in areas with long histories of antipathy toward the Indian population. Sometimes the public schools are a greater distance from home than the bureau day schools, and in some instances the federally supervised BIA school is superior to the local public school in facilities and staff, as well as in attention to the special needs of Indian children.

In addition, Indians have rarely been in a strong political position in their local communities, and thus have had little say over the design of programs and the allocation of funds received for their people by the local school districts. And again, in the light of the long history of Indian-white relations, transfer to public schools without approval of the local Indian community is suspected as a policy of reneging on the federal obligations to provide education.

Growing Indian political consciousness has led several Rio Grande pueblos to institute court actions charging misappropriations of federal funds by local public school boards; Indians are exercising their vote to elect school board members; and demands are being made that no school transfers take place without community approval.

Increasingly, nevertheless, the problems of Indian education are likely to be found in the public schools. Since World War II, growing numbers of American Indians, together with other rural Americans, have moved to the cities. Some have gone on their own, searching for jobs, others in urban relocation programs designed by the federal government to assist young Indians to move from the reservations to urban employment. One-third of the Indian population now lives in cities, although for many reservation ties remain strong and there is much moving back and forth.

For those Indian children who are recent migrants to the city, school generally means attendance at a large, inner-city slum school, where they are submerged among the rest of the "disadvantaged" children of the city. The absence of special programs to meet their particular needs, plus the high transiency rate typical of many, is not conducive to successful completion of school programs, and dropout rates are high. As members of the urban poor, they lose out in the competition with other larger and more powerful minorities as recipients of federal programs.

Virtually every critic of American Indian education has pointed to the urgent need to elevate the BIA, which is now a relatively low-level bureau within the Department of the Interior. Some, such as Alvin M. Josephy reporting to President Kennedy, have argued for transferring the BIA to the executive office of the President where it would be more visible and have a mandate for change. Others have urged that it be transferred to the Department of Health, Education, and Welfare, kept intact, and be placed under an Assistant Secretary or Administrator for Indian Affairs. Still others have proposed that the educational functions of the BIA be transferred to the Office of Education in HEW. A proposal for a more fundamental change was made in a Carnegie Corporation report that called for the creation of a federal commission to assume control of Indian education, with an explicit mandate to transfer this control to Indian communities within five years. The report was careful to state that it was not calling for termination, but rather the continuation of federal responsibility except with Indian control.

The recent Senate subcommittee report elected to retain the BIA in an elevated position within the Department of the Interior. Taking a strong stand in favor of fulfilling federal responsibilities to Indians, it urged that the federal Indian school system be developed into an exemplary system that can play an important role in improving education for Indian children. In addition, it recommended increased and extended funding to public schools, calling for the involvement of Indians in the planning, execution, and evaluation of the use to which the funds are put. Over and above the strengthening of existing schools, it urged policies that permit tribal governments and Indian communities to run their own schools.

In calling for the government to commit itself to a national policy of educational excellence for Indian children, the report emphasized the need for maximum participation and control by Indian adults and communities, more demonstration and experimental programs, and a substantial increase in appropriations to achieve these goals.

The 1960s was a period of intense search and evaluation concerning American Indian education. It began with great hope for change with President Kennedy's proposed task force to examine the problems, and ended with a call for a national commitment to excellence. In the interim, while termination practices have halted, little has happened to change the Indians' basic position of powerlessness, and Indian affairs have continued to take a back seat in Department of the Interior programs.

It is too soon to judge the policies of the 1970s, but certain aspects are clear. The myths of the vanishing and silent Indians have been shattered. Active participation and organization by American Indians themselves are growing, whether in the National Congress of American Indian Tribes, meetings such as the National Indian Education Conference, or the proliferating groups of organized college students and "Red Power" advocates.

Despite the pessimistic past there are still time and great promise for America. The heterogeneity of the Indian populations matches that of the nation. If we can be responsive to the education needs of culturally different groups, many of whose members resist loss of identity in a common, bland "melting pot," if we can provide flexible programs with massive federal funding that allows people themselves to engage in the educational enterprise and to develop the programs best suited for their children, we will have gone a long way in tackling the needs of all American education.

The old chiefs are gone; the young men are to be found in school rather than in the woods, but the lesson is clear. It is not just the Indian who has to learn from us, there is much to be learned from him—the values inherent in group identity; respect for nature; the right of men to participate in the institutions that affect their lives; and that no policy or program, regardless of how well intended, will succeed without his approval.

Intelligence and Achievement of the Indian Student

Robert A. Roessel, Jr.

Any thoughtful educator is concerned with the intellectual capacity of his students. Such questions as these are often asked: "Are Indian students innately inferior to non-Indians?" "Is there a difference between the achievement of Indians and non-Indians?"

Studies of the intelligence of Indians, prior to 1935, tended to show that Indians appeared to be less intelligent than white children.[1] After 1935 research studies tended to show that there appeared to be no difference in average intelligence between Indian and white children, except for such differences as were explainable on the basis of cultural differences.[2] These more recent testings studies on Indian children agree that the verbal component in tests of intelligence handicaps the Indian child. On the other hand, tests that are relatively "culture free," of a performance variety, appear to be considerably more appropriate for many Indian students than tests which require facility with the English language.

The University of Chicago conducted an extensive testing program with In-

From *Handbook for Indian Education*, Los Angeles, California: Amerindian Publishing Company, 1969, pp. 57–65.

[1]T.R. Garth, "The Intelligence of Full-blood Indians," *Journal of Applied Psychology*, IX (1925), 382–89. _____, *Race Psychology: A Study of Racial Mental Differences* (New York: McGraw-Hill, 1931).

W. S. Hunter and E. Sommermeier, "The Relation of Degree of Indian Blood to Score on Otis Intelligence Test," *Journal of Comparative Psychology*, II (1922), 257–77.

[2]Robert J. Havighurst and Rhea R. Hilkevitch, "The Intelligence of Indian Children as Measured by a Performance Scale," *Journal of Abnormal and Social Psychology*, XXXIX (1944), 419–33.

J. H. Rohrer, "The Test Intelligence of Osage Indians," *Journal of Social Psychology*, XIV (1942), 99–105.

Madison L. Coombs and others, *The Indian Child Goes to School* (Washington D.C.: Bureau of Indian Affairs, 1958).

dian children.[3] The Grace Arthur Point Performance Scale was used with 670 Indian children, ages 6 through 15, in communities of the Navaho, Hopi, Zuni, Zia, Papago and Sioux tribes. Non-verbal tests were used because it was felt by the researchers that tests requiring oral or written work in English would penalize the Indian children.

On the Grace Arthur test battery, most of the Indian groups gave almost exactly the same quality of performance that white children did. There were two Indian groups who fell substantially below the norms for white children—one Papago and one Navaho group—and these children also fell substantially below other groups from the same tribes. However, the Hopi groups performed definitely above the level of white children.

The results of this research indicate that Indian children do about as well as white children on a performance test of intelligence, and that differences exist between tribes and among communities within a tribe.

In a study made on Indian children of these same five tribes (Navaho, Hopi, Zuni, Zia, and Papago), another non-verbal test of intelligence showed a considerable superiority of Indian children over white children.[4] The test utilized was the Goodenough Draw-A-Man Test. This test requires the child to use a pencil to draw a figure of a man. The drawing is scored for accuracy in proportion and detail, and not for other esthetic qualities. It has been found that between the ages of 6 and 11 the scores on this test have been closely related to other measures of intelligence. Average I.Q.'s ranged from 117 (one of the Hopi groups) to 102 (one of the Sioux groups).

[Table 1][5] indicates the mean I.Q. scores for the Goodenough Draw-A-Man Test:

Havighurst concluded that from this study:[6]

1. Indian children from the tribes tested do better than white children on the Draw-A-Man Test.
2. Indian boys from Pueblo groups do better than girls on the Draw-A-Man Test.
3. The evidence points strongly to the conclusion that environment affects the performance of children on the Draw-A-Man Test.

TABLE 1   Mean Draw-A-Man I.Q.'s

Group	Hopi	Zuni	Zia	Navaho	Sioux	Papago	Midwest White
Number	78	42	32	47	53	74	66
Mean I.Q.	113.3	111.7	109.6	109.6	109.1	106.9	101.2

[3]Havighurst and Hilkevitch, loc. cit.
[4]Robert J. Havighurst and others, "Environment and the Draw-A-Man Test: The Performance of Indian Children," Journal of Abnormal and Social Psychology, XLI (1946), 50–63.
[5]Ibid., p. 56.
[6]Ibid., p. 62.

The results are best explained as due to cultural difference between Indian and white children. The Indian children, especially the boys, are stimulated culturally to take an active interest in the world of nature and are provided much opportunity to form and express concepts of natural objects, including the human body, on the basis of their observations.[7]

Let us briefly examine several other significant studies which discussed the matter of intelligence of Indian children.

The results obtained from Joseph's study on the Papago, which used the Grace Arthur intelligence test, showed a considerable difference in the average I.Q.'s of the western and eastern districts of the Papago Reservation.[8] The test performance of the eastern children was on the average about equal to that of the white children on whom the test was standardized. The average I.Q. of the white children was 102.5; while that of the eastern Papago children, 99.4. The western Papago children had an average I.Q. of 86.9. In analyzing the findings, Joseph stated that the western Papago communities are distinguished from those of the eastern area by their strong resistance to white influence and particularly to the introduction of schools.[9] The resistance to whites, on the part of the western Papago, may have produced an emotional resistance which is reflected in the test.

A second factor was felt to have been significant. The relatively limited school experiences of the western Papago children. School training as a factor possibly influencing the results of the Grace Arthur Test must be seriously considered.[10] [Table 2][11] illustrates the difference in average I.Q. scores on two different intelligence tests between two areas of the Papago reservation.

The mental capacities of Papago children as measured by the Goodenough Draw-A-Man Test appeared to be different from those measured on the Arthur Test. The Papago children scored appreciably higher on the Goodenough than they did on the Arthur. In fact, the average I.Q. of both eastern and western Papago children, as revealed by the Goodenough, was higher than that obtained by white children on whom the test was standardized (100.0).[12]

The Indian's power of observation, memory, alertness and attention to important details apparently combine to contribute to his better showing on the Goodenough Test because these are the traits scored in that test.

In summarizing the intelligence testing of Papago children, Joseph declared:

So far, it is clear that in average mental ability as indicated by tests, the Papago groups studied reveal differences between one another, on the other hand, and that specific

[7]Robert J. Havighurst, "Education Among American Indians: Individual and Cultural Aspects," *The Annals of the American Academy of Political and Social Science* (Philadelphia: American Academy of Political and Social Science, 1957), pp. 112–113.

[8]Alice Joseph, *The Desert People* (Chicago: University of Chicago Press, 1949), p. 186.

[9]*Ibid.* The eastern Papago communities have long been exposed to outside influences. They are the "progressives" among the Papago. The western communities are conservative and have retained more items of the traditional Papago culture. In other words, eastern Papago children are more familiar with white ways.

[10]*Ibid.*

[11]*Ibid.*, p. 189.

[12]*Ibid.*, p. 188.

TABLE 2 Average I.Q.'s Scored by Papago Children of Two Areas on Two Intelligence Tests

AREA	ARTHUR TEST	GOODENOUGH TEST
Eastern	99.4	108.5
Western	86.9	103.6

differences seem to be tied up with specific tests. This casts some doubt on the wisdom of accepting test results at face value and suggests certain hypothetical explanations, of which the influence of a different way of life appears to be of primary importance.[13]

Another major study on the intelligence of Indian children dealt with Navaho children and was conducted during the 1940's.[14]

This Navaho research supported the findings of the Papago study in that differences were observed between different Navaho communities. The community which scored the lowest on the Grace Arthur Point Performance Scale was also the community that was least exposed to white influence. Leighton stated:

The Navahos here (Ramah) have been much less exposed to white agencies, such as schools and missions, which deliberately set about to change their way of life than have the Navaho of the Reservation.[15]

The Navaho community which had the greatest amount of contact with whites and was considered the most sophisticated was Shiprock and interestingly these children had the highest I.Q. of all Navaho communities tested.

[Table 3][16] indicates the range of intelligence on the Navaho Reservation, as determined by this study:

Leighton and Kluckholm reported the results of further testing at Shiprock, the most acculturated Navaho community, and found that the Navaho did better on the Goodenough Draw-A-Man Test than on the Arthur Test. It will be remembered that the study of Papago children found the same difference. The reasons

TABLE 3 Number of Navaho Children Tested and Average I.Q.'s as Obtained from Different Communities

	GRACE ARTHUR POINT PERFORMANCE SCALE				
	Tribal Average	Shiprock	Ramah	Navaho-Mountain	Whites
Number of Children Tested	158	92	33	33	409
Average I.Q.	91.4	95.9	84.3	94.1	102.5

[13]*Ibid.*, p. 190.
[14]Dorothea Leighton and Clyde Kluckholm, *Children of the People* (Cambridge: Harvard University Press, 1947).
[15]*Ibid.*, p. 133.
[16]*Ibid.*, p. 149.

TABLE 4   Average I.Q.'s for Shiprock Navahos and Midwest White Children, 6 through 11 Years of Age, on Two Intelligence Tests

TEST	SHIPROCK NAVAHOS	MIDWEST WHITES
Arthur	94	113
Goodenough	110	101

for the Navaho's superiority on the Goodenough appear to lie in the habit of detailed observation which characterizes aspects of Navaho culture.

[Table 4][17] contrasts Navaho test scores with test scores for midwest whites: In summarizing the Navaho testing study Leighton stated:

It appears that neither of the tests employed gives a final and convincing evaluation of intelligence in all cases. In the case of the Arthur Test, children who have not been to school are penalized for their lack of experience, and in the case of the Goodenough so many Navahos do average or better work that they must have some advantage. In spite of these facts, and with these imperfect methods, Navaho children still show as a group nearly the same range and distribution of intelligence as was found in the group of white children on whom the Arthur Test was standardized.[18]

The most recent and perhaps the most outstanding study on achievement of Indian students was directed by Madison Coombs and resulted in the publication *The Indian Child Goes to School: A Study of Interracial Differences.*[19]

This book, published by the Bureau of Indian Affairs, is primarily a report on the school achievement of Indian children as compared with that of white students.

The California Achievement Tests were administered to 23,608 pupils attending Federal, public and mission schools in eleven states.[20] Fifty-eight percent of the pupils were Indian and 42 percent of them were white. Of the Indian pupils 8,564 or 62.6 percent were attending Federal schools; 3,144 or 23 percent were attending public schools; and 1,978 or 14.5 percent were attending mission schools.[21]

The children included in the study lived in these states: Arizona, New Mexico, Colorado, North Dakota, South Dakota, Nebraska, Montana, Wyoming, Oklahoma, Mississippi, and Kansas.

There were differences in average achievement among groups of pupils of different races attending different types of schools. The following clear-cut general hierarchy appeared.[22]

1. White pupils in public schools.
2. Indian pupils in public schools.
3. Indian pupils in Federal schools.

[17]*Ibid.,* p. 154.
[18]*Ibid.,* p. 155.
[19]Coombs, *The Indian Child Goes to School, op. cit.*
[20]*Ibid.,* IX.
[21]*Ibid.,* p. 2.
[22]*Ibid.,* p. 4.

4. Indian pupils in mission schools.

Before valid interpretation of this hierarchy can be made, Coombs cautioned:

There is a popular off-hand assumption that the quality of a school can be determined by the amount its pupils learn in a given period of time, by comparison with other pupils and other schools. This assumption is both persistent and pervasive. It is indulged in not only by the lay public, but also by teachers who should know better. It is as though all pupils were considered to be equally blank and equally impressionable sheets of paper which are sent to school and upon which no one is ever permitted to mark except the school itself. If such were the case, the school should indeed be held entirely accountable for the amount and rate at which students learn, but the facts are something quite different. The facts are that children do not learn everything they know in school, although some are far more dependent upon the school than are others; they do not all *start even* in point of ability, or interest, or experience, or health; and they certainly do not *remain even* throughout their school careers in terms of *learning advantages* outside the school. Most persons know, of course, that this is true of individual pupils, but they forget sometimes that whole groups of pupils may be characterized by such differences.

It is not to be wondered at, then, that the white pupils in the study, as a group, consistently made higher scores than Indian pupils, considering the great cultural advantage they enjoyed with respect to such things as language, motivation, and out-of-school learning opportunities. Nor is it surprising that the Indian pupils who attended public schools achieved better on the average than Indian pupils who attended Federal and mission schools since culturally they were more advanced.[23]

A comparison based on several skills revealed that the Indian pupils compared best in spelling and least well in reading vocabulary.[24] There was a wide difference between these two extremes, with the comparative achievement of the Indian pupils in spelling being significantly higher than for any of the other skills.

By comparison the Indian pupils were second highest in arithmetic fundamentals, and second lowest in arithmetic reasoning.[25] Coombs declared that spelling and computational skills in arithmetic are probably learned, by most children, largely within the school and by a rote method.[26] Word meanings, on the other hand, may be acquired by pupils in a wide variety of learning situations, outside the school as well as in. In other words, the pupil who is culturally disadvantaged in point of language or experience may suffer less by comparison with other pupils in the learning of skills over which the school has the greater control.

Careful analysis of the data, Coombs believed, reveals an amazingly consistent relationship between the degree of Indian blood and pre-school language on the one hand and the level of achievement on the other.[27] Generally, the smaller the amount of Indian blood in a group and the greater the amount of English spoken prior to school entrance, the higher the group achieved. To state it differently, the higher achieving race-school groups contained fewer full-

[23] *Ibid.*, pp. 4–5.
[24] *Ibid.*, p. 5.
[25] *Ibid.*
[26] *Ibid.*
[27] *Ibid.*, p. 6.

blood Indian pupils and more pupils who spoke only English, or at least a combination of English and some other language, prior to school entrance.

Coombs stated:

The writers do not believe that blood quantum and pre-school language, of and by themselves, are strong determiners of achievement. They do believe that these characteristics are two of the best indices of the degree of acculturation of a pupil and that the stage of acculturation which a pupil and his family have reached has a powerful influence upon his school achievement.[28]

The research confirmed opinion of many experienced teachers of Indian children by declaring that Indian pupils are, on the average, older for their grade than white pupils.[29] It appears likely that the observed over-ageness of Indian pupils is determined not only by late school entrance, but also by the necessity for a beginning year for many children where basic social and conversational English skills are taught, and by the fact of irregularity of attendance.

In addition, Coombs found that on the average pupils who are over-age for their grade do not achieve nearly as well in the basic skill subjects as do those who are at-age or under-age.[30]

Perhaps the single most comprehensive study dealing with the impact of cultural differences on intelligence is that of Eels, Davis, Havinghurst and others, entitled *Intelligence and Cultural Differences*.[31] This study analyzed the behavior of students from high and low social class backgrounds on more than 650 items in several widely used group intelligence tests. The principal purpose of the research was to provide answers dealing with the extent that cultural bias appears in intelligence tests and the effect of such cultural bias.

When the special high and low status groups are contrasted, the average I.Q.'s of the high-status students are from 8 to 23 I.Q. points higher than those for the low-status students.[32]

Practically all the test items which showed unusually large status differences were verbal in symbolism. Items which showed small differences were either non-verbal in symbolism or involved simple everyday words drawn from materials quite common to the experiences of all children.[33]

Dr. Ralph Tyler posed the question: "Can intelligence tests be used to predict educability?"[34] In discussing this provocative question, Dr. Tyler pointed out that the problem of educability can take one of two forms. The first form may be stated: Given our present American schools, with the ends which they accept and the means which they use, what characteristics of students can be used to predict success in schools? The second form can be stated in this manner: What characteristics of students can be identified which *could* be developed into

[28]*Ibid.*
[29]*Ibid.*
[30]*Ibid.*, p. 7.
[31]Kenneth Eels, Allison Davis, Robert J. Havighurst and others, *Intelligence and Culture Differences* (Chicago: University of Chicago Press, 1951).
[32]*Ibid.*, p. 53.
[33]*Ibid.*, pp. 54–55.
[34]*Ibid.*, pp. 39–47.

valuable behavior *if* school programs were planned and directed to capitalize on these abilities?

In regard to the first formulation, Dr. Tyler declared that from research we know that, of all characteristics which can be measured, facility in the use of words is most highly correlated with success in existing American schools.[35] Motivation to learn school tasks, or to do good work at school, also has a significant correlation with school success. Dr. Tyler cautioned that motivation to excel at school is not a universal characteristic of all people of all cultures. Another factor related to predicting success at school is parents' attitude toward the school. If the school is viewed as interfering with the home, a place in which children must remain until they are old enough to legally leave school and work, then it is extremely likely that the children's attitudes toward school will be negative and their motivation low.[36]

Tyler summed up his remarks, concerning whether it were possible to predict the success of students in existing schools, by stating that as long as American schools and colleges remain as they are, it will be possible to predict the success of individuals.

This present day ability to predict the success of students at school should not blind us to the fact that this is not a satisfactory formulation for a long-range program.[37] In his discussion of the second formulation; namely, what abilities of people can be identified which school programs could encourage and could develop, Dr. Tyler made several penetrating observations. In the first place, schools today are inadequate with reference to their real aims. He said,

By and large, although there are many noteworthy exceptions, American schools and colleges place primary emphasis on memorization of textbook content and on the development of certain limited subject skills, like computation in arithmetic, grammatical usage in English, and reading at the plain sense level of interpretation. The development of an intelligent person—one who is able to analyze problems, to think them through clearly, and to bring to bear on them a wide variety of information, who understands and cherishes significant and desirable social and personal values, who can formulate and carry out a plan of action in the light of his knowledge and values— is not the goal toward which schools and colleges are aiming in practice.[38]

Tyler added that the tendency of American schools to capitalize solely on verbal abilities does not take into account what could be gained by more adequately educating persons who have other talents which are needed, but which are often unidentified and untrained. Typical schools are doing an unimaginative job in providing learning opportunities for American students. Dr. Tyler concluded:

We have learned a great deal about educability for our present school programs, but we have hardly scratched the surface when it comes to understanding educability in the broadest possible framework of what American schools could be.[39]

[35]*Ibid.*, p. 40.
[36]*Ibid.*, p. 41.
[37]*Ibid.*, p. 42.
[38]*Ibid.*, p. 43.
[39]*Ibid.*, p. 47.

What are the findings of Eels' study that educators of Indian children should examine and consider? The author suggests at least these:

1. Intelligence tests, as they presently exist, may not be a true indication of a child's innate intelligence.
2. Intelligence tests may be culturally biased in favor of white middle class children, to the extent of over 20 I.Q. points.
3. Verbal items on intelligence tests are the most difficult for low status children.
4. Intelligence tests can be used to predict educability within the narrow limited concept practiced by schools today.
5. Many children are penalized because their culture and their class precludes their possessing the knowledge necessary to succeed at school.
6. Motivation is not everywhere the same and constant, but varies.
7. Present day schools should break the shackles that bind them and provide adequate educational programs for *all* children regardless of culture.

SUMMARY

Early research appeared to indicate that Indians were not as intelligent as non-Indians, as determined through the use of intelligence tests.

Recent research has disproved the concept that Indians were innately inferior to non-Indians in regard to intelligence. Research has shown that Indians do achieve at a lower level on intelligence tests which are primarily prepared for white middle-class Americans. It has been shown that the language or verbal handicap is a very real problem to many Indians.

Intelligence and achievement of Indians varies not only between tribes, but also within tribes. This appears to be due to the fact that tribes and communities within any single reservation varies as to the degree of acculturation.

Any standardized testing program carried on with Indian students must be carefully planned, carefully executed, and more carefully interpreted.

SUGGESTED READINGS

Coombs, Madison and others. *The Indian Child Goes to School.* Haskell Press, Bureau of Indian Affairs, 1958. This is an excellent account of the comparative achievement of Indian students by type of school and area: contrasts results with non-Indian students. A very important contribution to Indian Education.

Eels, Kenneth and others. *Intelligence and Cultural Differences.* Chicago: University of Chicago Press, 1951. This is one of the most outstanding books on this subject now available. It is thorough and comprehensive. It is not easy to read, but there is much food for thought stored between the covers of this book. A must for all schools enrolling bicultural children.

Havighurst, Robert J. and Neugarten, Bernice L. *American Indian and White Children: A Sociopsychological Investigation.* Chicago: University of Chicago Press, 1955. This book reports on the moral and emotional development of Indian children from six American Indian tribes: Hopi, Navaho, Papago, Sioux, Zia, and Zuni. It is difficult to read and not easy to understand, but contains much useful information.

Good Day at Rough Rock

Paul Conklin

On the northern flank of Arizona's Black Mountain, an experiment has been started that could change the entire structure and philosophy of Indian education in America. Here, in a bleak setting of desert, rock, and sagebrush, near the center of the country's largest reservation—25,000 square miles—that is home to 105,000 Navajos, Robert A. Roessel, Jr., director of the Rough Rock Demonstration School, is applying a community control approach that could hold promise for poor, uneducated people everywhere. His method—to work with the Indians, not on them. His thesis—that Indians ought to be able to be Americans and Indians, too. "Education as the Indian knows it on the reservation can best be characterized as the Either-Or type," says Dr. Roessel, a vigorous man with an unruly, greying thatch of hair:

One is either an Indian or a white man, and the way we have traditionally weighted things, the good way is always the non-Indian way and the bad is always the Indian. We tell Indian children they are superstitious and primitive and that their hogans are dirty. We try to impose our values and tell them they should eat green, leafy vegetables and sleep on a bed and brush their teeth. In short, we try to make white men out of Indians.

The Indian child listens and looks at himself and sees that he doesn't measure up. In his own eyes he is a failure. Education can be a shattering experience when one is taught nothing but negative things about himself for 12 years.

As he talks, Roessel occasionally squints through the window of his comfortable living room which, in keeping with his educational beliefs, is furnished in modern and Navajo. Outside, the wind blows incessantly, swirling sand against the panes and wearing away at the light-colored buildings that blend with the monochromatic landscape. In the far distance can be seen the looming red sandstone monoliths of Monument Valley.

From *American Education*, February 1967, pp. 1–5.

"Now Indians have begun to question whether it is necessary for them to lose their heritage in order to become citizens of the United States," he continues. "And so the Both-And—both white and Indian—approach to Indian education was born."

Rough Rock Demonstration School is a self-contained community within a scattered population of about 600. It has to be. The nearest paved road is 16 miles away and the nearest sizable town, Gallup, N. Mex., 120 miles. The school has its own water system and fire engine, a spacious classroom-office building with a gymnasium, a separate kitchen-dining room, and a boys' dormitory and a girls' dormitory, each with a capacity of 165 children. The staff are quartered in 36 houses and 8 apartments.

Roessel's expectations and hopes for the experiment come through clearly as he speaks of the school:

Rough Rock is the first school to have the tools and resources to see whether this new approach can be effective. We want to instill in our youngsters a sense of pride in being Indian. We want to show them that they can be Indian and American at the same time, that they can take the best from each way of life and combine it into something viable.

When I first came on the reservation as a teacher, I told children they had two legs, one being their Navajo heritage and the other the best part of the white world. They couldn't get along with just one leg, but needed both to be secure and whole.

The Rough Rock staff includes ten full-time classroom teachers, a remedial reading specialist, a speech therapist, an art teacher, a librarian, two TESL (Teaching English as a Second Language) specialists, and two recreation leaders. Fifteen members of the Volunteers in Service to America (VISTA) also work at the school. Of the 91 full-time people on the payroll, 46 are Indian, 35 of them from Rough Rock, a fact that illustrates a vital part of the Roessel philosophy—involving the local community in school life as much as possible.

The school laundry is a good example. Bureau of Indian Affairs schools typically contract their laundry out to private firms, which are usually located in towns many miles away. In the Rough Rock budget $5,000 was set aside for this purpose. Roessel spent $2,000 on washing machines and used the rest to hire two local women to operate them.

No opportunities are missed at the school to help the children understand themselves as Indians. Navajo motifs are freely mixed in with other classroom decorations. The library has a Navajo corner. Recordings of the Navajo music and rituals are played during the school day.

In the evening old men, the historians and medicine men of the tribe, come to the dormitories and tell Navajo folk tales and legends. The staff is preparing biographies of successful Navajos to give the students something on which to pattern their own lives.

Each day, 35 minutes of class time are set aside in the pre-school sections and lower three grades, and 45 minutes in grades three through six for "cultural identification" lessons. During the first six weeks the lessons cover the Navajo hogan—its history, how it is built, the ceremonies that surround it, and how life is conducted in it. The second six weeks cover farming and caring for livestock. The third period deals with reservation facilities, the land and climate, Navajo history and tribal government.

A crucial part of "cultural identification" at Rough Rock is the adult arts and crafts program, which has a twofold purpose: to revive dying Navajo handicrafts so that the children of the school can observe the process, and to produce more local wage-earners.

This is the domain of Dr. Roessel's wife, Ruth, who is Navajo. A graduate of Arizona State University and a member of the Governor's Advisory Committee on Indian Education, Ruth is one of the reservation's most skilled weavers. She has also proved herself an able recruiter. Ambrose Roanhorse, renowned as the most skillful silversmith, came to Rough Rock at her invitation. His first apprentices have already reached the stage where they are ready to market their jewelry.

Sharing the school's arts and crafts center with the silversmiths are a weaver and a moccasin maker. They will soon be joined by basketmakers, potters, leather craftsmen, and rawhide workers.

"This is not art for art's sake, although the Navajo puts great store in creating beautiful things. These skills are extremely marketable and we are training people who otherwise would have no income," Roessel explains. The Indians now eke out a precarious existence herding sheep.

At one time in most Indian schools the children were punished if they spoke Navajo. At Rough Rock they are encouraged and even forced to use their own language. Navajo is taught in the fourth, fifth and sixth grades for one hour three days a week. Also, for the first time on the reservation, portions of regular classes, such as arithmetic and social studies, are held in Navajo. The purpose is to see whether students find it easier to retain subject matter when taught in their native language, as research has suggsted may be the case.

Roessel provides evening tutoring lessons in Navajo for his staff members who do not speak the language. They find it tough going, since Navajo—a harsh, gutteral tongue—is classified by linguists as the world's second most difficult language.

Because of the importance the Both-And philosophy places on mastery of both English and Navajo, Rough Rock's TESL department is highly active at the school. English is taught formally twice a day, informally at all times. For example, as the children pass through the cafeteria line at noon they must ask for their food in English.

A teaching aid which TESL director Virginia Hoffman has found invaluable is the school's closed-circuit TV system. Once a month she writes a simple play, using staff members and VISTA personnel in the cast. A recent drama, "The Zegafferelebra," took place in a painted jungle. The message, spoken by animals with papier mache heads, dealt with correct intonation and the lengthening of vowels. Future productions will be concerned with gender, number, tense, "to be," and "is going to."

The idea for the Rough Rock experiment began to take shape at Arizona State University in 1959 and 1960 while Roessel studied for a doctor's degree. To gather raw material for his thesis, he visited over 100 Indian communities, talking to the elders about their needs and aspirations.

Much of what Roessel learned during that period was incorporated in a proposal which he and a number of Indian leaders later presented to the Office of Economic Opportunity (OEO) for the establishment of a different kind of Indian school. The result, in 1965, was the Lukachukai Navajo Demonstration School, which foundered after only one year, primarily because of an awkward administrative set-up. The school was funded by OEO, which superimposed a staff of academic and community development specialists on the existing staff of the Bureau of Indian Affairs (BIA) boarding school at Lukachukai, a hamlet not far from Rough Rock. The administrative dichotomy proved too much, and OEO reluctantly withdrew its support.

BIA and OEO, still mindful of the need for a new approach to Indian education and wary of repeating their mistakes at Lukachukai, put up money for another demonstration school that would be independent of them both. The funds, $335,000 from OEO and $307,000 from BIA, were awarded to a private, nonprofit corporation called Demonstration in Navajo Education, Inc.—whose Navajo acronym DINE means the Navajos, or "the people." Roessel was recruited as director and BIA turned over a brand new $3.5 million school which it had just built in Rough Rock.

At the time, Roessel was director of Arizona State University's Indian Community Action Center, one of three such centers established by OEO to provide technical assistance and training to reservation Indians under its Community Action Program.

His decision to go to Rough Rock was not easily made. "I was happy at Tempe, and felt important. I had real influence in the OEO Indian program and went to Washington every week. It wasn't easy to come out here where the roads are terrible and the phones never work. But I had been writing articles too long saying what was wrong with Indian education and Indian programs. Here was a chance to put into practice what I believed, or shut up."

Soon after Roessel's arrival, the people of Rough Rock elected one woman and four men to the school board. All were middle-aged Navajos and only one had ever had as much as a day of formal education. In a move that must have raised eyebrows in many quarters, control of the demonstration school was immediately passed over to the board.

"At least 50 schools on the reservation have their own boards, so in this respect Rough Rock is not unique," Roessel points out.

But the traditional Indian board has a housekeeping function: it builds roads, maintains buildings, and acts as a truant officer. It has no authority or decision-making power, and the superintendent really calls the shots. What we have here is local control in the true sense for the first time.

The greatest need of Indian education today . . . is to involve Indians. The belief persists that Indians have neither the desire nor the ability to manage their own affairs. It's the old "father-knows-best" approach that says it's up to me, an expert sitting behind my desk, to make policy for them. But the Both-And philosophy says that Indians are eager for responsibility and, if given a chance, they'll act creatively and assume leadership.

Roessel takes the principle of local control seriously. Once a week he and a few of his senior staff discuss a part of the master program with the school board, explaining the reasons the staff consider it important. In each instance the board has accepted the proposal, modifying it, however, and adding a Navajo cast to it. Roessel sees the modifications as strengthening the demonstration program. So strong is his faith in the board members that he is willing to scrap completely any part that they oppose.

It is not simply rhetoric when Roessel says of Rough Rock:

This is a community-oriented school, rather than child-oriented. In the past, Indian schools have taken little interest in their communities, but here we want to involve adults and teenagers, dropouts, people who have never been to school.

Rough Rock's school facilities—gym, kitchen, dormitories, shower rooms, library—are open to anybody who wants to use them. School fairs, movies, basketball games, talent nights have drawn crowds that increase steadily.

Rough Rock parents are encouraged to come to the school for board meetings, to spend time in the classrooms, to eat in the cafeteria, and to stay overnight in the dormitories. They sometimes come in team-drawn wagons, the men with stiff-brimmed hats and, if they are of the old generation, their hair drawn into tight knots at the back. The women wear long velveteen skirts, silver jewelry, and strings of turquoise and coral. Quiet and grave, they flit shyly about the school like old-fashioned ghosts.

"Our school board has told the parents of this district that they can't use the school as a dumping ground where they can leave their children and forget them. We believe the kids belong to their parents and not to the school. Instead of limiting the child to two or three visits home a year, as is the case in most schools, we let parents take their children home any weekend they want," Roessel says.

To make the dormitories more homelike and to avoid the usual ratio in dormitory staffing of one adult for every 60 children, Roessel employs eight parents to mend clothes, tell stories, help with the twice-a-week shower, and do a variety of other chores that parents know how to do best. For this they receive a dollar an hour. The parents change every six weeks; the school board handles recruiting. With help from instructional aides, parents, and VISTA workers, the Rough Rock adult-child ratio has dropped to 1 to 15.

Just as most Navajo parents know virtually nothing about the way reservation schools are operated, so, too, is it rare to find a teacher in the system who has any first-hand knowledge about how life is lived in the Navajo hogan. In a study conducted in 1963, the Indian Education Center at Arizona State University found that only 15 of 100 reservation teachers had ever visited an Indian home.

One of the reasons for this failure was that the heavy daily routine makes escape from the classroom almost impossible for the teacher. And often the teacher is afraid he will be unwelcome in the hogan. Rough Rock teachers visit the homes of all their students at least twice a year. They are accompanied by the child, and an interpreter when necessary, and tell the parents about their children's progress.

Roessel would also like each of his non-Indian teachers to live in a Navajo hogan for a week. "I want them to see what it means to haul water five miles, to chop wood for heat, to go to bed at dark because there is no light, to eat bread and coffee for a meal," he says.

By giving his staff an awareness of the peculiar texture of Navajo life, Roessel hopes to avert a repetition of the small-scale tragedy that resulted from a teacher's inexperience at another reservation school. The teacher was from the East. Her credentials were excellent, but she had never taught Navajo children before. She noticed one morning that the face and arms of one of her third grade boys were covered by something that looked like soot. In his hair was a substance that resembled grease. With a normal respect for cleanliness, the teacher asked the boy to wash himself. When he refused she took him to the bathroom and washed him.

The boy never returned to school. It turned out that his family had conducted an important healing ceremony on his sick sister, the "soot" and "grease" being part of the ceremonial painting. With her soap and water the teacher destroyed the healing powers of the ceremony. The girl died and the parents could not be shaken in their belief that it was the teacher's fault. No member of the family has set foot in a school since.

Programs for adults have claimed only the peripheral attention of Indian education officials in the past. Through a canvass of the 600 Navajos who live in the area of Rough Rock, it was learned that the men are most interested in auto mechanics instruction. Women want classes in cooking and nutrition. Both are interested in classes in basic literacy. They want to gain a rudimentary knowledge of money and how to make change so they will not be cheated when they buy at the store. They want to acquire a basic English vocabulary of about 50 words that can carry them through their trips to the local trading post and to the outside world.

"It is here in our work with adults that the most significant thrust is being made at Rough Rock. It is an area to which other demonstrations have not been directed, an area of little prior activity," Roessel says.

At Rough Rock the BIA and OEO have said to the Indians in effect, "This is your school. Make of it what you want. Develop a curriculum that will reflect what you think is important." This is an isolated, illiterate community where 95 percent of the people are uneducated, but I am convinced that they have the necessary vision and concern for their future.

It would be hard to find a more disadvantaged community than Rough Rock, where the average family of six makes $500 a year and where cultural life is utterly threadbare. Roessel believes that if Rough Rock can succeed—if these uneducated people can determine the educational needs of their children and their community—then it cannot be said that impoverished, uneducated people any place are unable to provide self-leadership.

"This is why Rough Rock is the most exciting thing going on in Indian education anywhere in the country," says Roessel. "This is why our program has ramifications far outside the Indian world."

School Problems of Indian Youth

Frederic R. Gunsky

A panel of six American Indians had just finished telling an audience composed primarily of educators from some of California's mountain counties about "The Schools as Indians See Them." During their presentation, they told the audience how difficult it is for many children from Indian homes to acquire an education and enter the world of work. Then the principal of an elementary school said:

I'm not afraid of segregation. If Indian children are often shy and insecure, wouldn't it be a good idea to put them in a separate class, at least for the first few years? They would gain confidence by staying in their own group, and the teacher could give them special attention.

The reaction of the Indians, three men and three women, was immediate. "No!" they said. In the context of the discussion, their meaning was clear: Separation and isolation are among the roots of the Indian child's lack of preparation for school experiences. Segregation in the early years of formal education would reinforce his negative self-image. If he needs compensatory education, he should obtain it in an integrated classroom.

This revealing exchange took place last fall in the auditorium of Sierra Union High School, near Tollhouse, Fresno County. About 70 persons met to explore school and career problems of California Indian youth. Among them were teachers, counselors, and principals from the high school and several of the elementary schools within the boundaries of Sierra Joint Union High School District, an area that extends from the foothills to the mountains of

From *California Education*, February 1966, Vol. 3, No. 6, pp. 1–3, a publication of the California State Department of Education, Sacramento. Reprinted by permission.

eastern Fresno and Madera counties. The offices of two county superintendents of schools were represented, as were antipoverty and other governmental and private agencies.

This meeting, which was called by L. T. Cook, Superintendent of Sierra Joint Union High School District, in cooperation with the State Commission on Equal Opportunities in Education and the State Department of Education, was held in an area in which Indians form a significant segment of the population. The area includes Big Sandy and Cold Springs *rancherias* and the towns of North Fork, Coarsegold, Friant, and O'Neals, all of which have large Indian populations. The conference, initiated by the Bureau of Intergroup Relations in the State Department of Education, was the first of its kind. Offices of county superintendents of schools and school districts in other parts of the state are considering similar meetings to bring teachers and administrators together with Indians and others concerned with the problems of this group of culturally different, disadvantaged children. In addition, Fresno State College and other state colleges are considering a series of summer institutes or workshops for the training of teachers of Indian children.

About 30 percent of the pupils enrolled in the North Fork Elementary School and perhaps 6 percent of those enrolled in the Sierra High School are Indians. Unlike high schools in some other parts of California, Sierra holds many of its Indian students until graduation. A few have gone on to higher education. Too often, however, Indian young people, there as elsewhere, drop out from school and never enter careers that seem to be open to them. The girls may find roles in marriage, but boys who do not fit into logging or laboring jobs may fail to find any responsible role in society.

The Indians who address the group—three mothers, a Navy chief petty officer, a barber, and an educator—asked the teachers and officials who were present to do one thing to improve the chances of their youngsters for a brighter future: *Try to understand them.*

An experienced school nurse said:

It isn't easy for a white teacher from a middle-class home and a big-city college to understand, but visit Indian families, as I have, and you'll begin to see that the children live in two worlds. The world that starts every morning when they get on the school bus and ends when they get off it every afternoon is totally different from their home world.

Poverty is only part of the difference. Culture, education, attitudes, dress, hygiene, diet—all these things set the life at home apart from the life at school.

A former public health worker, who has continued to advise and help Indian people, quoted approvingly an article from the October, 1965, *CTA Journal* on "The Dilemma of the California Indian":

Part of each day [the Indian student] is expected to conform to rules, regulations, and scholarship standards set up by a white American, middle-class society, and the rest of the day he lives in a squalid, overcrowded, unpainted house, or escapes to town, roaming the streets aimlessly. He cannot identify himself with a tribal culture or with a language and life clearly Indian, nor can he accept the aspirations and incentives of his "white" classmates at school. He feels lost, misunderstood, rejected.

In 88 Indian homes of the Sierra district studied in 1964 by the California League for American Indians, the conferees were told, welfare payments were being received for at least 50 of the 278 children. Many families were headed by a mother or grandmother, and perhaps a majority of the homes depended upon income of seasonal workers. These economic factors, combined with cultural differences, isolation, a heritage of distrust, and old antagonisms, raise formidable barriers to learning for Indian pupils.

These problems are compounded by racial discrimination. Prejudice apparently still exists in both the white and the Indian groups. It was agreed that a dark-skinned Indian has more difficulty than a light-skinned one in social, school, and job relationships. Indian children are psychologically conditioned by folklore and adult attitudes to "run from the white man." Wherever they live, Indians suffer from stereotypes out of an often misinterpreted past.

"The American tradition is one of equal opportunity for all," said conference Chairman J. Marc Jantzen, Dean of Education at the University of the Pacific and a member of the Commission on Equal Opportunities in Education. "Our problem," he said, "is to find out how to approach Indian youngsters so that they will be able to take full advantage of the educational opportunities offered them."

Sensitivity to the feelings and attitudes of the children would be improved, several speakers declared, by frequent teacher visits to Indian homes, involvement of Indians in parent-Teacher activities, parent education programs, promotion of community organization, and participation in efforts to preserve and appreciate Indian arts, traditions, and observances.

"The problem in a sense is one of morale," said a state consultant in education. "Like members of other minorities, children from disadvantaged Indian families tend to expect to fail, and the prophecy fulfills itself. They need encouragement, but of course it must be expressed in ways which they can accept."

A 14-point list, "Ways to Help Indian Pupils Improve Their Self-Image" was distributed at the conference. This list is available from the Bureau of Intergroup Relations, [California] Department of Education. It includes such suggestions as these:

- The Indian child should be helped to think of his people, not with shame or a sense of inferiority, but with pride because they had the strength to endure their ordeal and have survived.

- School libraries should contain books in which Indian children and adults figure realistically and prominently. In the classroom, teachers may read or recommend such books.

- Teachers and other school personnel should be screened carefully so that the Indian child has a minimum of exposure to adults who retain prejudiced attitudes toward Indians.

- If many children in a class are educationally disadvantaged, a smaller class will permit the teacher to take more time to deal with children as individuals. Any child who is accepted as an individual by an understanding adult will be helped to accept himself.
- Free preschool education will reduce the effects of helplessness and lethargy which are common in poverty-stricken homes. Operation Head Start and similar programs have proved helpful in preparing young children from such homes for school entrance.
- Close cooperation with the home and the coordination of compensatory education with parent and adult education will help the Indian child to see the school as being related to his family and friends. A source of poor self-concept is the inability to connect the values of the school and the world of work with those of a lower-class family.

The three women panelists stressed financial and family considerations which prevent girls, especially, from aspiring to higher education and careers. Early marriage interferes with careers even when girls have completed high school and acquired business skills, they observed.

All three Indian men had had experience or training as a result of military service which had helped them to see themselves as equal in ability to non-Indians, and to gain confidence to become qualified to compete for better jobs. One of them, assisted by the GI Bill, became a teacher and is now an administrator at Fresno City College.

Although some of the panelists had received part of their education in federal Indian schools, all agreed that the social and educational values of going to school with others made nonsegregated public schools preferable for their children.

A portion of the conference was devoted to discussion of the types of projects and programs under the Elementary and Secondary Education Act of 1965 and the Economic Opportunity Act which might assist California Indians in overcoming barriers to success in school and in career preparation. The following were among the suggested program components: preschool classes, teacher aides, parent education, tutoring, part-time work for students, expanded vocational education, inservice training of school personnel in dealing with cultural differences and educational handicaps of the disadvantaged, special counseling, school social workers, study trips, and guest speakers.

Indian pupils are always in the minority in schools of the Sierra district. Therefore, any program designed to help them, it was emphasized, would be equally available to and would benefit non-Indian pupils who need similar help.

5 THE ASIAN-AMERICAN HERITAGE

Anyone who has taught young Americans of Japanese heritage, from elementary school through graduate school, as have the editors, will very likely have been impressed by their sincere desire to become "100 percent American"—to be fully accepted, to be a "success" in the best American economic sense. Americans of Japanese heritage seem to have been able to make the schools work *for* them to a greater degree than have Americans of Chinese heritage, or Americans from the other minority groups we have been discussing.

While the assimilation process has been slower for all Asian-Americans than for white European immigrants, they seem to have made significant early gains in this direction. Some have hypothesized that Asian-Americans have enjoyed an advantage unavailable to other non-white minorities in that they have always possessed a proud sense of a noble and ancient cultural heritage. In many respects, according to this view, the Asian-American family and community have been able to cherish a proud concept of a civilization that rivals and in a number of ways surpasses the achievements of white western culture.

One might, of course, inquire to what extent a loss of cultural identity and individual pride has been required in order to accomplish this feat where it has occurred. And there is mounting evidence that the next generation of Americans of Japanese heritage want something other than what their people have been able to achieve thus far. The Asian-Americans, according to their own spokesmen, have a considerable number of demands to make of society at large, and especially of the schools.

In many quarters, a disconcerting degree of racism toward Asian-Americans remains. For many, it comes early in the schoolyard taunts—the eye jokes, the obsequious bowing, the fake accents and the "Ah so's!" For others there is no early initiation, only a much later shock to one having been brought up in good will: suddenly to feel new social and economic pressures subtly exerted against all who are "not white." Some young Asian-Americans try to guard against being stereotyped by showing that they are not like all other Asian-Americans: they choose a life style which gives a living denial of the stereotype. They are noisy, they refuse to eat rice, they are ashamed to be seen with "oriental" Orientals. Others, more militant, protest their white surroundings. They shout, "Accept me on my own terms! Don't try to make me over!"

This Part, then, contains an interesting admixture of material documenting successful acculturation, along with other material documenting failure. Some of the failure is traced in the opening article—an historical review by descendents of those whose history they are writing. The following piece, by Kitano, stresses the positive aspects of Japanese acculturation. Kitano points out, however, that the crucial problem today lies with the third and fourth generations who have less identification with their heritage. They are tempted to "make it" in the American middle class by denying their orientalness.

In a report on a contemporary Chinese urban community, Leary next illustrates how the Chinese, in contrast to the Japanese, have not become comfortably acculturated and she offers some interesting speculation as to why this may be true. With careful documentation, the Kitano piece which follows explores socio-psychological aspects of Japanese acculturation telling a moving story of a people fighting to keep an identity while trying to merge with the American middle class mainstream.

We have already noted the generation gap among third- and fourth-generation Americans of Japanese heritage. Existing among the Japanese in a mild form, this problem is becoming rampant among Chinese youth. The popular writer Tom Wolfe chronicles this vividly in "The New Yellow Peril," a no-holds barred article about San Francisco's Chinatown and Chinese and Japanese militants' disenchantment, frustration, anger, hatred, and ultimate confrontations with the San Francisco schools.

We end, then, on a note of action, for we believe that this is the keynote for the coming decade in America's schools. Our hope that teachers will become part of the action in a constructive sense has led us to assemble these selections designed to spotlight the multi-cultural populations in our schools.

Asians in America

Asian-Americans
of the Third World
Political Alliance

Chinese and Japanese, the most prominent of Asian-descended groups in America, are constantly held up as the successful minority groups. But little of their history and experience in the United States is known by the general public. And an awareness of this historical background is needed to understand the present situations of the two groups. In reality the "success" of Chinese and Japanese Americans is really very questionable, and in this respect, they are merely representative of all Asian-Americans who are given an ambiguous acceptance in American society. They are allowed to succeed economically, academically, and socially—but only to a certain extent. By an unspoken but real consensus, Asian Americans have not been completely acceptable regardless of how long they have been in this country.

Chinese have been in California for a little over one hundred years. As most European immigrants did, Chinese came pulled by the economic opportunities of America. The coincident discovery of gold in California with the outbreak of the Taiping Rebellion, drought, and famine in China propelled many Chinese to the United States. When they first came in 1850, they were warmly welcomed by a young state which was eager for the cheap labor Chinese workers could provide. Over 12,000 were employed on construction of the Central Pacific Railroad and a few thousand more toiled in agriculture, and land reclamation. Stories are abundant about the hundreds of stereotyped Chinese cooks and launderers who helped domesticize the wild West. California's first civil governor Barnett spoke of the initial Chinese laborers as "desirable acquisitions," and his successor McDougal cited them as the most valuable of newly-arrived citizens.

From *The Stevenson Libre*, Spring 1969, Year 2nd, No. 39, pp. 1–4, Stevenson College, University of California at Santa Cruz.

The warm welcome was short-lived. Almost from their arrival intense prejudice and discrimination ran high against the Chinese in the gold mines. White gold-seekers were incensed to find yellow foreigners "stealing" the gold of the United States of America. Chinese often hauled in $5 or $6 worth of gold per day, as compared to the average $30 of white Argonauts. Besides running Chinese off their claims and driving them from the mining camps, white miners also won the Foreign Miner's Tax in 1852 which levied a $20 per month fee directly at the Chinese. Many paid just to avoid trouble, but most quit the mines and swarmed into the cities.

Their reception there was hardly better. Too many available Chinese laborers cheapened the wage each could command. As a result, the Chinese probably worked the most for the least pay. They processed tobacco in the cigar factories, cleaned wool in clothing factories, laundered shirts for $5 a dozen instead of $8, sold cheaper-priced food in their small restaurants, and did just about anything else the white worker scorned. Though poorly-paid, the Chinese were at least working and many succeeded in their occupations. Then the business recession of 1872 struck. The average white laborer was out of a job. He would not work the same tasks as the Chinese, nor would he accept the same low wages. Venting his frustration, anger, and fear, these laborers followed the cry of Dennis Kearney who insisted "the Chinese must go!" Fierce anti-Chinese sentiments led to burned homes, looted businesses, assaults, and even murder. The West coast was clamouring for the exclusion of Chinese, which they finally won with the Chinese Exclusion Act of 1882 prohibiting further entry of Chinese laborers. Chinese already in the States retreated behind the walls of Chinatowns and there carried on a life almost completely apart from the American mainstream.

Although the official history of Japanese in America began after the Exclusion Act of 1882, the experiences of Japanese immigrants abroad began as early as 1868 when the first contracted laborers left Japan to work on Hawaiian plantations. Before that year Japan had maintained itself for over two centuries in self-imposed isolation characterized by tranquility and stability in a feudal society. During that period the Japanese government had been intensely isolationist, allowing few to leave or enter the country. But as feudalism collapsed, many peasants were unable to maintain subsistence level existences on the already overcrowded land. The Japanese government, extremely reluctant to allow its citizens to leave, eventually conceded because of the necessity to remedy the poor economic situation of so many people. The earliest emigrants migrated in great numbers to the Hawaiian islands where they were needed on plantations.

In the late nineteenth century, however, a shift in the migration pattern occurred as Japanese, both via Hawaii and directly from Japan, began to enter the United States. The labor shortage caused by the exclusion of Chinese created a demand for cheap labor; the Japanese were therefore welcomed, particularly in California, as railroad workers, domestics, and especially as "stoop" laborers, who did the tiring, back-bending work on farms.

In addition to acquiring the former occupations of the Chinese, the Japanese also inherited much of the prejudice against the Chinese. The first anti-Japanese movement, which was strong at the turn of the century, was led by American laborers who objected to the undermining of wage rates by Japanese (characteristic of the anti-Chinese movement which had culminated in the exclusion laws). Prejudice caused by the economic threat to laborers combined with local San Francisco politics and remnants of the general public's fear of "the yellow peril" so that anti-Japanese discrimination became the concern of both the American and Japanese national governments. Unlike China, Japan retained great concern for the welfare of her people in America. The American government, aware of Japan's potential as a power in Asia and as a world power, and concerned with its economic interests in Asia, intervened in an attempt to appease Japan and California. The result, in 1907, was the "Gentlemen's Agreement," in which both parties expressed a willingness that the Japanese government would not allow additional laborers to emigrate to the U.S.

The agreement, however, apparently pleased Californians for only a short time. Meanwhile, the Japanese, who like the Chinese had come to America with the hope of acquiring wealth in a short time and then returning to their own countries to live a better life, began to realize the impossibility of making the dream come true. Perhaps they also decided that the life in America, although not their native country, was better than what they could hope to attain in Japan. So, the Japanese men sent for "picture brides" who could legally enter the country under the "Gentlemen's Agreement;" they began to settle and raise families. Unlike the Chinese, they did not retreat fully into urban ghettos but tended to concentrate more in rural farming communities. Not content to remain laborers, the Japanese began to acquire small farms of their own which usually specialized in truck and berry crops. But this move toward occupational independence evoked reaction by small farmers, who felt threatened by economic competition, and by larger farmers hurt by the loss of a cheap labor supply. The result was the Alien Land Law of 1913, which prohibited ownership of land by non-citizens. When the law proved ineffective another was passed, in 1920, prohibiting the leasing of land. As the second law also proved relatively useless, and as a result of the prevalent anti-foreign mood of the 1920's, came the passage of the Alien Exclusion Act of 1924, which effectively prevented any immigration into the U.S.

Throughout this period of intense anti-Japanese feeling, a new stereotype had been forming: in addition to remnants of the traditional Chinese stereotype the Japanese acquired a reputation for craftiness, treachery, and subversiveness.

Reactivated during World War II, this stereotype led to the interment of all Americans of Japanese descent, including those who were American citizens, in "relocation centers," ostensibly for their own protection but actually as a result of the American fear of the Japanese "yellow peril." The relocation was carried out under the authority of an executive order in which respect for the constitutional rights of citizens was strikingly absent—and this order still exists today.

A significant result of the wartime encampment was that those of Japanese descent who were born and raised in America became aware of the vulnerable position they occupied, outside of American society yet not able to identify with Japan and its society. After the war, therefore, there was a great effort on the part of Japanese Americans to establish themselves as "real Americans;" the second generation as a whole worked very hard to attain economic security and consciously built a reputation for industriousness, honesty, and reliability.

The Chinese had been "good losers." Around the turn of the century they were no longer needed economically, and surely not wanted socially or politically. Forced into Chinatowns because of prejudice and discrimination, Chinese had nevertheless gone peacefully—if not also willingly to escape the hostile white environment. With the outbreak of World War II, though, Chinese labor was once more in demand. California's agribusiness, especially, needed the Chinese for farm labor, for the Japanese, who had previously supplanted Chinese farm workers, were now confined to concentration camps. Chinese returned once more to the fields. War industries such as aircraft factories and shipyards which previously had not even considered Chinese now began hiring Chinese engineers, technicians, workers, and even clerks. It was evident that if Chinese were to fill the labor shortage, the Exclusion Act had to be repealed. Besides, China herself was now an active Asian ally of America; complete trust and cooperation could not be established if Chinese exclusions was still a part of United States policy. In 1943, the historic exclusion laws were finally repealed by President Franklin D. Roosevelt. Instead, an annual quota of 105 was substituted.

Today the Chinese are still living within the situation imposed upon them by their history in America. Simple repeal of the exclusion laws could not suddenly transform Chinatowns born of years of withdrawal. Faced by hostility from outside, Chinatown had become an ingrown community, with economics at the base of the matter. Both locating jobs and conducting business outside of Chinatown were extremely limited; consequently social contacts were also restricted to the area. Fear kept the Chinese politically isolated from the American mainstream. No political party or labor union has been able to effectively organize in Chinatown since it began.

Thus cut-off from American society, the Chinese were prey for a new exploitation, which in fact began, and continues now, surviving on the fact that 20,000 new immigrants arrive each year to crowd into Chinatown and compete with one another for a living. Housing is extremely poor. A high rate of tuberculosis is one natural consequence. Seamstresses, waiters, cooks, busboys, and launderers often only make $60 per full seven-day work weeks. Immigrants have hard times learning English and adjusting to the American pace, which forces many of them into economic and social cul-de-sacs within Chinatown. Cultural conflicts are reflected in the rising rate of juvenile delinquency. These problems can no longer be contained, however. The sweeping minority protest is breaking into Chinatown and Chinese are affirming themselves. Among the youth there is an awakening. Political groups such as the Red Dragon Party are demanding that the Chinese elders lower their traditional veil of pride and take steps to solve problems which have long bred in Chinatown.

This reforming of Chinatown appears likely to bring its inhabitants and their culture more into the American mainstream. As they move out of Chinatown boundaries economically and socially, Chinese will face the conflicts of assimilation demanded by American society. If nothing else, withdrawal into the Chinese community has strongly preserved the cultural heritage and traditions of Chinese. Now the Chinese people are squarely faced with defining what exactly the term "Chinese-Americans" should mean in regard to ethnicity, individuality, and "Americaness." Not only those in the Chinatowns, but also the second and later generations of Chinese-Americans in the suburbs, must confront this question of identity among a people whose skin color will always tie them to the Chinese culture and the problems of other Chinese-Americans. For no matter how "Americanized" a Chinese may become, he cannot be accepted by whites as "one of their own kind." Chinese-Americans thus will probably need their culture and their fellow Chinese to fully possess an identity and sense of belonging.

Although there are certainly problems of "Little Tokyos" today, the economic situation for most Japanese-Americans is relatively good. The real problems are with the third and fourth generations of Japanese-Americans who have little identification with the Japanese part of their heritage. Although they identify strongly with American middle-class values, they must still face the reality of being members of a minority group which is recognized for certain virtues yet still not fully accepted as "American."

It is important, therefore, that Japanese-Americans too understand their heritage, for it both distinguishes them from the rest of society and keeps them from becoming completely accepted by it. It is to be hoped, however, that in the new awakening of Asian-Americans today, some way can be found whereby a people need not give up their right to and need of a full identity, in order to accomplish the process of assimilation.

The Remarkable Evolution of a Japanese Subculture

Harry H. L. Kitano

. . .

In a faculty lecture at UCLA a few years ago, I told the audience of a personal experience, by way of illustration:

> . . . I remember making another address approximately 19 years ago, similar in that I was doing the talking and similar because there was an audience. But there were many differences. I was much younger and it was a high school valedictory address, filled with words and ideas that only a high school youngster could comfortably espouse. And even more different was the audience and the setting; the audience was made up only of Japanese, for it was given at the graduation exercises in a war relocation camp, a euphemism for a concentration camp. Although I have difficulty in remembering the exact words of the address (for which I am thankful) I do recall declaring with all of the dramatic power that a naive high school youngster can: "I don't know why we're here, I don't know where we're going, but I'm sure that things will work out." . . . The question of where we were going was the crucial question. How could anybody have really guessed? For if I had thought that within the next two decades I was to be giving a lecture such as this as a member of the staff of UCLA to such an audience, it would have been just a matter of time that people in white jackets would have whisked me out of the war relocation center, and into another kind of institution for handling problems of people who had somehow lost touch with reality.[1]

Many other Japanese can recall similar stories.

The story of Japanese achievement is especially impressive if we recall the thinking of many Americans of an earlier era. For example, V. McClatchy, publisher of the *Sacramento Bee,* wrote of the Japanese in 1921:

From Harry H. L. Kitano, *Japanese Americans: The Evolution of a Subculture* © 1969. Reprinted by permission of Prentice-Hall, Inc., Englewood Cliffs, New Jersey.
[1] Harry H. L. Kitano, "The Japanese in America," Faculty Lecture Series: The Many Faces of Integration, UCLA, October 21, 1963.

The Japanese cannot, may not, and will not provide desirable material for our citizenship. I. The Japanese cannot assimilate and make good citizens because of their racial characteristics, heredity and religion. 2. The Japanese may not assimilate and make good citizens because their government claims all Japanese, no matter where born, as its citizens. 3. The Japanese will not assimilate and make good citizens. In the mass, when opportunity offered, and even when born here, they have shown no disposition to do so. . . . There can be no effective assimilation of the Japanese without intermarriage. It is perhaps not desirable for the good of either race that there should be intermarriage between whites and Japanese. . . . They cannot be transmuted into good American citizens.[2]

Obviously, the record of the Japanese has challenged the early racist claims that nonwhite groups can never become good American citizens.

It should also be mentioned that the Japanese comprise a remarkably successful immigrant population, whether in the United States or in other countries. It is extremely difficult to get a Japanese to move from his beloved island of Mt. Fujiyama and the cherry blossoms, but once he emigrates he adapts extremely well. Brazil, which has a Japanese population approximately equal in size to that of the United States group, has been good for the Japanese, and the Japanese have been good to Brazil.[3] Similar successes have been noted in other countries. But he appears to have progressed the furthest in the United States.

ASSIMILATION BY GROUP

The term *Japanese American* of course describes many different kinds of groups and individuals, and these different groups have sometimes acculturated, assimilated, or integrated in different ways. Referring back to Gordon's model, if we divide Japanese Americans along cultural, structural, marital, and identificational lines, the following pattern emerges. The Nisei and Sansei are fully acculturated; the Kibei and war brides have partially acculturated, and the Issei have not acculturated; the Kai-sha—students and visitors—have also been placed in the "no acculturation" classification, even though there is evidence that some individuals from this group are even more "American," or at least less "Meiji Japanese," than members of the other groups.

None of the identified Japanese groups has achieved widespread structural assimilation (primary friendship, dating, and marital patterns outside of the ethnic community and in the larger "American community"), although this generalization must be modified somewhat by the pattern of those Japanese residing outside of the large ethnic communities (see Table 1, page 379). Similarly, marital assimilation has been limited, except for the Japanese war bride. Finally, identificational assimilation, which refers to the hyphenated American (e.g., Japa-

[2]V. McClatchy, "Japanese in the Melting Pot: Can They Assimilate and Make Good Citizens?" *The Annals of the American Academy of Political and Social Science,* CCCXXII (Januray, 1921), pp. 29–34.
[3]*The Japanese Immigrant in Brazil* (Tokyo University Press, 1964).

nese-American), has also been limited. Identificational assimilation in Gordon's model refers to primary identification as an "American," without regard to nationality, race, or religion. The "hyphenated American," then, is one who has not yet achieved a full American identity. Individuals and groups do not achieve the identity instantly and the process is one which includes perceptions and attitudes from both the majority and minority groups. For some groups such as the Japanese, it is a long-term process—starting off as Japanese; then to a Japanese-American and possibly ending up in the future with the American label.

The process of achieving an identification may be hypothesized as following certain developmental guidelines. For example, Cohen, in tracing the process of identity for the Jew, describes a broad initial phase where the primary concern of certain Jewish organizations was the protection of their good name.[4] Associated concerns at this stage might include keeping a united front and not airing intragroup problems in public. A possible next stage might include the development of ethnic humor, not only for the ingroup, but now performed for the larger society. It would be symptomatic of a decreasing concern over the "image and goodness" of the group. Ethnic self-consciousness during this period would still be high, but of a much more objective and self-critical kind. Defensiveness may diminish. Finally, there may be a stage where references to the ethnic group depart completely from the conscious stream, to be replaced by the majority group identification. The desirability of this last step remains a value question.

From this perspective, neither the Issei nor the Nisei have fully achieved an American identification. Only the Sansei have moved significantly in this direction. The Sansei have few ties with Japan—nor do they retain a broader ethnic identification of being oriental, nor do they identify with skin color—consequently, many Sansei are insulted if referred to in any other terms but American. But the majority of the Sansei and the majority of Americans still perceive them as different, so that it is still accurate to indicate that they retain a hyphenated identity, but less so than their parents and grandparents.

ASSIMILATION BY AREA OF RESIDENCE

Table 1 summarizes the relationship between area of residence and cultural, social-marital, occupational, housing, and political assimilation. The reference point here is in terms of Nisei-Sansei participation in the majority society, appropriate to their age-sex-class status.

All Nisei-Sansei groups, no matter what the area of residence, have achieved cultural assimilation or acculturation. In the area of intermarriage (structural and marital assimilation), areas away from California have been ahead. One com-

[4]Nathan Cohen, private conversation. The writer is indebted to Professor Cohen, Dean of the Graduate School of Social Welfare at UCLA who served as a springboard and testing source for many ideas.

TABLE 1   Degree of Japanese Assimilation by Area and Type

	TYPE OF ASSIMILATION				
Area	Cultural	Social-Marital	Occupational	Housing	Political
California (West Coast)	Yes	No	Partly	Partly	Beginning
Chicago (Midwest)	Yes	Beginning	Yes*	Yes*	No
New York- New England	Yes	Partly	Yes*	Yes*	No
Hawaii	Yes	Partly	Yes*	Yes*	Yes

*Substantially yes.

mon-sense factor in this is numbers. Those Japanese in the Eastern part of the United States just do not have a population large enough to support marriages strictly within the group. There is also a selection and mobility factor. Many families who desire that their children marry only other Japanese either send their children to California or move the entire family there. Although Japanese comprise most of the nonwhite population of Hawaii, and Hawaii has been famous for the intermingling of races, Japanese there usually marry within the ethnic group. However, this pattern is changing.

Some indication of the feeling of the Japanese in the Los Angeles area can be gathered from a question concerning marital preferences. Ninety-seven percent of a sample of Nisei parents preferred that their children marry only other Japanese, although a high proportion conceded that the idea of marriage to a Caucasian was not as disturbing as it once seemed.[5]

In the occupational area, the opportunities for Japanese to find positions commensurate with their training and experience appear to be better away from California. Once again, numbers play an important role, and it is probable that even in the East, there is room at the top for only a small, select group of Japanese. There appears to be an unofficial quota system in operation; it would be unusual to see more than one person of Japanese ancestry in an executive position in the same American business, even on the East Coast. However, positions below the executive level remain plentiful for the Japanese American.

Occupational problems in Hawaii stem more from the type of economy, and from general overall employment patterns there. Many trained Hawaiians of Japanese descent emigrate to the mainland simply because of the better opportunities on the mainland.

Housing is not a major problem for the Japanese. There are still areas that practice covert discrimination but, in general, the Nisei and Sansei can buy homes in "desirable" neighborhoods, depending on their income and occupation. The progress in housing can be inferred from the mixed reaction of Nisei

[5]Harry H. L. Kitano, "Passive Discrimination: The Normal Person," The Journal of Social Psychology, LXX (1966).

and Sansei to Proposition 14, a controversial 1964 California ballot measure on discrimination in housing. Many Japanese took the side of the California Real Estate Association, which opposed fair-housing laws.

The political situation of the Japanese Americans today clearly reflects the power of numbers. The Nisei United States Senator and several elected members of the House are from Hawaii, and the successful Japanese-American candidates in California government are from areas, such as Gardena,[6] of heavy ethnic concentration. However, in spite of the few elected and appointed officials, most observers describe the Japanese American as extremely naïve politically. If we use knowledge of political issues, active participation in political organizations, and the like as criteria, the observations are correct. The Japanese American, at least at this stage of his acculturation, is an apolitical population.

SUMMARY BY GENERATIONS

In summarizing the acculturative history of the Japanese in America, we will find it most convenient, as well as most meaningful, to look once more at the differences among the three generations, Issei, Nisei, and Sansei. For it is by generation that progress along most variables is most clearly seen, and it is from the changes, generation by generation, that one may discern the probable direction of future changes, for predictions of social behavior, like any prediction, must rest upon past phenomena.

The Issei

The Issei, who by the 1960's were mostly in the over-70 age bracket, have changed but little in certain areas since their arrival in America at the turn of the century, except in those directions inevitable to advancing age. They were, and remain, products of a vanished Japanese era, conforming, hard-working, group- and family-oriented, clinging to old values, customs, and goals. Oddly enough, it is this, the most exotic Japanese group, that has been least studied, in spite of the fact that it possesses the most striking cultural differences. This is in part because its very life-style limits the use of quantitative instruments. An investigator, for instance, finds it difficult to receive answers that reflect anything other than what the Issei expects the investigator to want to hear, for this is the customary convention of conversation. There was a day, in Japan, when the great lord would chop off your head if, when he asked you if you could deliver him a million bushels of corn, you said no. You said yes whether you could or not.

The Issei culture itself is still a relatively classless one, even though its members may be economically distinct. Most of them, however, are in comfortable

---

[6]A suburb of Los Angeles.

circumstances and have retired both from their businesses and farms and from their positions as leaders of the Japanese community. Their problems are those of any aging group—the problem of leisure time and of finding useful family roles. They are concerned now not with their own children as much as with their grandchildren, and, again, as is typical of all peoples, seem to be mellower, more understanding and more indulgent of this generation than of the one whose upbringing was their direct responsibility. The American life styles of the Nisei and Sansei family do not allow the grandparent the same honor and responsibility he would have in Japan, but he has a definite and respected place nonetheless. His role may simply be that of guardian of Japanese ways; for many Sansei, a grandparent is his only contact with the land of his ancestors.

The Issei, for themselves, continue to cultivate their Japaneseness. Many retain a degree of nostalgic nationalistic feeling. Most participate in Japanese-oriented group activities through the church, Issei organizations, Japanese movies. The more affluent often take a trip to Japan, seeing for the first time since they left it at the turn of the century the motherland they had idealized for fifty years. This, predictably, is usually something of a nasty shock. The remembered values of politeness, calm, and honesty have been lost in the jostle of a great Westernized city. They admire the physical achievements and fine accommodations in Tokyo, but find themselves unable to understand the people, and are themselves laughed at and treated as quaint country cousins. Among rural Japanese they are able to find some of the mores they remember, but they are by now unable to tolerate the primitive rural living conditions. The author's mother, upon returning, much disillusioned, from such a visit, remarked that Japan is a nice place to visit, but one wouldn't want to live there.

Happily, the elderly Issei can usually find within the Japanese community and family here a fairly satisfying way of life. Most continue to live with or near their children, so that the extended family is maintained at least to a token extent. It is common for widows and widowers to live with their children. There are, of course, no elderly spinsters, but there is the small population of old bachelors, previously mentioned, for whom isolation and social interaction remain problems. As the number of their cronies diminishes, they are more apt than any other Japanese group to fall into the care of Japanese social welfare agencies and medical facilities.

But in general, the Issei population today has entered that period usually described as "golden," and the description is apt. Their complaints—that people pay too little attention to them, that no one really appreciates what they went through, that the younger generation is getting "soft"—are overbalanced by the manifest satisfactions of material well-being, and by the pleasure they feel in seeing the success of their children, for whom they had indeed sacrificed much. A comparison of their own circumstances and those of their children with the circumstances of those friends and relatives who stayed in Japan most likely confirms the wisdom of their choice to emigrate, and they have little to regret.

The Nisei

Most Issei, having considered the future of their children more important than the immediate satisfaction of their own wishes, today measure their success in terms of the success of the Nisei, and the Nisei in general have rewarded the sacrifices, in spite of the fact that their transitional position between the Japanese and American cultures has been a difficult one. A Nisei schoolboy found himself similar to Caucasian students on many levels and to his Japanese parents on others, but was considered "Japanese" by his American peers, and incomprehensibly American by his parents. But unlike the situation in some other immigrant cultures, where the transitional generation, most affected by culture conflict, has shown the highest degree of delinquency and mental illness and anomie, the Nisei have functioned successfully, producing what may legitimately be termed a Japanese-American community. Like the Issei, they have constructed an elaborate network of cliques and organizations, but these organizations are themselves designed according to American models. Family attitudes and concerns are American, yet the sophisticated observer would notice a subtle lack of verbal exchange, a faintly "Japanese" climate there. The college professor, used to giving seminars to Caucasians, would tear his hair at the docile silence of a group of Nisei, yet the cheering and fighting at the Nisei basketball game is as rowdy as at any other American game.

The Nisei have achieved a remarkable professional and educational record, comparable to or exceeding that of the majority community. Although this has tended to produce some class distinctions, these are still negligible. The gardener, the CPA, and the doctor may make up a threesome at golf. The fathers of Sansei debutantes are as likely to be nurserymen as lawyers—and very few perceive this as untoward social climbing.

Like any group of established, fairly affluent midde-aged people, the Nisei find themselves concerned with leisure and community service. Groups in Los Angeles play golf and take Las Vegas weekends. The women often spend a great deal of time in voluntary social work, and many take classes, particularly those which reflect an awakening interest, typical of ethnic groups, in Japanese traditional pursuits, such as flower arranging or Japanese dance. Bridge clubs are popular.

Nisei housing patterns reflect their transitional position. They tend to live at the fringes of the ghetto, in more prosperous circumstances, or to form new contiguous living groups in middle-class subdivisions. Few are to be found randomly scattered in other neighborhoods.

With more leisure and economic success, the Nisei have found time to examine problems of family life, and find there typically American role conflicts and generation conflicts. Some evidence points to an increase in separations and divorce, though this is far from typical. The appearance of several Japanese-American psychiatrists in the Los Angeles community is probably no coincidence. Few Nisei avail themselves of community mental health and guidance facilities, but the group shows good attendance at lectures on child rearing or understanding adolescents.

Finally, of course, it is necessary to consider the atypical but sizable Nisei group who have not achieved economic success and middle-class status. There are, of course, the Nisei gas-station attendants, janitors, and laborers. These individuals probably interact more than their middle-class peers with subgroups outside of the Japanese community, particularly with Negro and Mexican groups, and in a mild sense can be said to have assimilated, albeit into lower-class society, more than other Nisei. But, as is common with their middle-class Japanese peers, they have retained or modified their culture so that very few have incorporated the values and behaviors of the lower-class population.

The Sansei

What is true for the Nisei is also true of the Sansei generation, though some evidence suggests that deviant behavior is slightly increased in this group. The explanation lies, of course, in the fact that Sansei are, on most measurements of acculturation, completely identical to the Caucasian group. Their test results, achievement and interest preferences, and social values are typically American. They are members of Little League, fraternities, sororities, and other organizations designed upon American models, although these are still primarily ethnic in their membership. But even these structural barriers are breaking down. Sansei college students now sometimes join non-Japanese fraternities and sororities, and intermarriage is increasing, although the preference of most remains to marry within the group. In general, however, Sansei thinking and behavior are typically American.

It is difficult to say, however, that they are not still transitional. The college professor, giving a seminar to Sansei, will notice that, while these students are not as reticent as Nisei, they are still somewhat subdued and conforming. Their education is job-oriented; they enter "secure" professions. The fierce desire for upward mobility is occasionally frightening, and is more typical, perhaps, of an aspiring rather than a fully acculturated middle-class American. As has been mentioned, most prefer to marry other Sansei.

But there are built-in structural factors that will literally force a change. The increased differentiation and stratification among the relatively small number of Japanese will inevitably lead to increased interaction with non-Japanese groups on all levels. For example, if we fall back on our eth-gen-class model, the third-generation Japanese Ph.D. social scientist will probably, in looking for a wife, find few Sansei females with comparable background, interests, and values. The old model "just so long as she is Japanese," will no longer be satisfactory; the same point will hold true for the female Sansei liberal arts major with a strong bent for theater. And the same story will be repeated on all levels of the Japanese-American structure. The social expectations of group members will not be fully satisfied within the ethnic community. We have already seen how this change has operated to affect the ethnic occupational structures, with a generational move from in-community to out-community jobs.

This change will no doubt be slower in the West, where Japanese-American institutions and numbers are strongest and where resistance to structural crossing is probably the highest, but appears inevitable everywhere in time.

THE RACE QUESTION

This leads to a point of particular significance for the study of minorities in America, namely, the question of the assimilation and integration of a racially distinct group. Race is commonly thought to be an almost insurmountable social barrier. Programs for the integration of, say Negroes, almost always rest upon the tacit assumption that the biological distinction is to be maintained. "Would you want your daughter to marry one?" remains a fundamental, inescapable question.

But evidence, even that collected during the height of wartime passions, shows that a presumably rigid criterion such as race is not an absolute one. For example, O'Brien mentions that in the racially segregated city of Memphis, although the Chinese were buried in the Negro section of Elmwood Cemetery, the Japanese used the same section as whites.[7] We wonder what tortuous paths Hitler's Aryan policy must have gone through to include the Japanese nation as a full-fledged ally and partner. And the Japanese businessman, who is an extremely important factor in the current South African economy, is considered as "white," at least for business purposes, in that country. Therefore, historical, political, and economic factors apparently influence the definition of race in an interesting fashion.

Sixty years has produced a marked change in the attitudes of both the Caucasian majority and the Japanese minority in the United States. Marital preference remains ingroup, but the groups themselves are less rigid in their attitudes, and intermarriage brings little opprobrium. The results of the postwar occupation of Japan and the large numbers of Japanese warbrides are obvious. As a Caucasian airlines pilot once remarked to this writer, speaking of his Japanese bride, "No one pays much attention to us since there was that movie *(Sayonara)* with Marlon Brando." Perhaps this generalization sounds somewhat too "Hollywoodish," but there is little doubt that the general direction of assimilation, generation by generation, will include biological as well as social integration. An important but often overlooked integration variable also includes the desirability of the Japanese female from American eyes, although such an attraction may be somewhat overexaggerated. Another important point concerning race and acceptance for the Japanese was the factor of differential perception

[7]Robert O'Brien, "Selective Dispersion as a Factor in the Solution of the Nisei Problem," *Social Forces* (December, 1944), pp. 140–147.

and differential acceptance from the majority group. Although it may have seemed to the Japanese that most everybody in the United States was always against them (especially during certain periods), this was not so. There were regional differences; there were social class differences and there were always a number of influential "Japanophiles"—those who "loved" Japan and the Japanese. Therefore, he was not subjected to the well-nigh universal degree of constant hostility that has been the lot of other ethnic groups.

CULTURAL PLURALISM

This leads to a pertinent question: What has been the most significant factor in the Japanese acculturative process? The answer seems to be the pluralistic development of a congruent Japanese culture within the framework of the larger American society. If we may be permitted a somewhat elaborate metaphor, this development may be envisioned as two trees, sprung from different seeds but flourishing in the same soil, in identical climatic conditions, the younger of them springing up by the side of the older, so that although the two trunks, rooted in similar values and aspirations, nourished by similar factors of education and industry, are separate, their branches intermingle, and eventually, it may be difficult to distinguish the leaves of one from the leaves of the other. The organic and gradual nature of this metaphor is particularly appropriate to cultural pluralism, yet it must be emphasized that this mode of acculturation seems only to work when two cultures spring from relatively similar seeds. The exotic plant of some cultures seems not to flourish in American soil. For some groups it seems apparent that cultural pluralism hinders acculturation and assimilation simply because the discrepancies between the cultures seem to lead to increased divergence and intergroup tensions. In such cases, assimilation seems to require the dissolution of one of the cultures, and its substitution by more "American" patterns of behavior. Such a process inevitably requires more time, more conflict, raises critical questions of value, and creates more difficulties for the individuals and cultures caught in the process. Further, as we have mentioned in our opening chapter, there may be a functional order so that the smoothest method of adaptation follows an acculturatiin, integration, and assimilation sequence.

A comparison of cultural pluralism with other modes of acculturation immediately involves one in the subtleties of possible modes of selective cultural pluralism. For instance, a purely cultural-pluralistic development might imply, say, the retention of the native language as well as its customs and values. Yet the Japanese have quickly and almost completely discarded the Japanese language, and artificial attempts to preserve it (e.g., Japanese language school) have largely failed. In other dimensions, too, certain unwieldy Japanese customs were almost immediately supplanted by more efficient American ones. The potential inherent in cultural pluralism for retaining some elements of a distinctive way of life and discarding others is one of its most attractive elements. It is a cliché to say of America that it is a great melting pot, meaning, presumably, that the disparate elements that comprise it are eventually commingled in an amorphous brew labeled "the norm," and that this is desirable. Yet, surely, the distinctive contribution of Oriental, of Mexican, of African, and many other cultures, could greatly improve the savour of the bland American brew. The cultural-pluralistic development of the Japanese-American group so far provides another example of how the native and American may coexist.

STRUCTURAL PLURALISM

The problem of structural pluralism is a related issue. Followed to an ultimate extreme, it might describe a society with a vast number of independent groups maintained through restrictions on friendship, dating, and marriage. There is an obvious danger to the proliferation of such structures—the restriction of friendship and marriage to persons within one's own network could very well foster a strong "we" and "they" feeling, leading to less communication, more misunderstanding, more prejudiced attitudes and higher levels of discrimination.

The development of pluralistic structures for the Japanese was originally based more on necessity than choice—there was little opportunity for Japanese to enter into the social structure of the larger community. Currently, however, the matter of choice appears to be of a more voluntary nature—most Japanese can enter into the social structures of the larger society, although there is always the element of greater risk and possible rejection for those choosing this path. The continued existence of the ethnic structures, however, limits the opportunity for "risk-taking," and many Japanese who might otherwise have ventured into the larger society choose the easy way out through participation in the ethnic structures (even though these groups are as "American" as any). The comment of "being more comfortable and at ease with one's own kind" covers many situations. However, many Japanese still need the ethnic structures and the justification for the cradle-to-grave services (e.g., a Japanese doctor will be on hand at delivery; a Japanese priest will perform over the burial; and in between, one can live a life of friends, dating, and marriage primarily with other Japanese) provided by the ethnic community is important; however, the structures may be playing a negative role when their strength pulls back some who might venture into the larger society. This writer feels that social interaction based primarily on interest and achievement is healthier than one based on ethnicity.

Judged by most standards, the coexistence between the Japanese and American cultures has been successful. Education, productivity, and "Americanism" have been high, and crime, delinquency, and other forms of social deviance have been low. And if we remember that this has been accomplished by a nonwhite group, the progress appears even more remarkable.

Interestingly enough, the adaptation of the Japanese to the United States is similar to that of many European groups—what Park refers to as a natural history cycle.[8] A typical pattern of interaction between groups starts with contact, followed by competition, then by accommodation. Accommodation is usually accompanied by segregated ethnic islands, which eventually leads to the final stage of assimilation. When an observer takes a long-range historical view of the interaction between two cultures, the process as described by Park appears to have high validity. It must be added, however, that this model can function best when there are equal opportunities (e.g., especially in education and employment) and where there is a willingness on the part of both cultures to accommodate to each other.

The unusual part of the Japanese adaptation is that it is being accomplished by a "nonwhite" group and a population heretofore considered to be "unassimilable." In fact, the adaptation has been of such a quality that it has been termed a "model American minority."[9]

But we must also be reminded that the judgment of Japanese Americans as the "model American minority" is made from a strictly majority point of view. Japanese Americans are good because they conform—they don't "make waves" —they work hard and are quiet and docile. As in a colonial situation, there tends to be one set of prescriptions for those in power and another for the subject people. But, ideally, members of the ethnic community should share in any evaluation of the efficacy of their adjustment. For if the goals of the American society include freeing an individual for self-expression and creativity, and if social maturity includes originality, participation, and the opportunity for individuals to function at their highest levels, then certain questions may be asked about the Japanese. It may be a disservice to some of them to continue calling them "good" and reinforcing their present adaptation. The kind of goodness that led them to accept the wartime evacuation can, in the long run, be a drawback as well as a strength. Perhaps this is one group where emphasis on the self— the development of individual self and the satisfaction of ego needs—can be more highly emphasized.

However, it would be tragic if some of the strengths of the Japanese culture were to be forgotten. The ability to look beyond self and to act in relation to others is an admirable quality, and the ethnic identity, whether in terms of a nation and manifested as pride, or in terms of a community, helped the Japanese achieve a degree of cohesion and group loyalty that appears important for a meaningful life. Without an abstraction that leads beyond self, life may regress to self-indulgence and to self-gratification so that the accumulation of wealth and power—often associated with "success"—may only be an empty victory. Hopefully, the next generation of Japanese Americans will integrate the best of the Japanese and the American cultures so that their lives will reflect the richness of both. But, at the risk of being unduly pessimistic, the probability that

[8]Robert E. Park, *Race and Culture*, ed. E. C. Hughes, et al. (Glencoe, Illinois: The Free Press, 1950), pp. 138–151.
[9]William Peterson, *The New York Times Magazine*, January 9, 1966.

they may draw from the more negative elements of both the cultures is also a realistic prospect.

We have described a group that has been effective in social organization, effective in socialization, effective in controlling deviant behavior, and effective in "becoming successful" in American terms. When we look back on the past prejudice and discrimination faced by the Japanese, we find that even their most optimistic dreams have been surpassed. Such a story may give us some optimism for the future of race relations in the American society.

San Francisco's Chinatown

Mary Ellen Leary

The most aggrieved people in Chinatown are the least able to articulate demands: they cannot even speak English. They have long been victims of discrimination; often it has been brutal. Today, among all the minorities trying to find their own identity within America, those of Chinese heritage have perhaps the least instinctive savvy about how to use our political system to promote their welfare; they confront the greatest gaps between generations, between cultures, between languages.

Even their labor gets overlooked. When the centennial of the transcontinental railroad completion was celebrated at Promontory Summit, Utah, last May, Chinese representatives were included tardily only at the insistence of historians that the Western route never would have been built without the work of 12,000 Chinese. They then had to sit by while Transportation Secretary John A. Volpe orated: "Who else but Americans could have drilled ten tunnels through mountains in thirty feet of snow and chiseled a line through solid granite?"

WARM PLACE

To speak of Chinatown is to speak of the deprived. Countless Chinese have truly been assimilated as Americans, moved into middle-class or upper-class neighborhoods, bought homes, found jobs at every level, no longer send their children to Chinese school, and never read Chinese newspapers. But left behind in Chinatown are the elderly, the timid, the very poor, and that largest segment, the non-English speaking.

San Francisco's Chinatown is America's oldest continuous ghetto. It consists of a minority that has hovered together now for some ninety years for self-protection. "A ghetto may be poor, but it is a warm place to crawl into if the outside world is hostile," says one of Chinatown's third-generation sons. Here men hid in terror of their lives three quarters of a century ago. They were lightly dismissed from the American conscience with that solacing myth: "The Chinese take care of their own."

On December 16, 1943, a somewhat shamefaced U.S. government, out of belated consideration for a wartime ally, decided to abolish Chinese exclusion laws that had been on the books since 1882. Thus some Chinese came into the U.S. after World War II. More came under liberalized terms of the 1952 Walter-McCarran Act. But the real "wave" of new immigration began in 1962 after President Kennedy opened the doors to some 16,000 refugees from Red China. In 1965 there followed complete revision of immigration laws, wiping out restrictions on entry by race or place of origin. China, like other nations, might send a maximum of 20,000 a year into the United States. It hasn't, so far. Latest figures show 16,420 immigrants in 1968 and 19,741 in 1967.

There is debate over just how big the Chinese immigrant impact is or will be, particularly in San Francisco. One reason is that half of those recorded as being new entries are really Chinese already in the country, taking advantage of the law to regularize their status. And immigrants unsuccessful in making a go of it elsewhere come back to San Francisco as the nearest thing to home. At any rate, while San Francisco City Hall and welfare agencies term Chinese immigration a crisis, C. W. Fullilove, San Francisco district director of the Immigration and Naturalization Service, contends this is sheer hysteria.

By Mr. Fullilove's count, only 1600 new Chinese came into San Francisco in 1968. By city tally, 8000 came. The federal estimate of the persons of Chinese origin now living in San Francisco hovers a bit over 40,000. San Francisco's count is 62,000. This, if correct, represents a meteoric rise in the decade. The 1960 census numbered 36,445 Chinese, 4.9 percent of the population. If, as city statistics indicate, 25,500 more have come in since, a 70 percent jump, then Chinese have been increasing in San Francisco twice as fast as Negroes.

The Chinese themselves think this immigration marks the beginning of a new era for them in America. They anticipate that by 1972 the population of Chinatown will be 75,000—half of them non-English-speaking.

If the immigrant's plight and Chinatown's silent suffering are not enough to elicit help from city, state, or federal government, this community may become another U.S. minority able to bring remedy for its wrongs only by provocative violence. Cherry bombs tossed by the defiant Hwa Ching (Young Chinese), broken windows, muggings, street crime, and even murder of non-Chinese, all of which are stunningly new social disorders in a previously unruffled Chinatown, today express the dissent of the young with Chinatown's customary cool.

Many factors are working for change in Chinatown. One is the impact of the Office of Economic Opportunity. Money is a force the Chinese recognize, and federal money in anti-poverty efforts, despite complaints that results are negligible, did at least seed new sources of power. OEO undertook the first community organization on a democratic basis when it mustered committees among housing project tenants to speak out. It produced the first program to meet Chinatown's major needs when it developed proposals for language and medical centers. Mayor Joseph Alioto of San Francisco, and Chinese leadership thereafter, undertook a survey of that community's problems, the first time Chinatown's leaders ever came together to study their situation.

Out of the ferment have come a half dozen serious proposals to Washington in recent months, backed by wide-ranging studies, community response, and some political support. All emphasize that only a federal effort can meet Chinatown's need.

One of the most important of these proposals asks Health, Education, and Welfare to fund a language center capable of coping with the language disability of the whole community from pre-kindergarten to grandfather. Another proposes a central community health plan, embodying a great range of medical support from health education teams to patient care. Vocational training, youth centers, new job preparation, better police-community relations all are under study, and San Francisco has laid groundwork for a major master-plan to rebuild the whole area with a Model Cities grant, preserving the allure and cultural attractions while tearing down the dilapidated tenements.

CORE

The heart of Chinatown is a seventeen-block core squeezed within "greater Chinatown." The whole community lies between two sections of the highest priced land in the West, elegant Nob Hill and Montgomery Street, San Francisco's financial center. City statistics show that 231 persons per acre live in the core, compared with a city density elsewhere of 33 persons per acre. This is congestion second only to Manhattan. In some 30 surrounding residential blocks, population density is 147 per acre. The Chinatown core is a wedge which downtown San Francisco presses to devour, and the population now spills northward into the Italian sector.

Souvenir shops line Grant Avenue, the main thoroughfare, a street so narrow two cars can barely pass. Chinatown lies precisely where commercial San Francisco, the city of sea trade and gold seekers, first was formed. There, aglitter with tile fronts, top-floor balconies, gold paint, turquoise, yellow, and red adornment, are the headquarters of the vital family associations and district associations, displaying their enigmatic names: Kong Chow, Hing Yeung, Hop Wo, Sam Yup. Twenty-five percent of Chinatown's core area is owned by such all-important organizations, some based on family, some on the district within Canton from which the immigrants came.

Off Grant Avenue, Chinatown hasn't changed much in forty years. Fortune cookie manufacturers have multiplied. Mah-jongg games still clatter behind cur-tained windows. Eight herb shops still dispense Oriental medicines. And in winter's dusk children still trek off to Chinese language school.

In the thriving food import stores, older women come to shop, black hair pulled tight as satin from their brows, jade in their ears. The food has an exotic mystique of its own: gleaming white and delicate green of Chinese cabbage, the gnarled, earthy talo root, the great mounds of winter melon shipped in from Sacramento Valley, big as party balloons, piled ceiling high in the produce stores. In butcher shops dripping brown barbecued ducks hang by their feet, and amidst the fish great bowls of naked squid lie eyeing the passerby. There is in-credible trade in quail eggs, shark fins, jellyfish, preserved mustard greens, bird's nests for soup, bean curd canned in Hong Kong, bamboo shoots, green grass jelly, dry fungus, and the blanched white rice flour. And tea.

The restaurants seem countless. Actually, there are about eighty, from tiny teashops in unbelievably deep basements, to resplendent modern bars and ban-quet halls. All do a thriving business. Importers of modern teak furniture, of por-celain and pottery, of wooden puzzles, incense, children's toys, silk yardage, and food, especially Chinese food to be funneled across the continent to other Chinatowns, create a constant business world bustle.

Chinese newspapers flourish, Chinese movies, Chinese radio broadcasting, beauty shops, dress shops, barbers, hardware stores, jewelers, their windows full of jade and yellow gold. All attest to flourishing times in Chinatown. But none as much as the parade of banks and savings and loan companies along Grant Avenue, each caparisoned with pagoda roof or tile dragons or stone watchdogs, like money-temples.

And yet it is a slum, an extraordinary slum; probably the only glamorous slum in America. Within this area 40 percent of the families in 1960 were below the poverty line of $4000 income. The proportion is higher now. A recent city sur-vey showed that 75 percent of Chinatown's families earn less than $6000 a year; 13 percent are unemployed, twice the rate for the city as a whole; 82 percent of the families live in three rooms or fewer; 60 percent share bathrooms with other families or have none. In the core of Chinatown, 45 percent of the resi-dents never went to school (compared with 3 percent for the city as a whole). Median schooling is 1.7 years, though in surrounding "greater" Chinatown, resi-dents have had about 8 years in school. Median years schooling for San Fran-cisco as a whole is 12.

Of the housing, 67 percent in the core area and 51 percent in greater China-town is substandard. There is some public housing. Three clusters, built in the 1950s, with appropriate Oriental motif, are called Ping Yuen (Tranquil Gardens). They house 428 families. More than 500 other applicants are on file to succeed them. The only new housing going up in Chinatown is a high-rise condominium whose apartments will sell to residents for over $50,000.

More than 10,000 elderly live here, some still unaware of Medicare or old-age pensions, unable to manage alone and ashamed to admit want. The number needing medical care and unable to afford it, according to official community reports, is 16,000. Until a few months ago, a vacant basement laundry room of the housing project served as the city's tuberculosis clinic and family planning center. City health officials recently opened a new emergency hospital in the area, and gave the clinic space—an improvement, but far short of what is needed.

Psychiatrists call Chinatown "a refugee camp," in the sense that a large proportion of its population is suffering the effects of dislocation: disenchantment and psychological inability to adapt to the new terrain. San Francisco is notorious for a suicide rate three times the national average; Chinatown's suicide rate often climbs spectacularly higher. There are two over-worked bilingual Chinese psychiatrists. The mental health clinic which serves Chinatown (and a quarter of the rest of the city) is so inadequately financed and volunteer help is so scarce that Dr. Sanford Tom must sometimes mop out the place himself. That isn't his chief worry. What is, is the reluctance of the Chinese to admit emotional stress. They come instead with stomach pains.

Underemployment is a greater Chinatown problem than unemployment. Many families scrape by on half-wages. The Labor Department tries to police wage rates but it faces employers of uncertain literacy who claim that their workers are family members, and an employee class too fearful of being blackballed to protest. The ten-hour day and the seven-day workweek are common.

Chinatown now boasts but one industry: tiny, one-room storefront sewing shops, inconspicuous behind curtained windows on side streets. These mushroomed after World War II as San Francisco's garment industry expanded. Called "bundle shops," they take in truckloads of garments, usually inexpensive cottons, pre-cut at the manufacturer's, to be sewn under sub-contract agreements. By now more than 300 such shops hiring 8 to 15 women keep an estimated 3000 women employed at wages sometimes half the state's $1.65 minimum, and an ever-fresh supply of avid workers is available.

Labor constantly inveighs against these "sweatshops." The International Ladies' Garment Workers Union has been hammering at Chinatown for years. Its local agent, Cornelius Wall, terms the exploitation "worse than anything I ever saw in the South."

PYRAMID

The elder statesmen of Chinatown today are China-born, and often only Chinese-speaking. They constitute an "establishment" far more obdurate to pleas from the young than any moneyed urban leadership elsewhere in the United States. They cling to old village customs. Today newcomers from Hong Kong, worldly-wise, as refugees from that sophisticated scrap heap must be, find Chinatown twenty years behind the Orient in accommodation to new thinking.

Out of need for self-protection, Chinatown originally created its own internal governance. Family is the base. "Family Associations" were formed to unite all relatives, the Wongs, the Lees, the Chinns, and so on. In addition, "District Associations" were created, grouping Chinatown residents according to the Cantonese neighborhoods from which they originally came. A man may belong to both and rise politically in both. They are linked. Officers of district groups often are chosen by vote cast according to family strength.

These two structures are part of a pyramid, the top of which is the Chung Wai Wui Kwoon, or Chinese Consolidated Benevolent Association, known familiarly in San Francisco as the Chinese Six Companies (and erroneously, for there are seven). The Six Companies are commanded by a president's board, consisting of presidents of the seven district associations, and a board of directors. The organization, which can be traced back 100 years, was able to come to the aid of Chinese caught in the white man's law, to function as a court in disputes between district or family groups, and to dispense welfare as well. It established the Chinese Hospital in 1925 when the old herb dispensary gave way to Western medicine. It maintains Chinese schools (of varying quality) which still keep 50 percent of all Chinese youngsters two hours at the end of each day to learn the Chinese language and literature.

Nothing of consequence happens in Chinatown without the nod of Six Companies, which has been a formal "front" to the white community, placating it with generous contributions to local charities. But it is hardly structured to cope with today's community needs. It has no executive secretary. It changes presidents every two months. It has no continuity of policy and no means for long-range planning.

Intelligent young Chinese activists and unreasoning rebel teen-agers alike are protesting this feudal hierarchy. They want a share of power, and a chance to put the community into motion toward solving its own problems. But the Six Companies system was designed to prevent participation in community decisions by any except the elite.

In the past, Chinese culture pressured the young to conform. It emphasized honor and respect for the elderly. Reversal of such priorities in American culture is trying enough for the older generation. Now immigrant realities have increased tensions. Many old men in Chinatown who have worked their lives away for distant families now cannot afford to bring them to the United States, and they are cruelly lonely. But they may be the lucky ones. Others have brought over sons, wives, parents, grandchildren, brothers, or sisters, only to face opprobrium.

Men who slaved to send $100 a month to the Orient were in fact supporting their far-off families in considerable comfort, by Hong Kong standards. The new arrivals have been shattered to discover how little $100 is in America, and that getting it takes work. They are further demoralized to discover the low status of a parent who may be a laundry worker or cook. No one wants new bars to the reunion of these families. But there is need of better advance preparation, particularly since today's Chinese arrivals, unlike their forefathers, come determined to be Americans.

Young people have been particular victims of this lack of preparation. The chance America offers the young for free education and economic advance usually motivates a family's move to America, but it is a parental aspiration, not the children's own. For little children, adjustment will come. For teen-agers, it is hard. Most of these young Chinese came here unwillingly, torn from groups in Hong Kong with which they felt identity, and plunged at the sensitive and lonely period of adolescence into an alien land whose strange language forces successive failures in the classroom.

To the horror of a Chinatown that believes in self-discipline, a number of these teen-agers, perhaps 300, have become rebels, dropouts, runaways, street loiterers, petty thieves, even violent agitators. It was inconceivable to Chinatown that Chinese youth would adopt the public obscenities of the militant blacks, or join college demonstrations in the Third World Freedom Movement. When they did, it was blamed on a "Communist plot."

Last year a mimeographed sheet called "Red Guard Community News" was circulated in Chinatown. It featured an open declaration that "Mao Tse-tung is our leader" (and an adaptation of Black Panther rules to the yellow race). Chinatown was aquiver with rumor about Red Chinese subsidies pouring in to the disaffected young. Mao's sayings and posters have indeed turned up in youth hangouts in a Chinatown previously untroubled in its loyalty to Chiang. And clearly some sense of local youths' identity with Mao's cause originated in Hong Kong. (Other disillusioned young Hwa Ching reportedly are being cultivated by Chinatown tongs, protective associations lately quiescent but with a Mafia-like history, which are not beyond forming gangs of available young toughs.) But the basic explanation for the phenomenon of youthful outlawry which has so shaken Chinatown is simply frustration over the language barrier, and over Chinatown's reluctance to change.

Sociopsychological Aspects of the Acculturation of Japanese in America

Harry H. L. Kitano

COMPATIBILITY OF JAPANESE AND AMERICAN MIDDLE-CLASS VALUES

Caudill stresses the compatability of Japanese and American middle-class values. For example, politeness, the respect for authority and parental wishes, duty to the community, diligence, cleanliness and neatness, emphasis on personal achievement and on long-range goals, a sense of shame concerning nonsanctioned behavior, the importance of keeping up one's appearance, and a degree of "outer-directedness" are values shared by the two cultures.

However, from our evidence it appears that the acculturation of the Japanese has not been because their culture and the American middle class are the same, but rather because of the functional compatibility and interaction between the two. The Issei have not acculturated, and have retained most of the ways of the old culture. Even the Sansei retain a certain degree of Japaneseness. However, the differences often facilitate rather than hinder their adjustment to American society.

For example, Iga notes that success-aspiration and obligation, both of which the Japanese American values more highly than does the Caucasian, are ideal norms of an older Protestantism, and both values help the group to become successful in America.[1] Some other characteristics in which Japanese Americans are higher than Americans are conformity and compromise. Therefore, a complex of patterns of Japanese-American culture, wherein success-aspiration and regard for rapid socioeconomic success are coupled with deference,

---

From Harry H. L. Kitano, *Japanese Americans: The Evolution of a Subculture* © 1969. Reprinted by permission of Prentice-Hall, Inc., Englewood Cliffs, New Jersey.
[1]Iga, "Changes in Value Orientation of Japanese Americans."

conformity, and compromise, may explain why the group at the present time is doing well in America, but has not raised the hostility of the larger society.

An "Ethical" Culture

The American and Japanese cultures have different ways of viewing norms and goals. The American appears more goal-oriented—efficiency, output, and productivity are highly valued, and the primary object is to win or to achieve success. The Japanese system appears much more norm-oriented—the how, the style, and the means of interaction are important, so that playing the game according to the rules is as important as winning it.

The norm-oriented culture may prove to be quite adaptable to external changes (e.g., the Issei immigrant, or the behavior of the Japanese during the wartime occupation of Japan), provided that some social structure remains, because interrelationships have meaning in themselves. How to interact with others—superiors, inferiors, and equals—can be relatively easily transferred from one structure to another, so that such a system may be less stressful to its members than one that is more success-oriented in terms of goals. For when goals are blocked or are unreachable, or when the lack of success in terms of "output" are glaringly apparent, the individual in such a position may be placed under very high stress.

Our previous illustration of the employer-employee relationship provides an example of the possible difference between the two cultures. A Japanese firm will tend to keep an inefficient employee, since Japanese norms encourage the notion of obligation; the *oyabun* (parent) and the *ko-bun* (child) relationship obtains between employer and employee, and is a goal in itself. Conversely, an American firm will not hesitate to fire an unproductive employee—the goals of the system are productivity, and can be summarized in the familiar phrase, "I'm running a business, not a welfare agency."

In a similar vein, American baseball players who have played in Japan feel that the Japanese will never be major leaguers until they develop a greater will to win. By this the American means that Japanese pitchers should throw at batters more often; Japanese players should slide with spikes high, challenge umpires, and play a more aggressive game. There is little question that if the worth of a culture is measured in terms of efficiency and productivity, the American model is vastly superior, but one may also question the possible emotional cost of such a system to those who cannot "make it" there. However, there are indications that the modern Japanese business and economic world is rapidly moving toward the American model.

Assimilation of the American Culture

The present trend away from the Japanese culture in terms of norms, values, and personality means that in the near future there will be almost complete acculturation. For example, although Japanese and Americans have differed in the past in their collective and individualist orientations, the collectivity orientation has diminished among Sansei and at present is similiar to that of Caucasian samples. Egoistic behavior and the importance of self over others has developed to such an extent that, in a study discussed earlier, on a question dealing with the family and the nation, the Sansei held a more individualistic position than did the non-Japanese American! Similarly, standards of discipline, paternalism, status distinction and other parameters of the "American" value system show that the Sansei are for all practical purposes completely acculturated. Iga states:

Their [the Sansei] desire to be assimilated appears to be so complete and their knowledge of Japanese culture so marginal that we cannot anticipate their return to traditional Japanese cultural interests. The only factor which prevents them from complete assimilation seems to be the combination of their physical visibility, and racial prejudice on the part of dominant group members.[2]

But parts of the Japanese culture undoubtedly remain. The tea ceremony, flower arranging, ondos and other dances, sukiyaki and other Japanese dishes, have become firmly a part of the Japanese-American culture. Certain traditions are already lost. Nisei and Sansei remember fondly the public singing performances of their otherwise restrained Issei parents at festivals and picnics, but the self-conscious Nisei have not stepped in to fill the role. Some values—responsibility, concern for others, quiet dignity—will hopefully survive, but other less attractive aspects—authoritative discipline, blind obedience to ritual, extensive use of guilt and shame to shape behavior, and the submissiveness of females—will not be much regretted in their passing.

Finally, although most empirical tests indicate the similarity of the Sansei to his American peers, the groups are by no means identical. Hopefully, in a culturally pluralistic society, the Sansei will find an effective combination of Japanese and American values, a personal value system for maintaining a mature and responsible attitude toward themselves and the world.

.   .   .

RELATIONSHIPS AMONG CRIME, DELINQUENCY, MENTAL ILLNESS, AND SUICIDE

There is an oversimplified description of behavior that predicts a balance between "withholding" or "acting out." By this is meant that cultures may either value repression or suppression so that very few emotions or impulses are acted upon, or encourage the release of impulses so that feelings are "acted out." From this perspective, delinquency (e.g., "acting out") and mental illness (e.g., withdrawal) are looked upon as a single dimension so that a

[2]Ibid.

negative correlation is thought to exist between the two variables. Therefore groups who are high on one end of the continuum are assumed to be low on the other and vice versa. Obviously, the Japanese American does not fit into this model, at least according to official statistics.

Another oversimplified view sees deviance as an escape valve, analogous to the values on a steam engine, necessary to prevent explosions in the social system. If this were true, one would expect a monstrous explosion within the Japanese group, for there is little deviance. But there is no indication that such an explosion will occur. Even suicide, thought to be a typically Japanese form of release behavior, although frequent in Japan, is no more frequent in the Japanese-American population than in the American population as a whole. In general, the Japanese population simply minimizes "acting-out" behavior.

We do, however, describe other forms of acceptable "release" behavior among Japanese Americans. Most common is somatization—that is, the development of psychosomatic symptoms and undue concern with bodily functions. Although the evidence is only impressionistic, all that one knows of the Japanese group tends to support this observation. The widespread use of patent medicines, obsession with high blood pressure, hot baths, masseurs, the practice of acupuncture, and concern for the stomach and other internal organs is typical of Japanese whether in the United States or Japan.

Further, the rather formal, stylized social interaction among Japanese, with a minimum of personal affect, presents diagnostic difficulties. For example, one Japanese-American psychiatrist related:

Because of the relatively rigid, set ways for social interaction, it's often difficult to diagnose where the role-set ends and possible psychiatric symptomatology begins. The person who reacts to extreme stress with a pattern of unemotional and ritualistic behavior may be relatively easy to diagnose psychiatrically in another culture, but for the Japanese (especially the Issei), it's really hard to figure one way or the other.[3]

The choice of occupations is also protective for many Japanese. The stereotyped Japanese gardener has an occupation where the amount of social interaction can be held to a minimum and where *ki-chi-gai* or crazy behavior can be widely tolerated.

But possibly, the most relevant hypothesis concerning the Japanese and their overall lack of deviant behavior relates to their family and community structure; their "culture" and their ability to control marginality. Gordon writes that the marginal man, from the sociological perspective, is the person who stands on the borders or margins of two cultural worlds but is fully a member of neither.[4] Marginal positions may develop from mixed or interfaith marriages or from those who seek contact in worlds other than their ethnic culture.

Psychological indications of marginality, hypothesized but not empirically

---

[3]Kitano, "Japanese-American Mental Illness," p. 24 of original manuscript.
[4]Milton M. Gordon, *Assimilation in American Life* (New York: Oxford University Press, 1964), pp. 56–57.

validated, are possibly related to marginal sociological positions and would include symptoms such as anxiety, frustration, alienation, and anomie, as well as the commission of deviant acts.

The ability of the Japanese family and community to provide ample growth opportunities, to present legitimate alternatives, to provide conditions of relative tolerance and treatment, to provide effective socialization and control, as well as the relative congruence between Japanese culture and the middle-class American culture, has aided the group in adapting to acculturative changes with a minimal marginal population. Relatively few Japanese seek social friendships in the social cliques and organizations outside of their own ethnic group. And those who do seek outside contacts appear to have many of the necessary requisites for such activity—high education, good training, and adequate income.

We do not wish to infer that the marginal position is necessarily a negative one. For example, in a study of interethnic contacts (e.g., such as dating or marriage), those Japanese who were marginal in terms of ethnic identification and psychological orientation were found to be much more "liberal" in crossing ethnic boundary lines than their more "normal" cohorts.[5]

Of our cases of deviance—the mentally ill, the suicide, and the delinquent, a great many fall into the marginal classification. For example, Japanese delinquents can be differentiated from a matched group of non-delinquents on certain variables. The delinquent tends to be characterized by broken or conflict-ridden homes, a lack of ethnic identity and incongruent life-styles. Cases of suicide and mental illness also show a surprising degree of similarity. A recent suicide case involved a 35-year-old man from Japan who had little income or job security, was not a member either of the ethnic community or the majority community, had no close relatives or friends and finally killed himself over an unhappy love affair with a Caucasian divorcee. A recent case of mental illness that came to our attention involved a 40-year-old female, married to a non-Japanese, who, after the death of her husband, finding herself rejected by both families and unequal to the task of raising several young children by herself, had a psychotic break. A 22-year-old Sansei male, unable to get along with his parents, left home, married a Negro girl, and was recently arrested for robbery. Those are fairly typical patterns, and, it will be noticed, are similar to one another in most respects except the ultimate form of the expressive behavior.

The essential similarity of case histories of deviant Japanese appears to be more than coincidental. For this reason we feel that certain predictions can be made. It would seem to be relatively easy to differentiate between the "normal" and those with prospects for "deviant" behavior, so that most clinicians, in analyzing case histories, would be able to decide very accurately who is normal and who is potentially deviant. In other words, it will be relatively easy to

---

[5]Harry H. L. Kitano, "Passive Discrimination: The Normal Person," *The Journal of Social Psychology*, LXX (1966), pp. 23–31.

predict that many future deviants will come from the group that has been selected out on such variables as broken homes, lack of ethnic identity, and marginality. But it is more difficult to predict what direction the eventual deviance will take—whether an individual will become delinquent, criminal, or mentally ill—because these behavior patterns seem to derive from essentially similar histories. But finally, there are very few deviant individuals among the Japanese, because the ethnic community has been effective in providing a large enough umbrella to cover and control the development of a significant marginal group.

REASONS FOR [ACCULTURATION WITH A] SMALL MARGINAL POPULATION

Why have the Japanese been able to acculturate with such a small marginal population? Why have so many Japanese retained their ethnic identity? Why have so many remained with their ethnic community? Why have child socialization techniques been so effective? We have attempted to answer these questions in the broadest terms—the physical visibility of the Japanese; the difficulty they have had in entering the opportunity structures within the larger society; their relatively small numbers; the Japanese culture itself, with its cohesive family and community systems, and the effective enforcement of certain norms and values.

Some additional features of the Japanese culture also bear upon the problems of social control and social deviance. For example, the opportunities within that culture were open to virtually everybody with the correct ancestry, so that there was a place for everybody, no matter what his degree of talent, success, rank, or personality. If he was Japanese, he belonged. For instance, the typical Nisei basketball team of the 1930's included excellent, good, mediocre, and poor players who "belonged" equally—they bought the same club jackets, they shared in its activities, and they felt the same degree of club loyalty and acceptance. The current emphasis on winning is a recent phenomenon and brings with it selectivity, and small squads.

These changes surely reflect an important phase of acculturation. An American goal-orientation that values efficiency, success, winning, is taking over from a system more oriented toward ethical interaction, a system that valued means more than ends. And as the group changes from an inclusive system, in which most everybody belongs and which conduces to social control, to exclusive, where some are left out, it will face one common American dilemma—the maintenance of excellence and yet attempting to get everyone involved. It is difficult to retain social control over groups and individuals who feel no stake in the practices of that culture.

The New Yellow Peril

Tom Wolfe

suzie wong flower drum song no tickee no tong war no wonton no canton oriental pearly chop suey carry-out slanty-eyed family ties take care of our own charlie chan and his dragon dancers hoppy go bang-bang february red firecracker shredded fu manchu new year of rooster but none of your juvenile delinquency among our lilla fellas porcelain dolls almond-eye melon-seed miss chinatown my chinatown, and then an odd thing happened. One of our young Chinese tigers over here threw a cherry bomb at the stage. The damn thing landed on the chest of Dr. Robert Jenkins, Superintendent of Schools for San Francisco, and began rolling down his necktie. In that instant the bedlam in the auditorium actually died down. Everyone was fascinated, of course. A cherry bomb can blow the head off a parking meter, as quite a few souls in here already know. This particular cherry bomb is lit up with a weird silvery flame, like a party match. You can't take your eyes off it. . . . The moment begins to freeze. . . . Jenkins . . . thrust back stiff in his seat with his eyes bulging and peering straight down his nose at the sizzling little doom ball on his necktie. . . . His nose seems to have grown longer. . . . Whites—for the benefit of any who are interested in the local viewpoint—whites really have the noses; enormous, you might say. . . . Such a variety of bulbs and tubers . . . long and pointed like carrots, gibbous like green peppers, puffy like cauliflowers, hooked like a squash, hanging off the face like a cucumber. . . . They have protuberant eyes, too, whites do . . . they're tight in the lips, big in the hips, both men and women, and really inordinately hairy, most of them.

From *Esquire Magazine*, Decmber 1969, Vol. 73, No. 6, pp. 190-199 and 322. Reprinted by permission of the author c/o IFA. First published in *Esquire Magazine*, December, 1969.

. . . But just now it is the nose as the moment congeals, freezes . . . here in Chinatown, San Francisco. . . . Kung fu!

On November 27, 1968, the opening session of the "Free University of Chinatown Kids, Unincorporated" was held in a storage basement at 737½ Clay Street, just across from Chinatown's little public park, Portsmouth Square. Here they came, filing down the stairs for the F.U.C.K.U., about twenty Chinese student activists from San Francisco State and about thirty Chinese street youth, plus several whites from State and one odd guy in a raincoat. There were no windows down here and no way out except the way you came in. There were inscriptions on the walls and the overhead beams:

IF YOU'RE NOT INVOLVED IN THE STRUGGLE FOR YOUR PEOPLE, THEN YOU'RE OF NO USE TO YOURSELF, YOUR FAMILY, OR YOUR WOMAN—YOU'RE DEAD.

ENSLAVED PEOPLE OF THE WORLD NOW RISE TO DEMAND RECOGNITION OF THEIR HUMANITY: THOSE WHO JOIN THE MOVEMENT FEEL THE EMERGENCE OF NEW LIFE IN THEIR BLOOD, THOSE WHO WITHDRAW ARE SCREWING THE PEOPLE, THEIR FAMILIES, AND THEIR HUMANITY.

Also graffiti:

GO TO HELL YOU GOD DAMN MOTHERFUGGIN WHITE PIECE OF ALBINO NIGGER TOE ROACH.

Also a stack of picket signs:

WHY DO YOU SMILE WHEN WHAT YOU MEAN IS WHITE DEVIL?

And everybody wears yellow-and-black buttons reading:

YELLOW PERIL.

The Free University of Chinatown Kids, Unincorporated, is to have no faculty. Everyone is to learn from one another in the free university spirit. But with a man like George Woo around—well, he's formidable. He is in his thirties. He is bigger than most Chinese, husky, dressed in black, with long black hair and a full beard. He carries a silver-handled umbrella. He looks good and fierce . . . Kwang Kung-style! Just so.

They turn the lights out and the pictures start flashing up on the back wall. . . . "The history and problems of Chinatown." . . . *Yerba Buena Island, the immigration barracks, San Francisco's Ellis Island. . . .*

One of the kids in the dark: "Hey! it looks like a jail!"

George Woo: "Like a jail? Man, it is a jail."

. . . *A tinted drawing of Chinese working a gold mine in the 1850's. . . .*

". . . They let them work the abandoned mines, and then if they found any gold, the whites threw them out and took the mines back."

. . . *Chinese out in the scrublands building the transcontinental railroad. . . . The first Chinese policeman in San Francisco. . . .*

The kids start yelling: "Tom! He's a Tom!"

"Hayakawa!"

"He's got to go!"

"Off the mother!"

"No more Uncle Toms!"

"Right on!"

. . . So far they're right with the slide show, these boys. It's a laugh and a half . . . pictures of Ross Alley, Mason Alley . . . *Ross Alley,* man! Like, we could tell you about that freaking *Ross Alley* . . . and then Portsmouth Square, the little park in the center of Chinatown, jacked up over an underground parking garage. . . .

George Woo says, "It's named for a battleship, did you know that? It's named for an American battleship. . . ."

"Off the Portsmouth!"

"Right on!"

"On a good day, you'll see five hundred old men and a hundred fifty old women spending the day out in Portsmouth Square. If it rains, they have to crawl back in their holes in the rooming houses. . . ."

. . . *Cameron House,* the *Presbyterian mission in Chinatown* . . . an *old map of Chinatown.* Some of the boys begin to get restless. The white man in the raincoat starts picking up on that. . . . "How many slides you got?" he keeps saying.

A couple of Chinese turn around in the dark and tell him to shut his mouth. But he doesn't get it. "How many more slides you got? Show some topless, man! Show some movies!" Right! he's into that terrible bind where you're sure you have a laugh coming and you probe and probe and repeat and repeat. . . .

And then the voice of George Woo: "Shut up, honky!"

Well, now; the basement goes quiet except for the whirring of the slide machine and the voice of the white guy in the raincoat. He's still trying: "Bring on the Topless!"

In the light that seeps out of the side of the slide machine one can see George Woo closing in on the guy.

"Shut up or get out, honky!"

The fellow looks at George Woo in a really strange way. "What do you think you're doing, man?" The weird thing is, he really seems to mean it. He stands there blinking inside his raincoat—"You can't—"

"Bullshit!" says George Woo. "This is Chinatown, honky!"

The guy can't believe it . . . *honky!* . . . and hulking Genghis Khan in a beard. . . . He stares at George Woo a moment like he really can't figure it out . . . alone . . . in a basement in Chinatown with Chinese eyes pinned on him in the dark. . . .

"Well, now, wait a minute—"

"Bullshit!"

"—like, I mean, you know, the thing is, like, we're in this thing, and we're all here, and I mean, there's a *right,* you understand, and everybody's got to get his thing *together,* man! I mean, you can't—"

"Bullshit! If you don't get out of here, honky, I'll—"

"—get your thing together right on top of my *head,* like you're doing!"

"—throw you out!"

At this point, the white kid running the slide projector steps in. He's saying, to the white guy in the raincoat. "Listen, maybe you better go," and all of that business. He takes the guy's arm and steers him toward the stairs. Take my advice, friend—the guy is happy enough to have even ten percent of an out. He shambles up the stairs . . . the blue funk honky. . . .

This guy is a shambles and a shambler and a shaky drunk . . . but there it is! . . . *Honky* . . . sounding the black battle cry in Chinatown. . . .

The slide photographs keep flashing up on the wall . . . *Little Pete, Chinatown's number-one underworld character of the 1890's . . . An opium den. . . .*

And then the voice of George Woo, but distracted, as if he's thinking out loud: "I didn't call him honky because he was white. We have some white brothers who have done some of the things we should have done ourselves. I called him honky because he was a honky."

Over the next ten weeks it seemed like half the kids in Chinatown had started wearing the buttons saying

YELLOW PERIL

The F.U.C.K.U. had been part of the indoctrination phase of the movement. And now to see if the youth can be mobilized for the confrontation. On February 14, 1969, out in front of the San Francisco Unified School District administration building on Van Ness Avenue, fifty Chinese pickets were making the long picket loop and getting soaked for their trouble. . . . Mothering *rain,* friends. . . . Most of them were student militants from Berkeley and San Francisco State, plus a few liberals, and they were all looking up Van Ness for the Chinatown street youth to show. Like, where were the Wah Ching? That was one question. The Wah Ching, and the scores of Chinese high-school students who were presumably cutting out from school to come here and demand their rights. Everybody walked in the rain and looked up the avenue, up the six-lane hill, and all that happened was that the cardboard of the signs kept warping and rippling and getting that sopping sheen in the rain.

The cops looked on from under the portico over the main stairs. Man, despite all, despite all knowledge, it was still . . . a *bear* to see the Chinese into the protest thing.

On the picket line, every time the loop swung toward the hill on Van Ness, Alice Barkley looked for signs of the Wah Ching, the hard-core *machismo*. Alice Barkley was a slender Chinese woman, pretty, small-boned, delicate to look at, but such a demon organizer, such a terror when the heat is on—the Dragon Lady! She and George Woo and Kailey Wong had come closer than anyone to steering Chinatown's gang youth out of house jobs and all the rest of it and into political action. Alice Barkley had been studying architecture at Berkeley. Then she and her husband, Richard Barkley, a white, opened a coffee shop in Chinatown, on Waverly Place, called Il Piccolo. It started off as a coffee shop for "intellectuals" and became the Wah Ching's hangout. The Wah Ching—"Chinese Youth"—were about three hundred Hong-Kong-born street youth who made up Chinatown's largest and fiercest gang. Most spoke little or no English. They went for Il Piccolo. People like Alice Barkley and George Woo could speak Cantonese their way. Woo had come to Chinatown when he was fifteen. He had worked as a photographer but now began to concentrate more and more on the movement. Out of the long sessions at Il Piccolo had come the Wah Ching's big public meeting during the lunar New Year last year. It had been like a Black Power confrontation. The Wah Ching sounded the battle cry—*Bullshit!*—and threatened to burn down Chinatown, Watts style. They had protested that they could not get jobs, an education, or even a working knowledge of English and were desperate. George Woo did most of the talking for them. Their attack was not so much on the white "power structure," however, as on the Chinese "Establishment," the Six Companies. They said the Six Companies would not even use its influence, much less its wealth, to help them. It was like the Wah Ching were the Muslims of the Yellow Peril movement, the militant hard-core proles. The street revolution seemed to be starting. . . . But, friends, where were the Wah Ching today, at this moment, in the rain—

YELLOW LABOR CREATED CALIFORNIA . . . WHITE SHAME MARCHES TODAY . . . YELLOW PEOPLE NEED YELLOW EDUCATION . . . THE AVERAGE EDUCATION OF A CHINESE OVER TWENTY-ONE IS 1.7 YEARS . . . THE PRESENT SCHOOL SYSTEM MAKES YOU WHITE AS A SHEET . . . YELLOW? IMAGES? GOLD IS YELLOW . . . BORED OF EDUCATION . . . BORED OF EXPLOITATION . . . and Kailey Wong kept marching the loop. The rain poured down over his parka, his rimless glasses, his Fu Manchu beard. Like Alice Barkley, he was waiting for the street youth. Kailey Wong was twenty-three and the most independent and unusual leader among the Chinese youth. He was tied neither to the college activists, A.A.P.A. and I.C.S.A., nor a street gang. Until he was eighteen he was heavily into the street life and the gang life and went through many hassles with the police. Then he dropped out of high school and joined the Air Force for four years, two of them in Vietnam. He came back to Chinatown, started going to college at night and organized the Chinatown-North Beach Youth Council, pulling together members of gangs like the Chinatown Raiders and the Junior Wah Ching, but also straight groups such as the Cameron House youth. . . . Kailey Wong could almost hold onto the fantasy that the Chinese high-school students were ready to cut school and join the demonstration. For days they had been roaring through the halls of Galileo High School, throwing cherry bombs that exploded in the school corridors with the most terrific concussion. Chinese students had never dared wild stuff like that before, not even during the lunar New Year. But the mothering *rain!* Or might the youth of Chinatown be not so hot on the heels of the movement as the movement imagined. . . .

The rain was coming down and the time was running out. By now a few Leways—a coalition of some of the old American-born gangs—had shown up, and also a few of the junior-high-school youth, street types who were active in the Youth Council. Also there was a fairly large group of the Baby Wah Ching . . . boys in their early teens, born in America rather than in Hong Kong, who had adopted the name Wah Ching because the Wah Ching were the heaviest street characters in Chinatown. But as for the Wah Ching themselves—they hadn't shown.

Finally there was nothing to do but head inside the building. The police offered no resistance. In fact, they rather hospitably ushered the marchers down a long hall toward the school administration's main hall, Nourse Auditorium. In the huge 1930's-Grand auditorium the demonstrators were a lonesome band. The quiet and gloom of the place engulfed them. They had nobody to talk to but themselves. Ling-Chi Wang, one of the Berkeley intellectuals, took the microphone. He was a tall, scholarly Chinese with close-cropped hair.

"I understand that Dr. Jenkins is not around," he says, "but that Gordon Lau is trying to get Dr. Goldman and—"

"Hey, man, you too *polite!*"

What the hell is this? . . . a little contrapuntal jiving by the Baby Wah Ching in the first two rows.

"—Dr. Goldman and the other school administrators to come here—"

"Talk louder, man. . . . You too polite. . . ."

Alice Barkley jumps up from the audience and comes to the microphone and says: "Dr. Goldman is in the building but he refuses to come meet with us!"

This goes over better with the Baby Wah Ching. The catcalls start.

Alice Barkley goes on: "Gordon Lau is now upstairs trying to get the Acting Superintendent to come talk to this group . . . to the only ones in the school system who really know what's wrong—the people themselves!"

"The whole thing's wrong!" says a kid called Deerskin.

"Right on!"

"Get him down here!"

"Wellington Chew is in the building," says Alice Barkley, "and he is supposed to represent us in the school system, but he won't—"

"Get him down here!"

Ling-Chi Wang says: "I understand that two administrators, Dr. McElligott and Dr. Goldman, have agreed to appear before us. We must try to be orderly and put our point across."

"Burn it!"

"Shut it down!"

Wang says: "In the meantime I want to welcome the people from the adult-education classes, because they're the people who need our support the most, and—"

"Man, you too polite!"

Wang smiles in a melancholy way and says: "Perhaps that is my problem. I am too nice and too polite." But he says it so softly and calmly and directly to them that they don't say anything more.

Alice Barkley, who is back in the audience now, yells out: "They're upstairs listening!" She's pointing up toward the balcony. Way up in the balcony are two figures, a white man and Wellington Chew, the top Chinese school administrator. Shouts of derision. Alice Barkley gets up and says something to Bill Lee, Deerskin and Kailey Wong and points up at the balcony again. Bill Lee and Deerskin head up the aisle toward the rear doors. In a minute Lee returns. He has Chew with him. Chew is a slender man in a dark suit and a red tie. Alice Barkley jumps up:

"Wellington Chew is here. He isn't the man we wanted to talk to. We wanted *Jenkins* but Wellington Chew is here."

Chew turns out to be a cool one. The street youth are pinned on him for the first sign of weakness, but he is completely calm. "Of these twelve demands you have," he says, "I don't know the answer to all these questions. I have tried to set up . . ." and he moves immediately to very specific data about bilingual programs and so on, and while everyone is still trying to pick a point out of it all to challenge, he wraps it up and walks out of the hall unscathed.

Gordon Lau walks in with two school administrators, tall whites in grey suits. They're trying to keep the smiles of goodwill on their faces. Lau is a young Chinese lawyer who is running for the city Board of Supervisors as a liberal Democrat. He is a huge, powerful man, built like a Japanese Sumo wrestler. But he's quiet, almost as quiet as Wang. He introduces the whites, McElligott and Cobb, and says they have agreed to listen to the demands. He starts reading the demands. He talks about the need for education, especially in English, so Chinese will not be trapped in jobs like dishwasher and waiter.

"What job!" yells Deerskin. "I don't have any job! I'm hard core!"

Lau keeps on going, quietly, and some of the Baby Wah Ching start a stage-whisper chant: "Gung hay *fat* choy . . . gung hay *fat* choy . . ." which is Chinese for Happy New Year, but the way they're bearing down on the *fat* . . . obviously it's to needle Lau. Lau turns to McElligott and Cobb and says: "They're here to show their faces and show that they're not going to put us off. They assure us Dr. Jenkins will meet with us publicly very soon."

McElligott gets up to speak and leans into the microphone with a big smile of good fellowship on.

Voices from the crowd: "We can't hear you!"

McElligott breaks into a bigger, more anxious smile. The Baby Wah Ching have been waiting for a cat like this.

"Quit smiling!"

"You not happy, man! You scared!"

"I think it is a very appropriate and . . . forceful way that you have—"

"Quit smiling, man!"

"—that you have chosen to present your demands. I think there are some very fine points that you—"

"*All* of them are good, man!"

"Quit smiling!"

McElligott gets through the rest of it fast, and in no time he and Cobb are up and out of here and the demonstrators are left by themselves again.

Suddenly there is an outcry from Alice Barkley, in the rear: "I don't give a damn about the Six Companies and the Chinese Chamber of Commerce!" She's screaming at a white woman. The woman's about sixty. She has white hair. She's the type of old party who carries shopping bags and hangs around city bureaus as the concerned citizen. God knows what she's doing here . . . except staring back at Alice Barkley. Aghast is the word. . . .

"I don't give a damn!" says Alice Barkley. "We're tired of you white folks telling us what to do!" She turns toward the crowd: "She just told me we have the Six Companies and the Chinese Chamber of Commerce to represent us! She told me the white people pay all the taxes, and we have to be patient! We have people here who can't speak English and can't get any work or enough to eat, and she's talking to me about paying taxes and being patient! Well, Chinese have to pay taxes, too, even if they're only making seventy-five cents an hour!"

But the woman is so . . . *old*, man. . . . It doesn't get the job done. . . . Kailey Wong goes up front and takes the microphone.

"Hey, man!" he says, and the street youth swing around to the familiar tone. "You see, The Man gave you the shine job just now . . . see? . . . right. . . . The Chinese people are nice quiet cats . . . you know . . . So they figure they can come in here and shine us on . . . see? . . . and like, the only way they're gonna wake up is for us to have some Yellow Soul, man, some Yellow Soul—"

Emperor of Soul time . . . yes . . . the street youth are fascinated. . . . This Kailey Wong can turn it on any way he chooses, street, Soul, or straight. Right now the whole demonstration seems about to sink back into the sodden monsoon swamp from where it started. . . . This is a job for the Emperor of Soul.

"It's not enough to be Chinese . . . see? . . . You got to have some Yellow Soul. . . . That cat who was up here, he was Chinese . . . right? . . . But he's a Tom! man. . . . See, he's right out there . . ." and he points up the aisle to where Wellington Chew is standing just outside the door, ". . . he's a Tom in a three-button suit, and he's shining you on just like the rest of them who come in here with the three-button suits and the Big Shine!"

Two of the Baby Wah Ching start pointing at Gordon Lau:

"Hey! he's got the three-button suit!"

"You a *Tom,* man?"

"This cat's got a *three-button suit!*"

Gordon Lau just shakes his head.

After the demonstration Alice Barkley, Bill Lee, Gordon Lau and a few of the others had lunch at a Chinese restaurant called Ernie's, on Polk Street. Gordon Lau was still shaking his head. "Those Baby Wah Ching are something. . . . But I guess they can be amusing if they're on your side."

"They're looking for some action," said Alice Barkley. "I had to come on like I did, Gordon, I had to come on militant, because those kids were ready to tear that place apart. I had to do that to pacify them. That was the only way I *could* pacify them. They come all the way down to the school administration building, and nothing's happening. I had to have them bring Wellington Chew downstairs. We had to *do* something."

Bill Lee said: "I went up there and told him he had to come down and he kept saying: 'I don't know if I should say anything or not.' I told him if he didn't, they were ready to go up and pull Goldman downstairs bodily."

"Gordon," said Alice Barkley, "you can't talk to these kids like a lawyer. They've heard too much talk. If nothing happens, they'll make it happen."

Lau gave her a slightly ironic smile. "Maybe I'm too Americanized for what you're talking about."

"Sometimes I think you are, Gordon."

Of the three older spokesmen at the demonstration—Gordon Lau, Ling-Chi Wang and Alice Barkley—only Alice Barkley had really been at ease with the Black Soul style that was catching on among the Chinese youth. Gordon Lau was a successful lawyer with white partners and many white clients. He had grown up in Chinatown, now lived out in "The Avenues," a section of small but neat and genteel detached homes on San Francisco's west side. The Avenues were one step before the move to the suburbs. Lau had never learned Chinese; it was seldom spoken at home. Like a lot of middle-class Chinese who lived outside of Chinatown, he was amused by the way whites would ask him about esoteric details of Chinese culture . . . as if he carried Chinese culture around with him in his attaché case. Nevertheless, he was one of the few younger middle-class Chinese who had started working on Chinatown's latter-day problems. The idea of Yellow Soul, however, was foreign to him.

Ling-Chi Wang was at home, intellectually, on the New Left and with the "Third World" idea of an alliance between blacks and orientals—but psychologically he was the Chinese Scholar. In fact, that was what he studied and taught at Berkeley . . . the Chinese classics. The Scholar was the most revered figure in traditional Confucian culture. As in Christian culture up to a hundred fifty years ago, the scholar had a quasi-religious role as the repository of tradition. Wang always had the scholar's dignity and genteel bearing, qualities that often made him an effective buffer in the more complex dealings of the movement. But Soul was not his style, either. . . .

In fact, it was remarkable that the black style had caught on even among the youth in Chinatown. In terms of income, education and housing, Chinatown was as much a slum as the Negro districts like the Fillmore and Hunters' Point. But there the resemblance ended. The landlords in Chinatown were Chinese, not white. The merchants, from the smallest smoke shop to the largest import-export firm, were Chinese, not Jewish or anything else. And the police—the police had tended to leave Chinatown alone. The Chinese who came to California in the 1850's had been impoverished and often illiterate farm people, but psychologically they never really felt downtrodden. They were leaving the center of the civilized world, the Celestial Empire, to make their fortune out among the barbarians. Even in the late 1940's and '50's a Chinese boy was likely to grow up with his father talking about whites not as The Man, or anything like it, but as *lo fan* or *bok gooi*. *Lo fan* means *foreigner*. It is what the villagers in Kwangtung called the British when they invaded Canton in 1839, came sailing up to the Pearl River in gunboats. To many of the "overseas Chinese" in San Francisco after World War II, the 600,000-or-so whites in town were still the foreigners. Occasionally in the family they might call the whites "Americans," but that was the same thing. They, the whites, were the only Americans in America. Not that the concept was necessarily screwy. . . . *Bok gooi* had even more spin on it. Many a boy spent his early childhood thinking this term *bok gooi* was just Chinese for *white*, it was used so much, in such an offhand way. What *bok gooi* actually means is white devil. It comes from the Opium-War times in Kwangtung Province, too—the white devil, the barbarian, the Hun, the heathen, the uncultured, the primitive. There are plenty of Chinese restaurants today where the whites come in and sit down and order their won ton soup, sweet and sour pork, egg rolls, fortune cookies, and the waiter leaves the table and says to the busboy, "*Bok gooi* at table 16." On the immediate, practical level, it merely lets the busboy know that a party of whites just sat down and he should set up the table with forks instead of chopsticks. Yet some of the original scorn is still imbedded in the words. Any Chinese who sees those forks being laid out on the table instead of chopsticks —well, another silent insult for the *bok gooi*.

As for Negroes, they were the *hok gooi*, black devils. They weren't known as anything much, except dumb and strong. If you had to move a lot of heavy stuff around or haul it upstairs, it was good to call on the *hok gooi*. Intermarriage with whites was forbidden, but even fraternization with the *hok gooi*—it was almost too remote to think about.

The common word for a Chinese person was *T'ang jen*. Like if you're talking about something that happened on the street, and you want to indicate that one of the guys involved was Chinese, you say *T'ang jen*, which means T'ang person, son of the T'ang dynasty. Right! from the seventh century A.D. You grew up with the feeling that all of Chinatown was wired directly to Kwangtung Province of olden times. In a way it was. One of the main reasons was that although thousands of Chinese had come to San Francisco in the 1850's, only a few thousand children were born here before World War II. There had been no real "second generation." In hard times, village families in the Canton area would send their young men to Hong Kong, Macao, Shanghai, Singapore, the Philippines, Hawaii or California, to make money and send it or bring it back home. They left their wives and children behind and expected to return home rich enough to buy land. There were almost no women in Chinatown other than prostitutes. In 1884 there were 32,000 Chinese in San Francisco, but only 1400 females, and very few children. The Chinese Exclusion Act of 1882 ended immigration to Chinatown. Also, many Chinese returned to China. For one thing, anti-Chinese feeling in San Francisco had gone wild. Chinese were not permitted to testify in court. By 1920 the population of Chinatown had dropped to about 7000, with males outnumbering females three and a half to one. During the Twenties and Thirties, the proportion of women rose, due to an increase in illegal immigration. But by 1940 there were still only 18,000 Chinese in San Francisco, with males outnumbering females slightly more than two to one.

Strictly speaking, Chinatown's "second generation" was born during the Twenties and Thirties, but it wasn't big enough to change much of anything in Chinatown. Besides, many second-generation Chinese, if they had the money or the education, would move out of Chinatown. Chinatown was run by a clan system that had been transplanted straight from the villages. Back home the farm people had lived in houses packed together in compounds, sometimes surrounded by walls, and they went out from there in the morning to work in the fields. The clan elders ran everything in the village, from settling disputes to operating the schools. From the beginning Chinatown had a hierarchy of family and district associations—clan organizations—with the Six Companies at the top. The Six Companies were not a group of commercial firms, although they accumulated plenty of wealth, but a council of elders from all the major clans. They ran the whole system—just as in China. Most of the terrific buildings in Chinatown with the pagoda roofs and balconies and so on—they belonged to the family associations, the district associations, and the Six Companies—the clans —just as in China. In fact, the ties with China were direct. In 1912, after the Manchu dynasty fell and the Republic began, the Chinese in Chinatown cut off their queues—just as in China. Until after World War II Chinatown was really more old-fashioned, more nineteenth-century Chinese, than Canton itself.

The shortage of women was a fierce thing for a closed community like Chinatown. World War II brought some women, or at least indirectly it did. During the war the Exclusion Act was repealed as a kindly gesture to America's Chinese allies. Five thousand Chinese brides came to Chinatown, many from Hong Kong. In the Forties and Fifties Chinatown started having what was, for Chinatown, a baby boom. The population rose fast, but inside, there was the psychological hold of the whole old-country system, the Six Companies and all the rest of it. Outside, there was the anti-Chinese feeling of the whites. It wasn't as blatant as it had been before the war, but Chinese who didn't have an American education had almost no chance of getting jobs other than things like cleaning out ashtrays in the lobby of the Fairmont Hotel. Outside of Chinatown they couldn't even get jobs as waiters. Frankly, you never thought about anti-Chinese prejudice, it never hit you in person, until you were eleven or twelve and went to junior high school and got called Chink or Chinaman for the first time. The public elementary schools, like Commodore Stockton or Jean Parker, were ninety-five percent Chinese. The teachers were mostly white, white women, and the language was English, of course. But after public school let out for the day, you went to Chinese school, every day, for two hours, to learn to read and write Chinese . . . climbing those old brown steps in the Six Companies building on Stockton, up into those old brown halls, and the brown rooms, row on row, Chinese boys and girls, chanting the lessons out loud, in unison, singing them out, learning by rote. The Chinese teachers were always stricter than the white ladies, and they would whop you over the knuckles for cutting up or not doing the lessons or otherwise playing the fool.

The Chinese school! Every day! Practically every kid in Chinatown! But even there, in the bosom of Chinese culture, some of the . . . exotic complications . . . came in. The lessons were in Cantonese, which was the natural thing, since almost every family in Chinatown originated in the Canton area. But there are many different dialects of Cantonese, and the schools taught the most high-class dialect, the Sam Yup. So you take your lessons home and get your father to help, and you come back the next day, and you've got it all wrong! Your father, who speaks and reads Chinese, got it all wrong! Unbelievable! Then you discover that what your father speaks is See Yup, which next to Sam Yup is regarded as almost like, you know, *hick*. One of life's early downers, man. It was startling to find out that your father spoke the wrong dialect. Your father was the most important figure in your life. The cardinal Confucian virtue, filial piety, was the strongest thing a boy learned.

Came the time when you had to leave the shell of Chinatown, that was when you climbed on the Number 30 Stockton bus in the morning and first headed off to Galileo High School. There were all the placid white business types in their three-button suits and the white girls in their page-boy bobs, and packed in between them on the bus were a bunch of Chinese kids with epidemic tachycardia. You had to get off the bus at Bay and Polk and start climbing up the hill to Gal, which has walls around it like an Alamo. And up the hill . . . *they* would be waiting . . . the black kids over here and the Italian kids over here, the *hok gooi* and the *bok gooi*. And they'd start the stuff about Chink and Chinaman, and every day there was somebody who had to fight or be humiliated. Both the white kids and the black kids were bigger than the Chinese the same age, and half the time it was like the Terror. *Kung fu* wasn't going to help you, and your father wasn't going to help you. You could draw a map of Galileo High School, into the territories that each group occupied before school, during recess and after school, the black land, the white land, and the yellow land.

What the hell were you doing here? As far as the big-deal school activities went, like the football team and the basketball team and all that went with it, you might as well have been from Venus. No Chinese could make those teams or get into all that. That was all for the big whites and the big blacks and their girl-friend cheerleaders, and who cared if they won or lost. You'd end up half-way wishing they would get their asses kicked in. You were going to get yours kicked in, in any case, because after school the same stuff started all over.

It was really the whole high-school scene that first made you think about your father and your family and Chinatown in relation to the white status system. White kids might invite you over to their house or their apartment some after-noon—and you'd think these white kids must be millionaires. The *space* they lived in! Everybody had his own bedroom! They had dining rooms that weren't used for anything except meals! It was incredible. . . . Then you would find out that the kid's father was nothing but an insurance salesman or a construction foreman. This was just the way ordinary whites lived. It seemed like almost every kid in Chinatown had grown up in a household where everybody and everything was crowded into two or three little rooms. If a family had a twelve-by-twelve-foot square of open floor space, that was *Sunset* magazine stuff by Chinatown standards.

Even today, most of the Hong Kong immigrants, for example, can't afford anything more. The father is a dishwasher or a busboy at seventy-five cents an hour, and the mother is sewing dresses in the storefront sweatshops at fifty cents an hour, and the five of them, father, mother, two children, and the grandmother, are crowded into a couple of little rooms in one of the rooming houses that was built when there were nothing but men in Chinatown. There are twenty or thirty rooms to a floor and one bathroom and one kitchen. Now fifteen families are on one floor. They have to take turns doing the simplest things. They stand in line in the morning to go to the bathroom, holding their towels, toothpaste, toothbrush, razor, or whatever, in their hands and shuffle forward in the gloom to the tubercular beat of the toilet flushing. They have to stand in line for the kitchen. They eat standing up, because there aren't enough places to sit down. A lot of people take turns sleeping, "hot-bedding," sleeping shifts.

But even people who have some money—they will still live in two or three little rooms, in an apartment, or out back of their shop or laundry, or whatever they have. Nobody wants to blow money on rent, or on furniture, for that matter. Those photographs you see of beautiful Chinese furniture, the K'ang cupboards, the lute tables, the canopied beds, the Ming coffee tables, the carved screens, lohan chairs, painting tables, all that geometric carving and satiny wood and burled inlays and brass hinges and lake red lacquer—a lot of kids in Chinatown grow up thinking it is all in museums or in the front parlors of the Chinese landlords. You might have a small K'ang table or a rosewood chest in the apartment, but the rest of the place would be just stuff stacked up and pushed together, mattresses, electrical cords, ironing boards, a radio, a TV set, with a sewing machine out on the kitchen table between meals, suitcases with clothes packed in them because there aren't enough closets, and so on. The thing was, everybody was saving money to buy real estate or to send it back to relatives in China so they could buy real estate. That was the big goal in life, to own some land. It was a sound idea. But as with a lot of other things in Chinatown, this was something, this urge to own land, that went back to the villages of the Pearl River delta, where all of life had been a scramble to acquire more land for more crops. Three acres had been practically an estate. . . .

It got harder and harder for you to look up to your elders when you saw the kind of life a lot of the white kids led. The way they talked, the way they acted, the way they acted toward girls—they broke all the rules, but they still had everything. You wanted to bring up the whole school hassle to your father, in the hope that he would have the solution to the puzzle. But he would always have the same answer for everything—the eight Confucian ideals, starting with filial piety and going from there to moderation in all things.

If you made white friends in school, you were likely to be too embarrassed to invite them to your home. It was not just because you knew it would look shabby and cramped. It was more because the whole Chinatown thing would seem old-fashioned. It was like you had to live a split life if you wanted to make it in Chinatown and on the outside. And if a boy ever pushed it too hard on the outside and got into trouble with the police, that would be it. As likely as not his father would disown him, drum him out of the family, not even furnish bail, because he had dishonored the house. This went back to the Chinese villages, too—where the ultimate punishment within the family had been expulsion from the clan. In China that had often been tantamount to a death sentence, unless a youth had the moxie to become a bandit. In Chinatown there were always the gangs. They were just down the street.

It was funny in a way. At the very time the whites were building up their main fantasy about Chinatown—which goes: there is no juvenile deliquency in Chinatown, because the Chinese have such close family ties—at the very time the whites were enjoying this fantasy, namely, in the Fifties and early Sixties, the street gang thing was really building up in Chinatown. Nobody seemed to realize it, but Chinatown's first real "second generation" was now growing up. All the babies born during the war and just after were moving into their teens. And more and more families were moving into Chinatown from Hong Kong and Taiwan, but mostly Hong Kong. Immigration regulations were eased some more in 1962, and over the next seven years about 30,000 Chinese immigrated to San

Francisco. The population of Chinatown itself rose to about 50,000—and half of them were less than twenty-one years old. There were American-born gangs like the Raiders and the 895's, who later came together in the Leways, and foreign-born gangs like the Wah Ching. The American-born kids used to call the Hong Kong kids "Chinabugs," but they didn't keep that up very long, because the Wah Ching was the biggest gang in Chinatown, with about three hundred members, and the roughest.

But the whole gang thing, American-born or foreign born, was more like part of the general way Chinese youth were looking for a new, non-Chinese style of life. They seemed to try out a lot of things white kids had popularized five or ten years earlier. The Chinatown gangs were sort of 1949 New York Turf style, with the gang jackets, colors, pompadours, and the hard-bop gang girls with mini-skirts and beehive hairdos. One group of the Leways was heavy into the 1955 Southern California style of customized cars. They had a fleet of Chevrolets that were jacked up front and back, until they rose up about seven feet off the road and the grilles gaped over the street like they were about to roll over small cars and devour the mothers. . . . Later another group of the Leways went deep into the psychedelic thing, with all that went with it, including the heavy mysteries of the *I Ching,* which they seemed to prize not so much because it was Chinese, but because it was 1966 Hip Psychedelic. One of the few really local styles was the Bugs'. The Bugs were both Hong Kong kids and American-born—unified mainly by a common interest in house jobs. They were the wildest burglary gang that ever hit Chinatown, even wilder than the Wah Ching. They dressed entirely in black, including black pompadours, black jackets, black jeans and high black Tom Jones boots. They were mostly in their teens, but small, some of them less than five feet tall, slender, agile, renowned for their ability to slither through tiny openings, climb drains and roofs, and so on. There was something about the idea of tiny super-burglars that appealed to a lot of Chinese youth who had no interest in gang activities at all. The Bugs turned smallness of stature—one of the sore points when you were in high school—into a daring advantage, almost comic-book style . . . Micro-Man! All sorts of kids, including the most studious and well-behaved, began to adopt the Bugs' all-black look.

But the idea that Chinese youth would look to the Negroes for a way out, to the *hok gooi*—nobody would have bought that. If anything Chinese boys grew up feeling they were more like the Jews. Chinese culture had the same intense emphasis on education. Chinese parents drilled home the idea that a boy should never fight physically, only with his brain. Chinese families tended to be adept at business, even the village people. Even in the villages the arts of credit and accounting were well-known because moneylending had become a highly developed practice in the centuries-old scramble for land in an overpopulated country. In San Francisco it was as likely to be the Chinese as the Jews who operated the grocery stores in the Negro districts. Even socially the Chinese were somewhat like the Jews. White Christian families might frown on intermarriage with Chinese, but there was no horror at the thought as there was with the thought of Negroes. In fact, Chinese parents were likely to object more than white parents in the case of intermarriage. Whites were ten times more likely to adopt Chinese orphans than Negro orphans, and half-white half-Chinese orphans—"Eurasians"—were fairly easy to place with white families. Educated Chinese had fairly easy entry into white business firms in San Francisco at the middle levels, although not the upper . . . again, like the Jews.

There were other reasons for Chinese youth not to identify with the blacks. Serious warfare had erupted between black and Chinese street gangs in the early 1960's. It wound up with a black gang commandeering a city bus at the Aquatic Park turnaround and attempting to barrel into Chinatown like a blitzkrieg. . . . The cops headed them off. The Wah Ching fought it out with black gangs many times. The Wah Ching—even the ones who had never been near a school—used to descend on the school ground at Samuel Gompers High, the remedial school over in the Mission district, when trouble broke out between Chinese and blacks there. Yet curiously Gompers was one of the places where the black thing got its start among the Chinese youth.

In Chinatown, Gompers was known as a dumping ground where Chinese teen-agers who couldn't speak English got trapped with other outcasts of the school system, including the most bad-ass elements of the Negroes and the Mexicans. The Chinese teen-agers who ended up at Gompers, many of them immigrants from Hong Kong, found that Chinese culture—obedience, filial piety, hard work, self-respect—didn't mean a damn thing at Gompers. Being a cool and bad-ass cat, that was all that mattered. The gangs ran the show at Gompers, the bloods and the Mexicans, but mainly the bloods. They were loud, violent, sexually aggressive—stuff that really stunned most Chinese. But if it was the bloods who ran the show, maybe the thing to do was to get in on their thing. . . . That was when one really started seeing some exotic sights in Chinatown. Here came Chinese kids who really had the *gait,* man, down pat, that cooooool rolling gait, with the hips and the shoulders turning over like the wheels on a railroad engine. And for kids who spent any time in Juvenile Hall—well, the bloods *ran* Juvenile Hall, they ran the show, coined the slang, set the styles, and any kid, Chinese or not, who spent much time in there would come out macking around with the bloods' way of coming on.

But what really put the Soul thing over in Chinatown was the way San Francisco's young Negroes started swinging with Black Power. Negroes had rioted in the Fillmore and Hunters' Point sections in 1966, but it wasn't that. It was the way they had capitalized on the fear tremor the riots had kicked off in the whites. Heavy cats like Orville Luster had come walking into City Hall with gunnysacks full of knives, guns, Molotov cocktails, weaponry great and small, and dumped it on the buffered walnut conference table and announced: "This is just some of the stuff I was able to take off the boys yesterday, but I can't keep it cool down there forever, man." Pretty soon the City has people running down there with money waving from every fist, and social workers, youth workers, survey takers, Office of Economic Opportunity cats and God knows who all, lighting up the very darkness with their good shuck sunshine smiles. The blacks were truly getting their thing together, to use the parlance of the movement, and the lesson of how you do it was not lost on other groups in San Francisco, such as the Chicanos, the Samoans—right! Samoans—and the Chinese.

Even the oriental intellectuals at Berkeley began to see the significance of the hard times in Chinatown. The Chinese and Japanese intellectuals had always ignored Chinatown as backward and uncultivated. But now they formed the Asian-American Political Alliance and saw Chinatown as "the people," the Soul mass of the revolution. One of them was Alice Barkley, who had come to Berkeley from Hong Kong in 1957 to study architecture.

Other Chinese students were getting into the movement at San Francisco State College. Again, it was the blacks who set the style and the pace by starting the wild student strike that ended up with the Third World movement squared off against S. I. Hayakawa. The Chinese students at State started the Intercollegiate Chinese for Social Action. They were closer to the street youth of Chinatown than the Berkeley intellectuals were. They set up their basement headquarters at 737½ Clay, where the "free university"—F.U.C.K.U.—was held.

The black thing—Soul—began to seem like the way out for a lot of "good" Chinese kids at Galileo, too. *Soul* had music, dance, a whole vocabulary and a whole new way of looking at the world built into it. By late 1968 Galileo High School was just about seventy percent Chinese—more than double the percentage for 1960—but at the school dances, now run by the Chinese, the music was always Soul, and you would see kids doing Negro dances like the popcorn and referring to each other as "bloods" and slapping each other's palms in the bloods' approved Confidential Jive street greeting.

And down at the Leways'—some of the boys were ready to go the stone total way with the black thing. Leway was shorthand for "Legitimate Way." The implication, a couple of years ago, had been that here were the street youth going straight, forming a public-service club. Lim P. Lee, San Francisco's Chinese postmaster, and other prominent citizens, and various organizations, had backed them and helped them find space at 615 Jackson, where they set up a pool hall and a soda fountain, the Fountain of Youth. The Leways were not really "hard core." Many were middle-class by Chinatown standards and had the money to try out exotic life-styles like the customized cars and psychedelia. And now the entryway to the Leway pool hall had some new posters, alongside the psychedelic: portraits of Huey Newton and Eldridge Cleaver of the Black Panthers. Inside the pool hall itself, on the back wall, was a shoji screen covering a blind window. If you spun the screen around, there was the face of the chairman, Mao Tse-tung. The Leways were now in a factional fight over whether to keep on the psychedelic route or to go Red Guard. Red Guard, the radical vanguard of Red China itself. Clifford Tom, Raymond and Alex Hing, Al Wong, Ted Kajiwara and the others backing this idea didn't really have the Red Chinese model in mind, however. They looked to the Black Panthers, Soul Rebel heroes of the Bay Area. They were already tight with some of them, like Dave Hilliard, the Panther chief of staff. It was now Emperor of Soul time good and true.

One of our young Chinese tigers over here just threw a cherry bomb at the stage. The damn thing landed on the chest of Dr. Robert Jenkins, Superintendent of Schools for San Francisco, and began rolling down his necktie. In that instant the bedlam in the auditorium had actually died down. A cherry bomb can blow the head off a parking meter, as quite a few souls in here already know. This particular cherry bomb is lit up with a weird silvery flame, like a party match. You can't take your eyes off it. . . . The moment begins to freeze . . . Jenkins . . . thrust back stiff in his seat with his eyes bulging and peering straight down his nose at the sizzling little doom ball in his necktie. . . . His nose seems to have grown longer . . . the moment congeals, freezes . . . here in Chinatown, San Francisco, in the auditorium of the Commodore Stockton Elementary School, where Jenkins and five other administrators of the San Francisco United School District sit in a row at a table for a public forum on the educational needs of Chinatown . . . in their three-button suits . . . King fu!

The demonstration at the school administration building on Van Ness two weeks ago may have been no great deal in itself, but it had been enough to make Jenkins and his colleagues decide to come to Chinatown and hold this public forum. But did they know this was lunar New Year time in Chinatown? Not exactly the time to tempt fate in Chinatown. Wellington Chew must have known, and he was with them. . . .

One has to hand it to them, however; they did very well at first. There were a lot of friendly older Chinese faces in the center rows, also many white teachers, and the audience looked manageable. Lady schoolteachers in San Francisco look forward to retiring to Chinatown elementary schools, precisely because ninety-five percent of the pupils are Chinese, obedient little boys and girls with identical round black haircuts. Yes. . . . True, these young Chinese studs in the seats on the sides with all the insolent hair on their heads look a bit feisty. Could it be the fuses in their eyeballs? But the nerve gas seems to keep all pacified.

Jenkins and his colleagues started off with a grand drizzle of statistics and terminology. The *N.E.A. Journal* itself never did it any better.

". . . budget of eighty-two million dollars . . ."

". . . tax ceiling of ninety-seven million . . ."

". . . anticipated Federal moneys . . ."

". . . urban factor . . ."

". . . teacher-pupil ratio . . ."

". . . bad linkage with the State Labor Department. . . ."

They had everybody nodding off left and right. It was like nerve gas. The first hint of the shitfire came when a cherry bomb went off in a stairwell or bath-

room beyond the auditorium. Jenkins looked up. It truly startled him. One wonders how it looks to him as he looks up and out upon this spread of Chinese
faces. How much does he know? . . . Panthers! . . . Edging in through the doors
in the back of the auditorium were, like, Panthers, man . . . boys in field jackets
and Navy blue warm-up jackets and black pants wearing buttons reading YEL-
LOW PERIL. . . . One has to savor that a bit. . . . You couldn't tell if they were
just standing in the aisles because there were no more seats or if they were . . .
Panthers! . . . They had miles of straight black hair, these kids. With most of
them it was parted on the side and hung down straight over the forehead, the
sides, the back of the neck, in the current mode of Honest hangdown College
Hip. Al Wong—not that Jenkins ever heard of Al Wong—even had a beret and
shoulder-length hair in the old Sierra Maestra Che fashion. A few younger boys,
Baby Wah Ching, not more than fourteen or fifteen years old, had gone all the
way down front and were sitting on the edge of the stage itself, over to one
side. And then, from the rear, came the first cry of "Bullshit." . . . You would
think that all school bureaucrats would know the format by now. First, the
bureaucrats, or faculty, or school board, or whoever, come out on stage in their
three-button suits, and the charade of parliamentary give-and-take begins. They
try to be very reasonable, very specific, you understand, no bullshit, for The
Youth will no longer tolerate bullshit, just honest facts and figures in an earnest
drizzle. Then, nevertheless, comes, always, the cry, which is "Bullshit!" . . . But
in Chinatown? from our friends the Chinese? and in this weird spade accent?

"Bullshit! Don't try to shine us on with these *numbers,* man!"

"We're tired of the same old bullshit!"

"Right on! Right on!"

Each of these Bullshit solos receives a choral reprise of "Right on" from a
few militants in the rear like Raymond Hing here, of the Leway-Red Guard, but
also some are Chinese girls . . . quite an addition to the barricades. They have
long hair hanging straight down, steel-rim granny glasses, black bell-bottoms . . .
shouting "Right on!" which was originally a Negro shout-service response,
meaning You're right on the mark, brother, or on the case. One wonders what
the San Francisco Unified School District administrators think of this. These
Chinese kids don't have Chinese accents and they don't have the standard California white accent. In fact, if you close your eyes, these are the voices of bloods,
blacks . . . *shine job, right on, off the pigs, stone fascist, house nigger.* . . .

One guy—he happens to be Japanese, Ted Kajiwara, also of the Leways, but
no time for complicated distinctions just now—one guy yells out: "You're nothing but a bunch of white racist running dog house nigger—" pause for *le mot
juste* "—liberals!"

"Right on! Right on!"

"Off the pigs!"

"To the wall!"

Right on the case, boys, and stomping up and down most smartly. A tall
Leway jumps up on one edge of the stage and starts pointing at a white man in

the audience on the other side. "That's him! Let's hear him talk! That's him right there!"

The white man sits tight. One can't help but feel sorry for him. He has white hair, he wears glasses, he is thin, pale, and good and worried; a junior-high-school guidance counselor, as it turns out, named Leland McCormick.

"That's him right there, with the glasses on!"

McCormick takes his glasses off . . . very wily, these whites . . . as if *perhaps, if I am.* . . . That only prompts another kid, very big for a Chinese, to jump up on the stage and open up a grin to total copyrighted Black Panther grinning menace and start yelling:

"You *scared,* man! You scared!"

. . . Well, hell, yes. . . .

Suddenly a rangy Negro, a high-school student, is out of the aisle, yelling at Jenkins: "How can you sit there and tell these jive-ass hypocritical lies? You got this, like, jive-ass educational bullshit, and it's, like, one big jive-ass. . . ." This word jive-ass starts getting to the kid. It starts wrapping around him like a turban, like a flamenco sash, like an epiphyte, like a flag, like a python, an octopus, ". . . I mean, like, you *talk* jive-ass, man, then you *do* jive-ass, and this hypocritical jive-ass ain't relevant to the Third World peoples, it's just jive-ass, and you sit there with *both hands* on the jive-ass hypocritical jive-assing jive-ass!"

"Right on! Right on!"

At this moment a great roar from the rear: "Bullshit!" The ultimate pronunciamento, friends. . . . It's George Woo, which may mean nothing to Jenkins & Co., either . . . but one wonders . . . they have eyes . . . George Woo is barreling down the aisle, a big Chinese with the full Kwang Kung beard, carrying an umbrella in one hand and a piece of paper in the other. He jumps up on the stage and bangs the piece of paper down in front of Jenkins—"Look at this!"

Scores of our *T'ang jen* out in the aisles now, chanting the old refrains—Alice Barkley is in the aisle leading it like a cheer:

"On strike! Shut it down! On strike! Shut it down!"

"Right on!"

And . . . so . . . a cherry bomb loops up and lands on Jenkins' chest, the moment congeals, freezes, the air is sucked out . . . then the action spins forward, the cherry bomb keeps rolling and lands on the floor at Jenkins' feet . . . a *dud,* man. . . . Nevertheless, the hell with that. Jenkins and the administrators back up out of their chairs, grabbing sheafs of paper. Another cherry bomb sails over their heads and explodes behind them. Explosions and smoke. The air is full of miscellaneous shitfire, cherry bombs, firecrackers, eggs. Outside, in the dark, under the streetlamps, kids surround the exits. They let McCormick have it with the eggs. Screams, cops, cherry bombs, a regular madhouse. . . . A woman hits the sidewalk. . . . Three detectives pick this moment to try to arrest a member of the Leways for draft evasion. Other kids surround them and wrestle the kid away from them. The whole crowd goes running down Clay Street and into the traffic on Grant. . . . In Chinatown, man? In Chinatown? . . . It starts raining like hell.

And who might this Very Earnest fellow be, sitting in front of Dr. Dennis Wong? The first of the parade? Is there now to be a parade of white reporters coming to Chinatown to celebrate the troubles, the crisis, "the breakdown of the old order." . . . One can only take a deep breath. . . . Dennis Wong, Doctor of Pharmacy, proprietor of the Safety Pharmacy, and, currently, President of the Six Companies, can look from his desk out across the great nave of the Six Companies hall, out across the floor balustrades and great conference table, down the rows of lohan chairs, to the portraits of Sun Yat-sen and Chiang Kai-shek and the flags of the Republic of China and the United States there on the far wall . . . and all the time, in the foreground, just across his desk, is the reporter from New York, a young man with hair in his face and that Very Earnest look. . . .

To think it was only twenty years ago—only yesterday!—that the white press was running pictures of Albert Chow, former President of the Six Companies, smiling and shaking hands with his great friend, Harry Truman. Albert Chow was always identified in the captions as "unofficial Mayor of Chinatown." The unwritten caption was: "All is well. The Chinese know how to govern themselves. . . ." Of course, nobody in Chinatown called or even thought of Albert Chow as the Mayor of Chinatown, but that was all right. . . . The main thing was that, in fact, once, years ago, the Six Companies *did* govern Chinatown. . . .

. . . And now the youth are openly disobedient. Not many weeks ago some of them broke the windows of this building. Perhaps now is the appointed time for Dr. Dennis Wong. He is in his mid-thirties, the youngest president of the Six Companies, this council of elders, in anybody's memory. . . . Surely he knows the old ways and the new. . . . His father came to Chinatown forty years ago and went back and forth, San Francisco to Kwangtung Province, five times, and Dennis Wong was born in China, Toysan area, and grew up with the ideal of being like the great Dr. Chan, who had studied in Germany and returned to China to teach new sciences to the people and improve their lot. The Japanese wars, and then the Communist takeover, finally drove his family from China for good . . . but even now he travels to the Chinese settlements of Hong Kong with the medical missions of Project Concern. . . .

. . . But Chinatown! One wonders what the Chinese ways can do in this candy-fruit jungle of the U.S.A. . . . the Very Earnest reporter scribbles ceaselessly in his notebook as Wong talks: "These are critical times for Chinatown, I feel. . . ." Why does Very Earnest write so furiously? ". . . It is very apparent that some kind of change is bound to come, and the youth might be the spark or the catalyst to bring it about. There is no longer a wall around Chinatown, and now all the forces of American culture are invading the Chinese subculture, and the second generation, the young-timers, the young folk, try to alienate themselves completely from the old ways of revering your elders and listening to the other person. Then the older generation finds that the younger generation has become militant and disobedient, and these feelings pervade the Chinese-American community."

"When did you first notice this split developing?" says Very Earnest.

"Fairly recently, I would say. . . . Seven or eight years ago they didn't even keep records of Chinese law violations, there were so few. . . . I think the whole restlessness became very apparent after the Vietnamese war began. There are a lot of factors. Our children grow up seeing things like the anti-war movement and the civil-rights movement in the mass media, and they see that others can get away with disobedience, with violence, and they think: 'Why can't we?' The idea of respect means less and less to them. Even if you think your elders have not done well, I feel you must show them respect, because without them there would be nothing, you would have nothing. In the old Chinese family the children lived always together with two or three generations, their parents and grandparents, but today families more or less completely adopt the American way. There is less and less communication between the elders and the youngsters in the home. The father and mother of the family have to work long hours, and this can be related to lack of education and lack of skills, and the children are left unattended, and the boys go into the gang, and they look at television and see the Negroes and the whites in the civil-rights movement and the anti-war movement confronting society's last line of defense, the police, and doing things that not even gangs would have dared to do in the past, humiliating the police and getting away with it, and so they say, 'We can get away with it, too.' There was an incident on Grant Avenue—not long ago—a crowd of youngsters surrounded two policemen trying to arrest a boy, and they began throwing things at the police and obstructing them—fighting them!—and the boy escaped. So they say: 'See! We can get away with it!' Such a thing has never happened here before."

"Do you think the Six Companies can do anything to change the situation?"

"Well, certain things we can't change. We can't change this country. In some ways we are very naïve in this country. The American people should have learned some of the old culture from China rather than always experimenting with the new. We should go back to the old ways of love, understanding, compassion, perseverance, fidelity, instead of wanting everything now. There is a Chinese saying [Wong draws some characters on a sheet of paper]—'the bitter first, then the sweet.' The sweet is sweeter and more permanent if you put off immediate pleasure, and sacrifice and work hard and then enjoy the sweet after you have earned it. But this generation wants everything now, cars, girls, good times, and they are going to have the bitter later, and it is going to be very bitter. But it is very hard to talk to them about the old ways. . . . Certain things we can do in Chinatown, but we have never had a long-range plan for the youngsters or for the new immigrants. In certain things our ancestors had great foresight. We would never have had any of this [he motions around toward the expanse of the great hall] if they hadn't bought the buildings, year by year, all over Chinatown. The newspapers say the family associations own thirty million dollars' worth of real estate in Chinatown, and of course we could never buy a fraction of that today if we had to start out from zero. But it is true that we have not used that wealth to plan for the changes that have come such as the new immigration. In five years' time more than half the population of Chinatown will be foreign-born."

Very Earnest says, "Isn't that situation ready-made for the family associations and the Six Companies? Couldn't you bring these people into your organizations?"

Wong smiles . . . and hesitates. . . . "Well . . . there is another Chinese saying . . . 'Each one sweeps the snow from his own doorway, and never mind the frost on somebody else's roof.' . . . Many times if they did not join in the family association in Hong Kong or Taiwan, they do not join it here. . . . And we have not been charitable-minded enough to seek out those people who are coming in."

"Does this mean the militant groups will become more influential with the immigrants? What about the Wah Ching?"

"The Wah Ching are much quieter now," says Wong. "Some of the tongs are doing a good job of taking in these Wah Ching as members. After they have this kind of traditional companionship in the tongs, and someone shows them some concern, they are more ready to live in the traditional way. The tongs take in these youngsters and try to line up jobs for them, and so forth."

"So the tongs have been a good influence."

"Oh, yes. There are still many deep-seated problems, but the tongs are helping them to find a place in the community."

Very Earnest is still scribbling away in his notebook. . . . The streets are quiet. . . . The glow in the great hall is soft. . . It is about four p.m., and out in the hallway, from up the old brown stairs leading to the second and third floors, the sound of the recitations begins . . . up the old brown stairs through the old halls, from the classrooms, the chants of the lessons. . . . Another day's classes of the Chinese school. . . . Almost all Chinese children from age seven to eleven still come, every day, as soon as they finish at the public grade schools. . . . The Chinese school! . . . and the traditional way . . . chanting their lessons aloud, in unison, by rote . . . learning to use the Chinese brush, to show strength of character in the downstrokes. . . . That the final years, the high-school years, are now compressed into one room with one teacher and but a handful of students—this means . . . means what? . . . numbers! . . . what is a year? a decade? a century? . . . mere fractions in the millennial numerology of the one way. . . .

Wah Ching . . . there's a name for you, if you give it a little three a.m. movie pronunciation in the back of the throat. . . . Chinese tigers, fangs in the tong, tongs in the fog, hidden fury of the Orient. . . . Just now some of the whites who keep an eye on Chinatown affairs, such as the police, the school administration and the journalists, are deep into their Wah Ching theory. They've never gotten over the big Wah Ching meeting of last year, with George Woo raising the battle cry. According to this theory, as outlined by Police Chief Thomas J. Cahill, among others, Chinatown is now split down the middle between the conservative American-born Chinese and the new militants from Hong Kong . . . *Wah Ching!*

This is a very tidy fantasy. It explains almost all The Troubles in Chinatown. It explains the downfall of last year's fantasy, which went: There is no juvenile delinquency in Chinatown, because the Chinese have such strong family ties. It traces both the rise of gang outrages and New Left agitation to the same source: outsiders from Hong Kong. . . .

Yellow Peril!

At this moment one of the Wah Ching's two maximum leaders, Tom Tom, is in the Far East Restaurant on Jackson Street with Very Earnest. Very Earnest—one thing you have to say for the guy, he gets around. Very Earnest and Tom Tom are at a table in the Far East, drinking Scotch. Just to look at him, this Tom Tom strikes you as a happy-go-lucky fellow back from an outing at Disneyland. He is a slightly built guy, smiling, wearing black slacks, a black T-shirt and a black velour hat with a kind of ultra-streamlined Cardin snap brim with two Disneyland buttons on the front, one on each side. The buttons are the stereoptic kind that say one thing when you look at them from this angle and another thing from the other. One button has a picture of Goofy on it, and when you look at it from another angle it says: "I'm goofy about Disneyland." The other button has a picture of Tinker Bell and the message: "Disneyland—I think it's great!"

"I notice you wear your hair short," says Very Earnest. "All the other guys I see in Chinatown have long hair."

Tom Tom smiles. "We no follow anybody," he says. "We no wear our hair like the Leways or the hippies. We by ourselves. We not with anybody."

"What about politics? What about the meeting the Wah Ching had last year? Aren't you and the Leways on the same side?"

"We by ourselves. All we want is money and girls and be with our friends. The Leways talk about Mao and the Little Red Book—they crazy. We don't bother anybody unless they bother us. Then we beat the hell out of them."

"Such as who?"

"We used to fight the American-born Chinese all the time. They call us 'Chinabugs.' We say, 'Who you think you are?' They say, 'We American-born.' That's a joke. They Chinese same as us. We used to fight the Negroes. The first time—they beat us. They bigger. But we always come back. The first time, you bigger than me, you beat me, I lose. But you better not ever be alone again. Because we find you, two, three, four, five of us. Walk up to you on the street, one here, one here, one over here, not even look at you, not say a word —just rip you off. We never marched as a gang. We all came to the same place at the same time from every direction. One minute, nobody. Next—all there at once. You have to kill us to stop us. You split my head open—I get up, keep fighting. We all been to the hospital. I been three times."

"What did you use as weapons?"

"Axes and knives," says Tom Tom.

"Axes?"

"Yeah. They don't slice but they hurt plenty."

"You sure you don't mean sledge hammers?"

"No. Ax with short handle." Then he draws a picture of it on a napkin. It's an ax with a short handle, all right. A hatchet, in a word . . . too much *déjà vu* in Chinatown.

The tong warriors of the 1890's, all dressed in black, were known as precisely that, the Hatchet Men. And now, in the very moment when Chief Cahill and the others had their Wah Ching theory worked out, the Wah Ching had already split up into several factions, none of which was left in the New Left. They had gravitated into the old tongs.

Tom Tom and a lot of his boys had joined the Suey Sing tong.

Another group was headed by a thirty-three-year-old Hong Kong Chinese named Jack Hoey, of the Hop Sing tong. He had been a key figure in tong troubles that had flared up in 1957. Quite a little scare. . . . It hadn't done much for the postwar image of the tongs as kindly Elks Clubs for the old men of Chinatown . . . olden times in old Kwantung. . . . In fact, the tongs, which had raised so much hell in Chinatown in the 1890's, remained what they had always been: the direct outgrowth of the fraternities and secret societies that young men had founded in the Kwantung villages. And they performed the same function: which was, doing things that the respectable clans could not officially undertake—everything from providing rooms for card games to punishing malefactors and operating the rackets. Sometimes it seemed like history was just a cycle, as Confucius had written. A speedy one, too, at times. In 1900 it had gotten to the point where the hatchet men in black of the Hop Sings and Suey Sings were ripping each other off so fast and furious, one of the white newspapers had run box scores, on the order of: Today's Standings—Hop Sings, 3; Suey Sings, 2. . . . The very same. . . . And now the tremor running through Chinatown was that the same bad blood was about to flow again. It was no joke.

The Yellow Peril Movement had underestimated the pull of the old ways, too. After the big Wah Ching meeting of 1968, everybody kept looking to the Wah Ching as "the people," the revolutionary masses, the muscle of a real street movement. In his own way, Tom Tom had a social conscience. He worked for his boys in all sorts of scrapes, violent or otherwise. He tried to get the Wah Ching a meeting place and other aid from agencies like the Economic Opportunity Council. But in the end—it was like Tom Tom and the Wah Ching had an urge similar to many white and black gangs', for that matter, the urge to stay pure—not to get involved with the "middle-class mentality," whether the radical intellectuals' or anybody else's. The status split between the American-born and the Hong Kong youth still hung on, too. A lot of the Wah Ching felt more at home in . . . the tongs . . . and the old way. . . .

Man! Just how deep and how uncannily had the ancient ways and the history of the *T'ang jen* insinuated itself into every psyche . . . one never knew . . . until something like when Clifford Tom and Ted Kajiwara, Alex and Raymond Hing, Al Wong and some of the others of the Leways who pulled off the victory of the Cherry Bomb Night—until they went all the way and allied themselves with the Black Panthers and formed the Red Guard out in the open . . . the *Red Guard* . . . like, if they could have called it *anything* else, *anything* . . . the Red Dragon . . . the Red Tiger . . . the Red Eyebrows, which was a secret society that started revolution during the reign of Wang Mang, 1900 years ago. . . . Red Eyebrows. . . . But they had to go the stone total way and call it the Red Guard . . . and then take over a Sunday program in Portsmouth Square that was supposed to star Chou Tung-hua, the consul-general from Formosa. They bumped him and everybody else off the program, even a liberal and popular guy like Franklin Chow of the E.O.C., and stood out there under portraits of Mao with their Black Panther-Raoul-Che berets on and field jackets and red armbands that said "Red Guard" in Chinese. They lined up holding Red flag staffs out at stiff-arm attention and announced: "We want the freedom to make our own destiny! Chiang Kai-shek is ruling us through the Six Companies!" . . . while their Red Guard Girl Guerrillas with the granny glasses and the Tahiti Lagoon hair sold the Little Red Book from card tables. . . . Then they started stopping the white grand turismo tourist cars down on Grant, and gleamed the Peril down from under their sizzling berets and asked for contributions for their Children's Breakfast program. . . . The white turistas took one look and

YELLOW PERIL.

They forked it over. It was like the Red Guard was collecting admission tolls to Chinatown. All that stuff really shorted out a few brainstems in Chinatown! I can tell you that . . . but some of them were the boys in black themselves, "the people," the masses . . . who started taking off their Yellow Peril buttons, some of them, and staying away from the Leway pool hall. . . . For what reason! Who can figure it all out! . . . Part of it was that the police began hassling the pool hall almost daily, checking out I.D.'s and so on. Part of it was the feeling that the Red Guard had moved off too fast to the stone Soul radical edge. The pool hall would soon be forced out of business, and the Red Guards' days, as an organization, were numbered.

Ching
    Ming
       Chou
          T'ang
            Han
               Celestial dynasties go trooping down Kearny Street, banner by banner, also the board of presidents of the Six Companies in open Chevrolet convertible and Judge Harry Low and Postmaster Lim P. Lee and

Galileo High School band majorette prancing purple-and-orange-joined Negro girls with absolutely ferocious naturals . . . and those bad-ass kids on the tenement roofs on Commercial Street across from the Ruby Palace restaurant throw down so many firecrackers over the parade, they come down spluttering comets in midair . . . weird shit. . . . They always throw fireworks during the Chinese New Year Parade, all during the two weeks of the beano, in fact, and the cops always look the other way . . . but tonight, as dusk closes in, there is an . . . epidemic in the air, a malarial tremor. . . .

A boy in black with pompadour and a Leway button on runs along in front of the whites who have all the bleacher seats on Kearny, shouting in a shuck Charlie Chan voice:

"Hey! You buy cherry bomb? Go boom! Big boom!"

. . . More splutters, explosions, Chinese gongs, cymbals, floats with loudspeakers and music coming out in insane screels . . . the Old Movie Charlie Chan himself rides by in a convertible . . . the Veterans of China, Burma, India, all whites, of course, the Old China Hands, with caps on and pieces of uniforms and farflung-outpost gear, hauling their aging colloidal tissue out for one more march in friendly old cozy Chinatown . . . but jaysus! the hulking fireworks! . . . bunch of cherry bombs bad-ass kids throwing explode hulking concussion grenades Indochina '27. . . . The darkness closes in. . . . Whole vertebrae of firecrackers arch out of the thousands packing the street. . . . Madness and gunpowder. . . . The cops run their motorcycles along the curbing like herdsmen. . . . The white, black, yellow beast of a crowd throws firecrackers in their wake. . . . They throw them at the parade, at the high-school bands, at the little Chinese girls in imperial silks and empress headdresses from the St. Mary's Chinese Drill Team. . . . Right! let's see those little babies dance with a couple live firecrackers under their feet! . . . It's a sport! . . . It's insane!

"Hey! You buy cherry bomb? Go boom! Make big boom!"

The crowd on the sidewalk humps and bubbles like a great black sci-fi beast. . . . It explodes and flashes with firecrackers and cherry bombs . . . fire falls out of the sky. . . . It skids on the pavement. . . . The white families in the bleacher seats, three dollars a head, are starting to huddle together like the last holdouts of Khartoum. . . . They can't go forward and they can't retreat. . . . Shitfire fills the air. . . By the time the great annual Chinese New Year Parade dragon comes into view, it's chaos. . . . The Chinese swells up on the second floor of the Ruby Palace look down through the plate-glass windows. . . . The white swells in the bleachers look up. . . . Here comes the dragon. . . . Everyone's standing up. . . . No one can see. . . . Nothing but bodies and concussions and gunpowder. . . . The dragon is forty feet long, red, green and gold, with megawatt light bulbs for eyeballs and a battalion of Chinese youth in black pantaloons holding the train of its body and tail aloft and doing the dragon dance. . . . The beast-crowd pours out into the street around it . . . erupting concussions. . . . Kailey Wong is inside the dragon's head holding it aloft with his arms and jerking it up and down in the air to the—he can't hear the gong beats and the cymbals any longer. . . . The air—the world!—is one vast nut-house . . . fireworks at his feet . . . bouncing off the dragon's head. . . . The bastards have gone berserk! They're trying to *kill the dragon* . . . blow his legs off. . . . The dragon, the beast-crowd, the flashes and concussions—it's all one grand jumble in front of Portsmouth Square. . . . The Parade is over . . . de facto! . . . finished! . . . done for! . . . The crowd runs up the hill, toward Grant Avenue, to the heart of Chinatown. . . . Nothing is left to do but complete the chaos! . . . Go boom! . . . Make big boom!

Up the hill, in the heart of tourist Chinatown, thousands, mostly whites, many young drunks and Saturday-night big-timers, packed into Grant Avenue, the restaurants, the bars. They bought firecrackers from the street kids and had a rare time throwing them all over the main drag. Deerskin was on a corner pulling back his black jacket and pointing within to the inner lining and saying: "Want some firecrackers?" They jammed into the Street Fair on Waverly Place. For years the two blocks of Waverly Place, underneath the pagodas of the family associations, had been turned into a street fair with booths on both sides of the street. But this year, the Year of the Rooster—Power to the Rooster! . . . Some of the booths were the usual . . . Hit the Milk Bottle with a Baseball . . . Pop the Balloons with a Dart . . . Throw the Hoop . . . but—All Power to the Rooster! —there were other booths such as spun many heads out . . . the Third World Liberation booth—a great pile of debris daubed yellow and black and mounted with signs saying POWER TO THE PEOPLE . . . YELLOW POWER FOR YELLOW PEOPLE . . . OFF THE PIG! . . . and Chinese kids with ferocious hair smiled out at the crowds . . . I.C.S.A. had three booths in a row. The first had the literature of The People, such as the *Voice of Youth* and a huge poster of George Woo. At the second, one could buy a ticket and vote for "The Ten Worst Enemies of Chinatown." The tote board showed Reagan, Hayakawa and Kearney, the principal of Galileo, leading the field. The third was a dart game. The targets were posters of Ronald Reagan as a cowboy riding a horse and Hayakawa with bull's-eyes instead of glasses over his eyes. The Asian-American Political Alliance had a "Course in Becoming a Revolutionary." The Leways had a shooting gallery with drawings of pigs wearing police badges and N.R.A. targets on their sides and signs saying OFF THE PIG . . . The white crowds—weird mother this street fair was. . . . Cops drifted by on either end of Waverly Place. . . . A dozen Wah Ching, Jack Hoey's boys, stood in front of the Hop Sing Tong, on Jackson Street across from Waverly Place, just waiting. . . . On Grant Avenue the lunacy grew louder and louder. A white kid throws a firecracker at the feet of a cop. It explodes against his shoe. The kid just stands there grinning at him. It's like a dare. The cop glares at him, but nothing more. . . . Everybody is waiting. . . . By midnight the congestion was total. The cars were backed up on every street and the crowds spilled over the sidewalks. The Chinatown squad, half a dozen plainclothesmen, stood up at one end of Waverly Place in their Stingy-brim hats. . . .

An old Chinese came out of the Yee Jun Restaurant with a glass in his hand. . . . He threaded his way between the cars. One of the plainclothesmen came over and said, "What you got, Willie? Is that whisky?"

"Whisky!" says the old guy. "This tea. . . . You look."

The cop looks and sniffs and nods somberly. "It's tea. Okay, Willie."

A boy in black says: "They talk to him like a nigger, man!"

Another one yells at the Chinatown squad: "Hey man! You get a good cut on the firecrackers!"

By the time the Chinese-American Democratic Club banquet at Joe Jung's lets out . . . it's only a matter of which way the whole goddamn thing is going to blow. . . . The pols and dignitaries and postal employees come walking down Jackson Street. . . . Fights are breaking out on Grant. . . . Drunk whites are starting cherry-bomb battles with each other. . . . They throw the goddamn things head on. . . . They're out to lunch. . . . At Jackson and Grant a Chinese boy in black starts hassling a firecracker white crazy twice his size who doesn't even have time to swear . . . four boys in black roll over him from behind. . . . All disappear running into the alley. . . . The white boy sits on the sidewalk telling people: "They *jumped* me!" . . . Young Chinese from the Youth for Service organization move in to keep the peace, and the cops see *them* and hassle them up against the wall. . . . George Woo is in the middle of Jackson Street, amid the cars. . . . He's furious. . . . Here's a Cadillac full of whites. . . . They're middle-aged, they're panicked . . . they're blowing the horn . . . like, clear the way! . . . There's no way left to clear. . . . The Cadillac horn brays amid the shitfire. . . . Inside the car, they keep pressing all the buttons, like are you *sure* all the windows are up—

"Shut up, you white ass!"

It's George Woo. . . . He's just a foot away from them . . . only a pane of Cadillac Thermoglas between them and Armageddon. . . .

"This is Chinatown, honky! Go back to the Peninsula where you belong!"

Christ! . . . They'd like nothing better! you can bet on that. . . . They stare back . . . nothing but a ferocious bearded Chinese and a hurricane of shitfire between them and Palo Alto. . . . They have their heads pulled down under their clavicles . . . their eyes are like golf balls . . . *Cong!*

"Tell 'em, George!"

"Tell it like it is!"

"Right on!"

On Grant Avenue, under the pagodas and the dragon lampposts and the ten thousand Chinese signs, all wise Chinese burghers have gotten the hell out. The shops, bars, restaurants, kiosks, knick-knackeries, imports & exports—they're closed, shuttered, bolted . . . lights out! . . . The beast-crowd reigns! Power to the beast! . . . White hulks, herds of them, pack both sides of the street. . . . They're drunk on the beano and the gunpowder. . . . It's elemental. . . . It's this side against that side. . . . This side cuts loose with a barrage of cherry bombs. . . . The herd-hulk on that side lurches back against the shopwindows. . . .

Blam! Flash! . . . That side bursts apart, fires back. . . . Kaboom! . . . This side shrinks into a vast clot . . . a white kid with half his cheek blown open sits on the curb. . . . Blood, man, and he doesn't believe it . . . The police, the Tac squad, the riot cops, with plastic shields over their faces, riot sticks drawn, are trying to close in from both ends of Grant Avenue . . . So what! the beast-crowd breathes pure gunpowder! . . . The firecracker crazies are berserk! . . . They're diving, falling, ricocheting off the storefronts, rolling up into balls, springing out into pistons! throwing cherry bombs into the void! . . . At the Pacific and Grant the Tac cops try to collar a Chinese. . . . Boys in black surround them and drive them back with cherry bombs . . . Ted Kajiwara, of the Red Guards, runs down the hill on Jackson, past the Hop Sing Wah Ching, who still stand there, not making a move . . . Tom Tom's Wah Ching—they're staying out of it, too. . . . Ted Kajiwara says, "Listen, man! The pigs are ripping us off! They're busting people right and left!" He plunges into the chaos on Grant. At Grant and Clay the crowd feels the weird tremor. . . . The Tac squad is starting a sweep from the Pacific end. . . . They swing from the heels! No holds barred! . . . It's your ass! . . . The impact rolls through the herd hulk for two blocks. . . . Then the shrieks, and the whole crowd starts running. . . . They're shoving, falling, groping, pulling, baying, neighing, trampling each other. . . . A whole herd of white youths comes running up Jackson. . . . The first cop breaks through. He's huge! He's got his riot stick over his head, he's packing guns, bullets, cuffs, pads, blackjacks. . . . He's closing in on a big white boy from behind, running straight up the hill. . . . He jumps him, they go crashing to the sidewalk in front of the Yee Jun restaurant. . . . He picks the cat up and pins his arms back. . . . A detective runs up and bellies the guy from the front. . . . Two more detectives. . . . They knee him. . . . They take turns. It's like a ritual. The white boy looks out at . . . nothing, he's a blank, a poleaxed steer. . . .

Two white boys, both about eighteen, are walking up Jackson. The first one has an important-mission look on his face. . . . He's addressing one and all, lighting them up with his eyeballs. . . . He has a voice like a spieler, a barker. . . .

"Badge—! Remember that badge number, folks! Badge—, San Francisco P.D. Remember that badge number, ladies and gentlemen!"

The second kid is lurching up the sidewalk with a huge gimp. . . . He's hunched over and holding his groin with both hands and sprocketing his eyes over every living soul. . . .

"Holy shit!" he says. "Ho-leee *shit!*"

"Re-mem-ber that *badge number,* folks!" says the advance man. "Badge num-ber—! San Fran-cis-co P.D.! Next time it *could be you!*"

"Holy shit! Ho-lee *shit!*" . . . and he clutches his groin. . . .

It's a chorus . . . a reprise . . . a holy shit antiphony. . . .

On Grant the Tac squad has plowed a paddy wagon as far as Sacramento Street. . . . The white crazies have fled. . . . The Red Guard has mounted the barricades. . . . The battle has simplified. . . . It's the crowd versus the Tac squad. Boys in black surround the paddy wagon. Bottles, bricks and all sorts of shit rain down from rooftops. Cats are throwing cherry bombs dipped in glue and studded with broken glass . . . suzy wong flower drum song no tickee no tong war no wonton.

At Pacific and Stockton a squad car is half keeled over against the curb. . . . Somebody slashed the tires on the curb side. . . . Behind the car crouch two Tac squad cops with riot guns aimed at the roof of the Ping Yuen housing project. . . . Cars are still inching up Pacific to get the hell out of Chinatown. . . . At the corner people look out their car windows at the riot gun muzzles four feet away . . . *mothering crossfire!* . . . in Chinatown. . . .

no canton oriental pearly chop suey carry-out slanty-eyed family ties take care of our own charlie chan and his dragon dancers hoppy go bang-bang february red firecracker shredded fu manchu new year of rooster but none of your juvenile delinquency among our lilla fellas porcelain dolls almond-eye melonseed miss chinatown my chinatown.

CONCLUSION

Cultural diversity *is* the American way of life. We *are* a pluralistic society. Let us capitalize on it.

That is what we have been saying about American blacks, Puerto Ricans, Mexicans, Indians, and Asians throughout this book. America maintains a pluralistic school system—in theory if not in practice—in the belief that such diversity enriches all of us. When we see the means for greatly improving our handling of cultural diversity in the schools, bringing practice closer to our theory, then, we ought to explore them. They entail a few radical changes, to wit:

1. Encourage and preserve bilingualism as one of our most valuable assets—valuable both to Anglos and non-Anglos.

2. Provide instruction which consciously and deliberately emphasizes Hispanic, Indian, Negro, Oriental and other cultural contributions—again to the great benefit of the Anglo as well as his non-Anglo brother.

3. In all subject areas, bend over backwards, if necessary, to recognize the contributions of non-Anglos wherever relevant. Put greater emphasis in school and college curriculums on the literature, music, art, dance, games, sports, of minority cultures. Bring into the schools new instructors, new materials, and new methods which will increase the authenticity of the schools' coverage of minority cultures.

4. Expand and enrich adult education opportunities so that parents and children are exposed to acculturation at a more closely related pace.

5. Retrain Anglo teachers—particularly in the competencies implied by subject

433

matter in the first three recommendations above, and also in cultural sensitivity to and empathy with the various ethnic groups.

6. Provide special "paid to learn" recruitment and training programs for minority group teachers, teacher aides, teacher assistants, and other paraprofessionals for school service first among their own cultural groups, and as more trained personnel become available, to teach Anglo middle class children in isolated suburban pockets.

At issue is whether even those changes can be accomplished within the present school and college system as we now know it, or whether a new educational system has to evolve. Our own view is that the present system may accommodate these changes *too slowly* and *too late* unless we are inventive enough to establish some competing educational agencies, newly endowed, organized, and staffed to undertake the job at once as we know it must be done. One such agency, the voucher plan,[1] might well open up the elementary and secondary system. At the higher education level, the work might be accomplished through the kind of agency Stone describes in the essay that follows: Education Professions Institute—a school-college run of, by, and for the culturally unique community. America has become the economic marvel of the world because of competition in the presence of rich natural resources. We suggest it is high time to involve some of this grass-roots competition in the business of schooling.

This volume has focused upon multi-culturalism in America. In conclusion, we wish to emphasize that cultural differences and the need for cultural awareness by teachers know no national boundaries. Both are timeless and worldwide. But let's make the beginning here at home and perhaps we'll become one model for the rest of the world.

The time to act is now. Tomorrow will be too late.

[1]See page 4.

A New Model
for the Teacher
Preparation We Need

James C. Stone

In several previous publications we have pointed out the failure of traditional teacher education,[1] a failure that is particularly alarming with respect to our total lack of accomplishment in recruiting, training, and retraining ghetto teachers. This failure may be summarized as that of the colleges, the schools, the state, and the profession.

The Colleges

Most colleges—as institutions—have *not* taken seriously their responsibility to educate teachers. As institutions their efforts have been largely incidental—tangential to other (and more important) missions like preparing liberal arts graduates, or, at the professional level, doctors and lawyers. Certainly, in the present most crucial need of teacher training—preparing teachers of the disadvantaged —most colleges and universities are far removed from the problem. Since institutions of higher education have not taken seriously this social obligation of teacher training, since they cannot be forced into active social responsibility, and since the most significant aspect of this training should occur in the ghetto and in classrooms of disadvantaged children, why not move this unwanted stepchild from the colleges?

From James C. Stone, *Teachers for the Disadvantaged,* San Francisco: Jossey-Bass, 1969, pp. 197–207.

[1]James C. Stone, *Breakthrough in Teacher Education,* San Francisco: Jossey-Bass, 1968, pp. 178–180, Chap. 12, *passim,* and James C. Stone, "Reform or Rebirth?" *NEA Journal,* Vol. 57, No. 5 (May, 1968), p. 23. Also James C. Stone, "Whither Reform in Teacher Education?" *Educational Leadership,* Vol. 25, No. 2 (November, 1967), p. 127; reprinted in *The Education Digest,* Vol. XXXII, No. 5 (January, 1968), pp. 40–42.

The Schools

For years schools merely accepted teachers trained by the colleges, however adequate or inadequate, and sent them back to college for refresher courses and advanced degrees. Similarly the public schools have merely accepted student teachers and intern teachers and passively provided them with whatever laboratory experiences the college or university requested. In more recent times, aided and abetted by federal grants, school systems have developed their own in-service education programs that teachers have flocked to and generally applauded.

Building on this know-how, it would be logical for the schools also to become the pre-service educators of teachers, replacing the institutions of higher education. For the increasing numbers of public schools involved in internship programs, this would be a logical and simple step. Assistant superintendents in charge of staff development are being found with greater frequency in the schools; such persons are the individuals obviously qualified to direct and organize pre-service teacher education as they now successfully organize and direct in-service training. An obvious benefit would be to close the gap that has so long existed between pre-service and in-service education and which internship programs were expected to achieve but few have.

In publicly supported education this shift of responsibility would involve a simple transfer of funds from higher to public education. Such a shift would create in every school system a division of teacher education—in-service and pre-service—that is closer to the operational level and not so removed as present education departments and schools are now, bound up as they are in the bureaucracies, politics, and distractions in higher education. The teacher-education center previously described would be an example of this administrative model. Yet to expect public education—which has failed in the ghetto, bound up as it is by the inertia, irresponsive bureaucracy, middle-class traditions, over-legislation, underfinancing, and other distractions of public education—to mount and sustain such centers on a wide-scale basis and at high levels is to expect what is not and what is not likely to be.

The State

The education of teachers has long been recognized as a state responsibility. Originally states took this obligation seriously and provided special institutions—the normal school, the teachers college—as their prime vehicle for pre-service and in-service education. The last decade has seen the demise of these institutions. Most have evolved into state colleges interested in the education of all occupational groups, including teachers. Gradually teacher training has lost its importance in these institutions, their subsequent conversion to state universities has continued and hastened the decline of interest in teacher education on the collegiate level.

Meanwhile, state departments of education have been content with confining their teacher-education obligations to the certification of teachers and the accreditation of colleges and universities for teacher education. In most states the accreditation function amounts to an approval system based primarily on whether the institutions offer the specific courses prescribed by the certification office and, as a recent Teacher Education and Professional Standards (TEPS) publication points out, has failed to provide leadership.

Thus a no-man's land is created for the college . . . school function (of teacher training) which is typically characterized by dual administration, improper financing, and conflicting supervision.[2]

The Profession

World War II created a critical shortage of teachers and was followed by an unprecedented increase in the birth rate, which worsened the teacher shortage. Out of this crisis came the "professional standards movement" in which the NEA took the leadership through the formation of its Commission on Teacher Education and Professional Standards in 1946. While all of us connected with this movement over the past twenty-five years—at local, state, and national levels—can enthusiastically testify about its many accomplishments, the simple fact is that, despite these efforts, the average teacher still is disinterested in and uninformed about teacher education and the professional processes such as certification, accreditation, in-service training, personnel standards, and the like which undergird and support it. If you doubt this statement, look around at the next school conference you attend. Check how few general sessions are given over to the topic of teacher training. Visit the section meetings on Training, Certification, Accreditation, or Ethics and note the paucity of teachers at these section meetings in contrast to the standing-room-only signs on doors marked Salary, Negotiating Councils, Collective Bargaining, and the like. Check on who goes to conferences on teacher education—a few public school master teachers and personnel directors, yes, but mostly college or university professors of education. We can't blame the teachers—we've never really opened the doors of teacher education to them. When it comes to pre-service training, we college people have given a few supervising teachers a look inside, but we've not dared to let them get further than *recommending* the grade the student or intern teacher should receive. (We, the college supervisors, who only visit the student teacher about two or three times a semester are empowered with the final judgment!) When it comes to in-service training, teachers are merely the recipients of our ideas, seldom involved in the planning for what is *needed* and desirable for them!

We could open the door wider—make supervising teachers faculty members, give them pre-service teaching responsibilities for the whole professional se-

---

[2]"A New Order in Student Teaching," National Commission on Teacher Education and Professional Standards, NEA, Washington, D.C., 1967, p. 21.

quence instead of the student teaching problems seminars we typically toss to a few of them. We could set up procedures whereby teachers actually plan, organize, and conduct their own in-service training. Any such moves would be in the right direction, but there is scant hope that from these forms of tokenism, the profession will be moved to a concern for teacher education.

Social Institutions

All attempts to reform teacher training[3] have failed to recognize that the social institutions in which teacher education is embedded—the schools, the colleges, state departments of education—were created by society *not* for the purpose of bringing about change and innovation, but rather that of preserving the status quo. As guardians of the establishment, the schools, institutions of higher education, and state regulatory agencies were specifically created to see that change does not take place. The primary function of these educational agencies, in common with education since the days of primitive man, is to pass on the cultural heritage to the upcoming generation. Designed to preserve "what is," they have been staffed largely by those who are wholly committed to this end. Few teachers, for example, see their role as agents of change. The result is that reform efforts have done little to break the patterns of traditional teacher education.

As long as education and its handmaiden, teacher education, remain fixed in the concrete of college, public school, and state department traditions, both likely will remain substantially as they are now, and reform efforts will continue to come and go without making an appreciable impact on either higher education or public education, or on state departments of public instruction where teacher education has its roots.

If ever we hope to break what George Counts, writing some twenty-five years ago, called "the lock-step in teacher training," we must create new organizational structures; we must be willing to go one step further than modifying the present establishment. We need to cut the ties, plough over the old college-school ruts in which teacher training is quagmired, and begin fresh.

Our summation of the failures of teacher education and its traditional role in society brings to mind the statement by Felix Robb, the long-time former president of George Peabody College for Teachers, one of the two remaining teachers colleges still in existence in the United States:

If the successors to teachers colleges become mediocre and abandon their concern for teachers, another generation will have to start teachers colleges all over again.[4]

---

[3]There have been many reform efforts. Among the major attempts have been the Commission on Teacher Education of the American Council on Education (1938–1946); the NEA TEPS Commission (1946 to date); the Fund for the Advancement of Education (1950–59); the Ford Foundation's "Breakthrough Programs" (1960–66); NDEA, ESEA, and other Federal Grants (1964 to date).

[4]Henry C. Hill, "Wanted: Professional Teachers," *The Atlantic Magazine* (May, 1960), p. 39.

While not wishing simply to go back as Robb suggests, we do propose a new model that takes something from the past—the idea of a separate social institution for teacher training—while adding several new dimensions crucial for the education of teachers of the disadvantaged: training that is "planned and conducted from and at the grass-roots level" and intimately involving the local school and neighborhood—an agency controlled by the client-groups that comprise the local community.

We have called this new social institution an *EPI—Education Professions Institute*. We offer it as our major recommendation for training teachers of the disadvantaged, if not for all teachers. For those of us who have been in teacher education most of our professional lives, proposing an alternative and competing agency to the one that has nurtured us these many years is a difficult task. As Minnis has said: "No one likes to point out that the king is naked. If you are the tailor, it is especially difficult."[5]

EDUCATION PROFESSIONS INSTITUTE (EPI)

The EPI would be a separate agency of higher education with a distinct, unique, and differentiated function.[6] The unique purpose would be to provide professional training for teachers-to-be, teacher aides, associate teachers, intern teachers, regular teachers, master teachers, and teachers of teachers through the bachelor's and master's degrees. It would recruit adults of all ages from the ghetto community in which it was located as well as from the ranks of high school graduates, the junior colleges, four-year colleges, and universities. Those teachers and prospective teachers who had not themselves grown up in a ghetto would be expected to both live in and work in the local community for a significant part of their training period.

[5]Douglas Minnis, "Rebellion in Teacher Education: Requiem for a Fossil in White Tie and Tails," CASCD Conference Address (Nov. 21, 1968), p. 2 (mimeographed).

[6]Hobert Burns, a member of the Task Force of the NDEA National Institute for Advanced Study of the Disadvantaged and a key member of the California Advisory Committee for this Four-State Project, has arrived at a somewhat comparable idea to that of an EPI. Coincidentally, he hit upon his proposal, not from the results of this study, but through his concern for the problem of the disadvantaged, his impatience with present modes of teacher education, and his training as a philosopher. In an address to the California Council on the Education of Teachers, he stated: "It is no longer possible for colleges and universities, through the instrumentation of schools or department of education, adequately to prepare teachers within the relative isolation of the campus—even when that preparation involves, as it usually does, some cooperative efforts between the colleges and the public schools. The coalition between colleges and schools should be expanded to include representatives from student and community groups and, since neither the college nor the public school is able by itself to provide for that kind of extension of the teacher education coalition, the creation of new institutions responsible for the training of educational personnel. Put simply, the creation of quasi-governmental or multi-institutional consortia or corporations for the preparation of educational personnel. While such an institution must and would include schools and colleges it would also include other groups now excluded; and the full meaning of that, of course, is to suggest that the present school-college coalition surrender some of its present sovereignty over teacher education to a new quasi-governmental institution. . . ." [Hobert Burns, "The Public Schools as Trainers of Teachers: A (Modest) Proposal," California Council on the Education of Teachers, Yosemite, California, Oct. 31, 1968 (mimeographed).]

Fiscal support for the institute might come from a variety of sources. Some might be funded entirely by the state or the federal government, others might be supported in whole or in part by private foundations, industrial groups, or professional associations. *Initially, they would offer an alternative to present agencies of teacher training, thus providing healthy competition to existing college and university and school district operations. In time, the EPI might completely replace colleges and schools as the trainers of teachers.*

Regardless of source or sources of financial support, the EPI should be viewed as a natural extension of the state's responsibility for teacher education; better stated, it would be a case of the state's returning to itself the responsibility it has always had but has failed to exercise since the end of the teachers colleges. The institute would be accredited by the state for developmental and experimental purposes. Special and unique licensing provisions might be needed in some states for those completing EPI training. This is not to suggest a lowering of standards, but rather different standards for a different group to accomplish a purpose not now adequately served by any existing social agency.

The EPI would draw its faculty from the communities in which it was located, the local schools, adjacent colleges and universities, and other social, governmental and industrial agencies. While strictly a professional institution, the EPI might admit prospective teachers and paraprofessionals at any point in their college career when they were deemed ready to embark on a semester of professional education. During any semester of enrollment, the trainees would be paid by the state or the local school, or both, for rendering teaching or community services of various kinds. This "paid to learn" feature is especially significant in terms of recruiting from the ghetto community itself. In-service teachers would enroll in the institute for afternoon or evening workshops and seminars or summer colloquiums, conferences, institutes, sabbaticals, and the like, using scholarships provided by local, state, and federal governments, foundations, the business community, professional associations, and school district sabbatical leaves.

The single most distinguishing feature of the EPI would be that it is a *teaching* institution. Its educational style would be to "learn to teach by teaching" so all trainees would be involved in some form of teaching as the central focus of their learning activities.

The EPI is envisioned as a prestige agency, paying better salaries, for example, to its faculty than do traditional colleges, universities, or school systems. This would be a truly professional school analogous to the medical school, the law school, the divinity school. Its program for the education of teachers of teachers would encompass research focused on professional problems in the teaching-learning process.

There would be equality of status and prestige for those faculty having differentiated responsibilities for the so-called theoretical and practical aspects of teacher training since any one individual would be expected to be equally involved in both. The heart of the EPI would be an exemplary school or school system that it would adopt or organize. The institute and the school would be housed together. Professional education would grow out of the instructional problems of children. Laboratory experiences in classrooms and neighborhoods of the disadvantaged would be the central focus of the in-service and pre-service teacher-training program. The professional curriculum would be tailored to each individual and would be so organized that every trainee, during his stay at the institute, would be simultaneously involved in a stream of classroom or community experiences and a concurrent stream of theoretical seminars, both taught and supervised by a team of instructors working with a particular group of trainees. The EPI would have the advantage of being close to the schools, yet removed one step from the politics of local school systems. Though ultimately responsible to the state, it would be characterized by "home rule" from the local community and the trainees themselves. However funded, it would be administered by and for the local community and trainee clientele. The state department of education, the local school district, and adjacent institutions of higher education would have a cooperative and consultative relationship with the institute.

The EPI would be chartered by the state under a joint powers agreement (see Figure 1). This is a legal entity provided for in most states, but until now seldom used in education circles except in connection with the federally sponsored Research and Development Laboratories. The powers brought together to organize the EPI and to formulate policy for it (within broad state guidelines) would be (1) a local community, (2) the trainees, (3) a college or university, (4) a school system, and (5) the organized profession. These powers would establish an independent local board of control that would have fiscal and administrative authority to operate the EPI. The five powers initially comprising the governing board might appoint additional representatives, including the public-at-large.

Within state departments of public instruction, there would be a specific unit of higher education with responsibility to provide leadership for the EPI and coordinate their efforts. The permanent staff would be a small cadre of higher education and disadvantaged teaching specialists. This nucleus would be augmented by yearly appointments of a much larger number of consultants and faculty drawn from the institutes, the schools, colleges, communities, and other educational and social agencies.

The curriculum of the EPI would provide for a number of levels of training for a number of different roles. Thus mothers with the equivalent of a high school education might enter the EPI to become teacher aides; those with junior college preparation to become associate teachers; those with an AB degree, intern teachers; and those with teaching credentials, master teachers or teachers of teachers. Movement from one program and role to another would be provided. All would be paid during their period of training, for all would be serving in some capacity in the local school or community.

A school in the ghetto would be the "home" of the institute, with the local district supplying a room for seminars and an office for the staff. Academic

FIGURE 1
State Organization of Education Professions Institute (EPI)

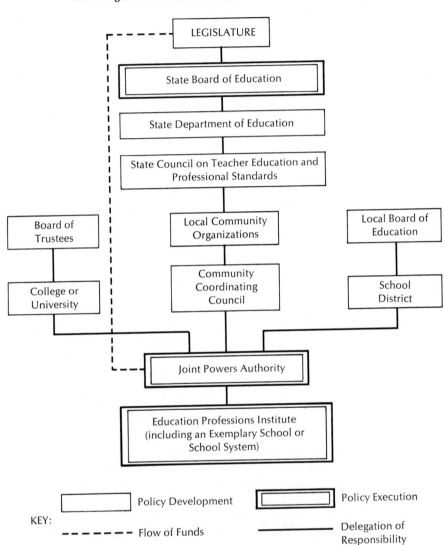

preparation needed by trainees would be provided by nearby colleges on a contractual or cooperative arrangement. In the vernacular of the times, the EPI would be "where the action is"—in the disadvantaged community. And it would stay there in the sense that it would be controlled in part by the local community. It would address itself solely to the problem that not only have our schools failed to help enough children from the lower classes to enter the mainstream of society, they actually have prevented many of them from doing so.

We are now educating students whose lives will be lived as much in the next century as this one, but our schools and colleges are . . . still based on structures, functions, and curricula more apropos of the last century than the next. . . . For many . . . the judgment has been made that the urban schools are failures because the present ends of the schools are not acceptable as the proper ends by . . . students and parents from impoverished or minority groups.[7]

And if our schools have failed, teacher training likewise has failed. Both are part and parcel of the present establishment. We teacher educators thus are admitted failures, but we can also be part of the solution through the EPI. We can draw a lesson from a parallel problem that has long been prevalent in rural America. Like the present ghetto, rural teachers have been and are in short supply. An attempt to solve the rural problem was made by recruiting from the country young women to be trained at colleges located in the towns and cities. Upon qualifying for teaching certificates, however, very few returned to the country to teach. The EPI would draw from its area many of those who were local residents but it would train them on the spot, with a greater likelihood of their remaining in the area after training to serve in the local schools.

Since the EPI is *the model* that emerges from our findings, we feel obligated to underscore and reiterate the fact that in an EPI the ghetto community and its trainees would be active participants in determining their own and their children's education. They clearly would have a stake in it—a piece, perhaps *the* piece, of the action. The growing belief by ghetto communities that schools and teacher-education institutions no longer are serving ends they believe in is the cause of the increasing demands and increasingly intense confrontations by black power, Mexican-American, Puerto Rican, and American Indian groups. In an EPI, the ghetto community and the trainees would have not only a *voice* but also a *vehicle* for remaking their own education and the education of their children.

No one doubts the difficulty of establishing such a new social institution, especially not those of us who have been "the tailors" (Minnis' term) for so many years of conventional training in traditional colleges and universities. Yet surely the times demand action, new approaches, radical departures, brave new worlds. Henry David Thoreau once wrote:

Why should we be in such desperate haste to succeed, and in such desperate enterprises? If a man does not keep pace with his companions, perhaps it is because he hears a different drummer. Let him step to the music which he hears, however measured or far away.

Let those of us who are committed to training teachers for ghetto communities and retraining present staffs who teach the disadvantaged be given the opportunity to march to a different drummer whom now we hear in ever increasing crescendo.

[7]Burns, pp. 11, 12.

Go ye therefore, and teach all nations.

—*Matthew, XXIII, 27*

Appendix   Sources on the Education and Study of Multi-Cultural Populations[1]

Bibliographies

A guide to studies in the education of the culturally different should be international and comparative in approach, yet little that is available at this time transcends national or even sub-national ethnic boundaries.

The United Nations Education, Scientific and Cultural Organization (UNESCO) annually publishes items such as *World Survey of Education* and the *International Yearbook of Education,* as well as monographs. Catalogues or lists of material available can be obtained from the UNESCO Publications Center (317 East 34th St., New York, N.Y. 10016).

Nations including New Zealand (Maori education), Mexico (bi-lingual education for native groups) and Israel (programs for low-income and culturally different groups) issue bibliographic materials through their respective ministries of education.

Bibliographies are more readily available for materials originating in the United States.

The National Reading Is Fundamental Program. *Guide to Book Selection.* (Smithsonian Institute, Washington, D.C. 20560).

> Includes a general list of paperbacks and other inexpensive books for the elementary grades and a special book list for ethnic groups. Graded groups include black elementary, black teenage and adult, Indian elementary, Indian teenage and adult, Spanish-speaking elementary and Spanish-speaking teenage and adult. Reading and interest grades serve as guides only in the broadest terms.

Elinor F. McCloskey. *Urban Disadvantaged Pupils* (Northwest Regional Laboratory, 710 S.W. Second Ave., Portland, Oregon).

> Lists 99 studies and books dealing primarily with education of culturally different urban children.

U.S. Office of Education, Educational Materials Center. *The Education of Disadvantaged and Culturally Different Children: A Bibliography.*

> Not exhaustive but does list some of the professional studies available, as well as teacher guides and reports published by local school districts and state departments of education.

Harvard Research and Development Center on Educational Differences. *Annotated Bibliography on School Racial Mix and the Self Concept, Aspirations, Academic Achievement and Interracial Attitudes and Behavior of Negro Children* (Monograph No. 3, Harvard Research and Development Center on Educational Differences, Cambridge, Massachusetts).

> A valuable compilation of educational research and with relevant socio-psychological studies pertinent to black education.

Anti-Defamation League. *The Research Annual on Inter-Group Relations.*

> A good source of information on minority group research in progress.

Several bibliographies of research reports and books dealing with American Indian education which have some applicability to the education of all culturally different populations have been issued. One prepared by the staff of the Bureau of Indian Affairs is distributed by the National Research Conference on American Indian Education (Pennsylvania State University, University Park, Pennsylvania). Large numbers of copies are not available.

Project True, Hunter College. *Urban Education and the Culturally Different, an Annotated Bibliography,* together with *Supplement I* (New York 1963).

---

[1] The authors are indebted to Jack D. Forbes of the University of California at Davis for use not only of his writings but also his extensive collection of bibliographic materials on the education of the culturally different. It is probable that some of the earlier sources cited here are no longer in print; we list them nevertheless, in case library copies may be available and also to suggest the range of approaches possible within the broad framework of the study of multi-cultural populations.

Journals

Many journals run articles and book reviews pertinent to the education of the culturally different.

Crisis
Current Anthropology
Daedalus
El Grito
Freedomways
Human Organization
Integrated Education
Journal of American Indian Education
Journal of Human Relations
Journal of Negro Education

Journal of Sociology of Education
Phylon
Saturday Review
Social Forces
Social Issues
Social Problems
Sociology and Social Research
UNESCO Courier
The Urban Review

The vast amount of new research data being accumulated on the culturally different will ultimately be available in a more manageable form from ERIC (Educational Resources Information Center). Currently available are:

Office of Education. *Research in Education.*
  Provides a monthly summary of educational research projects supported by the Office of Education.
Catalog of Selected Documents on the Culturally Different and Disadvantaged: A Number and Author Index (OE-37001, 65¢) and *Subject Index* (OE-37002, $3.00). Government and Printing Office, Washington, D.C. 20402.

Sources on the Effects of Conquest, Colonialism, and Cultural Change

Educators seeking a fuller understanding of the position of non-white populations in the U.S. will wish to acquire some familiarity with the effects of conquest, colonialism, and cultural change occurring within colonial or quasi-colonial contexts. Post-conquest and decolonization phenomena not only illustrate many aspects of non-white cultures, but they also provide insight into the ideological basis for much of the revolutionary strategy among minority-group members who believe that violent struggle is a necessary step in the psychological liberation of a colonialized people.

Fanon, Frantz. *The Wretched of the Earth.* New York: Grove Press, 1966.
  Born in Martinique of African background and trained in France as a doctor specializing in mental disorders, Fanon joined the Algerian rebels rather than serve with the French army. His book provides an understanding of the psychological as well as socio-political effects of conquest and "national liberation" processes, is basic to black radical thought. Written in Fanon's last year of life, at the age of 36, it should perhaps be read prior to reading the preface by Jean-Paul Sartre, which somewhat distorts Fanon's message.
Balandier, George. *Ambiguous Africa: Cultures in Collision.* New York: Pantheon, 1966.
  A specialist in African sociology explores the problems of decolonization.
Forbes, Jack D. *The Indian in America's Past.* Englewood Cliffs, New Jersey: Prentice-Hall, 1964.
  Chapter such as "The Conquered" and "Red Slavery" illustrate effects of conquest and colonialization.
Frazier, E. Franklin. *Race and Culture Contacts in the Modern World.* Boston: Beacon Press, 1965.
  An introduction to modern interethnic relations, Frazier's book contains valuable footnotes to other sources.
Josephson, Eric, and Mary (eds.). *Man Alone: Alienation in Modern Society.* New York: Dell, 1962.
  This early but still timely account deals with aspects of alienation including those resulting from interethnic confrontations.
Kardiner, Abram, and Ovesey, Lionel. *The Mark of Oppression.* New York: Norton, 1951.
  Explores the psychological effects of denigration.
Mavnier, Rene. *The Sociology of Colonies.* London: Routledge & Paul, 1949.
Memmi, Albert. *The Colonizer and the Colonized.* New York: Orion Press, 1965.
Price, A. Grenville. *White Settlers and Native Peoples.* Cambridge, England: University Press, 1950.
  A comparative study, Price's book examines European-native relations in areas such as North America, Australia, and New Zealand.
Turnbull, Colin. *The Lonely African.* New York: Anchor, 1962.
  An excellent portrayal of the effects of conquest derived from a number of life-histories.

More specialized interests in multi-ethnic societies may be served by the following classic works dealing with the acculturation of the culturally different.

Malinowski. Many studies, especially *The Dynamics of Culture Change*.
Beal. "Acculturation" (in Kroeber, *Anthropology Today*).
Hunter. *Reaction to Conquest: Effects of Contact with Europeans on the Pondo of South Africa*.
River. *Essays on the Depopulation of Melanesia*.
Herskovitz. Various works including *Acculturation: A Study of Culture Contact*.
Redfield. *The Primitive World and Its Transformations* and *Methods of Study of Culture Contact on America*.

During the last two decades a large body of literature relating to socio-cultural change and mental illness has developed. Much of this literature is theoretical in nature or is based upon insights gained in clinical psychology or in socio-anthropological field studies. Among the more general works in this growing body of literature, the following are noteworthy.

Wallace. Many studies, including his general *Culture and Personality* and his more technical "Stress and Rapid Personality Changes" (*International Record of Medicine*, V. 169, 1956), "Revitalization Movements" (*American Anthropologist*, V. 58, 1956), and "Mazeway Disintegration: The Individual's Perception of Socio-cultural Disorganization" (*Human Organization*, V. 16, 1957).
Leighton, Clausen and Wilson. *Explorations in Social Psychiatry*.
Beaglehele. "Cultural Complexity and Psychological Problems" (in Mullahy's *A Study of Interpersonal Relations*).
Thompson. "Attitudes and Acculturation" (*American Anthropologist*, V. 50, 1948).
Mead. "The Implications of Culture Change for Personality Development" (*American Journal of Orthopsychiatry*, V. 17, 1947).
M. K. Opler. *Culture, Psychiatry and Human Values* and *Culture and Mental Health*.
Nalzberg. *Migration and Education*.
Kluckhohn and Murray. *Personality In Nature, Society, and Culture*.
Linton. *Tht Cultural Background of Personality* and *Culture and Mental Disorders*.
Caudill. "Japanese-American Personality and Acculturation" (*Genetic Psychology Monographs*, V. 45, 1952).
Tooth. *Studies in Mental Illness in the Gulf Coast*.
Bakke. *Citizens Without Work*.
Erikson. *Youth: Identity and Crisis* and "Symposium of Alienation and the Search for Identity" (*American Journal of Psychoanalysis*, V. 21, 1961).

Socio-psychological studies of native American peoples may also be pertinent.

Spicer. *Cycles of Conquest*.
    This study is of value in dealing with acculturation, conquest, and resistance to conquest.
Kluckhohn and Leighton. *The Navaho*.
MacGregor. *Warriors Without Weapons*.
Unton (ed.). *Acculturation in Seven American Indian Tribes*.
Wallace. "Some Psychological Determinants of Culture Change in Indian Communities" (*Bureau of American Ethnology Bulletin*, V. 149, 1951).
Spindler (ed.). *Socio-cultural and Psychological Processes in American Acculturation*.

Sources on the Education and Study of Black Americans

Sources on African History and Culture

Source material on Africa is now becoming available in considerable quantity. Cited below are introductory works, some intended for use by secondary-level students, others by teachers, most of which contain bibliographies which will guide the reader to more technical or regionally-focused sources.

Beattie, John. *Bunyoro: An African Kingdom*. New York: Holt, Rinehart and Winston, 1960.
    A description of the history and culture of the Kingdom of Bunyoro in Uganda.
Chu, Daniel, and Skinner, Elliott. *A Glorious Age in Africa*. Garden City: Doubleday, 1965.
    An introduction to the ancient civilizations of Ghana, Mali, and Songhay.
Curtin, Philip D. *Africa Remembered, Narratives by West Africans from the Era of the Slave Trade*. Madison: University of Wisconsin Press, 1967.
Davidson, Basil. *Africa: History of a Continent*. New York: Macmillan, 1966.
    A very readable and accurate history of all of Africa.
——. *The African Genius*. Boston: Little, Brown, 1971.
——. *A Guide to African History: A General Survey of the African Past from Earliest Times to the Present*. Ed. Haskel Frankel. Garden City: Doubleday, 1965.

——. *A History of West Africa to the Nineteenth Century.* Garden City: Doubleday, 1966.
    A fairly detailed but nonetheless interesting history of the black peoples of West Africa.
——. *Black Mother: The Years of the African Slave Trade.* Boston: Little, Brown, 1961.
——. *The African Past: Chronicles from Antiquity to Modern Times.* Boston: Little, Brown, 1964.
——. *The Lost Cities of Africa.* Boston: Little, Brown, 1963.
DeGrant-Johnson, J. C. *African Glory: The Story of Vanished Negro Civilizations.* New York: Walker & Co., 1966.
    A history of Negro peoples.
Diamond, Stanley, and Burke, Fred G. (ed.). *The Transformation of East Africa: Studies in Political Anthropology.* New York: Basic Books, 1966.
Dobler, Lavinia, and Brown, William A. *Great Rulers of the African Past.* Garden City: Doubleday, 1965.
    A secondary level account of the lives of five African leaders of four hundred or more years ago.
Hallett, Robin. *Africa to 1875: A Modern History.* Ann Arbor: University of Michigan Press, 1971.
Kenyatta, Jomo. *Facing Mount Kenya.* London: Lecker and Warburg, 1938.
    An introduction to the Kikuyu people and to the Kenya independence movement.
Kilson, Martin. *Political Change in a West African State: A Study of the Modernization Process in Sierra Leone.* Cambridge: Harvard University Press, 1966.
Mair, Lucy. *Primitive Government.* Middlesex: Penguin Books, 1962.
    A good description of the native political institutions of African tribal groups with emphasis upon east Africa. Useful for students interested in comparative political institutions.
Oliver, R., and Fage, J. D. *A Short History of Africa.* Middlesex: Penguin Books, 1962.
Trimingham, J. S. *The History of Islam in West Africa.* New York: Oxford University Press, 1959.
Wauthier, Claude. *The Literature and Thought of Modern Africa.* Tr. by Shirley Ray. New York: Praeger, 1967.
    An introduction to "negritude" as evidenced in the writing of modern black Africa.

Sources on the Afro-American Past

General Bibliographies and Guides

——. *Bibliographic Survey: The Negro in Print.* Washington, D.C.: The Negro Bibliographic and Research Center, Inc.
    A carefully annotated survey, published six times a year.
Miller, Elizabeth W. *The Negro in America: A Bibliography.* Cambridge: Harvard University Press, 1966.
    A survey of recent writings.
Welsch, Erwin K. *The Negro in the U.S.: A Research Guide.* Bloomington: University of Indiana Press, 1964.
Work, Monroe N. *A Bibliography of the Negro in Africa and America.* New York: Octagon Books, 1965.

Some bibliographic guides are designed especially for schools:
——. *Integrated School Books: A Descriptive Bibliography of Selected Classroom Texts.* New York: National Association for the Advancement of Colored People, 1966. 18pp.
Kast, William. *Resource Unit on the Negro.* New York: Bantam, 1967.
    A handbook for secondary teachers for use in the social studies curriculum. Programmatic techniques, special units, resources, as well as bibliographic and audiovisual references.
Penn, Joseph E., Brooks, Elaine C., and Berch, Mollie L. (eds.). *The Negro American in Paperback.* Washington, D.C.: National Education Association, 1201 Sixteenth St., N.W., 1967. 35¢
    A selected list of paperbound books compiled and annotated for secondary school students.
Schatz, Walter. *Directory of Afro-American Resources.* New York: Bowker, 1971.
    Compiled by the Race Relations Information Center, this guide lists organizations holding research materials in Afro-American studies.

Books

Aptheker, Herbert. *American Negro Slave Revolts.* New York: International Publishers, 1963.
    A basic source.
——. *Documentary History of the Negro in the United States.* Vols. I & II. New York: Citadel, 1951.
    Contains valuable documents not found elsewhere. Together they provide deep insight into American Negro history.
Bennett, Lerone, Jr. *Before the Mayflower: A History of the Negro in America, 1619–1964.* Baltimore: Penguin, 1965.

A very readable history of the Negro from the great African empires to the civil rights movements of the early 1960's.

Botkin, Benjamin A. *Lay My Burden Down: A Folk History of Slavery.* Chicago: University of Chicago Press, 1945.
A collection of reminiscences of ex-slaves about slavery.

Broderick, Francis L. *W. E. B. DuBois: Negro Leader in a Time of Crisis.* Stanford: Stanford University Press, 1959.

Buckmaster, Henrietta. *Let My People Go.* Boston: Beacon, 1959.
Vivid story of the Underground Railroad.

Cronon, Edmund David. *The Story of Marcus Garvey.* Madison: University of Wisconsin Press, 1955.
The life of Garvey is particularly significant today, with black separatism growing strong again.

Davis, Allison, et al. *Deep South.* Chicago: University of Chicago Press, 1941.
Provides insight into the status of black people in the pre-World War II South.

Donnan, Elizabeth. *Documents Illustrative of the Slave Trade to America.* Washington: Carnegie Institute, 1935.

Douglass, Frederick. *The Life and Times of Frederick Douglass.* New York: Collier, 1962.
This classic American autobiography of the great Negro leader's life first as a slave, then as abolitionist writer and statesman, is indispensable reading.

DuBois, W. E. B. *Black Folk, Then and Now, an Essay in the History and Sociology of the Negro Race.* New York: Holt, Rinehart and Winston, 1939.
——. *Black Reconstruction in America.* New York: Meridian, 1962.
——. *Darkwater, Voices From Within the Veil.* New York: Harcourt, Brace Jovanovich, 1920.
——. *Dusk of Dawns: An Essay Toward an Autobiography of a Race Concept.* New York: Harcourt Brace Jovanovich, 1940.
——. *The Souls of the Black Folk.* New York: Fawcett, 1961.
A collection of essays that has become a classic in Afro-American literature. Considered by many the effective impetus of Negro militancy in the twentieth century.
——. *The World and Africa.* New York: Viking, 1947.

Dumond, Dwight L. *Antislavery.* Ann Arbor: Ann Arbor Publishers, 1961.
A basic source on the abolitionist movement.

Durham, Philip, and Jones, Everett L. *The Negro Cowboy.* New York: Dodd, Mead, 1965.

Elkins, Stanley M. *Slavery: A Problem in American Institutional and Intellectual Life.* New York: Grosset and Dunlap, Universal Library, 1959.
Skillfully utilizes the insights of social psychology to determine why American slavery was different from other slave systems and why its effects upon the Negro personality have been so severe and persisting.

Franklin, John Hope. *From Slavery to Freedom: A History of American Negroes.* New York: Alfred A. Knopf, 1956.
An objective scholarly history with an excellent bibliography.

Frazier, E. Franklin. *The Negro Family in the United States.* Chicago: University of Chicago Press, 1939.
A basic study.

Freyre, Gilberto. *The Masters and the Slaves.* New York: Alfred A. Knopf, 1946.
A history of the Negro in Brazil during the slave era.

Garfinkle, Norton (ed.). *Lincoln and the Coming of the Civil War.* Boston: Heath, 1959. (Heath American Studies Series)

Garvey, Marcus. *Philosophy and Opinions.* New York: Universal, 1925. Compiled by Amy Jacques-Garvey. Two volumes.
The views of the founder of the Universal Negro Improvement Association.

Goldwin, Robert A. (ed.). *100 Years of Emancipation.* Chicago: Rand McNally, 1963.
A collection of articles, mostly written by scholars.

Herskovits, Melville. *The Myth of the Negro Past.* Boston: Beacon, 1958.
A basic analysis of the origins and cultural legacies of Afro-Americans.

Holmes, S. J. *The Negro's Struggle for Survival.* Berkeley: University of California Press, 1937.

Hughes, Langston, and Meltzer, Milton (eds.). *A Pictorial History of the Negro in America.* New York: Crown, 1956.
Excellent use of pictures and facsimiles of documents.

Johnson, James Weldon. *Black Manhattan.* New York: Columbia University Press, 1956.

Katz, William Loren. *Eyewitness: The Negro in American History.* New York: Pitman, 1967.
——. *A Teacher's Guide to American Negro History Materials.* New York: Pitman, 1967.

Korngold, Ralph. *Citizen Toussaint.* New York: Hill & Wang, 1965.
A good biography of the famous black Haitian general.

Kugelmass, J. A. *Ralph J. Bunche, Fighter for Peace.* New York: Messner, 1952.

Litwack, Leon F. *North of Slavery.* Chicago: University of Chicago Press, 1961.

The best general study available on the Negro in the North before the Civil War.

Locke, Alain (ed.). *The New Negro: An Interpretation.* New York: Boni, 1925.

Logan, Rayford W. *The Negro in American Life and Thought.* New York: Dial Press, 1954.

———. *The Negro in the United States: A History to 1945.* New York: Van Nostrand Reinhold, 1970.

Logan, Rayford W., and Winston, Michael. *The Negro in the United States: The Ordeal of Democracy.* New York: Van Nostrand Reinhold, 1971.

———. *What the Negro Wants.* Chapel Hill: University of North Carolina Press, 1944.
A collection of essays.

Meier, August. *The Negro in American Thought, 1880–1915.* Ann Arbor: University of Michigan Press, 1964.

Meltzer, Milton, and Meier, August. *Time of Trial, Time of Hope: The Negro in America, 1919 to 1941.* Garden City: Doubleday, 1966.
Written for secondary students.

Olmstead, Frederick L. *The Slave States (Before the Civil War).* New York: Putnam, 1959.
A first-hand view of the South during the 1850's.

Pierson, Donald. *Negroes in Brazil.* Chicago: University of Chicago Press, 1942.

Quarles, Benjamin. *The Negro in the Making of America.* New York: Collier Books, 1964.
A brief history of the Negro's place in American history down to the Second World War. A good introductory chapter on Africa.

Redding, J. Saunders. *On Being Negro in America.* Indianapolis: Bobbs-Merrill, 1951.

Rowan, Carl T. *South of Freedom.* New York: Alfred A. Knopf, 1952.

Rozwenc, Edwin C. (ed.). *Reconstruction in the South.* Boston: Heath, 1952.
A collection of readings.

Stampp, Kenneth M. *The Peculiar Institution.* New York: Vintage, 1956.
A good introduction to slavery in the South.

Sterling, Dorothy, and Quarles, Benjamin. *Lift Every Voice.* Garden City: Doubleday, 1965.
The lives of DuBois, Terrell, Washington, and J. W. Johnson, written for secondary students.

Stowe, Harriet. *Uncle Tom's Cabin.* New York: Washington Square, 1962.
It would be fruitful to read this anti-slavery classic in conjunction with Baldwin's discussion of it, "Everybody's Protest Novel," included in *Notes of a Native Son.*

Tannenbaum, Frank. *Slave and Citizen: The Negro in the Americas.* New York: Vintage Books, 1946.
A comparative study of African slavery in the Americas which seeks to place the U.S. slave system in perspective.

Walker, David. *One Continual Cry: David Walker's Appeal to the Colored Citizens of the World* (with "Its Setting and Meaning" by Herbert Aptheker). New York: Marzani and Munsell, 1965.
The earliest bold attack upon slavery written by a black American.

Washington, Booker T. *Up From Slavery.* New York: Bantam, 1959.
Published in 1900, this autobiography remains a valuable source of information on Washington and his approach to race relations.

Wish, Harvey (ed.). *The Negro Since Emancipation.* New York: Prentice-Hall, 1964.

Woodward, C. Vann. *The Strange Career of Jim Crow.* New York: Oxford University Press, 1955.
An excellent study of segregation from its beginning in the post-Reconstruction South to present.

Wright, Richard. *Black Boy.* New York: Signet, 1945.

Ziegler, Benjamin M. (ed.). *Desegregation and the Supreme Court.* Boston: Heath, 1958.
A collection of essays.

Sources on Contemporary Issues

Materials for this subject are particularly liable to the flux of contemporary events. Black militancy, for example, is a movement constantly subject to change. In addition to consulting the bibliographies cited previously, therefore, the reader will depend somewhat more on periodical literature and pamphlets.

Books

Allport, Gordon. *The Nature of Prejudice.* New York: Doubleday, 1958. (Anchor Books).
A sound and comprehensive analysis of group prejudice.

Baldwin, James. *Nobody Knows My Name.* New York: Dell, 1961.

———. *Notes of a Native Son.* Boston: Beacon, 1957. New York: Bantam, 1964.

———. *The Fire Next Time.* New York: Dell, 1963.
It is said that this essay has had as significant an impact as *Souls of the Black Folk* did in 1903. All the above essays are basic reading.

Bennett, Lerone, Jr. *Confrontation: Black and White.* Baltimore: Penguin, 1965.
An historical discussion of the Negro struggle for equal rights from colonial times through 1965.

Broderick, Francis L., and August, Meier (ed.). *Negro Protest Thought in the Twentieth Century.* Indianapolis: Bobbs-Merrill, 1966.
A chronological sourcebook of documents ranging from Washington, Trotter, DuBois, and Garvey to Randolph, Wilkins, Farmer, and King.

Brown, C. *Manchild in the Promised Land.* New York: New American Library, 1966.
A powerful representation of ghetto life.

Cash, Wilbur J. *The Mind of the South.* New York: Vintage, 1960.
An exploration of attitudes of southern whites toward Negroes.

Clarke, John Henrik (ed.). *Harlem: A Community in Transition.* New York: Citadel, 1964.
A collection of essays, photographs, and poems.

Clark, Kenneth B. *Dark Ghetto.* New York: Harper and Row, 1965. Torchbook, 1967.
A probing study of the Negro "power structure" and the psychology of the ghetto. It describes the efforts of HARYOU (Harlem Youth Organization), which Clark directs, to combat the system that maintains ghettoes.

———. (ed.). *The Negro Protest: James Baldwin, Malcolm X, Martin L. King, Jr.* Boston: Beacon, 1963.
———. *Prejudice and Your Child.* Boston: Beacon, 1963.
A sound and incisive account of the broad and subtle ways children absorb racial prejudice and an examination of its effects.

Dollard, John. *Caste and Class in a Southern Town.* 3rd ed. New York: Doubleday, 1949.
An excellent source on race-relations in the small-town Deep South during the 1930's with a chapter on education. Out of date in some respects, it is still useful background reading.

Drake, St. Clair, and Layton, Horace R. *Black Metropolis: A Study of Negro Life in a Northern City.* (2 vol.) New York: Harper and Row, 1962.
A comprehensive study of Negro life in Chicago through the early 1940's, with appendices written in 1962.

Edwards, Gilbert Franklin. *The Negro Professional Class.* New York: Free Press, 1959.

Essien-Udom, E. U. *Black Nationalism.* New York: Dell, 1964.
An excellent survey of black separatist movements in the United States, focusing upon the Nation of Islam. Published first in 1962, the growth of separatism of non-Muslim varieties has already altered the book's subject but it still remains a valuable source with a good bibliography.

Frazier, E. Franklin. *Black Bourgeoise.* New York: Collier, 1962.
Although published in 1955, this work still remains a source for understanding the problems and goals of the Negro middle-class.

———. *The Negro in the United States.* New York: Macmillan, 1957.
A classic study of Negro society.

Ginzberg, Eli, and Eichner, A. S. *Troublesome Presence: American Democracy and the Negro.* New York: New American Library, 1964.
Discusses relationship of American politics to Negro discrimination.

Glazer, Nathan, and Daniel P. Moynihan. *Beyond the Melting Pot.* Cambridge: M.I.T. Press, 1965.
A study of New York's separate ethnic groups that have not been absorbed into the "melting pot." Good section on the Negro.

Goodman, Mary Ellen. *Race Awareness in Young Children.* New York: Collier, 1964.

Gordon, Milton M. *Assimilation in American Life.* New York: Oxford University Press, 1964.

Gregory, Dick, and Lipsyte, R. *Nigger.* New York: Pocket Books, 1964.

Grimes, Alan Pendleton. *Equality in America: Religion, Race, and the Urban Majority.* New York: Oxford University Press, 1964.

Handlin, Oscar. *The Newcomers: Negroes and Puerto Ricans in a Changing Metropolis.* New York: Anchor Books, 1959.

Hare, Nathan. *The Black Anglo-Saxons.* New York: Marzani & Munsell, 1966.
A black sociologist looks critically at the Negro middle-class.

Isaacs, Harold R. *New World of Negro Americans.* New York: Viking, 1964.

Jones, LeRoi. *Home: Social Essays.* New York: Morrow, 1966.
———. *Preface to a Twenty Volume Suicide Note.* New York: Citadel, 1961.
———. *System of Dante's Hell.* New York: Grove, 1966.

King, Martin Luther, Jr. *Stride Toward Freedom: The Montgomery Story.* New York: Harper and Row, 1958.
———. *Why We Can't Wait.* New York: New American Library, 1964.
Especially "Letter from a Birmingham Jail," an eloquent and provocative statement of the rationale for the non-violent civil rights movement. (Also published in pamphlet form by the American Friends Service Committee, Philadelphia.)

Kinzer, Robert H., and Sagarin, Edward. *The Negro in American Business: Conflict Between Separatism and Integration.* New York: Greenberg, 1950.

Lee, Irwin H. *Negro Medal of Honor Men.* New York: Dodd, Mead, 1967.
The story of black men in the U.S. armed forces.

Lincoln, C. Eric. *The Black Muslim in America.* Boston: Beacon, 1961.

Lomax, Louis E. *The Negro Revolt.* New York: New American Library (Signet Books) 1963.

A good summary of the civil rights movement between 1955 and 1962, although many sections are now out of date.

Malcolm X. *Autobiography*. New York: Grove Press, 1965.

Required reading for insight into ghetto life, black nationalism, and the life and mind of this extraordinary leader.

——. *Malcolm X Speaks*. New York: Grove Press, 1966.

McCarthy, Agnes, and Reddick, Lawrence. *Worth Fighting For*. Garden City: Doubleday, 1965.

A history of the Negro during the Civil War era, designed for secondary pupils.

McWilliams, Carey. *Brothers Under the Skin*. Rev. ed. Boston: Little, Brown, 1964.

Mendelson, Wallace. *Discrimination*. Englewood Cliffs, New Jersey: Prentice-Hall, 1962.

An overview of discrimination based upon the 1961 Report of the U.S. Civil Rights Commission.

Moore, Richard B. *The Name "Negro": Its Origins and Evil Use*. New York: Afro-American Publishers, 1960.

An attack upon the use of the term "Negro."

Parsons, Talcott, and Clark, K. B. (ed.). *The Negro American*. Boston: Houghton-Mifflin, 1966.

A collection of recent essays.

Reddick, Lawrence D. *Crusader Without Violence: Martin Luther King, Jr.* New York: Harper and Row, 1959.

Rose, Arnold. *The Negro in America*. New York: Harper and Row, 1944, rev. ed. 1962 with new 1963 introduction in latest edition. Torchbooks.

A condensation of Gunnar Myrdal's *An American Dilemma*, this study of Negro-white relations through the early 1940's is still valuable, although no longer "current" in every respect.

Sexton, Patricia Cayo. *Spanish Harlem*. New York: Harper and Row, 1965.

Contains valuable information on Puerto Ricans of African background.

Silberman, Charles E. *Crisis in Black and White*. New York: Random House, 1964.

A good analysis of the black-white racial confrontation in America.

Simpson, G. E., and Yinger, J. M. *Racial and Cultural Minorities: An Analysis of Prejudice and Discrimination*. New York: Harper and Row, 1953.

Thompson, Danial C. *The Negro Leadership Class*. Englewood Cliffs, New Jersey: Prentice-Hall, 1963.

Thompson, Edgar. *Race: Individual and Collective Behavior*, ed. Everett Hughes. Glencoe: Free Press, 1958.

Warner, W. Lloyd. *American Life: Dream and Reality*. Rev. ed. Chicago: University of Chicago Press, 1962.

Wilson, James O. *Negro Politics: The Search for Leadership*. Glencoe: Free Press, 1960.

Wright, Nathan, Jr. *Black Power and Urban Unrest: Creative Possibilities*. New York: Hawthorn, 1967.

A constructive look at the manner in which "black power" can be utilized as a basis for building a better America.

Fanon, Frantz. *Black Skin, White Masks*. New York: Grove Press, 1967.

A book which explores the psychological problems of being Negro in a white-dominated world.

Sources on Black Arts: Novels, Poetry, Drama, and Music

What can be said of all art is particularly true of black American art: It is an indispensable source of insight into the human condition.

Novels

The history of the black novel is mainly a history of protest fiction. Early Post-Reconstruction works sought to combat the prevailing "Sambo" clichés with counter-stereotypes of genteel or so-called "white" Negro characters. They are mostly out of print, but it would be worthwhile to find one or two in libraries, such as William Wells Brown's *Clotel* or J. McHenry Jones' *Hearts of Gold*, to get a sense of the middle-class "Talented Tenth" elitism that Harlem writers from the 1920's on were repudiating when they began to write about the common man. Two early successes recently reprinted are William Demby's *Beetlecreek* (New York: Avon, 1950) and James Weldon Johnson's *Autobiography of an Ex-Colored Man* (New York: Hill & Wang, 1960). Perhaps the most outstanding novel from this period is Gene Toomer's *Cane* (New York: Boni and Liveright, 1923). Since World War II novelists have been more concerned with art than protest and have cast the "Negro Problem" in a universal perspective, producing what are certainly major works:

Baldwin, James. *Go Tell It On The Mountain*. New York: Signet, 1953.

Ellison, Ralph. *The Invisible Man*. New York: New American Library, 1952.

Winner of the National Book Award.

Wright, Richard. *Native Son.* New York: Signet, 1962.

There has been a similar development in poetry, moving from genteel imitations of white verse to a superficial embodiment of folk dialect and slave themes, as exemplified by Paul Laurence Dunbar, to mastery of jazz and Negro urban idioms by Langston Hughes, and absorption of both ghetto reality and America's intellectual tradition, culminating thus far in the work of Pulitzer Prize-winning Gwendolyn Brooks, available in *Selected Poems* (New York: Harper and Row, 1963).

Sources of Black Poetry

> Bontemps, Arna (ed.). *American Negro Poetry.* New York: Hill & Wang, 1963.
> An excellent anthology.
> Hughes, Langston, and Bontemps, Arna. *The Poetry of the Negro, 1746–1949.* New York: Doubleday, 1949.
> The best collection of earlier poetry; includes poets from the Caribbean.
> Hughes, Langston. *Selected Poems.* New York: Alfred A. Knopf, 1959.
> ———. (ed.). *New Negro Poets: U.S.A.* (Bloomington: Indiana University Press, 1964.
> McKay, Claude. *Home to Harlem.* Pocket Books, 1928.

An outstanding example of black drama is:

> Hansberry, Lorraine. *Raisin in the Sun.* New York: Signet, 1959.
> A moving play about an urban Negro family. Winner of Critics Circle Award.

Secondary school teachers may wish to use with mature students more uncompromising contemporary plays like Ossie Davis' race-war satire, *Purlie Victorious,* LeRoi Jones' *Dutchman* and *The Slave* (Apollo, 1964), or James Baldwin's *Blues for Mr. Charlie* (Dell, 1964).

There are a large number of classic non-Negro works which deal with Negro subjects, such as Faulkner's *Intruder in The Dust* and *Light in August* (both in Modern Library paperback), Melville's *Benito Cereno* (in *Great Short Works* published by Harper and Row), O'Neill's *Emperor Jones* (Appleton), and more recent works, *A Member of the Wedding* by Carson McCullers (New Directions) and Harper Lee's *To Kill a Mockingbird* (Harcourt, Brace Jovanovich.)

Black Periodicals and Pamphlets

Periodicals dealing with black affairs, race relations, Africa, and other subjects are numerous, both in terms of those which are suitable for secondary-level classroom use and in terms of those which are useful for library use and teacher reference.

Black Dailies and Weeklies Published in the West

Alaska
> *Alaska Spotlight,* Anchorage, Alaska (weekly).

California
> *Berkeley Post,* Berkeley, California (weekly).
> *The Black Panther,* Box 8641, Emeryville Branch, Oakland, California (monthly).
> *California Eagle,* Los Angeles, California (weekly).
> *California Voice,* Oakland, California (weekly).
> *The Flatlands,* Box 10287, Oakland, California (monthly).
> *Los Angeles Herald-Dispatch,* Los Angeles, California (semi-weekly).
> *Los Angeles Record,* Los Angeles, California (weekly).
> *Los Angeles Sentinel,* Los Angeles, California (weekly).
> *The Movement,* 449 14th St., San Francisco, California (monthly).
> *Sacramento Observer,* Sacramento, California (weekly).
> *San Diego Lighthouse,* San Diego, California (weekly).
> *The Sun Reporter,* San Francisco, California (weekly).

Colorado
> *Denver Blade,* Denver, Colorado (weekly).
> *Denver Star,* Denver, Colorado (weekly).

Missouri
> *Kansas City Call,* Kansas City, Missouri (weekly).

Nevada
> *Las Vegas Voice,* Las Vegas, Nevada (weekly).

Oklahoma
> *Black Dispatch,* Oklahoma City, Oklahoma (weekly).
> *Oklahoma Eagle.* Tulsa, Oklahoma (weekly).

Eastern Black Newspapers

The Amsterdam News, New York, New York
The Baltimore Afro-American, Baltimore, Maryland
The Chicago Defender, Chicago, Illinois
Muhammad Speaks, Chicago, Illinois
The Pittsburgh Courier, Pittsburgh, Pennsylvania

Black Magazines

The Crisis (National Association for the Advancement of Colored People, 20 W. 40th St., New York, $1.50).
A monthly focusing on civil rights but containing also book reviews, articles on Negro life and history, and an annual list of books by black authors.
Ebony (1820 S. Michigan Avenue, Chicago, Illinois, $5.00).
A magazine of excellent quality which ordinarily serves as a voice for the Negro leadership elite and has a middle-class orientation.
Liberator (Afro-American Research Institute, 244 E. 46th St., New York, $3.00).
A monthly magazine which provides an outlet for black radical viewpoints of varying degrees. A necessary supplement to magazines of the *Ebony* type.
Negro Digest (1820 S. Michigan Ave., Chicago, Illinois, $3.00).
A monthly featuring original articles which generally strike a middle-ground between the *Ebony* and *Liberator* viewpoints.
Probe (a new magazine published in New York, at 136 W. 52nd St., New York City.)

Quarterlies Dealing with United States Negro History and Affairs

Freedomways (Freedomways Associates, Inc., 799 Broadway, New York, $5.00).
A quarterly which mixes together scholarly articles, essays, book reviews, and poetry.
Integrated Education (Integrated Associates, 343 South Dearborn St., Chicago, Illinois) bimonthly.
Interracial Review (Catholic Interracial Council of New York, 233 Broadway, New York, N.Y.)
Journal of Intergroup Relations (National Association of Intergroup Relations Officials (NAIRO), 49 Sheridan Avenue, Albany, New York) quarterly.
Journal of Human Relations, Central State College, Wilberforce, Ohio.
A quarterly composed of scholarly articles, essays and book reviews dealing with the broader issues relevant to inter-group relations.
Journal of Negro Education, Howard University, Washington, D.C.
Focuses attention upon educational issues relevant to black people.
Journal of Negro History, Association for the Study of Negro Life and History, 1538 Ninth St., N.W., Washington, D.C.
A major quarterly dealing with the history of Afro-American peoples.
Phylon: The Atlantic University Review of Race and Culture, Atlanta University, Atlanta, Georgia.
An excellent quarterly with historical and contemporary scholarly articles dealing with race relations.

Quarterlies and Journals Dealing with Africa

African Abstracts, International African Institute, St. Dunstan's Chambers, 10/11 Fetter Lane, London, E.C. 4.
A quarterly review of articles appearing in current periodicals. A guide to specialized journals.
African Forum, American society of African Culture, 720 Fifth Avenue, New York 10019.
A quarterly dealing with political, social, economic, and cultural developments of the African nations and the American Negro.
Journal of African History, School of Oriental and African Studies, Cambridge University Press.
The standard quarterly on African history.

Pamphlets and Mimeographed Materials

These materials reflect the concerns of the black community and comprise a significant set of resources for use in secondary-level social studies classrooms. National and regional headquarters of the major organizations may be able to supply material and local addresses.

Afro-American Research Institute, Inc. 244 E. 46th St., New York.
Black Panther Party for Self Defense, Box 8641, Emeryville Station, Oakland, California.
Congress of Racial Equality, 38 Park Row, New York 38, N.Y.
Lowndes County Freedom Organization, 125 Route 1, Haynesville, Alabama.
Mississippi Freedom Democratic Party, Box 275, Sunflower, Mississippi.
National Association for the Advancement of Colored People, 20 W. 40th St., New York.
Nation of Islam, 5335 So. Greenwood, Chicago, Illinois 60615.

Southern Christian Leadership Conference, 334 Auburn Avenue N.E. Atlanta, Georgia.
Student Non-Violent Coordinating Council, 8½ Raymond St., N.W. Atlanta, Georgia; and 449 14th St., San Francisco, California.
Urban League of the Bay Area, 1607 McAllister, San Francisco, California.

Sources of Audio-Visual Materials for Black Studies

The local Afro-American community ultimately comprises the best source for the greater part of audio-visual materials used in any given school. But no matter where such materials are acquired, they should be reviewed by representatives of the local community. Interaction with the local community will serve to prevent the kind of, perhaps, unconscious partisanship which sees middle-class school personnel posting pictures of Roy Wilkins and Whitney Young while failing to display poster-portraits of Malcolm X and Muhammad Ali.

The selective, annotated bibliography of materials on the Afro-American published by Bowker, *Multimedia Materials for Afro-American Studies,* compiled by Harry A. Johnson, includes a vast amount of data plus four position papers by black educators.

Recordings

The Afro-American population has played such a strong part in popular music in the United States that recordings of current black contributions are impossible to overlook. Other types of African and Afro-American music, however, along with speeches and poetry readings, are also available on recordings.

The Archive of Folk Song of the Library of Congress publishes a catalog of available recordings entitled *Folk Music,* available from the U.S. Government Printing Office, Washington, D.C. 20402 for 40¢, which lists records that can be ordered from the Library of Congress.

Columbia Records, Education Department, 799 Seventh Avenue, New York 10019, issues a brochure which lists the folk records available on the "Columbia" and "Epic" labels.

Folkways Records, (121 West 47th Street, New York) has an excellent selection of Afro-American recordings ranging from the poetry of Langston Hughes to civil rights documentaries to folk and freedom songs.

Similarly, write to Ethnic Folkways Records, 165 West 46th Street, New York, for information on their African recordings.

Wall Charts, Pictures, and Posters

Posters and illustrative material depicting current aspects of African, Afro-Caribbean, and Afro-Brazilian life may be obtained from the consulates of African and American governments as well as from airlines serving these regions.

Other sources for illustrative material or guides include the National Association for the Advancement of Colored People, Suite 703, 948 Market Street, San Francisco, California 94102; and the Association for the Study of Negro Life and History, 1538 Ninth Street, N.W., Washington, D.C. 20001; Friendship Press (475 Riverside Drive, New York 10027) has published a set of portrait-type reproductions of notable personages of African ancestry including such individuals as James Baldwin, Roy Wilkins, Robert C. Weaver, Martin Luther King, Jr., Althea Gibson, John Hope Franklin, and Carl Rowan. These may be supplemented by posters of Malcolm X available from *The Movement* (449 14th St., San Francisco, California) for one dollar each.

Illustrative material is to some degree available from commercial agencies serving the educational market, such as the illustrated booklet and wall-size mural on "The American Negro" published by Rand McNally and Company (P. O. Box 7600, Chicago, Illinois 60680).

Films and Filmstrips

The African Film Bibliography 1965, published by the African Studies Association, Indiana University, Bloomington, Indiana, is a useful guide to over three hundred films dealing with sub-Saharan Africa. The films are annotated in such a way as to make the guide especially useful for teachers, yet many of the films are products of agencies with a viewpoint to popularize (corporations with investments to protect, missionary organizations, governments, etc.) and the teacher must exercise caution in exposing her pupils to one-sided or propagandistic material.

The Educators Guide to Free Social Studies Materials contains references to films dealing with Africa and Afro-Americans, but the propagandistic element in these "free" films is apt to be extremely high.

Commercial concerns are producing films and filmstrips for the school market dealing with American Negro history, race relations, and the civil rights movement. The accuracy and acceptability of these commercial products is not uniformly high, and they should be previewed before purchase by persons familiar with current conditions and recent research, including especially individuals from the local black community.

The Oakland, California, schools have produced a "Resource Guide for Teaching About Contributions of Minorities to American Culture" (1966) which lists and describes some of the commercial educational films dealing with the above subjects. The Berkeley, California, Unified School District's unit on Negro history also contains reference to several filmstrips which their staff recommends for classroom use. Readers will also wish to check with their local educational television station for information on availability of television productions dealing with Africa and Afro-Americans.

Commercial films intended for television broadcast or theater viewing are sometimes especially to be recommended for school use at the secondary level. Among the excellent films of this type available are *Black Orpheus* (Orfeo Negro), a Brazilian production, and *Nothing But a Man*, A United States production.

Examples of other motion pictures of this type include

A Patch of Blue
Lilies of the Field
The Defiant Ones
Raisin in the Sun
Go Down Moses
Black Monday
Cry The Beloved Country

African and Afro-American Arts and Crafts

School personnel in metropolitan areas should have little difficulty in locating sources of Afro-American and African art, via museums, retail stores, importers, or local black organizations. Educators in more isolated regions may have to travel to the city after first checking the classified telephone directory for references to the above types of agencies. Letters to the embassies of African and Afro-Caribbean governments may yield addresses of sources for genuine arts and crafts products from individual countries.

Items produced by blacks in Mississippi can be obtained from Liberty House, P. O. Box 3193, Jackson, Mississippi.

For the most part, schools will have to be content with purchasing reproductions of African works of art. The following museums sell accurate reproductions and issue catalogues:

The British Museum, London, England, W.C.I.
Field Museum of Natural History, Chicago, Illinois.
Lowie Museum of Anthropology, University of California, Berkeley. Issues "African Arts," $3.50 per year.
Metropolitan Museum of Art, 5th Ave. and 82nd St., New York.
Museum of African Art, Washington, D.C.
Museum of Primitive Art, 15 West 54th St., New York. Issues twenty relevant publications.
Museum of the University of Pennsylvania, 33 Spruce, Philadelphia 19104.

A catalogue of art reproductions and where to get them is published by Scarecrow Press of New York.

Books of value in providing background information prior to the building up of a collection of reproductions, and useful in the classroom, include:

Fagg, William, and Plass, Margaret. *African Sculpture*. New York: Dutton, 1964.
Leuzinger, Elsy. *African Sculpture*. Zurich, Switzerland: Museum Rietberg Zurich, Atlantis Verlag, Zurich, 1963.
———. *Art of Africa*. New York: Crown Publications, 1965.
Radin, Paul, and Sweeney, James J. *African Folktales and Sculpture*. 2nd ed. New York: Pantheon Books, 1964.
  Teacher can read tales and show corresponding images.
Robbins, Warren. *African Art in American Collections*. New York: Praeger, 1966. ill. $12.50.
  All American museums are listed.
Segg, Ladislas. *African Sculpture*. New York: Dover, 1964. $2.00
Underwood, Leon. *Masks of West Africa*. New York: Transatlantic, 1948.

A film on "African Sculpture" is also available from Encyclopedia Britannica Films, 2494 Teagarden, San Leandro, California.

Books About the Black Man in America

Bennett, Lerone. *Pioneers in Protest*. Chicago: Johnson, 1968.
  Moving profiles of black revolutionists from the earliest days of nationhood to the present.
——. *What Manner of Man*. Chicago: Johnson, 1964.
  A biography of Martin Luther King, Jr.
Brink, William, and Harris, Louis. *Black and White*. New York: Simon and Schuster, 1967.
  A survey and analysis of white and Negro racial attitudes.
Brown, Claude. *Manchild in the Promised Land*. New York: Macmillan, 1965.
  An autobiography of a Harlem boy in the post World War II era.
Carmichael, Stokely, and Hamilton, Charles V. *Black Power: The Politics of Liberation*. New York: Random House, 1967.
  The authors argue that American racism makes existing political attitudes and institutions irrelevant and that blacks must form their own political organizations to effect needed social change.
Clark, Kenneth B. *Dark Ghetto, Dilemmas of Social Power*. New York: Harper and Row, 1965.
  A distinguished psychologist analyzes the Negro power structure and dissects the effectiveness and ineffectiveness of civil rights' strategies.
Cleaver, Eldridge. *Soul on Ice*. New York: McGraw-Hill, 1968.
  Essays and open letters from California's Folsom Prison in which the author tells of forces which shaped his life and which are currently molding our national destiny.
Conot, Robert. *Rivers of Blood, Year of Darkness*. New York: Bantam Books, 1967.
  The 1965 Watts rebellion in Los Angeles.
Dawson, Helaine S. *On the Outskirts of Hope*. New York: McGraw-Hill, 1968.
  An unorthodox approach to teaching youth from poverty areas.
Fairbairn, Ann. *Five Smooth Stones*. New York: Crown, 1966.
  The life of David Champlin, born in New Orleans during the Depression, and his service as a civil rights leader.
Fishel, Leslie. *The Negro American: A Documentary Story*. New York: William Morrow, 1968.
  Over 200 readings tracing the Negro American from his African background to his place in America today.
Frazier, E. Franklin. *From Slavery to Freedom*. New York: Alfred A. Knopf, 1967.
  The history of the Negro in the United States from his African origins to today.
Gaines, Ernest J. *Bloodline*. New York: Dial Press, 1968.
  Five dramatic stories drawn from the author's background as a Negro on a Southern plantation.
Gregory, Dick. *The Shadow That Scares Me*. Garden City, New York: Doubleday, 1968.
  Short articles critical of Negro and white attitudes toward the problem of civil rights.
Grier, William H., and Cobbs, Price M. *Black Rage*. New York: Basic Books, 1968.
  Two black psychiatrists reveal the full dimensions of the psychological conflicts and the desperation of the black man's life in America.
Griffin, John Howard. *Black Like Me*. Boston: Houghton Mifflin, 1961.
  A white man masquerades as a Negro and travels in the deep South.
Halasz, Nicholas. *The Rattling Chains*. New York: David McKay, 1966.
  A documentation of slave rebellion in the antebellum South.
Hersey, John. *The Algiers Motel Incident*. New York: Alfred A. Knopf, 1968.
  A fascinating reconstruction of events leading to and from the killing of three black youths by policemen during the Detroit rebellion of 1967.
Hughes, Langston. *Black Magic*. Englewood Cliffs, New Jersey: Prentice-Hall, 1967.
  A pictorial history of the Negro in American entertainment.
—— (ed.). *The Book of Negro Humor*. New York: Dodd, Mead, 1966.
  A selection from the wealth of Negro humor from old-time folk tales to the Cool Comics.
Jacobs, Paul. *Prelude to Riot*. New York: Random House, 1968.
  An analysis showing how police discrimination, poor schools, welfare corruption, bureaucratic indifference and political backwardness led to the Watts riots in 1965.
Jones, LeRoi. *Tales*. New York: Grove Press, 1967.
  Sixteen powerful stories about the black man's search for a black America.
Kardiner, Abran, and Ovesey, Lionel. *The Mark of Oppression*. Cleveland: World, 1962.
  The psychological effects of oppression on the American Negro.
Katz, William L. *Eyewitness: The Negro in American History*. New York: Pitman, 1967.
  Contributions of Negroes in every period of American history from the early explorers to today's champions of equality and civil rights.
King, Martin Luther, Jr. *The Trumpets of Conscience*. New York: Harper and Row, 1968.

Five talks reflecting the author's changing ideas about use of civil disobedience in the civil rights struggle.

——. *Where Do We Go From Here: Chaos or Community?* New York: Harper and Row, 1967.

Kohl, Herbert. *36 Children.* New York: New American Library, 1967.
A sixth grade teacher tries to communicate with 36 remote and resistant Negro children in a Harlem school.

Kozol, Jonathan. *Death at an Early Age.* Boston: Houghton Mifflin, 1967.
A white teacher laments the destruction of the hearts and minds of Negro children in the Boston Public Schools.

Lentz, Perry. *The Falling Hills.* New York: Charles Scribner's Sons, 1967.
A story about Negro Union troops in West Tennessee in 1864.

Mitchell, Loften. *Black Drama.* New York: Hawthorn Books, 1967.
The story of the American Negro in the theater.

Pope-Hennessy, James. *Sins of The Fathers.* New York: Alfred A. Knopf, 1968.
A study of the Atlantic slave traders, 1441–1807.

Stone, Chuck. *Tell It Like It Is.* New York: Trident Press, 1968.
Essays on the American racial scene by the well-known Negro journalist.

Styron, William. *The Confessions of Nat Turner.* New York: Random House, 1967.
A novel depicting one man's view of the torment of a slave.

Walker, Margaret. *Jubilee.* Boston: Houghton Mifflin, 1966.
The continuation of slavery in the minds of white men following the Civil War.

Williams, John A. *Beyond the Angry Black.* New York: Cooper Square Publishers, 1966.
Stories, articles and poems of twelve Negro and seven white writers.

——. *The Man Who Cried I Am.* Boston: Little, Brown, 1967.
A brilliant novel about a Negro dying of cancer who takes the reader through nearly 30 years of recent American history as the Negro sees it.

Sources on the Education and Study of Puerto Ricans[2]

Sociological and Anthropological Studies

Back, Kurt W. *Slums, Projects and People: Social, Psychological Problems of Relocation in Puerto Rico.* Durham: Duke University Press, 1962.

Berbusse, *The United States in Puerto Rico, 1898–1900.* Chapel Hill: University of North Carolina Press, 1966.

Bourne, James R., and Dorothy P. *Thirty Years of Change in Puerto Rico: A Case Study of Ten Selected Rural Areas.* New York: Praeger, 1966.

Brameld, Theodore. *The Remaking of a Culture: Life and Education in Puerto Rico.* New York: Harper and Row, 1959.

Cordasco, Francesco. *Puerto Rican Children in Mainland Schools.* Metuchen, New Jersey: Scarecrow, 1968.

Lewis, Gordon K. *Puerto Rico: Freedom and Power in the Caribbean.* New York: Monthly Press Review, 1963.

Steward, Julian H. (ed.). *The People of Puerto Rico.* Urbana: University of Illinois Press, 1956.

Tumin, Melvin M., and Feldman, Arnold. *Social Class and Social Change in Puerto Rico.* Princeton: Princeton University Press, 1961.

Puerto Ricans in the United States

Bibliography on Puerto Ricans in the United States (Migration Division, Commonwealth of Puerto Rico, April, 1959).

Glazer, Nathan, and Moynihan, Daniel P. *Beyond the Melting Pot.* Cambridge: M.I.T. Press, 1964.

Lewis, Oscar. *La Vida.* New York: Random House, 1966.

Monserrat, Joseph. *Puerto Ricans in New York City* (Migration Division, Commonwealth of Puerto Rico, 1967).

Padilla, Elena. *Up From Puerto Rico.* New York: Columbia University Press, 1958.

Senior, Clarence. *The Puerto Ricans: Strangers—Then Neighbours.* Chicago: Quadrangle, 1965.

Sexton, Patricia Cayo. *Spanish Harlem: Anatomy of Poverty.* New York: Harper and Row, 1965.

Wakefield, Dan. *Island in the City: Puerto Ricans in New York.* Boston: Houghton Mifflin, 1959.

[2] The editors gratefully acknowledge the assistance of Francesco Cordasco of Montclair State College in suggesting sources for this section.

Additional Selected Published Materials

Abrams, Charles. "How to Remedy Our 'Puerto Rican Problem'," *Commentary*, Vol. 19, No. 2 (February, 1955): 120–127.

Anastasi, Anne, and Cordova, Fernando A. "Some Effects of Bilingualism upon the Intelligence Test Performance of Puerto Rican Children in New York City," *The Journal of Educational Psychology*, Vol. 44, No. 1 (January, 1953): 1–17.

Berle, Beatrice B. *Eighty Puerto Rican Families in New York City.* New York: Columbia University Press, 1958.

"Bi-Lingual Problems in Puerto Rican Study," *Curriculum and Materials*, Vol. 11, No. 2 (February, 1948): 1–2.

Briggs, Frances M. "As Five Teachers See Themselves," *Educational Forum*, Vol. 28, No. 4 (May, 1964): 389–397. [reprinted by Migration Division, Commonwealth of Puerto Rico, 1965]

Burma, John. *Spanish Speaking Groups in the United States.* Durham, N.C.: Duke University Press, 1954.

Cebollero, Pedro. *A School Language Policy for Puerto Rico.* San Juan, 1945, 133 pp.

"The Challenge in Working with Puerto Rican Families," *Pathways in Child Guidance*, Vol. 2, No. 3 (April, 1960): 3–6.

Chenault, Lawrence R. *The Puerto Rican Migrant in New York City.* New York, 1938, 190 pp.

Collazo, Francisco. *The Education of Puerto Rican Children in the Schools of New York City.* San Juan: Department of Education Press, 1954, 14 pp.

Cordasco, F., and Covello, Leonard. "School and the Spanish Speaking Community," *Congressional Record* (June 12, 1962): A4322–A4323.

Cordasco, F. "The Puerto Rican Child in the American School," *Congressional Record*, Vol. 111, No. 195 (October 19, 1965): 26, 425–26.

——. "Nights in the Gardens of East Harlem: Patricia Sexton's *East Harlem*," *Journal of Negro Education*, 34 (Fall, 1965): 450–451.

——. "The Puerto Rican Child in the American School," American Sociological Association. *Abstracts of Papers* (61st Annual Meeting, 1966): 23–24.

——. "Studies in the Disenfranchised: The Puerto Rican Child," *Psychiatric Spectator*, 3 (November 1966): 3–4.

—— and Roederer, Louis. "Modern Languages and Modern Living," in Roucek, Joseph S. (ed.). *Changing Aspects of the Foreign Language Teaching in the United States.* New York: Philosophical Library, 1967.

Covello, Leonard, with D'Agostino, Guido. *The Heart Is the Teacher.* New York: McGraw-Hill, 1958, 275 pp.

Dossick, Jesse J. *Doctoral Research on Puerto Rico and Puerto Ricans.* New York: New York University, School of Education, 1967.

"Education of Puerto Rican Children in New York City," *The Journal of Educational Sociology*, Vol. 28, No. 4 (December, 1954): 145–192.

Elam, Sophie E. "Acculturation and Learning Problems of Puerto Rican Children," *Teachers College Record*, 61 (February, 1960): 258–264.

Entman, Frederick. "Our Puerto Rican Children: One School's Approach," *Strengthening Democracy* (May, 1955): 3, 5.

Fernos Isern, Antonio. "The Role of Puerto Rico and Its People in the Americas," *The Journal of Educational Sociology*, 35 (May, 1962): 397–401.

Guerra, Emilio L. "The Orientation of Puerto Rican Students in New York City," *Modern Language Journal* (October, 1948): 415–420.

Handlin, Oscar. *The Newcomers, Negroes and Puerto Ricans in a Changing Metropolis.* New York: Doubleday, 1962, 177 pp.

"The Integration Movement in Education," *Curriculum and Materials*, Vol. 18, No. 3 (Spring, 1964): 1.

Jaffe, Abraham J. (ed.). *Puerto Rican Population of New York City: A Series of Papers Delivered Before the New York Area Chapter of the American Statistical Association, October 21, 1953.* Bureau of Applied Social Research. January, 1954, 61 pp.

Kaufman, Maurice. *The Effect of Instruction in Reading Spanish on Reading Ability in English of Spanish-Speaking Retarded Readers.* Unpublished Ph.D. dissertation. New York University, 1966.

Klein, Woody. *Let in the Sun.* New York: Macmillan, 1963, 297 pp.

Lewis, C. "Some Puerto Rican Viewpoints," *Childhood Education*, 43 (October, 1966): 82–84.

Loretan, Joseph O. "Problems in Improving Educational Opportunities for Puerto Ricans in New York," *High Points* (May, 1963): 23–31.

Massimine, E. Virginia. "The Puerto Rican: Citizen of New York," *The Journal of Pi-Lamda Theta* (New York University) (April, 1950): 2.

Mayor's Advisory Committee on Puerto Rican Affairs in New York City, Sub-Committee on Education, Recreation and Parks. *The Puerto Rican Pupils in the Public Schools of New York City: A Survey of Elementary and Junior High Schools.* New York, 1951, 102 pp.

Menton, Seymour. "Teaching English to Puerto Rican Students," *High Points* (November, 1952): 67–70.

Messer, Helaine R. *The Puerto Rican Student in the New York City Public Schools: 1945–1965.* Unpublished M.A. dissertation. Columbia University, 1966.

Mills, C. Wright, Senior, Clarence, and Goldsen, Rose Kohn. *The Puerto Rican Journey.* New York: Russell, 1950, 238 pp.

Monserrat, Joseph. *School Integration: A Puerto Rican View.* San Juan, Commonwealth of Puerto Rico, Department of Labor, Migration Division, 1963, 16 pp.

——. "A Puerto Rican Family," *Natural History* (April, 1967), on Lewis's *La Vida.*

Passow, Harry A. (ed.). *Education in Depressed Areas.* New York, 1963, 359 pp.

Probst, Nathan, and Olmsted, Sophia A. "The Rising Puerto Rican Problem," *Bar Bulletin* (New York County Lawyers Association), Vol. 9, No. 5 (March, 1952): 5–12.

"Puerto Ricans Bid for More Schools," *New York Times,* August 6, 1967.

Puerto Rican Community Development Project: A Proposal for a Self-Help Project to Develop the Community by Strengthening the Family, Opening Opportunities for Youth and Making Full Use of Education. New York, Puerto Rican Forum, 1964.

"Puerto Rican Conference on City Needs," *New York Times,* April 17, 1967.

The Puerto Rican Forum, Inc. *Aspira.* 1965, 4 pp.

"Puerto Ricans and Inter-American Understanding," *The Journal of Educational Sociology,* Vol. 35, No. 9 (May, 1962): 385–440.

"Pupils from Puerto Rico," *The Elementary School Journal* (November, 1958): 74.

Rand, Christopher. *The Puerto Ricans.* New York: Oxford University Press, 1958, 178 pp.

Riessman, Frank. *The Culturally Deprived Child.* New York: Harper and Row, 1962, 140 pp.

Rogers, Melvin L. "For Puerto Rican Pupils: Crash Program in Reading," *The Elementary School Journal* (November, 1958): 87–89.

"Seek Better School Programs for NYC Puerto Rican Youth," *New York Teachers' News,* May 31, 1952, p. 4.

Senior, Clarence. "Schools, Newcomers and Community," *Problems and Practices in New York City Schools.* 1963 Yearbook of the Society for the Experimental Study of Education. Parts II and III, pp. 107–111. New York: Society for the Experimental Study of Education, 1963.

Slotkin, Aaron N. "The Treatment of Minorities in Textbooks: The Issues and the Outlook," *Strengthening Democracy,* Vol. 16, No. 3 (May, 1964): 1–2, 8.

Smith, Richard C. "This School Solves Its Own Problems," *The Elementary School Journal* (November, 1958): 75–81.

Weales, Gerald. "New York's Puerto Rican Dilemma," *The New Leader,* March 7, 1955, pp. 8–10.

Weitzman, Judy. "Reheating the Melting Pot," *The New Leader,* June 28, 1954, pp. 11–12.

Welfare Council of New York City, Committee on Puerto Ricans in New York City. *Puerto Ricans in New York City.* New York, 1948, 60 pp.

Wolk, E. "The Teaching of English as a Second Language in the Elementary Schools of New York City," *Hispania,* 49 (May, 1966): 293–296.

Young, Marguerite. "Schools in City Fit Courses to Puerto Ricans." Reprint. *The New York Herald Tribune,* November 16, 1947.

Sources on the Education and Study of Mexican-Americans

Educational Implications

Abraham, W. "The Bilingual Child, His Parents and Their School," *Exceptional Children,* 23 (November, 1956): 51–52.

Carter, Thomas P. *The Mexican American In School: A History of Educational Neglect.* New York: College Entrance Examination Board, 1970.

Chavez, S. J., and Erickson, T. L. "Teaching American Children from Spanish-Speaking Homes," *Elementary School Journal,* 57 (January, 1957): 198–203.

Coleman, James S., et al. *Equality of Educational Opportunity.* U.S. Department of Health, Education and Welfare, Office of Education. Washington, D.C.: Government Printing Office, 1966. See also the unofficial analysis of the Coleman document by Mayeske, George W. "Educational Achievement Among Mexican-Americans: A Special Report from the Educational Opportunity Survey." National Center for Educational Statistics, U.S. Office of Education. Technical Note 22, Washington, D.C., January 9, 1967.

Galbraith, C. K. "Spanish-Speaking Children Communicate," *Childhood Education,* 42 (October, 1965): 70–74.

Gordon, C. Wayne, et al. *Educational Achievement and Aspirations of Mexican American Youth in a Metropolitan Context.* Mexican American Study Project Educational Sub-Study, Center for the Evaluation of Instructional Programs, Graduate School of Education, University of California at Los Angeles, March, 1968. (Mimeographed.)

Heller, C. S. *Mexican American Youth: Forgotten Youth at the Crossroads.* New York: Random House, 1966. Chapter 4.

Manuel, H. T. *Spanish-Speaking Children of the Southwest: Their Education and the Public Welfare.* Austin: University of Texas Press, 1965. Chapters 11–17.

———. "Recruiting and Training Teachers for Spanish-Speaking Children in the Southwest," *School and Society,* 96 (March 30, 1968): 211–214.

Noreen, Sister, D. C. "A Bilingual Curriculum for Spanish Americans," *Catholic School Journal,* 66 (January, 1966): 25–26.

Parsons, Theodore W., Jr. *Ethnic Cleavage in a California School.* Unpublished Ph.D. dissertation, Stanford University, 1965.

Poulos, W. T. "They Learn Basic English Before School Starts," *Texas Outlook,* 43 (August, 1959): 15–16+.

Pucinski, Roman C. *The Federal Investment in Bilingual Education.* Speech delivered at the Third Annual TESOL Convention. Chicago, 1969, 11 pp.

   In this speech Congressman Pucinski reviews the outlook for bilingual education in the United States. He urges us to concentrate our efforts and resources on three major problems: changing state laws forbidding instruction in languages other than English, developing suitable bilingual materials, and preparing teachers to participate in bilingual programs.

Rodriguez, Armando. *Mexican-American Education: An Overview.* Speech given at Workshop To Develop Human Resources among Mexican-American Teachers in the Denver Metropolitan Area. Denver, Colorado, June 9–10, 1968, 9 pp.

Romero, Fred E. "A Study of Anglo-American and Spanish-American Culture Value Concepts and Their Significance in Secondary Education," *A Research Contribution for Education in Colorado.* Denver: Colorado State Department of Education, September, 1966, Vol. 3, No. 2, p. 7.

Sanchez, G. I. "History, Culture, and Education," in Samora, Julian (ed.). *La Raza: Forgotten Americans.* South Bend, Indiana: University of Notre Dame Press, 1966, pp. 1–26.

———. "Concerning Segregation of Spanish-Speaking Children in the Public School," Inter-American Education Occasional Papers, No. 9. December, 1951. Chapters 2 and 3.

Sonquist, H. D., and Kamii, C. K. "Applying Some Piagetian Concepts in the Classroom for the Disadvantaged," *Young Children,* 22 (March, 1967): 231–238+.

Spodek, Bernard. "Poverty, Education, and the Young Child," in Frost, J. L., and Hawkes, G. R. (eds.). *The Disadvantaged Child: Issues and Innovations.* Boston: Houghton Mifflin, 1966, pp. 183–188.

Teel, D. "Preventing Prejudice Against Spanish-Speaking Children," *Educational Leadership,* 12 (November, 1954): 94–98.

Tireman, L. S. *Teaching Spanish-Speaking Children.* Albuquerque, New Mexico: The University of New Mexico Press, 1948.

Valencia, Atilano A. *Bilingual/Bicultural Education: A Perspective Model in Multicultural America.* Albuquerque, New Mexico: Southwestern Cooperative Educational Laboratory, 1969, 24 pp. Bureau of Research Report.

   Bilingual/bicultural education, with its focus on the linguistic and cultural needs of America's multicultural population, is emerging as a potential type of educational curriculum. In this volume, nineteen models (some operative, some theoretical) and nine bilingual programs for Spanish-speaking children are presented to illustrate differences, similarities, and potentialities of the models for implementation elsewhere.

Wallace, A. "Bilingualism and Retardation," *Elementary English,* 33 (May, 1956): 303–304.

Wilson, Alan B. "Residential Segregation of Social Classes and the Aspirations of High School Boys," *American Sociological Review,* 24 (December, 1959): 836–845.

Zintz, Miles V. *What Classroom Teachers Should Know About Bilingual Education.* Albuquerque, New Mexico: New Mexico University, 1969, 57 pp. Bureau of Research Report.

   This classroom teacher's guide to bilingual education discusses cross-cultural education and English language learning, with illustrations from Navajo, Alaskan Indian, Zuni, and Mexican-American cultures. Materials for Spanish-English bilingual programs and selected bilingual readings for classroom teachers are listed. Annotated bibliographies of studies on cultures, language, vocabulary and TESOL texts are appended.

Sources on Mexican-American History and Culture

Barrett, D. N. "Demographic Characteristics," in Samora, Julian (ed.). *La Raza: Forgotten Americans.* South Bend, Indiana: University of Notre Dame Press, 1966. pp. 159–199.

Browning, H. L., and McLemore, S. D. *A Statistical Profile of the Spanish Surname Population of Texas.* Austin: The University of Texas, Bureau of Business Research, 1964.

———. "The Spanish-Surname Population of Texas," *Public Affairs Comment,* Vol. 10, No. 1 (January, 1964).

Burma, J. H. *Spanish Speaking Groups in the United States.* Durham, North Carolina: Duke University Press, 1954. Chapters 1 and 2.

Diaz, Bernal. *The Conquest of New Spain,* translated by J. M. Cohen. Baltimore: Penguin, 1963.

Fogel, Walter. *Education and Income of Mexican Americans in the Southwest.* University of California at Los Angeles Mexican American Study Project. Advance Report No. 1. Los Angeles: University of California at Los Angeles. Graduate School of Business Administration, Division of Research, 1965.

Grebler, Leo. *Mexican Immigration to the United States: The Record and Its Implications.* University of California at Los Angeles Mexican American Study Project. Advance Report No. 2. Los Angeles: University of California at Los Angeles, Graduate School of Business Administration, Division of Research, 1966.

——. *The Schooling Gap: Signs of Progress.* University of California at Los Angeles Mexican American Study Project. Advance Report No. 7. Los Angeles: University of California at Los Angeles, Graduate School of Business Administration, Division of Research, 1967.

Hayden, Robert G. "Spanish-Americans of the Southwest: Life Style Patterns and Their Implications," *Welfare in Review* (April, 1966).

Heller, C. S. *Mexican American Youth: Forgotten Youth at the Crossroads.* New York: Random House, 1966. Chapters 2 and 3.

Kibbe, P. R. *Latin Americans in Texas.* Albuquerque: The University of New Mexico Press, 1946.

Lamanna, R. A., and Samora, J. "Recent Trends in Educational Status of Mexican Americans in Texas," in Estes, D. M., and Darling, D. W. *Improving Educational Opportunities of the Mexican American: Proceedings of the First Texas Conference for Mexican Americans,* April 13–15, 1967, San Antonio, Texas; Austin: Southwest Educational Development Laboratory, 1968.

Lozano, R. R. *Viva Tejas: The Story of the Mexican-Born Patriots of the Republic of Texas.* San Antonio: Southern Literary Institute, 1936.

Madsen, William. *Mexican Americans of South Texas.* New York: Holt, Rinehart and Winston, 1964. Chapters 1 and 4.

Manuel, H. T. *Spanish-Speaking Children of the Southwest: Their Education and the Public Welfare.* Austin: University of Texas Press, 1965. Chapters 2–6 and Appendix.

McWilliams, Carey. "America's Disadvantaged Minorities: Mexican Americans," *Journal of Negro Education,* Vol. 20, No. 3 (1951): 301–309.

——. *North from Mexico: The Spanish-Speaking People of the United States.* 2nd ed. New York: Monthly Review Press, 1961.

Miller, H. J. "Historical Perspective of Mexican American Culture," *Americans of Mexican Descent —An In-Depth Study.* San Antonio, Texas: a publication of the Human Resources Development Institute, held July 17–28, 1967, at St. Mary's University.

Mettelbach, F. G., and Marshall, G. *The Burden of Poverty.* University of California at Los Angeles Mexican American Study Project. Advance Report No. 5. Los Angeles: University of California at Los Angeles, Graduate School of Business Administration, Division of Research, 1966.

Morin, Raul. *Among the Valiant: Mexican Americans in WW II and Korea.* Los Angeles: Borden Publishing Company, 1963.

Myers, J. M. *The Alamo.* New York: Bantam Books, 1966.

Parkes, H. B. *A History of Mexico.* 3rd ed. Boston: Houghton Mifflin, 1960. Chapters 4 and 6.

Rubel, A. J. *Across the Tracks: Mexican Americans in a Texas City.* Austin: University of Texas Press, 1966. Chapter 2.

Sanchez, G. I. "The Culture of the Spanish-Speaking People of the Southwest," in Moseley, J. E. (ed.). *The Spanish-Speaking People of the Southwest.* Council on Spanish-American Work, 1966.

——. "History, Culture, and Education," in Samora, Julian (ed.). *La Raza: Forgotten Americans.* South Bend, Indiana: University of Notre Dame Press, 1966. pp. 1–26.

——. "Spanish-Speaking People in the Southwest—A Brief Historical Review," *California Journal of Elementary Education,* 22 (November, 1953): 106–111.

Simmons, Ozzie G. "The Mutual Images and Expectations of Anglo-Americans and Mexican Americans," *Daedalus* 90 (1961).

Singletary, O. A. *The Mexican War.* Chicago: The University of Chicago Press, 1960.

A Guide to Further Reading and Study About Mexican Americans[3]

Barker, George C. *Pachuco, An American-Spanish Argot and Its Social Functions in Tucson, Arizona* (University of Arizona, Tucson, Social Science Bulletin, Vol. 21, No. 18, January, 1950). A study of the "pachuco" language.

Bernal, Ignacio, and Soustelle, Jacques. *Mexico: Pre-Hispanic Paintings* (United Nations Economic and Social Council, World Art Series, No. 10, 1958).

Caso, Alfonso. *The Aztecs: People of the Sun* (Norman, 1958).

Clark, Margaret. *Health in the Mexican-American Culture: A Community Study* (Berkeley, 1959). A study of San Jose, California.

[3] From Jack D. Forbes, *Mexican Americans: A Handbook for Educators.*

Clincy, Everett Ross. *Equality of Opportunity: Latin Americans in Texas* (Ann Arbor, 1954).

Cline, Howard F. *The United States and Mexico* (Cambridge, 1953).

Council of Mexican-American Affairs, *First Annual Report on Mexican-American Education Conference Proceedings* (Los Angeles, 1956).

Covarrubias, Miguel. *Indian Art of Mexico and Central America* (New York, 1957).

Dworkin, Anthony Gary. "Stereotypes and Self-Images Held by Native Born and Foreign-born Mexican-Americans," *Sociology and Social Research*, Vol. 49, No. 2 (January, 1965).
  Part of a larger study conducted under the direction of Dr. Paul Sheldon of Occidental College, Los Angeles.

Edmonson, Munroe. *Los Manitos—A Study of Institutional Values* (New Orleans, 1957).
  An anthropological study of values carried out in New Mexico.

"The Eye of Mexico," *Evergreen Review*, No. 7 (New York, 1959).
  A collection of translations of works by Mexican authors.

Gamio, Manuel. *The Mexican Immigrant—His Life Story* (Chicago, 1931).
  A still-timely study of the new arrivals to the United States.

——. *Mexican Immigration to the United States* (Chicago, 1930).
  The best study of Mexican immigration.

Garibay K., and Angel M. *Historia de la Literatura Nàhuatl* (Mexico, 1953–4).

——. *Llave del Nahuàtl* (Mexico, 1940, 1961).
  The above are for those who seek a better knowledge of ancient Mexican thought and of the Mexican language.

Gillmore, Frances. *Flute of the Smoking Mirror, a Portrait of Nezahualcóyotl, Poet-king of the Aztecs* (Albuquerque, 1949).

Griffith, Beatrice. *American Me* (Boston, 1948).
  A fine study of Mexican-American youth.

——. "The Pachuco Patois," *Common Ground* (Summer, 1947).
  A part of the above book, but focusing upon the development of the Pachuco idiom.

Gruening, Ernest. *Mexico and Its Heritage* (New York, 1928).
  A volume still valuable for its coverage of the Mexican revolutionary era.

Kibbe, Pauline R. *Latin Americans in Texas* (Albuquerque, 1946).
  A somewhat dated book, but still useful in providing background for recent developments.

Kurath, Gertrude Prokosch. *Dances of Anahuac: The Choreography and Music of Precortesian Dances* (Chicago: Aldine, 1966).

León-Portilla, Miguel. *La Filosofía Nàhuatl* (Mexico, 1956). Translated as *Aztec Thought and Culture* (Norman, 1963).
  A "must" for an understanding of the Mexican heritage.

Manuel, Herschel T. *The Education of Mexican and Spanish-Speaking Children in Texas* (Austin, 1930).

——. "The Educational Problem Presented by the Spanish-Speaking Child . . . ," *School and Society*, Vol. 40 (1934).
  Although somewhat dated, these two studies still have implications for today.

——. *Spanish-Speaking Children of the Southwest; Their Education and the Public Welfare* (Austin: University of Texas, 1965).

McWilliams, Carey. *North from Mexico: The Spanish-Speaking People of the United States* (New York, 1949).
  Although dated, this work represents the closest that any author has come to making a general survey of Mexican-American history and development.

"Mexican Issue," *The Texas Quarterly*, Vol. II (Spring, 1959).
  A presentation of modern Mexican literature, art, philosophy and culture.

Ortega, Joaquin. *The Compulsory Teaching of Spanish in the Grade Schools of New Mexico* (Albuquerque, 1941).

Parkes, Henry B. *A History of Mexico* (Boston, 1950).
  Out of date but still useful as an introductory work.

Pinkney, Alphonso. "Prejudice Toward Mexican and Negro Americans," *Phylon*, 1st Quarter (1963).

Romanell, Patrick. *Making of the Mexican Mind* (Lincoln, Nebraska, 1952).
  This work surveys the world of Mexican intellectual development.

Sanchez, George I. *Forgotten People: A Study of New Mexicans* (Albuquerque, 1940).
  The sections on education are still especially pertinent.

Saunders, Lyle. *Cultural Differences and Medical Care: The Case of the Spanish-Speaking Population of the Southwest* (New York, 1954).

——. *A Guide to Materials Bearing on Cultural Relations in New Mexico* (Albuquerque, 1944).

——. *Spanish-Speaking Americans in the United States: A Selected Bibliography* (New York City, 1944).

Samora, Julian (ed.). *La Raza: Forgotten Americans* (Notre Dame, 1966).
  A collection of essays and articles aimed at achieving an understanding of contemporary Mexican-American affairs.

Southwest Conference. *Proceedings,* various years, Occidental College, Los Angeles.
    These Proceedings often contain articles of significance, but they are not listed separately because they are difficult to obtain.
Taylor, Paul S. *An American-Mexican Frontier* (Chapel Hill, North Carolina, 1934).
    An excellent study, providing insight into present-day issues.
———. "Mexican Labor in the United States," *University of California Publications in Economics,* Vol. VI, 1927–1930.
    Excellent background, including information on educational issues.
Toor, Frances. *A Treasury of Mexican Folkways.* (New York, 1947).
Tuck, Ruth. *Not With the Fist* (New York, 1946).
    A study of Mexican-Americans in California.
Yanovski, E. *Food Plants of the North American Indians* (U.S. Department of Agriculture, Miscellaneous Publications, No. 237).
    Provides information on Mexican agricultural contributions to modern society.

Examples of Supplementary Materials Available for Classroom Use

Published Materials for Secondary-level Use

Paperbound Books

Astrov, Margot (ed.). *American Indian Prose and Poetry.* New York: Capricorn, 1962.
    Includes Mexican material.
Galarza, Ernesto. *Merchants of Labor: The Mexican Bracero Story.* Santa Barbara: McNally and Loftin, 1964.
Heller, Celia S. *Mexican American Youth: Forgotten Youth at the Crossroads.* New York: Random House, 1966.
    A useful introduction to some problems of Mexican-American youth.
Idell, Albert, trans. *The Bernal Diaz Chronicles.* Garden City, New York: Doubleday, 1956.
    A classic account of the Spanish conquest.
Lewis, Oscar. *Tepoztlàn: Village in Mexico.* New York: Holt, Rinehart, and Winston, 1960.
Madsen, William. *Mexican-Americans of South Texas.* New York: Holt, Rinehart and Winston, 1964.
Peterson, Frederick. *Ancient Mexico.* New York: Capricorn, 1962.
    An excellent survey of ancient Mexican history.
Pozas, Ricardo. *Juan the Chamula.* University of California, 1962.
    Explores the life of a group of modern day Mexican Indians.
Ruiz, Ramon (ed.). *The Mexican War.* New York: Holt, Rinehart and Winston, 1963.
    A good introduction to the U.S.-Mexican War.
Séjourné, Laurette. *Burning Water: Thought and Religion in Ancient Mexico.* Evergreen Grove Press, 1960.
    An excellent introduction to ancient Mexican philosophy and religion.
Simpson, Lesley B. *Many Mexicos.* University of California Press, 1952.
    A useful survey of Mexican civilization.
Soustelle, Jacques. *The Daily Life of the Aztecs.* Baltimore: Penguin Books, 1964.
Vaillant, George C. *Aztecs of Mexico.* Baltimore: Penguin Books, 1966.
    An excellent study of Aztec culture and history.
Von Hagen, Victor W. *The Aztec: Man and Tribe.* New York: New American Library, 1958.
    A popular introductory work.
———. *World of the Maya.* New York: New American Library, 1960.
    A popular introductory work.

Spanish-language Paperbacks

Spanish-language studies in all disciplines are available from sources such as the Libreria Universitaria, Ciudad Universitaria, Mexico 20, D. F., and the Instituto Nacional de Antropología e Historia, Mexico D. F. Write for catalogues.

Other Printed Material

Mexican-American groups often publish pamphlets, newsletters, et cetera, which may enrich classroom discussions. It will be necessary to contact the Mexican American Political Association, Community Service Organization, League of United Latin American Citizens, Political Association of Spanish-Speaking Organizations, American G. I. Forum, or other groups in order to ascertain what is currently available. The Mexican Government from time to time issues special publications of value for an understanding of Mexico. The nearest consulate or branch should be contacted for information. *Religious groups* sometimes have material available, but it is often slanted toward sectarian interests. Government agencies in the United States have issued special publications on Mexican-Americans. Consult the government publications section of the nearest large public library for information. *The Mexican-American Study Project* at the University of California, Los Angeles, also issues publications of interest. Interested individuals or groups may be added to their mailing list.

Published Materials for Elementary Use

Few elementary-level books which deal specifically with Mexican-Americans, but numbers of books deal with Mexicans living in Mexico or with children from other Spanish-speaking countries. In general, many are unsatisfactory because based upon stereotypes and a style of life which disappeared years ago or which has retreated to isolated, rural areas. Teachers and librarians should avoid books which utilize the stereotypes of a rural Mexican family wearing big sombreros and serapes, living in a hut, and using donkeys for transportation. Other categories of books which need to be examined closely are those which feature stories of poverty-stricken Mexican children who achieve success because of Anglo philanthropy, stories of the U.S.-Mexican War written with an Anglo bias, and stories which use the term "Spanish" where Mexican would be more correct.

A few books which seem acceptable under the above criteria follow:

> Brock, Virginia. *Piñatas*. Nashville: Abingdon, 1966.
> A how-to-do-it and historical book for upper elementary or junior high.
> Geis, Darlene (ed.). *Let's Travel in Mexico*: Chicago: Children's Press, 1965.
> An interesting book about Mexico for upper elementary or junior high.
> Wilson, Barbara Ker. *Fairy Tales of Mexico*. New York: Dutton, 1960.
> A collection of excellent stories for upper elementary grades.

Audio-Visual Materials

Transparencies

Sets of transparencies are available from the Instituto Nacional de Antropología e Historia, Mexico, D. F.

> 50 sets of six transparencies each, focusing primarily upon ancient Mexican civilization but with some sets on more recent monuments and places (Serie 1 through Serie 50).
> Two sets of twelve transparencies illustrating the various human racial types of Mexico, from the Museo Nacional de Historia del Castillo de Chapultepec. (Serie 51 and Serie 52). Excellent for courses in social science, anthropology, world history, southwestern history, and biological science.

The Archivo y Laboratorio Fotografico of the Instituto Nacional de Antropología e Historia also has more than 200,000 photographs and 20,000 other color transparencies available. Write to the above at Córdoba 45, Mexico 7, D. F. for catalogues.

Reproductions of Ancient Mexican Ceramic Statues

The Instituto Nacional de Antropología e Historia has a number of reproductions (statues, etc.) available at reasonable prices (ranging from one to sixteen dollars). These would be excellent classroom and display items for schools.

Imitation statues, et cetera, are also available in shops throughout the Southwest and along the border. Prices are relatively high, however, even when dealing at "wholesale."

Phonograph Records

Records of Mexican folk music are available from the Museo Nacional de Antropología, Instituto Nacional de Antropología e Historia. The cost is about $1.20 per record.

Commercial phonograph records featuring various styles of Mexican and Mexican-American music are available throughout the Southwest. Contemporary Mexican-produced commercial records are usually available in music or appliance stores serving Mexican-American neighborhoods.

Southwestern Mexican folk music is sometimes available on records from museums or historical societies. The Southwest Museum, Los Angeles 42, has a collection of Indian and Hispano-Mexican folk music from the California region.

Films

Unfortunately, many films which deal with Southwestern history are inaccurate and/or biased, usually in a pro-Spanish or pro-Anglo direction. Films dealing with the "Mission

Period" are often derogatory in their treatment of native Indians, for example. Those dealing with Mexico must be examined for stereotypes or for a failure to illustrate the diversity of modern Mexico, if they deal with contemporary conditions.

Sources of Materials and Additional Information

Babin, Patrick. *Bilingualism: A Bibliography.* 1968 (ED 023 097).
> This bibliography, available from ERIC (Educational Resources Information Center of the U.S. Office of Education) is a selected listing of books, monographs, journal articles, unpublished papers, and bibliographies focusing on bilingualism.

Harrigan, Joan. *Materiales Tocante Los Latinos: A Bibliography of Materials on the Spanish-American.* Denver, Colorado: Colorado Department of Education, Division of Library Services (Colorado State Library), October, 1967.

Heathman, James H., and Martinez, Cecilia J. *Mexican-American Education, A Selected Bibliography.* University Park, New Mexico: New Mexico State University, 1969, 58 pp. Bureau of Research Report. (ED 031 052).
> Documents of the subject of Mexican-American education which have been indexed and abstracted in *Research in Education* are cited, as are publications dealing with research findings and developments in bilingual compensatory education for the Spanish-speaking.

Ibarra, Herb. *Bibliography of ESL/Bilingual Teaching Materials.* San Diego City Schools, California, 1969, 31 pp. (ED 028 002).
> Four hundred six books, articles, and instructional realia published between 1945 and 1968 are listed in this bibiliography for teachers and students of Spanish-speaking and bilingual students. Though emphasis is placed on English as a second language, textual materials for all levels of education from primary to adult, lists of materials such as kits and visuals for music and science also appear.

Macnamara, John (ed.). "Problems of Bilingualism," *The Journal of Social Issues,* 23 (April, 1967), 137 pp. Available from Acme Printing and Reproductions, 611 South Maple Road, Ann Arbor, Michigan.
> This issue of *The Journal of Social Issues* is devoted to nine articles on the topic of bilingualism written by authorities in the fields of linguistics, anthropology, sociology, psychology, and education.

Messinger, M. A. *The Forgotten Child: A Bibliography with Special Emphasis on Materials Relating to the Education of "Spanish-Speaking" People in the United States.* Austin, Texas: Twenty-four mimeographed sheets from the Department of History and Philosophy of Education, the University of Texas, July, 1967.

Montelores Studies Center Staff. *Bibliography: Professional Library and Instructional Materials.* Cortez, Colorado: Center for Multi-Cultural Studies and Educational Resources, 1967.

National Education Association. *The Invisible Minority. Report of the NEA-Tucson Survey on the Teaching of Spanish to the Spanish-Speaking.* Washington, D.C., 1966, 45 pp. (ED 017 222).
> The major findings of a survey that investigated the Southwest for programs on teaching Spanish to the Spanish-speaking. A reading list for an advanced literature course for native speakers on the eleventh- or twelfth-grade level is supplied, as well as a basic system for literary criticism in advanced courses.

Office of Economic Opportunity. *Bibliography of Completed Research Projects Funded by Project Head Start, Division of Research and Evaluation.* Washington, D.C.: Five mimeographed sheets from Project Head Start, Community Action Program, Office of Economic Opportunity, June, 1967.

Office of Economic Opportunity. *Equipment and Supplies: Guidelines for Administrators and Teachers in Child Development Centers.* Washington, D.C.: Project Head Start, Community Action Program, Office of Economic Opportunity, 1967.

Sanchez, G. I., and Putnam, H. *Materials Relating to the Education of Spanish-Speaking People in the United States: An Annotated Bibliography.* Austin, Texas: The University of Texas, Institute of Latin American Studies, 1959.

Texas Education Agency. *Preschool Instructional Program for Non-English Speaking Children.* Austin, Texas, March, 1964.

University of California at Los Angeles, Graduate School of Business Administration, Division of Research. *Mexican American Study Project, Advance Report 3: Bibliography.* Prepared by the Staff, February, 1966.

Sources on the Education and Study of American Indians

A Guide to Further Reading and Study

Aurbach, Herbert A. (ed.). *Proceedings of the National Conference on American Indian Education.* Kalamazoo, Michigan: Society for the Study of Social Problems, 1967.

Benedict, Ruth. *Patterns of Culture*. Boston: Houghton Mifflin, 1934.

Berry, Brewton. *The Education of American Indians: A Survey of the Literature*. Washington, D.C.: U.S. Department of Health, Education and Welfare, 1968.

Lesser, Alexander. *Education and the Future of Tribalism in the United States: The Case of the American Indian*. New York: Phelps-Stokes Fund, 1961.

Underhill, Ruth. *Red Man's America. A History of the Indians of the United States*. Chicago: University of Chicago Press, 1953.

Wax, Murray, and Rosalie. "Formal Education in an American Indian Community," *Social Problems*, 11 (Spring, 1964).

Wax, Rosalie, and Thomas, Robert K. T. "American Indians and White People," *Phylon*, 32 (1961): 305–317.

California Indians

American Friends Service Committee. *Indians of California, Past and Present*. San Francisco: American Friends Service Committee, 1960.

Anderson, Gene. *The Chumash Indians*. Banning, California: Malki Museum Brochure, 1968.

Bean, Lowell, and Lawton, Harry. *The Cahuilla Indians of Southern California*. Banning, California: Malki Museum Brochure, 1965.

Downs, James F. *The Two World of the Washo*. New York: Holt, Rinehart and Winston, 1966.

Heizer, R. F., and Whipple, M. A. (eds.). *California Indians*. Berkeley: University of California Press, 1951.

Johnston, Frank. *The Serrano Indians of Southern California*. Banning, California: Malki Museum Brochure, 1965.

Kroeber, Alfred L. *Handbook of the Indians of California*. Bureau of American Ethnology, Bulletin 78, 1925.

Miller, Ron, and Dean, Peggy. *The Chemehuevi*. Banning, California: Malki Museum Brochure, 1967.

Underhill, Ruth. Indians of Southern California. B.I.A. Department of Interior. Order from Publications Service, Haskell Institute, Lawrence, Kansas. 1941.

Iroquois Indians

Fenton, William N. *An Outline of Seneca Ceremonies at Coldspring Longhouse*. Yale University Publications in Anthropology, No. 9. 23 pp. 1936.

——. *Problems Arising from the Historic Northeastern Position of the Iroquois*. Smithsonian Miscellaneous Collections, vol. 100, pp. 159–251. 1940.
    Important for Iroquois history and locations. Out of print.

——. *Masked Medicine Societies of the Iroquois*. Smithsonian Institution Annual Report for 1940, pp. 397–430, 25 pls. 1941. Out of print.

——. *Symposium on Local Diversity in Iroquois Culture*. Smithsonian Institution Bulletin 149. 187 pp. illus. 1951.
    Eight important articles on various aspects of Iroquois customs and beliefs. Out of print.

——. *Symposium on Cherokee and Iroquois Culture*. Smithsonian, Bulletin 180. 292 pp., bibliog. 1961.
    A collection of articles by specialists, especially see numbers 2 (linguistics); 4 (archaeology); 9 (community types); 14 (Handsome Lake religion); 18 (music and dance); 20 (diagnosticians); and 25 (culture history).

Morgan, Lewis Henry. *League of the Ho-De-No-Sau-Nee or Iroquois*. 2nd edition, H. M. Lloyd, Editor, 2 vols., 338, 332 pp. illus., maps, Dodd, Mead, New York. 1901. (Reprinted 1954 by Human Relations Area Files, New Haven. (The standard work on Seneca customs, first published in 1851; weak on history.)

Ritchie, William A. *Indian History of New York State. Part II: the Iroquoian Tribes*. Educational Leaflet Series No. 7. 20 pp., illus. New York State Museum and Science Service, Albany, 1963.
    Summary of history, customs and artifacts, written for school and general public. Free copy available to N.Y. state teachers; others, 25¢. Available from New York State Museum and Science Service, State Education Dept., Albany, N.Y. 12224.

Shimony, Annemarie A. *Conservatism Among the Iroquois at the Six Nations Reserve*. 302 pp., 19 figs. bibliog. Yale Univ. Pubs in Anthropology 65. 1961.
    A thorough description of the conservative customs in the largest modern Iroquois community.

Speck, Frank G. *The Iroquois: a Study in Cultural Evolution*. 94 pp., many illus. Cranbrook Institute of Science Bull. No. 23. Bloomfield Hills, Mich. 1945.
    Popular account of Iroquois customs and artifacts.

Tooker, Elisabeth. *An Ethnography of the Huron Indians*. 1615–1649. 183 pp. appendices, bibliog., index. Smithsonian Bulletin 190, 1964.

Wallace, Paul A. *The White Roots of Peace*. 57 pp. University of Pennsylvania Press. Phila. 1946.
    The Iroquois legend of the founding of their League.

Waugh, F. W. *Iroquois Foods and Food Preparation*. 235 pp., illus., Canada Dept. of Mines.

Geological Survey. Memoir 86. Anthropological Series No. 12. 1916.

Wilson, Edmund. *Apologies to the Iroquois*. With a study of the Mohawks in High Steel, by Joseph Mitchell. 310 pp., illus. Farrar, Straus and Cudahy, N.Y. Paperback reprint: Vintage Books. 1960.

> A superb evocation of conservative Iroquois ceremonies, plus a good account of modern Iroquois political problems; Mitchell describes Mohawk specialization in high steel construction work.

Wright, Gordon K. *The Neutral Indians: A Source Book*. 95 pp., illus., bibliog. Occasional Papers of the N.Y. State Archaeological Assn. No. 4. Rochester, 1963.

Other Tribes

Dozier, Edward P. *Hano: A Tewa Indian Community in Arizona*. New York: Holt, Rinehart and Winston, 1966.

Drucker, Philip. *Cultures of the North Pacific Coast*. San Francisco, Chandler, 1965.

Hoebel, E. A. *The Cheyennes*. New York: Holt, Rinehart and Winston, 1960.

Kluckhohn, Clyde, and Leighton, Dorothea. *The Navaho*. New York: Doubleday, 1962. The Natural History Library.

Lowie, R. H. *Indians of the Plains*. New York: McGraw-Hill, 1954. American Museum of Natural History Handbook Series, No. 1.

Wallace, E., and Hoebel, E. A. *The Comanches: Lords of the South Plains*. Norman, Oklahoma: University of Oklahoma Press, 1952.

Indian Stories, Myths and Poetry

de Angulo, Jaime. *Indian Tales*. New York: Hill and Wang, 1962.

Astrov, Margot (ed.). *American Indian Prose and Poetry*. New York: Capricorn, 1962.

Clark, Ella E. *Indian Legends of the Pacific Northwest*. Berkeley: University of California Press, 1960.

Day, A. Grove (ed.). *The Sky Clears*. Lincoln, Nebraska: University of Nebraska Press, 1964.

James, Harry. *The Cahuilla Indians*. Los Angeles: Westernlore Press, 1960.

Kroeber, Theodora. *The Inland Whale*. Bloomington, Indiana: University Press, 1959.

——. *Ishi in Two Worlds*. Berkeley: University of California Press, 1961.

Lawton, Harry. *Willie Boy*. Balboa Island, California: Paisano Press, 1960.

Sources on the Education and Study of Asian-Americans

Bosworth, Allen H. *America's Concentration Camps*. New York: Bantam, 1968.

Eaton, Allen H. *Beauty Behind Barbed Wire: The Arts of the Japanese in Our War Relocation Camps*. Harper and Row, 1952.

Gordon, Milton M. *Assimilation in American Life*. New York: Oxford University Press, 1964.

Kitano, Harry H. L. *Japanese Americans: The Evolution of a Subculture*. Englewood Cliffs, New Jersey: Prentice Hall, 1969.

Smith, Bradford. *Americans from Japan*. The People of America Series. New York: Lippincott, 1948.

Index

Ability, extremes of, 216
Ability to Understand Spoken English (USE)
  Test, 145
Abortion, 125
Abstraction, great American, 154–5
Acceptance, 177
Accommodations, 255
Acculturation, 190–4
  of Japanese-Americans, 370, 396
  of small marginal populations, 401
Accumulated social assets, 131
Achievement, 182, 245, 348–56
  academic, 216
  educational, 44, 113
  scholastic, 69
Activists
  Chinese-American, 394
  Indian-American, 319
Activities
  classroom, 270
  extracurricular, 74, 78
  school-sponsored, 212
Actors, Negro, 96–7
Acts, accommodatory, 248
Adaptation
  of Japanese-Americans, 386–7
  proper, 336
Adjustment, 146
Administrators
  and Anglo stereotypes, 211
  Mexican-American, 207
  suggestions for, 89–93
Adolescents, 221
Adults, 91–3
  domination by, 171
  working, 116
Advantage, expectancy, 235–6
Advisory board, 93
Affluent society, 311
Africa, 34
  cultural legacy from, 30
  literature of, 90
  as site of first human, 32–5
Afro-Americans, 10, 89–93
  cultural legacy, 30–1
  heritage of, 24–106
  identity of, 29–35
  militancy of, 24
  population statistics of, 32
  schools for, 16
  significance of, 29–35
  studies about, 25
  see also Blacks; Negroes
Agencies, for funding, 279–80, 282
Ages, 93, 115
Aggression, 120
Agnew, Spiro T., 323
Agregados, 133, 209, 226
Agriculture, 273, 295–6

Aid
  federal, 4, 127, 222–3 237, 281, 322
  municipal, 136
Albuquerque (N.M.) 316, 324, 327
Alcatraz, 286, 318–9
Alcohol, 311, 314–15, 321
Alienation, 8, 147
  gradual, 7
  recognition, 11–12
Alien Exclusion Act (1924), 373
Alien Land Law (1913), 373
Alioto, Joseph, 391
Allegiance, peer, 226
Allen, James E., Jr., 6, 16
Ambivalence, 226
Amendment, "sleeper," 20–2
Amendments, constitutional, 316–17
America, 18
  Asians in, 371–5
  identity in, 84
  Japanese-Americans in, 396
  see also United States
American Anthropological Association, 14
American dream, 107
American Indian Development Workshop,
  292
American Indians, see Indian-Americans
American Indians Movement, 322
American Indians United, 322
Americanization, 277, 326
Americans, 411
  hyphenated, 378
  legacy of, 31
  opinion of, by Puerto Ricans, 125
  Puerto Ricans as, 120
Americas, 30–2, 34
Ancestors, white, of Negroes, 95
Ancestry, African, 32
Anglo-Americans, 9–13, 89, 107, 179, 228, 240,
  253–4
  acceptance of Mexican-Americans, 194
  busyness of, 182
  discrimination by, 176
  flight of, 205
  interaction with, 209
  intermarriage with, 193
  medical concepts of, 183–4
  passion for planning, 181
  as peers, 246
  stereotypes of, 178, 211
  suspicion and mistrust of, 192
  ways of, 163–4
  see also Whites
Anthropologists, 294, 303, 321
Apaches, 297, 303, 327
Apartments, 114
Appearance, Negroid, 30
"Apples," 322
Areas, metropolitan, 66, 245

Arithmetic, 69, 149, 353
Arizona, 242, 295, 330, 358
Arizona State University, 360–61
Arts, 91, 298–9
Asia, 34
Asian-Americans, 369–432
Asians, in America, 371–5
Aspira, 149
Aspirations, 217
Assimilation, 1, 19, 255, 384
　by area of residence, 378–80
　by group, 377–8
　Japanese-American, 378–88
Assistant Commissioner of Indian Affairs, 326
Association on American Indian Affairs, 14
Associations
　family and district, 391, 393–4
　Negro, 60
　play, 171
Atrocities, 154
Attendance, 241
Attitudes, 53, 217
　dying, 155
　toward education, 254–5
　of Puerto Rican community, 139
　scale of, 254
　of teachers, 345
Attocknie, 329
Attributes, "inferior" cultural, 286
Attucks, Crispus, 75
Authoritarianism, 221–2
Authority, 58, 117, 134, 170
　aggression toward, 120
　male, 134
　structure, 227
Automobiles, 115
Aztecs, 291

Baby Wah Ching, 410, 420
Backwardness, 9
Baker, Gene, 87
Balance, racial, 58–9
Baldwin, James, 25, 80
Baltimore, 61
Banks, Ernie, 87
Banneker Group, 69–70
Baptism, 173
Barkley, Alice, 406–10, 421
Barriers
　language, 189–90
　psychological, 189
　social class, 212
Baseball, 87–8
Behavior, 97, 223–8, 248
　"acting out," 398–9
　antisocial, 227
　changing, 155
　patterns of, 59
　"release," 399
Bellecourt, Clyde, 322
Bennett, Robert, 335
Berlin, I. N., 7
Bey, Faith, 99
Bibliographies, 75
Bigotry, 154–5

Bilingual American Education Act (1967), 4, 223
Bilingual Education Program, 23
Bilingualism, 3–4, 22–3, 157–8, 160, 187, 189–90, 221–2, 250
Birth control, 125, 137
Birth rate, 124, 137
Bitterness, 84
Black, Hugo L., 313
Black
　as color of skin, 94–8
　as state of mind, 94–8
　what it's about, 94
Blackness, 97
Black Panthers, 103, 105, 395, 418–19
Black Power, 100, 417
Black revolution, 26
Blacks
　African, 35
　appearance, 106
　culture quotient about, 27–8
　degree of color, 96
　demands of, 104
　election of, 104–5
　experience of, 98
　freedom, 97–8
　heritage of, 24–106
　identity of, 98
　as laborers, 83
　looks of, 95–6
　militant, 97, 99–106
　as revolutionaries, 105
　work of, 95–6
　see also Afro-Americans; Negroes
Black Soul, 410
Blatchford, Herbert, 325–9, 331, 336
Bloom, Benjamin, 67
"Blooming," 235
Boards of education, local, 160
Bok gooi, 411, 416
Bookstores, 93
Border states, 51
Boulder (Colo.) 292
Braceros, 179
Brain drain, 206
Bram, Joseph, 108, 130
Bravery, 98
Brewster, Kingman, Jr., 105
Bridgeport (Conn.), 158–9
Brightman, Lehman, 319
Brightman, Trudy Felix, 320
Broadway, 96
Brooklyn, 60; see also New York City
Brown v. Board of Education of Topeka (1954), 57–8, 66
Brown, Rap, 102
Brussel, Charles B., 165, 169, 247
Bryde, Father John F., 6, 292
Buffalo, 102
Bunche, Dr. Ralph, 76
"Bundle shops," 393
Bureau of Indian Affairs, 290, 295, 298, 301, 312, 315, 319–20, 341–3, 346, 352, 359, 361, 364
Bush, George W., 75

Business, 50
  small, 322
Busing, 61, 66
"Busy work," 270
Byler, William, 6, 14
Bythe, Jarrett, 314

Cafeteria, 231
California, 7–8, 188, 200–4, 208–10, 218, 221,
    224–8, 230, 241–2, 245, 265, 365–8,
    371–432 passim
California Achievement Tests, 352
California Inter-Tribal Council, 322
California League for American Indians, 367
California School Boards Association, 203
Cameron House, 404
Campanella, Roy, 88
Canton and Cantonese, 391, 413
Care, medical, 128
Carlisle Indian School (Pa.), 341
Carmichael, Stokeley, 100
Carter, Robert, 60
Carter, Thomas P., 164–5, 197, 272
Cases, hard-core, 119
Caste, 37
Castro, Fidel, 85–6
Catholics, 183; see also Roman Catholics
Caucasians, 382–4, 396, 400; see also Anglo-
    Americans
Caucasoids, 32–4
Celebrations, ethnic, 91
Census of 1960, 131, 161
Centers, urban, 65
Chalk, Roy, 124
Change, 109, 181, 200
  ordeal of, 51–4
  in Puerto Rican family life, 139
  in the schools, 281–3
  social, 273
  in society, 283–4
Charity, 136
Charles, Jack, 286, 311
Cherokees, 313–14, 340
Chew, Wellington, 407–9, 419
Chiang Kai-shek, 427
Chicago, 40, 60, 159–60, 322, 330, 332
Chicanos, 164, 167–8
Children
  Anglo, 188, 190
  bilingual, 158
  caring for, 170
  chances of, 215
  changing, 279–80
  civilizing of, 80
  consciousness of, 81
  "crippling" of Mexican-American, 198
  cultural identity of, 20
  culturally deprived, 13, 70
  culturally handicapped, 68
  culture of Indian, 294–310
  deprived, 9
  disadvantaged, 13
  discipline of, 113
  early years, 67
  English-speaking, 258
  failure of, 4

"good and sufficient," 197
  illegitimate, 137
  limited backgrounds of, 70
  as losers, 148–62
  loved and attended, 171
  lower-class, 234
  low-status, 229
  Mexican-American, 164
  Mexican-American, tracks of, 215, 217, 219
  middle-class, 228
  middle-track, 235
  minority-group, 20, 229, 234, 236, 245
  motivation of, 57
  names of, 224
  Negro, 59, 85
  non-English-speaking, 20–1
  "normal," 276
  older, 235
  operational level of, 259
  ordinary, 235
  "phasing-in" Mexican-American, 280
  pressures on, 227
  problem, 186
  problems of Mexican-American, 239
  processing of, 16
  Puerto-Rican-American, 108–9, 121, 141–7,
    149–54, 256–7
  Puerto-Rican-American, saving of, 160
  rearing of, 45, 290
  roles, 210
  school attendance, 201
  segregation of Mexican-American, 188
  self-identity of, 224
  self-image of, 57
  slow-track, 235
  Spanish-speaking, 144, 232, 247–59, 262–71
  special, 235
  testing of Indian-American, 349–56
  training, 45
  younger, 235
"Chinabugs," 416, 425
Chinatowns, 14, 374–5, 389–95
  core of, 391–3
  number in, 392
Chinese-American Democratic Club, 430
Chinese-Americans, 10, 12
  in California, 371–95, 402–32
  deprivations of, 389–90
  foods of, 391
  housing, 392
  lack of acculturation, 370
  living conditions, 414
  militancy of, 403, 405, 426, 428–9, 430–2
  second-generation, 413
  standards of living, 394
Chino, Wendell, 328
Choctaws, 329, 341
Chow, Albert, 422
Christianity, 84
Chung Wai Wui Kwoon, 394
Church, 49, 114, 316
Cities, 63, 319
  finances of, 127
Citizenry, 81
Citizens

American, 107, 200
  middle-class, 233
Citizens' Councils, 51
City Planning Commission (N.Y.C.), 126
Civil rights, 105, 283–4
Civil Rights Act (1964), 52–3, 316–17
Civil rights movement, 203
Civil War, 75
Clark, Kenneth, 21, 38, 66–7, 154
Classes (school)
  adult, 92
  compensatory, 213
  large, 244
  open, 92–3
  organization of, 145
  special education, 218, 220
Classes (social), 179
  barriers, 212
  and the community, 36–54
  socioeconomics of, 214
Classrooms, slum, 6
Cleanliness, 231
Cleavage, ethnic, 210–13
Cleaver, Eldridge, 418
Climate, 114, 132
Clothing, 115, 297–8
Coleman Report, 150
Colleges
  community, 63
  and education of teacher, 435
  Negro, 71
Collier, John, 341
Colonia, 175
Color, 95–6, 98
Colorado, 207, 218, 241, 265
Comanches, 329
Commager, Henry Steele, 75
Commission on Equal Opportunities in Education, 367
Commissioner of Indian Affairs, 315, 335, 341
Committee on Fair Employment Practices, 104
Communication
  ability for, 262
  problems of, 144
Communism, 85–6, 395
Communities, 146, 160
  adult, 91
  black, 89
  and class realities, 36–54
  exclusion and subordination in, 177
  Mexican-American, 192
  Negro, 50
  organization in, 122
  and school-sponsored activities, 212
Community Education Centers, 92
Compadrazgo, 173
Competence, scholastic, 227
Competition, 305, 321
Comradeship, 125
Conant, James B., 7, 12
Concepts, 229
Conflict, 120, 226, 232
  marital, 113
Conformity, 226, 238
Confucianism, 415

Congress, 4, 6, 20–21, 104–5, 312–13
Conklin, Paul, 287, 358
Connor, Fred, 321
Conscience, 85
Conservatism, 307–8
Constitution, guarantees of, 200
Constitutionality, 217
Context, social, 147
Contraception, 137
Control, principle of local, 362
Controls, behavioral, 223–8
Cook, L. T., 366
Cooking, 91
Coombs, Madison, 352–4
Coparenthood, 173
Cordasco, Francesco, 2–3, 19, 108, 141, 148
Counseling, 227
Counselors, 225
  guidance, 145–6
Country, founding of, 84
Counts, George, 55, 438
Courses, elective, 77
Courts, 217
Crafts, 91, 298–9
Creed, American, 177
Criticism, 289
Crowding, 128
Cruz, Juan, 154
Cubberly, Ellwood, 20
Cultural ambience, 143
Cultural distinctiveness, 276
Cultural ethnocentrism, 305
Cultural relativism, 305
Culture quotient, 167–8
Cultures, 77
  Afro-American, 90–2
  American, 223
  American, assimilation by Japanese, 397
  Anglos, 252
  "bad," 246
  basic differences, 307
  components of, 295–306
  in conflict, 197, 223–5, 245
  defined, 294
  denial of, 193–4
  "ethical," 397
  exclusion from, 220–32
  failure of, 233–4
  folk, or rural, 191
  home and school, 230
  "ideal," 228
  of Indian children, 294–310
  Japanese compared with American, 382, 386–7, 398
  learning of other, 217
  Mexican, 227–8, 275
  middle-class, 230
  multiple, 19
  Negro, 77
  popular, 85
  Puerto Rican, 147
  slum, 111–40
  of Spanish-speaking, 179
  urban, 191
Curandero, 185

Curiosity, intellectual, 235
Curriculums, 228–32
    components, 228
    enriched, 63
    guides and texts, 229
    inhibiting learning, 197
    innovations in, 92
    integration of, 73–9
    promoting culture conflict, 197
    racism in, 76
    of slum schools, 67
    special, separation by, 213–20

Dallos, Robert, 94
Dancing, 90, 121
    Indian, 303
Dartmouth, 339
Dating, interethnic, 212
Davis-Elis Test of General Intelligence or
    Problem-Solving Ability, 256
Dawes Act (1887), 341
Deep South, 53
Defender, Mrs. Adelina Toledo, 14–15
Deficiencies, of Mexican-American children,
    213
Delgado v. The Bastrop Independent School
    District, 189, 200
Deloria, Vine, Jr., 319, 336
Democracy, 65
Democratic party, 122
Demonstration Guidance Project, 69
Demonstration in Navajo Education, Inc., 361
Demonstrations, by Chinese, 407–10, 420–2
Dentler, Robert, 60
Denver, 320
Department of Defense, 6
Department of Health, Education and Wel-
    fare, 22–3, 346, 391
Department of the Interior, 319, 346
Department of Labor, 6
Deprivation, 56
    cultural, 9, 17, 233, 239
    of Puerto Ricans, 142
Desegregation, 49, 51, 53
    of schools, 24, 57–60, 62, 204
Detroit, 50, 70
Deutsch, Martin, 68
Deviance, 400
Dialects, 90
Diaspora, Puerto Rican, 161-2
Differences
    cultural, 179–86, 233
    individual, 21
Dining rooms, 88, 96
Dinos, Carmen, 155
Diplomas, 143
Disadvantaged, 9, 58
    culture of, 120
Discipline, 45, 170–1, 289
    classroom, 228
Discrimination, 3, 56, 117, 176–9, 277, 284,
    372
    ethnic, 114
    in housing, 40–2
    by tracking, 217
Disease, 128, 183–6

Dislocation, 393
Disorder, 160
Dispersion, 141
Dissatisfaction, "grass-roots," 5
Distortion, 74
Districts
    and curriculum, 73–9
    two-school, 205
Diversification, linguistic, 291
Diversity, cultural, 1–3, 13, 17, 433
Divorce, 137
Doctors, Anglo, 185
Douglas, William O., 314
Dozier, Edward P., 285, 289
Dramatism, 182
Dress, codes of, 224
Drew, Charles, 76
Drill, 267–8
Dropouts, 3–4, 7, 113, 151–2, 205, 285
Drunkenness, 318, 321–2
Du Bois, W. E. B., 99, 101
Due process, 217
Dumont, Robert, 7, 9, 11, 13, 227
Duncan, Otis Dudley, 41
Durslag, Melvin, 25, 87, 128
Dwight, Ben, 329

Earnings, nonwhite, 48
East Harlem, see Spanish Harlem
East Harlem Reform Democrats, 119
Eating, 231
Economic Opportunity Act (1964), 20, 368
Economy, of Indian-Americans, 290
Educable Mentally Retarded (EMR), 219
Education
    American, 81
    as answer to national problems, 55
    bilingual, 3–4, 22–3
    "Both-And" approach, 359
    compensatory, 8
    cross-cultural, 164
    data of, 201
    "Either-Or" approach, 358
    federal aid for, 23
    formal, 326
    goals of, 17
    higher, 182
    and income, 116
    of Indians, 339–47
    inferior Negro, 56
    innovative response by, 5–18
    level of formal, 143
    levels of, 46
    minority, 43
    paradoxes of, 85
    programs for Puerto Rican children, 144–6
    as promoting mobility, 192–3
    purpose of, 80
    slum, 42
    of Spanish-speaking, 197
    special, 219
    statistics, 143
Educational complex, 62–3
Educational park, 63
    costs, 64

Education Professions Institute, 434, 439–443
 structure of, 441
Educators, 275
 American, 1
 favoring tracking, 215
 middle-class contacts of, 10
 Puerto Rican, 263
 Southwestern, 226
 suggestions to, 296–9, 301–2, 304, 306, 356
Edwards, G. Franklin, 25, 36
Egalitarianism, 155; see also Equality
Einstein, Albert, 304
El Barrio, 119, 123, 126–7
Elders, 328, 393
Elementary schools, 43, 62, 68, 200, 207, 209, 222–3, 270, 366
 minority, 202
Elementary and Secondary Education Act (1965), 20–3, 368
Elizade, Felix, 164
Emigrants and emigration, 111, 137; see also Migration
Empacho, 231
Empiricism, 234
Employment, of Puerto Ricans, 139
English, 3, 11, 19, 69, 113–14, 138–9, 149, 164, 187–8, 222, 251, 320
 for bilinguals, 268
 for five-year-olds, 264–5
 problems of teaching of, 270–1
 program for teaching, 265–6
 as second language, 145, 262–71, 279
 standard, 90, 266–7
 value of, 268
Enlightenment, educational, 19–23
Enrollment, 218
 Negro, 50
 open, 61
 school, 161–2
Environment
 learning, 229
 of schools, 67, 90, 198, 223
Envy, 184
Equality, 52–4, 177
Equal Protection of the Law, 217
Erikson, Erik H., 290
Espiritu, 185
Establishment
 among Chinese-Americans, 393
 among Indians, 330
Estevanico, 75
Ethnic groups, concentration in schools, 201
Ethnocentrism, 19
Ethos, individual, 173–4
Eurasians, 416
Europe, 30, 34, 36
Europeans, 35, 38
Evers, Medgar, 100
Evil eye sickness, 184
Examinations, medical, 225
"Exchange" system, 66
Exclusion, 177, 224
 of Chinese, 374
 cultural, 220–32
Exclusion Act (1882), 372

"Expecters," 238–9
Expenditures, for schools, 241
Experience, 98
 black, 26, 95
 learning, 229
 negative school, 245
Expulsion, 222

Facilities, 232–45
 physical, 242
 quality of, 240–5
Faculty, 93
Failure, 4, 228, 233
 academic, 237
 of Mexican-Americans, 278
Fallen fontanel, 184
Families
 American, 42
 as center of adult obligations, 126
 changes in, 139
 Chinese-American, 392
 disabilities of Negro, 52
 distinction between biological and social, 299
 extended, 300
 father as disciplinarian in, 170
 income, 128
 independence in, 113
 lower-status Puerto Rican, 108, 130–40
 low-income, 23
 loyalty to, 174
 Mexican-American, 169–94
 minority-group, 226
 on move, 159
 multi-problem, 46
 Negro, 42–50
 New York, 112
 nuclear, 169, 172
 Puerto Rican, 138
 sanctions by neighbors against, 174
 size of Puerto Rican, 115
 traditional Mexican-American, 226
 unity of, 43
 very-low-income, 215
Fantasy, 85
Fatalism, 180, 182
Father, as disciplinarian, 170
Fear, 126
Features, 95–8
 human, 33
Federal Bureau of Investigation, 102
Feelings, negative, 226, 239
Females, 225
 in the home, 170
Finch, Robert H., 22
Finns, 12
Firearms, 316
Fischer, John H., 25, 55
Fleeing, 238
Food, 231
Forbes, Jack D., 2, 5, 29, 89
Fourteenth Amendment, 188, 200
Franklin, Benjamin, 339
Franklin, John Hope, 76
Frazier, E. Franklin, 37, 47
Freedom, 97–8

Free University of Chinatown Kids, 403, 405
Friendship, 180
Fright sickness, 185
Frustration, 149, 226, 234
Fuchs, Estelle, 286, 339
Fulfillment, 178
Fullilove, C. W., 390
Funds, withholding of, 281
Furniture, 114

Galileo High School (San Francisco), 413–14, 418, 428–9
Gallup (N.M.), 321, 332, 359
Gangs, 416
Gannon, Diane, 17
Gates Reading Test, 145
Generations, Japanese, 380–4
Genes, exchange of, 34
Genetic pool, 33–4
"Gentlemen's Agreement," 373
George Peabody College for Teachers, 438
Ghettoization, 20
Ghettos, 10, 38, 42, 47, 65, 67, 82, 103–4, 389–90, 440–2
    life in, 41
    Negro, described, 40
    pathology of, 39
"GI Bill" for the poor, 284
Giunsky, Frederic R., 365
Goals, 17, 45
God, 181, 183
Goodenough Draw-a-Man Test, 250, 256, 349–51
Government, 204
    do nothingness about, 85
    and minority groups, 283–4
Governor's Committee on Public Education (Tex.), 243
Grace Arthur Point Performance Scale, 349–51
Grades, 150
    level, 229
    repeating, 234
    segregation according to, 200
Graduates, 70, 241
Grammar, 269
Graves, Theodore, 320
Great Depression, 83
Great Society, 5
Groups, 12, 33, 171
    Anglo and Mexican-American, 254–5
    assimilation by, 377–8
    cultural, 217
    ethnic, changes in, 139
    ethnic peer, 226–7
    immigrant, 37
    middle-class peer, 227
    minority, 1, 8, 14
    minority, occupations open to, 284
    normative, 258
    Spanish-speaking, 177–8
Guidance Testing Associates, 258
Guides, curriculum, 229

Habits, speech, 269
"Happy slave" perspective, 236–7

"Hard core" families, 46
Harlem, 17, 69, 81
Harvard, 339
Harvey (Ill.), 78
Hatred, 82
Havighurst, Robert, 60
Hawaii, 379–80
Hayakawa, S. I., 404, 418
Hazing, 199
Head-Start, 6, 8, 20
Healing ceremony, 363
Health, 193–6
Heritage
    American, 18
    Asian-American, 369–432
    black, 24–106
    cultural and linguistic, 3
    identity with, 289
    Indian-American, 285–368
    Mexican-American, 163–284
    Puerto Rican-American, 107–62
Herskovits, Melville, J., 299
Hickel, Walter, 319
Hickerson, Nathaniel, 11
Higher Horizons Program, 69
High Schools, 63, 92, 151, 209, 222–5
    minority, 202
Hispanos, 125
History, 75–6
    Afro-American, 77, 92, 101
    American, 85, 92, 101, 103
    Negro, 74–8, 83
    United States, 73–8
Hoagland, Hudson, 128
Hoboken (N.J.), 155
Hoffman, Virginia, 360
Hoffman Bilingual Scale, 254
Holly, Ellen, 26, 94
Home economics, 231
Home Loan Bank Board, 40
Homes, 68, 170
    average, 228
    conflict with school, 245
    "deficient," 276
    Indian, 295–7, 367
    "normal," 276
    purchase of, 129
    rejection of, 246
    and school, 223
Hong Kong, 394, 414–15, 417, 425–6
Hoover, J. Edgar, 105
Hopis, 294, 297, 303–4
Hostility, 78
Hotels, 87–8
Households
    goods and expenses, 113
    large, 176
    nuclear, 111
    size, 111
Housing, 39
    discrimination in, 40–2
    Indian, 296–7
    Japanese-American, 379–80
    low-income, 127
    poor conditions, 114
    public, 119

segregated, 63
shortage, 129
tenement, 122
tight market, 40
values, 41
Hughes, Langston, 76
Humphrey, Hubert H., 316
Hunt, James McVicker, 67, 247–8, 255, 257
Hurt, N. Franklin, 78
Hypocrisy, 56

Ideals, assumed, 230
Identity
of country, 83–4
ethnic, 117
with one's heritage, 289
of youth, 290
Idiosyncrasies, 289
Illness, 186; see also Disease
Images, confused, 10
Immigration and immigrants, 36–7, 142, 397
of Chinese, 371–2, 375, 390, 414–15, 424
of Japanese, 372–4
Immorality, 212
Implementation, challenge of, 15–18
Income
annual, 131
and education, 116
low, 112
low nonwhite, 44
median annual, 113
median family, 128
Indebtedness, 113
Indian Arts and Crafts School (Santa Fe), 343
Indian Community Action Center (Ariz. State Univ.), 361
Indian Education Center (Ariz. State Univ.), 363
Indian Reorganization Act (1934), 341
Indian-Americans, 9, 285–368
Americanization of, 326
arts and crafts, 298–9
bitterness of, 318–19
children, 294–310
contrasted with whites, 291
culture of, 292, 294–309
divisions of culture, 307–9
dropout rate, 285
education, 326–7, 339–47
history, 285
housing, 296–7
initial contact with whites, 292
intellectual achievement of, 348–57
involvement of, 362
lands of, 312–17
language, 304
living conditions, 286, 315–16
median school years for, 285
the new Indian, 324–38
number in schools and colleges, 326–7, 340–2
number of tribes, 295
plight of, 318–23
reduction in population, 285
religion, 303–4
renaissance, 285

rights of, 331
school problems, 365–8
social organizations, 299–301
as students, 289–93
traditionalists, moderates and progressives, 307–9
urbanization of, 319–21
values of, 291, 305–6
vital statistics, 311
wrongs toward, 311–17
Individuals
dignity of, 289
equilibrium of, 184
fate and fortunes of, 180
roles in family, 169
Industrialization, 137
Inferiority, 178
of Puerto Ricans, 117
Inheritance, genetic, 177
Insecurity, 226
Institutions
educational, 274
middle-class, 242
social, 299, 438
status quo, 278
Instruction, bilingual, 222
Instructors, and elective courses, 93
Instruments, psychometric, 215, 219
Integration, 24, 384
acceptance of, 58
of curriculum, 73–9
of hotels and restaurants, 87–8
scales, 202
of schools, 59, 64
Intelligence, 348–56
fixed, 247
increase in, 248
new viewpoints concerning, 247
Intelligence quotient, 67, 70, 219, 234–6, 250
average Indian, 349–56
dropping off of scores, 249
English verbal, 190
high, 351, 354
increase in, 69, 235
low, 252
scores, 247
testing, 249–50, 255
Intelligence tests, 249–59, 346–56
and bilingualism, 250
content of, 255
interpretation of, 257
nonverbal, adequacy, 255–6
as predicting educability, 354–5
standardized, 258
standardized on Anglos, 251–2
translated, 251, 256
see also Intelligence quotient
Interaction, 209
equal-status, 246
organism-environment, 255
Inter-American Tests of General Ability, 258
Intermarriage, 35, 193
International Ladies' Garment Workers Union, 393
Inter-Tribal Ceremony, 332

Intimidation, of Negroes, 51
Involvement, of Indians, 362
Irish, 12
Iroquois, 290
Irrelevancy, curricular, 230, 232
Isenberg, Barbara, 286, 318
Isolation, 198–220
Issei, 380–3, 397
Italians, 12, 120–2, 128
  organization among, 122

Jackson, Andrew, 313
Jacobson, Lenore, 4
Jantzen, J. Marc, 367
Japan, occupation of, 397
Japanese
  in America, 372–4
  interment of, 374
Japanese-Americans
  acculturation of, 396
  defined, 377
  economic situation, 375
  heritage, 369
  subculture of, 376–88
Javitz, Jacob K., 22
Jealousy, 138
Jenkins, Robert, 402, 408, 419–20
Jews, 12, 378, 416–17
Jibaros, 132–6
Jobs
  for Indians, 320–1
  low-prestige, 116
  for Puerto Ricans, 124
Job training, of Indians, 319–21
Johnson, Carroll F., 78
Johnson, Henry, 76
Johnson, Lyndon B., 8, 55, 316
Josephy, Alvin M., 346
Junior high schools, 69, 215, 224–25, 231

Karelsen Frank E., 13
Katz, William Loren, 75–6
Kearney, Dennis, 372
Kennedy, John F., 40, 312–13, 346–7, 390
Kennedy, Robert F., 22
Kindergarten, 63, 264
King, Martin Luther, Jr., 76, 99–100, 105
Kinship and kinsmen, 172–3, 180
  ritual, 173
Kinzua Dam, 312–13
Kitano, Harry H. L., 370, 376, 396
Klamaths, 342
Ku Klux Klan, 51
Kurzband, Toby K., 14
Kwangtung Province, 411, 426

Labor, 44, 83
  black, 31
  Chinese, 371–2, 389, 406
  distribution of force, 49
  Japanese, 374
  shortage, 372–3
Laboratory, 267
Lado, Robert, 268
LaGuardia Neighborhood House, 120
Land, ownership of, 133

Language, 11–12, 22–3, 90, 181, 250–1, 291,
    304, 353
  ability, 262
  barrier, 189–90
  difficulties, 151
  disability, 391
  English and Spanish, 186–90
  environment, 267
  foreign, 3, 4
  handicap, 256
  problems of, 145, 186–90
  program, 265–8
  second, 18, 262–71
Language arts, 70
La Raza, 190–4
Latinos, 164
Lau, Gordon, 408, 410
La Vida, 111
Law, 4, 21, 105, 135–6, 217
  Chinese violations of, 423
Lawlessness, 114
Leaders and leadership, 50, 120, 191, 274, 301,
    330
  Mexican-American, 15
League of United American Citizens, 265
Learning, 197
  better, 58
  by Puerto Ricans, 149–54
  and verbal mediation, 252–3
Leary, Mary Ellen, 370, 389
Legal Defense Fund, 105
Legislation, civil rights, 105
Leighton, E. Robby, 330
Levels
  of education, 46
  of teaching, 229
Lewis, Hylan, 45
Lewis, Oscar, 107, 111
Liberals, 97
Lieberson, Stanley, 41
Life
  affective and cognitive, 253
  Afro-American, 100–1
  American, 36–7, 42–3, 56, 92
  views of Spanish-speaking toward, 179
Ling-Chi Wang, 407–8, 410
"Little Tokyos," 375
Living, standard of, 117
Long, Ralph, 266
Looney, Ralph, 316
Lorca, Garcia, 123
Lorge-Thorndike Nonverbal Test, 145
Los Angeles, 202, 319–22, 379, 382
Los Angeles Indian Center, 320
Lounge, social, 92
Love, Nat, 76
Lukachukai Navajo Demonstration School,
    361
Lurie, Nancy O., 292
Luster, Orville, 417
Lutherans, 316
Lynching, 105

Machismo, 174
Mainland, 142
Major, Ronald W., 8

Majority, Anglo-American, 9
Maladjustment, 223
Malcolm X, 24, 100–1, 103
Males
  irresponsibility of, 45
  Mexican, 170
  Negro, 46
Manhattan, see New York City
Mann, Horace, 65, 71
Manners, 245
Manpower Retraining Program, 46
Manuel, Herschel T., 5, 165, 262
Manuelito, 325
Manufactures, of Puerto Rico, 124
Mao Tse-tung, 395, 418
March on Washington, 99, 100
Marginality, 399–401
Margolis, Richard J., 108, 148
Marqués, René, 133
Marriage, 117, 128, 138
  as career, 170
  consensual, 137
  mixed, 138
Marshall, Thurgood, 76
"Marshall Plan" for Negroes, 47
Massachusetts, 22
"Massacre of the Black Desert," 335
Materials
  reference, 76
  supplementary, 76
Matzeliger, Jan, 76
Mayor's Advisory Committee on Puerto Rican
    Affairs (N.Y.C.), 144
McClatchy, V., 376–7
McGrath, Earl J., 71
McKay, Claude, 101
McKenzie, Richard, 336
Meador, Bruce, 327
Meals, 231
Meanings, word, 353
Mediation, verbal, 252–3, 256
Medicare, 392
Medicine, concepts of, 183
Melting pots, 3, 122, 347
Meltzer, Milton, 76
Membership, peer-group, 227
Memphis (Tenn.), 384
Men, see Males
Mendez v. Westminster School District, 188
Mentally retarded, see Retarded
Menus, 231
Meredith, James, 100
Meriam Report (1928), 341
Merriam, J. L., 268
Methods, teaching, 228
Metropolitan Achievement Test Battery, 256
Metropolitan Applied Research Center, 104
Metropolitan areas, 66, 245
Mexican-Americans, 15, 163–284
  acceptance by Anglos, 194
  acculturation of, 190–4, 220–32
  Americanization, 220
  anglicization, 193, 212
  appearance, 224
  attitude toward Anglos, 253–4
  attitudes of, 254–5

childlike ways of, 237
considered dirty, 231
culture, 220–1
customs, 170–6
disadvantaged and subordinate status, 272
discrimination toward, 176–8
ethnic attitudes, 253
ethnic values, 225
failure in school, 228
first names of, 224–5
future of, 272–84
health concepts of, 183–6
heritage, 219
home and culture as source of school
    problems, 276–9
increasing population, 274
intelligence quotients of, 190, 249–59
isolation and separation of, 198–228
language difference, 186–90
low-status, 227
modesty of, 225
number in the United States, 163
problems of, 21, 175
as rowdies, 237
school experiences, 186–90
schooling of, 275–83
in schools, 197–246
as second-class citizens, 272
segregated from Anglos, 176
socioeconomic and educational status, 275,
    277
in special classes, 218
status of, 209
stereotypes of, 176–9, 211
values of, 227
"Mexicanness," 220, 223
Mexico, 191, 291
  culture of, 227–8
Middle class, 10–18, 47–8, 179, 191, 193, 223,
    228, 239, 383, 396–8
Middle-school parks, 63
Migration, 112, 123, 141–2
  of Indians, 319–21
  of Negroes, 45
Militancy, 99–106
  of Afro-Americans, 24, 97, 99–106
  black, defined, 101–2
  Chinese-American, 403, 405, 426, 428–9,
    430–2
  in United States, 100
Miller, Theresa M., 11
Mind, in prejudice, 94–8
Minneapolis, 322
Minnesota, 316
Minorities
  forgotten, 163
  linguistic, 2
  "model American," 387
Minton, Charles, 329–30
Mintz, Sidney, 137
Misnomers, "Indian," 339
Mistrust, 192
Mobility, 192
  social, 37
Mobs, 105
Model Cities, 322

Moderatism, 308–9
Modesty, 225
Money, Indian attitudes toward, 321
Mongoloids, 32–5
Mores, 230
  legislating of, 283
Morison, Samuel Eliot, 75
Mortality, infant, 128
Mothers, 134
Motivation, 57
  and drill, 267
Mulatos, 31, 96–7
  number, 32
Munoz, Luis, 124
Music, 90, 121
Mythology, 84–5, 92, 303–4

Names, Angloization of, 224–5
Narcotics, 119
National Advisory Committee on Civil Dis-
  orders, 105
National Advisory Council on the Education
  of Disadvantaged Children, 8, 13
National Association for the Advancement of
  Colored People, 8, 77, 101–5
National Congress of American Indians, 319,
  328–9
National Congress of American Indian Tribes,
  347
National Council for Indian Opportunities,
  323
NEA-Tucson Survey Group, 187–8, 193
National Education Conference, 347
National Equal Rights League, 102
Nationalism
  Indian, or red, 331, 333, 340
  of Issei, 381
Nationality, 117
National Scholarship Service Fund for Negro
  Students, 71
National Teacher Corps, 8
National Urban League, 47
Navah(j)os, 18, 294–5, 301–3, 305, 324–6, 342,
  349, 358–60, 363
  number in schools and colleges, 327
  testing of, 351–2
Negativism, 240
Neglect, educational, 197–246
Negroes, 10, 118–29, 143, 150, 179, 201, 217,
  390, 411
  African, 95
  American, 95
  in American history, 73
  appearance of, 95–8
  as artisans, 31
  attitudes toward, 38
  characteristics, 29–30
  concentration, 39
  considered uneducable, 67
  decorated, 75
  deprived of heritage, 73
  displacement of, 38
  enhancing status of, 71
  entertainers, 95
  group characterizations, 37
  heritage of, 24–106, 219
    homes of, 129
    hostility of Puerto Ricans toward, 114
    integration of, 66
    isolation of, 38, 42
    middle-class, 47–8
    migration of, 45
    northern, 98
    occupations, 48
    opinions of, by Negroes, 125
    oppression and persecution, 38, 44
    population, 32
    professional, 48–9
    right to education, 71
    rural, 98
    segregation, 37
    social life, 50
    southern, 98
    Spanish, 121
    urbanization of, 47, 98
    values of, 81
    see also Afro-Americans; Blacks
Negroids, 34–5
Negro Revolution, 5, 41
Neighborhoods, 82
  ghetto, 108
  Puerto Rican, 111–29
Neighborhood Youth Corps, 20
Neighbors
  minority, 118–27
  sanctions by, 174
Nevada, 333
Newark, 155
Newcombe, Don, 87–8
New Deal, 341
New Frontier, 5
New Left, 425
New Mexico, 210, 218, 230, 234, 242, 305, 316,
  321, 324
Newspapers, 114
New Yellow Peril, 402–32
New York City, 60–2, 68–9, 81–2, 107,
  111–29, 131, 143–5, 149, 160–2, 216,
  255
  poverty in, 127
New York City Board of Education, 6, 144
New York City Welfare Department, 124
New York State, 19
New York State Education Commission, 6
  Advisory Committee on Human Relations
    and Community Tensions, 60
Niagra Movement, 102
Night Riders, 51
Nisei, 377–83
Nixon, Richard M., 104
Nondiscrimination, 58
Nonwhites, 66
Norms, middle-class, 239, 245
North America, 290, 292
North Carolina, 314
Northwest, 290
Nudity, 225
Nursery schools, 63, 92
Nutrition, 231

Oakland, 103
Objectives, long- and short-term, 279

O'Brien, Robert, 384
Occupations, 44, 47–8, 112–13, 379
   of Chinese-Americans, 413–16
   choice of, 399
   clerical, 124
   higher-level, 284
Oceania, 34
Office of Economic Opportunity, 6, 319, 322,
   361, 364, 390
Office of Education (U.S.), 6, 23, 268, 327, 346
Officer, James, 326
Oklahoma, 313–14
Oneidas, 313
Open Housing Act (1968), 317
Operation Head-Start, see Head-Start
Opportunities, 82
   educational, 43, 202
   equality of educational, 279
   language, 266–7
Opposition, 52
Oppression, 38
Optimism, 236
Oregon, 342
Organizations, social, 299–301
Orientals, 12, 38; see also Asian-Americans
Orientation
   community, 147
   value, 179–86
Other Teaching Positions (OTP), 145
Otis Self-Administering Test of Mental Abil-
   ity, 250

Padilla, Elena, 125
Pain, 186
Paired Associates Learning task, 252
Pairing, 62
Paiutes, 333–5
Palomillas, 171
Panaceas, 8–9
Paranoia, 98
Parents, 45, 93, 200, 205
   beliefs of, 182
   care by, 161
   Negro, 59
   participation of, 158–9
   Puerto Rican, 158–60
   reaching, 158–60
   respect and obedience toward, 171
Parent-Teachers' Associations, 158
Paternalism, 179–80
Payne, Mrs. Mary Lou, 6
Peace Corps, 91
Peers, as Anglos, 246
Perceptions, 232–45
Performance
   contracts, 4
   differential standards, 49
Permissiveness, 221, 290
Permits, emergency, 243
Personalism, 169, 179–80
Personalities, 234
   warped, 289
Personnel
   certified, 209
   school, 91, 210
Pessimism, 236

Peyton Place, 94
Philadelphia, 155, 160
Philosophies, contemplative, 291
Physical education, 225
Piaget, Jean, 247–8, 253, 255
Pickerring, Timothy, 312
Pictures, in testing, 253
Pimas, 295
Pittsburgh, 70
Placement
   pattern, 207–8
   techniques, 215
   by tracking, 214–20
Planning, 181
Plants, school, 243
Pluralism
   cultural, 385–6
   structural, 386–8
Pochismos, 187
Point Scale of Performance Test, 249–50
Poles, 12
Police, 135–6, 230–1, 431–2
Policies, 58
   free choice, 61, 205–6
Political systems, 301–2
Politics
   corruption in, 181
   United States, 117
Poor
   new, 122
   urban, 135
Popagos, 295, 297, 303, 349
   testing of, 350–1
Population, 131
   balanced, 63
   characteristcis of, 244
   heterogeneous, 2
   multi-cultural, 165
   Negro, 65
   Puerto Rican, in America, 161–2
   Puerto Rican, described, 135
   of Puerto Rico, 136–8
   small marginal, 401
   statistics, 32
Poverty, 19, 56
   culture of, 116–17
   in East Harlem, 127
   in Harlem, 123
   in Puerto Rico, 131–6
Power, dilemmas of, 21
Practice, 267
Predestination, 180
Prediction, of ability, 354–5
Pregnancy, 128
Prejudice, 117, 122, 154–5, 284, 372
   toward Chinese, 413
   toward Puerto Ricans, 138
   score, 254
Prekindergarten, 63
Preschooling, 92
Press, "white," 98
Pressures, 140
   governmental, 204
Prices, of staples, 132
Primary Mental Abilities Test, 256
Princeton Plan, 62

Principals, 151, 207, 225, 240
Privacy, 128
Problems
  of Indians in schools, 365–70
  of language, 187–90
  school, 275–9
  of the Spanish-speaking, 174–90
  of teaching English, 270–1
Professions, 48–9
  teaching, 437–8
Programs
  community relations, 160
  compensatory educational, 202, 213
  continuous day, 92
  educational, 279
  for education of Puerto Rican children,
    144–7
  for the educationally disadvantaged, 8–9
  enriched, 63
  family-limitation, 46
  federal, 237
  language, 265–8
  preschool, 68
  primary, 63
  remedial, 154
  urban renewal, 39
Progress, 181
  technological, 71
Progressivism, 309
Projective Test of Racial Attitudes, 253–4
Project Keep Moving, 6
Promotion, 229
Pronunciation, 269
  nonstandard, 269–70
Prophecies, Indian, 336–7
Protestants, 12, 183, 396
Psychologists, 219, 224
Puberty, 171, 303
Puberty ceremony, 303
Pueblos, 290–1, 303, 327, 329, 349
Puerto Rican Coordinators, 145
The Puerto Rican Study, 145, 146
Puerto Rican-Americans
  adjustment of, 146
  birth rate, 137
  children, 141–7
  culture, 147
  dispersion, 141
  enrollment in public schools, 161–2
  ethnic identity, 117
  families, described, 130–40
  features, 120, 138
  fondness for children, 136–40
  gregariousness of, 126
  identity, 147
  increase in, 119
  intelligence quotients of, 256–7
  leadership, 120
  level of education, 143
  marriage, 138
  middle-class, 117
  migration of, 123, 141–2
  mobility, 159
  and Negroes, 150
  and Negroes and whites compared, 150
  opportunities of, 138
  population, 141
  population in America, 161
  rating of, 125
  religion, 124
  segregation, 40
  sentiments, 126
  spending and saving patterns, 115
Puerto Rico, 114–17, 142, 256–7, 263
  colonial status of, 124
  described, 123–4
  jobs in, 124
  migration from, 161–2
  population of, 136–7
Punishment, 222
Pupils
  Afro-American, 89–93
  anti-school and anti-establishment, 11
  capacities of, 69
  disadvantaged, 9
  and literature, 90
  maturation, 69
  minority group, 8
  non-English speaking, 146
  performance, 69
  ranking of, 235–6

Qualla Indian Reservation, 314
Quitting, 226

Races
  human, 32
  hybrid, 35
  "inferior," 200
  Negroid, 34
  question of, 384–5
  and reconciliation, 55–72
  separate, 34, 41
  types, 32–35
  universal, 30
Racine (Wisc.), 68
Racism, 121, 238
Randolph, A. Philip, 104
Rapport, 12–14
Reaction Time Test of Bilingualism, 250
Reading, 69–70, 149, 229
  ability, 236
  mature materials for, 270
Reading circles, 214
Realities, of class, 36–54
Rebellion, 3
Reconciliation, and race, 55–72
Reconstruction, 83
Red China, 390, 395, 419
Red Dragon Party, 375
Redfield, Robert, 292
Red Guard, 418, 427
"Red Guard Community News," 395
Red men, see Indian-Americans
Red Muslims, 327
"Red Power," 347
Refugees, 390, 393
Rejection, 233
Relationships
  employer-employee, 397
  inter- and extra-familial, 173–4
  loose individual, 171

school-community, 92
  social, 41, 169
Relatives, 172–3, 299–300
Relief, government, 136
Religion
  and fatalism, 181
  of Indians, 303–4
Relocation, of Indians, 319–23
Rents, high, 114
Requirements, of system, 239
Research, 234
Reservations, 315, 318
Residential dissimilarity, index of, 176
Respect, 12–13
Response, lack of, 7
Responsibility, 245
Restaurants, 88
  Chinese, 392
Retarded, 143, 218–19
Revised Stanford-Binet Scale, 256
Rezoning, 62
Riesman, Frank, 13
Rights, constitutional, 53
Rillieux, Norbert, 75
Riots and rioting, 102, 105
Ritual, religious, 182
Robb, Felix, 438–9
Robert Williams Case, 103
Roberts, Needham, 76
Rodriguez, Percy, 94, 96, 98
Roessel, Robert A., 286–7, 294, 359–64
Roessel, Ruth, 360
Roles, 214
  of children, 210
  intra-familial, 169–73
Roman Catholics, 12, 124, 137
Rooms, Mexican, 218
Rosenthal, Robert, 4
Rough Rock Demonstration School (Ariz.),
  358–64
Rural areas, 132–3
Rusco, Elmer, 7

St. Louis, 69, 87
St. Paul (Minn.), 249
Salk, Erwin A., 77
Samora, Julian, 7
Samuel Compers High School (San Francisco),
  417
San Carlos Apaches, see Apaches
San Francisco, 7, 234, 319, 370, 389–95, 402–32
San Francisco State College, 403, 418
San Francisco United School District, 419–20
San Juan (P.R.), 112
Sansei, 377–81, 383–4, 398
Santa Fe (N.M.), 327, 343
Saving, 115
Scale
  integration, 202
  social, 191
Scalping, real estate, 312–17
Scarsdale (N.Y.), 74
Scheuer, James H., 22
Schizophrenia, 81
Scholarships, 93
School-Community Coordinators, 145

School, starting, 300
School districts, 207–8, 243
  Mexican-American, 204–5
"Schooling," 161
Schooling, for five-year-olds, 265
Schools
  ability of Mexican-Americans to use, 277
  acceptance of teachers, 436
  action from outside, 160–1
  advantaged Anglo, 228
  allocating status and roles, 214
  American, 141–7, 340
  American, enrollment, 161–2
  American, Puerto Rican children in, 148
  Anglo-American, 12–13
  Anglo-dominated, 239
  attendance, 201, 241
  authorities of, 58, 238
  authority structure of, 227
  barrio, 226, 240, 242
  belonging to people, 89
  changing, 278, 281–3
  Chinese, 413, 424
  church, 325
  city, 64–5
  and community, 91
  conflict with home, 245
  control of, 15–16
  desegregated, 51, 203–4
  disadvantaged, 228
  dropout rates for, 7
  enrollment, 57
  and environment, 67
  failure of, 233
  ghetto, 16, 66
  and home, 223
  humaneness of, 160
  imbalanced, 61–2
  as inappropriate, 198
  Indian, 341, 347
  Indian, described, 358–64
  inferior, 200
  inflexibility and rigidity of, 232
  influence of, 67
  integrated, 51, 59, 64, 66
  intercultural, 14
  lack of care by, 161
  as ladder of social mobility, 107
  mainland United States, 142–4
  majority, 208–9
  mass-produced, 18
  Mexican, 200, 215, 242
  and Mexican-Americans, 197–246
  middle-class, 67
  middle-class oriented, 224
  minority, 208–9, 242
  mixed, 208–32
  monocultural, 17
  negative feelings toward, 226
  Negro, 57, 59
  neighborhood, 64
  New York City, 143
  number of Indians in, 326–7
  operated by B.I.A., 342–3
  and parents, 158–60
  parochial, 12

personnel of, 210
position on Mexican-Americans, 275–9
power of improvement of, 59
practices, 245
Puerto Rican segregated, 60
quality of, 199, 242
reflecting society, 197
with rigid practices, 282
role of, 55–72
rural, 64
segregated, 62, 200, 203
separate, 188, 316
separate Mexican, 199
separate unequal, 57
significance and meaningful, 234
slum, 6–7, 42, 67–8, 228
and society, 273–9
southwestern, 199–246
suburban, 64–5
suggested changes for, 433–4
target, 202
Texas, 230
traditional, 198
types, 202
ultraconformist, 228
School systems
Indian, 347
pluralistic, 433
School year, 232
Scores, intelligence test, 250–1
Segregation, 40–1, 49, 117, 147
de facto and de jure, 199–204
indices of, 37
maintained by free-choice policy, 206
residential, 175–6
as retarding acculturation, 191
in schools, 57
by tracking, 215
urban, 65
Selective Service tests, 7
Self-concept, 91, 217
Self-image, 57
improvement of Indians', 367–8
Senecas, 312–13
Sentiment, 126
Separation, 198–220
in mixed schools, 209–20
spatial, 175–6
by special curriculum, 213–20
Serial Learning task, 252
Services
educational, 46
remedial, 63
social, 46
Sex, 121, 171
Sexes, 212
Sexton, Patricia Cayo, 107, 118
Shaman, 290
Sharecroppers, 133–4
Shiprock (N.M.), 351
Shock, massive cultural, 318
Shriver, R. Sargent, 6
Siblings, 171–2
Sicilians, 122
Sierra Union High School District (Calif.),
365–6

Silberman, Charles, 46
Silent majority, 104
Silver, James, 37
Sioux, 7, 9
Situations, extended family, 300
Six Companies, 394, 406, 409, 412–3, 422–3,
427
Skills, 124, 271
Slavery, 31, 75, 81, 97, 102
Sloan, Irving, 74–6, 78
Slums 42, 56, 111–29, 135, 392
in East Harlem, 127
housing in, 39
schools in, 6
Smilansky, Moshe, 17
Social distance, 193
Socialization, 175
Social scientists, 221
Social studies, 78
Social workers, interviewed, 224
Societies, 80–6
American, 37, 56, 65
atomistic, 169–94
backward, 85
changes in, 81
changing of, 283–4
democratic, 65
distrust of, 174
dominant, 229
matrilineal, 299
Negroes' place in, 56
patrilineal, 299
pluralistic, 433
revolutionary, 80
and the schools, 273–84
wants of, 81
war with, 85
Sociologists, 311–12
Soul, 418
South, 15, 31
South Dakota, 292
Southeast, 290
Southern Regional Council, 104–5
Southwest, 16, 21, 165, 176, 199, 200–46, 262–
71, 272–84, 326–38
ethnic peer groups, 226–7
Southwest Conference on Social and Educational Problems of Rural and Urban
Mexican-American Youth, 15
Southwestern Association on Indian Affairs,
329
Southwestern Regional Youth Conference,
329, 333
Spanish, 21, 114, 130, 151, 155, 159, 164,
186–90, 250–1, 257, 262
case for and against, 263
and English compared, 268–9
prohibition of, 221–2
used in teaching of English, 270
value of, 263
"Spanish detention," 222
Spanish Harlem, 107, 118–29
characteristics, 169–94
Spanish-speaking
cognitive functioning of, 247–59
fatalism of, 180–1

intellectual functioning of, 247–59
  problems of, 169–94
  teaching of English to, 262–71
Speech, 269–70
  errors in, 270
  of Mexican-Americans, 189
  as reflecting value orientations, 187
Spelling, 269
Spending, 115
Spindler, George, 292
Spindler, Louise, 292
"Spurting," 235
Stability, societal, 274
Staffs
  Anglo, 222
  inservice reeducation of, 282–3
Standford-Binet Intelligence Test, 249–51, 257
State system, 127
Status
  on ascription not proscription, 214
  equal, 209
  lower, 239
Steiner, Stanley, 286, 324
Stereotypes, 176–9, 246, 281, 373–4
Stevens, Ernest, 322
Stimulation, environmental, 248
Stocks, human, 32–5
Stone, James C., 434–5
Strategy, 89
Strikes, 421
Structures, behavior and thought, 248
Students
  appearance, 224
  breaking down ethnic distinctions, 212
  culturally different, 221
  effect of criticism and discipline on, 289
  Indian, 289–93, 348–57
  isolation of, 60
  lower-class, 212
  lower-status, 57
  low-track, 217
  Negro, 69, 78
  non-English speaking, 142
  number of Indian, 340, 342
  placement pattern, 207–8
  rank of Negro, 67
  social class of, 228
  with Spanish surnames, 218
  teenage, 92
  transferal of, 61
Studies, of Indian children, 352
Subcultures, Japanese-American, 375–88
Subjects, integration of, 77–8
Submissiveness, 120
Subordinates, 210
Subordination, 177
Subsistence, 295–6
Substitute Auxiliary Teachers (SAT), 145
Success, 191
Suffering, 186
Suicide, 400
Superintendents, 240
Superordinates, 210
Support, financial, 440
Supreme Court, 24, 57, 76, 313–16

Surnames, Spanish, 205, 208–9, 218
Suspension, 222, 224
Suspicion, 192
Sweatshops, 393
Swedes, 12
Syndrome, acute stress, 128
"System beaters," 238–40
Systems, age-grading, 93

Taeuber, Alma, 38
Taeuber, Karl, 38
Taft Neighborhood Development Committee, 119
Taiwan, 415
T'ang jen, 412, 427
Tax, Sol, 330
Taylor, Paul S., 5
Teacher Education and Professional Standards (TEPS), 437
Teachers, 80–6, 93, 225
  acceptance by schools, 436
  Anglo, 238
  and Anglo stereotypes, 211
  attitudes, 245
  bilingual, 207, 238
  certified, 209
  changing of, 154–5
  cultural differences with Indians, 293
  culture and values of, 289
  without degrees, 243
  divergent personalities or philosophies, 238
  effective, 67
  environments of, 239
  ethnic groups of, 239
  expectations of, 235
  failure of, 234
  of foreign descent, 22
  helping of children, 239
  high expectations of, 239
  identifying with students, 240
  of Indian students, 289–93, 343
  in- and pre-service training, 441
  inservice work, 77
  interviews with, 210–11
  knowledge of Spanish, 263
  low expectancies of, 237
  Mexican-American, 206–9, 237–40
  and Mexican-American children, 236–40
  minority-group, 434
  mobility of, 239
  model for preparation, 435–43
  monolingual, 16
  Negro, 52–3, 70, 239
  noncertified, 243
  number, 208–9
  obsession with cleanliness, 231
  payment of, 155
  perceptions of children, 70, 234
  pessimism and optimism, 236
  preparation of, 281–2, 435–43
  preservice and inservice training, 282
  proposed conditions for, 439–43
  in Puerto Rico, 159
  ratio with students, 244
  roles of, 238
  salaries, 343

seminars, 155
shortages of, 244, 437
southwestern, 233, 238
Spanish-speaking, 155, 158
with Spanish surnames, 238
suggestions for, 89–93
teaching of, 76–7
tours for, 155
training of, 233
as troublemakers, 244
views of, 233–7
Teaching
craftsmanship in, 271
of five-year-olds, 264–5
methods, 228
a second language, 262–71
of skills, 229
and student rejection, 237
team, 70
techniques, 268–71
Teaching English as a Second Language
(TESL), 359–61
Teenagers, 92–3, 223, 228
Television, 96, 266, 360
Tellicoe Dam, 314
Tenants, New Yorkers as, 129
Tenants' Council, 126
Tennessee, 314–15
Tennessee Planning Commission, 314–15
Tennessee Valley Authority, 314
Tennessee Writers' Association, 314–15
Tense, 187
"Termination," 341
Testing, 150
and life chances, 215
Tests, English, 91
Texas, 19–23, 199–200, 202, 205, 215, 222, 224,
228, 230, 240–2, 244, 265
Textbooks, 74, 229, 247
elementary, 229
inadequate, 75–6
integrated, 77
Third World Freedom Movement, 395, 418,
421
Thom, Mel, 330–1, 333–5, 338
Thoreau, H. D., 443
Thorpe, Jim, 341
Thought, 248
Afro-American, 101
Thurmond, Strom, 316
Time, 182
Indian concept of, 304, 321
Tireman, L. S., 268
Title I Programs, 20
Tolerance, 154–5
Tollhouse (Calif.), 365
Tom Tom, 425
Tongs, 395, 424
"Total" inservice reeducation, 282–3
Tracking, 214–20, 246, 281
constitutionality of, 217
effects of, 216
low tracks, 219
of Mexican-Americans, 237
Traditionalism, 307–8
Training, 45

Transfer, 61, 151
Transport, public financed, 61
Trauma, 186
Treaties, with Indians, 316
"Triangle," 119, 127
Tribes and tribalism, 33, 290–1, 295, 301, 322,
333–4
Truman, Harry S., 422
Tuberculosis, 128
Turner, Nat, 101
Tyler, Ralph, 354–5
Types, human, 33–5

"Uncle Tomahawks," 322, 330
Uncle Toms, 404
Underachievement, 8
Underemployment, 44, 393
Understanding, 155
Unemployment, 44, 113, 116
Unions, labor, 83, 112, 116
United Native Americans, 319
United States, 5, 26, 30, 64, 89, 137, 140,
263, 312–17, 341, 377
founding of, 84
identity of, 83–4
multi cultures in, 3
Unity, of family, 43
Universities, life in, 326–7
University of Arizona, 330
University of Chicago, 330–48
University of New Mexico, 324, 327, 329
Upper class, 179
Upward Bound, 20
Urban areas, 45, 132
Urban Indian Development Association, 322
Urbanization, 47, 65, 192, 319
pressures of, 321
Urban League, 102
Urban renewal, 39

Vacuum, cultural, 163
Values, 81
American, 36
American and Japanese, 398
ethnic, 225
of Indians, 291, 305–6
Japanese and American middle-class, 396–8
Mexican-American, 227
middle-class, 239
of migrants, 126
Vasquez, Joe, 320
Venereal disease, 128
Verbal competency, level of, 257
Very Earnest, 425
Vietnam, 2
Violence, 105
Vision, strong, 184
Volpe, John A., 389
Volunteers in Service to America (VISTA),
91, 359–60
Voters, Negro, 53
Voting, of Indians, 302, 315
Voting Rights Act (1965), 52–3, 104
Voucher system, 4

Wages, 372, 393

Wah Ching, 395, 405–7, 410, 416–17, 424, 426–7, 429
Walker, David, 102–3
Walker River Reservation, 333–4
Wallace, George, 85
Walter-McCarran Act (1952), 390
Warfare, 290
  internecine, 98
War of 1812, 312
War on Poverty, 6, 45
Washington, Booker T., 103
Washington, George, 312
Washington D.C., 217
Washington State, 338
Watson, Goodwin, 13
Wax, Murray, 7, 9, 11, 13, 227
Wax, Rosalie, 7, 9, 11, 13, 227
Wechsler Intelligence Scale for Children, 190, 250, 256
Western hemisphere, 258
Westminster School District et al. v. Mendez et al., 188, 200
"Where It's At," 97–8
White Anglo-Saxon Protestants (WASPS), 9
"Whitelisting," 96
White Plains (N.Y.), 78
White problem, 92
Whites, 26, 30, 411; see also Anglo-Americans
"Whitey-watching," 97
Wilcox, Preston, 120
Wilkins, Roy, 99
William and Mary, 339
Williams, Daniel Hale, 76
Williams, Robin, 37, 41

Wilson, James, 319
Wirth, Louis, 20
Withdrawal, 7–8
"Withholding," 398
Wolfe, Tom, 370, 402
Women, see Females
Wong, Dennis, 422–4
Woo, George, 403–5, 421, 425, 430
Work and workers
  agricultural, 133
  Chinese, 389
  nonwhite, 48
  Puerto Rican, 112
  relationships with employers, 135
  value of work, 182
  white workers, 48
Workshops, community-teacher, 93
World War I, 47
World War II, 54, 200, 273, 327, 341, 374, 390, 412
Wovoka, 334
Wrongs, civil, 311–17

Yarborough, Ralph, 21–2
Yellow Peril Movement, 426
Young, Whitney, 46
"Young intellectuals," 324–38
Youth
  culturally disadvantaged, 8–9
  and identity, 290
  Mexican-American, isolation of, 217
  militancy of, 403, 405, 426, 428–9, 430–2
  turbulence of, 335
Youth Council, 333–4, 336